1990

To My Uncle Patrick

HAPPY CHRISTMAS

from your friend Rupert.

SOUTH AFRICAN
DESPATCHES

SOUTH AFRICAN DESPATCHES

Two Centuries of the Best in South African Journalism

Edited by
Jennifer Crwys-Williams

Foreword by
Lord Deedes of Aldington,
former editor, *The Daily Telegraph,* London

ASHANTI
PUBLISHING LIMITED
A DIVISION OF ASHANTI INTERNATIONAL FILMS
GIBRALTAR

Copyright © 1989 Jennifer Crwys-Williams

ISBN 0620099542

First edition, first impression 1989

Published by Ashanti Publishing (Pty) Ltd.,
P.O. Box 10021,
Rivonia 2128.
Johannesburg.

Designed by Photo-Prints, Long Street, Cape Town
Cover Design by Axel Adelbert, of Adelbert and Rens, Cape Town

Set in Garamond 11 point
by Photo-Prints, Long Street, Cape Town
Printed and bound by
Interpak, Pietermaritzburg.

Acknowledgments

No book is the product of one person and *South African Despatches* is not an exception. It is no exaggeration to say that without the unstinting help of Natasha Younghusband, Jackie Ault and Andrea Steenkamp, *Despatches* would still be in the newspapers from which it was drawn. Special thanks are due to Lord Deedes of Aldington, former editor of *The Daily Telegraph,* who unhesitatingly agreed to write the Foreword to this book.

Sincere thanks are owed to Mr G. Johnson, chief librarian, Mail Newspaper, Mr F.B. Singleton, librarian, Guardian Newspapers, Mr C.P. Wilson, chief librarian, *The Times* and Mr J.G. Entwisle of Reuters, all of whom helped generously and with enthusiasm. Thanks, too, are owed to the library of *The New York Times* for its assistance.

Librarians bear a special burden when a book such as *Despatches* is researched. Arlene Fanarof and the staff of the Reference Section, South African Library, were endlessly helpful and extraordinarily patient. The Africana Museum allowed itself to be used like a bus station, and Carol Leigh, head librarian of the Strange Library of Africana, provided an endless source of information. *The Star*'s syndications department and archives deserve thanks, particularly Norman Fairbairn, archivist, as does the Killie Campbell Museum of Africana, De Beers' library and the South African Museum of Military History.

Special thanks are due to Rykie van Reenen, who not only coped with most of the translations, but made valuable suggestions. Charles Barry of *The Star* and Glynis Horning of *The Natal Mercury* were constantly asked for help and constantly provided it, as did Joel Mervis. David Beresford, *The Guardian*'s man in South Africa, introduced me to a new and valuable field of research, for which many thanks are due.

Thanks, too, are due to the various editors who responded to requests for information with apparent pleasure. The journalists themselves went out of their way to help me sort through their articles, thus eliminating many hours of research, and were moderately patient when asked for details of stories long forgotten; Rex Gibson allowed himself to be interviewed no fewer than three times on the closing of the *Rand Daily Mail* without apparent irritation.

Without the support, encouragement and uncharacteristic patience of Peter Younghusband, this book would not have been completed.

Editor's Prologue

When South Africa's first independent newspaper, *The South African Commercial Advertiser,* was launched on Wednesday, 7 January 1824, newspapers the world over were struggling, not so much to print, but to print free from governmental control. Indeed, the very term 'newspaper' had only recently come into everyday use.

Modern newspapers are the descendants of gazettes and journals. These were frequently of no more than two pages and were produced under strict licence from the state. A gazette was a paper, usually of political news, drawing its material from a catholic variety of sources; a journal covered a specific area of interest, be it science, the arts or social news. Neither was permitted to deviate from their licensed areas of interest without incurring the wrath of the government in question, sometimes with severe penalties (one British reporter, for instance, was charged in 1737 with ridiculing five Acts of Parliament. He was fined 200 marks, imprisoned for five years, had to put up two sureties of £250 in addition to his own surety of £500, and placed on good behaviour for life).

The newspaper of today emerged slowly from these 16th, 17th and 18th century gazettes and journals, but it emerged only after protracted struggles with government. In many instances, these struggles continue today. South Africa was, and is, no exception. It was thanks to the pioneering work of British, Dutch and American newspapers that the concept of freedom of the press came slowly and unwillingly to be accepted.

The history of newspapers in South Africa was just as controversial as in other countries. The first newspaper, *The Cape Town Gazette and African Advertiser,* was in effect, published by the government; the second, *The South African Commercial Advertiser,* was banned, the first of many to suffer this fate. The battle to publish freely and without official constraints continues.

But behind all of this, and hidden by the type on the front pages, there runs the story of the men and women who make the papers, who get the stories, who write them, sometimes at great cost to themselves and certainly without great financial reward, and who see the results of their work read once and then discarded. The story of newspapers and the people who write them is a romantic one.

South African Despatches is an attempt to capture some of that romance, some of that excitement. It is not a history of newspapers in this country — that is a task for someone else. *Despatches* is a history of some of the great despatches which have been written from this country, published both nationally and internationally, and, wherever possible, of the journalists who wrote them.

The book had its inception some three years ago. Foreign correspondent Peter Younghusband had long mulled over the idea of writing a book of this kind, but pressure of work prevented him from doing so. At a memorable lunch in Cape Town, he asked me to take the concept of the book, to develop it, research it and write it. At that stage, I had no idea of the avenues down which I would have to travel in order to complete the most fascinating assignment I have ever been offered.

There were several stipulations: the despatches must have emanated from South Africa, they must all have come from newspapers (be they local or foreign), and they must all have been written by journalists. The keyword in the selection of despatches was quality of writing.

The stipulations immediately eliminated large areas of research. Military communiques, fascinating though they are, were excluded from the book. So, too, were articles, frequently of a high calibre, written by people who were not journalists (the only exceptions to this rule were Rudyard Kipling, who began his career in journalism and who briefly edited a South African newspaper, and Arthur Conan Doyle, who was a writer who contributed extensively to local papers during the Second Anglo-Boer War). And many despatches, newsworthy though they might have been, were written in such a pedestrian manner as not to come within the confines of the quality clause which dominated the selection of the despatches.

Thus it became immediately apparent that *Despatches* could not be compiled on the basis of historical events, although it was obviously to landmark events in the nation's past that I initially turned. The book is therefore neither a history of newspapers nor a history of events: it is a history of outstandingly-written despatches or examples of a particular *genre* of newspaper writing.

Until the Anglo-Zulu War of 1879, the reporting of events was, in the main, faithfully (and minutely) covered, but without much heed paid to the quality of writing which can make even an ordinary event a pleasure to read. The war changed, to a large extent, the parochial writing, for it brought to this country some of the most outstanding journalists of the day, covering this particular part of the British Empire for their mother newspapers. Faced with competition from foreign correspondents, local writers improved their copy, sharpened their techniques and vied successfully with international reporters. The Second Anglo-Boer War, studded as it was with correspondents of the calibre of Winston Churchill, Leo Amery and J.B. Atkins, further improved the quality of writing.

In many instances, the stories behind the original despatch are more interesting than either despatch or event. The chapter on Archibald Forbes — who opens this book with his amazing scoop on the Battle of Ulundi — the Reuter scoop on the relief of Mafeking, and Edgar Wallace's scooping the Second Anglo-Boer War peace talks are all examples of the story overshadowing the despatch.

Much perforce has had to be omitted. I have not covered such intriguing papers such as *Chiao Sheng Pao,* a Johannesburg Chinese newspaper which ran from 1931 to 1938. Nor have I included anything from *The Robben Island Times* (1886-1887) or, sadly, the entirely hand-written *Ladysmith Bombshell,* published during the siege of that town and full of the most execrable schoolboy jokes I have ever read. And fine journalists have been omitted solely for reasons of space. Their time will come in another volume.

Inconsistencies galore abound in *South African Despatches.* Wherever possible, archaic spellings for places and names of people have been faithfully reproduced; in some of the early despatches, however, the reporter was catholic with his use of names, sometimes spelling them in two or even three different ways. These have been rationalised, without, I hope, taking the charm away from the original. The variance in style (in newspapers, a 'style' book is issued to all reporters and is transgressed only on pain of death) which appears in different despatches has been left as it was in the original.

South African Despatches is, in a modest way, a salute to a highly individual, largely dis-organised, infuriatingly sceptical and totally dedicated group of people. Singling any one of today's journalists out for special recognition is probably asking for trouble. But I would like to dedicate this book to John O'Malley, as fine a journalist as one is likely to meet anywhere.

Foreword by Lord Deedes of Aldington

Journalists are not good historians. They like to deal in bright colours, and much of history is grey. But properly assembled they can convey wonderfully well the flavour of a country. They have been admirably assembled here by Jennifer Crwys-Williams, and so we get the true flavour of South Africa. Observe that amid the dramas and disasters, triumphs and tragedies, room has been found for half a dozen sporting essays. An anthology of this kind which left out the Springboks would not be a true portrait of South Africa at any time.

We are reminded how many English writers have relished the flavour of the country. One of them was John Buchan, later Lord Tweedsmuir, whose name here is linked to the Battle of Delville Wood in July 1916. Buchan belonged to that small and now forgotten company, Milner's young men. South Africa entered his bloodstream. The hero of his novels, Richard Hannay, had made his pile in South Africa. Not a bad thing, in passing, to remind the world that in that Battle of Delville Wood, the bloodiest of many costly Somme battles, the South Africans fought alongside us.

Naturally Winston Churchill is here; and so, I am glad to see, is that underrated genius Edgar Wallace. I missed him by only a year or two when I joined the old *Morning Post* in London; and was brought up on the story, included here, of how he scooped the peace talks for the *Daily Mail* in 1902. Another of that company of correspondents who made their name during the Boer War was H.A. Gwynne, then correspondent for Reuters, and later my editor on the *Morning Post* until 1937. Rudyard Kipling joined this company for a while, but I fancy he was more spiritually at home in India than South Africa.

Although there is a long professional kinship between South Africa's and Great Britain's journalists, there is one distinguishing mark between them, which is clearly signalled in this collection. South Africa's reporters have experienced — are experiencing now — censorship in peacetime. In half a century or more of journalism I have never been called upon to take the sort of decision Donald Woods had to take as editor of *The Daily Despatch* before printing his editorial in 1972 — "The whole bloody world will rejoice".

No mean feat to secure its inclusion among these pieces.

Woods, and Tony Heard and Allister Sparks later on, certainly convey the flavour of a journalist's life in South Africa in the 1980s. I do not always agree with what they write, but I admire them for writing more freely than I would dare to do under repression. Come to think of it, the first part of this anthology reminds us of men who made their reputations by circumventing war-time censorship; in the second half we find men who made their names by making the truth shine in the twilight of peacetime censorship. That is the harder feat.

Yes, this is a pretty faithful portrait of a country of which the outside world now knows very little. The days of glory are here, as well as the days of shame; the days of international sporting triumphs, as well as sad days when South Africans must walk onto their playing fields alone.

The true value of this collection is that it transcends prevailing prejudices. I first learned of South Africa from my father, who had gone there as a boy of 17 to fight in the Boer War. He gave me a feeling for the country which has been with me all my life. It is rekindled by reading through these pages. Those who love the country for its own sake have reason to rejoice that, notwithstanding all the little local difficulties, Jennifer Crwys-Williams has been able to give us such a rich collection to turn over in the mind's eye.

Contents

'Bloody with spurring, fiery red with haste'

Archibald Forbes' Ride, Zululand, 1879

If Archibald Forbes felt a sense of *déjà vu* while covering yet another battle in yet another country, he concealed it well.

On the evening of 3 July 1879, at the age of 41, he was in a military camp deep in the heart of Zululand, surrounded not only by British troops, but by some of the most famous special correspondents of the day. On the morrow, they hoped to witness the conclusive defeat of the Zulu army at the hands of the British under the command of Lord Chelmsford. Commander of the British army in Natal until Sir Garnet Wolseley had taken over as Commander-in-Chief, Chelmsford had marched 10 000 soldiers and a clutch of special correspondents across the width of Natal.

For Chelmsford it was a search for the final, successful confrontation with the Zulus, as well as avenging the killing of the Prince Imperial; for Forbes, it was a search for one more story, one more scoop.

He was no stranger to either. Like many other war correspondents, he had entered journalism more by chance than by design. His story, recounted at length over the years, went something like this:

With an inheritance of £2 500 in his pocket, Forbes decided to go to Canada to seek fame and fortune. Instead he found love. But it was both unrequited and expensive, and Forbes had to return to England not only broken-hearted but empty-pocketed, travelling as a sailor to Liverpool and then, in order to get to London, selling his field-glasses to pay for the train fare. In London, virtually destitute, Forbes went to a lecture. The subject was 'The Charge of the Light Brigade', the speaker none other than William Howard Russell, *The Times'* great war correspondent. Russell spoke with fire, he spoke with colour and, above all, he spoke with passion. Forbes was entranced. A passionate man, he responded by enlisting immediately with the Royal Dragoons, and spent the next five years in the army.

He wrote the occasional piece from the occasional battlefield, but nothing outstanding came from him in those years. Leaving the army because of ill health, and because he thought he could write, he decided to go into journalism, and promptly opened his own newspaper, the *London Scotsman,* and, with typical Scottish parsimony (he was born near Aberdeen and educated in Edinburgh) staffed and ran it himself. It was not an outstanding success.

Forbes' luck began to change for the better when he went to talk to James Grant of the *Morning Advertiser,* to which journal he had contributed modest articles. Grant, short of reporters and with the Franco-Prussian War recently declared, offered Forbes a job as a war correspondent,

1

leaving him to choose the side on which he wanted to report. Forbes chose the German side, and sent back some outstanding despatches from the battlefront. His first scoop was more by dint of luck than enterprise, although in his long career he was to lack neither.

Coming out of his hostelry before six o'clock one morning, Forbes spotted the figure of Bismarck on horseback, and together with a reporter from the *Glasgow Herald,* decided to follow him. Shortly after Bismarck had moved off, an open carriage with four French officers came past. One was 'as impassive and sphinxlike as ever, but with those lines drawn and deepened as if by some spasm' — it was the Emperor Louis Napoleon of France on his way to sign the French surrender. Forbes and the *Glasgow Herald* man were therefore the only civilians to see the surrender at the little weavers' cottage where the talks took place.

But, in his own words, Forbes was a journalistic tramp. He got his despatches through,

Archibald Forbes, war correspondent to the London Daily News. *At 45, he was to say, 'my nerve is gone and my physical energy but a memory'.*

but not in an organised fashion; his financial arrangements were always haphazard and, when he received a flesh wound in his leg which turned gangrenous (he continued working during this time, walking around with a sponge soaked in vinegar in his mouth which was supposed to act as an antiseptic but which must have somewhat restricted his interviewing), decided to return to England for treatment and a rethink.

Cured, and determined to create a more structured working life for himself, Forbes returned to the battlefront, and witnessed the fall of Paris. As usual, he had his fair share of adventures. Leaping onto the back of a half-starved horse in order to deliver a despatch to the nearest telegraph station, he was only mildly concerned when it collapsed beneath him. He got off, urged the beast to its feet and through the barricades, climbed back into the saddle and somehow made it walk and trot 32 km before he reached the telegraph station and sent his story.

On his return to London, with the news of the fall of Paris in his notebook, he found the *Morning Advertiser* less grateful than it should have been. Piqued, he offered the story to *The Times,* which told him to write it, and it would then decide whether to take it. Even more piqued, Forbes went to the *Daily News* and offered it the story. It took it unseen, snatching folios from him the moment the sheet was filled and coming out the next day with the first news of the fall of Paris. 'In those days,' Forbes recalled, 'I had the gift of writing like a whirlwind, and I always found that the faster I wrote the better I wrote.'

He was to cover many wars for the *Daily News,* but it was his experiences in the Zulu War of 1879 and, in particular, the Battle of Ulundi, which were to bring him his greatest (and final) fame. As a writer, he had great powers of description. He visited the battlefield of Isandhlwana months after the massacre, to find the dead still lying where they had fallen. His description of the field of battle is a haunting one. 'All the way up the slope I traced, by the ghastly token of dead

Archibald Forbes, 'the bold, unwearied, dauntless, solitary horseman, bloody with spurring, fiery red with haste,' as he was depicted on the front page of The Illustrated London News, *9 August 1879.*

men, the fitful line of a flight. It was like a long string with knots in it, the string formed by a single corpse, the knots of clusters were the dead where, as it seemed, little groups must have gathered to make a hopeless, gallant stand, and so die.'

Together with other correspondents, including the indomitable Melton Prior, war artist to *The Illustrated London News,* he was present when the body of the Prince Imperial of France, son of the man he had seen surrender in the weavers' cottage nine years before, was discovered in a donga. The day after the prince's body left camp for its long and slow journey down to Durban, and thence by sea to England, he set out for Ulundi, the Zulu king's great kraal, with Lord Chelmsford and his forces.

The logistics of Chelmsford's journey were formidable: by the time he was some 65 km from Ulundi, deep in the heart of Zululand, he had 10 000 soldiers, 700 wagons and 12 000 oxen — and the first Gatling gun to be fired in the field. It was imperative for Chelmsford, personally and professionally to bring the Zulu war to its conclusion: personally, because he wanted the credit and glory, and professionally, because his reputation had been blemished after the defeat at Isandhlwana and the death of the Prince Imperial while in his care.

He travelled with the usual retinue of war correspondents, the most prominent representing London newspapers. Apart from Forbes, there was Francis Francis of *The Times,* Melton Prior of *The Illustrated London News,* and, the greatest of them all, the man responsible for getting Forbes into both the army and journalism, William Howard Russell, now lamed for life and, inexplicably, after years on *The Times,* writing for *The Daily Telegraph.* The memorial to him in the crypt of St Paul's Cathedral states simply: 'The First and Greatest of War Correspondents'.

Severely restricted in their ability to send despatches from the middle of the bush, the main telegraph station at Landman's Drift receded ever further into the distance with each day and required a system of runners (or riders) to reach. Reports filed at this time were brief, and were amplified later. As it was, news did not usually reach London until three to four weeks later, telegraphed despatches being taken on board one of Her Majesty's ships bound for Britain and re-telegraphed to London at the first opportunity, which was the underwater cable at Madeira.

Camping on the Durban side of the White Umfolozi River, Chelmsford viewed Ulundi, only six kilometres distant. It was 3 July, and the day, as Forbes was to report in a brisk, unemotional and brief despatch, was not exactly uneventful, thanks to Redvers Buller and the Zulus.

> Camp, Umvoloosi River, July 3.
> The Zulus took no advantage of the grace granted to them until midday to-day. We until then remained supine on the hither bank. Soon after midday Colonel Buller took out his Irregular Horse on a reconnaissance, to support which guns were moved out in front of the camp. All the morning Zulu stragglers from the rocky hillock on the opposite side of the river were firing at us. One man was wounded. This hillock was shelled while Buller's men crossed to its right, lower down the stream, bent to the left, took the hillock in reverse, and chased the Zulus, who ran into a military kraal named Delanyo, shooting several. Sweeping round to the left of this kraal, and leaving a detachment to cover the retreat by holding the hillock in the rear, the horsemen galloped across the open towards a larger kraal named Nondjueno, about 200 Zulus retiring before them. No more were visible, and an easy success seemed awaiting Buller as he galloped by the Nondjueno kraal and headed straight on Ulundi, but a deep hollow intervened. The body he was pursuing was merely a decoy. Suddenly from a hollow sprang up a long line of Zulus, 2,000 strong, confronting him in front and flank. He held back, but frequently turned at bay. Meanwhile the whole plain had suddenly sprung into life. Quite 10,000 Zulus closed on his lines of

retreat, intent upon cutting him off. He made good his retreat, fighting all but hand to hand, with a loss of three wounded. Lord William Beresford greatly distinguished himself, killed Zulus with his sabre in single combat, and rescuing a wounded sergeant from under a heavy fire. I understand that Lord William Beresford will be recommended for the Victoria Cross. The Zulus were much elated by Buller's retreat. The whole force crosses the river tomorrow, intent upon penetrating to Ulundi. The 24th Regiment remains to garrison the laager. We shall probably fight our way in and out of Ulundi.

In spite of the confrontation, and in spite of peace overtures from a confused Cetshwayo — which included the return of the Prince Imperial's sword, brought by his attackers to Ulundi — Chelmsford committed himself to battle on the evening of 3 July. Determined to bring the Zulu forces to battle in the open, and thus prove that the disaster at Isandhlwana had not been the fault of ill-disciplined or ill-trained troops, but the fruit of bad deployment, Chelmsford decided to stand in the classic outward-facing square.

At daybreak on 4 July, more than 5 000 men, including the correspondents, crossed the Umfolozi River. Guarded by Lancers and Dragoons, they formed a huge red-coated square, with men standing four ranks deep. In the centre were 50 ox-wagons laden with supplies (which included ammunition boxes, the restraining bands which had proved such a hindrance at Isandhlwana six months before) well loosened. The huge square moved slowly forward onto the plain on which Ulundi stood, all 220 hectares of it, and, at a spot chosen the previous day, halted facing outwards.

'The Battle of Ulundi', 4 July 1879, by Melton Prior. The original was carried by Forbes on his epic ride to Landman's Drift and Pietermaritzburg, and printed by The Illustrated London News *one week before any other despatch or illustration reached Fleet Street.*

They could see the Zulus — some 20 000 strong — massing on the low rises, and moving towards them, their assegais drumming against their hardened war shields. Archibald Forbes had taken a £100 bet that morning that the troops would not be brought to battle: he was to lose his money.

Together with the other correspondents and Melton Prior with his sketching materials, Forbes was in the centre of the square. The cavalry, taunting the impis, drew the Zulus towards the square. Almost at the last moment it opened briefly to let them in, and then, with bayonets fixed, began firing on the hordes.

Prior, busy sketching and determined to provide *The Illustrated London News* with another of his scoops, noted Archibald Forbes striding around the enclosure, making notes and seemingly unperturbed either by the loss of his £100 or by the Martini-Henry bullets which flew overhead.

But the Zulus, although numerous, did not attack with the force they had used at Isandhlwana or Rorke's Drift. They had lost a lot of senior men in both battles and they were understandably apprehensive about their ability to carry the day against what was a visibly well-armed and disciplined force.

The battle lasted little over 30 minutes. When Chelmsford judged the time to be right, he ordered the Lancers and Dragoons to charge and, the square opening to let them out, cheered as they ran the fleeing Zulus down. Melton Prior, leaving the square with the other correspondent, paced the distance between the closest fallen Zulu to the British lines: he counted nine paces, although *The Daily Telegraph* stated that it was 28. By midday, all was over: the royal kraal was fired and the troops recrossed the Umfolozi to laager for the night. Chelmsford had broken the power of the Zulus.

The correspondents sat down to write their despatches. Chelmsford, too, sat down to write his despatch of the battle. The difficulty lay not in the writing, but in the delivery. Landman's Drift was now more than 160 km away through hostile country. Learning that Chelmsford did not intend sending out his despatch until the following day, Forbes realised that here was another opportunity for scoring one of his scoops.

He was an old war-horse by now, and not unaware of his own importance: 'To have held once and again in the hollow of my hand the exclusive power to thrill the nations; to have looked into the very heart of the turning points of nations and dynasties! What joy equal to the thrilling sense of personal force, as obstacle after obstacle fell behind one conquered, as one galloped from the battle with tidings our people awaited hungeringly and tremblingly!' he wrote. Allowing himself 30 minutes to make ready, Forbes told Prior that if he could finish his sketch in time, he would take it with him. He took personal messages from Chelmsford's staff but not, as *The Illustrated London News* was to claim, and Chelmsford indignantly to deny, official despatches from him to Wolseley. Promising to hand out information on the battle wherever appropriate, and with Prior's sketch safely packed, Forbes spurred his horse into the late afternoon of the Zululand thornveld.

By any standard, Forbes' ride was an astonishing feat of endurance and determination, and one of the most celebrated deliveries of a despatch in modern journalism. The country was swarming with hostile Zulus, few of whom would have heard, or cared, about the battle so recently lost. Four days earlier, following the same indistinct wagon track made by Chelmsford's men on their march to Ulundi, Lieutenant Scott-Douglas and Corporal Cotter, on their way to rejoin Chelmsford after sending a message from Mtonjaneni on his behalf, had lost their way and been killed.

Undeterred, and with only one lead-horse, Forbes galloped through the night, riding past burnt-out kraals and figures silhouetted against the dying flames of still-burning huts. He lost his way in the dark and the fog, but somehow managed to find his way back onto the track. He stopped briefly at Forts Evelyn and Newdigate to pass on the news and change his horses and crossed the Blood River at dawn. Before noon he was at Landman's Drift and, haggard with tiredness after his twenty-hour ride, had filed his story for the *Daily News,* in which it appeared on 26 July. A telegram only, it was brief and to the point — but it was news:

July 4.

At daybreak this morning the whole force was waiting for the order to advance again. Buller's Horse, to the front, crossed above and below the hillock, gained it, and found the country abandoned. The whole force passed the drift and through the bush clear of the Delanyo kraal. The formation consisted of a great square. The 80th formed the front; the 90th and 94th the left face; the 94th the rear; the 58th and 13th the right face. Inside, ready for action, were the Artillery, the Engineers, the Natives, &c. We had passed the Nondjueno kraal, and all was quiet as yet. The enemy was visible in one considerable straggling column moving parallel with us. Another was crowning and descending the eminence on the left rear, towards Nondjueno. Another was visible fitfully in various directions on our left. A fourth great mass was moving down on the right from Ulundi. It was impossible to tell how many lay in dongas on and about the direct front. Buller was continually stirring them up, and a brisk fire was exchanged. The Zulus began to close on us on all sides. The guns were moved out on their flanks and into action. Buller's Horse resisted as long as possible, and then galloped back into the square. In a short space of time the guns alone were in action; but, the Zulus coming on swiftly, the Infantry opened fire first, the closest on our right front. The artillery practice was beautiful, but it failed to daunt the Zulus, who rushed into the Nondjueno kraal, which had not been burnt, utilising the cover. Then men with white shields streamed with great daring against the right and rear of the square, where were two companies of the 21st, and two nine-pounders. The Zulus dashed with great bravery into close quarters amidst the deadly hail of the Martini bullets and volleys of canisters, and stubbornly assailed us on all four faces of our square, which stood like a rock. The whole affair was in a small compass, which made it seem more animated. The Zulus fired half Martini and half round and jagged bullets, which rent the air above our soldiers, who observed a stern purposeful silence. At the first shell fired, at 9.30, there rose a mighty cheer from the right flank and rear, the enemy giving way. A responding cheer came from the left; and then the front square opened to emit the Lancers and Buller's Horsemen, who burst like a torrent upon the broken enemy. The Lancers dashed towards the rear, caught a number of men in the long grass, and cut them down with their sabres and lances. Several officers of the Lancers killed four Zulus each. Two received assegai wounds. Captain Wyatt Edgell was killed, and two officers were slightly wounded. The British cavalry effectually vindicated its reputation. The enemy were driven widely distant. Their dead lay thick all round the square, most of them facing the 21st. I estimate that 400 Zulus lay dead. After a slight halt, the cavalry moved to the front and burnt Ulundi and the neighbouring military kraals. The whole force advanced close to Ulundi, and halted to eat. About two o'clock the force marched back to laager. The success of the day is unquestionable. Its bearing on the conclusion of peace is not clear. It is estimated that about 10,000 Zulus were engaged. Our loss was ten killed and about fifty wounded, exclusive of natives.

At Landman's Drift Forbes also took the time to write news of the Battle of Ulundi to both Sir Bartle Frere and Sir Garnet Wolseley. Frere despatched it to London, where it was read in both

7

the House of Commons and the House of Lords. It was, said *The Times,* 'a proud moment for the confraternity of special correspondents'.

Then the man, described by *The Illustrated London News* as 'the bold, unwearied, dauntless, solitary horseman, bloody with spurring, fiery red with haste,' set out for Pietermaritzburg, to catch the post for Melton Prior. When he reached there, 50 hours after he had left the White Umfolozi, his clothes were in tatters, and he was exhausted almost beyond caring.

The English press hailed his astonishing ride as the 'Ride of Death', and it was suggested that Forbes be awarded a Victoria Cross. (He was not entitled to one, being a civilian.) 'If he cannot have the Victoria Cross . . . let him have the Order of St Michael and St George, which is usually bestowed on civilians for services rendered in any of the British colonies or foreign possessions,' wrote *The Illustrated London News,* which had cause to be grateful, having run Prior's sketch of the battle a full week before anyone else.

But Forbes was to receive no decoration. He was also not to write anything spectacular again. He died quietly in London in 1900, and a tablet with a medallion portrait of him was placed in the crypt of St Paul's Cathedral. His ride and his achievements, if not unique among the loosely-fashioned brotherhood of journalists, was at least extraordinary and worthy of honour.

He was 'The Nilghai, the chiefest, as he was the hugest, of the war correspondents,' wrote Kipling. 'And his experience dated from the birth of the needle-gun . . . there was no man mightier in the craft than he, and he always opened the conversation with the news that there would be trouble in the Balkans in the spring.'

Introduction

It is appropriate that the real history of journalism (and journalists) in South Africa should begin with *The South African Commercial Advertiser,* founded in Cape Town on 7 January 1824 by an English emigrant printer, George Greig.

The South African Commercial Advertiser, hailed to this day as the newspaper which fought for the right to print news which it deemed the populace had the right to read, was not the first newspaper to be published in this country — but it was the first independent newspaper to be printed free of the restraining shackles of government intervention.

The first paper to be published in South Africa was *The Cape Town Gazette and African Advertiser,* published in Cape Town on 16 August 1800 by Messrs Walker and Robertson on a

small press established on 1 February 1800 at 35 Plein Street. From the paper's inception, following a petition to the Governor of the Cape Colony, Sir George Yonge, no political news of any kind was permitted to appear on its pages, which became a cheerful mélange of shipping reports and parochial social events interspersed with advertisements.

Even that was an achievement. The need for a printing press, let alone a newspaper, had been sorely evident in the colony. Unsuccessful requests for the importation of a press had been made to the Dutch authorities in Amsterdam in 1783 and 1786. The first press to operate commercially in South Africa was run by Johan Christian Ritter, who obtained a wooden press by devious means and who printed 'trifles', such as almanacs, handbills and advertisements until Walker and Robertson petitioned the Governor for permission to start a newspaper.

Even under the more liberal rule of the British, the right to publish anything purporting to be news was non-existent. Within eight months of the launch of *The Cape Town Gazette and African Advertiser,* the sole right of printing was vested, not with an independent newspaper, but in the government of the colony, and the *Gazette* was henceforth printed from the Castle. In 1826, two years after the founding of *The South African Commercial Advertiser* and the advent of press freedom (which came in 1829 with the publication of Ordinance 60 of 1829, South African newspapers' Magna Carta), the *Gazette*'s title changed to the *Cape of Good Hope Government Gazette.* It was the forerunner of today's *Government Gazette.*

Thus, the story of newspapers, however lightly touched upon in this book, and the despatches printed in them, begins, and rightly so, with the pioneering *The South African Commercial Advertiser.* Archibald Forbes and his magnificent ride were a long way in the future.

'So, Sir, you are one of those who dare to insult me and oppose my government!' (Lord Charles Somerset)

The first press censorship, 1824

Little did Thomas Pringle know when he arrived at Algoa Bay, South Africa, on 15 May 1820, that within four years he would not only have clashed violently with the Governor of the Cape, Lord Charles Somerset, but would also have laid the foundations for the freedom of the press in this country.

A Whig, a poet and a Scot, not necessarily in that order, Pringle quickly established a reputation for himself as an independent-minded man of letters. Of gentle but stubborn persuasion, he wrote to fellow Scot John Fairbairn, suggesting he too emigrate to South Africa. There, said Pringle, the two of them would set up in business together to run a teaching academy — schools and education in general being in woefully short supply in Cape Town. (By this time Pringle had moved to Cape Town, his efforts at farming at Baviaansrivier having been unsuccessful.)

Fairbairn, who was politically ambitious and who later became leader of the Lower House, arrived in Cape Town in 1823. So too did the doughty George Greig, an immigrant with a printing background. Shortly after his arrival, Greig set up shop in Longmarket Street, Cape Town and printed and published South Africa's first independent newspaper from his premises on 7 January 1824 on a wooden press loaned by the London Missionary Society.

While it cannot be said that the first issue of *The South African Commercial Advertiser,* a full eight pages and carrying advertisements in English and Dutch, contained articles of outstanding literary merit, there were some quaint pieces. (One advertisement under a Private Sale heading, offered a property watered by the Liesbeeck River, with 63 000 vines, together with 'Some Male and Female Slaves used to House Work and Field Labour').

With a shrewd understanding of subliminal advertising, Greig inserted 'The Paper', a mercifully brief poem, between an article dealing with 'The Surprise of the Trocadero — The Submission of Cadiz &c', and another poem, written under the pseudonym 'Timothy Torrid', on page four.

11

THE SOUTH AFRICAN COMMERCIAL

A D V E R T I S E R.

No. I.   WEDNESDAY, JANUARY 7, 1824.   Terms—4 Rds. per Quarter—16 Rds. per Ann.; or 3 Sks. the Single Number

THAT this, the *First Attempt* to establish a Medium of general Communication at the CAPE OF GOOD HOPE, should take place at the opening of a fresh season—at a time when the mind is naturally disposed to look forward with hope, that the events of the succeeding year may atone for the disappointment of the last—we cannot but think an auspicious circumstance: and, as the gradual influence of the genial Seasons rears and protects the rising blossom until the full fruit is matured—so we cannot but hope, that the Patronage of our fellow-Subjects will attend our progress, and finally crown our efforts with that reward which alone will compensate our labours—the confidence and approbation of a discerning public.

IT is the privilege of reason to view the scene of life with all its events, not merely in the light which the moment of their actual occurrence may shed upon them, but with the eye of retrospect to what has passed, and of caution for what is to come; and, surely, if there be a time more favourable than another, at which a reasonable being would feel disposed to look back with reflection on the past, it must be at the commencement of a new season, when another year has been spared to his existence, another period added to that account which he must sooner or later be called upon to render.

THE last year has been an eventful one. Our late allies, the Spaniards, have been exposed to the inroad of foreign troops; which, without entering into the discussion of a political question, we are not so destitute of British feelings as to hesitate in designating a gross violation of a people's dearest right—that of regulating their own mode of Government. The troops of France are still in the field, and the Continental nations are more or less agitated by this state of affairs: and, while we cannot but express our abhorrence of the principles which led to this disgraceful invasion, we fervently hope that peace and tranquillity will eventually be restored.

AMID these scenes of trouble and disquiet, how stands our native Land? Happy, thrice happy, do we feel whilst enabled to state, that, by the manly prudence and cautious forbearance of her councils, she keeps aloof from the dissensions which pervade the Cabinets of her neighbours, and nobly refuses to enter into a contest with which she has no right to interfere. Britain values too highly the blessings of her own constitution to deny to other states the liberty of making their own laws; and, while she disdains to listen to the cant of disaffection and anarchy, knows too well the value of a Representative Government to prevent any nation from lawfully striving to obtain it. What may be the result of the scenes now exhibited in Spain, or how rightfully the forces of France may have been employed in entering that ill-fated country, we shall not stop to inquire: but we do wish our fellow-subjects to turn their attention to their native land, and ask themselves, whether they have not reason to be thankful for the blessings of the past year, and whether the peace and prosperity which Great Britain enjoys, do not afford a pleasing contrast to the turbulent scenes we have alluded to.

PROTECTED by the invaluable ramparts of her unrivalled Constitution, and guided by Councils of justice and moderation, Great Britain has added another year of peace and gradual prosperity to that long period of tranquillity with which we hope the Almighty Ruler of Events will crown the efforts she has made for the protection of the Rights and Liberties of herself and her Confederates.

DURING the last year, in consequence of retrenchments not more forcibly recommended in her Parliament, than more readily adopted by her Ministers, the expenditure of the nation has been reduced within its income; and we have now the cheering prospect of lessening the debt, incurred in the preservation of all that is dear to us, by gradual Instalments, which whilst they may imperceptibly abate the pressure of the Interest, will not distress the Country by too suddenly withdrawing from circulation a species of property which has become essential to its existence.

IF our Gazettes no longer teem with the news of victory, still we have ample reason to rejoice in the intelligence which reaches us of the general diffusion of knowledge—especially of that which surpasses human invention—the knowledge of the Revealed Religion of CHRIST in all parts of the World: nor can we cease to rejoice, when we perceive the British flag, which heretofore waved the signal of victory wherever it was unfurled, now

The front page of South Africa's first independent newspaper, The South African Commercial Advertiser. *Printed and published by George Greig, it was edited by Thomas Pringle and John Fairbairn.*

THE PAPER

In gown and slippers loosely drest,
And breakfast brought, a welcome guest;
What is it gives the meal a zest?

> The Paper.

When new-laid eggs the table grace,
And smoking rolls are in their place,
Say what enlivens evr'y face?

> The Paper.

In vain the urn is hissing hot,
In vain rich Hyson stores the pot,
If the vile Newsman has forgot.

> The Paper.

What is't attracts the optic pow'rs
Of Ensign gay, when fortune show'rs
Down prospects of "a step" in "ours"

> The Paper.

What is't can make the man of law
Neglect the deed or plea to draw,
Ca.Sa—Fi.Fa.—Indictment, Flaw?

> The Paper.

What is't can sooth his Client's woe,
And make him quite forget John Doe,
Nor think on Mister Richard Roe?

> The Paper.

What is't informs the country round,
What's stol'n or stray'd, what's lost or found,
Who's born, and who's put under ground?

> The Paper.

What tell's you all that's done and said,
The fall of beer and rise of bread,
And what fair lady's brought to bed?

> The Paper.

What is't narrates full many a story,
Of Mr. Speaker, Whig, and Tory,
And heroes all agog for glory?

> The Paper.

What is it gives the price of Stocks,
Of Poyais Loans, and patent locks,
And Cape Wine at West India Docks?

              The Paper.

Abroad, at home, infirm or stout,
In health, or raving with the gout,
Who possibly can do without

              The Paper.

Its worth and merits then revere,
And since it now begins the year,
Forget not 'midst your Christmas cheer,
Nor think you e'er can buy too dear

              The Paper.

Apart from extracts lifted from *The Observer of London,* the nearest thing approaching a news report was an article written by Mr Thompson, of the firm Cooke and Thompson. On an up-country visit to John Moffatt, the missionary, Thompson observed a general assembly of the tribes making up the Bechuana nation, which was called together at Kuruman to meet the threat of the advancing Mantatees. Thompson's first-hand report, his idiosyncratic spelling, notwithstanding, makes good copy, but its effect was somewhat blunted by its being broken off abruptly with the note: '(Press of Matter obliges us to defer the remainder of this article till our next.)'.

"At Sun-rise, thousands of the Warriors assembled, and the War-hoops was mingled with the discordant cries of the women and children; after which the Warriors formed into parties, and retired to the outskirts of the town, where they appeared to discuss the object of the assembly; they then advanced to the place of meeting, accompanying their march with the War Song and Dance, and occasionally exhibiting their dexterity in sham fighting.

Before ten o'Clock, the whole of the Population were assembled in a Kraal, in the centre of the town, appropriated to such meetings. It formed a circle of about 150 yards in diameter: on the one side were seated the old men, women, and children; and on the other the Warriors, bearing before them a shield, the handle of which was well stored with hassagais, and on their shoulders a quiver full of poisoned arrows, a bow, and a battle-axe; from their backs hung the tails of Tigers, and plumes of Feathers waved in their Heads.

In the centre a sufficient space was left for the Privileged (those who have killed an enemy in battle) to dance and sing, in which they exhibited more violent and fantastic gestures that can be easily imagined, but which drew forth clamarous applaus from the surrounding spectators.

After about an hour had been spent in these exercises, 'Mateebe', commanding silence, proceeded to his stand in front of the centre of the Warriors, and, taking a Hassagai from his shield, pointed it towards the North-east (the quarter whence the 'Mantatees' were advancing), imprecating a curse upon them, and declaring war, by repeatedly advancing his Hassagai in that direction, as if in the act of plunging it into an enemy; — this was repeated by the warriors, who joined in a loud whistle, in token of approval. He then turned his Hassagai to the South and South-west, imprecating a curse on the Ox-Eaters (Bushmen), and, having repeated his warlike gestures, he returned the

14

Hassagai to its place, and calling each tribe by its name — which was answered by each with a low hollow groan, indicating attention — he addressed the whole to the following effect."

John Fairbairn (Cape Archives)

Sensing that a newspaper is no place for amateurs, Greig wisely decided to put the editorship and management of *The South African Commercial Advertiser* into professional hands, and called in the services of Pringle and Fairbairn. Pringle was already involved in editing his own magazine, *The South African Journal,* whilst Fairbairn, together with 'a copy of Euclid, some of Gray's Arithmetic, a few of the more elementary books in Geography, French, Latin and Greek', requested by Pringle before he joined him in Cape Town, was involved with the Classical and Commercial Academy they had jointly founded in December 1823. Both men were to become famous for their efforts to obtain a modicum of press freedom in South Africa.

They were to edit the newspaper from its second issue to its eighteenth, and last issue, with a sturdy independence and pride in their work, which did not promote the relationship the paper had with the government of the day.

Under the dictatorial High Tory hand of Lord Charles Somerset, the then Governor, any publication operating with a semblance of independence was suspect. Both Pringle and Fairbairn knew full well that they had to be careful with their editorial content, and avoided controversial subjects such as personality interviews, slavery and, for some reason, Maoris. They did, however, report on law cases, and came to grief on one involving William Edwards, an attorney, and the government, the report of which the Governor insisted be suppressed.

Somerset was determined that the government would remain, in the eyes of the public at any rate, in a good light, and insisted either that Greig deposit security of 10 000 rix-dollars lest he should publish anything untoward, or that *The South African Commercial Advertiser* be submitted to censorship prior to publication.

The eighteenth issue, published on Wednesday 5 May, almost four months after the paper's first issue, carried a strap line immediately below the headline, quoting Dr Johnson: 'The mass of every People must be barbarous where there is no printing.' Its first report, on the front page, written at 01h00 that day, told the public that the paper had been brought out under conditions amounting to censorship — but that nothing in the paper had been altered.

POSTSCRIPT. WEDNESDAY MORNING, One o'Clock.

HIS MAJESTY'S FISCAL having assumed the CENSORSHIP of *"The South African Commercial Advertiser,"* by an Official Order, sent to the Printing Office, by a Messenger

15

late in the evening before Publication, Demanding *Proof Sheets* of the Paper for next day [this day] and prohibiting its being struck off "till we had received his further directions thereon" — we find it our duty, as BRITISH SUBJECTS, under these circumstances, to discontinue the Publication of the said Paper *for the present* in this Colony, until we have applied for redress and direction to His Excellency the Governor, and the British Government.

Our numerous Subscribers will, we trust, require no farther explanation at present of this distressing interruption. They, and the rest of the world, shall be speedily put in possession of a full statement of all the facts: — one of which is a demand from the Fiscal of Two Securities, on or before Friday next, to become bound under a penalty of TEN THOUSAND RIX-DOLLARS, that nothing offensive shall appear in any future Number — such as Extracts from the experienced work of the Civil Servant, a work PUBLISHED in this Colony, this year, by W.W. BIRD, Esq. *Comptroller of Customs,* and *Assessor of the Court of Appeals.*

We will only mention further, at present, that not a word of this our last Number has been written or altered in consequence of the above-mentioned transaction, excepting this Notice.

The Business of the Commercial Printing Office will be carried on as usual.

Nonetheless, it was not a situation which could be tolerated by the three principals. The forthright Greig gave notice to the governor that the paper would cease publication until he had had a ruling from the British government. This did not endear him to Somerset, who was further incensed when Greig impertinently printed a four-page paper, 'FACTS Connected with the STOPPING of the *SOUTH AFRICAN COMMERCIAL ADVERTISER',* which carried the correspondence between the two parties and which did not greatly redound to the government's credit.

Somerset's response was to give Greig one month to leave the colony. He also seized his presses in case he should try to continue printing.

Pringle's magazine was next to fall foul of Somerset. 'I found him,' he wrote later, 'with the Chief Justice, Sir John Truter, seated on his right hand, and the second number of our *South African Journal* lying open before him. There was a storm on his brow, and it burst forth at once upon me like a long-gathered South-Easter from Table Mountain. "So Sir!" he began "you are one of those who dare to insult me, and oppose my government!" and then launched forth into a long tirade of abuse . . .'

Pringle's magazine was also forced to cease publication, but he petitioned the Crown to grant the right of establishing a free press

Thomas Pringle (Africana Museum)

in the colony, an objective which was finally achieved in July 1828 when John Fairbairn returned from London with the freedom of the South African press guaranteed by the British government.

Thomas Pringle moved to London, where he continued his work with emancipation in its broad sense, working for the Anti-Slavery Society and editing small publications. He died in London on 5 December 1835, much mourned by Fairbairn. On the anniversary of his death in 1970, Pringle then returned to the Cape in a lead coffin and was reinterred by his descendants in a church on the family farm near Bedford, in the Cape Province.

Fairbairn outlived Pringle by nearly thirty years, dying in Cape Town on 5 October 1864, a noted politician, editor and educationalist.

'The outraged feelings of a community'

The Anti-Convict Association, 1849—1850

On a chill, rainy 4 July 1849, in front of the Commercial Exchange building in the Heerengracht, Cape Town, 7 000 people stood for seven hours listening to a series of speakers expounding on the convict problem.

It was indeed a problem: from 1841 on, the British government had been stating its intention of sending convicts to the Cape Colony. The citizens of Cape Town had mounted a remarkably vigorous protest campaign. Appalled at the prospect of what would happen if shiploads of convicts were to make their eventual homes on Cape soil, a committee of the Commercial Exchange met on 10 May 1849 to see what could be done 'in view of Earl Grey's continued determination to make this Colony a penal settlement'. On 31 May, 38 of Cape Town's leading commercial men formed the Anti-Convict Association. The association was to dominate life not only in Cape Town, but in the rest of the colony until the February of the following year.

Its first step was to launch a campaign, abetted through the medium of John Fairbairn's

The Thomas Bowler painting of the great anti-convict meeting held in front of the Commercial Exchange, Cape Town. To the right is what is now Adderley Street. (Cape Archives E4169)

newspaper, persuading people to boycott any ship arriving in the colony with felons on board, and to refuse to house, feed or clothe the convicts or the crew. So powerful was the association's campaign, that people refusing to sign the pledge (a verbal promise to abide by its rules was not enough) were ostracised, banks and businesses refusing to do business with them, shopkeepers refusing to serve them for fear of being boycotted themselves, and, in some cases, suffering physical violence at the hands of a singularly united populace.

It did not matter that the convicts were, for the most part, convicts in name only: most were Irishmen captured after the 1848 'potato-patch rebellion'. 'There is nothing in the papers from beginning to end but about convicts,' wrote Sir Theopholus Shepstone sourly in October 1849.

The Governor of the Cape, Sir Harry Smith (who bore with equanimity his nickname, 'Hurry-along-wackalong-smite'), tried to calm the bristly and militant colonists, and assured them that their views would be put to the Secretary of State for the Colonies, Earl Grey. Moreover, he personally undertook to ensure that until the earl had given a ruling on the situation, no convict would be landed at the Cape. The colonists nonetheless continued their protest campaign.

The press, always pleased to bring sacred idols down a peg or two, had a field-day during the campaign, at its height from July 1849 to late February 1850, and reported events with gusto.

The bilingual (English-Dutch) *De Zuid Afrikaan* carried the following emotional report on 12 July 1849:

A report having gone abroad that Messrs Letterstedt, Cloete and De Smidt had refused to accept the seats offered to them, in deference to the popular wish, the very large concourse of people present on the above occasion, were not a little staggered and indignant at their appearance to take the usual oath and assume their seats; the consequence of which was, that prior to and at the conclusion of the sitting they were thoroughly and continually hissed.

On the announcement of an adjournment, the audience withdrew and gathered in the yard, in front of the Council Room, where, after a short while, his Excellency the Governor made his appearance, leaning on the arm of his aide-de-Camp, followed by some other gentlemen, amongst whom were the new unofficial creatures. His Excellency saluted the crowd by 'how are you all gentlemen? I am glad to see you; my heart is with you. Depend upon it that in all my measures I aim at your welfare.' This called forth a universal shout of approbation, but was at the same time the signal for renewed hisses, cries and shouts, attended by general shoving, thumping and kicking of the three new officials. Laurence Cloete made his escape, after being rather roughly handled about the posteriors. Abraham de Smidt took shelter in the office of the Central Road Board, and Jacob Letterstedt in the Council Room. After the latter had remained here for a considerable time, he was attended to the street door by the Attorney General, and accompanied to his offices in Plein Street by Messrs. Lynar and Fitzpatrick. A very large crowd followed him, and he was incessantly hissed and hooted, and thrown with mud and other missiles. From hence a few persons proceeded to the Heerengracht, and accidentally meeting Mr Ebden, they immediately stopped and three loud and long cheers at once collected a crowd of about 2000 persons. They now proceeded down the Heerengracht, and when arrived at Mr Robertson's, a Chair was procured upon which Mr Ebden was put and carried to the Commercial Hall where he was placed on the table. The cheers now were most deafening. Silence was at length procured, and after the spectators had been addressed by Mr Ebden, Sr., Mr Sutherland and Mr Adv. Ebden, the crowd separated, after having again and again cheered the worthy patriot, for his manly resolve to resign his situation, and thus cutting off all connexion with a Government incapable to protect its own honor.

* * * *

At an early hour in the evening a vast number of people assembled on the Grand Parade, and publicly burnt a figure destined to represent Abraham de Smidt, amidst groans and imprecations; they then separated, but again assembled about 8 o'Clock, when the process of burning two figures representing Lawrence Cloete and Jacob Letterstedt was resumed. They then proceeded to the town residence of Abraham de Smidt, in Hottentot's square, to the Stores of Jacob Letterstedt in Ziske-street, his house in the Heerengracht, and his mill near the North Jetty, the glasses and windows of every one of which were successively smashed, in fact such was the thorough battering at the mill, that even the cast iron frames were broken.

At Letterstedt's stores in Zieke-street the whole of the police force interfered. But the manner in which this interference took place is, we say with tenfold emphasis, the most disreputable act of cowardice and shame imaginable, and should not be allowed to rest here. The force came down Shortmarket-street, and just as they reached the corner of Zieke-street, without any warning or admonition, without the Riot Act being read, — the word was at once given to 'charge' and the crowd assailed by a host of staves and drawn swords. The consequence was, that several people, inoffensive people, who either stood at a distance, or had occasion to pass that way, were shamefully cut and wounded, some even dangerously.

Feelings continued to run high. In the same issue of *De Zuid Afrikaan* (kindly referred to in *The African Journal* as 'that "Dutch drop" in the Literary Ocean — that chronicler of small beer and sheep's tail fat'), correspondents sent in commendably brief despatches, mostly from the Cape Town area, in which the brevity is outweighed only by the obvious pleasure in reporting (and publishing) the events:

Mr Abraham de Smidt, we have this from himself, is no longer an *honourable;* he had not been twenty-four hours in possession of the title, when he resigned it, *in deference to the feeling of the public.*

Will his *honourable* example be followed up by Messrs Letterstedt, Cloete and Cock, or do they intend to defy the public feeling and maintain their offensive position? We trust a little reflection will bring them to their senses.

We have been informed that the Municipality, indignant at the conduct of Mr de Smidt, has at once paid off to him a debt of £1500.

* * * *

Since writing the above we have been informed on the best authority that Mr Letterstedt has resolved to send in his resignation this morning.

* * * *

The following is said to be a speech delivered by Mr. Hendrik Cloete, at Sir John Wylde's ball, on Tuesday Evening last, (addressing Lady Smith,) 'I will never leave de Governor. I will be firm to de Governor. When people take dis body and cut off dis head, and de blood goes over Lady Smith, den I will resign my seat in Council, and leave de Governor.' It need scarcely be said that this speech was loudly cheered by all who heard it, as being excessively loyal and patriotic.

* * * *

A Correspondent informs us that Mr. Cock is in a fix, as the directors of the Phoenix will not take him back to Algoa Bay. The Governor considered, as he said in Council, that the Phoenix did good work in bringing Mr. Cock to his assistance. She is going to improve her work, by leaving him on the Governor's hands.

* * * *

Two great Public Meetings against the introduction of Convicts, have been held on the Frontier, on the 4th instant, — one at Graham's Town, the other at Port Elizabeth.

The Dutch Border Farmers will hold an Anti-Convict Meeting at the Kaga, on Wednesday the 18th instant.

* * * *

Sir Harry appears to be equally perplexed and wavering as his master, my lord Grey, with regard to the Convict question. Every now and then he hits on some other plan. At first the valuable cargo was destined for Amsterdam Battery; subsequently it was Robben Island; and of last it is to be transferred to the Ship Seriagapatash.

Feelings were running high throughout the Colony. John Fairbairn, in his position as editor of *The South African Commercial Advertiser,* was a staunch advocate of the Anti-Convict Association (of which he was a member). His particular contribution to the cause was to publish the names of people, particularly those with businesses, who did not support the association.

On 19 September 1849, the *Neptune,* with 300 'ticket-of-leave' convicts on board, cast anchor off Simonstown. In spite of the good records of the convicts — some of whom, in spite of their personal dilemmas, were supportive of the colonists' stance against British authority — public feeling was such that the Cape Town municipality despatched four of its most prominent citizens to Simonstown to ensure that no one from the ship disembarked. To add to the drama, all church bells and fire alarms were rung at daybreak the following morning.

From 19 September 1849 to 21 February 1850, the *Neptune* lay isolated in Simon's Bay. Sir Harry Smith kept his word that, until he had heard from the Secretary of State for the colonies, Earl Grey, on the colony's vehement opposition to the landing of convicts, no one would be landed. Grey acceded to the wishes of the citizens and instructed the *Neptune* to sail for Tasmania. Barely believing their success, the citizens of Cape Town indulged in a positive frenzy of self-congratulation and celebration.

'Helpless as logs of timber'

The Great Gale of 1865, Cape Town

'There is a lurid light in the sky on my left, a reflection of the fire they have kindled on Green Point . . . the sky is black, the wind blowing with greater freshness than ever. How terrible is the sea!' wrote *The Eastern Province Herald*'s correspondent on 17 May 1865.

The Great Gale of 17 and 18 May hit Cape Town with unprecedented ferocity. With no breakwater, the harbour was prey to a violent north-wester which had been preceded by weeks of unseasonally dry and warm weather.

The harbour was studded with ships, some steam-driven, but mostly sail. *The Argus'* report, unlike the highly colourful despatch published in *The Eastern Province Herald,* was business-like but descriptive. Written and updated throughout the day as the wind blew and the number of shipwrecks steadily increased, the story was complete at 21h00. Comprehensive though it was, it did not include the most dramatic story of all — the loss of the Union Line Royal Mail steamer, *Athens,* with all hands on board.

TERRIFIC GALE IN TABLE BAY.
Seventeen Ocean-going Vessels Wrecked.
NINE MEN DROWNED.
GREAT DESTRUCTION OF CUTTERS AND BOATS.

Yesterday, Table Bay was visited by one of the most severe gales from the north-west which has been known for many years, and in the course of the day no fewer than seventeen ocean-going vessels were wrecked, and nine gallant boatmen met with watery graves in addition to which it is estimated that no less than thirty cutters and boats have been stranded. While we write, the storm has not abated, and it is questionable whether the night will close without additional disasters. The beach beyond the Castle presents a mournful spectacle. The waves, which come rolling in in immense volume, break upon the wrecked vessels, causing them to pitch and grind with fearful violence. The wind blows with unusual force, while the rain which descends every few minutes in torrents adds to the desolation around. Some of the stranded ships, with their forward sails set, stand perfectly upright, and would almost appear to be sailing into harbour, while others again, which have taken the beach broadside on, are drenched by the green seas which wash over them. Others, again, have lost masts and bowsprits, and are helpless as logs of timber. As far as can be ascertained at present, we believe that most of the stranded ships are on the sands, so that no danger of their breaking up need be anticipated for the

22

present, and as communication by means of ropes has been established with all, the people on board may be considered as being in comparative safety.

We must, however, endeavour to give our readers some account of yesterday's storm. Up to Monday last the weather had been unusually warm for the season, and fears were entertained that the continued absence of rain would tell with a damaging effect on the country. On Monday, however, the wind blew strongly from the westward, and in the evening heavy rains fell. Tuesday also was showery, with the wind still blowing from the same direction as on the previous day, but in the course of the night a change took place and a gale commenced from the north-west. By daylight yesterday a tremendously heavy sea was setting in, while the wind came down in terrific gusts, and the vessels anchored in the bay rolled and pitched with great violence. As soon as there was sufficient light for the purpose, a signal was made from the Port Office, directing the vessels in harbour to strike topgallant masts, and to point yards to the wind. As daylight increased several cargo-boats put off with anchors, and two or three vessels, which had parted, were supplied with extra holding gear. At half-past eight an anchor was run to the brig *Esther*. The sea, however, continued to rise, and many of the larger boats which were at their moorings parted, and were driven on shore. Between nine and ten o'clock one of these was observed to be adrift, when one of the Water Police, a young man named Charles Bryce, who had gone on board the police boat near the North Wharf, for the purpose of throwing out the ballast, conceived the idea of going to her assistance. With this view he got into a dingy, and pushed off, but before reaching the cargo-boat, the dingy was

Some of the wrecked ships after the great gale of 1865. The site of the photograph is today's Duncan Docks, the lion-headed gateposts leading into Victoria Base (Cape Archives E8007).

23

capsized, and the unfortunate fellow was thrown out. The accident was witnessed by some hundreds of people, and an attempt was at once made to render him assistance; it was seen that he had struck out manfully and was making for the Central Causeway, but owing to his being burdened with his oilskin his progress was slow. Efforts were made to launch a fishing-boat from the front of the Sailors' Home, but it was discovered that no oars were to be obtained. In the mean time a couple of life-buoys were procured from the Port Office, and were conveyed to the end of the Causeway, and a gallant fellow named, Maderosse, stripped himself and plunged into the waves from the beach. Most gallantly did he breast the waves, dipping his head on the approach of the breakers, and when he had accomplished about one fourth of the distance from the beach to the point at which the drowning man was struggling, the people on the shore saw the latter go down. He had battled hard for life, but was at length overcome and perished within sight of hundreds anxious to render him assistance.

Shortly after this, the cargo-boat *Stag,* which was off with an anchor, was capsized while in the act of going about and it is feared that out of a crew of nine men two only were saved. The accident happened not far from the steamer *Dane,* and it was seen from the shore that the life-boat of the steamer was at once lowered and put off. She was however, upset, and it was feared that a loss of life would have resulted from this cause. The boat was afterwards righted, and was seen to be pulling about for a considerable time, and on her return to the steamer, and in reply to a signal from the shore, she replied "all right." It is hoped from this that the remainder of the crew of the *Stag* have been saved; two of them having in the mean time been picked up by another anchor-boat. About eleven o'clock, the brig *Galatea* parted, and commenced drifting towards the beach. The life-boat, under the command of Assistant Port Captain Jackson, put off to her, and gave such instructions as led to her being put in a favourable position on the sandy shore beyond the Castle. The life-boat then proceeded to the brig *Jane,* which had shown signals of distress, and having taken the crew out of her landed them on the beach, where the life-boat was hauled up. The *Galatea* was shortly joined by the brig *Jane* and the cutter *Gem,* and before two o'clock five other vessels were on shore; they were the bark *Star of the West,* the schooner *Fernande,* the schooner *Clipper* (the latter having dragged her anchors), and the bark *Frederick Bassil.* About two o'clock, the barks *Alacrity* and *Deane* also parted and drifted down upon the steamer *Dane.* The former carried away the steamer's boat, and the latter her jib boom, losing her own top-mast, and sustaining other injuries. Both vessels then drifted helplessly down upon the beach. Later still they were followed by the bark *Royal Arthur,* which took the ground near the south wharf, and she again was followed by the brig *Kehrweider.* The wind was still falling and the barometer is on the rise. At noon the mercury stood at 29.48, at three at 29.49 while it has now reached 29.51. The prospect is not as bad as it was an hour or two since.

9 o'clock p.m.

The wind has freshened somewhat, and the swell is tremendous. Another vessel, supposed to be the brig *Esther,* has parted. The night is intensely dark, and huge bonfires have been lit upon the beach, as some guide to vessels which may still part. It is rumoured that the mail steamer *Athens* is on the rocks at Sea Point. The rain is falling in torrents: *The City of Peterborough* is said to be breaking up.

*   *   *   *

The *Athens* and her sister ship, *Briton,* both under 1 000 tons, were at anchor in Table Bay when the north-wester struck. For some hours the *Athens* held fast but the wind and huge seas finally dragged the anchor. Captain Smith could see the fate which awaited vessels driven ashore and, determined not to have a wreck on his hands (he was due to sail the following day for Mauritius with the 'overland' mail for the United Kingdom), Smith decided to take his ship out to sea and, if possible, make for Simon's Town.

As light began to fade, the *Athens* headed out to sea. Just past Mouille Point she was over-whelmed by enormous seas and wind, and water poured in through the skylights, extinguishing the fires in the engine room and effectively putting the vessel out of control. She was swept towards Green Point. *The Cape Argus* reported:

7 o'clock p.m.

The mail steamer *Athens* is now attempting to steam out. She had previously parted and signalized that her last anchor was gone. From some lights which are now seen in the bay, it is believed that she has failed in her efforts to round the point.

One hour later the news was confirmed: the *Athens* was ashore.

LATEST INTELLIGENCE. WRECK OF THE STEAMER 'ATHENS', AND SUPPOSED LOSS OF ALL HANDS.

10 o'clock p.m.

At five minutes to eight, a messenger arrived in hot haste at the Cape Town Police Station with information that a vessel, supposed to be the steamer *Athens,* was on shore at Green Point, and that loud cries were heard on shore coming from on board for assistance. Sub-Inspector Evans at once proceeded on horseback to the spot where the wreck was lying, between the two lighthouses, and found a crowd of Green Point residents assembled, with lights, ropes, and life-buoys for the purpose, if possible, of rendering assistance, but quite unable to do so. The ship was lying sixty or eighty yards from the shore, grinding heavily on the rocks with every sea, and evidently fast breaking up, for pillow cases and cabin doors were washing ashore, so as to leave no doubt that the wreck was complete. No dead bodies could, however, be found on the beach but in the face of the tremendous seas and the boiling surf, it appeared impossible that any single one of the unfortunate people on board could reach the shore alive. It was supposed that the hands had taken to the shrouds, but the darkness was too intense to allow them to be seen. Occasionally, however, as the heavy sea struck the ill-fated vessel, loud wails of anguish were heard proceeding from it, and the effect upon the crowds of spectators was terrible.

Mr. Evans sent for Capt. Wilson, Port Captain, but that gentleman was not at home, and if he had been, he would not probably have been able to render any efficient aid. No boat could live in such a surf, and it would have been barely possible to draw the crew ashore by means of life lines.

That the vessel is the *Athens* there can be no doubt. She steamed out of the bay when her anchors parted about six o'clock, and the pillow cases washed ashore, were marked with the initials "U.S.S.C."

The *Athens* carried about thirty hands, including Captain Smith and officers. She was to have sailed for Mauritius yesterday, and some fear is entertained that part of her

25

passengers embarked on Tuesday. This, however, is hardly likely to have been the case, and embarkation yesterday was impossible.

The storm still rages with unabated violence; and the probability is that at daylight not a vestige of the *Athens* will be left above water.

11 p.m.

We have since learned that the steamer has entirely broken up, and that not one of her crew has come ashore either alive or dead. The wind continues to blow fiercely.

The following day the report on the fate of the *Athens* was further amplified by *The Eastern Province Herald*'s correspondent, who spent much of the gale watching from the warm comfort of his apartment as boats beached themselves in front of his eyes.

After losing her last anchor, the *Athens* endeavoured to steam out of the Bay. She was seen passing the Breakwater under a full pressure of steam, and apparently making headway. Whether her engine broke down, or whether, when she got to the mouth of the Bay and endeavoured to wear to the westward, the tremendous sea that was rolling in overpowered her, is not known, and never will be known. But certain it is that at about seven o'clock she was carried broadside on against the Green Point reef, and very rapidly broke up. The calls for help of those on board of her could be distinctly heard upon the shore amid the roar of the breakers; but the crowd of persons whom those cries attracted were powerless to aid. All that those on shore could do was to light a fire, and thereby indicate to those on board that their peril was known. There was not a rope or lantern at the lighthouse; no rockets nor Manby apparatus within a mile or two of the spot. And yet for two hours a continued wail of anguish and appeals for help came from the steamer, which, it occasionally could be seen, was broken-backed, but still above water, with masts standing until after nine o'clock. Fragments of wreck washing ashore then bore testimony that the ship was rapidly breaking up. About ten o'clock the cries ceased, and thick darkness gathered o'er the scene.

This morning nothing remains of the vessel except her engines and boilers, which have been carried some distance from the place at which she is believed to have originally struck, and nearer to the Mouille Lighthouse. All the way from the reef to the break-water the shore is strewn with fragments of wreck. Even the masts and yards have been snapped into short lengths; and the lighter portions of the ship have been literally smashed into matchwood. Two bodies have been recovered — one washed up at the breakwater, the other at the south wharf. Both were much bruised from pounding against the rocks, and both were stripped, with the exception of under-drawers, showing before taking their final plunge the unhappy men had calmly prepared themselves for a last struggle for life.

'Whoever dreamed of an Afrikaans newspaper?'

Rev. Stephanus du Toit and the Afrikaans language movement, 1876

The first independent newspaper to be published in Afrikaans was *Die Afrikaanse Patriot.* Founded by the fiery Reverend Stephanus Jacobus du Toit of Paarl, *Die Patriot* was first published on Saturday, January 15 1876 and was an integral part of the first Afrikaans language movement.

Prickly, passionate, a visionary, Stephanus Jacobus du Toit was born on the farm Kleinbosch, outside Paarl, on 9 October 1847. A student at the Paarl Gymnasium, he evinced early in his scholastic career a strong Afrikaans patriotism. In November 1874, while a student at the Theological Seminary, Paarl, Du Toit published seven spelling rules for Afrikaans in *De Zuid Afrikaan* and, in 1875, became joint founder of the first Afrikaans language movement, the Genootskap van Regte Afrikaners.

Du Toit's determination to foster the Afrikaans language led to his founding *Die Afrikaanse Patriot,* to writing several books on the subject of the language and becoming a formative influence in the founding of the Afrikaner Bond. Amid much controversy, he also later translated the Bible into Afrikaans.

With its plea, familiar to modern editors, for readers to dig deep into their pockets and shell out five shillings for a year's subscription, *Die Patriot* was to last just under thirty provocative years, closing in 1904. Fiercely pro-Afrikaner, the newspaper grew steadily from its original 50 subscribers to 633 subscribers in 1877 and 950 the following year. Because of its political stance and support of Boer policy in the First Anglo-Boer War (1880-1), *Die Patriot*'s influence spread far beyond Paarl.

Although the paper's editorials were stirring, the most popular column contained verses from the public, with people from all walks of life contributing, including General Piet Joubert. The five editors who served the paper (Du Toit served as editor twice) wrote under the engaging pseudonym 'Oom Lokomotief'. 'If ever anything should come of the language movement,' wrote Du Toit, 'then *Die Patriot* will have been the chief contributor.'

Du Toit was appointed superintendent of education in the Transvaal in 1881 where he refused to recognise English as a teaching medium in schools. In 1883 he went with Paul Kruger and General Nicolaas Smit to London in an effort to obtain greater freedom for the Transvaal Republic.

The Rev. du Toit finally fell out with President Kruger and returned to Paarl, editing *Die Patriot* until it ceased publication. He died, and is buried, on the farm on which he was born, on 28 May 1911.

DIE
Afrikaanse Patriot.

"Eert uwen vader en uwe moeder, opdat uwe dagen verlengd worden in het land dat u de Heere uw God geeft."—*Het vijfde Gebod.*

Deel I.]   SATURDAG, 15 JANUARY, 1876.   [No. 1.

"DIE AFRIKAANSE PATRIOT."

Een Afrikaanse koerant! Wie het dit ooit gedroom! Ja, Afrikaanders! een koerant in ons ei'e taal! Dit het baiang moeite gekos om so vêr te kom; dit kan ek julle verseker, want die meeste Afrikaanders is nes steeks pêrde, hulle wil mos nie glo dat ons een ei'e taal het nie. Die ou'e Patriotte hou vas, en klou vas, an die *Hollans* taal; die jong mense vind die *Engelse* taal weer so danig mooi, en o'ertui'e gaat net so moeilik, as om steeks pêrde te leer pronk in die voortuig. Ons wil nou met ons "Patriot" an die wereld wys, dat ons wel de'entlik een taal het waarin ons kan sê net wat ons wil.

"AFRIKAANSE PATRIOT,"

Ja, dit is die naam van ons blad! Een beter naam kan ons nooit kry nie, want een *"Patriot"* is een flukse vent, en so wil ons ons koerant ook maak:— klein, maar fluks.

Op die 15 van ider maand kan julle een besoek van die "Patriot" verwag, en ek is seker, hoe meer julle hom lees, hoe liewer julle hom sal kry. En hoe meer intekenaars julle ver hom sal besorge, hoe meer jul julle dankbaarheid sal betoon! Ek sê: *teken in! dis maar 5 sielings in die jaar! Sê an al julle vrinde, teken in ver die* "Patriot," *dis mar 5 sielings in die jaar!* Myn skepsels! wat is 5 sielings ver een "Afri-

The front page of the first Afrikaans newspaper, Die Afrikaanse Patriot, *published on January 15, 1876 under the editorship of the Rev. S J du Toit.*

"DIE AFRIKAANSE PATRIOT."

Een Afrikaanse koerant! Wie het dit ooit gedroom! Ja, Afrikaanders! een koerant in ons ei'e taal! Dit het baiang moeite gekos om so vêr te kom; dit kan ek julle verseker, want die meeste Afrikaanders is nes steeks pêrde, hulle wil mos nie glo dat ons een ei'e taal het nie. Die ou'e Patriotte hou vas, en klou vas, en die *Hollans* taal; die jong mense vind die *Engelse* taal weer so danig mooi, en o'ertui'e gaat net so moeilik, as om steeks pêrde te leer pronk in die voortuig. Ons wil nou met ons "Patriot" an die wereld wys, dat ons wel de'entlik een taal het waarin ons kan sê net wat ons wil.

"AFRIKAANSE PATRIOT,"

Ja, dit is die naam van ons blad! Een beter naam kan ons nooit kry nie, want een *"Patriot"* is een flukse vent, en so wil ons koerant ook maak: klein, maar fluks.

Op die 15 van ider maand kan julle een besoek van die "Patriot" verwag, en ek is seker hoe meer julle hom lees, hoe liewer julle hom sal kry. En hoe meer intekenaars julle ver hom sal besorge, hoe meer jul julle dankbaarheid sal betoon! Ek sê: *teken in! dis maar 5 sielings in die jaar! Sê an al julle vrinde, teken in ver die "Patriot," dis mar 5 sielings in die jaar!* Myn skepsels! wat is 5 sielings ver een "Afrikaanse Patriot?" . . . . . . Een mens gé in een jaar tyd meer oulappe en stuiwers ver syn kinders om tammeletjes en ander lekkergoed te koop. Nooit en te nimmer sal julle daar spyt van kry dat julle intekenaars is van die "Afrikaanse Patriot" nie.

Ons vra: *"Agente in die buitendistrikte"* ver ons "Patriot." Hulle kry een koerant verniet ver hulle moeite, as hulle ons een party intekenaars besorg!

Afrikaanders! vraag julle altemitters wat daar in die koerant sal te lees wees, of, in andere woorde, hoe ons die blad sal inrig? Kijk dan, hier is die plan:

1. Een Inleiding.
2. Afrikaanse Correspondensie.
3. Afrikaanse Geskiedenis.
4. Afrikaanse Gedigte.
5. Afrikaanse Taalkennis.
6. Een Maandelike O'ersig van die voornaamste nuus.
7. Vrae en andwoorde.

No. 1. *Die Inleiding* skryf ons selwers o'er belangrike sake.

No. 2. *Afrikaanse Correspondensie* is ver julle om te skrywe. Julle kan Afrikaanse

The Rev S J du Toit, instigator of the first Afrikaans language movement (Africana Museum).

briewe en stukke stuur. Druk op dat dit help! Die grootste gros van ons nasie was tot nog toe so's doofstomme gereken. Dis hulle vertel, "julle het geen taal nie!" En in een seker sin was dit so. Want die meeste Afrikaanders het nie so veul Hollans of Engels geken dat hulle daarin goed kan praat of skrywe nie, want dis ver ons twe vreemde tale, en ons het nog geen tyd en skole gehad om vreemde tale te leer nie. En ons ei'e taal was nog nie erkend nie. So moes meer as een Afrikaander wat *verstand en gees* het stil bly, omdat hij *geen taal* het waarin hij hom kon uitdruk nie. En die Hollanse of Engelse taal wat hij daartoe wou gebruik, kom hom net so sleg te pas as Sauls wapenrusting ver David. Né, jonge Afrikaanders! goi nou weg die vreemde wapenrusting nes David! Vat julle slinger! En goi elke vyand, al is hij so groot as Goliath, teun die grond. Ja, nou kan elke Afrikaander skrywe wat hy wil in syn ei'e taal. Wat traak ons verder met Hollanse Spraakkuns of Engelse Woordenboek. Nou skryf ons nes ons praat, en seg net wat ons wil. Kom nou voor'n dag, verborge pêrels en diamante! Waarom langer onder die vreemde stof begrawe en met vreemde voete vertrap? Kom uit nou, Afrikaanders! en laat ons sien of Afrikaanders nie net so veul gees het as eenig ander nasie op die wereld nie! Waarom moet ons hart langer die graf wees van ons gedagte? Kom uit! Skrywe julle taal! Hulle skryf wel Kaffertaal en Boesman-geklap te'enwoordig. Waarom ons taal dan gesmoor? Kom uit! Ons weet daar is gees genoeg; dis net nog mar verborge!

No. 3 Is ook ver julle — Ons sal saam werk. Julle moet, maskie klein brokkies, van die Geskiedenis van ons voorouwers by makaar maak en ver ons stuur. Als julle wil weet hoe, kijk dan na die stuk van Ware Afrikaander o'er die Hugenote — dis die manier!

No. 4 Is ook ver julle. Julle kan nou rym en dig dat dit nie maklik is nie. Jonge Afrikaanders! julle kan mos fluks rym! Stuur julle gedigte, kerels! Stuur mar! Die wat een beter gedig stuur as ons "Volkslied," die kry van ons een pluimpie. En die wat foute maak, dis niks nie, ons sal hom reg help.

No. 5 Is ver julle en ver ons same, om te skrywe o'er ons taal. Een taal is een ding wat nie soemar kant en klaar uit die hemel val nie. Kijk mar Hollans en Engels, hoe't hulle dit eers geskrywe, en hoe nou! Daarom moet ons oek begin te skrywe oer ons taal.

No. 6 Blyf ver ons. Omdat:

(a) Baiang Afrikaanders lees geen koerante nie.

(b) Baiang lees dit mar half.

(c) Baiang kan nie onthou wat hulle lees nie, veral in verband met die gebeurtenisse.

No. 7 Is ver ons Intekenaars. Elke intekenaar het reg om eenige vraag in ons blad te doen, en elke intekenaar het reg om eenmaal daarop te andwoorde, mits alles onder toesig van die Redaksie. Die hou reg op die laaste woord. Ek sal ver dees keer die eerste vraag en andwoord opgé, om Afrikaanders op die weg te help. Vraag: "Waarom het ons in die Afrikaanse taal mar *één verleden* en *vier toekomende ty'e?*" Andwoord: "Omdat ons nog amper geen verleden, mar wel een toekoms het!"

Is daar nog Afrikaanders wat vra wat ons doel is! Ons andwoord is: "OM TE STAAN VER ONS TAAL, ONS NASIE EN ONS LAND."

Is daar spotters? (daar is zeker baiang). Spot mar fluks op! Ons troos ons daarmé, julle spot uit DOMHEID! Alle dinge word bespot. Stoom is mé gespot. Gaslig is mé gespot, enz. En sou die Afrikaanse taal dan vryloop? Een Regte Afrikaander sal nie spot nie, en dis ver Regte Afrikaanders, Afrikaanders met Afrikaanse harte, wat ons skrywe, en nie ver spotters!

Ons sal an al die Hollanse koerante in die land ons "Patriot" stuur. Wil hulle ver ons oek so dan en nou een koerant stur, ons sal dit dankbaar ontvang. Wil hulle van ons stukke o'erneem, hulle is welkom.

Ons sal an die Editeur van die *"Zuid-Afrikaan en Volksvriend"* altyd dankbaar wees ver die hulp en vrindskap wat hy ons betoon het en nog bewys.

En nou: Klein begin,

Anhou win. Dis tog mar een al te ware woord. Een babetje kan een reus worde; en waarom sou die *"Afrikaanse Patriot"* nie een Afrikaanse reus kan worde nie? Waarom sou ons intekenaars nie later alle da'e een koerant kan ontvang in plaas van alle maande? Ons wil die beste hoop en die beste wens. En met die gegronde hoop, en die welgemeende wens, stuur ons die eerste nommer van die *"Patriot"* die wereld in. En skree al wat ons kan, en roep ider "Regte Afrikaander" toe om ook saam te skree: "Hoerê ver die *"Afrikaanse Patriot!"*

"Afrikaanse Patriot" bo'e!!"

"Hip, hip, hip, hoerê!!!"

The above copy translates as follows:

"DIE AFRIKAANSE PATRIOT"

An Afrikaans newspaper! Who ever dreamt of that! Yes, Afrikaanders! a newspaper in our own language! It took a lot of doing to get this far; that I can assure you, because most Afrikaans people are like jibbing horses, they won't believe, as you know, that we have a language of our own. The old Patriots hold onto, cling onto the *Dutch* language; the young people, again, find *English* so frightfully fine a language, and to convince (them) is as difficult as teaching jibbing horses to prance in the front harness. With our "Patriot" we now want to show the world we well and truly have a language in which we can say whatever we please.

"AFRIKAANSE PATRIOT"

Yes, that's the name of our paper! A better name we could never find, for a "Patriot" is an energetic fellow, and that's what we want to make our paper too; — small but energetic.

On the 15th of every month you can expect a visit from the "Patriot", and I'm sure the more you read him, the more you'll love him. And the more subscribers you get him, the better you'll be showing your gratitude. I say: *subscribe, it's only 5 shillings a year! Tell your friends, subscribe to the "Patriot", it's only 5 shillings a year!* My (good) creatures! What is 5 shillings a year for an "Afrikaanse Patriot"? . . . . . . One gives one's kids more pennies and ha'pennies in one year to buy stickjaw candy and other sweets. Never ever will you regret that you're subscribers to the "Afrikaanse Patriot".

"We're looking for *"Agents in the country districts"* for our "Patriot". They get one newspaper free for their trouble, if they find us some subscribers!

Afrikaander people! are you asking, perhaps, what there'll be to read in the newspaper, or, in other words, how we're going to put the paper together? Then look at this, this is the plan:

1. A leading article.
2. Afrikaans Correspondence.
3. Afrikaans History.

31

4. Afrikaans Poetry.

5. Afrikaans Language Studies.

6. A Monthly Review of the most important news.

7. Questions and Answers.

No. 1 *The Leading Article* we write ourselves, about prominent affairs.

No. 2 *Afrikaans Correspondence,* is for you to write. You can send in Afrikaans letters and items. Come on, go to it with a will! The largest part of our nation has up to now been taken for deaf and dumb. They've been told: "you have no language!" And, in a sense, this was so. For most Afrikaanders didn't know enough Dutch or English to speak or write well in it, because these two are for us foreign languages, and we haven't had the time or the schools to study foreign languages. And our own language was not yet recognised. So more than one Afrikaander *of spirit and intelligence* had to remain *silent* because he had no language in which to express himself. And the Dutch or English language which he wanted to use for the purpose fitted him as ill as Saul's suit of armour did David. Isn't that so, young Afrikaanders? throw away the foreign suit of armour now, like David did. Take your sling. And hurl every adversary to the ground, be he as big as Goliath. Yes, now every Afrikaander can write what he likes in his own language. What further do we care for Dutch grammar or English dictionary? Now we write as we speak and say whatever we like. Come to the light now, you hidden pearls and diamonds! Why longer be buried under foreign dust and trodden underfoot by foreign feet? Come out now, Afrikaanders, and let's see whether Afrikaanders haven't got just as much spirit as any other nation in the world! Why must our thoughts longer be buried in our hearts? Come out! Write your language! They do write Kaffir language and Bushmen clacks these days. Why, then, is our language smothered? Come out! We know there is spirit enough; it's only still hidden!

No. 3 This is also for you — We'll work together. You must collect even if short fragments of the History of our ancestors and send it to us. If you want to know how, look at Ware Afrikaander's piece about the Huguenots — that's the way.

No. 4 Also for you! You can now rhyme and versify with all your might. Young Afrikaanders! you can rhyme vigorously, can't you! Send in your verses, you chaps! Go on, feel free to send them along! Whoever sends a better poem than our "Volkslied", gets a feather in his cap from us. And who makes mistakes, never mind, we'll put him right!

No. 5 Is for you and us together, to write about our language. A language isn't something that falls ready-made from the heavens. Just look at Dutch and English, how they wrote it before, and how now! That's why we must also start writing about our language.

No. 6 Remains for us. Because:

(a) Many Afrikaanders read no newspapers.

(b) Many don't read them thoroughly.

(c) Many can't remember what they read, especially concerning what happened.

No. 7 Is for our Subscribers. Every subscriber has the right to put any question in our paper, and every subscriber has the right to reply to that once, all under supervision of the Editorial staff. They keep the right to have the last word. To show Afrikaanders the way, I'll this time put up the first question and answer. Question: "Why has our Afrikaans language *only one past tense* and *four future tenses?*" Answer: "Because we have hardly any past yet, but certainly a future!"

Are there still Afrikaanders who ask what our aim is? Our reply:
"TO STAND FOR OUR LANGUAGE, OUR NATION AND OUR COUNTRY."

Are there mockers? (there probably are many). Go ahead, mock away! We console ourselves with this, you mock out of IGNORANCE! Everything is mocked. Steam was mocked. Gaslight etc. was mocked. And could the Afrikaans language escape? A Real Afrikaander will not mock, and it's for Real Afrikaanders, Afrikaanders with Afrikaander hearts, that we write, not for mockers!

We'll send the "Patriot" to all Dutch papers in the country. If they'll also send us a paper now and again, we'll receive it with thanks. If they want to take over items, they're welcome to do so.

We'll always be grateful to the Editor of the *"Zuid-Afrikaan en Volksvriend"* for the help and friendship he offered us and continues to show.

And now: a small beginning,
            but doggèd does it! That's all too true a saying. A baby can become a giant; and why shouldn't the *"Afrikaanse Patriot"* become an Afrikaans giant? Why shouldn't our subscribers get a paper every day instead of once a month? We would hope for the best, and wish for the best. And with this grounded hope and well-intentioned wish we send the first number of the *"Patriot"* into the world. And shout as hard as we can, and call on every "Real Afrikaander" to join in shouting "Hurrah for the *'Afrikaanse Patriot'!"*

  "Afrikaanse Patriot" tops!!"
  "Hip, hip, hip, hurray!!!"

'Let his life and death be a warning to you'

Death of Sandile of the Gaika, 1878

Sandile was the last paramount chief of the Gaika, a tribe which lived on the troubled Kei frontier during the period of English settlement and expansion. Discontent on both sides of the Kei — from the Xhosa on the one side and the British on the other — invariably involved either land or cattle.

Born in 1820, a son of the Great House of Gaika or Ngqika, Sandile commanded the territory between the Kei and Keiskamma Rivers. Although not opposed to the presence of limited numbers of settlers, Sandile was naturally concerned about the pressure on the land and the steady flow of new immigrants to the area. Five years after he became paramount chief (1841), Sandile reneged on an agreement with the Governor of the Cape, Sir Peregrine Maitland, which allowed British forts to be built west of the Keiskamma River. Tension on the frontier was heightened when one of Sandile's tribesmen stole an axe from a shop in Fort Beaufort and fled with it.

Sandile refused to hand the man over to the colonial government, resulting in the Seventh Frontier War, or the War of the Axe. The war ended with a defeated Sandile seeing his territory annexed by the British and renamed British Kaffraria, and his position usurped by appointed commissioners. In 1850 the Eighth Frontier War broke out, ending in 1853 with the deposition of Sandile and the movement of his people to a more distant part of British Kaffraria.

In spite of the deliberately low profile he maintained, Sandile was inexorably drawn into the Ninth Frontier War (commonly known as the Gaika Rebellion) which broke out in August 1877. In command of both the Galeka and Gaika armies, Sandile was brought to battle at Kentani on 7 February 1878. The colonial forces' superior firepower and inter-tribal treachery contributed to Sandile's decision to withdraw his men across the Kei. Remnants of his army took refuge in the Pirie Bush, some 19 kilometres from an understandably jittery King William's Town.

At bay, and with the Fingoes harassing his men, Sandile saw his men slipping away. Starving, cold and almost without hope, the Gaikas retreated into the heart of the Pirie Bush. On 20 May 1878, Sandile was mortally wounded, probably by a Fingo in the pay of the British. He did not die immediately. His post mortem established that he had lived for several days after the soft-nose lead bullet had penetrated his right side and, expanding, broke two ribs and destroyed his liver.

The remnants of Sandile's bodyguard dragged their dead chief into the thickest undergrowth they could find in a vain effort to prevent his being discovered by the hated Fingoes.

A British patrol, led by Guba, a Gaika who claimed to have been with Sandile when he fell,

34

discovered the dead chief deep within the Pirie Bush. He was naked but for a simple necklace and a blood-soaked walking stick. The left side of his face and his right arm had been eaten by animals.

Unmentioned in the despatch which follows was Sandile's decapitation, which followed his post mortem. In 1934, it was revealed that his bleached skull had been taken back to England, together with other less grisly trophies of the Frontier Wars, by Sir Richard Carrington, the officer commanding in the area at that time. The skull sat on his mantelpiece in Cheltenham, Gloucestershire, for many years until it was finally buried in a lead casket, the grave marked by a stone with the inscription 'Here lies the head of Sandilli, killed in the Peeribush, King William's Town, 1878'.

The first reporter on the scene after Sandile's death was the 'special correspondent' for *The Cape Mercury.* His name unknown, he wrote a long, colourful despatch, marked as much for its attention to detail as its omission of paragraphs. The article was widely syndicated in the Cape Province. Taken from *The Eastern Star* of 14 June 1878, this was the final version of the story:

HOW WE BURIED SANDILLI

Having received a kind invitation from Captain Landrey to "come out and see the burial of Sandilli," on Sunday morning, some time before six o'clock, I in company with two or three others were in the saddle and on our way. At first it was tolerably chilly, but by-and-by the sun rose and we had a beautiful mild summer's day, making riding perfectly enjoyable. A couple of hours cantering brought us to Frankfort, where we enjoyed the hospitality of Mrs. Landrey, and after breakfasting ourselves, and the horses having been fed, we mounted, and were off across country to Isidenge, which lay about fifteen miles off. But first let me not omit to mention that we had the pleasure of inspecting the only things that were found on Sandilli's person or with the body. They were few in number, simply a common beadnecklace of large round black beads with white marks upon them; an article of Kafir apparel, which I do not know how to spell; and a walking stick covered with his blood. He had nothing else near him, and though many articles will doubtless be produced as having belonged to the renowned Chief, they will not have been taken from the body. Hunted from place to place, he appears to have lost almost all he had, and probably those who were with him during his last hours took away with them everything of value or of interest. The body was found naked and without even a blanket. There have been many stories of the finding of the body, but I think that the following is correct in every particular. Many persons will remember that a Kafir named Juba came to Peelton on Wednesday last, and gave the information that Sandilli had been wounded and had died from the effects of his wound. His story was that he was with the Chief when he received the shot, which was fired by one of three men in European clothing, but whether white or black he could not say; that he had remained with about twenty others until Sandilli died, when he left in company with two men and went towards Izeli, where he lay down to sleep at the edge of the bush; when he awoke in the morning he found that his companions had gone, and so he resolved to go to Peelton and give himself up to Captain Stevenson, which he did. Many persons disbelieved his statement, and bets were freely made as to whether it would turn out correct or not. However, Captain Landrey being in town, he received verbal instructions to proceed to the place indicated by the prisoner, who was to accompany him and point out the spot. Accordingly, on Friday he went to the bush, near Fort Merriman, to prosecute the search, accompanied by forty men of the Kaffrarian Rangers under Captain Gorman

'The Gaika Kaffir Chief, Sandilla — The Withered Leg' (The Illustrated London News).

and Lieutenant Simpson, to assist. Juba was handcuffed, and after being warned by Captain Landrey, that if this were a trap, he would be the first to fall, the troop were extended in skirmishing order, and entered the bush. After searching some time, and only finding the bodies of two or three Kafirs, Juba appeared to get confused; he said he remembered certain trees and other landmarks, and the body should be somewhere thereabouts. After some more fruitless searching, a young private of Gormon's troop, named E. Dye, who was on high ground, shouted out to Captain Landrey, "There's a dead nigger." "Where?" cried the Captain. "Under the big rock close to you," was the answer; and pushing aside the brushwood, Captain Landrey found the dead body of the man who has cost the country so many lives and such a vast sum of money. Catching hold of Sandilli's withered leg, he exclaimed, "It's Sandilli;" and Juba answered "Yes; that's him, and there is his stick." Mr. Landrey at once shouted out for the men to come on and carry him out; first detaching the articles we have before mentioned, and cutting off a lock of hair from his forehead. The body was found in capital preservation, and appeared well nourished. Some animals had already gnawed away the flesh of the right arm, and a small portion of the left side of the face. The place where he was found was most retired, and there is evidence which seems to show that the body was slipped down the rocks from where he died, and then left to rot. Here, let me mention that, during the whole war there have been only one or two instances of the rebels burying their dead, and in every case it was done to what are termed school-Kafirs. One was a petty Chief, whose grave was found in the Perie Bush, another was the noted Dukwana, whose body is to be unearthed for identification, by order of the Government. After requesting Captain Gorman to have the body conveyed to Commandant Schermbrucker at the Isidenge, Captain Landrey proceeded to Kabousie, where he telegraphed the success of his mission to Mr. Innes, the Civil Commissioner.

Slung over a horse, the body of the once redoubtable Kafir Chief was taken to Isidenge, where it was received with a *feu de joié.* Here it was recognised by number of persons, natives and others, and on Saturday evening Mr. Wright, the Resident with Sandilli, officially identified the body, and on the same day Dr. Everitt, Captain of the Tarkastad Volunteers, made a *post mortem* examination, and reports that it is evident, from the appearance of the body, that death had taken place about four days previously. The left eye and side of the face, together with the right arm, and smaller patches about the body, had been eaten by animals. A Snider bullet had entered the side, above the right loin, fracturing the seventh and eighth ribs, passing right through the body, and causing death. From the inflammation that existed, the doctor judged that the wound was received some days before his death. This is the substance of the official report.

We had a couple of hours riding through most lovely country, consisting of open glades, and gentle slopes of grass covered land, with deep valleys filled with dense forest. Much has been said of the Amatolas as seen from the Perie, but, to my thinking, this portion of that range is by far the most beautiful, and from the high table lands on gets a magnificent view of the country, including King Williamstown, the Railway line, and Kei Road Station, and stretching away mile after mile of country, with houses and farms dotted about here and there, adding a charm to the natural beauty of the landscape, while in the far distance the blue sea can be distinctly seen if the atmosphere is at all clear. From Kei Road Station to Isidenge is what Captain Landrey laughingly calls his hunting ground; and over the open space which intervenes between the Amatola Bush and the forests which extend to Thomas River, there are a fair number of skeletons that attest the skill of the Frankfort Police. Unostentatiously they have done valuable work, and though occasionally in difficult places, with a savage foe all round them, strange to say they have never had a casualty. They form part of the Amatola Division, under the command of Commandant Schermbrucker. At about half-past ten we reached the Isidenge, and found that we were still in time to see the corpse. Inside of a wooden shed, stretched stark and stiff, on an old wagon sail, lay the naked body of the once dreaded Gaika Chief. It needed but a glance to satisfy one of its being the remains of Sandilli, the features were unchanged, though perhaps it was fancy that led me to imagine that he wore a hunted and wearied expression on his face. There was the small leg and foot that looked by the side of the other as though it should have belonged to a youth of sixteen; and there in his side was the bullet wound which laid him low. His body had been so disposed as to hide the portion of face that had been eaten, and one had to bend over to see it. His hands were crossed over his body, the right arm being without flesh, though the hand and wrist were still intact. This then was the end of the man who had taken the chief part in two wars, and twice had a price put upon his head! Once at his back ten thousand men would have armed themselves to plunder and murder their hated conquerors: now not a single Gaika is near him. The Fingoes pass in and out, and jeer and laugh as they pass. Stripped of his power, his savage grandeur gone, he lies before us simply as the carcass of a dead rebel; the tangible proof of the white man's superiority. The last time I saw him he was erect amidst his councillors — the haughty Chief of a proud tribe who knew that they had never been properly beaten, and fancied themselves invincible if once in possession of those mountain fastnesses which lay so close at hand. Sandilli was then telling Mr. Brownlee that he had no wish to go to war again. He said — "What have I to gain by war?" He forgot his own words, and all he has gained is a permanent occupation of six feet of ground on the slopes of Isidenge. Standing over his body, and looking at the awful wound in his side, one could not help wondering what were his thoughts during those four days of intense suffering — for wounded on Thursday, the 31st, at three o'clock, he did not die until ten o'clock on Tuesday morning. He must have thought of the misery he had brought about, his friends killed, his tribe broken up, and he himself dying. Even the friends of those Englishmen who have fallen in his bloody war, could scarcely wish him a harder fate. His sin was great and his retribution just.

The only trophy that was obtainable was some of the hair from his head; and having begged Lieutenant Sheehan to use the scissors on my behalf, I left the shed the happy possessor of a lock of a dead savage's hair and a piece of his white whisker. When he was buried a more hairless man could only have been found among the incurably bald.

At the request of Commandant Schermbrucker, all who were present, including Fingoes, walked through the shed to satisfy themselves that the body was that of Sandilli, after which it was rolled up in the canvas, tied up with rope, and borne upon the guns of eight Fingoes, to the grave, which had been dug near an apple tree at the corner of a garden. The followers were the Kaffrarian Rangers, the True Blues, and the Fingoes of the Amatola Division. I shall not call it a mournful procession, because all present felt that in the death of Sandilli a blow had been struck at the tap root of the war, and memory would call up the names of Tainton, Brown, McNaughton, Donovan, and many others who had fallen victims to Kafir bloodthirstiness. Those who gathered round the grave were there from motives of curiosity rather than of sympathy. A detachment of the 2-24th Regiment, the Kaffrarian Rangers, the Frankfort Police, the True Blues, and the

Fingoes of Streatfield and Dereling, were drawn up so as to form a hollow square. The Fingoes were chanting a sort of hymn in praise of their own prowess in the field, and reviling the "Tiger of the Forest" that had been killed. This was the only funeral service held over the open grave of Sandilli. As a rebel he died, and as a rebel he was buried. Before the filling in of the grave, Commandant Schermbrucker made a short speech, the substance of which was as follows: — "Men of the Amatola Division, you have gathered together to-day, not to do honour to Sandilli, but to witness an historical event — the burial of the Gaika Chief; he rebelled against his Queen and country, and this is the consequence. He has been killed by our Volunteers, and has been denied the honours which are usually accorded even to an enemy. Had he fallen on the side of his Queen, and not as a rebel, he would have been buried in a manner befitting his rank. This is the last Chief of the Gaikas; let his life and death be a warning to you. The man who lifts arms against his Queen will sooner or later meet a fate like this. Sandilli has been laid low, his tribe dispersed, scattered, and stripped of all they once possessed; instead of being lords and masters in the country they once owned, they will now be servants. Let those who are present communicate through the length and breadth of South Africa the fact that Sandilli, the great Gaika warrior, has been brought low by the might of Great Britain, and in two months his tribes have been driven from strongholds which they deemed impregnable. Let this teach you that if any native has a complaint to make to do so in a proper manner. Any man who lifts his hand against his Queen is a rascal of the deepest dye, and deserves the fate and burial of Sandilli." The speech was principally addressed to the Fingoes and natives present, and was interpreted for their benefit.

Beside the grave of Sandilli are those of poor Hillier and Dicks, who fell in the struggle for mastery between the white man and the black, between the savage and civilised. In death friend and foe lie side by side.

After the interment I accepted the kind invitation of Commandant Schermbrucker to tiffin. After the tiffin was over, and the consumption of beer was at an end, most of the visitors rode off, and in the quiet conversation that ensued over our tobacco, I learned the story of Sandilli's death as follows:—

On Thursday, the 31st May, Lonsdale's Fingoes made an attack upon some Kafirs they saw in a bush near Fort Merriman. After they had been fighting some time, three of Schermbrucker's Police — a corporal and two privates — went towards the upper end of the bush, and seeing two natives, shot at them, and upon their return reported that they had killed two Kafirs, having no suspicion of one being Sandilli. A rebel Kafir turns up at Greytown a few days afterwards, and told this tale: — "I was with Sandilli when he was shot, the two of us were together, and we were making our way out of that bush to get into the next. I saw three white men in drab uniform come up, and fire at us, and Sandilli was hit in the side. I then stayed with him until he died, when I came here." It has since transpired that the loyal Kafirs went from Fort Merriman to attend upon Sandilli. That Chief was amongst the last to leave the Perie, and was endeavouring, with about a hundred followers, to make his way to the Thomas River, when he met with his death.

Interesting though the reports of the different Frontier Wars and endless skirmishes were (and providing something other than small town news for the newspapers of the area such as the *Cape Frontier Times* and *The Grahamstown Journal*), the stories paled into insignificance before the first really big news that came from the fledgling country: the Zulu wars.

The need for the Imperial forces of the Crown to subdue the Zulus in the face of settler expansion in the colony of Natal led to a series of vividly described confrontations which culminated in the defeat of the Zulu army at the Battle of Ulundi on 4 July 1879.

The battles which marked the war against the Zulu king Cetshwayo were notable not only for their ferocity, but for the string of despatches written by some of the great British correspondents, drawn to the conflict. Their arrival and their reports dwarfed the sometimes naive writing of local reporters and, for the first time, put journalism from South Africa on the front pages of many of the world's great newspapers.

'We saw the soil that it was red'

Massacre at Isandhlwana, 1879

On the morning of 22 January 1879, Captain George Shepstone and a detachment of mounted men were scouting for Zulus on the Nqutu Plateau, some six kilometres from the army camp at Isandhlwana. The Zulu army was thought to be in the vicinity, making its way towards the Zulu capital, Ulundi.

Lord Chelmsford, Commander-in-Chief of the British army in South Africa, had invaded Zululand with the Central Column on the same day (11 January) that war against the Zulu king, Cetshwayo, had been declared. The camp, pitched in the shadow of the stark mountain, Isandhlwana, was intended to be used as a base while the area around was searched for the Zulu army. Taking a large body of men with him — including Charles 'Noggs' Norris-Newman, the only English correspondent in Zululand — Chelmsford left almost 1 800 men at Isandhlwana under the command of Brevet Lt-Colonel Pulleine, an officer of 24 years' army experience.

Shepstone, like everyone else, was keeping a wary eye open not just for the Zulu army, but for individual Zulus who might indicate that force's whereabouts. From a distance, he saw a group of cattle being driven towards a dry ravine, and ordered one of his men to investigate both cattle and drover. Reigning his horse in on the edge of the ravine, the soldier saw, to his horror, the silent 20 000-strong Zulu army under the command of General Tshingwayo.

The Zulus had not intended giving battle that day. The previous day, the Zulu hierarchy had decided that when they met the Central Column they would go into battle in the classic horned advance.

They put their plans into immediate effect, pouring over the rim of the ravine and, forming a crescent nearly three kilometres wide, stormed towards the camp, despatching a section to deal with Shepstone and his men.

Ordering Lieutenant Charles Raw to hold off the enemy for as long as possible, Shepstone galloped towards the camp to give news of the impending attack to Pulleine. Pulleine scribbled off a note to Chelmsford: 'Report just come in that the Zulus are advancing in force from left front of the camp.' The message reached Chelmsford at 09h30. He decided that it indicated no more than a skirmish and went on with his day's work. Norris-Newman, who had left his tent pitched and his belongings under the supervision of his servant at the camp, noted the message and continued with his day.

For Pulleine, there was no immediate cause for alarm. Although the camp, contrary to Chelmsford's orders, had not been protected by a laager, he had, in addition to the Imperial Infantry, the foot levies and the 'casuals', two field guns, a rocket battery and ample supplies of ammunition. Organising the camp by stringing out the three companies of Imperial Infantry (two from the 1st Battalion under Captain Wardell and Lieutenant Porteous and one from the 2nd Battalion under the distinctively monocled Lieutenant Charles D'Aguilar Pope) across a broad front, there was one man every three metres.

There was no panic as the Zulus approached. Firing steadily, the troops of the Central Column kept the army at bay, but, as their ammunition began to run low, the firing became slower. The quartermasters, adhering to procedural regulations in the midst of battle, sent men away from the ammunition wagons empty-handed. When ammunition was finally passed out into the hands of desperate men, it came too little and too late.

Realising there was a decrease in fire power, the Zulu impis, in battalions eight deep, roaring 'uSuthu,' charged forward, breaking the line. One eye-witness account, in a report published in *The Natal Mercury* on 3 February, noted that the members of the leading regiment wore tall red feathers in their hair — a truly terrifying sight.

With the Zulus upon them, little or no ammunition and barely time to fix bayonets, the men were massacred where they stood. But the fight was fierce. The Zulus later recounted that in order to reach the soldiers they picked up their own dead warriors as shields, impaled them upon the British bayonets and then closed in for the kill. The few men who managed to escape the main thrust of the Zulu attack made for the Buffalo River, in spate from heavy rains and fordable only in a few places. They were either killed on their way or speared in the water itself.

An oil on board painting of Isandhlwana, sketched on the spot by Lt-Col. J. North Crealock on the evening of January 22, 1879. Crealock arrived there with Lord Chelmsford's column on the evening of the massacre. "The day wandered, and the night hung over the hill," he wrote, "when we reached the last ridge, beyond which lay what had been our camp . . . in silence we marched down into the gloom below, where lay, shrouded by a merciful pall, the horrors of the past day." (Africana Museum).

Nineteen kilometres away and close to 12h30, Lord Chelmsford heard the sound of gun fire from the plateau. A soldier, climbing a tree and using an eye glass, could see the flashes of exploding shells. When the noise died down, Chelmsford assumed that the skirmish had been successfully repelled. He received a further message: 'For God's sake come back with all your men; the camp is surrounded and must be taken unless helped.' But he assumed all was now under control.

By 15h00, a disbelieving Chelmsford was in possession of the truth: the camp and all in it had been lost. Britain had suffered its worst defeat of an army in the field against a 'native' army.

Charles Norris-Newman did not have to try for his scoop: he was the only reporter with Chelmsford. Special correspondent for the London *Standard,* and stringer for the *Times of Natal* and *The Cape Standard and Mail,* he assembled with Chelmsford's tired troops who, in failing light and battle order, advanced with dread towards Isandhlwana.

Norris-Newman's story of the approach to the now dark field of battle and the tense night spent in the midst of the unseen, but imagined dead, makes gripping reading. He was not to write his despatch immediately. Rising before dawn on the 23rd (Chelmsford did not want his men to see what had happened and issued orders that no one was to break away from the column in order to see the camp), Norris-Newman marched with the troops towards Rorke's Drift, from which, during that fell night, they had seen a deep red glow.

Norris-Newman, ever the intrepid reporter, was among the first group of mounted men to go into that devastated settlement. He was determined to break the news to the outside world and galloped for Pietermaritzburg — in a ride not dissimilar to Archibald Forbes' — spreading the news at military outstations as he changed horses.

He wrote his despatch and the in-depth stories which were used by every major South African newspaper, in a state of exhausted elation once he reached the pretty little red brick village of Pietermaritzburg. For a short while, such is the fickleness of the public, he was hailed as the hero of the hour. His despatch was put on board the *Dunrobin Castle* and sent from the southernmost part of the submerged cable at Madeira, from where it reached London on 11 February.

The despatch reproduced here filled an entire page of the *Times of Natal* and has of necessity been shortened. It appeared on 27 January, a mere five days after the massacre at Isandhlwana and the heroic defence of Rorke's Drift.

It was quite four o'clock when the rest of our reconnoitring Column rejoined us, and the order of march for our whole force was established as follows: — The four guns were placed in the centre, with a half battalion of the 2-24th extended in line on each flank, that on the right being commanded by Colonel Degacher, that on the left by Major Black; on either side of them were eight companies of the 3rd N.N.C.; and the cavalry outside of all, on the flanks; Major Dartnell, in command of the Mounted Police and Volunteers, on the left; and Colonel Russell, with his Mounted Infantry, on the right. The ambulance and waggons followed the guns, with a small guard closing up the rear. Before the march was commenced the General briefly addressed the men, saying that the camp had fallen into the hands of the enemy, who had captured it in overwhelming force during our absence; but that he relied upon them to retake it, and so reopen our communications with Natal. Then the advance was made in the above order — with fear in our hearts as to the events that might have taken place, but nevertheless with a stern determination to recapture the position, even in the increasing darkness, and whatever might be the cost.

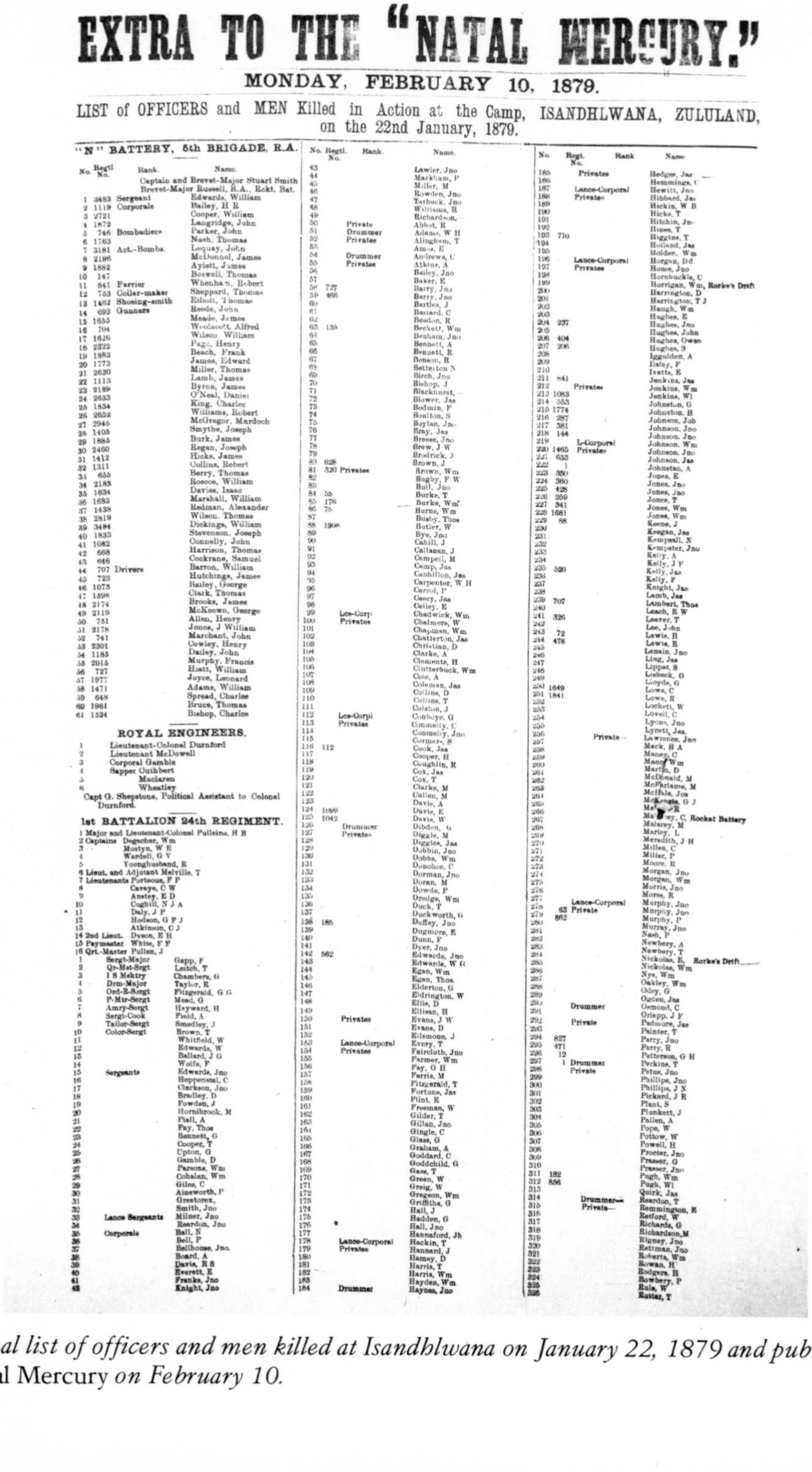

EXTRA TO THE "NATAL MERCURY."

MONDAY, FEBRUARY 10, 1879.

LIST of OFFICERS and MEN Killed in Action at the Camp, ISANDHLWANA, ZULULAND, on the 22nd January, 1879.

"N" BATTERY, 5th BRIGADE, R.A.

Captain and Brevet-Major Stuart Smith
Brevet-Major Russell, R.A., Rckt. Bat.

No.	Regtl. No.	Rank.	Name.
1	3483	Sergeant	Edwards, William
2	1119	Corporals	Bailey, H R
3	2721		Cooper, William
4	1872		Langridge, John
5	746	Bombadiers	Parker, John
6	1763		Nash, Thomas
7	3181	Act.-Bombs.	Lequay, John
8	2196		McDonnel, James
9	1882		Aylett, James
10	147		Boswell, Thomas
11	841	Farrier	Wheuham, Robert
12	753	Collar-maker	Sheppard, Thomas
13	1462	Shoeing-smith	Elliott, Thomas
14	692	Gunners	Reede, John
15	1655		Meade, James
16	704		Woolacott, Alfred
17	1626		Wilson, William
18	2322		Page, Henry
19	1883		Beach, Frank
20	1773		James, Edward
21	2630		Miller, Thomas
22	1113		Lamb, James
23	2189		Byrne, James
24	2633		O'Neal, Daniel
25	1834		King, Charles
26	2652		Williams, Robert
27	2945		McGregor, Murdoch
28	1405		Smythe, Joseph
29	1885		Burk, James
30	2460		Regan, Joseph
31	1412		Hicks, James
32	1311		Collins, Robert
33	655		Berry, Thomas
34	2183		Roscoe, William
35	1634		Davies, Isaac
36	1683		Marshall, William
37	1438		Redman, Alexander
38	2819		Wilson, Thomas
39	3484		Dickings, William
40	1833		Stevenson, Joseph
41	1082		Connelly, John
42	668		Harrison, Thomas
43	646		Cockrane, Samuel
44	707	Drivers	Barron, William
45	723		Hutchings, James
46	1073		Bailey, George
47	1598		Clark, Thomas
48	2174		Brooks, James
49	2119		McKeown, George
50	751		Allen, Henry
51	2178		Jones, J William
52	741		Marchant, John
53	2301		Cowley, Henry
54	1185		Dailey, John
55	2015		Murphy, Francis
56	727		Hiatt, William
57	1977		Joyce, Leonard
58	1471		Adams, William
59	648		Spread, Charles
60	1961		Bruce, Thomas
61	1524		Bishop, Charles

ROYAL ENGINEERS.

1 Lieutenant-Colonel Durnford
2 Lieutenant McDowell
3 Corporal Gamble
4 Sapper Cuthbert
5 Maclaren
6 Wheatley

Capt G. Shepstone, Political Assistant to Colonel Durnford.

1st BATTALION 24th REGIMENT.

1 Major and Lieutenant-Colonel Pulleine, H B
2 Captains Degacher, Wm
3 Mostyn, W E
4 Wardell, G V
5 Younghusband, R
6 Lieut. and Adjutant Melville, T
7 Lieutenants Porteous, F P
8 Cavaye, C W
9 Anstey, E D
10 Coghill, N J A
11 Daly, J P
12 Hodson, G F J
13 Atkinson, C J
14 2nd Lieut. Dyson, E H
15 Paymaster White, F F
16 Qrt.-Master Pullen, J

No.	Regtl. No.	Rank.	Name.
1		Sergt-Major	Gapp, F
2		Qr-Mst-Srgt	Leitch, T
3		I S Msktry	Chambers, G
4		Drm-Major	Taylor, R
5		Ord-R-Sergt	Fitzgerald, G G
6		P-Mtr-Sergt	Mead, G
7		Amry-Sergt	Hayward, H
8		Sergt-Cook	Field, A
9		Tailor-Sergt	Smedley, J
10		Color-Sergt	Brown, T
11			Whitfield, W
12			Edwards, W
13			Ballard, J G
14			Wolfe, F
15		Sergeants	Edwards, Jno
16			Heppenstal, C
17			Clarkson, Jno
18			Bradley, D
19			Fowden, J
20			Hornibrook, M
21			Piall, A
22			Fay, Thos
23			Bennett, G
24			Cooper, T
25			Upton, G
26			Gamble, D
27			Parsons, Wm
28			Cohalan, Wm
29			Giles, C
30			Ainsworth, F
31			Greatorex,
32			Smith, Jno
33		Lance Sergeants	Milner, Jno
34			Reardon, Jno
35		Corporals	Ball, N
36			Bell, P
37			Bellhouse, Jno.
38			Board, A
39			Davis, R S
40			Everett, E
41			Franks, Jno
42			Knight, Jno
43			Lawler, Jno
44			Markham, P
45			Miller, M
46			Rowden, Jno
47			Tarbuck, Jno
48			Williams, R
49			Richardson, —
50		Private	Abbot, R
51		Drummer	Adams, W H
52		Privates	Alingham, T
53			Amos, E
54		Drummer	Andrews, C
55		Privates	Atkins, A
56			Bailey, Jno
57			Baker, E
58	727		Barry, Jno
59	466		Barry, Jno
60			Bartles, J
61			Bastard, C
62			Beadon, R
63	135		Beckett, Wm
64			Benham, Jno
65			Bennett, A
66			Bennett, R
67			Benson, R
68			Betterton N
69			Birch, Jno
70			Bishop, J
71			Blackhurst, —
72			Blower, Jas
73			Bodmin, F
74			Boulton, S
75			Boylan, Jno
76			Bray, Jas
77			Breese, Jno
78			Brew, J W
79			Brodrick, J
80	628		Brown, J
81	320	Privates	Brown, Wm
82			Bugby, F W
83			Bull, Jno
84	55		Burke, T
85	176		Burke, Wm
86	75		Burns, Wm
87			Busby, Thos
88	1908		Butler, W
89			Bye, Jno
90			Cahill, J
91			Callanan, J
92			Campell, M
93			Camp, Jas
94			Canhillon, Jas
95			Carpenter, W H
96			Carrol, P
97			Casey, Jas
98			Ceiley, E
99		Lce-Corp	Chadwick, Wm
100		Privates	Chalmers, W
101			Chapman, Wm
102			Chatterton, Jas
103			Christian, D
104			Clarke, A
105			Clements, H
106			Clutterbuck, Wm
107			Cole, A
108			Coleman, Jas
109			Collins, D
110			Collins, T
111			Colston, J
112		Lce-Corpl	Conboye, G
113		Privates	Connelly, C
114			Connelly, Jno
115			Cormers, S
116	112		Cook, Jas
117			Cooper, H
118			Coughlin, R
119			Cox, Jas
120			Cox, T
121			Clarke, M
122			Cullen, M
123			Davis, A
124	1069		Davis, E
125	1042		Davis, W
126		Drummer	Dibden, G
127		Privates	Diggle, M
128			Diggles, Jas
129			Dobbin, Jno
130			Dobbs, Wm
131			Donohoe, C
132			Dorman, Jno
133			Doran, M
134			Dowde, P
135			Dredge, Wm
136			Duck, T
137			Duckworth, G
138	185		Duffey, Jno
139			Dugmore, E
140			Dunn, F
141			Dyer, Jno
142	562		Edwards, Jno
143			Edwards, W G
144			Egan, Wm
145			Egan, Thos.
146			Elderton, G
147			Eldrington, W
148			Ellis, D
149			Ellisan, H
150		Privates	Evans, J W
151			Evans, D
152			Eilsmone, J
153		Lance-Corporal	Every, T
154		Privates	Faircloth, Jno
155			Farmer, Wm
156			Fay, G H
157			Ferris, M
158			Fitzgerald, T
159			Fortune, Jas
160			Flint, E
161			Freeman, W
162			Gilder, T
163			Gillan, Jno
164			Gingle, C
165			Glass, G
166			Graham, A
167			Goddard, C
168			Goddchild, G
169			Gase, T
170			Green, W
171			Greig, W
172			Gregson, Wm
173			Griffiths, G
174			Hall, J
175			Hadden, G
176			Hall, Jno
177			Hannaford, Jh
178		Lance-Corporal	Hackin, T
179		Privates	Hannard, J
180			Hamey, D
181			Harris, T
182			Harris, Wm
183			Hayden, Wm
184		Drummer	Haynes, Jno
185		Privates	Hedges, Jas
186			Hemmings, C
187		Lance-Corporal	Hewitt, Jno
188		Privates	Hibbard, Jas
189			Hickin, W B
190			Hicks, T
191			Hitchin, Jno
192			Hines, T
193	710		Higgins, T
194			Holland, Jas
195			Holden, Wm
196		Lance-Corporal	Horgan, Dd
197		Privates	Home, Jno
198			Hornbuckle, C
199			Horrigan, Wm, Rorke's Drift
200			Harrington, D
201			Harrington, T J
202			Haugh, Wm
203			Hughes, E
204	237		Hughes, Jno
205			Hughes, John
206	404		Hughes, Owen
207	206		Hughes, S
208			Iggulden, A
209			Ilsley, F
210			Ivatts, E
211	841		Jenkins, Jas
212		Privates	Jenkins, Wm
213	1083		Jenkins, Wl
214	553		Johnston, G
215	1774		Johnston, H
216	287		Johnson, Job
217	381		Johnson, Jno
218	144		Johnson, Jno
219		L-Corporal	Johnson, Wm
220	1465	Privates	Johnson, Jno
221	633		Johnson, Jas
222	1		Johnstan, A
223	350		Jones, E
224	360		Jones, Jno
225	428		Jones, Jno
226	259		Jones, T
227	341		Jones, Wm
228	1681		Jones, Wm
229	88		Keene, J
230			Keegan, Jas
231			Kempsall, N
232			Kempster, Jno
233			Kelly, A
234			Kelly, J F
235	520		Kelly, Jas
236			Kelly, F
237			Knight, Jas
238			Lamb, Jas
239	707		Lambert, Thos
240			Leach, R W
241	326		Leaver, T
242			Lee, John
243	72		Lewis, H
244	478		Lewis, R
245			Lenain, Jno
246			Ling, Jas
247			Lippet, S
248			Lisbeck, G
249			Lloyde, G
250	1649		Lowe, C
251	1841		Lowe, R
252			Lockett, W
253			Lovell, C
254			Lyons, Jno
255			Lycett, Jas.
256		Private —	Lawrence, Jno
257			Mack, H A
258			Maney, C
259			Mann, Wm
260			Martin, D
261			McDonald, M
262			McFarlame, M
263			McHale, Jos
264			McKenzie, G J
265			Ma[illegible] R
266			Ma[illegible]ey, C, Rocket Battery
267			Malarey, M
268			Marley, L
269			Meredith, J H
270			Millen, C
271			Miller, P
272			Moore, R
273			Morgan, Jno
274			Morgan, Wm
275			Morris, Jno
276			Morse, R
277		Lance-Corporal	Murphy, Jno
278	63	Private	Murphy, Jno
279	862		Murphy, P
280			Murray, Jno
281			Nash, P
282			Newbery, A
283			Newbery, T
284			Nickolas, E, Rorke's Drift
285			Nickolas, Wm
286			Nye, Wm
287			Oakley, Wm
288			Odey, G
289			Ogden, Jas
290		Drummer	Osmond, C
291			Orlapp, J F
292		Private	Padmore, Jas
293			Painter, T
294	827		Parry, Jno
295	471		Parry, R
296	12		Patterson, G H
297	1	Drummer	Perkins, T
298		Private	Petus, Jno
299			Phillips, Jno
300			Phillips, J N
301			Pickard, J R
302			Plant, S
303			Plunkett, J
304			Pallen, A
305			Pope, W
306			Pottow, W
307			Powell, H
308			Procter, Jno
309			Prasser, G
310			Prasser, Jno
311	182		Pugh, Wm
312	856		Pugh, Wl
313			Quirk, Jas
314		Drummer—	Reardon, T
315		Private—	Remmington, E
316			Retford, W
317			Richards, G
318			Richardson, M
319			Rigney, Jno
320			Rettman, Jno
321			Roberts, Wm
322			Rowan, H
323			Rodgers, H
324			Rowbery, P
325			Rule, W
326			Rutter, T

The dismal list of officers and men killed at Isandhlwana on January 22, 1879 and published in The Natal Mercury *on February 10.*

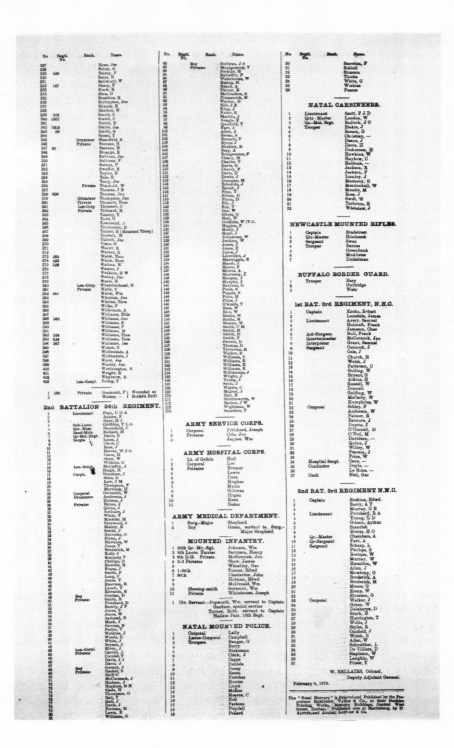

No	Regtl. No.	Rank.	Name.
327			Ryan, Jas
328			Salter, G
329	529		Sainey, F
330			Sears, H
331			Sellwood, W
332	147		Sharp, F
333			Shaw, R
334			Shea, D
335			Sheather, H
336			Shrimpton, Jno
337			Silcock, R
338			Skelton, W
339	806		Smith, C
340	1867		Smith, C
341			Smith, E
342	1903		Smith, Jas
343	58		Smith, G
344			Speed, T
345		Drummer	Stansfield, S
346		Private	Stevens, H
347	20		Stevens, W
348			Strange, E
349			Sullivan, Jno
350			Sullivan, P
351			Sutton, P
352			Swaffer, R
353			Taylor, E
354			Tate, R
355			Terry, Jas
356		Private	Theobald, W
357			Thomas, J B
358	636		Thomas, Jno
359		Drummer	Thompson, Jno
360		Private	Thomett, Thos
361		Lce-Corp	Thrassell, C
362		Private	Tillisard, H
363			Tuneny, T
364			Todd, G
365			Townsend, J
366			Trottmann, D
367			Turner, E (Mounted Troop)
368			Trowell, W
369			Tullett, Jas
370			Vines, G
371			Waller, E
372			Walker, E
373	285		Walsh, Thos
374	493		Walsh, Thos
375	596		Walhen, W
376			Warner, J
377			Watkins, H W
378			Watley, Jno
379			Watts, H
380		Lce.-Corp.	Wheatherhead, H
381		Private	Webb, T
382	861		Welsh, Wm
383			Wheelon, Jno
384			Whelan, Thos
385			Wilks, F
386			Wilkinson, A
387			Williams, Ellis
388	582		Williams, Jno
389			Williams, E
390			Williams, P
391			Williams, M
392	534		Williams, Thos
393	624		Williams, Thos
394	267		Williams, Jas
395			Wilson, S
396			Wolfendale, A
397			Wolfendale, J
398			Wood, Jas
399			Wooley, Jno
400			Worthington, E
401			Wright, R
402			Whybrow, E
403		Lce.-Corpl.	Young, T

No	Regtl. No.	Rank.	Name.	
1	568	Private	Desmond, P	Wounded at
2			Waters, —	Rorke's Drift

2nd BATTALION 24th REGIMENT.

No	Regtl. No.	Rank.	Name.
1		Lieutenant	Pope, C D A
2			Austen, F
3			Dyer, H J
4		Sub-Lieut.	Griffiths, T L G
5		Qtr.-Mstr.	Bloomfield, E
6		Band-Mstr.	Bullard, H
7		Qr-Mst. Srgt.	Davis, G
8		Sergts.	Lines, J
9			Chew, C
10			Ross, J
11			Reeves, W J G
12			Carse, H
13			Shaw, W
14			Wilkins, G
15		Lce.-Sergt.	McCaffry, J
16			Haigh, H
17		Corpls.	Henshaw, J
18			Sims, G
19			Low, J M
20			Thompson, T
21			Mortlock, H
22		Corporal	Greenhill, W
23		Drummers	Anderson, J
24			Holmes, J
25		Privates	Byrne, J
26			Quinn, J
27			McGuire, J
28			White, T
29			Mockler, M
30			Sherwood, S
31			Malley, E
32			Smith, J
33			Horrocks, G
34			Flynn, J
35			Hawkins, W
36			Jones, T
37			Broderick, M
38			Kelly J
39			Kennedy T
40			Phillips, D
41			Howells, R
42			Evans, J
43			Smith, P
44			Long, C
45			Jones, T
46			Emerson, R
47			Lynch, T
48			Edwards, E
49		Boy	Gordan, D
50		Privates	Smith, R
51			Pritchard, D
52			Buerly, J P
53			Jones, T
54			Jones, W
55			Sathand, B
56			Mack, J
57			Stevens, R
58			Pedler, T
59			Watkins, J
60			Woods, G
61			White, J
62			Bryant, J
63		Lce.-Corpl.	Elvey, J
64		Privates	Carroll, J.
65			Cornish T
66			Davis, J J
67			Davis, J
68		Boy	Gurney, J
69		Privates	Hacker, S
70			Hall, C
71			McCormack, J
72			Hudson, J
73			Hopkins, R H
74			Slade, H
75			Thompson, G
76			Ball, T
77			Hall, J
78			Davis, J
79			Fortune, M
80			Lewis, E
81			Williams, G

No.	Regtl. No.	Rank.	Name.
82		Boy	McEwan, J S
83		Privates	Montgomery, T
84			Perkins, H
85			McCaffry, P
86			Waterhouse, W
87			Bishop, H
88			Byard, A
89			Turner, B
90			McCracken, S
91			Fitzpatrick, M
92			Watson, G
93			Hill, J E
94			King, J
95			Nobes, R
96			Machin, J
97			Neagle, T
98			Quelford, T
99			Farr, A
100			Allen, J
101			Bevan, S
102			Bennett, T
103			Byrne J
104			Buckley, R
105			Bray, A
106			Bridgewater, F
107			Cleary, M
108			Charles, T
109			Davis, G
110			Cherry, F
111			Davis, D
112			Dowie, J
113			Donegan, M
114			Edwards, J
115			Earish, J
116			Finn, T
117			Fitton, G
118			Flynn, D
119			Fry, J
120			Fox, T
121			Gee, W
122			Ghost, G
123			Hall, W
124			Griffiths, W (V.C.
125			Hughes, F
126			Healy, J
127			Hunt, J
128			Johnstone, W
129			Jenkins, W
130			Jones, J
131			Jones, E
132			Jones, J
133			Llewellyn, J
134			Martingale, E
135			Marsh, J
136			Moore, F
137			Morris, A
138			Morrissey, J
139			Morgan, J
140			Murphy, J
141			McDoon, G
142			Poole, S
143			Popple, S
144			Price, H
145			Price, J
146			O'Keefe, T
147			Rees, W
148			Rice, W
149			Roche, W
150			Roche, M
151			Sheane, W
152			Smith, C M
153			Smith, H
154			Smith, D
155			Smith, F
156			Ferrett, D
157			Thomas, D
158			Treverton, R
159			Walker, S
160			Williams, E
161			Williams, E
162			Williams, E
163			Williams, E
164			Williamson, J
165			Wright, J
166			Young, J
167			Scott, J
168			Waters, C
169			Mulroy, J
170			Hall, B
171			Shuttleworth, W
172			Barton, J W
173			Wightman, W
174			Saunders, T

ARMY SERVICE CORPS.

1	Corporal	Pritchard, Joseph
2	Privates	Cole, Jno
3		Jaques, Wm

ARMY HOSPITAL CORPS.

1	Lt. of Ordrls	Hall
2	Corporal	Lee
3	Privates	Kremer
4		Lewis
5		Dean
6		Hughes
7		Munn
8		Giliman
9		Hogan
10		Keen
11		Baker

ARMY MEDICAL DEPARTMENT.

1	Surg.-Major	Shepherd
2	Boy	Green, servant to Surg.-Major Shepherd

MOUNTED INFANTRY.

1	80th Qr.-Mr.-Sgt.	Johnson, Wm
2	9th Lncrs. Farrier	Sampson, Henry
3	6th D.G. Private	McStravick, Jno
4	2-3 Privates	Shaw, James
5		Wheatley, Geo
6	1-24th	Turner, Edwd
7	80th	Chesterton, John
8		Holman, Edwd
9		McDonald, Wm
10	Shoeing-smith	Seymour, Wm
11	Private	Whitehouse, Joseph

1 Civ. Servant—Popworth, Wm. servant to Captain Gardner, special service
Turner, Robt. servant to Captain Hallam Parr, 13th Regt.

NATAL MOUNTED POLICE.

No.	Regtl. No.	Rank.	Name.
1		Corporal	Lally
2		Lance-Corporal	Campbell
3		Troopers	Banger, G
4			Berry
5			Blakeman
6			Clark, J
7			Capps
8			Daniels
9			Dorey
10			Eason
11			Fletcher
12			Hunter
13			Lloyd
14			McRae
15			Meares, C
16			Neil
17			Parsons
18			Pleydell
19			Pollard
20			Secretan, F
21			Siddall
22			Stimson
23			Thicke
24			White, C
25			Winkles
26			Pearce

NATAL CARBINEERS.

1	Lieutenant	Scott, F J D
2	Qrtr.-Master	London, W
3	Qr.-Mst. Srgt.	Bullock, J C
4	Trooper	Blakie, J
5		Borain, G
6		Christian, —
7		Deane, J
8		Davis, H
9		Dickenson, H
10		Hawkins, W
11		Hayhow, C
12		Haldane, —
13		Jackson, R
14		Jackson, F
15		Lumley, J
16		Macleroy, G
17		Mendenhall, W
18		Moodie, M
19		Ross, J
20		Swift, W
21		Tarboton, E
22		Whitelaw, J

NEWCASTLE MOUNTED RIFLES.

1	Captain	Bradstreet
2	Qtr-Master	Hitchcock
3	Sergeant	Swan
4	Trooper	Barnes
5		Greenbank
6		McAlister
7		Dinkelman

BUFFALO BORDER GUARD.

1	Trooper	Eary
2		Guttridge
3		Wehr

1st BAT. 3rd REGIMENT, N.N.C.

1	Captain	Krohn, Robert
2		Lonsdale, James
3	Lieutenant	Avery, Samuel
4		Holcraft, Frank
5		Jameson, Chas
6	Act-Surgeon	Bull, Frank
7	Quartermaster	McCormick, Jno
8	Interpreter	Grant, Samuel
9	Sergeant	Connock, J
10		Cole, J
11		Church, H
12		Welsh, J
13		Patterson, C
14		Golling, W
15		Bryant, G
16		Atkins, H
17		Russell, W
18		Donnell
19		Golding, W
20		McCarty, W
21		Humphries, W
22	Corporal	Sibley, F
23		Anderson, W
24		Palmer, R
25		Balmore, J
26		Dupris, J
27		O'Connell, D
28		O'Neil, M
29		Davidson, —
30		Quinn, J
31		Willey, W
32		Pearson, J
33		Price, W
34	Hospital Sergt.	Cane, —
35	Conductor	Doyle, —
36		Le Roue, —
37	Cook	Neil, Geo

2nd BAT. 3rd REGIMENT N.N.C.

1	Captain	Erskine, Edwd.
2		Barry, A T
3		Murray, O E
4	Lieutenant	Pritchard, R A
5		Young, L D
6		Gibson, Arthur
7		Standish
8		Rivers, H O
9	Qr.-Master	Chambers, A
10	Qr-Sergeant	Farr, A
11	Sergeant	Schaap, L
12		Phillips, S
13		Brebner, W
14		Murray, W
15		Hamilton, W
16		Allen, J
17		Mowbray, G
18		Broderick, A
19		Broderick, M
20		Moore, G
21		Kemp, W
22		Elverson, G
23	Corporal	Walker, J
24		Green, W
25		Delaharpe, D
26		Sturk, H
27		Harrington, T
28		Willis, J
29		Styles, R
30		Caufield, J
31		Welsh, E
32		Allen, W
33		Schneither, L
34		De Villiers, D
35		Stapleton, W
36		Laughin, W
37		Pitzer, T

W. BELLAIRS, Colonel,
Deputy Adjutant General.

February 6, 1879.

The "Natal Mercury" is Printed and Published by the Proprietors ROBINSON, VAUSE & Co., at their Machine Printing Works, Mercury Buildings, Central West Street, Durban. Published also at Maritzburg, by D SATTER, and ADAMS, LONDON & Co.

When we arrived within two miles of the camp, advanced guards were sent forward, but nothing was seen of the enemy. Our route was continued in the same order and with all precautions; the daylight dying away more and more, until, when the water-wash to the south of the camp was crossed, it was as dark as it ever became throughout that memorable night. At a distance of within a mile, where the ground rose to the site of the camp, we could see, by the shadows against the horizon, on the top of the neck of land, where our road ran back to the Bashee Valley, and so on to Rorke's Drift, that the enemy had dragged numerous waggons, so as to place a sort of barrier across our only road back. And from behind this we thought we could hear the hoarse cries of the enemy, and the rattle of their knob-kerries and assegais against their shields. A halt was therefore made to allow the guns to pour four rounds of shrapnel into the barricade, when the advance was resumed. Meanwhile Major Black received orders to gain possession, at all risks, of the kopje on the left of the ridge; as those holding it would then be enabled to protect our flank effectually, and to command the ridge itself with a destructive fire. As the gallant Major moved off in the dark on this hazardous errand, apparently one of almost certain death, I heard him call out to his men, "No firing, but only one volley, boys, and then give them the cold steel." After a short advance by the main body a second halt took place, and the shrapnel-fire was repeated. Afterwards all was silence, and we resumed our onward march. The 2-24th on the right were ordered to fire a few rounds, with the object of drawing the fire of the enemy, if any, but fruitlessly; and then, in silence and darkness, we moved on once more.

A little farther on, and we began to stumble over dead bodies in every direction, and in some places, especially where from the formation of the ground there was a ditch or anything like shelter, the men were found lying thick and close, as though they had fought there till their ammunition was exhausted, and then been surrounded and slaughtered. When within a few hundred yards of the top of the ridge, with the large and grotesque form of the Isandhlwana Mountain looming up in front of us, and showing clearly against the sky in the dusk of evening, we heard a ringing British cheer from hundreds of throats. We thus learnt that Major Black and his men of the 2-24th had gained the kopje without any resistance, and therefore that the enemy had retired still farther, though between us and Rorke's Drift. It was 8 or 9 p.m. by the time our little force had ascended the ridge; we received orders to bivouac where and as we were, on the field of slaughter, and only to move forward by daylight in the morning. Such precautions as were possible were taken to guard against a surprise; for it was known that a large force was following in the rear; and the victorious enemy were believed to be in close proximity to our front and flanks.

But oh! how dreadful were those weary hours that followed! while all had to watch and wait, through the darkness, with what patience we could muster, for the dawn of day; with the knowledge that we were standing and lying amid and surrounded by the corpses of our late comrades — though in what fearful numbers we then but little knew. Many a vow of vengeance was breathed in the stillness of the night; and many and deep were the sobs that came from the breasts of men who, perhaps, had never sobbed before, at discovering, even by that dim light, the bodies of dear friends, brutally massacred, stripped of all clothing, disembowelled, mutilated, and in some cases decapitated. How that terrible night passed with us I fancy few would care to tell, even if they could recall it. For my own part, I felt both reckless and despairing — reckless at the almost certain prospect of an overwhelming attack by the enemy, flushed with victory — despairing, because of the melancholy scene of horror which I felt awaited us at daybreak. During the night we noticed fires constantly burning on all the surrounding hills; and in particular one bright blaze riveted our attention throughout, as it seemed to be near Rorke's Drift, and we feared for the safety of those left in that small place, knowing how utterly powerless we were to aid them in any way before morning. Happily, in this instance, our fears were in vain.

After lying down for a while close to the General and his Staff, I arose at about an hour before daylight, for the purpose of taking a quiet look around, to see the state of matters for myself, and recognise what bodies I could. Nothing but a sense of duty could have induced me to undertake the task, or sustained me in its execution so as to go through with it. Not even on the recent battle-fields of Europe, though hundreds were lying where now I saw only tens, was there ever a more sickening or heart-rending sight! The corpses of our poor soldiers, whites and natives, lay thick upon the ground in clusters, together with dead and mutilated horses, oxen and mules, shot and stabbed in every position and manner; and the whole intermingled with the fragments of our Commissariat waggons, broken and wrecked, and rifled of their contents, such as flour, sugar, tea, biscuits, mealies, oats, Xc., the *débris* being all scattered about, and wasted as in pure wantonness on the ground. The dead bodies of the men lay as they had fallen, but mostly with only their boots and shirts on, or perhaps a pair of trousers or a remnant of a coat, with just sufficient means of recognition to determine to which branch of the Service they had belonged. In many instances they lay with sixty or seventy empty cartridge cases surrounding them, thus showing that they had fought to the very last, and only succumbed and fallen, after doing their duty without flinching, and when all means of resistance were exhausted. It seemed to me, at the time, that it was really wonderful that so small a force had been able to maintain such a desperate resistance for so long. There were, indeed, only about 900 men in camp, exclusive of our natives, who ran away, and of Colonel Durnford's mounted men, under Captain Barton; and yet, fighting in the open, without defensive works, protection or cover, they kept at bay for hours the almost overwhelming army of Zulus, by whom they were attacked and surrounded. Captain Barton subsequently told me that his mounted men really fought well at their first charge, and until all their ammunition was exhausted; they were then compelled to fall back on the camp, where they sought for a fresh supply of ammunition. Unfortunately, this was refused them by the officer in charge, who said it would all be required by the infantry themselves. This was assuredly a fatal error of judgment, inasmuch as a large quantity of ammunition unused fell into the hands of the enemy, together with more than 1,000 Martini-Henry rifles and carbines. Perhaps, however, though the defence might have been prolonged, the disastrous issue could not have been averted, considering the strength of the enemy. So far as I could judge, from what I saw through my field-glass, combined with all the reliable information which could possibly be obtained at the time, and careful computation, the line of Zulu warriors, which came down from the hills on the left, must have extended over a length of nearly three miles, and consisted of more than 15,000 men. And another large body, of at least 5,000, was held in reserve, remaining on the crest of the slope and taking no part in the first onslaught. They took part in the work of spoil and plunder at the camp, and aided in driving off the captured cattle and such waggons as had not been wrecked. Most of the bodies of their dead were also removed by them in the waggons, so that not many were found by us on the field; this makes it difficult to form any accurate estimate of the total loss on their side, which must have been considerable. Assuming that our troops had seventy rounds each, and allowing for the effective execution of many rounds of shrapnel and cases from the two guns, as well as the rockets, discharged into the dense masses at close quarters, I think the Zulus' loss may fairly be set down at not far short of 2,000, an estimate which has been considered low by military men well qualified to judge.

I had scarcely returned from my melancholy round, when just as daylight began to appear, preparations for the advance were completed, and the word was given to march. Formed in fours, not in line this time, we proceeded rapidly on our return route, with strong advance and rear guards, and feeling well on our flanks. On nearing the farther side of the plain, where the neck of land gives access to the Bashee valley, we saw in the distance on our left a returning Zulu *impi,* numbering many thousands. Judging from the numerous evidences of burning kraals bordering the Buffalo river itself, we concluded that this was a part of the victorious army which had set out from Isandhlwana, attacked the post at Rorke's Drift, and were now on their way back to Ulundi, after raiding the Border. This sight served to intensify our anxiety, and caused us to hurry onwards. We quickly reached the brow of the hill overlooking the Buffalo river and Rorke's Drift, with our previous camping ground on the opposite bank; but the sight of buildings in flames at the station by no means allayed our fears. Before we quite reached the river I carefully examined the house at Rorke's Drift through my field-glass, and thought I could distinguish the figures of men on parts of the wall and roof of the large building, and one of them seemed to be waving a flag. The attention of the General having been called to this, Colonel Russell, with some of his mounted infantry and myself, at once crossed the river and galloped up to the station at full speed. Much to our delight and relief, we were greeted with a hearty English cheer, showing that here at least no irreparable disaster had befallen. We quickly dismounted, and found the place had been temporarily defended by a barricade of empty biscuit-boxes and mealies in sacks, while outside numerous bodies of dead Zulus were lying all around. The little garrison, it appeared, had received timely warning from the fugitives escaped from the camp at Isandhlwana, and they were thus enabled to make some slight preparations for the antici-pated assault, so that they successfully withstood, and repulsed with severe loss to the enemy, a body of over 4,000 Zulus, that had commenced the attack on them at five on the previous (Wednesday) evening, and continued almost unintermittently till daybreak, only retiring upon the approach of our little column. The small garrison consisted of only about 130 men, under Lieutenant Chard, R.E., and Lieutenant Bromhead, 2-24th. Major Spalding, D.A.Q.M.G., had been left in command of the post, but had gone away to Helpmekaar late on the Tuesday afternoon preceding. The following officers were also present at the post and rendered material aid in the defence: Dr. Reynolds, 1-24th, Lieutenant Adendorff, 1-3rd N.N.C., Messrs. Dunne, Dalton, and Byrne, of the Com-missariat Department, as also the Rev. Mr. Smith, Protestant Chaplain to No. 8 Column.

It seems that several parties of men, escaping from the scene of the massacre at Isandhlwana, some of them strong in numbers, passed by Rorke's Drift; but it must be said, much to their discredit, they would not remain to aid the little garrison, but con-tinued their flight to Helpmekaar. The conflagration which we had seen was in a detached building, used as a hospital, at some little distance away from the house; this though at first defended, could not be held, and had therefore been evacuated.

The rest of the Mounted Infantry, and the General with his Staff, speedily also arrived at the station; and the gallant defenders, on relating the particulars of their heroic resistance, were warmly commended and deservedly congratulated. The remainder of the Column in the meantime crossed the river and encamped temporarily close by. Shortly afterwards, by the General's orders, the entire force was set to work to clear the ground around the station of all cover for an enemy's attack, to reconstruct and strengthen the barricade, and to mount the four guns, one at each corner. The roof of the house, being a thatch, was also stripped from it, to prevent further peril of fire. The two battalions of the N.N.C. were posted on the large hill at the back, to prevent any enemy occupying it to fire down on the station, and also to keep guard on the river. These preparations were necessary, as precautions against any possible attack, as the General had decided to remain for the time at Rorke's Drift; and they occupied the whole morning. Not till they were completed were the rations served out. It will readily be conceived what a boon this was at last, to men who had been out for two days and nights,

"At about 6.30 am we reached Rorke's Drift and saw smoke rising from the Post. Too late! Too late! But no — from amidst the smoke we saw the figures gesticulating; then a flag waved . . . we were not too late. There were 351 dead bodies found lying around the house and between it and the hill: and 60 around and in the burning hospital which they had succeeded in firing." Illustrated (and written) by Lt-Col. Crealock who, with Lord Chelmsford, was part of the 'relief' column which had spent the night on the battlefield of Isandhlwana and, before dawn, had set out to find what had befallen Rorke's Drift (Africana Museum).

who had had during that time absolutely nothing to eat but a little biscuit and tinned meat, and nothing to drink except bad water, while undergoing the fatigues of marching and skirmishing, and the wretched anxiety of such a miserable bivouac as our last.

Dramatic as Norris-Newman's despatch was (he was described as a 'smart fellow but wary' by Lt John Maxwell of the Natal Native Contingent, who had the ghastly experience on the night of the battle of slipping on the rocky hillside and landing with his hands inside the slit stomach of one of the dead and being unable to wash his hands until he reached Rorke's Drift the following morning), for sheer dramatic description it was exceeded by that of Muziwento.

A youth who lived nearby, Muziwento and his friends visited the silent battlefield three days after Chelmsford had left it for Rorke's Drift. His story was recounted to *The Natal Mercury,* from which newspaper this fraction of the interview is reproduced:

> "We arrived early in the morning. We saw the soil that it was red . . . we saw a single warrior dead, staring . . . his war shield in his hand . . . We saw countless things dead. Dead was the horse, dead too, the mule, dead was the dog, dead was the monkey, dead were the wagons, dead were the tents, dead were the boxes, dead was everything, even to the very metals . . ."

Almost four months to the day later, on May 21, after dining with Archibald Forbes, 'the *Daily News* special', Norris-Newman returned to Isandhlwana with a party of mounted volunteers under the command of General Marshall to visit the camp, bury the dead and retrieve any remaining relics.

Norris-Newman was able to visit his own tent and sift through his papers. He was not, of course, the only correspondent to have visited the melancholy site in the months that the dead had lain unburied. Both Melton Prior, *The Illustrated London News* artist who was a more than passable writer, and, notably, Archibald Forbes, had written moving accounts. In his guise of Special War Correspondent to the *Times of Natal,* Norris-Newman wrote the following account which put the full-stop on the stories emanating from the battlefield:

> Harness, accompanied by a detachment of the Army Service corps with seventy-five pairs of led horses, crossed the river at daybreak, and advanced in open order up the hill the other side. Nothing of any interest occurred, and no signs of any enemy were seen until we reached the last valley before reaching Isandhlwana. But immediately upon our descending this, signal fires were seen on our right, and these were quickly followed along the river line to the Inshlasagazi Mountains. On our left we could trace the advance of Colonel Davy Lowe's Brigade, and also that of Major Bengough's Native Battalion, by the smoke arising from the burning kraals, orders having been given to burn every kraal round about. We could also see our own native scouts racing up the hill so as to reach the scene first. We pushed on very steadily and carefully, and at half-past nine our advance guard was on the ridge overlooking the valley beyond Isandhlwana. There it lay, a magnificent stretch of country, with undulating plains for miles, only broken by dongas, and small rises, and bordered by high hills on each side. Who would have thought, looking down on the quiet scene, that it had witnessed one of the most terrific fights and disasters of modern times? The grass had grown up over the whole site of what had once been our camp, and was thickly intermixed with mealie stalks and oathay, green and growing yet. Among these lay the bodies of our poor soldiers scattered

50

The gallant defence of Rorke's Drift by Lieutenants Chard and Bromhead and 137 men — the scene at daybreak the following morning (Africana Museum).

about in all postures, and in all stages of decay; while the position of our tents were indicated by the broken remains of boxes, trunks, tins of preserved meats, remnants of the tents themselves, and masses of disordered papers, books, and letters, &c. the only thing, however, that at once drew the attention of a casual observer was the broken remains of wagons, and the skeletons of horses and oxen. Everything else was hidden at first sight, and required searching for to be noticed. One thing we had observed coming along the road was the fresh spoor of a wagon or two, and we conjectured that it had been recently used in conveying crops from Sirayo's valley away into the strongholds further inland. The spoor of two mounted Kafirs, and one on foot, was also traced by the scouts fresh that morning; one of the horses was shod all round, and these men were evidently of the party left by the enemy to watch the coming of our troops. For some time after our arrival, and while preparations were being actively carried out to harness the horses to the best wagons, all the men, except those on vidette or other duty, were allowed to wander over the scene of the disaster. The Carbineers, under Captain Shepstone, made immediately for their camp, and tried to find any relics of their dead brethren. Nothing of any consequence was, however, found near their lines; but upon searching over the ground where the bodies of some of them had been seen on the night after Isandhlwana, Captain Shepherd came upon the bodies of Colonel Durnford, Lieut. Scott, and nearly all the Carbineers, except London and Bullock, and those few who were killed along the fugitive path. Poor Durnford was easily recognisable, and he had on his mess waistcoat, from the pocket of which Shepstone took a small pocket knife with his name on it. Two rings were also taken, and are with the knife to be sent home in memoriam to the Colonel's father. Durrant Scott lay partially hidden under a broken piece of a wagon, and had evidently not been mutilated or touched after his death. He had his patrol jacket on, buttoned across, and although the rest of the body was only a skeleton, yet strange to say, the face was like in life, all the hair being still on, and the skin strangely parched and dried up, although perfect. Both these bodies lay right in the midst of the rest of the young colonists who fell gallantly in defence of their country, and judging from the position in which they all were, they must have made one last gallant stand, and have been killed altogether. None of these so found had attempted to run, but had stuck together in life as we found them in death. Knowing all of them well, and how they did their duty, I felt it almost impossible to examine any, and had to leave the scene for another one. I can only add that Durnford's body was wrapped in canvas and buried in a kind of waterwash, while all the others were covered over with stones, &c., and their names written in pencil, on wood, or a stone close by thorn.

The bodies of the Royal Artillery and Natal Mounted Police were also buried, the only ones left untouched being those of the 24th Regiment, which was done at the express desire of Colonel Glyn and the officers, in the hope of their being able some day to do it themselves. This appeared, however, very strange to us, and many remarks were made about the seeming dishonour to part of our brave dead. However, let us hope that some day, not far distant, we may be able to return to that once blood-red field and bury all the bodies, bones and relics that may be left. Great numbers of wagons have undoubtedly been taken away, as also everything of value in the camp, and many bodies have been, through one cause or another, either wholly or partially removed or disturbed, so as to effectually prevent recognition. I myself did not move far out of camp, and, therefore, may be a bad judge; but from what I saw there cannot have been more than 200 bodies in camp itself, and out of these not 25 Kafirs. Doubtless had I gone out to where the fighting first commenced, I should have found many more bodies, but I am glad for my own sake that I did not do so. Others who have had not perhaps so many bitter feelings, or sorrowful remembrances of those lying round us, went further and saw more, although I cannot hear of anyone having recognized any more bodies of officers, except those of the Hon. S. Vereker, and young Gibson, both lieutenants in the Native Contingent. I had the melancholy satisfaction of seeing my own tent, or rather the remains of it, with all my papers, letters, and books lying about torn up, but nothing of value was left, and I only succeeded in bringing away with me a few letters from my wife, a book containing some tales written by me, and a photo that had just reached me two days before the massacre. The skeletons of my servants and horses lay just behind my tent, as I was in the habit of having them picketed in that place. Many interesting relics were found, and brought away by others, and I know of a few cases where letters addressed to relatives at home from those among the killed, were found complete, and will be sent home to be held in loving regard by the living, but will cause many sores scarce healed to be reopened. The General was anxious, for more reasons than one, to get away, and therefore, as soon as the wagons were ready, we made a start back at 12, and reached Rorke's Drift at half-past three, without any hitch whatever. Immediately on getting back I went enquiring about among the different parties who had been over that day, and gleaned some other interesting facts from them. One officer in the Dragoon Guards, while out with his squadron burning kraals, found in one signs of very recent occupation, and the staff of the Queen's colour of the 1-24th. He also later on came across a kraal full of skeletons of Zulus, and this fact, taken in conjunction with a statement made in a former letter that the Zulus did not move their dead bodies, and as the kraal was some two miles off where skeletons were found, they probably also moved them in our wagons. The forty wagons we brought away included two water carts in good preservation, one gun limber, a rocket battery cart, and three Scotch carts. All that we left behind, in number not more than twenty, were in a partially or entirely disabled condition. Counting all there, therefore, there are still sixty or seventy wagons missing, which have been taken away at different times.

On Thursday morning General Marshall left with his staff for Dundee, and the cavalry were to have a day's rest before returning; while two companies of the 2-24th, under Major Bromhead, left for Dundee to join two already there. Last week, when Colonel Black and other officers visited Isandhlwana, in coming home by the Fugitives' Drift, they came across the body of Major Stuart Smith, who was killed just before reaching the river. They were not able to bury him on that occasion, being fired upon; but the morning after our visit, a squadron of Lancers, with some Artillery under Colonel Harness, went down one side of the river, crossed over at the Fugitives' Drift, and buried the body, returning in the afternoon.

The men of the 24th Regiment were finally buried in late June, their shallow graves joining those of their comrades beneath the shadow of Isandhlwana.

It was a shadow which stretched long: in England, fired by the disaster of Isandhlwana and the heroism of Rorke's Drift, the Prince Imperial of France volunteered for service in the troublesome colony. His was to be the next big story.

'Slain by savages'

Death of the Prince Imperial, 1879

On 11 July 1879, at 21h00 on a late summer's evening, a troop of English soldiers riding four abreast and with sabres drawn, preceded a gun carriage draped with the colours of France and England through the High Street of Chislehurst, Kent. Within the coffin lay the body of the young Prince Imperial of France, 22-year-old Napoleon Louis Eugene Jean Joseph, with 17 assegai wounds, mostly on his arms, chest and right eye.

On the following day, with the grey charger he had bought in Durban, Natal, three months before walking behind the gun carriage, and in the presence of Queen Victoria, the Prince was laid to rest beside his father, the late Emperor Louis Napoleon, in the Roman Catholic chapel and, with him, were buried the last hopes of the restoration of the French monarchy.

'He is a fine young fellow,' the Duke of Cambridge wrote to Lieutenant-General Lord Chelmsford, Commander of the British forces in South Africa, as the young Prince, fired by the battles of Isandhlwana and Rorke's Drift, departed on *The Danube* for Cape Town and Durban, 'full of spirit and pluck . . . my only anxiety on his account is that he is too go-a-head and plucky.'

In Durban, the Prince met M. Deléage, correspondent of *Figaro*, who was to follow his every move but not, alas, those of his last day, and bought Percy, his charger, and another horse, Fate. Together with his valet, his groom and the two horses, the prince arrived with Lord Chelmsford at Landsman's Drift, near the Buffalo River, Natal, on 29 March 1879.

For the fiery and impetuous Prince, the next two months were frustrating. Expressly forbidden by Queen Victoria and his mother, the Empress Eugenie, to take part in active warfare, he spent his time sketching reconnaissance maps. It was not what he had come to Africa for. He carried with him Napoleon's sword, and it was no secret that he wanted to use it on active duty. But Chelmsford, mindful of his charge's importance and the consequences should any harm come to him, kept him on a short reign.

On 1 June, however, the Prince Imperial persuaded Lieutenant Jahleel Carey to take him out on a reconnaissance party and, out of sight of the camp, to hand over effective command to him. Before setting out, the Prince penned a note to his mother the Empress, handing it to a correspondent on his way to Pietermaritzburg with a batch of despatches.

He left behind in the camp at Landman's Drift a group of distinguished British correspondents: Francis Francis of *The Times* (later fishing editor of *The Field*), Melton Prior, *The Illustrated London News'* artist who had arrived in South Africa on 6 April, F.R. MacKenzie of the London *Standard,* Phil Robinson of *The Daily Telegraph* and M. Deléage of *Figaro.* Although aware of the Prince's departure, as far as the correspondents were concerned it was just another reconnaissance party and as such not particularly newsworthy.

Too impatient to wait for the arrival of the six Basotho who normally accompanied such parties, the Prince, Lieutenant Carey and six troopers of Bettington's Horse, set off into the bushveld of Natal. They were armed with Martini-Henry carbines and a hunting knife each. A Zulu guide went with them.

The Prince Imperial and his party dismounted at a newly-deserted Zulu kraal owned by a petty chief, Sabuza. Dogs were still nosing around the empty huts, but a cursory search indicated that the area around the kraal was free of Zulus. From the kraal, a deep donga ran down to the Ityotyosi River. It was 15h00, and the Prince gave the order to off-saddle. He sat down to sketch the terrain. Neither he nor Lieutenant Carey posted look-outs.

At 15h45, a restive Lieutenant Carey suggested that the horses be fetched. The Prince, still sketching, was in no hurry to go. The guide reported a Zulu on the opposite hill, and the horses were gathered immediately.

The Prince got to his feet and gave the order: 'Prepare to mount.' No one was later certain who gave the following order: 'Mount!', but it was either Carey or the Prince Imperial, for the Zulus, creeping through the long grass, were upon them, yelling 'uSuthu' and brandishing a mixture of rifles and assegais.

The Prince's charger bolted. A brilliant horseman, he chased after it, caught it by the holster and ran with it for a hundred yards, struggling to mount. But the leather strap gave way and the horse disappeared into the donga. The Prince's sword, once carried by Napoleon himself was lost. (It was returned to Lord Chelmsford during peace negotiations prior to the Battle of Ulundi.) Drawing his revolver (from which he fired two shots), the Prince was last seen by the fleeing troopers as he ran into the donga, pursued by the Zulus.

Langalabalele threw an assegai which hit the Prince on the thigh; Xamanga, of the uMbonambi regiment, who was to lose his life at the Battle of Ulundi, was the next to spear him.

Carey and four men were the only survivors. They caught the Prince Imperial's horse, Percy, and, deciding there was little they could do against overwhelming odds, galloped for the distant camp.

Carey blurted the news to an incredulous Lieutenant-Colonel Richard Harrison, who in turn informed Lord Chelmsford that the Prince Imperial was missing and presumed dead. Aghast, Chelmsford asked for reports from the surviving troopers and ordered a large force to set out the following morning.

Deléage, almost beside himself, and having difficulty understanding the nuances of the English language, confronted Chelmsford and Carey. The news was confirmed. Forbes, Francis, Robinson and MacKenzie vied with each other to get at the telegraph. But they were not in full possession of the facts — no one was — and the first report was confused and merited no more than one paragraph in *The Natal Mercury* of Wednesday, 4 June:

THE ZULU WAR
Much excitement and anxiety prevailed throughout the town yesterday in consequence of the report telegraphed from Maritzburg that the Prince Imperial had been shot, but that his body had not been found. How the manner of the Prince's reported death could be known, if his remains had not been discovered, it is not easy to understand, and for some time we were not disposed to attach credence to the story. Any misfortune happening to the brave young prince who so gallantly cast in his lot with his old comrades in arms, at a critical juncture, would be intensely deplored by every colonist, by every citizen of the empire, and by every admirer of generous and courageous conduct.

More than 1 000 men set out at 07h00 on the morning of 2 June to find the Prince. He was found naked except for a gold chain with a medal of the Virgin and Napoleon's seal around his neck.

The death of the Prince Imperial, based on eye-witness accounts, and reproduced from Le Monde Illustre. On the brow of the hill the disappearing troopers and the Prince's riderless horse are just visible (Africana Museum).

56

We could recognise, even from a distance, the small white and well-knit body, in which the grace of form did not interfere with strength and activity [wrote Deléage in *Figaro*]. The Prince was lying on his back; his arms, stiffened by death, crossed a little above the chest; the features showed no sign of pain, or any contraction whatever; the left eye was half-closed, the right eye had been destroyed by an assegai stab. The chest was pierced by 17 wounds and according to their custom, the Zulus had cut open the stomach, but the incision was only a small one, and the viscera had been spared.

Melton Prior had brought his materials, and quickly sketched the place of the Prince's death and the Prince himself, his unmistakable profile illustrated from the left. The sketches were sent off from the camp the following day, enabling *The Illustrated London News* to be the only paper to publish eye-witness illustrations. As soon as they were able to after returning to the camp, the correspondents sent out telegrams confirming the death.

The Natal Mercury reported:

"MERCURY" TELEGRAMS.
THE PRINCE IMPERIAL
(Times to Mercury)

Having on receipt of the reported death of the Prince Imperial, wired for information, the following reply, dated Maritzburg, 10.45 a.m., reached us at 4 p.m.:—

Tuesday, 4 p.m.

It was reported yesterday that the Prince Imperial had been shot while off-saddling in a mealie garden. General Clifford has up to the present received no official information from Lord Chelmsford or from any other source on the subject; but has copy of a telegram from the front from the Hon. Bourke, correspondent of the *Daily Telegraph*. Will telegraph further information as soon as it is received from official or other authentic source. From private source we learn that another telegram to the same effect has been received.

At a late hour last night we received the following:

Ladysmith, June 8, 10 a.m.

News has just come that the Prince Imperial has been killed by Zulus. He and a few mounted men were out sketching a few miles from the column, when the Zulus fell on them, killing the Prince and two others.

Although the news was still sketchy, the *Times of Natal, The Natal Witness, The Natal Mercury* and the *Cape Times* were at least able to confirm the death of the Prince on 5 June:

THE ZULU WAR.

"MERCURY" TELEGRAMS.
THE PRINCE IMPERIAL
(From Times of Natal to Mercury.)

Mercury Office, Wednesday,
June 4th, 4.35 p.m.

The following special order has been issued by General Clifford:—

Wednesday, June 4th.

The Inspector-General of Lines of Communication and Base has received from His Excellency the Lieut.-General Commanding official confirmation of the calamity which has befallen the forces under his command, by the death, on duty in the field, of the late gallant young soldier the Prince Imperial, Louis Napoleon, who having in his military training been associated with the British army, came out to this country to take part in the Zulu campaign.

The Inspector-General feels that he is carrying out the wishes of His Excellency the Lieut.-General commanding, now in Zululand, by thus recording the feelings of deep sorrow and sympathy, experienced by every officer and man whose duty keeps him at his post in the colony, with the loss thus sustained.

The body of the unfortunate Prince will arrive here probably on Monday next, the 9th inst., *en route* to England. Arrangements will be made to receive it with all due respect and expression of sorrow.

Natal Mercury Office,
Wednesday, June 4, 10.30 a.m.

The news of the death of the Prince Imperial is officially confirmed. General Clifford has received a telegram, stating that he was killed, with two troopers.

The *Times* this morning says he was out sketching at the time. His body has been recovered, and will be brought to Maritzburg on Monday.

The Death of the Prince Imperial

The following telegram with regard to the sad death of the Prince Imperial of France reached us yesterday. It is intended to send the body to England; and it will be seen that the escort in charge of the remains arrived at Ladysmith yesterday.

ARRIVAL OF THE BODY AT LADYSMITH.
(BY ELECTRIC TELEGRAPH.)
(From our Special Correspondent)

Ladysmith, Wednesday, 3.15 p.m.

The escort with the remains of the late Prince has just arrived, and is to proceed this evening.

The Natal Witness amplified *The Natal Mercury*'s report, although information was still scanty:

Pietermaritzburg, 5.50 p.m.

Last Monday *Witness* telegram startled Maritzburg into agitation, being headed "Death of Prince Imperial," stating that whilst out patrolling he and his companions off-saddled near mealie field, from which soon after a volley was fired, as they were about remount. The Prince was first to fall. But news came in so tardily, that doubts grew, hopes fathering such doubts. Upon enquiry at General Clifford's, so late as eleven p.m. yesterday, no official confirmation had been received. *Telegraph* and other correspondents only too strongly confirm facts however. Shortly after leaving General Clifford the official telegram arrived, unknown to us though until this morning. The Prince and two troopers had fallen before a volley from hidden Zulus. Prince's body had been recovered, and will be conveyed to Pietermaritzburg, where it is expected to arrive on Monday. It is said Prince was sketching. Apart from political feelings, his death is much mourned by all — the man, if not the Prince.

Mule cart left Dundee for Maritzburg, containing body of Prince Imperial.

Archibald Forbes had telegraphed the London *Daily News* that the Prince was 'slain by savages in an obscure corner of a remote Continent . . . a miserable end truly for him who was once the Son of France'. But it wasn't until 11 June that full details of the Prince's death were published. They ran side by side with the account of the passing of the Prince Imperial's cortège from Ladysmith to Pietermaritzburg and then to Durban where, in the Roman Catholic cathedral, the coffin lay overnight, a tricolour and the Prince's sword and helmet upon it.

An abridged version of Phil Robinson's report to *The Daily Telegraph* was carried by the *Cape Times* after first appearing in *The Natal Witness:*

Pietermaritzburg, Saturday evening.
Cull following from Phil Robinson's account of Prince's death. Huts near which party off-saddled betrayed no signs of recent occupation, but two or three dogs still lingered about. Between it and river stretched luxuriant growth of Tambookie grass, five feet in height, interspersed with mealies and Kafir corn. Party sent their Kafir to river for water and made coffee. Concealed the while by deep donga were forty to fifty Zulus, who, creeping afterwards along river banks hidden by rank vegetation, must have been surprised by the Kafir crossing river and running away. Kafir returned to party and gave the alarm. In a few minutes the party was ready for starting; all stood to their horses awaiting order to mount. The word was hardly spoken when with a startling crash there burst from the cover a volley from forty rifles; the distance was not twenty yards, and the long grass swayed to the sudden rush of Zulus, as, with tremendous shout they charged towards Prince and companions. Horses, all swerved at suddenness of tumult, and some broke away. Rogers, of Beddington's Horse, was shot before he could recover his horse; and the Prince was unable to mount his charger, a grey 16 hands high always difficult to mount, and on this occasion frightened by firing. One by one party galloped past the Prince in vain endeavouring to mount. He was passed by Private Lecocq, *Depechez vous si vous plaît, Monsieur,* he cried as he dashed past only across his saddle, but the Prince made no answer, and in a minute he was alone. Zulus burst out from covert, yelling and firing after fugitives. Prince's horse followed, and Prince was seen by Lecocq holding stirrup leather with left hand and saddle with right trying to keep up with horse and mount. Must have made one desperate effort to leap into saddle by help of holster, and holster must have given way, and then he fell. Horse trod upon him. Prince regained feet and ran after fast retreating party. Lecocq turned in his saddle and looked behind. Prince was running on foot, some twelve or thirteen Zulus few feet behind him, all had assegais in their hands. No one saw the dreadful end. They galloped on to Wood's camp; after some three miles met Wood himself and Colonel Buller, made their report and those officers looking through their glasses saw Zulus leading away horses. Body is expected here (Pietermaritzburg), to-morrow.

Under the heading 'Obsequies of the Prince Imperial', *The Natal Mercury* of 6 June wrote:

We understand that the lamented Prince's remains are expected to reach Durban on Wednesday next. Major Butler, G.B., A.Q.M.G., and the Mayor yesterday arranged preliminarily the ceremonies to be followed on this sad occasion. The joint programme will be before the Town Council this afternoon. As the burgesses would no doubt wish the ceremony to be one befitting Durban, the Mayor will be glad meanwhile to receive communications and suggestions from public and private individuals wishing to co-operate. As at present advised Wednesday will probably be the day.

This was followed by:

The Late Prince Imperial

It has been arranged that the body of His Highness the Prince Imperial of France shall be taken down to Simon's Bay in H.M.S. *Shah.* Orders were received yesterday for that man-of-war to be got in readiness for the reception of his remains. At Simon's Bay, the coffin containing the remains will be transhipped to H.M.S. *Orontes,* which proceeds home at once. At Simon's Bay a temporary mausoleum will be fitted up on board the *Orontes.*

On the afternoon of 10 June, the prince's cortège arrived in Durban. *The Natal Mercury* of 11 June carried a step-by-step account of the passage of the cortège. One cannot help but feel that the citizens of Durban rather relished the event.

THE PRINCE IMPERIAL
Arrival of the Remains in Durban
THE PROCESSION FROM THE BEREA TO THE
CATHOLIC CHURCH

The scene witnessed yesterday afternoon as the cortège with the remains of the late lamented Prince Imperial of France, moved down the Berea to the Roman Catholic Church, was one which will never be forgotten by those who saw it. It was well known that great preparations had been going on at the instance of the military and civil authorities to receive the remains with due ceremony, but few expected to see such a spectacle as that which took place. From the time of the arrival of the sad news of the death of the Prince in Durban, flags have been hung at half mast, and yesterday after-noon, as soon as it was announced that the remains had arrived at the toll gate, there was scarcely a staff in town, without its flag so hoisted. It was expected that the body would reach the borough boundary near the toll bar, at the latest by noon yesterday, but the Mayor received a telegram from the Colonial Secretary stating that through some unavoidable delay on the road, it could not reach the toll gate until four o'clock; and an hour previously the whole of the troops in garrison, including every officer and man in each department, sick and on duty excepted, marched from the camp for the top of the Berea. These troops consisted principally of drafts of different regiments now stationed in the garrison, and included officers and men of the 24th, 58th, and 80th regiments, Army Service Corps, Ordnance Department, and Army Hospital Corps. A very large crowd of persons followed the troops to the Berea, and on arrival at the toll gate they were drawn up in angle ranks, the front and rear ranks facing each other. The troops numbered altogether 600, and the whole were under Major Huskisson, the commandant of the garrison. They were at first formed in angle rank on either side of the road, below the toll gate but were subsequently moved to the other side, and the two lines reached very nearly to the summit of the hill. At a quarter to four Major Butler, C.B., A.Q.M.G., accompanied by Major Huskisson, Major Graves, Captain Brunker, and Captain Kell arrived, all of course in full uniform. The usual salute was given, and the quick movement of the arms startled Major Graves' horse, a very spirited animal, which threw its rider. The Major fell heavily to the ground, but soon picked himself up, and within a few minutes was mounted again, his horse, which had bolted having been caught just beyond the toll-gate. It was now nearly four o'clock, and a large number of persons went to the other side of the road to see if the cortège was approaching. They had not gone far before they learnt that the mournful party had arrived at the bottom of Cato's Hill, where the horses were being changed. This occupied about a quarter of an hour, and before a fresh start had been made a number of French gentlemen posted themselves along the road and Capt. Baynton, of the Union Steamship Company, whose guest the Prince was during his short stay, drove up, and from his carriage alighted M. Delage, and M. Uhlman, the deceased Prince's trusty attendants, who remained in Durban when his Imperial master went to the front, to await his then probable return. Both appeared deeply affected, especially the latter, who is a very old servant of the Prince's father. In a few minutes an officer who had been despatched to the bottom of Cato's Hill to ascertain when the *cortège* might be expected, returned with the information that it was then moving. Just at this time an elderly man riding a grey horse, and leading a small bay, came slowly up the road, and the fact of his weeping bitterly caused many to make enquiries as to who he was. It was ascertained that he was an old groom whom the Prince had brought with him from Chiselhurst, and the grey horse he was riding was the one which his master was using on the day he met with his tragic end. The gun carriage with the coffin on it, preceded by an advance guard of the Natal Mounted Police, was next seen ascending the hill, followed by the Government mule wagon, in which was the Hon. the Colonial Secretary (Major Mitchell, C.B.) and other high officials. The coffin was covered with a tricolour, and the Prince's helmet and sword were placed on top of it. There were also several beautiful wreaths of flowers both on top, and hanging on the side of the coffin. Here Father Baudry, joined Father Sabon, who was walking behind the coffin, and M. Delage, and M. Uhlman took their places in the rear. Before reaching the top of the hill several French gentlemen joined the procession, and it was not long before the two lines of troops were reached. A body guard of one captain, one subaltern and 50 men of the general depot was here drawn up to receive the remains and escort them to the Roman Catholic Chapel; and whilst this was being done, Major Butler, Major Huskisson, Major Graves, Captain Brunker, and Captain Riley (who although suffering from the effects of a recently fractured arm, had marched with the body down from Maritzburg, and will accompany the remains home to England), Commissary-General Strickland, Commodore Richard (H.M.S. *Boadicea*), Capt. Bradshaw (H.M.S. *Shah*), Mr. Carlisle (Commodore's secretary), and others took their places in rear of the coffin. At the toll gate the Mayor and Corporation who had been driven to the Berea, and several other gentlemen, were in waiting. The band had struck up a slow march, and as the gun carriage was passing the gate, the gentlemen named joined in the procession. Over the gate there was a festoon of black drapery, hanging from which were white crosses, and the scene was very imposing. The procession made its way slowly down the Berea Hill in this order: —

ADVANCE GUARD.
BAND.
GUN-CARRIAGE AND COFFIN.

INFANTRY ESCORT.
MOURNERS.
MAYOR AND CORPORATION.
THOSE IN OFFICE AND OTHERS.
ARMY SERVICE CORPS.
ORDNANCE DEPARTMENT.
TROOPS OF THE GARRISON.
GENERAL PUBLIC.
PRIVATE CARRIAGES.

As the procession neared the Musgrave Road, at the entrance of which, as at all the lanes, a large crowd of persons had assembled, the band ceased playing the Dead March in Saul, and the order "quick march" was given. This was kept up until reaching the Durban side of the Vlei, from which spot the procession extended to some little distance up the Berea hill. Slow time was now resumed, and the band struck up a very beautiful march. The firing of the Durban Volunteer Artillery had been heard for some short time previously, and this was continued as the *cortège* passed the cemetery towards West Street. The little Roman Catholic Church at the top of West Street was soon reached, and the tolling of the bell added much to the solemnity of the occasion. Outside a very large crowd had assembled, and we do not recollect having before seen such a concourse of people at a given point in our streets. There were numerous carriages filled with ladies, many of whom were moved to tears as the mournful party escorting the remains entered the sacred edifice. The church was speedily crowded, and amongst those both outside and inside, there were evident feelings of deep emotion. There was a short service in the Church, prayers being offered up by the Rev. Father Sabon.

The procession it should be stated had left Pinetown at a quarter to eleven. The good people of that place had arranged to turn out, and march some distance up the road to meet the *cortège*, but it arrived an hour before it was expected, viz, a quarter to nine, instead of a quarter to ten o'clock; and Mr. McRoberts was the first to bring in the disappointing news that the small party was approaching. A change of horses took place at the camp, and at a quarter to eleven the procession started on its way. The Pinetown people were determined to show a last mark of respect, and the whole of the inhabitants turned out. The French flag floated at numerous places, and the Town Guard turned out and presented arms as the *cortège* passed. Westville was reached at one o'clock, and after a stay of an hour and a half, the procession again started, and arrived at Cato's Hill at four o'clock.

As above stated the remains rested last night in the Catholic Church, and during the night an immense number of persons flocked to the building to get a glimpse of the coffin of the beloved Prince. The place was most beautifully decorated, and neither trouble nor expense had been spared. We have not space this morning to refer to the decorations, but shall do so in to-morrow's issue.

It is estimated that 4000 people, at the least, turned out yesterday.

MAJOR BUTLER'S ADDRESS

We reprint with much pleasure the admirably expressed "special order," issued by the Assistant Adjutant-General. The fond style of the writer is manifest in every line.

The mortal remains of Prince Louis Napoleon will be carried to-morrow, at half-past 9 a.m., from the Roman Catholic Church, in Durban, to the Wharf, at Port Natal, for embarkation in H.M.S. *Boadicea* to England.

In following the coffin, which holds the body of the late Prince Imperial of France, and paying to his ashes the final tribute of sorrow and of honour, the Troops in garrison will remember: —

First: That he was the last inheritor of a mighty name, and of a great military renown.

Second: That he was the son of England's firm ally in dangerous days.

Third: That he was the sole child of a widowed Empress, who is now left throneless and childless, in exile, on English shores.

Deepening the profound sorrow, and the solemn reverence that attaches to these memories, the Troops will also remember that the Prince Imperial of France fell fighting as a British soldier.

W.F. Butler, A.A. General.

Durban, Natal,
Base of Operations.

South Africa.

On 17 June the *Cape Times* published a 'Telegram from our Special Correspondent' at Simon's Town. The reporter was almost overcome by the occasion which, for all its poignancy, had begun to assume the proportions of a techni-colour Victorian melodrama.

Sunday, June 15, 6 p.m.

Boadicea has come in well to her time. She was signalled as being off Cape Point at noon. The men of war in the Bay topped their yards — a foreign fashion, I understand — the crossing of the yards giving at a distance the appearance of numerous crosses. The *Orontes* has been arranged with the greatest care. She is painted dark grey, with black boot top. The line around the upper portion of the bulwarks is black. Some idea of the preparation of the vessel may be gleaned from the fact that over two hundred yards of black cloth have been used in draping the apartment set off for the reception of the body. Over the main hatch of the *Orontes* has been built a mortuary chapel, about 60 feet in length, by 12 wide, and 10 feet high. In recess in the forepart of the chapel is an altar with all the adornments of Roman Catholic faith; the chapel has panels worked out with white silk braiding, forming a Latin cross, in the centre of which are either monograms or wreaths of everlasting flowers. Facing the altar is the monogram so familiar to the world of the Imperial dynasty of the Napoleons. To the raised dais which receives the coffin are steps, and on these steps are placed boxes, in which are violets that should grow throughout the voyage. The Imperial violet is the colour of the curtains which hang over the doors. The Prince Imperial at least sleeps well if loving hands and thoughtful care can contribute anything towards that other mortuary chapel at Chiselhurst. The *Boadicea* came around Miller's Point which looking from Simon's Bay is even with the Roman Rock Lighthouse, at a quarter past one; the day was gloriously fine, alas that so bright an African sun should shine on such a scene! On board of the *Boadicea* the mortuary chapel was the Commodore's cabin. It was draped with black and the Imperial Monogram in white was the only relief to the sombre drapery. The coffin of solid mahogany was without ornament, leaving I suppose to Chiselhurst to decide what shall be written of the last of his race. The coffin was brought in by the pinnace, which was towed by a steam launch from *Boadicea* to *Orontes,* the cortège passed through the line of boats the crew of which were standing uncovered with the oars tossed; the strain launch arriving alongside the *Orontes* the coffin was hoisted in and was met by the Roman Catholic Bishop and priests immediately behind whom were His Excellency the Governor and staff, the heads of the Naval and Military, the Ministers, the officers of the Dutch Squadron, and others. After the coffin, enveloped in the French flag, had been lowered on the shoulders of British sailors, the funeral service was read whilst the *Active* was firing minute guns; the funeral service completed, the body was removed to the mortuary chapel. The coffin was covered with a magnificent pall cloth made of black velvet fringed with silver and white silk and having in its centre a silver cross beautifully worked. When the coffin was placed Lady Frere laid on it a handsome cross of palm leaves and everlasting flowers, and the Misses Frere, assisted by Mrs Wright, covered the steps with camelias and other beautiful flowers. The *Orontes* leaves to-night. I have seen many events in this country but none so sadly grand as this one I have witnessed to-day. Nothing that dignity could add to the solemnity of the occasion was omitted and it was most apparent how deep was the grief of the Governor and Lady Frere.

Immediately after he had seen the Prince Imperial's cortège on its slow way to Pietermaritzburg, Lord Chelmsford hastened to the Zulu capital, Ulundi, where he defeated the Zulus and Archibald Forbes made his greatest ride. No sooner had the Zulu war been concluded than the first Anglo-Boer War broke out in 1880. The short war was highlighted by one major battle: Majuba.

'Indescribable sufferings of wounded'

Majuba, 1881

The roots of the First Anglo-Boer War lay in the annexation of the Transvaal by the British on 12 April 1877, and in the slow deterioration of relations between Briton and Afrikaner which followed. In December 1880, five thousand Boers met at Paardekraal, where the Volksraad was reconvened and executive powers given to Paul Kruger, Piet Joubert and former President M.W. Pretorius. War broke out shortly afterwards.

Three thousand British soldiers were trapped in the Transvaal. The route from Natal to the Transvaal, through Laing's Nek, was controlled by a force of 2 000 Boers. Major-General Sir George Pomeroy Colley, High Commissioner for South-East Africa and Commander-in-Chief of the British forces in South Africa set himself the task of breaking through the frequently mist-shrouded pass and relieving the British troops in the Transvaal.

He established a base camp at Mount Prospect, close to Laing's Nek and shadowed by a flat-topped mountain, Majuba. Colley's troops — the Natal Field Force — consisted of 1 145 foot soldiers and 191 cavalrymen.

Telegraph links from Mount Prospect to the nearest sizeable town, Pietermaritzburg, enabled the special correspondents accompanying Colley and his men to file copy to their news-papers. John Cameron of the London *Standard,* Thomas Hay of the London *Daily News* and Carter of the *Natal Times,* were the three most prominent reporters. Melton Prior, the indefatigable *Illustrated London News* artist whose contribution to the pictorial history of South Africa over a period of fifteen years cannot be underestimated, was also in the camp, his beloved whisky hidden in boxes marked 'Drawing materials', together with his thousand cigarettes.

Unbeknown to the special correspondents, whose presence as men of substance had caused no small stir in Natal, in the area was the figure of Arthur Aylward, former editor of *The Natal Witness* (described by one exasperated correspondent as 'clever but quite unbalanced') and now correspondent to the London *Daily Telegraph.* The latter seemed, somehow, to cope with his fervently pro-Boer stand. Aylward had assigned himself to the Boer forces of Piet Joubert, camped in strength in the vicinity of Laing's Nek.

Colley was rebuffed twice in his efforts to get through Laing's Nek. His third attempt to break through the mustered forces of Joubert and his 800 men came at 20h00 on the evening of Saturday, 26 February 1881 when, together with almost 600 men, Colley set off to scale Majuba, which he had rightly decided commanded the approach to Laing's Nek.

'General Colley has the reputation of being a "strong man" who will act with discretion and vigour, but his conduct in the campaign thus far has scarcely been such as to inspire the army,' noted *The Eastern Province Herald.* The same article, ironically printed in the same issue of

The Natal Witness that carried the first disjointed news of the slaughter on Majuba, wondered whether Colley was even aware that 'every Boer is strictly instructed to shoot down *every officer first,* and on no account to expose himself to the fire of the enemy'. And why, continued the article, were the troops so conspicuously dressed? 'It will be absolutely necessary for General Colley to use extreme caution and advance only with a considerable force established of cavalry.'

Colley and his men reached the saucer-shaped summit of Majuba before 04h00 on the morning of Sunday, 27 February. On the mountain with Colley's forces were two correspondents — Cameron and Carter, Hay having fallen behind the column and subsequently missing most of the ensuing drama. Covering the story from the Boer lines was the pugnacious Arthur Aylward.

As daybreak lifted the dark from the mountain, Piet Joubert and his men saw with alarm the British soldiers, bright in their scarlet uniforms, against the skyline. At 06h00, 150 Boer volunteers, in their inconspicuous dun clothes, began to climb the mountain. The British, pitifully easy to see, were unaware of their presence until they opened fire. The British were at an immediate disadvantage. Apart from their bright uniforms, they had been issued with only 70 rounds of ammunition per man. The Boers picked them off one by one.

The despatches, among some of the most dramatic in South African newspaper history, reflect the complete confusion which reigned. It fell to Hay (Carter and Cameron being trapped on the mountain) to send off the first reports of the battle. As the garbled news arrived in the camp together with the first survivors, the despatches were telegraphed to Pietermaritzburg, sometimes at 20-minute intervals. Terse and urgent, they were printed in *The Natal Witness* the following morning.

General Colley moved out with Six Companies and the Naval Brigade.

Guns returned to Camp.

Firing Going On.

(From our Special War Correspondent.)

Mount Prospect, Feb. 27, 10 a.m.

General Colley, with two companies each of the 92nd and 60th, 58th, and the Naval Brigade, left Camp last night, taking three days' rations. The troops are now on the hills commanding the enemy's camp. Guns returned to Camp. Firing going on.

Boers Approaching Camp.

Our Men Laagering.

Artillery Playing on the Enemy.

Mount Prospect, Sunday, 3.25 p.m.

The Boers are approaching the camp, and the men are laagering. Vibart is firing on the enemy with two nine-pounders.

Majuba, painted from Colley's camp at Mount Prospect, by Edward Hutton, a soldier-artist who served in the Zulu War of 1879 and in the Second Anglo-Boer War, 1899-1902. He became a lieutenant-general and was knighted (Africána Museum).

A DISASTROUS BATTLE.

Amaguba Hill Retaken by Boers.

Only Seven Men of the 58th Left.

The 60th Fight their Way Back to Camp.

The Highlanders much Cut up.

British Fortifying the Camp at every Point.

Mount Prospect Camp, Sunday, 4 p.m.

Our men are now coming trooping in from the Amaguba Hill to the left front of our Camp. As wired, they took the hill last night. When morning broke the Boers, seeing the state of affairs, opened a heavy fire but seemingly, without serious effect, until a short time ago, when a large force of Boers came rushing on and poured a murderous fire into our fellows. Ammunition gradually fell short, and the slaughter was fearful. At last the English made a desperate rush. It was too late, and the battle is all but over. The Boers triumphed at almost every point, firing with deadly effect, knocking down our men on all hands.

Stragglers are still coming in. The 60th are fighting gallantly their way back to camp, but are hotly pressed on all hands. It is stated that only seven men are left of the 58th. The Highlanders are much cut up. Firing is now going on heavily, and the men in camp are engaged fortifying it at every corner. I will wire later, giving reliable news. The loss must be something fearful.

General Colley Reported Killed.

Commander Romilly, Capt. Morris and Lieut. Maude Killed.

Mount Prospect, Feb. 27, 4.20 p.m.

A survivor reports Colley shot through the head. All 60th officers escaped, loss of men not known; supposed to be slight. Other regiments suffered badly, both in officers and men. The following were seen dead:— Commander Romilly, Lieut. Maude, and Captain Morris. Reported — Singleton and Hay badly wounded. Lucy and Hill, 58th, missing.

Stragglers Still Coming In.

Guns Safe in Camp.

Firing Ceased — Flag of Truce.

Men still straggling in; many wounded. 60th got back well. Others suffered heavily in coming down steep hill. Boers keeping up heavy fire into them. Highlanders and 58th suffered very heavily.

Bagington, with flag of truce, gone out for wounded. Firing now ceased. Guns brought within camp. Fortifying still going on.

Throughout the long day (the British troops had reached their positions at 04h00), Carter and Cameron had paid as much attention to their own survival as to the battle. Few correspondents can have had more dramatic material from which to work. Positioned about 650 metres at ten-pace intervals above the Boers, they had been under heavy fire since 09h00. Out-gunned and out-manoeuvred, the troops with Carter and Cameron among them struggled to get off the mountain alive and back to the comparative safety of the camp.

Both men survived the rout, although they were captured by General Joubert's men and released on condition that they return to his camp the following day with copies of their despatches: he wanted to be kept informed. No sooner had a badly shaken Carter reached camp than he sent off the first eye-witness reports. He had been under fire for over 10 hours:

General Colley Dead.

Shot at the close of the Engagement.

No Staff Officer returned to Camp.

Rain Falling.

Indescribable Sufferings of Wounded.

300 Killed and Wounded.

Boer Loss said to be Slight.

The Camp considered Safe.

Mount Prospect, Monday, 7.15 a.m.

Our Special wires: I have just returned from the field. There are large numbers of wounded lying high up the mountain, a farmhouse being used as Hospital.

Sir George Colley was shot just at the close of the engagement, whilst giving orders to cease firing. The bullet struck him on the forehead. His helmet has been brought to camp; but the body is supposed to be still lying where he fell. No reliable news yet of the staff officers. None have returned to camp. Rain now falling heavily for hours and sufferings of wounded lying on the field something indescribable. I met Major Hay, who was shot through the leg and arm. He was got into camp with great difficulty. Our loss must be very heavy indeed, because the number returned is so small. I think there must be at least 300 killed and wounded. The Boers loss is admitted by our officers to have been slight.

General Sir George Colley at the Battle of Mount Majuba just before he was killed on February 27, 1881. The engraving, by Melton Prior, was published in The Illustrated London News, *May 14, 1881.*

Latest from the Camp

(From our Special War Correspondent.)

Mount Prospect, Feb. 28, 9.5 p.m.

Lieutenant Bruce Hamilton left here with General's despatch, to meet Sir Evelyn Wood at Newcastle.

The 2-60th, now at Newcastle, were to have come here to reinforce, but Wood stopped them, and the men here must keep to the camp.

105 of the 58th reported missing.

No news of Stewart, Fraser, and MacGregor. It is feared that all the staff have perished.

Burying parties leave to inter dead, and wounded must have suffered fearfully during cold wet night.

It is hoped that some men hiding in bushes may arrive during the day. The medical staff worked gallantly all night, accompanied by parties of men, searching for wounded and bringing them to hospital.

Heavy mist hanging over the scene of the fight, so cannot see whether the enemy is still in possession of the field.

Colonel Bond taken command of troops here. Every preparation is made to defend the camp should the Boers attack it.

The death of the General is greatly lamented on all sides. I am told that the party of Boers finding the body were so elated that they fired a volley in the air, and danced round it.

The 92nd fought bravely to the last. When ammunition became exhausted, kept the Boers back from the trench with stones, cans of meat, and canteens, until shot down. Wonder is, considering steady fire of Boers, and flanking, that any man escaped from the field.

Commander Romilly has been brought in, still alive. Lucy and Hill returned to camp last night.

Hornby not dead as reported, presumed along with Miller, Stanton, MacGregor (Staff), Singleton, and Field, (conductor.)

At about 09h00 the Boers opened fire: their marksmanship was immediately effective. Carter wrote through the long night. The lengthy despatch which follows was sent by telegraph to Pietermaritzburg before 09h00 the following morning, well before the full implications of the rout were apparent, and was printed in *The Natal Witness* the same day, 28 February. His despatch was sent in two parts, the second of which is reproduced below.

Camp, Mount Prospect,
February 28, 9 a.m.

It was about one o'clock that of a sudden a most terrific fire came from our left. Immediately every available man of reserves was hurried up to meet it, and they answered it well for ten minutes. There were men of the Naval Brigade, Highlanders, and 58th Regiment all firing as best they could — perhaps fifty in all against 200 Boers. The Boer fire was now very telling; our men were shot right and left at this point as they exposed themselves. No man could show his head without a dozen shots being fired at him. In ten or fifteen minutes the men wavered and broke, but in answer to shouts of

71

officers "Rally on your right" (that would bring them more to the left rear, where the General and about fifty men were) — they did rally and came up to the crest of the hill at the point I indicate. Colonel Stewart, Major Fraser, Captain MacGregor — staff officers — and indeed every officer present, now revolver and sword in hand, encouraged the men by word and action.

The whole of the Boer fire was now concentrated on our present and last point of defence on the left rear. Crowded as our men were by the necessity of finding cover at all behind this small clump of stones on the ridge, the officers called and directed them to deploy slightly right and left, to prevent us being flanked on our rear direct. The other side of the hollow basin was at this time only held by some fifteen or twenty men, our direct front by a score more, but they sent word to say that there were not many Boers there. In our direct rear the ground was so precipitous that no one could scale it. To the front it was also free to a certain extent of cover for the enemy. The Boers had evidently made up their mind to take points of the crest in detail, and now all their efforts were concentrated on the left. Major Fraser sang out, "Men of the 92nd, don't forget your bayonets!" Col. Stewart added, "And the 58th and the Naval Brigade" came from another officer, Capt. MacGregor, I think — the General at the same time directing movements as cooly as if at a review. The men did fix their bayonets, and standing shoulder to shoulder in a semi-circle, poured volleys back for the volleys fired by the enemy. Numbers of our poor fellows now fell, and they could not be carried far, for there was no shelter of any great safety to take them to. The stand made at this last stage lasted perhaps ten minutes, and then our men fell short of ammunition. It must be remembered that there were only the 70 rounds carried by our men in their pouches. At the same time a party of Boers crept up to the couple score of men holding our true front and extreme right and rear, and they poured in volleys at the little band of defenders, who fixed bayonets and charged down on the enemy. Perhaps not more than three or four ever came within thrusting distance, so hot was the fire on them as they charged the twenty yards separating them from their foes. To return again to where the General and Staff and main body were, now not more than 100, of our men, the officers still encouraged the men "to fire low, and only when the Boers jumped up to pour volley in, given them the bayonet next time after they have fired," was the last command I heard given, and in a moment our poor fellows broke and rushed for the crest in our rear. I ran with them, being only four or five yards behind the line that had made the last stand. How any one gained the ridge at the rear and escaped to Camp, down the precipice there, a fall of 30 feet clear, and then on and over enormous boulders and bush, a good quarter of a mile further yet to go before the foot of the hill was reached under the bullets that rained on us from all sides — I don't know. Four men dropped by my sides as I ran with the crowd across the basin, before even reaching the head of the precipice. Fortunately there was a kind of heather growing out of the side of the precipice. I can now only speak for myself, and I managed to save myself from injury in jumping down by catching at this herb. Then immediately I found I was with two or three others, who came after me, exposed to a dreadful fire as we scrambled over the rocks. The bullets rained on the stones, and several poor fellows, panting and bleeding, were struck as they tried to scramble away. I determined to give up running, as I could tell by the way the bullets came that Boers were all round us, though I could not see them myself, having thought best to follow a donga shrouded in bush, taking shelter as best I could in a dry gulley covered with slabs of rock. I determined to wait till nightfall, and then try to reach Camp.

All the while, and for at least half-an-hour after we had made a rush away, the bullets of the enemy pelted incessantly in the bush and on the rocks in every direction, as I could hear by the sound of powder and lead; then I heard big guns firing and took hope, thinking a party from Camp with artillery had been pushed to the base of the hill to cover the flight of fugitives. Half-a-dozen shots from big guns, and the fire of the Boers above my head and right and left ceased, and I heard a voice speaking in English and several others in Dutch close round us. Knowing that they must be searching for their enemies, I came out of my hiding-place and sang out to them. "Have you any gun?" The reply was, "No, I have no gun, I am not a soldier." "Then come up here, we will not shoot you." I accepted the invitation and clambering back up the rocks through the bush, saw a gentleman who said he was a Field Cornet. I told him my business and asked to see the General. Hearing an English voice, a dozen of our poor fellows who had been hiding within twenty yards of me sang out for help, and I told them to come out as the Boers would not hurt them. Crawling as best they could (everyone was wounded) they clambered up, delivered up their arms, those that had them, and we all went to the crest again, finding on the way Lieut. Hill, of the 58th, with his arm injured by a bullet wound, but as cheerful under the misfortune and as quiet as though nothing was the matter. This is the gentleman who distinguished himself, by carrying wounded from under fire at Laing's Nek. Seeing Mr. Smit, the General, I told him who I was. He said there had been six correspondents to him already. There happened to be only a correspondent of *Daily News, Standard,* and myself in this action. I showed my pass and got leave to return to camp, on condition I would send them copy of my account of the fight. First he asked, "Who is the officer killed?" I said. "Take me to him, and I will tell you if I can." I accompanied him to spot where our final stand was made. There lay a body — its face covered with a helmet by the clothing, I recognised it at once. Lifting the helmet up I made sure that it was our poor General, the bravest of the day; a gentleman who has shewn me many kindnesses since I have been in camp here; a Commander who was loved, and admired by every man under him, from highest to lowest. Knowing I would be first to carry this sad news back to camp, I wanted some token to bear out my information, but could find none about the body, save a white handkerchief, and that not marked. The Boers doubted me when I said: "It is the General." But when they questioned me again and again "Do you know him? Are you sure you know him?" I replied, "I give you my word of honour it is General Colley"; they were satisfied, no word of exultation escaped their lips when they learnt this. I said. "You have killed the bravest gentleman on this field," and they answered, "He was a very nice gentleman, he dined in my house when he went to Pretoria," and said another, "He did not think we were wrong but he was a soldier and he must obey orders." Others remarked, "It was no use fighting against men who had right on their side." Round the General laid the dead and wounded, Com. Romilly, Naval Brigade, and Lieut. Maude (lately joined the 59th) I myself was amongst the former, but I hurried away with the guide and the white flag past the enemy's videttes, and accompanied by Cameron, of the *Standard,* whom they picked up on the way down. Our guide took us safely outside the Boer lines, down the road we came up previously. Before we got far, we saw the Boers on horseback, to the number of two or three hundred galloping round the base of our hill, to the laager made by the Highlanders at the foot. Shots were exchanged, and then the guns at camp opened on the Boers, and kept them in check until the garrison of the laager had fallen back on camp, defiling through a narrow pass. This we saw as we descended the rocky slope. And also still more painful, we saw at every twenty or thirty paces our poor fellows either dead or wounded. They dotted the ground as far as the last ridge we passed. Poor Capt. Morris of the 58th, attended by his servant, was wounded in the shoulder. Cameron and I hurried on anxious to give the information we had, so that help might be sent to the suffering. A mile from camp, Cameron knocked up, and I trudged on, promising to send a horse for him. Close to camp an artilleryman coming out gave me his horse to ride, and so I arrived at camp.

In the confusion and emotion which surrounded Majuba, Carter had mistakenly sent over the wires the information that Commander Romilly was dead. Both the *Cape Times* and *The Natal Witness* had printed the news. Appalled at his carelessness, Carter hastened to rectify the error, and sent a lengthy despatch from Mount Prospect at 18h00 on Tuesday, 1 March to the *Cape Times,* where it was received on Wednesday at 16h20 and, too late for publication that day, was printed on the Thursday.

Commander Romilly, explained a chastened Carter in his despatch, had *looked* very dead when he saw him on the field, 'motionless and pale as marble. I asked one of the Naval Brigade men standing at his side, "Is your commander dead?" "Yes," was the reply, "he has been shot twice since he was first wounded." I considered the evidence sufficient without examining closely the body, and this morning wired you accordingly.'

In terms of their agreement with General Joubert, Carter and Cameron decided to honour the terms of their release and, armed with copies of their despatches and mounted on a couple of 'nags' with a flag of truce prominently displayed, set off for Laing's Nek. After an hour's wait, General Joubert appeared, accompanied by an extremely belligerent Arthur Aylward who had assumed the role of doctor as well as journalist.

Not wanting to make a second error in one day, Carter whipped out his notebook and took down, as far as he was able, the conversation between Joubert, Aylward and the *Standard*'s Cameron, whose indignation at Aylward's attitude rapidly overcame any tendency he may have had to remain unbiased. The article was reproduced word for word in the *Cape Times* of 3 March.

At last Joubert and Gen. Smidt, the Chaplain preacher, as they call him, and half-a-dozen staff officers came down to us; riding in front was Mr. Aylwood, late Editor of the *Witness,* with whom I had a slight acquaintance in Pietermaritzburg. I was rather astonished to see Mr. Aylward, and greeted him with "Hullo Aylward, what the deuce are you doing here?" He replied, "I am a Correspondent of the *Daily Telegraph,* and doctor here. Last night I attended to all your wounded men, took off a shoulder of one of our men. How are you? Let me introduce you and your friend" (Correspondent). The introduction took place promptly. "I have lots of information for you," added Mr. A, and he read the following, which he informed us had been sent by telegram to Lady Colley through the wire at the Mount Prospect camp (I have since learnt that message though handed in here, was regarded as improper for transmission to its intended destination):— "Gen. Joubert, Lange Nek, 28th February, to Lady Colley, Pietermaritzburg. I regret extremely the sad death of Col. Colley, who fell in action at one o'clock, February 27th, in attempting to hold mountain fortress forming right of Boer position. Regret he should have fallen in a war, the outcome of a policy which he had not caused, also that he should fall in such an unprovoked and unholy war against the Boer people struggling for freedom. Can only aid you in your sorrow by giving every facility for the removal of the corpse of your gallant husband."

74

I find on reading my notes of this document, taken on a slip of paper in pencil, that some of the characters are almost illegible. I will not guarantee in every word strict accuracy, therefore, so far as this particular telegram goes, since some of the words are nearly obliterated by wear. As regards the following transcript of notes, they have been taken in a notebook, and therefore well preserved, I will answer for their correctness *verbatim et literatim.* Information given by Aylward in presence of General Joubert, and confirmed by Joubert. The body of the General, (H.E. Sir G.P. Colley) is lying now in our headquarters camp and watched over by an English guard of Highlanders taken prisoners by us, and the circumstances of his death are these: When the Boer right attack drove in the English to the centre, Col. Colley, after the troops broke, himself began to fly. He was about eight paces in the rear, when he was shot. He was the last officer turned.

Telegram from General Joubert, Lange Nek, to President Brand, Bloemfontein, O.F.S.: "Your letters received about peace negotiations nearly lulled me into an unwise unsuspiciousness. (The reporter: "Is that right?" Aylward: "Yes; only these fellows can't write English.") But General Colley on Sunday morning attacked us as we were writing to you and him. He attacked our right and got possession of high natural fortress, built schanses and walls. Boers gallantly stormed; in five hours total defeat over British troops. Governor shot dead. Seven officers and one company in our hands prisoners. Will negotiate but not make submission or cease opposition." The next information given us was a list of prisoners and wounded in their hands. As this has been communicated to the officer in command here, and will certainly reach you by wire from official sources, I need not give it except this. Casualties on Boer side: Beeker killed, five wounded, and two horses killed. Next, Mr. A. obliged us with an account of the battle. I will only transcribe the parts that will afford information to the public. Five companies of Boers, three of which had been mounted and brought their horses to foot of precipice, and two of which were on foot, brought in position, but the first shot had been fired earlier, at 6.30 a.m., and a signalman had been taken prisoner by us after being wounded. The chief leaders of the most advanced storming parties were Commandants Roos and Ferreira (not the Ferreira taken prisoner by us). About twelve minutes past one the Highlanders, having completely given way on the north front, General Colley was seen attempting to rally, when he fell with two mounted officers.

Reporter: There were no mounted men on the field.

Joubert: Yes, there were three or four.

Reporter: I beg your pardon, there was no animal except one dog on the mountain top.

Aylward: Oh, you were there, were you?

Reporter: Yes.

Joubert: Then we must have taken two or three men standing together to be horses.

The Boer storming force, having completed the recovery of the summit of the hill, fired down the south side of the berg, and fire was suddenly opened on them from a laager held by a company of Rifles and a company of Highlanders. A volley was fired on us but failed to kill or wound one of our men. Francis Joubert stormed the redoubt, and the English fled. Later on some English cavalry, that had come out apparently with reserve ammunition and provisions, we attacked close to the Pass and drove them back, taking one prisoner. We charged them — that is to say, we rode up to within close shooting distance of them. Several of them we shot, and we brought a good many of their swords to our camp. The total force on the north side either storming or held in reserve for the right attack was 450 men. This last statement we took particular care to ask Joubert to endorse, and he did so in an emphatic manner.

Correspondent, who evidently did not fall in love with Mr. Aylward during the foregoing recitation, was addressed by that gentleman. Do you want to know anything more? It is all in the *Daily Telegraph.*

Correspondent: No sir, not from you, I came to speak to General Joubert. To Joubert: Is there anything you, sir, would like to say which you would wish published in England? If so, as it is possible, you may be misunderstood there, I shall be most happy to give full publicity to it.

Joubert: I don't think if the truth comes from our side it will be believed. Everything I can say is already put in writing to Governor and Ministers in England; nothing will help now. God may hear my prayer; England does not.

Correspondent: Would you accept Confederation?

Joubert: In what way?

Correspondent: With independence in the Transvaal as a part of the South African Empire.

Joubert: We have explained it thoroughly to the Government, to the Governor, and to everyone we could urge to consider a scheme of Confederation with all the other countries of South Africa. We have put it down clear, we have put in our proclamations again and again and said all that can be said about it. Do you believe that England — I would not say the honest people don't — do you think or believe that the Government of England as they were informed by their servants have, by their high men here, want the welfare of South Africa?

Correspondent: Well people have different notions. Of course, as a British subject, I am of the opinion that the war must go on, but I think it a great pity. If you had not taken up arms you would have been in the right, but perhaps in England they are not acquainted with all sides of the question. But now we have been defeated, the war must go on. Perhaps at the end of it you may get all you want, because by the end of the war the English people may probably know the rights and wrongs of the whole affair. There will however be a terrible loss of life before then. We can always go on; though our men have been beaten here, they won't always be beaten.

Joubert: Will they go on until the Transvaal is beaten and destroyed?

Correspondent: Of course, they can't destroy the Transvaal, but they will go on until you lay down your arms.

Joubert: Oh, yes, that is the way — you shoot us first and then say, "Lay down your arms."

Correspondent: But you fired the first shot at Pretoria.

Joubert: Oh, no, you did.

Correspondent: But our people there say you did.

Aylward: Just like the liars. I know the English.

Correspondent: The report, sir, comes from English, who *are gentlemen.*

Joubert: Just so. What is the good of us saying anything? How can we be believed?

Correspondent: Well, you see we have had all these wars in South Africa, we thought we had to fight the Zulus, because they were threatening you.

Joubert: Oh, we could have fought them well.

Cameron: But then the Secocoeni war. You must admit you utterly failed to fight Secocoeni.

Joubert: Then if you say that, what is the good of talking? How can you say England wants the truth? (excitedly). England does not want the truth from us, they want their own truth — that truth which will suit the scheme of their own Ministers; that is the truth for them, and whatever we say that is not the truth. We Boers want peace, and we would never try to fight England or her troops, but we will die all, every one of us, for our liberty; we will die for our liberty.

Correspondent: I answer, you can get your liberty without dying. You have a lot of brave fellows here, I see. Why should they die?

Joubert: Listen, now, President Brand wrote me a letter, asking if we could not have negotiations for peace. I sat up all night to consider, and write a letter about it, and just when I had concluded my letter I was attacked by your troops. I sent my letter to your Governor and I sent it to President Brand for advice, and again I am attacked. I am now tired. I don't see any other way than for me to be killed, and I *will* fight to the end. I know England will fight for honour, for predominance, and we will fight for liberty till we die.

I myself took no part in this political discussion. I am no great believer in politics of any kind, perhaps because I have had the fortune or misfortune to hear too many political discussions. Having a desire to get some facts, I began questioning the General: —

How many men had he at the Schuinshoogte Fight?

Joubert: I will tell you the truth plainly. When the battle began we had about 160 men, with patrols 200. After nearly all the fight was over I sent 100 reinforcements, and in the night another 70 men, and the day after I came myself with 60 men more.

And how many did you lose there, General?

We lost eight men killed and nine wounded.

In the course of further conversation with members of the staff, we learnt that the Boers were greatly surprised to find us on the hill above them, and particularly because it was Sunday, but we made them fight on Sunday, and they made up their minds to drive us out of the position. How they managed to do so they could not tell, except that God fought for them. Though they expected to take the position, they did not expect it would be so early in the day.

During the latter part of the interview, Correspondent and Aylward were not improving their acquaintance with each. Correspondent at last remarked, I raise my hat (suiting the action to the word) to you, gentlemen. You are brave men and fighting for your country, but to a renegade like that (pointing to Aylward) I wish to say nothing. Aylward made remarks about "the impertinence of that fellow," &c., &c., and I thought it was time the interview closed. I told Aylward I understood some time ago he had gone over the Border, but did not know it was in the capacity of correspondent and doctor. He replied he was aware of the reports about, but he would be quite ready to give an account of himself if required. Correspondent chiming in, advised Mr. Aylward not to be taken alive by the British, and Mr. Aylward indignantly dared his advisers to threaten him there. When on the point of leaving, after shaking hands all round, save with Mr. Aylward, a note came from the Rev. Ritchie to General Joubert, asking that the body of the General might be given up. This note was read by Aylward aloud, and then Aylward advised Joubert it was not right that "a parson" should make such a request; only the officer in charge of the camp could do such a thing. The General seemed impressed with this idea, and Aylward penned at once a reply, in language which would, I think, hardly have been palatable to any gentleman in this camp.

I appealed to Aylward not to make a fuss about such a matter, as no slight was intended. At the same time correspondent began to argue that the request was perfectly in order. Aylward had his say about the impertinence of that fellow daring to instruct General Joubert and his Staff. Things looked unpleasant; at last we prevailed on Joubert to have the language of the reply modified since he would not concede the point. The Rev. Ritchie was the right person to make such a request. We had on our side as peace-maker at this juncture the Chaplain of General Joubert. Taking the reply back to camp, we found that two requests, one from Col. Bond, and one from Major Essex had been sent to the General for the body. But, unfortunately, they had not reached him owing presumably to the fact that the messengers had taken the road to the hill where the fight took place, whereas they should have gone direct to the Nek. Another messenger and wagon was immediately dispatched this time in the right direction.

The story of Majuba had a little way to run yet. At O'Neill's farmhouse, at the base of Majuba, a peace conference had gathered on 31 March 1881. Waiting impatiently outside for news of peace were the correspondents. Melton Prior, whose illustrations of the battle, based upon amateurish sketches and descriptions given to him by Cameron, were the only authentic ones of the battle and thus yet another scoop for *The Illustrated London News,* had befriended the aide-de-camp.

Determined to return Cameron's favour, Prior asked the aide-de-camp to let him know when the terms of peace had been agreed upon and, strolling over to Cameron, quietly told him to have his horse at the ready out of sight of the other correspondents, and to wait for his signal, which would be his lifting his helmet briefly.

The aide-de-camp emerged from the farmhouse to light a cigarette, and told Prior in an aside that the treaty had been signed. Prior casually lifted his helmet, Cameron walked out of sight, leapt on his horse and galloped from the camp at Mount Prospect, wiring the news of peace to the *Standard* before the wires were closed, enabling his paper to publish the news of the end of a sorry war before the British government itself had had the news confirmed.

'Payable gold reefs have been discovered'

Discovery of gold on the Witwatersrand, 1886

Fred Struben, the son of a Ladysmith magistrate, discovered gold on the Witwatersrand on 18 September 1884. But the Confidence Reef, as he called his discovery, was not part of the 500 km arc of gold deposits which were to make South Africa wealthy. The real discovery of the main reef is generally credited to George Harrison and George Walker. Working on the Widow Oosthuizen's farm 'Langlaagte' in February 1886, Harrison noticed an outcrop of rock which contained distinctive white pebbles.

He took a sample of the rock to the Struben mill: the main reef had been discovered. It took a while for the news to filter out to the rest of the world. The first somewhat garbled reports appeared in *The Diamond Fields Advertiser,* founded in 1878 to report the news in the rumbustious mining town of Kimberley. But it was only years later that a coherent but still exciting account of the discovery of gold on the first paying reef on the Witwatersrand was recounted to the *Rand Daily Mail* by Fred Struben. Interviewed by Dr William MacDonald at Struben's home in South Devon, the article — only part of which is reproduced here — was published on 19 December 1929.

HOW FRED STRUBEN FOUND THE "CONFIDENCE REEF"

LONELY PROSPECTOR OF THE VELD

In the study of Spitchwick Manor, overlooking the lovely dales of Devonshire, with his original map of the Witwatersrand spread out before us, Mr. Struben related for the first time in simple but poignant language the story of his epoch-making discovery of the Rand.

"Leaving camp," he said, "soon after breakfast, I was fossicking about for several hours without finding anything of value. The sun was pouring down from a cloudless sky, and I was tired of tramping over the rough and rocky ground, and carrying the various samples I had collected on the way. I determined, however, to keep moving, and about mid-day I was down in the valley that runs at the bottom of the range.

"Suddenly, I looked up against the southern range, and saw that a disturbance had taken place to the rocks. I immediately conceived the idea of the possibility of a reef in that formation. The thought gave me new life and vigour.

"All depression and tiredness left me, and, I moved quickly forward to the spot. I was not wrong in my opinion, for there I found a reef cutting right through the displaced strata. Hastily I broke off a piece of the surface rock and took it to a stream nearby which ran down the valley only some fifty yards away. I crushed the stone on a large flat rock, slipped it into the pan I always carried with me and panned it.

A TEASPOONFUL OF GOLD

"Imagine my joy when out of that little bit of rock there came almost a teaspoonful of gold, the pan being literally covered with it. I was so astonished at the quantity of metal, which was of a light yellowish tint, that I was still doubtful whether it was really gold. I set off at once at rapid pace to my camp, and tested it with chemicals, and also by heating. It was then I realised I had found a vein of remarkable richness and of great value.

"I stood at my tent door alone. There was no one to speak to in the vast solitude of the silent veld. Years of suffering, ridicule, and disappointment came before me in a flash at that moment. I remembered that the only thing that was left to me through it all was that strange, unconquerable confidence within me that one day I would strike a rich gold field."

The main farms which made up the central Witwatersrand gold fields were proclaimed public diggings in September 1886. But by then gold fever had already set in: more than 3 000 people, mostly diggers, were hard at work on their claims.

Diamond magnates from Kimberley, anxious not to lose out on another fortune, were among the thousands who visited the Reef early on. The excitement of the times was captured by *The*

Gold mining in the early days of the Witwatersrand: drilling in a mine (Barnett Collection, The Star*).*

Diamond Fields Advertiser well before the September proclamation, when gold seemed to be everywhere.

On Saturday 14 August 1886, under the heading 'The Latest Gold News', the paper reported:

Another "Banket" Reef.

Movement of Kimberley Capitalists.

(From Our Special Correspondent.)

Pretoria, Monday.

Mr. Knight has been at Witwatersrand. He says it is nonsense to talk of the average yield being from six to ten ounces to the ton. He has seen the best reefs, and his conclusion is that the average yield is one ounce. He does not doubt that patches or pockets here and there show several ounces, but believes that practical working will show no more than one ounce. That will, he says, pay companies with large blocks of say one hundred claims to erect machinery, but not less.

The Member of the Raad for Potchefstroom has reported to Government that the Banket or Almond reef, the same as Witwatersrand, has been discovered in large quantities at Schoonspruit, 36 miles on the other side of Potchefstroom.

A Paarl syndicate, consisting of the editor of *Die Patriot* and Hendrick Schooman, have secured 100 claims, in proximity to Mr Robinson's property, for £1 500 per annum for mining rights only, other rights being secured by others, at £300 per annum.

Wellington, Malmesbury and Bloemfontein syndicates have been formed.

Ikey Sonnenberg has got an order to have his case heard on 26th inst.

A richer reef at Sheba is reported here and is confirmed by private intelligence. The wash-up is eagerly looked forward to by spectators at Witwatersrand.

Bentje's ground, at Struben's Hill, is finished, but the results are kept secret, and are not supposed to be encouraging.

Messrs Goch, Stead, Rhodes, Sauer, Rudd and Caldecot are at Witwatersrand, Messrs Robinson, Knight and English are here. Messrs A.B. Taylor, Wolhuter, Watson and Rhodes (attorney) leave tonight for Kimberley. Messrs. Rawe, Dalton and Rogers left to-day for Barberton.

MODIFIED GOLD NEWS

Two Kimberley Men Stuck

(From Our Special Correspondent)

Pretoria, Tuesday

Mr Knight's opinions have been wired here. He has been told to go to Barberton, where the average yield is greater. I have heard privately on the best authority that the wash-up at Struben's gave about half an ounce.

Great disappointment, Messrs. Rhodes and Rudd touched nothing.

81

The Diamond Fields Advertiser on 30 August ran a lengthy, colourful report dealing with gold-field events. More like a running diary than anything else, chatty and intimate in tone, it is reproduced here in greatly abridged form:

Pretoria, August 23, 1886

Everybody here is out of doors. I mean everybody in search of fortune-making specs, all over the Church Square principally lounging, chatting, waiting, alert, expectant, and interested to learn how the Government intends to act in the matter of granting mining leases or 'miga facht,' as they are termed, to those who, coming like the early bird, first on the Gold Fields of Witwatersrandt, secured certain farms or portions of farms on which gold was known to exist in more or less quantities. The scene is unchanged and there are still groups of persons to be seen here or there discussing gold intelligence, and it is as remarkable as during the last fortnight when half of Kimberley seemed to be for the nonce inhabitants of the Transvaal. As I have stated all along the intentions of the Government has always been the same in regard to Witwatersrandt to throw the Fields open to the public. They never thought of doing anything else although people were credulous enough to believe that nothing could be further from their intentions. But the Government's chief object in doing so is not evidently to protect the ignorant Boer from the machinations of his more intelligent rivals as was at first imagined: rather to increase the revenue of the country by all the means possible in their power. The first official notice appeared in the *Staats Courant* or *Government Gazette.* It runs as follows: "Whereas many people have given notice to the Government that in part of Witwaters-randt, district of Heidelberg, payable gold reefs have been discovered and as it appears from the report of the Commissioner delegated thither that on the farms Roodepoort, Vogelstruisfontein, Paardekraal, Langelaagte, Turffontein, and parts of Doornfontein, Elandsfontein, and Driefontein that gold reefs have been discovered, so it is that His Honour the President with the advice of the Executive, hereby notifies to all proprietors and parties lawfully interested in the above farms, that Government wishes to throw open for public diggings these grounds, either wholly or partly, according to law, so that they will have to assure themselves of their rights which the Government has allowed to grant them within a month from this date (August 17th).

A meeting of proprietors and those lawfully interested was held at the residence of the President, for the purpose of ascertaining from him what the Government intended to do in the matter. Messrs. Robinson, Rhodes, Van der Heuven, Douthwaite, Struben, and others, were present, and were treated by the President in a most cordial manner.

It will have been observed that the measurement usually followed in marking out claims has been departed from, and that two morgen on the reef are given to one morgen across it, which is advantageous to owners who have to pay only 5s. per morgen per annum.

As reported previously, Mr. Knight has entered into an agreement with Messrs. Robey and Son, to provide two gold reef crushing batteries with fifty head of stampers each, the same to be in working order before the end of the present year. The extent of gold-bearing area which Mr. Knight has secured, is very considerable, running for miles along the best auriferous reefs in Witwatersrandt. He will, I understand, see to the proper working of it himself, and, as in most things with which he has to do, is sure to be a success in the first degree.

Mr. Goch has secured to himself some excellent properties in this district. The scientific assay of a piece of reef in one of them, has not yet been completed, but when it has, I shall be in a position to inform you readers of the result. Mr. Goch bought into the Potchefstroom Syndicate very cheaply, but his entrance into that very select body of large property holders (and undoubtedly they do possess an immense tract of auriferous soil), is a happy one compared with others whose names are familiar with the Diamond Fields public. I could mention one or two who are now lamenting their misfortune.

I hear that Mr. Bray with his characteristic honesty has been looking up his old creditors and paying them the same he owed them with interest. Altogether they total from £14,000 to £15,000, but I am informed that there is one person to whom he owes not a trifle, who is demonstrating how awfully mean it is possible for some people to be. Mr. Bray offered the principal sum in full together with six per cent interest from the time payment was due, but this creature to whom I refer has actually had the audacity to claim ten per cent on the amount. I say audacity because it is notorious that none of Mr. Bray's liabilities can be legally claimed. He has refused payment under the circumstances and the High Court is, I understand, to decide the equity of the matter.

Horse-sickness is prevailing in Barberton.

The Transvaal Gold Exploration Company (Benjamin's) will throw open their alluvial deposits about the commencement of September, with the intention, presumably, of attracting an influx of people from Barberton to Pilgrim's Rest.

There are a number of Government officials leaving their billets, no doubt with the intention of bettering their financial position. Among them I know of the Postmaster of Potchefstroom, Landdrost's clerk, Heidelberg, and the Landdrost's clerk, Middelburg. The President of the Republic is very angry at so many taking their departure from the Service, and says that those who leave in search of fortune will never be taken back again.

How awfully stupid of the Government to commence, as they have done, the construction of the telegraph to Potchefstroom before first linking Barberton with the capital!

Mr. J. Geldenhuys gave out a number of claims on Saturday on his farm, which is situated two hours from Pretoria. This farm is the same as that on which Messrs. Vorstmann and Zeederberg found alluvial deposits nine months ago. Claims were also given out on the farm belonging to Jan De Beer, but the exact situation of it I have not been able to learn.

The "Edinburgh" Hotel, now vacant, is being inquired after. The proprietor (Mr. Van der Heuven) wants £200 a month for it after it has been repaired and finished in style: but in the dilapidated condition in which it now stands he will take £50 a month.

One-eighth of the Potchefstroom Syndicate belonging to Mr. Pretorius was sold the other day by him for £1,000, I believe to Mr. J.B. Robinson. It originally cost, with expenses, £22. He was offered £1,200 three days ago but did not accept.

The township of Witwatersrandt is to be at Doornfontein, on old Mr. Bezuidenhout's farm. The water rights, however, are Mr. J.B. Robinson's.

Two well known men, one belonging to Pretoria and the other to Wellington, have gone stark mad; the one over share speculation at Witwatersrandt and the other over something not definitely known. They are both, it is said, hopeless lunatics.

Mr. Tremlett on Friday showed me the result of a crushing and wash-up of a piece of auriferous stone weighing about four pounds, taken from a place (farm Welgegund) 20 miles from Pretoria. The mountain from which the stone was taken runs due east and west, and the farm adjoining that on which the gold-bearing reef was discovered has been secured by Mr. Tremlett, who traced the reef also on this farm. When I say "secured", I mean that he has acquired on easy terms the option of purchase or lease of the property, provided he finds payable gold upon it. The reef is composed of a hard, solid, semi-crystalised stone of a whitish nature. The wash-up was splendid, taking the statements with references to it as being of course *bona fide,* which most people would do coming from the source they do. The gold was not of that fine powdery description found at Witwatersrandt, but of a heavy gritty character.

The peace of mind of lessees and owners was considerably upset on Saturday, when it was generally bruited about that the State Attorney of the Transvaal had given it as his opinion that all contracts and leases entered into by capitalists with the owners of farms on which precious minerals were known to exist, would be null and void as soon as the gold fields were thrown open to the public.

I have heard that the Government on Saturday passed the resolution, that everyone who has claims on Witwatersrandt will be protected, i.e., claims by power of attorney, &c.

Mr. Von Brandis (clerk to State Attorney) is to assume the responsible position of Magistrate at Witwatersrandt. Mr. Eekhout, second clerk to the Gold Commissioner at Barberton, is to be Landdrost's Clerk at Barberton.

Mr. Tosel of Kimberley, has, I hear, purchased the Edinburgh Hotel for £4,500.

'As tough as leather, as nimble as a springbok'

The Couper—Bendoff fight, 26 July 1889

Sports coverage became an important part of South African newspapers in the early 1880s. Before then snippets of news appeared on an irregular basis and were usually presented with a faintly patronising air.

In the robust mining camps of Kimberley, Barberton and Johannesburg, sport was taken a great deal more seriously, however, and soon newspapers throughout the country began to give daily coverage. News, interspersed with items of comment and gossip, was invariably unsigned. It is for this reason that the identity of the reporter who covered this country's first sports event of national and international importance so well for *The Star* nearly 100 years ago, is not known.

The event was the fight-to-the-finish between James Robertson Couper, who was born in Scotland but had settled in the Transvaal, and Wolff Bendoff, a well-known London prizefighter.

It took place on Friday morning, 26 July 1889 near Eagle's Nest mine at Baragwanath, some few kilometres south of Johannesburg. There was such enormous interest in the fight that the Stock Exchange and most of the commercial establishments closed their doors for the occasion. The bout was to be contested in skintight gloves for a winner-take-all purse of £4 500 sterling, a fortune for the time.

Under the enterprising editorship of Francis Dormer, *The Star* made elaborate arrangements to give their readers full coverage of the event. Relays of cyclists rushed the copy from the ringside to *The Star*'s works, where the compositors waited.

The fight began at 09h45, more than two hours after the scheduled time, and Couper forced his opponent to surrender in the 26th round (Under the prevailing London Prize Ring rules, a round ended when one of the contestants went down from a throw, a knockdown, a slip or any-old-how.) The actual duration of the fight was only a little over 30 minutes.

The Star's first edition, carrying seven columns on the fight, hit the streets shortly after noon. The second edition, with an even more comprehensive report, went on sale at 14h00, and at 16h00 another edition saw the light, this time with the winner's comments added. Loser Bendoff had his say in a fourth edition published just after 18h00.

All four editions were sold out, and Dormer decided to reprint everything in a special supplement which he sold with his Saturday edition the next morning.

The selling power of major sport was proved conclusively and every successful South African editor since has remembered the lesson.

The unsigned report as it appeared in the first edition of *The Star* is reprinted here, uncut and with the original headlines.

The Prize Ring.

FIGHT FOR THE CHAMPIONSHIP.

The Biggest Stakes on Record.

COUPER WINS,
And Takes the £4,500:

26 Rounds in THIRTY MINUTES.

Bendoff Severely Punished!

Hurrah for Bonnie Scotland!

In truth it was a "merry mill". There were more early breakfasts in camp this morning than have ever been partaken of in Johannesburg before. The battle, so it was understood, would open at half-past seven o'clock. Long before that hour the road to Booysen's and beyond was thronged as on a Derby Day, and with such a collection of carts and horses as could not possibly be got together anywhere in South Africa save on the Rand. It was a bright and nipping morning. Shares and everything pertaining to them were left behind, and the most hopeless *habituees* of the market declared that, for this forenoon at all events, they would resign themselves to sport. Right away in the Eagle's Nest, six miles or thereabouts from Johannesburg, a stout enclosure of corrugated iron had been formed, with an excellent pitch in the centre. The enclosure, which was a hundred feet square, was eleven feet high, and was supposed to have been made stout enough to prevent any undesired inroad if the police should, at the last moment, change their minds, and *not* go to the racecourse to wait until "the parties" came. Subsequent events proved, however, that it was not stout enough. It was seven minutes after nine before the ringing cheers of the crowd outside announced that Couper had left his quarters. The curiosity of those who had not secured tickets of admission could no longer be kept within bounds. There were about five hundred people within the enclosure, and more than twice as many without. First a single sheet of iron was wrenched away. This was the signal for cries of "Turn them out"; but then a dozen others were started in every direction, and as the odds were in favour of the outsiders if a collision had taken place, prompt recognition was accorded to the wisdom of letting the intruders in. So in they came, and behaved themselves with the utmost decorum throughout the fight. The friends of Couper, never confident that he would be able to dispose of such a giant as Bendoff, were "getting a little bit anxious" during the past few days. On Wednesday morning their man was reported to be in the pink of condition; but on that day he had a nasty attack of diarrhoea, due to a change of quarters, and his weight went down more than six pounds in less than three days. Tommy Harris, to whom the training of the champion had been entrusted, looked anything but gay; the leading backers of Bendoff confidentially said that it was a 20 to 1 business; and there were even reports, right up to the moment when Couper threw his cap in the ring, that the event would not come off. But it was Bendoff who was late at the trysting-place. When five minutes had elapsed, Couper (who appeared in the face to be a little fine-drawn) began to get visibly impatient.

When seven minutes had flown without Bendoff putting in an appearance, Mr. Lowenthal, who acted as second to Couper, said, "This is cruel," but the friends of the gentleman from London said it was not cruel at all; they had been ready since eight o'clock.

It was fifteen minutes after nine by the clock before Bendoff stepped into the ring. The physical advantage appeared to be so much with him, and his air was so cool, not to say jaunty, that Couper at once receded in the betting to 5 to 2, at which a certain amount of business was done, though there was singularly little betting on the ground. A critical view of the favourite, however, soon revealed the fact that he was weak and disproportionate everywhere below the belt; and when Couper stripped, and disclosed his magnificent condition, it began to be whispered that the fight was not such a sure thing for the gentleman from London after all. Couper had affixed the tartan of his clan to one of the middle posts; but this was a courteous formality with which Bendoff dispensed, so that there were at the finish no "colours", save his own, for the victor to bear away. Whitaker, who had Bendoff in hand, said that his man was as fit as man could be, so that in point of condition when they were brought to the scratch, as well as in the other respects already mentioned, the advantage did not lie with the champion of Bonnie Scotland. Mr. L. Cohen acted as umpire for Bendoff, and as he lost the toss, Couper had the chance of corners, and naturally took that which did not bring the sun into his face. It was 9.23 a.m. when time was first called, and the battle lasted for about thirty minutes, twenty-six rounds in all being fought. Couper's obvious disadvantage brought popular sympathy to his side; but it soon became apparent that he had no need of artificial aid. His tactics were beautiful; he never hesitated to go down before a blow; but it was only to come up again smiling and to plant a real beauty with his left hand, which did not fail to leave its mark behind. Bendoff concentrated every nerve upon the endeavour to knock his man out of time; but Couper could have taken punishment even if he got it, which was not the case except in a very trifling degree. Bendoff's backers had been confident that the superior weight of their man was so great that it would be a murderous business, perhaps not more than a couple of rounds. If, however, Couper should live through the first ten minutes, they granted that he might have a chance! Live! Why he danced about like a kitten; his temper visibly improved as the fight proceeded, while the spirits of his rival, after the twelfth encounter, became proportionately depressed. It is said that an accident happened in the last round which broke, or nearly broke, Wolff Bendoff's arm; but it was patent to all observers that something else was broken too. The man may have the frame, but he has not the "heart" — as distinguished from courage — which would enable him to last out "a well-stricken field". Couper is not only a "good plucked 'un"; but he is just as hard as nails, and his condition may be judged from the fact that, after Bendoff threw up the sponge, he was just beginning to dance a hornpipe when the crowd of enthusiastic admirers broke in upon the ring, and bore the good old Champion away.

The combatants having entered the ring, the Referee stepped forward and said: — We have assembled here to-day to witness a contest for the championship of South Africa, to take place between Wolff Bendoff, of London, and J.R. Couper, of Johannesburg (cheers). The selection of officers and all other arrangements have been carried out to the satisfaction of the combatants, and it will only now remain for you, gentlemen, to give us every assistance to carry out this fight in such a way that it will be a credit to Johannesburg in particular and to South Africa in general. I may tell you we have a

The Couper-Bendoff fight, 1889, as depicted on the front cover of Famous Fights *(Africana Museum).*

strong representative Press here to-day, and I can only hope that there will be no necessity for these gentlemen to note anything that is unfair. Let us rather give occasion for giving them an opportunity of saying to the world that we in Johannesburg understand and appreciate the meaning of the words "fair play" (loud cheers). The stakes fought for to-day are the largest that have ever been fought for in the world. I shall now introduce J.R. Couper, of Johannesburg, and Wolff Bendoff of London, and I hope the best man will win (cheers). Gentlemen, I wish you both luck.

DETAILS OF THE FIGHT

1st Round. — Both men sprang up to the scratch, and Bendoff commenced hostilities by catching Couper a swinging left-hand full in the stomach. Couper replied with one at the face. Bendoff lunged forward, and made a heavy drive, but Couper fell. On Bendoff retiring to his corner blood was observed to be trickling from his nose, and at once a mighty shout went up 'Couper's drawn first blood'.

2nd Round. — Couper received a nasty smack on the nose without much retaliation on his part. Bendoff's blows were terrific, and his weight had tremendous effect.

3rd Round. — Couper had the first look in, and planted a brower, nimbly retreating out of the reach of Bendoff's righthander. Bendoff followed him up, however, and catching him on the left ribs, knocked him down — the first knock-down blow.

4th Round. — Bendoff again made for the stomach, but Couper ducked, and came up again on his left eye, which he punished badly, the round ending in the little man slipping.

5th Round. — Couper landed with his left on the face, upon which Bendoff hit out with his left; Couper ducked, and Bendoff not being over strong on his legs, tumbled over him, and the pair rolled in the ring amidst frantic cheers from Couper's backers.

6th Round. — Couper was again to the front with a magnificent stomacher, following up with a nasty one from the right on his man's temple. Up to this the fight was considered Bendoff's own, but the Londoner now showed signs of severe punishment, and the betting turned slightly in favour of the local man.

7th Round. — Bendoff forced the fighting, but Couper, watching his opportunity, came in with another facer, and Bendoff's eyes became smaller by degrees. The heavy man replied by a swinging blow from the right, Couper adroitly slipping and avoiding punishment.

8th Round. — On being tapped on the shoulder, Couper went down, Bendoff crying out — "Down without a blow, again." The Referee on being appealed to declare no foul.

9th Round. — Bendoff drove his man clean against the ropes, catching him as he came up again with a telling smack. The men closed, but only for a moment, Couper slipping on his left knee, and gravely kissing his hands to his friends, who cheered until they were hoarse.

10th Round. — Bendoff opened with a magnificent hooker, Couper replying with an equally magnificent left hander, catching his antagonist on the right ear. The little man slipped, and ended the round.

11th Round. — Bendoff laid his whole strength into a left-hander full on to Couper's ribs; but it was no more than a staggerer. Bendoff fought with difficulty, for his eyes were badly painted; whilst Couper was as fresh as air, and thoroughly good-tempered.

12th Round. — Bendoff again led, full at Couper's face, but his man ducked, and got in splendidly on Bendoff's mouth. The round ended by the new comer falling over the old champion. Both men were badly punished in this round.

13th Round. — Couper started with another between the eyes. Bendoff ran him round the ring, but failed in his object. Betting was now even.

14th Round. — Couper danced round his man, and got in again; but was sent away with a blow from Bendoff's right, and again slipped near the ropes.

15th Round. — Bendoff was ready for his man; but Couper did a little more jumping, and almost immediately planted another nose-ender. Bendoff returned the compliment by a severe blow in the pit of the stomach. Couper showed excellent staying powers, notwithstanding Bendoff's sledge-hammer blows.

16th Round. — Bendoff drove his man clean against the ropes in a twinkling, a fall ending the round.

17th Round. — Couper having received a tap on the left shoulder again slipped.

18th Round. — Bendoff tried the upper cut; but Couper ducked under his left, and planted a fearful blow on the eye. Bendoff replied with a rib rattler from the right, and as Couper slipped he again attempted the up strike.

19th Round. — Couper got well in with his left against Bendoff's nose, but at considerable peril, for he narrowly escaped a knacking down.

20th Round. — Couper, game as ever, watched his opportunity, and brought his right round with tremendous force against Bendoff's cheek bone. From this point, the fight was entirely Couper's. Bendoff's eyes were gradually being closed. Odds were offered on Couper, but Bendoff's friends would not take at any price; amidst loud shouts of "Well done, Couper," the unbeaten one again faced his opponent.

21st Round. — Couper got in with a right hander, which Bendoff palpably did not like, and retired to his corner.

22nd Round. — Couper was once again in evidence with his left, receiving in return a sharp one on his ribs.

23rd Round. — Couper feinted, and Bendoff's left went harmlessly over his shoulder. Bendoff followed this up with a blow on Couper's left arm, and drove him against the ropes, the little man bringing the round to a close by slipping under the strings.

24th Round. — Not caring for punishment, Couper did his best with his opponent's face, which swelled visibly.

25th Round. — Couper again led off with his left, receiving as he did so a tap on the chest. He smiled as he retired to his second's knee, and his heart and temper were obviously better than Bendoff's. Two to one was now offered on Couper but there were no takers.

26th Round. — Bendoff went pluckily forward, but only to receive a jawbreaker from Couper's left, the only blow (struck during the round). The giant having retired to his corner, his second threw up the sponge, and the fight terminated with ringing cheers from the crowd for Couper.

The Committee for the occasion consisted of Messrs J.B. Barnato, MLA, Abe Bailey, A.L. Lawley, H. Samuels, G.H. Farrar, and L. Cohen. The Umpires were Messrs Lowenthal (for Couper) and L. Cohen (for Bendoff), Mr C.D. Webb acting as Referee. The stakes were held by Mr. W.P. Taylor, and to Mr. C.D. Webb, who was Honorary Secretary to the Committee, much credit for the excellence of the arrangements belongs.

THE CHALLENGE

The fight originated in this way: Wolff Bendoff, on arriving in the Colony four months ago advertised as follows:— "Wolff Bendoff, who has just arrived from England, hearing of the boxing abilities of Professor J.R. Couper, champion of South Africa would like to box him in any style he likes, for £1,000 up to £5,000 a side. Bendoff hopes he will come to the point like a solid man and defend his title."

THE REPLY

Couper replied in the following terms:— "J.R. Couper, though having advertised for some time his retirement from the pugilistic profession, would say in answer to Mr. Bendoff's pressing challenge, that he would be glad to meet him in a light boxing match with small gloves to a finish for any stake for £2,000, on condition that he (J.R. Couper), whose weight is 144 lbs, gives no more than 8 lbs. away."

THE REJOINDER

Bendoff replied that he was astonished that Couper, who gave so much weight away in his battle with the Ladies Pet, should let a few pounds of flesh stand in the way when called upon to defend the title he then so gallantly won. It was impossible for Bendoff to come down to Couper's demands, and he claimed that Couper should either meet him or resign the Championship to him.

THE ISSUE JOINED

Couper ultimately accepted the challenge, and found friends to back him for £2,000 against £2,500 plunked down by the supporters of Bendoff.

THE CHAMPION

Couper looked remarkably fit when our representative called upon him yesterday. A little seediness which was apparent the day before had entirely worn away, and the Professor expressed himself as being in excellent health. He presented a striking contrast to Bendoff. He is 35 years of age; his height is not more than 5 feet 6 inches; he scaled 150 lbs., and measures 37¾ inches round the chest; but he possesses qualities which, in the eyes of a good many, are of infinitely greater consideration in forecasting the issue of a meeting of this description than those which his antagonist enjoys. He is tight and compact, and a wonderful tactician. He has no loose limbs. From the crown of his head to the sole of his foot, he is as tough as leather, though he is as nimble as a springbok. His legs differ from Bendoff's in that they are splendidly developed, and can be used to advantage. His thigh measures 22 inches; calf 14 in.; forearm 12 in.; biceps 1¼ in.; waist 20 in. and neck 15 in. Add to these important considerations the pluck and tenacity of a bulldog, and a nature that must be exhausted before he acknowledges defeat, and you will have a man who will always take a good deal of beating.

IN TRAINING

Couper is most conscientious in training. Allowing himself a course of ten weeks' preparation for a big event, he divides the time into three stages, or as he prefers to call them, degrees. The first degree lasts between two and three weeks, and is undertaken with the view of getting up his strength. During this time Couper is "dead off" drinking and smoking; indulges moderately in tennis, football, jumping, fencing, dumb-bell working, in fact every kind of exercise calculated to improve his condition. During the second degree the work is pretty much the same, except that it is harder. For the purpose of wind, he takes occasional sprints, and has longer walks. This lasts about five or six weeks. For three weeks prior to the fight, he is very careful. Rising at half-past six, he goes for an hour's walk, subsequently breakfasting off grilled chops and milk. Tea and coffee are rigidly eschewed. After resting an hour-and-a-half (which takes the form of lying on a bed or couch, reading some interesting book), Couper either goes for a long walk with occasional sprints, or has free exercise, such as ball punching for forty minutes, varied by turns with the skipping rope. Lunch is partaken of at half-past one, the meal consisting mostly of roast beef and mutton, vegetables, and a pint of Bass. The exercise after lunch is very much the same as that before lunch. Dinner, which is eaten at half-past six, varies little from lunch, and after this meal he plays a game of billiards, has a short walk, and goes to bed at half-past nine. This programme is varied by a day's complete rest now and again, whilst he does no work at all on Sundays. Couper has done most of his training for this event at the Half-Way House; but on Tuesday he removed to Booysen's Hotel, where he completed his preparations.

HIS IDEA OF BENDOFF

What is your idea of the fight? Queried our representative.

One cannot say. Bendoff is eight years my junior, 5½ inches taller, has a longer reach, and has had an excellent experience.

But you do not despair?

By no means; but I think the betting, instead of being two to one on Bendoff, should be three to one on him. Still, we shall see, he added significantly.

HIS RECORD: EARLY LIFE

Couper is the son of a gentleman, and was born in Scotland in the year 1854. He is well connected, and has relatives in both branches of the British Service. Early in life Couper acquired a strong liking for athletics, and was particularly fond of boxing in which department of sport he excelled. He received a sound education, and when a youth undertook a journey to India. His subsequent travels in New Zealand and America did him a power of good.

NEW ZEALAND

His first trip abroad in the interests of sport was to New Zealand. Here he travelled as an amateur, and here also he set up as a teacher of the manly arts. He was well patronised, and did well; but he possessed a roving spirit, and a year later he came to this country.

SOUTH AFRICA

On his arrival here, he accepted a commission in a volunteer force raised during the Basuto war, through which he served with great credit. At the conclusion of the hostilities, Couper, like another great personage, found his occupation gone, and he had to cast about for other means of living. His fistic experience now stood him in good stead, and he opened an establishment in Plein-street, Capetown, for the teaching of boxing and other exercises. This he continued for some time, and he did well by his profession.

At that time Couper received a large number of letters from gentlemen residing at Kimberley, begging him to enter the lists with Coverwell, who was described as a coloured bully, whose brute force led to the white population being insulted with impunity by off-coloured people. The professor was not at all anxious to come out as a prize-fighter; but his desire to "take down" such a person overcame his scruples in this respect, and he entered the P.R. for the first time. The result of this battle is too well known to need recapitulation. At that time, there was a great to-do in Kimberley over the knocking out qualities of P. O'Connor, and a meeting was accordingly arranged. O'Connor weighed 198 lbs., with a 44-inch chest, and Couper balanced with 155 lbs. This affair, as is well known, ended in a perfect *fiasco*. During the first round of three minutes duration, O'Connor showed himself devoid of all skill and science, and was the veriest novice at defensive tactics. During the second round, Mr Barnato, the referee, declared the match to be an unequal one, and stopped it.

DON'T LIKE PRIZE FIGHTING

"I don't like prize-fighting," said Couper, "and I never intended becoming a pugilist. This is my second fight, and, win or lose, it shall be my last."

'Is there not a man in Johannesburg who will lead a revolution?'

The Jameson Raid, December 1895

Dr Leander Starr Jameson stood in his camp at Pitsani, Bechuanaland, 5 km from the Transvaal border on the afternoon of 28 December 1895, and read his men a letter: 'Thousands of unarmed men, women and children of our race will be at the mercy of well-armed Boers, while property of enormous value will be in the greatest peril . . . we guarantee any expenses that may reasonably be incurred by you in helping us, and ask you to believe that nothing but the sternest necessity has prompted this appeal.'

The undated letter, signed by five members of the pro-Rhodes, pro-British Reform Club, Johannesburg was all the excuse Jameson needed to launch his men across the border and, after a headlong dash, to relieve Johannesburg from the 'yoke of Kruger and the Boer oppressors' and bring the city under British rule.

But the letter was a fake — undated, but written in early November. Not a ruse, however, was a Reuter telegram from that agency's chief agent in South Africa, M.J.M. Bellasyse. Dated 28 December 1895, it reported that Johannesburg was agitated by rumours of warlike preparations, and that women and children were leaving the Rand.

With these two epistles in his hand and seemingly oblivious that news of the impending raid had been widely reported in the local press and was most certainly known to President Kruger ('I shall wait until the tortoise puts out its head, then I shall cut it off'), Jameson, together with almost four hundred mounted Rhodesian police armed with Lee-Metford carbines, a 12½-pounder field gun, six Maxims and two seven-pounders, set off with his invasion force shortly after 17h00 on 28 December 1895.

News of their coming sped before them. The telegraph wires should all have been cut, but the one to Pretoria was left intact. At Krugersdorp, some 32 km from Johannesburg, Jameson and his exhausted men, constantly harried by Boer snipers on their journey across the South African Republic, were defeated by the well-positioned Boers. Jameson was led away weeping.

Almost the entire Krugersdorp scene had been viewed by *The Times'* special correspondent to South Africa, Captain Francis Younghusband. Younghusband had arrived in Johannesburg in mid-December and taken up lodgings in Colonel Frank Rhodes' house, through which passed, in endless conspiratorial huddles, members of the Reform Club. Younghusband kept himself aloof from the intrigue, but allowed himself to be persuaded by the Reformers, whose ardour towards the armed uprising in Johannesburg was cooling rapidly, to go to Cape Town, see Cecil Rhodes and persuade him to postpone the raid.

He was already well-known, not for his writing, but for his exploration of far-flung lands, mostly in the Far East. Born on 31 May 1863 in Murree on the Kashmir border, Younghusband's childhood and his education were spent in England. Educated at Clifton College ('It was drilled into all of us that our main aim must be CHARACTER'), Younghusband applied to Sandhurst and was accepted in 1881. In 1882 he was posted to the King's Dragoon Guards and was stationed at Meerut, India. It was here, in the country of his birth, that Younghusband's passion for exploration was to some extent satisfied with notable expeditions to the Himalayas, a trip from Pekin to Tientsien and another across the Gobi Desert. His first expedition to the Himalayas was a modest affair — Younghusband, a retriever, a Shikai and two mules; his last included 1 200 fighting men.

Admitted to the Royal Geographical Society as its youngest Fellow in May 1888, Younghusband left the army and was approached by *The Times* to undertake special missions. The first of these was as special correspondent to Chitral, in the Foutier Province, and, late in 1895, to South Africa, where he covered the Jameson Raid and a wide range of events relating to the South African situation of the time.

'I told Rhodes,' wrote Younghusband, 'that the Johannesburgers were not for it and wanted Jameson stopped. He said, "What! do you mean to say that there is not a man in Johannesburg who will get up and lead a revolution and not mind if he's shot?" "Apparently there isn't," I replied. "Would you do it yourself?" he asked. "Certainly not," I replied.'

(Younghusband was not the only newsman to become involved in the machinations leading up to the raid. Frederic Hamilton, editor of *The Star* and a member of the Reform Club, the aim of which was a reformed republic rather than its overthrow by agents purporting to represent Britain, went to visit Rhodes shortly before the raid to reiterate the Reform Club's stand. Rhodes paid little heed).

Younghusband passed the gist of this conversation on to the Reformers when he returned to Johannesburg, but within days came the news that Jameson, ignoring all messages, was on his way.

Their coming was no secret, not only to the Boers and the patient Kruger, but to the rest of the world as well. Berlin received a Reuter despatch which contained all the information in the proverbial nutshell.

> January 1, 1896
> (Reuters) Berlin, Tues.

> An alarming telegram has been received here from Pretoria.

> According to this despatch an armed force of the British South Africa Company (led by Dr. Jameson), numbering 800 men, with 6 Maxim and other guns, is reported to have entered Transvaal territory.

> The band is stated to be already in the vicinity of Rustenburg and to intend marching upon Johannesburg.

> The despatch adds that an armed conflict appears inevitable.

Together with a Dutch-speaking companion, Captain Younghusband rode out of Johannesburg towards Krugersdorp on 2 January 1896 to find Jameson and see what was happening. His notes, scribbled in the field, differ from the despatch he sent to *The Times* that evening, but contain the main elements of his article:

> Galloping over the grassy plains about twelve miles out we met a Boer patrol, who pointed their rifles at us in an unpleasant manner; but we held up our hands to show that

we were unarmed, and they let us pass on. On cresting a ridge we suddenly saw beneath us, near the hamlet of Vlakfontein, two bodies of men who we thought were on the point of attacking each other, till one party turned round and slowly marched back towards Krugersdorp. By the regularity of its movements we knew it could only be Dr Jameson's force. . . . We then rode straight into a Boer Commando, and I went up to the Commandant, Cronje, told him I was Correspondent of *The Times*, and asked for news. He said the news was that Jameson had just surrendered, and that I might go and see him and his men being marched off. We were allowed to ride up to the retiring column, but not to converse with the officers and men, who were riding along in their shirt-sleeves unarmed between escorts of Boers. They looked terribly tired, but were as hard and determined a lot as could be brought together, and the bravery which they had displayed earned the unstinted admiration of the Boers.

The report used by *The Times,* which had adopted a pro-Rhodes stance under its manager, Mr Moberley Bell, was brisk and businesslike, and was notable for its lack of anti-Boer sentiment.

Galloping over the rolling open grassy downs in search of Dr. Jameson's force which was expected to arrive at Johannesburg at any moment, my companion Heygate and myself saw between us two forces, both stationary. Then one began to move away and from the regularity of its movement we recognized that this must be Dr. Jameson's trying to round the opposing Boer forces. We found a Boer guard holding the only ford across the stream; so going up to the Commander we asked for news. He, after questioning us, told us all that had occurred.

Rhodesian mounted police belonging to Rhodes' Chartered Company, on kit inspection at Pitsani, Bechuanaland, before invading the South African Republic on the ill-fated and ill-conceived Jameson Raid. (Barnett Collection, The Star.*)*

Dr Leander Starr Jameson, leader of the ill-fated and ill-conceived Jameson Raid (Africana Museum).

He was a field-cornet from Potchef-stroom, and leader of one division of the Boers. He said that yesterday, January 1, Dr. Jameson had attacked the Boer force at the George and May Mine, two miles north-west of Krugersdorp, a small mining township twenty-one miles west of Johannesburg. Fighting took place from three in the afternoon to eleven at night. Dr. Jameson making three principal attacks, and doing great damage with his artillery, which the Boers, having then no guns, were unable to reply to.

My informant, the Boer leader, said that both then and to-day Dr. Jameson's men behaved with great gallantry, and he also said that admirable arrangements had been made at Krugersdorp for nursing the wounded on both sides.

The morning the Boers took up a position at Vlakfontein, eight miles on the Johannesburg side of Krugersdorp, on a circuitous road to the south by which Dr. Jameson was marching. The Boers in the night had been reinforced by men and with artillery and Maxims. Their position was an exceedingly strong one on an open slope, but along a ridge of rocks cropping out of it. It was a right-angled position and Dr. Jameson attacked them in the re-entering angle, thus having fire on his front and flank.

To attack this position his men had to advance over a perfectly open gently-sloping grassy down, while the Boers lay hid behind rocks and fired with rifles, Maxims, and artillery upon their assailants. The Boers numbered from 1,200 to 1,500, Dr. Jameson's force about 500, and the position was practically unassailable.

Dr. Jameson, after making a desperate effort to get through, surrendered, and as we stood we saw his brave little band riding dejectedly back again to Krugersdorp with their arms and surrounded by a Boer escort.

We were allowed to ride close up, but were refused permission to see Dr. Jameson. It is therefore impossible to state his full reasons, but it is known that he was made aware that it was impossible to send assistance from here, and this may have influenced him in giving up the contest when he found the enemy's position so strong that in any case it would have been no disgrace to have been beaten by superior numbers of such a brave foe as that Boer force which I saw in the very position they had fought in. It was evident that probably no one had ever started on a more desperate venture than had this daring little force, and they gained by their gallantry the adoration, not only of the Boer burghers who spoke to me, but of the whole town of Johannesburg.

These Boers — rough, simple men, dressed in ordinary civilian clothes, with merely a rifle slung over the shoulder to show they were soldiers — spoke in feeling terms of the splendid bravery shown by their assailants. They were perfectly calm and spoke without any boastfulness in a self-reliant way. They said, pointing to the ground, that the thing was impossible, and hence the present result.

The total loss of Dr. Jameson's force is about twenty. Major Grey was, they said, the principal military officer, and they thought that no officer was killed, and that the report that Sir John Willoughby had been killed was unfounded. He and Dr. Jameson have been taken to Pretoria.

Even Younghusband, in spite of all his contacts, was not able to interview, or even meet, Dr Jameson, incarcerated in Pretoria gaol before being ignominiously shipped to Britain by Kruger where he stood trial and was briefly imprisoned. The eighteen-year-old Reuter man in Pretoria, Roderick Jones, who was later to become head of Reuters, was the only journalist Kruger would permit to see Jameson.

Although the Second Anglo-Boer War was to break out only three years later, the Jameson Raid, with the unresolved ill-will it caused, was one of the contributing factors. 'The Jameson Raid was the real declaration of war in the Great Anglo-Boer conflict,' wrote Jan Smuts in 1906.

Immediately after the raid, Younghusband, who was to show a detached warmth in his writings about the crusty Kruger, interviewed him for *The Times*:

My interview with Kruger was especially interesting, for he is an altogether unique personality. In the old Puritan days there may have been men similar to him; but certainly at the present day no one like him exists, and perhaps no one of his peculiar stamp will ever appear again. . . . Undoubtedly the principal impression given me was the rugged strength of the man. Here was one who had as a boy left the Cape Colony in the Great Trek of 1836, and spent his whole life in a struggle for independence. Personally brave and with a force of character which has bent the people who made him their leader to do his will, he has first made his country and then kept it intact from aggression. Uneducated in all else save the knowledge of human nature, he has skilfully guided his people through dangers which would have overcome most others. And if his constant reference to Biblical texts give a stranger an impression of sanctimoniousness, this may be explained by the fact that the Bible is probably the only book he has ever read.

President Kruger cannot be numbered among the most enlightened and progressive rulers of the earth, and he has never shown indications of any feverish ambition to push his country higher up on the scale of civilization; but he is astute, strong and firm; he has one or two fixed ideas which he never departs from. . . .

On the present occasion I told him that I had seen and heard of the preparations which were being made, and I asked him what assurances he could give me on the subject. Sitting there in his well-known attitude in an upright armchair, smoking a huge pipe and expectorating profusely, he thumped upon the table at his side and bellowed back his answer, *that as long as his country was not attacked he would attack no one.* His people were scattered farmers and had no desire for the hardships of military service. If their country were invaded they willingly assembled for the defence, but they were in no way aggressively inclined. He acknowledged that his government was making considerable military preparations, but the Transvaal had been wantonly invaded once, and he must guard against its being similarly invaded again. . . . As he rose to say good-bye, he again

Francis Younghusband, shortly before setting out on his momentous journey to Lhasa, Tibet.

repeated to me most emphatically that I might tell people in England that unless we attacked him he would never attack us.

I asked him if he could hold out any hopes of granting the Uitlanders the franchise. Yes, to all who were loyal to the State. What, I asked, was his test of such loyalty? The taking up of arms in its defence. He distrusted the ordinary Uitlanders and especially the burghers of the city. They had once torn down the Transvaal flag, and had even hooted him, he said. That, to a man in Kruger's stamp, is unforgettable; conciliation would not be his line, but rather dogged opposition and isolation. When I remarked that the Uitlanders furnished about five millions sterling out of the five-and-a-half millions which the revenue produced, but were not allowed one single word in regard to its expenditure, he simply said that they were at any rate free to make as much money as they pleased, and he asked me to name any people who were less heavily taxed than they were. When I showed him that the Uitlanders of the Transvaal paid about ten times as much as the people of Great Britain, he merely said that he had not heard it before.

In two major articles for his newspaper, Younghusband sketched the history of the country leading up to its present unsettled state — made even more so by the raid, unsuccessful though it had been. Part of his second article, printed in *The Times* of 14 January 1896 foreshadows the conflict to come:

THE TRANSVAAL

II

(From our Own Correspondent)

JOHANNESBURG, Dec. 16 1896

At the close of my last letter I had brought the history of the Transvaal down to the time when gold had been discovered in the country and numbers of fortune-seekers, keen business men and spectators, had flooded into this quondam pastoral State till they had outnumbered the original Boer settlers in the proportion of three to one. This once remote country of undulating grassy downs, the typical country for a pastoral people who only desired to be left alone, hidden from the rest of the world, had suddenly been invaded by a host of the keenest men in the three continents of Europe, America, and Australia — men whose faculties and energy had been sharpened and developed by life spent where competition and the struggle for existence was severest. There is little wonder, therefore, that the situation grew strained, that a people at least two centuries behind the rest of the world showed themselves incapable of absorbing the antipathetic material suddenly thrust upon them, and that some radical change from the present state of affairs is confidently predicted here.

Everywhere, in the train, in the hotel, in the club, and in the newspapers the same story is told. The pushing, energetic "Uitlander" frets under the restrictions placed upon his enterprise by the stolid Boer rules of the country. He chafes at their hopeless immobility and complete inability to provide the proper administration for a great mining and business centre. And he insists that even if it comes to the use of force the Boers must be made to change their present attitude of *non possumus*. On the other hand, the Boers, strong in their sense of independence, mindful that they have but recently regained it, and endowed with natures diametrically opposed to those of the business men so urgently clamouring for their rights, present a front of blank opposition. They say the country is theirs, and they mean to keep it. If they cannot keep outsiders from entering it they may at least tax them and get all they can out of them. But as to according the Uitlanders any of the privileges of citizenship, any voice in the administration of the country, any voice even in the municipal control of the towns these Uitlanders have made, they return a dead, disheartening negative. Remembering only their victories of 15 years ago, and failing to appreciate the magnanimity of the act by which the British Government, when it had 16,000 troops at hand to pour into the country, yet from a sense of justice refrained from striking the blow, they openly — even in the Volksraad — express their contempt for the British, and their President in public speaks of the Uitlanders as "rotten eggs." He says in reply to a speech setting forth the claims of the Uitlanders that such privileges will only be obtained over his dead body, and he asserts as his reason for adopting this attitude of obstinate resistance that as in a dam in which a little hole had been pierced the water eventually comes rushing through till all is cleared away before it, so if the Uitlanders are granted but one concession they will surely gain the whole control of the country.

In this view he is undoubtedly right. The only question which arises is, has he a dam powerful enough to stop the flood? Can an impassive, backward people keep in check a vigorous, energetic population who to-day outnumber them by three to one, and without the present rate of immigration will in a few years' time outnumber them in a still greater proportion? Obviously the dam must give way sometime — those who have examined it say it may even do so within the next month or two — and then the injury done may be far greater than if the stream had been allowed to flow through in its own natural course. In any case, however, the eventual result must be the same. The Transvaal must be swamped by foreign, that is, principally, British, enterprise.

And now what are the claims of the Uitlanders? What is it they are aiming at?

They wish to obtain a suitable voice in the affairs of the country . . . they contribute nine-tenths of the income of the State, whereas they form by far the largest portion of the white population of the country and whereas in Cape Colony under precisely similar conditions the Dutch population are accorded the same privileges as the British, yet here under the South African Republic the non-Boer population are steadily refused the franchise, they are subjected to a taxation which makes the cost of living unwarrantably heavy, and their enterprises are constantly impeded by such restrictions as those which are placed upon the supply of native labour, with the scarcely veiled object of increasing the difficulties in working the mines and so stopping the flow of immigration into the country.

But a short time since the State was on the verge of bankruptcy, and 12 years ago cases even occurred of Government officials being paid in gunpowder and then given leave of absence to dispose of the same hunters on the high veldt. The Government were too poor to print stamps, so that persons paid in their money at the post-office and the letter was marked as paid. Now the revenue has increased tenfold, the State has more money than it knows what to do with, and all fear of bankruptcy is absolutely at an end. The State is able to build railways out of the money derived from the mining industry and all the means necessary for the development of this promising country. And this is due not to any enterprise on the part of the Boer population, not to any skill or energy displayed by them, but to the vigour and resource and bold initiative shown by the first British pioneers of the gold mining industry, and their numerous successors who form what is known as the Uitlander population. Millions of pounds have been sunk in the country. A vast industry has been started by which new gold to the value of nearly eight million pounds is annually extracted from the mines, and capitalists feel that the control of such an industry cannot be left in the hands of a partially educated people wholly ignorant of the civilized world of the present day. The Uitlander capitalists can neither proceed in the further development of the undoubtedly vast resources of the country, nor feel sure that what they have already accomplished may not be disturbed. The untrained Boer is not capable of grappling with such a situation and the Uitlander feels he must in some manner or other gain a control in what so vitally affects his interests.

President Kruger justifies his policy of obstruction by saying that the Uitlander does not come here to settle, but only to make money and return to his own country. He considers himself perfectly right, then, in bleeding the bloated Uitlanders as much as he possibly can while he is in the State. But President Kruger's is not a fair statement of the case. When only ten years have elapsed since the first great influx of immigrants it is hard to say whether men mean to stay or go. Some of the largest capitalists undoubtedly do not mean to stay. They can conduct their business better from the capitals of Europe, where they remain in touch with the great money markets of the world. But even from these the State derives immense advantages, for it is they who direct the flow of money which enables the resources of the country to be developed. These men, however, are only very few in number. The greater proportion of the Uitlander population is composed of the smaller capitalists, tradesmen, shopowners and keepers, mechanics and miners, who in a country with all the advantages of climate and of soil which the Transvaal possesses are as certain to settle in it as similar classes have done in British colonies. And one of the most striking arguments showing that this is likely to be the case is afforded by the fact that the Johannesburg Chamber of Mines, composed of these very capitalists who are accused of only desiring to make all the money they can and carry it off to Europe, have just adopted a scheme whereby over £30,000 is to be spent in the establishment of schools for the education of the children of mineworkers, stating that "unless the children who are now here are properly trained they will have no chance of becoming useful and industrious citizens, but will rather prove a source of danger to the community." It is clearly expected, then, by those hard-headed business men that the community will remain here. They are already beginning to provide for the next generation, and another indication pointing to the same conclusion is the fact that in the last ten months there have been applications submitted for the building of no fewer than

2,259 houses, offices, &c., in Johannesburg alone. So even if a few do come merely to make their fortunes and go away, still there are large sums of money being invested in the country, and there is a steady flow of immigrants, a considerable proportion of whom do mean to stay there.

These men it is who are now agitating for more freedom — a share in the administration of the country in which they intend to settle, and the same privileges for their children as they would enjoy in other countries. Against this strong tide of feeling President Kruger can no longer with safety preserve his present attitude. We may pity the Boers — pity them for the fate which has led them to choose as the place of their final retirement from the world just that very country whose recently discovered mineral resources have drawn to it the type of immigrant most distasteful to them and the least easy for them to absorb. We may admire their sturdy love of independence and in their rugged characters see much that is manly. We may even at times feel our sympathies more with them than with their rivals engrossed in money making. But the one party works and the other does not. And the one which works will win. In trying to shut themselves off so completely from contact with other people, the Boers have shut themselves off from the conditions which make for progress, and they will inevitably suffer the consequences. They have fled from the competition with other races, and now they are brought into the most severe of all competition — the industrial struggle — with a people who, by such competition, have been brought to the highest state of efficiency. Men who have worked hard and risked much are now demanding the full rewards of their labour. And the time is fast approaching when their voice must be heard and the stout but indolent Boer give way. The Uitlanders have petitioned for the franchise, and the petition was signed by 32,500 of them. But it was rejected with derision and even with taunts by the Volksraad. And now the feeling in Johannesburg is that the limit of patience has been reached and the time for action arrived.

Johannesburg — dubbed 'Judasburg' by the intensely pro-Rhodes editor of the *Cape Times,* Edmund Garrett, after its citizens had shown great disinclination to join Jameson and his men and overthrow the Boer yoke — was shortly to be visited by a man-made calamity which would push the Jameson Raid and its consequences, for a time at least, off the pages of the newspapers.

Captain Francis Younghusband left South Africa within months of the Jameson Raid to return to his first love, exploring. His expeditions were mirrored by a stream of books which found a ready market in Britain.

On 3 August 1902, Colonel Francis Younghusband reached Lhasa, Tibet, after an eight-month expedition across the roof of the world from Darjeeling, India. The first Englishman to walk through the portals of the Dalai Lama's residence, the Potala, since 1811, Younghusband established a British mission in the city, and left Tibet to acclaim and a knighthood — and fame as one of the great Victorian explorers and writers.

Younghusband received a knighthood after the Lhasa expedition in 1904. He spent his time writing (he was vice-president of the Royal Society of Literature) and delving into religion. 'Tibet' Younghusband died in August 1942.

'Half of Fordsburg
is practically laid low'

The dynamite train explosion, Braamfontein, 1896

The train load of dynamite that arrived in Johannesburg on Sunday, 16 February 1896 was a normal delivery. It contained almost 60 tons of dynamite stored in two closed trucks and in open trucks covered by tarpaulins. The train was shunted into the Braamfontein siding, 300 m from the main station and encompassed by Fordsburg, Braamfontein and the shanty town of Vredendorp.

The following morning the company which held the monopoly on the transportation of goods to and from the railway, the Spoorweg Besteldiens Maatschaapy, despatched a labourer, Klem, and three mule trolleys, to the station at 09h40. It took half an hour for each trolley to be loaded and one hour for the mules to drag the vehicles to the magazine at Lipperts' Dynamite Company. But when the trolleys arrived there at 11h30, the magazine keeper's assistant, William Langley, and his assistant, Alexander Powell, had disappeared for lunch. (They both later hotly disputed this.) Piqued, Klem returned the dynamite to the station and reloaded everything back onto the railway trucks.

Because of his action, there was a row about the wasted cartage. By the time the dispute had been resolved, the trucks had stood in the open for three and a half days. During that time no one had checked to see whether the dynamite had leaked.

After lunch on Wednesday, 19 February, the dynamite was again offloaded, onto seven trolleys pulled by teams of four mules. The first two trolleys left the siding without incident.

The points connecting the siding where the trucks of dynamite stood to the main line had been stolen, and therefore could not be locked. Joseph Williams, a shunter, duly closed the points to the siding as his engine passed to collect empty trucks. It took 45 minutes to assemble 31 trucks. The driver of the shunting engine, Jacob Bom, couldn't see much: the front of his train was 200 m away around a curve in the tracks.

The train went past the crossing, reached the unlocked points and, instead of going past the siding, moved onto the same track as the train of dynamite. As the track straightened, Blom saw the trucks in front of him. He applied the brakes, but it was too late: the train crashed into the stationary trucks.

The explosion which followed could be heard in Klerksdorp 200 km away. The shock was felt in Pretoria. Houses eight kilometres from the blast lost all their windows, and a piece of steel one metre long landed at Crown Mines five kilometres away.

Reporters from *The Star* were on the spot almost immediately. Confusing though the situation was (for a start, they were confronted by a hole 61 m long, 15 m wide and 8 m deep), they put together a good outline of what had happened in time for the third edition at 17h30.

103

Terrible Explosion

OF DYNAMITE

THIS AFTERNOON

(LATER NEWS)

At the Hospital

The Wounded and Dying

Harrowing Details

The Hospital, 4.20 pm — In the whole history of the Hospital there has never been anything like this. Already the court-yard is filled with carts, and the corridors are gradually filling up with dying and wounded people, and every single nook and corner which can be utilised is being so.

Immediately on the news of the disaster being received, Drs. Russel and Van Niekerk,

The hole left by the explosion which devastated Braamfontein, Fordsburg and the shanty town. The hole was 61 m long, 15 m wide and 8 m deep. In the background can be seen the twisted railway line (Barnett Collection, The Star*).*

assisted by everybody in the place who was capable of giving aid, turned out in readiness for the emergency.

At present the scene is simply indescribable. Here you come across a doctor soothing the last few moments of a dying person. A few yards away you see a nurse engaged in the same sad task with another sufferer.

The injuries of the wounded, who include numbers of women and children, are appalling.

Everything that can possibly be done is being done. Chemists are sending up supplies of bandages &c, and all who can render aid in any way are doing so willingly.

Mining magnate Abe Bailey was one of the first on the scene. Appalled at the carnage, which affected mostly women and children, he ordered carriages for the wounded, announcing he would pay all costs. The hospital, from which harrowing scenes were to emerge onto the pages of *The Star* in an almost minute-by-minute update, couldn't cope with the numbers, and sent the injured to Wanderers and Crown Reef, where doctors and nursing staff were organised.

DEATHS AT THE HOSPITAL

PITIFUL SCENES

THE SUFFERERS

LARGELY CHILDREN

The Hospital, 4.45 — Four of the injured have died here — all coloured people.

* * * *

The Hospital, 4.50 pm — Up to the present, between 90 and 100 have been brought into the Hospital. Of these the majority are coloured people, while the rest are made up of the poor Dutch class of the Brickfields character, and Coolies and Chinamen.

Something like one half of the total number are children. One little white girl has had a piece of iron driven right through her head, and the injuries are indescribable. Another little white girl who has been brought in, is also terribly mutilated.

The wounded are now being taken to Wanderers, where volunteers are urgently needed.

Inconceivable Damage

Number of Casualties

The terrible nature of the explosion may be judged from the fact that it has excavated a colossal trench 200 feet by 50 feet while by 25 feet deep.

The whole of Lingham's timber sheds are completely wrecked.

The diagonal shaped engine shed is a heap of ruins.

Half of Fordsburg is practically laid low, and the native locations are simply a heap of iron.

AUCTIONEERS' STORES

Messrs. Lezard & Company's auction mart has suffered severely, the whole of the back wall coming down and bringing with it all the sideboards, glasses, wardrobes, ornaments, &c., stored in that side. Messrs. Lezard estimate their loss from damage at £500. Both the partners narrowly escaped, the wall falling all round them.

Mr. Morkel's mart had the whole of the plate-glass window blown through. Mr. Morkel and his clerk also narrowly escaping.

IN THE CIRCUIT COURT

Counsel was arguing in a case when the report of the explosion was heard. The Court was filled with dust, window panes broke and people started out in dismay. His Lordship made an undignified descent from the bench and the Court was in a moment cleared.

Sixty-seven bodies and 20 coffins of assorted limbs 'whether human or animal it is not possible to determine' were collected, while 200 casualties, some of them with wounds the reporters were unable (and unwilling) to describe, filled the hospital and Wanderers. President Kruger visited the hospital on Thursday, 20 February. Visibly distressed, he was almost unable to talk. The third edition of *The Star* carried the report of his visit and then continued filling in details, not only of how the disaster had occurred but of miraculous escapes — and continuing scenes in hospital.

THE DISASTER

(LATER NEWS)

ARRIVAL OF THE PRESIDENT

THIS AFTERNOON

VISIT TO THE HOSPITALS

SYMPATHETIC SPEECHES

TO THE SUFFERERS

Punctually at the time announced, 12.55, the special train containing His Honour, the President drew up opposite the site of the disaster. The Presidential party consisted of Messrs. Wolmarans, Kock, Loveday, Erasmus and Tjaart Kruger, and Commandant Van Niekerk. An armed guard of the Pretoria Police also accompanied the party and two armed burghers remained in close attendance on the President, who was received by Mr. Van der Merwe, the Mining Commissioner, Mr. Van den Berg, Mr. Hancock and members of the Sanitary Board, and numerous officials. His Honour walked up through a guard of mounted police to the edge of the huge chasm caused by the explosion, where Commandant Schutte explained the details. His Honour looked on in silence and spoke not a word. Thence the party drove round the devastated area and inspected the ruins.

The party then drove to the Wanderers where His Honour inspected the coffins and was shown some of the remains. He then took each of the wards in turn and spoke to several of the sufferers. At the conclusion Mr. Van den Berg read a letter of thanks from the Dynamite Relief Committee for the visit, and mentioned the amount collected. His Honour made a short speech, couched in sympathetic and religious language. A move was then made to the Hospital, where all the wards were visited, and His Honour addressed consolatory words to the sufferers. His Honour then partook of refreshment, and awaited his departure, which will take place at 4.15. His Honour was very much moved, and spoke with very great difficulty.

THE HOSPITAL THIS MORNING

NATURE OF THE WOUNDS

SUFFERERS MOSTLY DUTCH

PROPORTION OF CHILDREN

DOCTORS INTERVIEWED

A reporter who called at the hospital this morning found that four more cases had ended fatally making ten in all at the Hospital. Of these, four were helpless from the start. Indeed, the people were dying when brought in.

During the night the medical men, of course, had been busy operating. The magnitude of their task will be understood when it is said that they were constantly at work in four operating theatres, three of which had been improvised for the occasion. In them about forty operations were performed. Most of the operations were major operations.

At first, owing to the blackened state of the bodies, it was thought that the majority were blacks. This view was erroneous. The great majority were whites, the Sisters in charge of the kaffir ward only having had three blacks under their care.

About a third of the sufferers were white children.

Dr Davies and other medical men were asked if any feature in common existed with regard to the wounds. They said the only common characteristic was THE TREMEN-DOUS SEVERITY of the wounds. Those who were hurt were hurt badly. One little boy's brains were protruding: another had a piece of bone 2 inches long sticking from his leg. The doctors said that on this occasion, as on most others, Chinamen and Coolies bore their pain with least fortitude. They united in praise of the endurance of the Dutch, men and women. "I never saw such astounding pluck in my experience," one doctor said.

The doctors were unanimous in saying that both Sisters and lay nurses worked like heroines, and proved fully equal to every call.

AT A FORDSBURG CHEMIST'S

A representative this morning called upon Messrs. Heymann and Cohn, the well-known chemists of Fordsburg, who had since yesterday afternoon ministered gratis to the wants of over two hundred sufferers. They were able to furnish some interesting details. The majority of the injuries of those attended to by them were cuts inflicted by glass or wood. The cuts were very deep, and those on the head were particularly ghastly.

Mrs. Tucker had a most miraculous escape. She was standing at the toll-house, only a few yards from the trucks which exploded. She was not even stunned, and was perfectly uninjured; whilst her two little girls (one of whom was a baby three months old) had, sad to relate, their lower limbs smashed.

Three men from the Rand Timber Company's works were also brought to the chemists. One of them had been standing in the centre of the circular saws, but marvellous to tell, was uninjured, except for a slight bruise in the back. The man standing next to him was killed.

Mrs Matthews sustained very severe injuries to the neck, but her life is safe.

Mr. Eastes, a one-legged man, had his arm broken.

A Dutch woman had her two little sons, who were in the same house with her, killed. She was uninjured.

The other casualties were of a minor nature.

SOME INCIDENTS

Stories of narrow escapes are just now of frequent narration, and a good many people have escaped with slight wounds from falling glass, who stood a very good chance of being seriously injured. In one case a man was riding in the direction of the scene of the explosion and, when it occurred some five hundred yards distant, he was thrown from his horse, some distance, but picked himself up hardly bruised; but the force of the concussion was such that the skin of the chest of the horse and one of the fore legs was split open and bleeding profusely. Another close shave was that of a man who was standing nearly a thousand yards away when the blow-up took place, and a piece of iron weighing some seven or eight pounds, apparently portion of the boiler plates of the engine fell within a foot of him and embedded itself in the soil. It was so hot that he could not touch it, but eventually he recovered it and kept it as a memento of the occurrence.

A portion of one of the truck wheels is said to have been found at Auckland Park.

An affecting scene was witnessed yesterday morning when an aged Dutchman, living in the vicinity of the disaster, and who had lost his wife and several children, was bemoaning the wreck of his house and his personal bereavement. There were men working endeavouring to recover the bodies when one of them came across a piece of carpet rolled up, and in this was found his youngest child, about three or four years old, who had by some miraculous means escaped injury and had lain thus all night. The emotion of the father, as he folded all that was left of his family to his breast, was contagious to the spectators.

'Natuurlijk weer die witte vlag' ('Again, naturally, the white flag')

The Battle of Elandslaagte, 21 October 1899

Dr Frans Vredenrijk Engelenburg arrived in South Africa from Holland in 1889. The product of a wealthy Dutch family, Engelenburg was the holder of a doctorate in law from the University of Leyden and had worked as a journalist on a paper in The Hague.

A letter of introduction to President Kruger led to his being offered the editorship of the Pretoria newspaper *De Volksstem* (founded on 8 August 1873, firstly as a weekly newspaper and, from 1885, published four times a week with two editions in English and two in Neder-duits. It also published a regular French edition), a position he was to hold with distinction and only a brief break in tenure, until 1929.

Under the editorship of Engelenburg, *De Volksstem* was staunchly pro-Kruger, and supported Generals Botha and Smuts until the 1912 Afrikaner split, after which it supported Smuts alone. The paper, in spite of the erudition of its editor, carried reports which can only be called naive. Nonetheless, it brought a second dimension to the reporting of the Boer War. Earnest and at times downright funny, *De Volksstem* repeatedly cocked a snook at the English during the early days of the war, crowing over Boer successes and reporting, in subdued tones, the failures.

War was declared at 17h00 on 11 October 1899. In the early hours of 12 October, watched by *The Times* special correspondent, Leo Amery, 6 000 Transvaal Boers under the command of Commandant-General Piet Joubert set out from Sandspruit, 19 kilometres from the Transvaal-Natal border, to wrest Natal from the British.

Two days later, *De Volksstem,* price 3d, ran a brief report in both English and Afrikaans, which nicely illustrates the paper's insouciant style. The English version alone is reproduced here:

> The time for British subjects to leave has been extended to Wednesday next 6 p.m.
> Bishop Hicks died at Maseru last night, aged 59 years, deeply regretted.
> Flags are half-masted in town for the loss of a distinguished prelate. Scotchmen will read this week's *Gazette* with mixed feelings. The names of the first batch of loyal Scotchmen is published. They must return and perform duties as burghers or pay the penalty. Serve them right!

The Battle of Elandslaagte as depicted by The Illustrated London News' *special correspondent, Mr G. Lynch. As the 5th Lancers began their charge across the veld, one of the Boers stood up and continued firing until the cavalry were within 20 metres of him. He jumped up behind a mounted compatriot and a British corporal of the 5th Lancers ran them both through. But he couldn't withdraw his lance and was himself killed shortly afterwards. Mr Lynch was taken prisoner by the Boers a few days after despatching his illustration. It appeared in* The Illustrated London News *on 2 December 1899 (Africana Museum).*

The paper's headlines, too, were colourful and explicit and had a pleasing spontaneity, the English and Dutch versions not necessarily matching — but who cared? Thus, in a special edition to *De Volksstem,* on Saturday, 4 October 1899, bilingual readers would have noted:

Natuurlijk weer de witte vlag	The White Flag again
Een hele gepant- serde trein genomen	A whole Armoured train captured
Zij schoten met grof geschut zonder sukses	Heavy Firing without Success
Een Engelse kapitein en act soldaten gewond	An English Captain and 8 Soldiers wounded
Dum-Dum-kogels	Long live Oom Koos!
Mafeking Belegerd	Bravo Burghers!
Leve Ook Koos!	
Bravo Burgers!	

Shortly after the beginning of the war, Engelenburg left Pretoria for the Natal front, where he both reported and edited the paper, many of the issues consisting of one page only and handed out free. Because of his difficulties in the field, there were occasions when the system broke down and the paper appeared either without Afrikaans-Dutch copy or without English. The paper's report on the Battle of Elandslaagte, a major disaster for the Boers, was issued free on Sunday, 23 October 1899 and did not carry an Afrikaans report.

The battle itself took place on 21 October about three kilometres from Elandslaagte Station. After holding their own for some time (and, according to reports, holding up a white flag and then promptly firing on the soldiers) the Boer forces under General Johannes Kock were charged three times by the Dragoons and Lancers, to devastating effect. Watched by a group of British correspondents, who included Steevens of the London *Daily Mail* and Bennet Burleigh of *The Daily Telegraph,* the battle of Elandslaagte was the first major reverse for the Boers and was reported in a subdued manner by *De Volksstem.*

THE FIGHT AT ELANDSLAAGTE

OUR MEN SUCCUMB TO A SUPERIOR FORCE

A BRAVE DEFENCE

REPORT FROM OUR CORRESPONDENT, WHO WAS PRESENT

(spec.) Newcastle, Saturday Yesterday morning at about eight o'clock the English artillery with eight cannon, who were situated on a hill to the northeast of Ladysmith, fired the first shot upon the Boer forces, who had taken possession of Elandslaagte Station.

The Boers retreated from the station to a position behind the hills opposite to the enemy. The Transvaal artillery with two cannon returned the fire, and the third shot fell in the battery.

One of the shells of the enemy burst in the camp of the burghers without, however, causing any personal injury.

The Transvaal artillery endeavoured to prevent the arrival of further reinforcements from Ladysmith, but alas without success.

After a few shots the enemy ceased to fire, and retired with the artillery in an easterly direction. A few of the Boers captured a cannon which was in a position deserted by the enemy.

Dr Frans Engelenburg, editor of De Volksstem *1899-1929* (Africana Museum).

Trains from Ladysmith brought reinforcements for the enemy, who took up a position in the mountains further removed from the forces of the Boers.

At two o'clock in the afternoon the enemy suddenly began to fire from a position more to the south-east. The cavalry of the enemy under the protection of the artillery stormed our position with maxims from that side.

From a distance of about 140 yards the maxims opened a heavy fire upon the left flank of the Boers, who were compelled to retreat to the right.

The Boers had not sufficient protection behind rocks from the hail of grape shot and the explosive bombs.

The fire of the enemy was overwhelming.

About five o'clock the German cavalry under Commandant Schiel appeared near the western flank of our forces from the direction of Picklesburg. Commandant Schiel fell almost immediately. A heavy rain now began to fall.

At six o'clock the English cavalry came also in full charge from the western side, and the Boers were surrounded. Many fled in the direction of Picklesburg, and were fired upon from behind by the enemy, thus killing many of our men.

At six o'clock the English were nearly master of the hill, behind which the Boers had concentrated their forces.

The loss on both sides were considerable, especially amongst the Germans. There are also some wounded men of the Hollander Corps.

COMMANDANT SCHIEL IS KILLED

and also Commandant Potgieter. (This must be Fieldcornet Potgieter. — Ed. V.)

The numbers of the enemy were estimated to amount to 10,000.

Our forces consisted of the Johannesburg commando, the German detachment under Commandant Schiel, the Hollander Corps, and a few Free Staters, estimated in all to be about 1,000 men.

I left the scene of the fight at six o'clock.

• • •

THE GREAT FIGHT

THE ENEMY EMPLOYS DUM-DUM BULLETS

MANY FUGITIVES ARRIVED IN NEWCASTLE

Dannhauser, Sunday

Yesterday an engagement took place near Elandslaagte station between the forces of General Kock and the English.

The commando under General Kock consisted of the Johannesburgers under Commandant Viljoen, the Hollander Corps under Commandant Lombard, and the German Corps under Commandant Schiel.

The Boers numbered about 700, the English several thousand. During the morning our men held their own and compelled the enemy to retreat, but in the afternoon the forces of the enemy were strengthened by the arrival of 16 cannon, which at once opened fire upon the portion of our forces where the Hollanders were stationed near the two cannon. The English stormed our position, and drove our men back by the force of superior numbers with a loss of about 100 killed and wounded, many of whom fell during the retreat.

The reports concerning General Kock are still uncertain. It is reported that Commandant Schiel was killed. So far the following are reported amongst the wounded: Gerritsen, Van Cittert, and Lieut. Uyenes of the Hollander Corps.

Amongst the killed are: Jan Rummeling, Otto, Dyksterhuis, Hoornblazer, and Fieldcornet Potgieter.

Commandant Jan Lombaard has just arrived and is greatly praised for his bravery by the Hollanders.

Many have been taken prisoners, and the loss in the enemies' side must be very great. Many of our men have escaped to Newcastle. Those who participated in the fight maintain that the English used dum-dum bullets.

• • •

(From the Editor)
THE WHOLE LADYSMITH GARRISON
ASSISTS IN THE ATTACK.

TRAIN WITH PROVISIONS RECAPTURED.

A BRAVE STAND.

GENERAL KOCK WOUNDED.

150 PRISONERS.

Dannhauser, 6.45 p.m.

Later reports respecting the Elandslaagte fight show that a small number of our men fought desperately. The fight commenced in the morning with British troops, which were reinforced by the whole force from Ladysmith, and after a heavy cannon fire their infantry stormed our position.

In the morning an English train with provisions and clothing was held up, but this has

Commandant of a mounted commando addresses a group of English soldiers standing in their shirts.
Commandant: **'Nou kan julle maar weer die pad vat en loop haal nog van daardie goed en breng dan banje amnisie saam. Loop sê ver Kitchener: hij moet ons perde stuur.'* (Africana Museum).

The artist was Johannes Adriaan Pott, an official in the office of the Staat-Secretaris of the ZAR. He served with Boer forces in the Second Anglo-Boer War, was wounded at Ladysmith, and accompanied President Kruger to Europe. He remained with Kruger until his death in 1904, when he returned to South Africa. Pott died near Pretoria in 1926.

* 'Now you can get back on the road and fetch more of that stuff, and bring a lot of ammunition with you. Go and tell Kitchener he must send us more horses.'

114

been recaptured by the enemy owing to the fact that our forces were compelled to fly with the loss of several men, chiefly caused by the charge of the artillery.

Captain Robertson and Commandant Viljoen have just arrived, and testify to the brave stand made by our men against 5,000 English.

General Kock was wounded in the chest, Fieldcornet Potgieter was killed by a shot through the head, and Commandant Schiel was killed by a shot through the abdomen. The younger Robertson is also killed. The expedition under Kock was intended as a hazardous attempt upon Ladysmith.

It is said that about 150 of our men have been taken prisoners.

The Hollander Corps was represented by about ninety men, of which number many escaped.

It is difficult to give with any certainty the names of the killed beyond the few which have been mentioned, and whose death is borne out by eye-witnesses.

• • •

MORE SATISFACTORY REPORTS
600 OF THE ENEMY KILLED

From reliable sources, we are informed that Commandant Viljoen, with 300 burghers belonging to the Commando under General Kock, has arrived at Dannhauser.

There is no cause for great unrest. The number of killed is about 50. About 600 of the enemy have been killed. Capt Schiel is killed, and also Commandant Joubert.

Further particulars are expected.

• • •

When Dr Engelenburg left for the front, he was accompanied not merely by his personal baggage but a wooden treadle press as well. On 27 October 1899 he issued the first in a series of field editions printed on the press, which was installed in a carriage of a moving armoured train.

De Volksstem thus made history by becoming the first — if not only — newspaper to go to war in South Africa, moving its editors, correspondents and printing press from battlefield to battlefield, reporting, editing, printing and publishing in the very thick of the fray, distributing among the Boer fighters the tales of their own exploits hot from Engelenburg's wooden treadle press within hours of the events having occurred.

As the siege of Ladysmith had confined some 14 000 British soldiers, for a time the press was able to function fairly normally, but as General Sir Redvers Buller's army began to build up, it became more and more difficult to print. However, Engelenburg, fired by patriotism and the challenge of the situation, continued to issue free daily editions of *De Volksstem*.

Paper was in short supply and editions had perforce to be printed on what was to hand. Frequently this meant that the newspaper was printed on paper normally reserved for railway notices. In a variety of colours, therefore, *De Volksstem,* sometimes with wobbly print or with uncorrected copy as befitted a paper brought out in conditions of guerrilla warfare, reached its readers on paper which ranged from deep orange to a noxious pink, blues ranging from indigo to powder, and a pale, subtle yellow.

After bringing out the famous field editions of his paper in Natal during the early part of the war, Engelenburg returned to Pretoria, where he was arrested by the British authorities — he refused to compromise in his support for Kruger and his policies — and banished from South Africa.

Engelenburg returned to the country he had learnt to love so fiercely in February 1903 and immediately resumed the editorship of *De Volksstem*. (Gustav Preller, who served as an artilleryman and war correspondent for *De Volksstem* during the war succeeded him briefly in 1924, but his tenure was short and Engelenburg once more stepped into the chair.)

Apart from his distinguished career in journalism, Engelenburg designed Pretoria's municipal coat of arms, was one of the founders of *Het Volk* and was also a founder member of the Zuid-Afrikaanse Akademie voor Taal, Letteren en Kunst. He died in Pretoria on 21 August 1938.

'For this relief much thanks'

Siege of Ladysmith, October 1899-February 1900

'We have a bad time before us and the Empire is about to support the greatest strain put upon it since the Mutiny,' wrote Sir Alfred Milner, British High Commissioner at the Cape shortly after hostilities began in the Second Anglo-Boer War.

Milner, one of the chief architects of the war, wrote more truly than he knew. Within a week of the outbreak of war and the sieges of Kimberley and Mafeking began. Within two weeks Ladysmith, with 14 000 British soldiers trapped inside, was similarly beleaguered. It was clear almost from the outset that the war would not be over by Christmas, as the British War Cabinet anticipated.

General Sir Redvers Buller, appointed Commander-in-Chief of the English forces in South Africa, had embarked for South Africa on the *Dunottar Castle* on 14 October, a sprig of Devonshire violets in his buttonhole. It was to be Buller's last carefree gesture for many a month.

Observed by Leo Amery, chief war correspondent for *The Times,* 21 000 Boers, fresh from celebrating Kruger's birthday on 10 October, and fired by their belief in their cause, wound their way down through the Drakensberg and into Natal the day after the war began. Their aim was to trap the 13 000 British soldiers then in Natal and take the little towns of Dundee and Ladysmith in northern Natal.

By the time the *Dunottar Castle* arrived in Cape Town to a rapturous welcome from a jingoistic crowd, one general had been killed in action, and Lieutenant-General Sir George White, VC, General Officer Commanding Natal until Buller's arrival, had lost 1 272 men in the routs of Nicholson's Nek and Ladysmith and had retreated in confusion into the Ladysmith garrison.

On the night of Sunday, 29 October, still flush with the success of Elandslaagte, White decided to meet the Boer forces amassing around Ladysmith in an attempt to ward off the by now inevitable siege. Against the advice of his staff officers, White ordered a night march to Nicholson's Nek under the command of Lieutenant-Colonel Carleton. The following morning, with Carleton and his men attacking from the rear, White sent out two infantry brigades to storm Pepworth Hill, on which the Boers could be seen building a large gun platform. That day — 20 Monday — which he saw as being so successful, turned out to be 'Mournful Monday' and the start of Britain's Black Week. Carleton's march did not go well, and nor did his day. *The Natal Mercury* of 1 November reported briefly on the débâcle:

SIR G. WHITE'S ACCOUNT

Latest Particulars

Maritzburg, October 31 (Reuter's Special Service) — Sir George White has issued a statement explaining the capture of a force, consisting of the 10th Mountain Battery, four half companies of the Gloucester Regiment, and six companies of the Royal Irish Fusiliers, the whole under Lieut. Col. Carleton, with Major Adye, D.A.A.G. as staff officer.

The force was despatched at ten p.m. on the 29th inst. to march by night up Bells Spruit and seize Nicholson's Nek, or some position, thus turning the enemy's right flank.

The circumstances which attended the movements of the column are not yet fully known, but from the reports received, the column appears to have carried out its night's march unmolested until within two miles of Nicholson's Nek.

Most of the correspondents were billeted in pleasant red-brick houses on the town's perimeter. During the day, however, it was necessary to avoid shelling, so 'bomb-proofs' were built. White, putting a brave face on his military ineptitude, refused to use his. The correspondents had no such qualms. Their bomb-proofs, tunnelled into the hillside facing the Klip River, allowed them to view the occasional shells and the movements of the 18th Hussars on the opposite bank, with comparative insouciance. This illustration, by Melton Prior of The Illustrated London News, *was used in a special supplement on Ladysmith and published on 7 April 1900 (Africana Museum).*

At this point two boulders rolled down from the hill and a few rifle shots stampeded the infantry ammunition mules.

The stampede spread to the battery mules, which broke from their leaders, and bolted with practically the whole of the gun equipment.

The greater portion of the regimental and A.A. reserve was similarly lost. The infantry battalions, however, fixed bayonets, and accompanied by the personnel of the battery, seized the hill on the left of the road two miles from the Nek, with but little opposition. There they remained unmolested until dawn, the time being occupied in organising the defence of the hill, and constructing stone dongas and walls, as cover from fire.

At dawn a skirmishing attack on the positions was commenced by the enemy, but they made no way until 9.30 a.m. Then strong reinforcements enabled them to push the attack with greater energy.

The fire became very searching and two companies of the Gloucesters in an advanced position were ordered to fall back.

The enemy then pressed on at short range, the losses on our side becoming very numerous.

At two p.m. our ammunition was practically exhausted. The position was captured, and the survivors of the column fell into the enemy's hands.

The enemy treated our wounded with great kindness and humanity.

The Government is informed that no blame whatever is attached to the troops, as the position was untenable.

De Volksstem, in a special edition issued at 13h00 on Tuesday, 31 October 1899, was cock-a-hoop with victory. The English and the Dutch-Afrikaans articles on the rout at Nicholson's Nek and the Battle of Ladysmith, which had taken place at more or less the same time, ran side by side in the paper, but did not follow each other slavishly, and contained snippets of *De Volksstem*'s particular brand of sarcasm. The reporting was carried out under great pressure within the confusion of serious skirmishes.

BEZONDERHEDEN VAN HET TELEGRAM

ONZE ARTILLERIE SLAAT DE ENGELSE TERUG

OOM LUKAS STORMT EEN KOPJE, EN KIJK IN LADYSMITH

DE IERSE BRIGADE VERDEDIGT HET GROTE KANON

(spec.) Modderspruit, Maandag.

Als vervolg op mijn telegram van heden morgen kan ik nog het volgende melden: Nadat het kanonvuur aan beide zijden tot ongeveer 12 uur aangehouden had, moesten de Engelsen hun twede positie ook opgeven en in wanorde trokken de Engelse bye (sic) Ladysmith: de Boeren waren meester van het slagveld. De Engelsen zijn bij grote getalen doodgeschoten en zwaar gewond. Intussen hadden een gedeelte van het Pretoria kommando en de bereden politie, waarbij zich later een afdeling Vrijstaters voegde, ongeveer 1400 man infanterie vastgekeerd op de linker vleugel en na een kort maar hevig gevecht met gering verlies aan onze zijde en 140 doden en zwaar gewonden aan de zijde van de vijand, staken de Engelsen een witte vlag op, waarvan zij blijkbaar een grote voorraad medegenomen hebben uit Engeland en onze mensen maakten twee mazims buit en namen 1170 manschapen en 42 offisieren en hoofdofficieren gevangen, waaronder een Luitenant-Kolonel en een officer van Generaal White's staf. De gevangenen werden na een kleine rust doorgestuurd naar Pretoria.

Generaal Meyer, gesteund door Generaal Berger, had inmiddels op de rechter vleugel ook niet stil gezeten: maar had, het zware bombardement van de Engelsen trotserend, een kopje nabij Ladysmith met sukses bestormd, vanwaar de Boeren nu tot grote angst van de Engelsen in Ladysmith kijken. Het bericht van de volkomen overwinning van de Boeren zal helpen de pijn van hunne wonden te verzachten. De "Irish Brigade" onder Kolonel Blake, waaronder ook uw twee korrespondenten waren, hadden het zwaar te verantwoorden. Van de kleine honderd man sneuvelden er vier, terwijl de Kommandant en een twaalftal anderen zwaar en licht gewond zijn. De meeste schoten zijn door de benen en de armen, terwijl drie een stuk bom in het hoofd kregen. De "Irish Brigade" lag op ongeveer 150 wards van het grote kanon, waarop de Engelse artillerie het gevigst geschoten heeft.

A WONDERFUL VICTORY

THIRTEEN HUNDRED PRISONERS

THE COMMANDING OFFICER SERIOUSLY WOUNDED

(spec.) Modderspruit, Monday night

The number of prisoners captured at Ladysmith amounts to 1215 with 45 officers. It appears that our cannon have caused a terrible slaughter amongst the enemy.

The estimate of the officers of the Royal Artillery is that the number of British killed and wounded by our artillery fire is 500, while those killed by the rifle fire is much larger.

The troops have now returned to town.

One of the captured officers state that General Sir G. White, is severely wounded.

The prisoners are now being disarmed by General Erasmus, and will be immediately taken to one of the captured towns.

The reports from General Meyer are also satisfactory. He has driven the enemy from one kopje to another, and has met with general success. Further particulars are yet to come in. So far as we are aware our loss is very slight. Reports are still awaited from a couple of commandos.

*   *   *

THE FIGHT NEAR LADYSMITH

FULLER PARTICULARS

LUCAS MEYER IN ACTION

BRITISH RETREAT

CAPTURE OF PRISONERS

(spec) Modderspruit, Monday

(Per despatch rider from headquarters camp near Ladysmith, Monday, 1 p.m.)

This morning a battle was fought in the vicinity of Ladysmith between large bodies of troops and the Boer forces. Fire was opened by the British artillery precisely at five o'clock, with the object of occupying and holding our position. The enemy's position was to the north-east of the town, about two miles distant. When all dispositions had been made a protracted artillery duel ensued. Shells were hurled into our position, but the British did not succeed in substantially checking the fire from our quick-firing guns, which were handled with superior efficiency. Meanwhile separate bodies of troops engaged with Lucas Meyer to the south-east and with the Free State forces in the direction of Van Reenen's Pass. This was followed by a hail of rifle and artillery fire. By 12 o'clock the position of affairs was such that the British were in a fair way of being badly beaten. The front of the enemy's main advance was checked, and the field forces retired on Ladysmith, accompanied by the artillery. At this moment our guns are pounding away at the town with a sullen roar, and the retreat is final. The prisoners taken are Surgeon Jackson and 17 men.

THE FIRE REOPENED
THE ATTACK LESS SEVERE ON GENERAL MEYER

(spec.) Modderspruit, Tuesday

Day had scarcely dawned before the English, who felt their position in Ladysmith to be uncomfortable, marched out of the town, evidently with the object of capturing the siege gun, and occupying the position taken up by General Meyer. The fire on both sides is less severe than it yesterday was, and it is generally believed that a decisive fight will take place to-day.

A fuller telegram will follow.

* * *

FURTHER PARTICULARS

OUR ARTILLERY DRIVES THE ENGLISH BACK

LUCAS MEYER STORMS A HILL
AND LOOKS INTO LADYSMITH

THE IRISH BRIGADE PROTECTS
THE CANNON

(spec.) Modderspruit, Monday

In continuation of my telegram of this morning I can state as follows:

After the cannon fire had lasted on both sides till about 12 o'clock, the English were

Ladysmith,
Jan 16th 1900

My dear Sir.

My Kaffer runners with tracings of the Battle of Cesars Camp went out to get through the Boer lines but together with all the other correspondents runner had to return – I sent him out again and now hear he was shot on the road. – I have therefore made more tracings, & send them on again, & trust this Kaffir will be more successful At the end of the Siege I shall send you over 40 Originals, (tracings of which I have sent you) – in the event of your not having received them all.

Yours very sincerely
Melton Prior

A letter from the artist, Melton Prior, smuggled out of Ladysmith by a runner, was printed on 3 March 1900, shortly after the siege had ended, but penned a full month before Buller and his troops relieved the town (**Africana Museum**).

driven from their second position, and had to fall back upon Ladysmith in great disorder.

The Boers remained in possession of the field.

Great numbers of the English are killed and wounded. In the meantime the Pretoria commando and the mounted police, assisted by a contingent from the Free State, had succeeded in cornering a number of the infantry, about 1400, on the left wing, after a heavy fight. There was but a small loss on our side, but the enemy lost about 140 killed and wounded. The English then hoisted a white flag, of which article they seem to have a large supply, probably brought with them from England. Our men took two maxims, and 1170 men and 42 officers as prisoners. Amongst these was a Lieut.-Colonel and one of the staff of Sir George White.

The prisoners were after a short rest sent on to Pretoria.

In the meantime General Meyer, assisted by General Burger had not been idle. They had under heavy bombardment from the English succeeded in taking a hill near Ladysmith after storming the position. From this point the Boers can now to the distress of the English overlook Ladysmith.

The news of the Boer victory will help to assuage the smart of their wounds. The Irish Brigade under Colonel Blake, amongst whom were your two correspondents, had a very heavy responsibility.

Of the small corps of scarcely a hundred men four were killed.

The Commandant and some twelve of his men were more or less slightly wounded. Most of the shots were through the arms and legs, while three men were wounded by portions of a shell in the head.

The Irish Brigade lay about 150 yards from the siege gun, upon which the fire of the English was mainly directed.

And *The Natal Mercury* on 1 November, almost as a postscript, reported from Ladysmith:

The Present Position.

Further Bombardment Probably.

Wounded Brought In.

Boer Humanity.

(From our Special Correspondent with the British Forces.)

Ladysmith, November 1. — Hitherto there has been firing.

To-day the Boers are occupied with fixing guns in position in the neighbouring hills, and are perhaps awaiting larger guns, possibly with a view to renewed bombardment to-night and early to-morrow.

About 70 of the Gloucester Regiment wounded have been brought in after Monday's disaster at Bell's Spruit. They all speak of the Boers' humanity and consideration for them during the night, the Boers themselves having no food but bringing them water.

The military authorities have taken over both banks here. No cash is obtainable. The books have gone to Durban.

Bennet Burleigh, *The Daily Telegraph* correspondent, rushed into Ladysmith in the midst of the troops' stunned retreat and commandeered the telegraph office, sending one of the last despatches from the town before the military took charge of everything. 'We are beaten and it means investment . . .' he wrote.

'They came back slowly, tired and disheartened and sick with useless losses,' Henry Nevinson wrote in the London *Chronicle.*

At 14h30 on 2 November the telegraph lines were cut and the siege of Ladysmith began, with almost 14 00 soldiers and 5 400 civilians (amongst whom was Dr. Leander Starr Jameson, who served as a doctor for the duration of the siege) trapped within its 22 km perimeter.

As in the Kimberley and Mafeking sieges, getting despatches out was a problem. The correspondents, in their special bomb-proof dugouts on the banks of the Klip River, relied largely on runners who, with a goodly appreciation of the risks they were taking, charged about £70 for a trip. After all, they had nothing to lose but their heads. If the weather was all right and if the authorities permitted, the correspondents were able to use the heliograph, but this was usually limited to very short despatches — 30 words was considered a reasonable length.

George Steevens, the *Daily Mail*'s correspondent, died of typhoid shortly after Christmas. Told that he was going to die, Steevens received the news with equanimity, and died two hours later, fretting about deadlines.

Richard Harding Davis, one of the correspondents who survived the siege, and who took over from George Steevens, sent two despatches shortly after the siege was lifted which not only bear the stamp of the time, but of his own rich prose. They were published in the London *Daily Mail* in early March. Ladysmith had been relieved on 28 February.

SIEGE IMPRESSIONS.

SOME HUMAN DOCUMENTS IN LADYSMITH.

HURRIED DEPARTURE OF THE LAST BOER TRAIN.

(From Our War Correspondent)

Pietermaritzburg, March 3

The signs of the siege of Ladysmith are not read in the shell holes, nor in the shattered walls, nor in the cellars used for bomb-proofs, but in the faces of the people.

Passing down the street is like walking through the wards of a fever hospital. The faces of the besieged are yellow, the skin is drawn sharply over the cheekbones, the uniforms hang in wrinkles, the eyes are hectic and staring, but there is so much more pluck in them than fever that one does not dare to sympathise.

They carry their suffering jauntily, but under the mask of habitual British indifference. One has only to offer an officer a cigar, or a biscuit to a Tommy, to find a starving man. Some of the prices of things sold at auction on February 21 are interesting.

Twelve matches brought thirteen shillings, condensed milk went to ten shillings a tin, but a quarter pound tin of Capstan tobacco brought three pounds, and a threepenny packet of cigarettes twenty-five shillings. A bottle of jam cost £1 11s., and cigars 5s. each.

The meeting between General Buller and Sir George White was eminently characteristic. It might have been a chance meeting on a field day at Aldershot. There was no cheering, no demonstration.

In London bands may be playing, people cheering, and flags waving, but here officers are saluting punctiliously and greeting old comrades as though they had met in Piccadilly.

The column followed Buller so smartly that one hour after he entered Ladysmith I was able to heliograph from here to the mail through the signal corps on Umbulwana, where only twelve hours before, the Boers' Long Tom had stood and shelled Ladysmith, and that since the last days of October.

In the morning the Imperial Light Horse rode into the abandoned camp on Ambulwana, and found fifty tents, some ammunition and live stock, and many cigars.

A force of artillery, Dragoon Guards, Natal Police, and Gordons rode out on a reconnaissance, after the retreating Boers, who however escaped on the railway, destroying two culverts behind them.

Rations are coming in to-morrow, and the next event will be the state entry of General Buller and part of the relief column. To-night everyone is cheerful. Officers are watching for their first cigarette in two months, and taking turns in reading the few papers brought in. Ladysmith's spirit is voiced in her siege song, "For this relief much thanks."

Melton Prior, war artist to The Illustrated London News, *illustrated the scene in Ladysmith shortly after the relief troops had marched in on 28 February 1900. General Sir George White called for three cheers for the Queen. 'The crowd, consisting of ladies, troops and civilians in all kinds of costumes, frantically cheered the Queen,' wrote Prior. The picture was published in* The Illustrated London News, 7 *April 1900* (Africana Museum).

125

BULLER'S ENTRY.

"AS MAGNIFICENT AS THE CZAR'S ENTRANCE INTO MOSCOW."

A MOVING SPECTACLE.

(From Our War Correspondent.)

Ladysmith, March 4

The entrance of General Buller and his column into Ladysmith this morning was one of the most splendid and moving spectacles I have ever witnessed.

It was as affecting as the Jubilee procession, as magnificent as the Czar's entrance into Moscow, as full of enthusiasm as Admiral Dewey's welcome to New York.

Twenty-two thousand Tommies — lance, foot, and the gunners, Irregular Horse, Colonials, bluejackets, and Indians — blistered and tanned, caked with mud and bloodstains, as ragged as sweeps — passed for three full hours before General White, cheering, laughing, shouting and tossing their helmets.

The emancipated, yellow-faced garrison, whose loose khaki told of the weeks of starvation, cheered them in return.

The Gordons piled for them, and the women and children to whom they brought relief waved and cheered with the men.

General Buller's arrival was hailed tumultuously.

The two battalions of Devons, who had separated last in India five years ago, broke ranks and rushed at old comrades.

After the march past the civilians put General White in a landau and dragged it by ropes to headquarters.

What the reports did not mention was the cost, in human lives, of relieving Ladysmith. It took the battles of Vaal Krantz, Colenso and Spion Kop — not to mention Redvers Bullers' reputation — before the little town was relieved. Winston Churchill, war correspondent to London's *Morning Post,* was involved in the melée in Natal.

'We do not catch lords' sons every day'

Winston Spencer Churchill, prisoner of war, 1899

At 04h30 on the morning of 15 November 1899, Winston Churchill, war correspondent to the *Morning Post,* and Leo Amery, *The Times'* chief war correspondent, were woken in their tent outside Estcourt, Natal, by an Indian servant. They were due to go on a reconnoitring mission with Captain Aylmer Haldane and two companies of men on an armoured train known as 'Wilson's death trap'.

Amery looked out of the tent, saw that it was raining heavily and philosophically went back to sleep. Churchill, with some misgivings, went on board. He was carrying a Mauser, two clips of dum-dum bullets and a pair of field glasses.

The train was ambushed by Louis Botha and 500 Boer commandos just outside Frere. Churchill helped to move the 50 wounded into the engine and tender and, seeing it on its way back to Estcourt, returned to help the remaining men. Alone in a shallow cutting, Churchill, to his astonishment, was fired upon by two Boers. 'Two soft kisses sucked in the air,' he later wrote, 'but nothing struck me.'

Although he was to write virtuously that he 'was a press correspondent without arms of any kind', he had the dum-dum bullets in his pockets (the Mauser and field glasses having being left in the engine cab in the confusion of battle) when he was captured. Churchill managed to get rid of one clip, but his captor, noticing him fumbling, took the other from him, looked at it contemptuously and threw it away. For the first — and last — time in his life, Winston Spencer Churchill had surrendered.

The first indication that Churchill had been captured came in a brief report written by Spencer Wilkinson, correspondent for the *Morning Post,* and published in the second edition of that newspaper at 06h25 on 17 November, 1899:

THE TRANSVAAL WAR.

ARMOURED TRAIN TRAPPED.

MR. CHURCHILL CAPTURED.

HIS COOLNESS AND BRAVERY.

FURTHER DETAILS.

COLENSO RAILWAY CUT.

LADYSMITH FIGHTING.

BOERS DEFEATED.

From Our War Correspondent.

DURBAN, Nov. 15, 10.25 a.m.

The armoured train arrived at Chieveley, where a few Boers were seen.

Two miles on the return journey the line was found thrown out of gauge.

The front truck turned over, and the enemy opened fire from a kopje with 9-pounders.

They got the range accurately, and hit the waggons and the engine, but did no damage to the vital parts of the locomotive.

The Naval gun on the train fired twice and was then put out of action.

Mr. Winston Spencer Churchill, with bravery and coolness which are described as magnificent, got a party of men to clear the overturned train.

Finally the engine passed over the degauged section.

The Dublins and the Volunteers, fighting an unequal battle, thrice drove the enemy back.

The wounded men's comrades put them back on the tender.

The engine and the tender with the wounded finally returned.

The men who left the trucks retired fighting, taking advantage of the cover.

It is hoped that the relief party will assist them in getting back safely.

The Boer fire was so severe during the bombardment that the telegraph wire poles were torn down.

The trucks were hit continually.

The Boer guns were posted on the kopjes and covered by the brushwood, and the sharpshooters were hidden in the dongas and behind the boulders.

Mr. Churchill remained with the retiring party.

The ambulance train which went out has now returned with only one wounded.

The doctor on the train got to the Boer lines and was informed that the wounded could not be recovered without orders from Joubert.

It is reported that a few men of the retiring party have arrived in camp.

Mr. Churchill is still missing, and I fear he is a prisoner.

I start for Estcourt to-night.

The story of Churchill's capture and his incarceration with other prisoners of war at the State Model School, Pretoria had to wait until after his escape. Churchill wrote up his capture while a prisoner of war. The following account of the skirmish and his subsequent capture was published on page 5 of the *Morning Post* on 1 January 1900:

WAR LETTERS

from

WINSTON S. CHURCHILL

Our War Correspondent

"WITH HEADQUARTERS"

FATE OF THE ARMOURED TRAIN.

PRETORIA, Nov. 19.

Now I perceive that I was foolish to choose in advance a definite title for these letters and to think that it could continue to be appropriate for any length of time. In the strong stream of war the swimmer is swirled helplessly about hither and thither by the waves, and he can by no means tell where he will come to land or, indeed, that he may not be overwhelmed in the flood. A week ago I described to you a reconnoitring expedition in the Estcourt armoured train, and I pointed out the many defects in the construction and the great dangers in the employment of that forlorn military machine. So potent were these to all who concerned themselves in the matter that the train was nicknamed in the camp 'Wilson's death trap'.

On Tuesday the 14th, the Mounted Infantry patrols reported that the Boers in small parties were approaching Estcourt from the directions of Weenen and Colenso, and Colonel Long made a reconnaissance in force to ascertain what strength lay behind the advanced scouts. The reconnaissance, which was marked only by an exchange of shots between the patrols, revealed little, but it was generally believed that a considerable portion of the army investing Ladysmith was moving, or was about to move, southwards to attack Estcourt and endeavour to strike at Pietermaritzburg. The movement that we had awaited for ten days impended. Accordingly certain military preparations, which I need not now specify, were made to guard against all contingencies, and at daylight on Wednesday morning another spray of patrols was flung out towards the north and north-west, and the Estcourt armoured train was ordered to reconnoitre as far as Chieveley. The train was composed as follows: an ordinary truck, in which was a 7-pounder muzzle-loading gun, served by four sailors from the *Tartar*; an armoured car fitted with loop-holes and held by three sections of a company of the Dublin Fusiliers; the engine and tender, two more armoured cars containing the fourth section of the Fusilier company, one company of the Durban Light Infantry (volunteers), and a small civilian breakdown gang; lastly, another ordinary truck with the tools and materials for repairing the road; in all five waggons, the locomotive, one small gun and 120 men. Captain Haldane, DSO, whom I had formerly known on Sir William Lockhart's staff in the Tirah Expedition, and who was lately recovered from his wound at Elandslaagte, commanded.

THE DEPARTURE

We started at half-past five and, observing all the usual precautions, reached Frere Station in about an hour. Here a small patrol of the Natal Police reported that there were no enemy within the next few miles, and that all seemed quiet in the neighbourhood. It was the silence before the storm. Captain Haldane decided to push on cautiously as far as Chieveley, near which place an extensive view of the country could be obtained. Not a sign of the Boers could be seen. The rolling, grassy country looked as peaceful and deserted as on former occasions, and we little thought that behind the green undulations scarcely three miles away the leading commandos of a powerful force were riding swiftly forward on their invading path.

All was clear as far as Chieveley, but as the train reached the station I saw about a hundred Boer horsemen cantering southwards about a mile from the railway. Beyond Chieveley a long hill was lined with a row of black spots, showing that our further advance would be disputed. The telegraphist who accompanied the train wired back to Estcourt reporting our safe arrival and that parties of Boers were to be seen at no great distance, and Colonel Long replied by ordering the train to return to Frere and to remain there in observation during the day, watching its safe retreat at nightfall. We proceeded to obey and were about a mile and three-quarters from Frere when on rounding a corner we saw that a hill which commanded the line at a distance of 600 yards was occupied by the enemy. So after all there would be a fight, for we could not pass this point without coming under fire. The four sailors loaded their gun — an antiquated toy — the soldiers charged their magazines, and the train, which was now in the reverse of the order in which it had started, moved slowly towards the hill.

The moment approached; but no one was much concerned, for the cars were proof against rifle fire, and this ridge could at the worst be occupied only by some daring patrol or perhaps a score of men. 'Besides,' we said to ourselves, 'they little think we have a gun on board. That will be a nice surprise.'

THE ATTACK

The Boers held their fire until the train reached that part of the track nearest to their position. Standing on a box in the rear armoured truck I had an excellent view through my glasses. The long brown rattling serpent with the rifles bristling from its spotted sides crawled closer to the rocky hillock on which the scattered black figures of the enemy showed clearly. Suddenly three-wheeled things appeared on the crest, and within a second a bright flash of light — like a heliograph, but much yellower — open and shut ten or twelve times. Then two much larger flashes; no smoke nor yet any sound, and a bustle and a stir among the little figures. So much for the hill. Immediately over the rear truck of the train a huge white ball of smoke sprang into being and tore out into a cone like a comet. Then came the explosions of the near guns and the nearer shell. The iron sides of the truck tanged with the patter of bullets. There was a crash from the front of the train and half a dozen sharp reports. The Boers had opened fire on us at 600 yards with two field guns, a Maxim firing small shells in a stream, and from riflemen lying on the ridge. I got down from my box into the cover of the armoured sides of the car without forming any clear thought. Equally involuntarily it seems that the driver put on full steam. The train leapt forward, ran the gauntlet of the guns, which now filled the air with explosions, swung round the curve of the hill, ran down a steep gradient, and dashed into a huge stone which awaited it on the line at a convenient spot.

THE DISASTER

To those who were in the rear truck there was only a great shock, a tremendous crash and a sudden full stop. What happened to the trucks in front of the engine is more interesting. The first, which contained the materials and tools of the breakdown gang and the guard who was watching the line, was flung into the air and fell bottom upwards on the embankment. (I do not know what befell the guard, but it seems probable that he was killed.) The next, an armoured car crowded with the Durban Light Infantry, was carried on twenty yards and thrown over on its side, scattering its occupants in a shower

"I had five dangerous days — continually under shell and rifle fire and . . . feather in my hat was cut through by a bullet. But in the end I came serenely through." Winston Churchill, writing to Pamela Plowden from South Africa, 28 January 1900 (Africana Museum).

on the ground. The third wedged itself across the track, half on and half off the rails. The rest of the train kept to the metals.

We are not long left in the comparative peace and safety of a railway accident. The Boer guns, swiftly changing their position, reopened from a distance of 1,300 yards before anyone had got out of the stage of exclamations. The tapping rifle fire spread along the hillsides until it encircled the wreckage on three sides, and a third field gun came into action from some high ground on the opposite side of the line.

THE DRIVER'S EXPERIENCE

The armoured truck gave some protection from the bullets, but since any direct shell must pierce it like paper and kill everyone it seemed almost safer outside and, wishing to see the extent and nature of the damage, I clambered over the iron shield and, dropping to the ground, ran along the line to the front of the train. As I passed the engine another shrapnel shell burst immediately, as it seemed, overhead, hurling its contents with a rasping rush through the air. The driver at once sprang out of the cab and ran to the shelter of the overturned trucks. His face was cut open by a splinter, and he complained in bitter futile indignation. He was a civilian. What did they think he was paid for? To be killed by bombshells? Not he. He would not stay another minute. It looked as if his excitement and misery would prevent him from working the engine further, and as only he understood the machinery all chances of escape seemed to be cut off. Yet when this man, who certainly exhibited lively symptoms of terror, was told that if he continued to stay at his post he would be mentioned for distinguished gallantry in action he pulled himself together, wiped the blood off his face, climbed back into the cab of his engine, and thereafter during the one-sided combat did his duty bravely and faithfully — so strong is the desire for honour and repute in the human beast. I reached the overturned portion of the train uninjured. The volunteers who, though severely shaken, were mostly unhurt, were lying down under such cover as the damaged cars and the gutters of the railway line afforded. It was a very grievous sight to see these citizen soldiers, most of whom were the fathers of families, in such a perilous position. They bore themselves well, though greatly troubled, and their major, whose name I have not learned, directed their fire on the enemy; but since these, lying behind the crests of the surrounding hills, were almost invisible I did not expect that it would be very effective.

ATTEMPTS TO CLEAR THE LINE

Efforts were now made to clear the line completely of the wrecked trucks so that the engine and the two cars which still remained on the rails might escape. Meanwhile Captain Haldane endeavoured to keep down the enemy's artillery fire by the musketry of the infantry in the rear armoured truck. The task of clearing the line would not perhaps, in ordinary circumstances, have been a very difficult one. But the breakdown gang and their tools were scattered to the winds, and several had fled along the track or across the fields. Moreover, the enemy's artillery fire was pitiless, continuous and distracting. The affair had, however, to be carried through.

The first thing to be done was to detach the truck half off the rails from the one completely so. To do this the engine had to be moved to slacken the strain on the twisted couplings. When these had been released the next step was to drag the partly-derailed truck backwards along the line until it was clear of the other wreckage and then to throw it bodily off the line. This may seem very simple, but the dead weight of the iron truck half on the sleepers was enormous and the engine wheels skidded vainly several times before any hauling power was obtained. At last the truck was sufficiently far back, and volunteers were called for to overturn it from the side while the engine pushed it from the end. It was very evident that these men would be exposed to considerable danger. Twenty were called for, and there was an immediate response. But only nine, including the major of volunteers, and four or five of the Dublin Fusiliers actually stepped out into the open. The attempt was nevertheless successful. The truck heeled further over under their pushing and, the engine giving a shove at the right moment, it fell off the line and the track was clear. Safety and success appeared in sight together, but disappointment overtook them.

COMPLICATIONS

The engine was about six inches wider than the tender, and the corner of its footplate would not pass the corner of the newly overturned truck. It did not seem safe to push very hard lest the engine itself should be derailed. So time after time the engine moved back a yard or two and shoved forward at the obstruction, and each time it moved a little. But soon it was evident that complications had set in. The newly derailed truck became jammed with that originally off the line, and the more the engine pushed the greater became the block. Volunteers were again called on to assist, but even though seven men, two of whom, I think, were wounded, did their best the attempt was a failure.

Perseverence, however, is a virtue. If the trucks only jammed the tighter for the forward pushing they might be loosened by pulling backwards. But now a new difficulty arose. The coupling chains of the engine would not reach by five or six inches those of the overturned truck. Search was now made for a spare link. By a solitary gleam of good luck, one was found. The engine hauled at the wreckage, and before the chains parted, pulled it about a yard backwards. Now, certainly, at last the line was clear. But again the corner of the footplate jammed with the corner of the truck, and again we came to a jarring halt.

A THRILLING EXPERIENCE

I have had, in the last four years, the advantage, if it be an advantage, of many strange and varied experiences, from which the student of realities might draw profit and instruction. But nothing was so thrilling as this: to wait and struggle among those clanging, rending iron boxes, with the repeated explosion of the shells and the artillery, the noise of the projectiles striking the ears, the hiss as they passed in the air, the grunting and pulling of the engine — poor, tortured thing, hammered by at least a dozen shells, any one of which, by penetrating the boiler, might have made an end to all — the expectation of destruction, the realisation of powerlessness, and the alternations of hope and despair — all this for seventy minutes by the clock with only four inches of twisted iron work to make the difference between danger, captivity and shame on the one hand — safety, freedom and triumph on the other.

Nothing remained but to continue pounding at the obstructing corner in the hopes that the ironwork would gradually be twisted and torn, and thus give free passage. As we pounded so did the enemy. The driver was adjured to be patient and to push gently, for it did not seem right to imperil the slender chance of escape by running the risk of throwing the engine off the line. But after a dozen pushes had been given with apparently little result a shell struck the front of the engine, setting fire to the woodwork, and he therefore turned on more steam, and with considerable momentum we struck the obstacle once more. There was a grinding crash; the engine staggered, checked, shore forward again, until with a clanging, tearing sound it broke past the point of interception, and nothing but the smooth line lay between us and home.

Brilliant success now seemed won, for I thought that the rear and gun trucks were following the locomotive, and that all might squeeze into them, and so make an honourable escape. But the longed-for cup was dashed aside. Looking backward, I saw that the couplings had parted, or been severed by a shell, and that the trucks still lay on the wrong side of the obstruction, separated by it from the engine. No one dared to risk imprisoning the engine again by making it go back for the trucks, so an attempt was made to drag the trucks up to the engine. Owing chiefly to the fire of the enemy this failed completely, and Captain Haldane determined to be content with saving the locomotive. He accordingly permitted the driver to retire along the line slowly, so that the Infantry might get as much shelter from the ironwork of the engine as possible, and the further idea was to get into some houses near the station, which were about 800 yards away, and there hold out while the engine went for assistance.

SAVING THE WOUNDED

As many wounded as possible were piled on to the engine, standing in the cab, lying on the tender, or clinging to the cowcatcher. And all this time the shells fell into the wet earth throwing up white clouds, burst with terrifying detonations overhead, or actually struck the engine and the iron wreckage. Besides the three field guns, which proved to be 15-pounders, the shell-firing Maxim continued its work, and its little shells, discharged with an ugly thud, thud, thud, exploded with startling bangs on all sides. One I remember struck the footplate of the engine scarcely a yard from my face, lit up into a bright yellow flash, and left me wondering why I was still alive. Another hit the coals in the tender, hurling a black shower into the air. A third — this also I saw — struck the arm of a private in the Dublin Fusiliers. The whole arm was smashed to a horrid pulp —

bones, muscles, blood, and uniform all mixed together. At the bottom hung the hand, unhurt, but swelled instantly to three times its ordinary size. The engine was soon crowded and began to steam homewards — a mournful, sorely-battered locomotive — with the woodwork of the firebox in flames and the water spouting from its pierced tanks. The infantrymen straggled along beside it at the double.

ESCAPE OF THE ENGINE

Seeing the engine escaping the Boers increased their fire and the troops, hitherto somewhat protected by the iron trucks, began to suffer. The major of volunteers fell shot through the thigh. Here and there men dropped on the ground, several screamed — this is very rare in war — and cried for help. About a quarter of the force was very soon killed or wounded. The shells which pursued the retreating soldiers scattered them along the track. Order and control vanished. The engine, increasing its pace, drew out from the thin crowd of fugitives and was soon in safety. The infantry continued to run down the line in the direction of the houses, and, in spite of their disorder, I honestly consider that they were capable of making a further resistance when some natural shelter should be reached. But at this moment one of those incidents — much too frequent in this war — occurred.

The armoured train which was ambushed outside Frere by Louis Botha, leading to Churchill's capture and his subsequent tales of derring-do (Africana Museum).

134

THE SURRENDER

A private soldier who was wounded, in direct disobedience of the positive orders that no surrender was to be made, took it on himself to wave a pocket handkerchief. The Boers immediately ceased firing, and with equal daring and humanity a dozen horsemen galloped from the hills into the scattered fugitives, scarcely any of whom had seen the white flag, and several of whom were still firing, and called loudly on them to surrender. Most of the soldiers then halted, gave up their arms, and became prisoners of war. Those further away from the horsemen continued to run and were shot or hunted down in twos and threes and some made good their escape.

MR. CHURCHILL'S CAPTURE

For my part I found myself on the engine when the obstruction was at last passed and remained there jammed in the cab next to the man with the shattered arm. In this way I travelled some 500 yards, and passed through the fugitives, noticing particularly a young officer, Lieutenant Frankland, who with a happy, confident smile on his face was endeavouring to rally his men. As I thought that only the wounded should be carried by the engine and that sound men should run, I jumped on to the line, and hence the address from which this letter is written, for scarcely had the locomotive left me than I found myself alone in a shallow cutting and none of our soldiers to be seen. Then suddenly there appeared on the line at the end of the cutting two men not in uniform. "Platelayers," I said to myself, and then with a surge of realisation, "Boers". My mind retains a momentary impression of those tall figures, full of animated movement, clad in dark flapping clothes, with slouch, storm-driven hats poising on their rifles hardly a hundred yards away. I turned and ran between the rails of the track, and the only thought I achieved was this, "Boer marksmanship." Two bullets passed, both within a foot, one on either side. I flung myself against the banks of the cutting. But they gave no cover. Another glance at the figures; one was now kneeling to aim. Again I darted forward. Movement seemed the only chance. Again two soft kisses sucked in the air, but nothing struck me. This could not endure. I must get out of the cutting — that damnable corridor. I scrambled up the bank. The earth sprang up beside me, and something touched my hand, but outside the cutting was a tiny depression. I crouched in this, struggling to get my wind. On the other side of the railway a horseman galloped up, shouting to me and waving his hand. He was scarcely forty yards off. With a rifle I could have killed him easily. I knew nothing of white flags, and the bullets had made me savage. But I was a Press Correspondent without arms of any kind. There was a wire fence between me and the horseman. Should I continue to fly? The idea of another shot at such a short range decided me. Death stood before me, grim sullen Death without his light-hearted companion. Chance. So I held up my hand, and like Mr. Jorrocke's foxes, cried "Capivy." Then I was herded with the other prisoners in a miserable group and about the same time I noticed that my hand was bleeding, and it began to pour with rain.

Two days before I had written to an officer in high command at home, whose friendship I have the honour to enjoy: "There has been a great deal too much surrendering in this war, and I hope people who do so will not be encouraged." Fate had intervened, yet though her tone was full of irony she seemed to say, as I think Ruskin once said, "It matters very little whether your judgments of people are true or untrue, and very much whether they are kind or unkind," and repeating that I will make an end.

'The position of a prisoner of war is painful and humiliating,' wrote Churchill at the beginning of his next despatch (also printed in the *Morning Post* of 1 January 1900). His natural fears at being captured were somewhat allayed when, after several hours' walking in an uneven column of captured British soldiers, guarded by armed Boers, one of them threw him a cap — belonging to the Irish Fusiliers — to replace the one he had lost during the battle. 'So they were not cruel men, these enemy.'

It did not take long before Churchill was recognised. "'You are the son of Lord Randolph Churchill?' said a Scottish Boer abruptly. I did not deny the fact . . . 'I am a newspaper correspondent,' I said, 'and you ought not to hold me prisoner.' The Scottish Boer laughed. 'Oh,' he said, 'we do not catch lords' sons every day.'"

The first night of Churchill's imprisonment was spent wrapped in a blanket given to him by one of the Boers, within the shelter of a shed. There, he wrote, at the conclusion of his despatch,

> "I could not sleep. Vexation of spirit, a cold night and wet clothes withheld sweet oblivion. The rights and wrongs of the quarrel, the fortunes and chances of the war, forced themselves on my mind. What men they were, these Boers! I thought of them as I had seen them in the morning riding forward through the rain — thousands of independent riflemen, thinking for themselves, possessed of beautiful weapons, led with skill, living as they rode without commissariat or transport or ammunition column, moving like the wind, and supported by iron constitutions and a stern, hard, Old Testament God who should surely smite the Amalekite hip and thigh. And then, above the rain storm that beat loudly on the corrugated iron, I heard the sound of a chaunt. The Boers were singing their evening psalm, and the menacing notes — more full of indignant war than love and mercy — struck a chill into my heart, so that I thought after all that the war was unjust, that the Boers were better men than we, that Heaven was against us, that Ladysmith, Mafeking and Kimberley would fall, that the Estcourt garrison would perish, that foreign powers would intervene, that we should lose South Africa, and that that would be the beginning of the end. So for the time I despaired of the Empire, nor was it till the morning sun — all the brighter after the rain storms, all the warmer after the chills — struck in through the windows that things reassumed their true colours and proportions."

Churchill's escape from the State Model School, Pretoria, was no less controversial than his capture. The Boers had refused to accept his vociferous claim that he was a war correspondent and therefore a non-combatant, and as such should be entitled to an immediate release. He bombarded the authorities with letters eloquent and angry, refuting the charge that he had played an active part in the battle around the ambushed armoured train.

Giving up hope of being released, Churchill and two fellow-officers planned to escape and make their way to Lourenço Marques. He escaped — leaving his companions behind, resulting in bitter accusations as to his selfishness and disregard for others — on 12 December, ironically, one day before Commandant-General Joubert relented and ordered his release.

From Lourenço Marques, once his escape was assured, Churchill telegraphed the *Morning Post:* 'I am very weak but I am free. I have lost many pounds but I am lighter in heart. I shall also avail myself of every opportunity from this moment to urge with earnestness an unflinching and uncomprising prosecution of the war.'

Not mentioned in the despatch which covered his escape and train journey to the east coast was the part played by a mine manager near the coal mining town of Witbank, who sheltered

Churchill for six days and organised his train ride to safety. The *Morning Post,* mindful that Churchill was, apart from being their South African war correspondent, a national hero, gave prominence to this report, published in the paper on Wednesday 24 January 1900:

HOW I ESCAPED FROM PRETORIA,

and

My subsequent adventures on the road to Delagoa Bay.

written by

Winston Spencer Churchill,

our war correspondent.

How unhappy is that poor man who loses his liberty! What can the wide world give him in exchange? No degree of material comfort, no consciousness of correct behaviour, can balance the hateful degradation of imprisonment. Before I had been an hour in captivity I resolved to escape. Many plans suggested themselves, were examined and rejected. For a month I thought of nothing else. But the peril and difficulty restrained action. I think that it was the news of the British defeat at Stormberg that clinched the matter. All the news we heard in Pretoria was derived from Boer sources, and was hideously exaggerated and distorted. Every day we read in the *Volksstem* — probably the most amazing tissue of lies ever presented to the public under the name of a newspaper — of Boer victories and of the huge slaughters and shameful flights of the British. However much one might doubt and discount these tales they made a deep impression. A month's feeding on such literary garbage weakens the constitution of the mind. We wretched prisoners lost heart. Perhaps Great Britain would not persevere; perhaps foreign powers would intervene; perhaps there would be another disgraceful, cowardly peace. At the best the war and our confinement would be prolonged for many months. I do not pretend that impatience at being locked up was not the foundation of my determination; but I should never have screwed up my courage to make the attempt without the earnest desire to do something, however small, to help the British cause. Of course, I am a man of peace. I do not fight. But swords are not the only weapons in the world. Something may be done with a pen. So I determined to take all hazards; and, indeed, the affair was one of very great danger and difficulty.

THE PRISONERS' HOME IN PRETORIA

The State Model School, the building in which we were confined, is a brick structure standing in the midst of a gravel quadrangle and surrounded on two sides by an iron grille and on two by a corrugated iron fence about 10 ft high. These boundaries offered little obstacle to anyone who possessed the activity of youth, but the fact that they were guarded on the inside by sentries armed with rifle and revolver fifty yards apart made them a well-nigh insuperable barrier. No walls are so hard to pierce as living walls. I thought of the penetrating power of gold, and the sentries were sounded. They were incorruptible. I seek not to deprive them of the credit, but the truth is that the bribery market in this country has been spoiled by the millionaires. I could not afford with my slender resources to insult them heavily enough. So nothing remained but to break out in spite of them. With another officer who may for the present — since he is still a prisoner — remain nameless I formed a scheme.

After anxious reflection and continual watching, it was discovered that when the sentries near the offices walked about on their beats they were at certain moments unable to see the top of a few yards of the wall. The electric lights in the middle of the quadrangle brilliantly lighted the whole place, but cut off the sentries beyond them from looking at the eastern wall. For behind the lights all seemed by contrast darkness. The first thing was therefore to pass the two sentries near the offices. It was necessary to hit off the exact moment when both their backs should be turned together. After the wall was scaled we should be in the garden of the villa next door. There our plan came to an end. Everything after this was vague and uncertain. How to get out of the garden, how to pass unnoticed through the streets, how to evade the patrols that surrounded the town and above all, how to cover the two hundred and eighty miles to the Portuguese frontiers, were questions which would arise at a later stage. All attempts to communicate with friends outside had failed. We cherished the hope that with chocolate, a little Kaffir knowledge and a great deal of luck we might march the distance in a fortnight, buying mealies at the native kraals and lying hidden by day. But it did not look a very promising prospect.

We determined to try on the night of 11 December, making up our minds quite suddenly in the morning, for these things are best done on the spur of the moment. I passed the afternoon in positive terror. Nothing has ever disturbed me as much as this. There is something appalling in the idea of stealing secretly off in the night like a guilty thief. The fear of detection has a pang of its own. Besides, we knew quite well that on occasion, even on excuse, the sentries — they were armed police — would fire. Fifteen yards is a short range. And beyond the immediate danger lay a prospect of severe hardship and suffering, only faint hopes of success, and the probability at the best of five months in Pretoria Gaol.

The afternoon dragged tediously away. I tried to read Mr Lecky's *History of England,* but for the first time in my life that wise writer wearied me. I played chess and was hopelessly beaten. At last it grew dark. At seven o'clock the bell for dinner rang and the officers trooped off. Now was the time. But the sentries gave us no chance. They did not walk about. One of them stood exactly opposite the only practicable part of the wall. We waited for two hours, but the attempt was plainly impossible, and so with a most unsatisfactory feeling of relief to bed.

Tuesday, the 12th! Another day of fear, but fear crystallising more and more into desperation. Anything was better than further suspense. Night came again. Again the dinner bell sounded. Choosing my opportunity I strolled across the quadrangle and secreted myself in one of the offices. Through a chink I watched the sentries. For half an hour they remained stolid and obstructive. Then all of a sudden one turned and walked up to his comrade and they began to talk. Their backs were turned. Now or never. I darted out of my hiding-place and ran to the wall, seized the top with my hands and drew myself up. Twice I let myself down again in sickly hesitation, and then with a third resolve scrambled up. The top was flat. Lying on it I had one part glimpse of the sentries, still talking, still with their backs turned; but, I repeat, fifteen yards away. Then I lowered myself silently down into the adjoining garden and crouched among the shrubs. I was free. The first step had been taken and it was irrevocable.

It now remained to await the arrival of my comrade. The bushes of the garden gave a good deal of cover, and in the moonlight their shadows lay black on the ground. Twenty yards away was the house, and I had not been five minutes in hiding before I perceived that it was full of people; the windows revealed brightly-lighted rooms, and within I could see figures moving about. This was a fresh complication. We had always thought the house unoccupied. Presently — how long afterwards I do not know, for the ordinary measures of time, hours, minutes and seconds, are quite meaningless on such occasions — a man came out of the door and walked across the garden in my direction. Scarcely ten yards away he stopped and stood still, looking steadily towards me. I cannot describe the surge of panic which nearly overwhelmed me. I must be discovered. I dared not stir an inch. But amid a tumult of emotion, reason, seated firmly on her throne, whispered, 'Trust to the dark background'. I remained absolutely motionless. For a long time the man and I remained opposite each other, and every instant I expected him to spring forward. A vague idea crossed my mind that I might silence him. 'Hush, I am a detective. We expect that an officer will break out here tonight. I am waiting to catch him.' Reason — scornful this time — replied: 'Surely a Transvaal detective would speak Dutch. Trust to the shadow.' So I trusted, and after a spell another man came out of the house, lighted a cigar, and both he and the other walked off together. No sooner had they turned than a cat pursued by a dog rushed into the bushes and collided into me. The startled animal uttered a 'miauw' of alarm and darted back again making a horrible rustling. Both men stopped at once. But it was only the cat, and they passed out of the garden gate into the town.

"AT LARGE" IN PRETORIA

I looked at my watch. An hour had passed since I climbed the wall. Where was my comrade? Suddenly I heard a voice from within the quadrangle say quite loud 'All up.' I crawled back to the wall. Two officers were walking up and down the other side jabbering Latin words, laughing and talking all manner of nonsense — amid which I caught my name. I risked a cough. One of the officers immediately began to chatter alone. The other said slowly and clearly: '. . . cannot get out. The sentry suspects. It's all up. Can you get back again?' But now all my fears fell from me at once. To go back was impossible. I could not hope to climb the wall unnoticed. Fate pointed onwards. Besides, I said to myself, 'Of course, I shall be recaptured, but I will at least have a run for my money.' I said to the officers: 'I shall go on alone.'

Now, I was in the right mood for these undertakings — that is to say that, thinking failure almost certain, no odds against success affected me. All risks were less than the certainty. I said to myself, *'Toujours l'audace'*: put my hat on my head, strode out into the middle of the garden, walked past the windows of the house without any attempt at concealment, and so went through the gate and turned to the left. I passed the sentry at less than five yards. Most of them knew me by sight. Whether he looked at me or not I do not know, for I never turned my head. But after walking a hundred yards I knew that the second obstacle had been surmounted. I was at large in Pretoria.

I walked on leisurely through the night humming a tune and choosing the middle of the road. The streets were full of burghers, but they paid no attention to me. Gradually I reached the suburbs, and on a little bridge I sat down to reflect and consider. I was in the heart of the enemy's country. I knew no one to whom I could apply for succour. Nearly three hundred miles stretched between me and Delagoa Bay. My escape must be known at dawn. Pursuit would be immediate. Yet all exits were barred. The town was picketed, the country was patrolled, the trains were searched, the line was guarded. I had £75 in my pocket and four slabs of chocolate, but the compass and the map which might have guided me, the opium tablets and meat lozenges which should have sustained me, were in my friend's pockets in the State Model School. Worst of all, I could not speak a word of Dutch or Kaffir, and how was I to get food or direction?

But when hope had departed, fear had gone as well. I formed a plan. I would find the Delagoa Bay railway. Without map or compass I must follow that in spite of the pickets. I looked at the stars. Orion shone brightly. Scarcely a year ago he had guided me when lost in the desert to the bank of the Nile. He had given me water. Now he should lead me to freedom. I could not endure the want of either.

After walking south for half a mile I struck the railroad. Was it the line to Delagoa Bay or the Pietersburg branch? If it were the former it should run east. But as far as I could see this line ran northwards. Still, it might be only winding its way out among the hills. I resolved to follow it. The night was delicious. A cool breeze fanned my face and a wild feeling of exhilaration took hold of me. At any rate I was free, if only for an hour. That was something. The fascination of the adventure grew. Unless the stars in their courses fought for me I could not escape. Where was the need for caution? I marched briskly along the line. Here and there the lights of a picket fire gleamed. Every bridge had its watchers. But I passed them all, making very short detours at the dangerous places, and really taking scarcely any precautions.

As I walked I extended my plan. I could not march three hundred miles to the frontier. I would go by train. I would board a train in motion and hide under the seats, on the roof, on the couplings — anywhere. What train should I take? The first, of course. After walking for two hours I perceived the signal lights of a station. I left the line and, circling round it, hid in the ditch by the track about 200 yards beyond it. I argued that the train would stop at the station and that it would not have got up too much speed by the time it reached me. An hour passed. I began to grow impatient. Suddenly I heard the whistle and the approaching rattle. Then the great yellow headlights of the engine flashed into view. The train waited five minutes at the station and started again with much noise and steaming. I crouched by the track. I rehearsed the act in my mind. I must wait until the engine had passed, otherwise I should be seen. Then I must make a dash for the carriages.

The train started slowly but gathered speed sooner than I had expected. The flaring lights drew swiftly near. The rattle grew into a roar. The dark mass hung for a second above me. The engine driver silhouetted against his furnace glow, the black profile of the engine, the clouds of steam rushed past. Then I hurled myself on the trucks, clutched at something, missed, clutched again, missed again, grasped some sort of handhold, was swung off my feet — my toes bumping on the line, and with a struggle seated myself on the couplings of the fifth truck from the front of the train. It was a goods train, and the trucks were full of sacks, soft sacks covered with coal dust. I crawled on top and burrowed in among them. In five minutes I was completely buried. The sacks were warm and comfortable. Perhaps the engine driver had seen me rush up to the train and would give the alarm at the next station; on the other hand, perhaps not. Where was the train going to? Where would it be unloaded? Would it be searched? Was it on the Delagoa Bay line? What should I do in the morning? Ah, never mind that. Sufficient for the day was the luck thereof. Fresh plans for fresh contingencies. I resolved to sleep, nor can I imagine a more pleasing lullaby than the clatter of the train that carries you at twenty miles an hour away from the enemy's capital.

DARING LEAP

How long I slept I do not know, but I woke up suddenly with all feelings of exhilaration gone, and only the consciousness of oppressive difficulties heavy on me. I must leave the train before daybreak, so that I could drink at a pool and find some hiding place while it was still dark. Another night I would board another train. I crawled from my cosy hiding place among the sacks and sat again on the couplings. The train was running at a fair speed, but I felt it was time to leave it. I took hold of the iron handle at the back of the truck, pulled strongly with my left hand, and sprang. My feet struck the ground in two gigantic strides, and the next instant I was sprawling in the ditch considerably shaken but unhurt. The train, my faithful ally of the night, hurried on its journey.

It was still dark. I was in the middle of a wide valley, surrounded by low hills and carpeted with high grass drenched in dew. I searched for water in the nearest gully and soon found a clear pool. I was very thirsty, but long after I had quenched my thirst I continued to drink that I might have sufficient for the whole day.

Presently the dawn began to break, and the sky to the east grew yellow and red, slashed across with heavy black clouds. I saw with relief that the railway ran steadily towards the sunrise. I had taken the right line after all.

THE VULTURE'S COMPANIONSHIP

Having drunk my fill, I set out for the hills, among which I hoped to find some hiding-place, and as it became broad daylight I entered a small group of trees which grew on the side of a deep ravine. Here I resolved to wait till dusk. I had one consolation: no one in the world knew where I was — I did not know myself. It was now four o'clock. Fourteen hours lay between me and the night. My impatience to proceed doubled their length. At first it was terribly cold, but by degrees the sun gained power, and by ten o'clock the heat was oppressive. My sole companion was a gigantic vulture, who manifested an extravagant interest in my condition, and made hideous and ominous gurglings from time to time. From my lofty position I commanded a view of the whole valley. A little tin-roofed town lay three miles to the westward. Scattered farmsteads, each with a clump of trees, relieved the monotony of the undulating ground. At the foot of the hill stood a Kaffir kraal, and the figures of its inhabitants dotted the patches of cultivation or surrounded the droves of goats and cows which fed on the pasture. The railway ran through the middle of the valley, and I could watch the passage of the various trains. I counted four passing each way, and from this I drew the conclusion that the same number would run at night. I marked a steep gradient up which they climbed very slowly, and determined at nightfall to make another attempt to board one of these. During the day I ate one slab of chocolate which, with the heat, produced a violent thirst. The pool was hardly half a mile away, but I dared not leave the shelter of the little wood, for I could see the figures of white men riding or walking occasionally across the valley, and once a Boer came and fired two shots at birds close to my hiding place. But no one discovered me.

REFLECTION AND PRAYER

The elation and the excitement of the previous night had burnt away, and a chilling reaction followed. I was very hungry, for I had had no dinner before starting, and chocolate though it sustains does not satisfy. I had scarcely slept, but yet my heart beat so fierce and I was so nervous and perplexed about the future that I could not rest. I thought of all the chances that lay against me; I dreaded and detested more than words can express the prospect of being caught and dragged back to Pretoria. I do not mean that I would rather have died than have been retaken, but I have often feared death for much less. I found no comfort in any of the philosophical ideas that some men parade in their hours of ease and strength and safety. They seemed only fair weather friends. I realised with awful force that no exercise of my own feeble wit and strength could save me from my enemies, and that without the assistance of that High Power which interferes more often than we are always prone to admit in the eternal sequence of causes and effects, I could never succeed. I prayed long and earnestly for help and guidance. My prayer, as it seems to me, was swiftly and wonderfully answered. I cannot now relate the strange circumstances which followed, and which changed my nearly hopeless position into one of superior advantage. But after the war is over I shall hope to lengthen this account, and so remarkable will the addition be that I cannot believe the reader will complain.

The long day reached its close at last. The western clouds flushed into fire; the shadows of the hills stretched out across the valley. A ponderous Boer waggon, with its long team, crawled slowly along the track towards the town. The Kaffirs collected their herds and drew around their kraal. The daylight died, and soon it was quite dark. Then, and not till then, I set forth. I hurried to the railway line, pausing on my way to drink at a stream of sweet, cold water. I waited for sometime at the top of the steep gradient in the hope of catching a train. But none came, and I gradually guessed, and I have since found out that I guessed right, that the train I had already travelled in was the only one that ran at night. At last I resolved to walk on and make, at any rate, twenty miles of my journey. I walked for about six hours. How far I travelled I do not know, but I do not expect it was very many miles in the direct line. Every bridge was guarded by armed men; every few miles were gangers' huts; at intervals there were stations with villages clustering round them. All the veldt was bathed in the bright rays of the full moon, and to avoid these dangerous places I had to make wide circuits and often to creep along the ground. Leaving the railroad I fell into bogs and swamps, and brushed through high grass dripping with dew, and so I was drenched to the waist. I had been able to take little exercise during my month's imprisonment, and I was soon tired out with walking, as well as from want of food and sleep. I felt very miserable when I looked around and saw here and there the lights of houses, and thought of the warmth and comfort within them, but knew that they only meant danger to me. After six or seven hours of walking I thought it unwise to go further lest I should exhaust myself, so I lay down in a ditch to sleep. I was nearly at the end of my tether. Nevertheless, by the will of God, I was enabled to sustain myself during the next few days, obtaining food at great risk here and there, resting in concealment by day and walking only at night. On the fifth day I was beyond Middelburg, as far as I could tell, for I dared not inquire nor as yet approach the stations near enough to read the names. In a secure hiding place I waited for a suitable train, knowing that there is a through service between Middelburg and Lourenço Marques.

Meanwhile there had been excitement in the State Model School, temporarily converted into a military prison. Early on Wednesday morning — barely twelve hours after I had escaped — my absence was discovered — I think by Doctor Gunning, an amiable Hollander who used often to come and argue with me the rights and wrongs of the war. The alarm was given. Telegrams with my description at great length were despatched along all the railways. A warrant was issued for my immediate arrest. Every train was strictly searched. Everyone was on the watch. The newspapers made so much of the affair that my humble fortunes and my whereabouts were discussed in long columns of print, and even in the crash of the war I became to the Boers a topic all to myself. The rumours in part amused me. It was certain, said the *Standard and Digger's News,* that I had escaped disguised as a woman. The next day I was reported captured at Komati Poort dressed as a Transvaal policeman. There was great delight at this, which was only changed to doubt when other telegrams said that I had been arrested at Brags-bank, at Middelburg and at Bronkersspruit. But the captives proved to be harmless people after all. Finally it was agreed that I had never left Pretoria. I had — it appeared — changed clothes with a waiter, and was now in hiding at the house of some British sympathiser in the capital. On the strength of this all the houses of suspected persons were searched from top to bottom, and these unfortunate people were, I fear, put to a great deal of inconvenience. A special commission was also appointed to investigate 'stringently' (a most hateful adjective in such a connection) the causes 'which had rendered it possible for the war correspondent of the *Morning Post* to escape.'

MILL "ON LIBERTY"

The *Volksstem* noticed as a significant fact that I had recently become a subscriber to the State Library, and had selected Mill's essay *On Liberty.* It apparently desired to gravely deprecate prisoners having access to such inflammatory literature. The idea will, perhaps, amuse those who have read the work in question.

All these things may provoke a smile of indifference; perhaps even of triumph after the danger is past; but during the days when I was lying up in holes and corners waiting for a good chance to board a train, the causes that had led to them preyed more than I knew on my nerves. To be an outcast, to be hunted, to be under a warrant for arrest, to fear every man, to have imprisonment — not necessarily military confinement either — hanging overhead, to fly the light, to doubt the shadows — all these things ate into my soul and have left an impression that will not perhaps be easily effaced.

BACK TO THE RAILWAY TRUCK

On the sixth day the chance I had patiently waited for came. I found a convenient train duly labelled to Lourenço Marques standing in a siding. I withdrew to a suitable spot for boarding it — for I dared not make the attempt in the station — and, filling a bottle with water to drink on the way, I prepared for the last stage of my journey.

The truck in which I ensconced myself was laden with great sacks of some soft merchandise, and I found among them holes and crevices by means of which I managed to work my way into the inmost recess. The hard floor of the truck was littered with gritty coal dust, and made a most uncomfortable bed. The heat was almost stifling. I was resolved, however, that nothing should lure or compel me from my hiding place until I reached Portuguese territory. I expected the journey to take thirty-six hours; it dragged out into two and a half days. I hardly dared sleep for fear of snoring.

FREE ONCE MORE

I feared lest the trucks should be searched at Komati Poort, and my anxiety as the train approached this neighbourhood was very great. To prolong it we were shunted on to a siding for eighteen hours either at Komati Poort or the station beyond it. Once indeed they began to search my truck, but luckily did not search deep enough so that, providentialy protected, I reached Delagoa Bay at last, and crawled forth from my place of refuge and of punishment, weary, dirty, hungry but free once more.

Thereafter everything smiled. I found my way to the British Consul, Mr Ross, who at first mistook me for a fireman off one of the ships in the harbour, but soon welcomed me with enthusiasm. I bought clothes, I washed, I sat down to dinner with a real tablecloth and real glasses; and fortune, determined not to overlook the smallest detail, had arranged that the steamer *Induna* should leave that very night for Durban. It is from the cabin of this little vessel, as she coasts along the sandy shores of Africa, that I write these lines, and the reader who may persevere through this hurried account will perhaps understand why I write them with a feeling of triumph, and better than triumph, a feeling of pure joy.

To the disgust of other correspondents, whose non-combatant position he jeopardised, the now-famous Churchill, back in the Natal war zone, persuaded General Sir Redvers Buller to commission him as a lieutenant in the South African Light Horse. Always with his eye on the main chance, Churchill retained his status as the *Morning Post*'s correspondent, at a salary of £1 000 for his first months in South Africa, thereafter receiving £200 a month, all expenses paid and the option to retain copyright on his despatches.

After witnessing the battle of Spion Kop, the relief of Ladysmith and Lord Robert's drive to Pretoria, Churchill left the wagon in which he followed the troops (it contained nearly a metre-deep layer of tinned provisions and alcohol) and returned to Britain and a political career.

Winston Churchill in the uniform of the South African Light Horse granted to him by Sir Redvers Buller (Africana Museum).

'That acre of massacre'

The Battle of Spion Kop, 24 January 1900

General Sir Redvers Buller was undoubtedly the most important man to set sail for South Africa from Southampton Docks on Saturday, 12 October 1899. Sailing with him on the *Dunottar Castle* were two young men who were to form a lifelong friendship: war correspondents Winston Churchill (*Morning Post*) and John Black Atkins (*Manchester Guardian*).

On the face of it, Atkins was an unlikely candidate for journalism. Educated at Marlborough and Pembroke College, Cambridge, he had emerged from university with a Theological Tripos and a desire to take Holy Orders. He was diverted from this course, however, by a leader writer for the *Manchester Guardian,* who persuaded Atkins that his future lay in journalism rather than in the church. Thus did Atkins, 27 years old at the time he sailed for South Africa, come to cover the Turco-Greek war (1897) and the Spanish American war (1898), and to earn a reputation as a war correspondent who was at the same time a poet. Atkins possessed a natural passion for words and their rhythm, and his strong narrative skills rose on occasion to a rare and memorable lyricism.

It was Atkins who, with fellow correspondent Leo Amery (*The Times*) followed the sound of gunfire outside Estcourt to discover that their colleague Winston Churchill, the only one to rouse himself from bed on that rainy morning, had been ambushed and captured.

Atkins and Filson Young, the other *Guardian* man in South Africa, had been instructed by the newspaper, in a burst of parsimony, to send very short news telegrams and to follow these with in-depth reports by mail three or four weeks later. The news reports printed in the paper were, therefore, brief to the point of being terse. Atkins' report of the armoured train ambush ran to only 36 lines and was heavily leaded to give it the appearance of being longer.

Together with Bennet Burleigh (*The Daily Telegraph*) and Winston Churchill, freshly back from his escape and, contrary to the rules governing correspondents and the wearing of military uniform, was resplendent as a lieutenant of the South African Light Horse, Atkins accompanied Buller on his push across the Tugela with the relief of Ladysmith as the goal.

Of the three military setbacks the unfortunate Buller was to receive (Colenso, Spion Kop and Vaal Krantz) as he battled his way towards Ladysmith, Spion Kop, like Majuba, was to become a byword both for horror and for military ineptitude.

The hill of Spion Kop stands some 475 metres above the Tugela which runs to its south. '(Spion Kop) was undoubtedly the key to the Boer positions,' wrote Amery, 'but to use a key in order to open the door just wide enough to get one's hand in, and then to leave it there, is deliberately to invite having one's fingers crushed.'

In order to join up with Buller's forces in a two-pronged attack that would sweep all before it on the open veld towards Ladysmith, Buller's senior subordinate, Lieutenant-General Sir Charles Warren, had to break through the range of hills of which Spion Kop was the key, and which, once taken, would allow Warren's force of 10 600 infantry and over 2 000 mounted troops to breach the Boer lines to the west. But Warren's progress, like his thought processes, was ponderous, and by the time he finally got himself into position, the alerted Boers had increased their forces, according to British intelligence, to almost 7 000 men.

Warren decided to commit his men to a night attack on Spion Kop. At 19h30 on the evening of 23 January, the 2 000 troops assigned to this task assembled. Each carried a rifle and 150 rounds of ammunition. They were allocated 20 shovels and 20 picks to dig the trenches. Lieutenant-Colonel A. Thorneycroft, commanding officer of the mounted infantry, was to emerge as the hero of the day. He addressed his men before setting off on the march: 'We are about to attack Spion Kop. Make no noise. It's bayonet work only. No shots are to be fired. No smoking. No talking. Keep in close touch with one another. The honour of the regiment is in your hands. I can trust you all to do your duty.'

In dense mist, the soldiers reached the crest of Spion Kop around 03h00, displacing

John Black Atkins, war correspondent to the Manchester Guardian.

the Boer picket at the cost of ten men wounded. The sappers began to dig the crescent-shaped line of trenches on what they took to be the crest of the hill but which was, in fact, 200 yards short. But only 45 cm beneath the stony topsoil they struck a layer of rock. Piling rocks and stones in front of the depression, they waited for the mist to rise.

Just before 08h00, against a clear sky, the eleven-hour ordeal of the men despatched so casually to take and hold Spion Kop began when they came under the fierce gunfire of Boer volunteers under the command of Louis Botha. (The volunteers included the 17 year-old Deneys Reitz.) Raked by the Boers' fire and confined to an area little more than 400 metres in width by 600 in length, the suffering of the men was appalling.

The war correspondents watched from below, but were not at first aware of the extent of the carnage nor, indeed, of what was actually happening on the hill. Of the 2 000 men who had scrambled up Spion Kop on the night of 23 January, 243 died on the hill, many of them horribly mutilated by the concentration of gunfire and lying three deep in the shallow trenches. Another 500 were wounded, many of whom later died. The fact that any of them lived at all must, in some part, be attributed to Winston Churchill.

At about 16h00, unable to watch the hill any longer without knowing exactly what was happening, but with the memory of Majuba imprinted on his mind, Churchill decided to climb Spion Kop. 'Streams of wounded met us and obstructed our path,' he wrote. 'Men were staggering along alone, or supported by comrades, or crawling on hands and knees, or carried on stretchers. Corpses lay here and there . . .' He hurried down the hillside, greatly agitated. 'For God's sake,' he called out to Captain Levita, 'don't let this be a second Majuba Hill.'

Churchill volunteered to go back up the hill again, this time with a message for the redoubtable Thorneycroft. (At one stage in that terrible day, a handful of British soldiers, tormented almost

146

beyond endurance by the gunfire and thirst, leapt to their feet and tried to surrender. Thorneycroft, a big man, jumped up in turn and met the astonished oncoming Boers. 'You may go to hell!' he told them. 'I command here, and allow no surrender. Go on with your firing.' The Boers retreated and Thorneycroft's men resumed their positions.) Churchill asked Thorneycroft for his views on the situation. Thorneycroft felt his position was untenable and begged Churchill for advice. Churchill supported Thorneycroft in his decision to withdraw. The hill was left to the Boers.

After sending his brief and factual despatch on the battle to his paper, John Atkins, in his rich prose and with chilling imagery, described the battle in a fuller report, written from Spearman's Farm Camp on 30 January 1900.

If you looked up from the Tugela to the hills where Sir Charles Warren fought, you would say that they rose in a continuous slope to the top. But South African hills are like the sea; at a distance they seem smooth, but look close into them and you will find unexpected valleys and crests. Nothing on the face of South African nature is what it seems. You see the British trenches up there seeming to lie immediately under the Boer trenches, but if you go up you will find that they are on different hills and a deep valley lies between them. You see troops march out on to a sheer plain, and when they have disappeared suddenly on their march you learn for the first time that the plain is no plain, but is full of dips and rises, dongas and unremarked kopjes. From the river it seemed for almost a week that Warren's troops were within charging distance of the crest of all those hills; really they remained from the crest the distance that separates a victory from a retirement.

Spion Kop, properly used, was the key of the position, and the key that would open the door of Ladysmith. Patrols had reported that there were only a few Boers on it. Soon after dusk on Tuesday a party set out to make a night attack on the hill. It was a hand-and-knee march up the southern face — a climb over smooth rock and grass. It was necessarily slow; it is to the great credit of the party that it was steady. The force was three-quarters of the way up before it was discoverd. Then a Boer sentry challenged it for the password. "Waterloo!" said an officer. The sentry turned to flee, but fell bayoneted where he turned. "Fire and charge," came the order. The Fusiliers went forward at the deliberate conventional trot; Thorneycroft's, with the untrained, admirable enthusiasm of volunteers, rushed forward in a frenzy. Only a picket was behind the sentry and it vanished. But the crest was not reached till dawn. When dawn came the party found that it was in the clouds. It could see nothing but the plateau — 400 yards across — on which it stood. Trenches were made, but it was difficult to determine the right place for them. The Boers were invisible; our own troops below were invisible; for three hours the party lived on a fog-bound island in the air. At last the mist lifted.

The curtain rose upon the performance of a tragedy. The Boers — need I say, upon another ridge of Spion Kop? — began to fire heavily, and our men seemed to have no sufficient protection in the trenches. The space was small; they were crowded together. I will describe the scene as I saw it from below. I shall always have it in my memory — that acre of massacre, that complete shambles, at the top of a rich green gulley, with cool granite walls (a way fit to lead to heaven), which reached up the western flank of the mountain. To me it seemed that our men were all in a small, square patch; there were brown men, and browner trenches, the whole like an over-ripe barley field. As I looked soon after the mist had risen (it was nine o'clock, I think) I saw three shells hit a certain trench within a minute; each struck it full in the face, and the brown dust rose and drifted

147

Sorting the living from the dead: dawn on Spion Kop, 23 January 1900, the aftermath of the battle depicted in The Illustrated London News *of 3 March 1900. The reality was far worse. Men were piled three deep in the shallow trench and most of them were in pieces. The Boers, among whom was the young Deneys Reitz, stood in tears after they had taken possession of the hill* (Africana Museum).

148

away with the white smoke. The trench was toothed against the sky like a saw — made, I supposed, of sharp rocks built into a rampart. Another shell struck it, and then — heavens! — the trench rose up and moved forward. The trench was men; the teeth against the sky were men. They ran forward bending their bodies into a curve, as men do when they run under a heavy fire; they looked like a cornfield with a heavy wind sweeping over it from behind. On the left front of the trenches they dropped into some grey rocks where they could fire. Spout after spout of dust bunched up from the brown patch. So it would go on for perhaps half an hour, when the whole patch itself bristled up from flatness; another lot of men was making for the rocks ahead. They flickered up, floated rapidly and silently across the sky, and flickered down into the rocks, without the appearance of a substantial beginning or end to the movement. The sight was as elusive as a shadow-show.

The Boers had three guns playing like hoses on our men. It was a triangular fire. Our men on Spion Kop had no guns. When on earth would the artillery come? Guns were the only thing that could make the hill either tenable or useful. When on earth would they come? No sign of them yet; not even a sign of a mountain battery; and we who watched wriggled in our anxiety. The question was whether enough men could live through the shelling till the guns came. Men must have felt that they had lived a long life under that fire by the end of the day, and still the guns had not come. From Three Tree Hill the gunners shelled the usual places, as well as the northern ranges of Spion Kop where the Boer riflemen were supposed to be. Where the Boer guns were we did not know. If only they had offered a fine mark, like our own guns, we should have smashed them in five minutes. The British gunner is proud of the perfect alignment and the regular intervals which his battery has observed under the heaviest fire; the Boer gunner would be sorry to observe any line or any interval. He will not have a gun in the open; he is not proud, but he is safe. You might say that in this war the object of the Boer gunners is to kill an enemy who cannot see them; that of the heroic British gunners is to be killed by an enemy whom they cannot see. The European notion of field guns is that they should be light enough to be moved about rapidly in battle and not hamper the speed of an army on the march. Now, does it not appear that the Boers will change all that for us? They have dragged heavy long-range guns about with them and put them on the top of steep hills, and we, of all people, know that they have not hampered the speed of their army. Some dunderhead, perhaps, proposed that such guns should be taken by the army into the field — some fellow who had never read a civilised book on gunnery. But how many fools in history have led the world? Let us make ourselves wise men by adding another to the list.

Reinforcements were ordered to Spion Kop. They were needed. The men on Spion Kop were crying out for them. I could see men running to and fro on the top, ever hunted to a fresh shelter. Some Boer riflemen crept forward, and for a few minutes fifty Boers and British heaved and swayed hand to hand. They drew apart. The shelling did not cease. The hollow rapping of the Maxim-Nordenfelts was a horrid sound; the little shells from them flapped and clacked along the ground in a long straight line like a string of geese. But the reinforcements were coming; already a thin line corkscrewed up the southern slope of Spion Kop. Their bayonets reflected the sun. Mules were in the column with ammunition, screwing themselves upwards, as lithe as monkeys. The Dorsets, Bethune's, the Middlesex, the Imperial Light Infantry — volunteers destined to receive a scalding baptism — were on the climb. From left to right of the field, too, from west to east, infantry moved. Hildyard's Brigade and the Somersets emerged from behind Three Tree Hill in open order, and moved towards the Boer line on the north and towards the west flank of Spion

Kop. The Boers sniped into them. A man was down — a shot rabbit in the grass with his legs moving. The infantry went a little way further east and north, halted and watched Spion Kop for the rest of the day. General Woodgate had been hit over the left eye about ten o'clock in the morning; the command came by a natural devolution to Col. Thorneycroft. And this big, powerful man, certainly the best mark on the hill, moved about fearlessly all day and was untouched. The reinforcements poured up the steep path which bent over suddenly on to the plateau at the top. It was ten steps from shelter to death. The Scottish Fusiliers came over the east side of the hill from Potgieter's. The men were packed on to the narrow table under the sky; some were heard to say that they would willingly go forward or go back, but they could not stay where they were. But no order was given to go forward. If there were few orders, it was because the officers had dwindled away. In the Lancashire Fusiliers only three officers were unwounded; in Thorneycroft's eleven were hit out of 18. Of Thorneycroft's men only about 60 came down unwounded out of 100. Late in the afternoon the 3rd battalion of the King's Royal Rifles advanced up the eastern slope of Spion Kop from Potgieter's and seized two precipitous humps. The left half battalion took the left hump; the right half the right hump. Never was anything more regular, and seldom more arduous. One hundred men were lost in the brief advance. I did not see it, and I am told I missed the most splendid thing that day. English people are fond of praising, with a paradoxical generosity, the deeds of Irish and Scottish regiments. Here is a case for praise, without affectation, of an English regiment.

Night fell, and still no guns. The shell fire continued and the sniping. The Boers still had the range. At eight o'clock Colonel Thorneycroft decided to retire. We were to give up the key to the position and the key to Ladysmith — and no one will ever be able to find anything but praise for what Colonel Thorneycroft did that day. He had been sitting on a target for thirteen hours, and now he was going. It was necessary. Some men had fought there for twenty-one hours without water. In England you have not the physical proof of what that means. The Mountain Battery was already up; two naval 12-pounders were half way up. But Thorneycroft was going; it was necessary. When dawn came the officer in command of the naval guns on Mount Alice looked through the long telescope. He looked long before he answered someone who asked how our men were on Spion Kop. "They are all Boers or Red Cross men there," he said. That was the first we who had slept at Potgieter's knew of the retirement; it was the first the Headquarters Staff knew of it. In a few hours Warren's force was coming back across the Tugela. 'The way round' had failed. No; let me say one of the ways round has failed; another must be found.

John Black Atkins reported the battle of Vaal Krantz and the relief of Ladysmith and returned to Britain one month after the relief of Mafeking. (His book, *The Relief of Ladysmith* was published while he was still in South Africa, less than two months after the event.) He was appointed London editor of the *Manchester Guardian,* served as assistant editor of *The Spectator* for 19 years and, from 1931 to 1936, edited the *Manchester Guardian.*

Among his many achievements, Atkins founded a movement called Poetry in Pubs (designed to provide high-class but not high-brow pub entertainment) and was a member of the Council for the Study of Inebriety. His friendship with Churchill intact, Atkins died on 16 March 1954.

'A despatch rider captured, natives turned adrift'

The siege of Kimberley, 14 October 1899 — 15 February 1900

The siege of Kimberley had been expected as early as September 1899. Apart from the civilian population, which numbered 20 000, including 10 000 Afrikaners, and the singularly baleful presence of Cecil John Rhodes himself, the garrison consisted of less than 5 000 men, the majority of whom were volunteers.

Kimberley was under the command of Lieutenant-Colonel Robert Kekewich, commanding officer of the 1st Loyal North Lancashire Regiment. His task was an arduous one: not only did he have to conduct the defence of the town, but he had to deal with Rhodes' bullying and machinations. Kekewich and his men had to defend a 13½ mile perimeter with no more than six old 2½ inch guns, no match for the Boers' Long Tom, which arrived shortly before the siege was lifted, or for their 9-pounders, which began firing on 9 November. The Boers, under the command of General Piet Cronje, engaged in no hostilities on Sundays.

The correspondents within Kimberley occupied their time by finding ways and means of getting their copy out, usually with the help of black runners. The Reuter special correspondent, in a waspish despatch he got out of town by rider at 14h40 on 6 November, noted that the place was not, as one hack had inferred, 'as safe as Piccadilly.' That statement, he concluded, 'is considered ridiculous.'

Difficulties the correspondents may have had, but they were as nothing compared to those experienced by the hapless George Green, editor of *The Diamond Fields Advertiser*, owned by Rhodes, who had conceived a violent and contemptuous hatred for Kekewich and his conduct of the defence. Green was bludgeoned into writing an inflammatory leader, in which he ranted at the inefficiencies of Kekewich and his men. Livid, Kekewich demanded to see him, only to discover that Green had been ignominiously but prudently hidden by Rhodes down a mine shaft, an unusual way of escaping the consequences of an editorial. Green survived that, and other indignities to become, in 1910, editor of *The Argus*.

The Boers, 5 000 strong, were well dug in beyond Kimberley's defences. They had an altogether different kind of siege, enlivened only by the clashes at Magersfontein and Modder River. In uncomfortable, temporary shelters and in relentless heat, they were unbearably bored.

De Volksstem's correspondent, writing from the Boer camp, was obviously hot, uncomfortable — and very homesick. His despatch, printed in English and Dutch-Afrikaans on 10 November 1899, refers obliquely to a situation all too familiar to most reporters: chronic boredom. His story was printed uncorrected, the English version running side by side with the Dutch-Afrikaans.

Cecil John Rhodes, immured within Kimberley, depicted by The Illustrated London News *of 21 March 1900. He stands, watching the effect of 'Long Cecil' on the enemy's trenches. The gun was made in three weeks at De Beers works — the tools used in its manufacture having to be made first. The shells were also made at De Beers' works to the design of a Frenchman, M. Labram, who was sadly killed by the last 100 lb shell to be fired into Kimberley by the Boers* (Africana Museum).

During the siege of Kimberley — the Rt. Hon. Cecil Rhodes and party at Fort Rhodes, Kenilworth (Africana Museum).

LEWE ONZE TELEGRAFIST.
EEN RAPPORTGANGER GEVAT.
EEN RAPPORT IN GEHEIM SCHRIFT
HET ZWART GOED
WEGGEZONDEN.
ZENDT ONS NIEWS.

(Spec) Hoofdlager Kimberley,

Woensdag

Dinsdag is het telegraafkantoor hier in ons lager geopend. Het is natuurlik een groot gerief voor allen. Onze telegrafist heeft het erg druk. Zijn kantoor bestaat uit een gewone tent en dat het daar des daags ondragelik warm kan worden, is goed verstaanbaar, als men een paar dagen hier in deze zandvlakten doorgebracht heeft.

Dinsdag werden

TWEE PERSONEN GEVANGEN

de een een rapportrijder en de andere een gewoon Engelsman zonder enige rang. De eerste is een Afrikaander en beweert onbewust te zijn dat hij rapporten bij zich had. Mijnheer de aanvoerder Kekewich had hem met paard, zadel en toom uitgerust en gezegd dat hij in de richting van Groot Rivier moest rijden, tot aan Klipsdam, alwaar hij iemand zou ontmoeten die ook te paard was; diens paard, zadel en toom moest hij nemen en dadelik naar maar hij werd door onze wachten gevangen, voordat hij weer in Kimberley was. n het lager gekomen werd hij onderzocht, maar men vond niets. Het omruilen van paard, zadel en toom scheen echter zeer suspicieus en de Generaal beval om zijn zadel te onderzoeken. Na lang zoeken vond men tussen het leder en de kussens van het zadel.

EEN GESCHRIJF

dat helaas onleesbaar was. Het was misschien ook weer het geheim schrift op die wijze der reformers van 1895 en 1896, dat ze tans weer in gebruik wilde brengen. Het geschrijf is opgezonden naar Pretoria en men

(Not corrected.)
TELEGRAPH OFFICE OPENED
A DESPATCH RIDER CAPTURED
NATIVES TURNED ADRIFT
SEND US NEWS

Kimberley, Wednesday

A telegraph office was opened in our lager on Tuesday. It is naturally a great convenience to everybody. Our telegraphist has plenty of work. His office consists of a tent, and you will readily understand that he finds this unbearably warm in the daytime, especially when it is remembered that we are in the middle of the sand flats.

On Saturday we captured two prisoners, one a despatch rider, and the other without any rank of any kind. The first named is an Africander, and professes not to have known that he was carrying despatches. Colonel Kekewich had supplied him with a horse, saddle, and bridle complete, and had told him to ride in the direction of Groot River, as far as Klip-dam, where he would meet another man also on horseback. He was to exchange saddles with this man, and then return to Kimberley. He had succeeded in doing this, but is now captured on his way back to Kimberley. When he was brought into the lager he was searched, but nothing was found on him. The exchange of his mount seemed a suspicious circumstance, and the General decided to examine his saddle. After a long search we found between the leather and the cushions of the saddle a letter, which was unfortunately unintelligible. It was probably written in cipher, as was so much of the correspondence at the time of the Jameson Raid in 1895 and 1896. The letter has been sent to Pretoria, and an attempt will there be made to decipher it. The man says that his name is Hamer, and there is no reason so far as I can see why we should not believe him. They are both here in safe custody. The enemy fired three shells on our guard at Kampersdam, but they all fell too short.

zal trachten het daar uit te werken en uit te vinden wat het bevat. De man zegt Haman te heten en waarom zal men heim niet geloven. Ze zijn beiden nog hier in het lager in bewaring.

De vijand schoot

DRIE BOMMEN
OP ONZE WACHTEN

te Kampersdam; maar allen tekort. Door onze veldtelegrafie werd heden Woensdag morgen bericht ontvangen van het Vrijstaatse lager, ten oosten van K. dat de vijand bewegingen scheen te maken om uit te komen. Dadelik werd opgezadeld en reden wij naar de zijde van de Vrijstaters. Weldra gewaarden we in de verte een grote zwarte massa. Nader gekomen bleek het een grote troep kaffers te zijn die uit Kimberley kwamen. Zij vertellen dat de Engelsen ze uitgezonden hadden, zeggende dat ze hier niets konden doen en alleenlik de kost hielpen opeten.

Verder vertellen ze dat voedsel in Kimberley schaars was. Ze kregen

NAUWELIKS GENOEG
OM TE LEVEN

Hun uiterlik bewijst ook dat ze het maar schraal hebben. Het feit zelf dat ze uitgezonden zijn kwam het vermoeden bij ons dat het niet te volop is in Kimberley nog helpen versterken. Volgens hun gezegde heeft de vijand op zeer vele plaatsen dinamiet, een andere afgod van de Engelsman, begraven en dienen we dus voorzichtig te zijn. De Hoog Ed Krijgsraad besloot om ze allen weder direkt naar Kimberley terug te zenden en dit werd dadelik gedaan. Zo zijn ze Kimberley weer in en hoe het nu verder binnen gaan zal, is wel moeilik te zeggen. Misschien doen de kaffers nog goed werk voor ons in de stad, in welk opzicht dan ook. Hun getal bedroeg ongeveer 600. Onze geachte Generaal en kommandant waren uit om de

A report was received this morning from our field telegraph that the Free Staters on the east side of Kimberley were expecting an attack from the enemy, as their movements were very suspicious. We at once rode in their direction, and in the distance we could see a dark mass of human beings moving towards us out of Kimberley. On a nearer approach it turned out to be a number of kaffirs who were sent out of the town by the British. They had been informed that they were of no use in the town, and that they only assisted to consume the food. They also informed us that food was very scarce in Kimberley, and that they scarcely had enough to live upon. Their appearance was quite in keeping with this statement. The fact that they had been sent out was sufficient proof that there is not much food in the town. They say that the English have laid dynamite trains in several places, and we are thus compelled to be careful.

The War Council decided to return them at once to Kimberley, and this was done. They are now there, and what the result will be is not easily seen. Perhaps they will be able to do something to help us. They numbered about 600.

Our General and Commandant have been on a visit to the Free State General, Mr Wessels, and did not return to the lager until late. Everything is well, with the exception of the sand, which is very undesirable. The heat is almost unbearable. We are greatly in need of rain. The burghers are very anxious for news here, but we require something more reliable than that. Please send us copies of the "Volksstem" even if they are old.

VRIJSTAATSE GENERAAL WESSELS

te ontmoeten en keerden eerst laat terug. In het lager gaat het verder goed, alleenlik het zware zand hier kan iemand mismoedig maken en de hitte is onuithoudbaar. Alles verlangd naar regen. De burgers verlangen erg naar niews en vragen aan de "Volksstem" om toch meer koeranten te zenden. Het publiek hier in Grikwaland West woonachtig is overstopt met Engelse koerante, die natuurlik vol valse berichten zijn en verlangen naar juiste tijdingen, al zijn het exemplaren van vroegere datum, ze zullen zullen welkom zijn.

The 'dark mass' to which the despatch refers were the 10 000 black mine workers made temporarily redundant by the siege, whom Rhodes wanted out of town. Without referring to Kekewich, he simply turned 3 000 Basotho into the veld. They met the Boers, who promptly sent them back again.

'Vat jou goed en trek, Ferreira'

Rudyard Kipling's war

When the Boer War broke out and Kipling determined to visit South Africa to do his bit for the war, he was no stranger to the country.

On his first visit to Cape Town, in 1891, Kipling was befriended by Cecil John Rhodes and by Olive Schreiner. Rhodes built Kipling a house on his Cape Town estate and Kipling stayed there each year, between November and April, until 1908.

Besides being no stranger to the country, Kipling was no stranger to journalism. His literary career had begun in Lahore, India, in 1882, when he became a reporter on the *Civil and Military Gazette.* Kipling deserted journalism in 1889 when he returned to England from India and, rich with the experience of the Indian subcontinent, wrote *Barrack-room Ballads,* which was published in 1892 and gained him instant celebrity. His reputation as a literary giant, as the embodiment of the Empire and all it stood for, went before him.

Kipling was well versed in the ways of South Africa — from the Englishman's point of view. Before President Kruger's 11 October 1899 ultimatum expired, Kipling sent an open telegram to the Colonial Secretary, Joseph Chamberlain. It nicely illustrated his attitude to the forthcoming war. He declared that Britain had an overwhelming case for intervention in South Africa because 'thousands of British subjects were kept permanently in the position of helots' by the Boers. (In spirited return, Kipling and Rhodes were contemptuously described by F.W. Reitz, President of the Orange Free State from 1889-1895 as 'Gods of the Jingo'.)

Kipling arrived to winter in Cape Town in 1899 to some considerable fanfare, not the least of which was an embarrassingly laudatory poem of welcome, written by Edgar Wallace, then working as a medical orderly in an army hospital, and printed in the *Cape Times.* Kipling flung himself into the war effort with gusto, visiting the troops at the Modder River railhead in February 1900 and travelling back in the ambulance train with the wounded. He wrote a letter home for a man whose arm had been amputated: the letter was published, much to Kipling's fury.

Field Marshal Lord Roberts and his army entered the small, undefended town of Bloemfontein on 13 March 1900. The press corps came too, including such luminaries as Prevost Battersby of the *Morning Post,* H.A. Gwynne of Reuters in South Africa, Percival Landon of *The Times,* 'Banjo' Paterson of the Australian contingent, representing *The Sydney Morning Herald* and Julian Ralph of the *Daily Mail.* (Arriving in the Orange River battle zone, Ralph had driven into the veld in a hired buggy only to find the British camp deserted; driving through it, he encountered the casualties resulting from the ambush of a reconnaissance patrol. He went on to cover the battles of Modder River and Magersfontein).

Rudyard Kipling (Africana Museum).

On 15 March, Lord Roberts closed down the pro-Boer newspaper *Express* and, using that paper's presses, started *The Friend*, using the correspondents as part-time contributors. Kipling arrived in Bloemfontein in March and served as associate editor of *The Friend* from 21 March to 1 April 1900. The content of the paper was unquestionably jingoistic and contained war news, 'home' news, poetry (by Kipling) and stories rich with the scent of South Africa.

Long Tom, which began firing at 11h00 on 7 February, fired its last shot at lunchtime on 15 February. With Lieutenant-General John French and the army sweeping towards Kimberley and its relief after a 124-day siege, Cronje and his men withdrew. Now there was just Mafeking to deal with.

The Way That He Took

The guns of the field-battery were hidden behind white-thorned mimosas, scarcely taller than their wheels, that marked the line of a dry nullah; and the camp pretended to find shade under a clump of gums planted as an experiment by some Minister of Agriculture. One small hut, reddish stone with a tin roof, stood where the single track of the railway split into a siding. A rolling plain of red earth, speckled with loose stones and sugarbush, ran northwards to the scarps and spurs of a range of little hills — all barren and exaggerated in the heat-haze. Southward, the level lost itself in a tangle of scrub-furred hillocks, upheaved without purpose or order, seared and blackened by the strokes of the careless lightning, seamed down their sides with spent watercourses, and peppered from base to summit with stones — riven, piled, scattered stones. Far away, to the eastward, a line of blue-grey mountains, peaked and horned, lifted itself over the huddle of the tortured earth. It was the only thing that held steady through the liquid mirage. The nearer hills detached themselves from the plain, and swam forward like islands in a milky ocean. While the major stared through puckered eyelids, Leviathan himself waded through the far shallows of it — a black and formless beast.

"That," said the major, "must be the guns coming back." He had sent out two guns, nominally for exercise — actually to show that there was artillery near the railway if any patriot thought fit to tamper with it. Chocolate smears, looking as though they had been swept with a besom through the raffle of stones, wandered across the earth — unbridged, ungraded, unmetalled. They were the roads to the brown mud huts, one in each valley, that were officially styled farm-houses. At very long intervals a dusty Cape-cart or a tilted wagon would move along them, and men would come to sell fruit or scraggy sheep. At night the farm-houses were lighted up in a style out of all keeping with Dutch economy; the scrub would light itself on some far headland, and the house-lights twinkled in reply. Three or four days later the major would read bad news in the Cape Town papers thrown to him from the passing troop trains.

The guns and their escort changed from Leviathan to the likeness of wrecked boats, their crews struggling beside them. Presently they took on their true shape, and lurched into camp amid clouds of dust.

The mounted infantry escort set about its evening meal; the hot air filled with the scent of burning wood; sweating men rough-dried sweating horses with wisps of precious forage; the sun dipped behind the hills, and they heard the whistle of a train from the south.

"What's that?" said the major, slipping into his coat. The decencies had not yet left him.

"Ambulance train," said the captain of Mounted Infantry, raising his glasses. "I'd like to talk to a woman again, but it won't stop here. . . . It *is* stopping, though, and making a beastly noise. Let's look."

The engine had sprung a leaky tube, and ran lamely into the siding. It would be two or three hours at least before she could be patched up.

Two doctors and a couple of nursing sisters stood on the rear platform of a carriage. The major explained the situation, and invited them to tea.

"We were just going to ask *you*," said the medical major of the ambulance train.

"No, come to our camp. Let the men see a woman again!" he pleaded.

Sister Dorothy, old in the needs of war, for all her twenty-four years, gathered up a tin of biscuits and some bread and butter new cut by the orderlies. Sister Margaret picked up the teapot, the spirit-lamp, and a waterbottle.

"Cape Town water," she said with a nod. "Filtered too. I *know* Karoo water." She jumped down lightly on to the ballast.

"What do you know about the Karoo, Sister?" said the captain of Mounted Infantry, indulgently as a veteran of a month's standing.

She laughed. "This is my home. I was born out there — just behind that big range of hills — out Oudtshoorn way. It's only sixty miles from here. Oh how good it is!"

She slipped the nurse's cap from her head, tossed it through the one car-window, and drew a breath of deep content. With the sinking of the sun the dry hills had taken life and glowed against the green of the horizon. They rose up like jewels in the utterly clear air, while the valleys between flooded with purple shadow. A mile away, stark-clear, withered rocks showed as though one could touch them with the hand, and the voice of a herdboy in charge of a flock of sheep came in clear and sharp over twice that distance. Sister Margaret devoured the huge spaces with eyes unused to shorter ranges, snuffed again the air that has no equal under God's skies, and, turning to her companion, said: "What do *you* think of it?"

"I am afraid I'm rather singular," he replied. "Most of us hate the Karoo. I used to, but it grows on one somehow. I suppose it's the lack of fences and roads that's so fascinating. And when one gets back from the railway. . . ."

"You're quite right," she said, with an emphatic stamp of her foot. "People come to Matjesfontein — ugh! — with their lungs, and they live opposite the railway station and that new hotel, and they think *that's* the Karoo. They say there isn't anything in it. It's *full* of life when you really get into it. You see that? I'm *so* glad. D'you know, you're the first English officer I've heard who has spoken a good word for my country?"

"I'm glad I pleased you," said the captain, looking into Sister Margaret's black-lashed grey eyes under the heavy brown hair shot with grey where it rolled back from the tanned forehead. This kind of nurse was new in his experience. The average sister did not lightly stride over rolling stones, and — was it possible that her easy pace up-hill was beginning to pump him? As she walked, she hummed joyously to herself, a queer catchy tune of one line several times repeated:

Vat jou goed en trek, Ferreira,
Vat jou goed en trek.

It ran off with a little trill that sounded like:

Swaar dra, al aan die een kant;
Jannie met die hoepel been!

"Listen!" she said, suddenly. "What was that?"

"It must be a wagon on the road. I heard the whip, I think."

"Yes, but you didn't hear the wheels, did you? It's a little bird that makes just that noise, 'Whe-ew'! she duplicated it perfectly. "We call it" — she gave the Afrikaans name, which did not, of course, abide with the captain. "We must have given him a scare! You hear him in the early mornings when you are sleeping in the wagons. It's just like the noise of a whiplash, isn't it?"

They entered the major's tent a little behind the others, who were discussing the scanty news of the campaign.

"Oh, no," said Sister Margaret coolly, bending over the spirit-lamp, "the Transvalers will stay round Kimberley and try to put Rhodes in a cage. But, of course, if a commando gets through to De Aar they will all rise — "

"You think so, Sister?" said the medical major, deferentially.

"I know so. They will rise anywhere in the Colony if a commando comes actually to them. Presently they will rise in Prieska — if it is only to steal the forage at Van Wyk's Vlei. Why not?"

"We get most of our opinions of the war from Sister Margaret," said the civilian doctor of the train. "It's all new to me, but, so far, all her prophecies have come true."

A few months ago that doctor had retired from practice to a country-house in rainy England, his fortune made and, as he tried to believe, his life-work done. Then the bugles blew, and, rejoicing at the change, he found himself, his experience, and his fine bedside manner, buttoned up in a black-tabbed khaki coat, on a hospital train that covered eleven hundred miles a week, carried a hundred wounded each trip and dealt him more experience in a month than he had ever gained in a year of home practice.

Sister Margaret and the captain of Mounted Infantry took their cups outside the tent. The captain wished to know something more about her. Till that day he had believed South Africa to be populated by sullen men and slack-waisted women; and in some clumsy fashion betrayed the belief.

"Of course, you don't see any others where you are," said Sister Margaret, leniently, from her camp-chair. "They are all at the war. I have two brothers and a nephew, my sister's son, and — oh, I can't count my cousins." She flung her hands outward with a curiously un-English gesture. "And then, too, you have never been off the railway. You have only seen Cape Town? All the *skel* — all the useless people are there. You should see *our* country beyond the ranges — out Oudtshoorn way. We grow fruit and vines. It is much prettier, *I* think, than Paarl."

"I'd like to very much. I may be stationed in Africa after the war is over. What a night it is, Sister!" He'd dwelt lovingly on the last word, as men did in South Africa.

The soft darkness had shut upon them unawares and the world had vanished. There was not so much breeze as a slow motion of the whole dry air under the vault of the immeasurably deep heavens. "Look up," said the captain; "doesn't it make you feel as if we were tumbling down into the stars — all upside down?"

"Yes," said Sister Margaret, tilting her head back. "It is always like that. I know. And those are *our* stars."

They burned with a great glory, large as the eyes of cattle by lamp-light; planet after planet of the mild southern sky. As the captain said, one seemed to be falling from out the hidden earth sheer through space, between them.

"Now, when I was little," Sister Margaret began very softly, "there was one day in the week at home that was all our own. We could get up as soon as we liked after midnight, and there was the basket in the kitchen — our food. We used to go out at three o'clock sometimes, my two brothers, my sisters, and the two little ones — out into the Karoo for all the day. All-the-long-day. First we built a fire, and then we made a kraal for the two little ones — a kraal of thorn-bushes, so that they should not be bitten by anything. You see? Often we made the kraal before morning — when those" — she jerked her firm chin at the stars — "were just going out. Then we old ones went hunting lizards — and snakes and birds and centipedes, and all that sort of nice thing. Our father collected them. He gave us half-a-crown for a *spoegslang* — a kind of snake. You see?"

"How old were you?" Snake-hunting did not strike the captain as a safe amusement for the young.

"I was eleven then — or ten, perhaps, and the little ones were two and three. Why? Then we came back to eat, and we sat under a rock all afternoon. It was hot, you see, and we played — we played with the stones and the flowers. You should see our Karoo in spring! All flowers! All our flowers! Then we came home, carrying the little ones on our backs asleep — came home through the dark — just like this night. That was our own day! Oh, the good days! We used to watch the meerkats playing, too, and the little buck. When I was at Guy's, learning to nurse, how home-sick that made me!"

"But what a splendid open-air life!" said the captain.

"Where else *is* there to live except the open air?" said Sister Margaret, looking off into twenty-thousand square miles of it with eyes that burned.

"You're quite right."

"I'm sorry to interrupt you two," said Sister Dorothy, who had been talking to the gunner major; "but the guard says we shall be ready to go in a few minutes. Major Devine and Dr Johnson have gone down already."

"Very good, Sister. We'll follow." The captain rose unwillingly and made for the worn path from the camp to the rail.

"Isn't there another way?" said Sister Margaret. Her grey nursing gown glimmered like some big moth's wing.

"No. I'll bring a lantern. It's quite safe."

"I did not think of *that*," she said with a laugh; "only *we* never come home by the way we left it when we live in the Karoo. If any one — suppose you had dismissed a servant, or got him sjamboked, and he saw you go out? He would wait for you to come back on a tired horse, and then . . . You see? But, of course, in England where the road is all walled, it is different. How funny! Even when we were little we learned never to come home by the way we went out."

"Very good," said the captain obediently. It made the walk longer, and he approved of that.

"That's a curious sort of woman," said the captain to the major, as they smoked a lonely pipe together when the train had gone.

"*You* seemed to think so."

"Well — I couldn't monopolize Sister Dorothy in the presence of my senior officer. What was she like?"

"Oh, it came out that she knew a lot of my people in London. She's the daughter of a chap in the next county to us, too."

The general's flag still flew before his unstruck tent to amuse Boer binoculars. But the general himself had gone to join an army a hundred miles away; drawing off, from time to time, every squadron, gun and company that he dared. His last words to the few troops he left behind covered the entire situation.

"If you can bluff 'em till we get round 'em up north to tread on their tails, it's all right. If you can't they'll probably eat you up. Hold 'em as long as you can."

So the skeleton remnant of the brigade lay close among the koppies till the Boers, not seeing them in force on the sky-line, feared that they might have learned the rudiments of war. They rarely disclosed a gun, for the reason that they had so few; they scouted by fours and fives instead of clattering troops and chattering companies, and, where they saw a too obvious way opened to attack they, lacking force to drive it home, looked elsewhere. Great was the anger in the Boer commando across the river — the anger and unease.

"The reason is they have so few men," the farmers reported, all fresh from selling melons to the camp, and drinking Queen Victoria's health in good whisky. "They have no horses — only what they call Mounted Infantry. They are afraid of us. They try to make us friends by giving us brandy. Come on and shoot them. Then you will see us rise and cut the line."

"Yes, we know how you rise, you Colonials," said the Boer commandant above his pipe. "We know what has come to all your promises from Beaufort West, and even from De Aar. *We* do the work — all the work — and you kneel down with your parsons and pray for our success. What good is that? The president has told you a hundred times God is on our side. Why do you worry Him? We did not send you Mausers and ammunition for *that*."

"We kept our commando horses ready for six months — and forage is very dear. We sent all our young men," said an honoured member of local society.

"A few here and a few servants there. What is that? You should have risen down to the sea all together."

"But you were so quick. Why did not you wait the year? We were not ready, Jan."

"That is a lie. You want to save your cattle and your farms. Wait till *our* flag flies from here to Port Elizabeth and you shall see what you will save when the president learns how you have risen."

The saddle-coloured sons of the soil looked down their noses. "Yes — it is true. Some of our farms are close to the line. They say at Worcester and in the Paarl that many soldiers are always coming in from the sea. One must think of that — at least till they are shot. But we know there are very few in front of you here. Give them what you gave the fools at Stormberg, and you will see how we can shoot rooineks."

"Yes. I know that cow. She is always going to calve. Get away. I am answerable to the president — not to the Cape."

But the information stayed in his mind, and, not being a student of military works, he made a plan to suit. The tall koppie on which the English had planted their heliostation commanded the more or less open plain to the northward, but did not command the five-mile belt of broken country between that and the outmost English pickets, some three miles from camp. The Boers had established themselves very comfortably among these rock-ridges and scrub-patches, and the 'great war' drizzled down to long shots and longer stalking. The young bloods wanted rooineks to shoot, and said so.

"See here," quoth the experienced Jan van Staden that evening to as many of his commando as cared to listen. "You youngsters from the Colony talk a lot. Go and turn the rooineks out of their koppies to-night. Eh? Go and take their bayonets from them and stick them into them. Eh? You don't go!"

"Jan — Jan," said one young man appeallingly, "don't make mock of us."

"I thought that was what you wanted to badly. No? Then listen to me. Behind us the grazing is bad. We have too many cattle here. To-morrow, by the sky's look, it will blow a good wind. So, to-morrow early I shall send all our cattle north to the new grazing. That will make a great dust for the English to see from their helio yonder." He pointed to a winking night-lamp stabbing the darkness with orders to any outlying picket. "With the cattle we will send all our women. Yes, all the women and the wagons we can spare, and the lame ponies and the broken carts we took from Andersen's farm. That will make a big dust — the dust of our retreat. Do you see?"

They saw and approved, and said so.

"Good. There are many men here who want to go home to their wives. I shall let thirty of them away for a week. Men who wish to do this will speak to me to-night. These men will look after the cattle and see that they make a great dust for a long way. They will run about behind the cattle showing their guns, too. So *that,* if the wind blows well, will be our retreat. The cattle will feed beyond Koopman's Kop."

"No good water there," growled a farmer who knew that section. "Better to go on to Zwartpan. It is always sweet at Zwartpan."

The commando discussed the point for twenty minutes. It was much more serious than shooting rooineks. Then Jan went on:

"When the rooineks see our retreat they may all come into our koppies together. If so, good. But it is tempting God to expect such a favour. *I* think they will first send some men to scout." He grinned broadly, twisting the English word. "Almighty! To scout! They have none of that sort of rooinek that they used at Sunnyside." (Jan meant incomprehensible men from a place called Australia across the southern seas who played what they knew of the war game to kill.) "They have only some mounted infantry," — again he used the English words. "They were once a red-jacket regiment, so their scouts will stand up bravely to be shot at."

"Good — good, we will shoot them," said a youngster from Stellenbosch, who had come up on a free pass as a Capetown excursionist just before the war to a farm on the border, where his aunt was taking care of his horse and rifle.

"But if you shoot their scouts I will sjambok you myself," said Jan, amid roars of laughter. "We must let them *all* come into the koppies to look for us; and I pray God will not allow any of us to be tempted to shoot them. They will cross the ford in front of their camp. They will come along the road — so!" He imitated with ponderous arms the army style of riding. "They will trot up the road this way and that way" — here he snaked his hard finger in the dust — "between koppies, till they come here, where they can see the plain and all our cattle going away. Then they will *all* come in close together. Perhaps they will even fix their bayonets. *We* shall be up here behind the rock — there and there." He pointed to two flat-topped koppies, one on either side of the road, some eight hundred yards away. "That is our place. We will go there before sunrise. Remember we must be careful to let the very last of the rooineks pass before we begin shooting. They will come along a little careful at first. But we do not shoot. Then they will see our fires and the fresh horse-dung, so they will know we have gone on. They will run together and talk and point and shout in this nice open place. Then we begin shooting them from above."

"Yes, uncle, but if the scouts see nothing and there are no shots and we let them go back quite quiet, they will think it was a trick. Perhaps the main body may never come here at all. Even rooineks learn in time — and so we may lose even the scouts."

"I have thought of that too," said Jan, with slow contempt, as the Stellenbosch boy delivered his shot. "If you had been *my* son I should have sjamboked you more when you were a youngster. I shall put *you* and four or five more on the nek (the pass), where the road comes from their camp into these koppies. You go there before it is light. Let the scouts pass in or I will sjambok you myself. When the scouts come back after seeing nothing here, then you may shoot them, but not till they have passed the nek and are on the straight road back to their camp again. Do you understand? Repeat what I have said, so that I shall know."

The youth obediently repeated his orders.

"Kill their officers if you can. If not, no great matter, because the scouts will run to camp with the news that our koppies are empty. Their helio-station will see your party trying to hold the nek so hard — and all that time they will see our dust out yonder, and they will think you are the rear-guard, and they will think *we* are escaping. They will be angry."

"Yes — yes, uncle, we see," from a dozen elderly voices.

"But this calf does not. Be silent! They will shoot at you, Nicholaas, on the nek, because they will think you are to cover our getting away. They will shell the nek. They will miss. You will then ride away. All the rooineks will come after you, hot and in a hurry — perhaps, even, with their cannon. They will pass our fires and our fresh horse-dung. They will come here as their scouts came. They will see the plain so full of our dust. They will say, "The scouts spoke truth. It is a full retreat." *Then* we up there on the rocks will shoot, and it will be like the fight at Stormberg in daytime. Do you understand *now?*"

Those of the commando directly interested lit new pipes and discussed the matter in detail till midnight.

Next morning the operations began with, if one may borrow the language of some official despatches — 'the precision of well-oiled machinery'.

The helio-station reported the dust of the waggons and the movements of armed men in full flight across the plain beyond the koppies. A colonel, newly appointed from England, by reason of his seniority, sent forth a dozen mounted infantry under command of a captain. Till a month ago they had been drilled by a cavalry instructor, who taught them 'shock' tactics to the music of trumpets. They knew how to advance in echelon of squadrons, by cat's cradle of troops, in quarter column of stable-litter, how to trot, to gallop, and, above all, to charge. They knew how to sit their horses unremittingly, so that at the day's end they might boast how many hours they had been in the saddle without relief, and they learned to rejoice in the clatter and stamp of a troop audible five miles away.

163

They trotted out two and two along the farm road, that trailed lazily through the wind-driven dust; across the half-dried ford to a nek between low stony hills leading into the debatable land. (Vrooman, of Emmaus, from his neatly bushed hole noted that one man carried a sporting Lee-Enfield rifle with a short fore-end. Vrooman, of Emmaus, argued that the owner of it was the officer to be killed on his return, and went to sleep.) They saw nothing except a small flock of sheep and a herdsman who spoke broken English with curious fluency. He had heard that the Boers had decided to retreat on account of sick and wounded. The captain in charge of the detachment turned to look at the helio-station four miles away. "Hurry up," said the dazzling flash. "Retreat apparently continues, but suggest you make sure. Quick!"

"Ye-es," said the captain, a shade bitterly, as he wiped the sweat from a sun-skinned nose. "You want me to come back and report all clear. If anything happens it will be my fault. If they get away, it will be my fault for disregarding the signal. I love officers who suggest and advise, and want to make their reputations in twenty minutes." '

"Don't see much 'ere, sir," said the sergeant, scanning the bare cup of the hollow where a dust-devil danced alone.

"No? We'll go on."

"If we get among these steep 'ills we lose touch of the 'elio."

"Very likely. Trot."

The rounded mounds grew to spiked koppies, heartbreaking to climb under a hot sun at four thousand feet above sea level. This is where the scouts found their spurs peculiarly useful.

Jan van Staden had thoughtfully allowed the invading force a front of two rifle-shots or four thousand yards, and they kept a thousand yards within his estimate. Ten men strung over two miles feel that they have explored all the round earth.

They saw stony slopes combing over in scrub, narrow valleys clothed with stone, low ridges of splintered stone, and tufts of brittle-stemmed bush. An irritating wind, split up by many rocky barriers, cuffed them over the ears and slapped them in the face at every turn. They came upon an abandoned camp fire, a little fresh horse-dung, and an empty ammunition-box splintered up for the firewood, an old boot, and a stale bandage.

A few hundred yards farther along the road a battered Mauser had been thrown into a bush. The glimmer of its barrel drew the scouts from the hillside, and here the road, after passing between two flat-topped koppies, entered a valley nearly half a mile wide, rose slightly, and over the nek of a ridge gave clear view across the windy plain north-ward.

"They're on the dead run, for sure," said a trooper. "Here's their fires and their litter and their guns, and that's where they're bolting to." He pointed over the ridge to the bellying dust cloud a mile long. A vulture high overhead flickered down, steadied herself, and hung motionless.

"See," said Jan van Staden from the rocks above the road, to his waiting commando. "It turns like a well-oiled wheel. They look where they need not look, but *here,* where they should look on both sides, they look at our retreat — straight before them. It is tempting our people too much. I pray God no one will shoot them."

"That's about the size of it," said the captain, rubbing the dust from his binoculars. "Boers on the run. I expect they find their main line of retreat to the north is threatened. We'll get back and tell the camp." He wheeled his pony and his eye traversed the flat-

164

topped koppie commanding the road. The stones at its edge seemed to be piled with less than Nature's carelessness.

"That 'ud be a dashed ugly place if it were occupied — and that other one; too. Those rocks aren't five hundreds yards from the road, either of 'em. Hold on, sergeant, I'll light a pipe." He bent over the bowl, and above his lighted match squinted at the koppie. A stone, a small roundish brown boulder on the lip of another one, seemed to move very slightly. The short hairs of his neck grated his collar. "I'll have another squint at their retreat," he cried to the sergeant, astonished at the steadiness of his own voice. He swept the plain, and, wheeling, let the glass rest for a moment on the koppie's top. One cranny between the rocks was pinkish, where blue sky should have shown. His men, dotted down the valley, sat heavily on their horses — It never occurred to them to dismount. He could hear the squeak of the leathers as a man shifted. An impatient gust blew through the valley and rattled the bushes. On all sides the expectant hills stood still under the pale blue.

"And we passed within a quarter of a mile of 'em! We're done!" The thumping heart slowed down, and the captain began to think clearly — so clearly that the thoughts seemed solid things. "It's Pretoria gaol for us all. Perhaps that man's only a look-out, though. We'll have to bolt! And I led 'em into it! . . . You fool," said his other self, above the beat of the blood in his eardrums. "If they could snipe you all from up there, why haven't they begun already? Because you're the bait for the rest of the attack. They don't want you *now*. You're to go back and bring up the others to be killed. Go back! Don't detach a man or they'll suspect. Go back all together. Tell the sergeant you're going. Some of them up there will understand English. Tell it aloud! Then back you go with the

Rudyard Kipling's father was an artist, whose son inherited some of his talents. This was the novelist's allegorical view of the chase of De Wet, which occupied the British forces for some considerable time. The gentleman in question can be seen, out of reach, galloping away on horseback (Africana Museum).

news — the real news."

"The country's all clear, sergeant," he shouted. "We'll go back and tell the colonel."
With an idiotic giggle he added, "It's a good road for guns, don't you think?"

"Hear you that?" said Jan van Staden, gripping a burgher's arm. "God is on our side
to-day. They *will* bring their little cannons after all!"

"Go easy. No good bucketing the horses to pieces. We'll need 'em for the pursuit
later," said the captain. "Hullo, there's a vulture! How far would you make him?"

"Can't tell, sir, in this dry air."

The bird swooped towards the second flat-topped koppie, but suddenly shivered side-
ways, and wheeled off again, followed intently by the captain's glance.

"And that koppie's simply full of 'em, too," he said, flushing. "Perfectly confident they
are, that we'd take this road — and then they'll scupper the whole boiling of us! They'll
let us through to fetch up the others. But I mustn't let 'em know we know. By Jove, they
do *not* think much of us! Don't blame 'em." The cunning of the trap did not impress him
until later.

Down the track jolted a dozen well-equipped men, laughing and talking — a mark to
make a pious burgher's mouth water. Thrice had their captain explicitly said that they
were to march easy, so a trooper began to hum a tune that he had picked up in Cape
Town streets:

> *Vat jou goed en trek, Ferreira,*
> *Vat jou goed en trek;*
> *Jannie met die hoepel been, Ferreira,*
> *Jannie met die hoepel been!*

Then with a whistle:

> *Swaar dra — al aan die een kant —*

The captain thinking furiously, found his mind turn to a camp in the Karoo, months
before; an engine that had halted in that waste, and a woman with brown hair, early
grizzled — an extraordinary woman . . . Yes, but as soon as they had dropped the flat-
topped koppie behind its neighbours he must hurry back and report: . . . A woman with
grey eyes and black eyelashes . . . The Boers would probably be massed on those two
koppies. How soon dare he break into a canter? . . . A woman with a queer cadence in her
speech . . . It was not more than five miles home by the straight road —

"Even when we were children we learned not to go back by the way we had come."

The sentence came back to him, self-shouted, so clearly that he almost turned to see if
the scouts had heard. The two flat-topped koppies behind him were covered by a long
ridge. The camp lay due south. He had only to follow the road to the nek — a notch,
unscouted as he recalled now, between two hills.

He wheeled his men up a long valley.

"Excuse me, sir, that ain't our road!" said the sergeant. "Once we get over this rise,
straight on, we come into direct touch with the 'elio, on that flat bit o' road there they
'elioed us goin' out."

"But we aren't going to get in touch with them just now. Come along, and come
quick."

"What's the meaning of this?" said a private in the rear. "What's 'e doin' this detour
for? We sha'n't get in for hours an' hours."

"Come on, men. Flog a canter out of your brutes, somehow," the captain called back.

For two throat-parched hours he held west by south, away from the nek, puzzling over a compass already demented by the ironstone in the hills, and then turned south-east through an eruption of low hills that ran far into the re-entering bend of the river that circled the left bank of the camp.

Eight miles to eastward that student from Stellenbosch had wriggled out of the rocks above the nek to have a word with Vrooman of Emmaus. The bottom seemed to have dropped out of at least one portion of their programme; for the scouting party were not to be seen.

"Jan is a clever man," he said to his companion, "but he does not think that even rooineks may learn. Perhaps those scouts will have seen Jan's commando, and perhaps they will come back to warn the rooineks. That is why I think he should have shot them *before* they came to the nek, and made quite sure that only one or two got away. It would have made the English angry, and they would have come out across the open in hundreds to be shot. Then when we ran away they would have come after us without thinking. If you can make the English hurry, they never think. Jan is wrong this time."

"Lie down, and pray you have not shown yourself to their helio-station," growled Vrooman, of Emmaus. "You throw with your arms and kick with your legs like a rooi-nek. When we get back I will tell Jan and he will sjambok you. All will yet come right. They will go and warn the rest, and the rest will hurry out by this very nek. Then we can shoot. Now you lie still and wait."

"Ere's a rummy picnic. We left camp, as it were, by the front door. 'E 'as given us a giddy-go-round, an' no mistake," said a dripping private as he dismounted behind the infantry lines.

"Did you see our helio?" This was the colonel, hot from racing down from the helio-station. "There were a lot of Boers waiting for you on the nek. We saw 'em. We tried to get at you with the helio, and tell you we were coming out to help you. Then we saw you didn't come over that flat bit of road where we had signalled you going out, and we wondered why. We didn't hear any shots."

"I turned off, sir, and came in by another road," said the captain.

"By another road!" The colonel lifted his eyebrows. "Perhaps you're not aware, sir, that the Boers have been in full retreat for the last three hours, and that those men in the nek were simply a rear-guard put out to delay us for a little. We could see that much from here. Your duty, sir, was to have taken them in the rear, and then we could have brushed them aside. The Boer retreat has been going on all morning sir — all morning. You were despatched to see the front clear and to return at once. The whole camp has been under arms for three hours; and instead of doing your work you wander all about Africa with your scouts to avoid a handful of skulking Boers! You should have sent a man back at once — you should have —"

The captain got off his horse stiffly.

"As a matter of fact," said he, "I didn't know for sure that there were any Boers on the nek, but I went round it in case it was so. But I *do* know that the koppies beyond the nek are simply crawling with Boers."

"Nonsense. We can see the whole lot of 'em retreating out yonder."

"Of course you can. That's part of their game, sir. I saw 'em lying on the top of a couple of koppies commanding the road, where it goes into the plain on the far side. They let us come in to see, and they let us go out to report the country clear and bring you up. Now they are waiting for *you*. The whole thing is a trap."

"D'you expect any officer of my experience to believe that?"

"As you please, sir," said the captain hopelessly. "My responsibility ends with my report."

'Great as our readers know him in literature, we know him to be even greater as a man,' eulogised the new editor when Kipling took his leave of *The Friend*.

His Boer war stories and journalism were rich with imperial sentiment and irony, redolent with the smell of Africa at that time. If they never reached the heights of his India-inspired work, it is probably because, after Kipling's initial trip up-country to the battle zone, he was never able again to stomach the business of war, and his grudging respect for the Afrikaner and his plight gradually tempered his more jingoistic prose.

After the war, Kipling's affection for South Africa became more apparent. He advised the English in South Africa to 'be quiet, stop prating about that loaded rifle and work.' He wrote Rhodes' obituary poem in 1902, declined the Order of Merit three times and a knighthood once, won the Nobel Prize for Literature in 1907 and died in London on 18 January 1936.

'Sixty-three shells fired and only one dog hit'

The siege of Mafeking, 14 October 1899 — 15 May 1900

There were five members of the international press corps in Mafeking when the telegraph lines with the outside world were cut on 14 October 1899 and the siege of Mafeking began. They were Vere Stent of Reuters, Angus Hamilton of *The Times*, E.G. Parslow of the *Daily Chronicle*, Emerson Neilly of the *Pall Mall Gazette*, and F.D. Baillie of the *Morning Post*. They were later joined by Lady Sarah Wilson who was correspondent for the *Daily Mail* during the siege of Mafeking, although she was not a professional journalist.

After approximately 30 days of the siege (it was to last 217), feeling that their services could be better employed elsewhere, several of them approached Colonel Baden-Powell and asked for his permission to escape through the Boer lines. Baden-Powell, who had no great admiration for the Fourth Estate, refused immediately: 'I consider it best they should not thus evade Censorship by a staff officer, and spread all the gossip of the place in "interviews" on reaching Cape Town.' After that, they resigned themselves to the siege and, like every other able-bodied man in the dusty little town, carried arms which they would use only in defence of their lives and Mafeking itself.

Like everyone else, the correspondents knew that the odds were against them. To the Boers' 6 000 men, nine field guns and a 94-pounder Long Tom, Mafeking could produce but 300 white men, 20 imperial officers, less than 700 men of the Protectorate Regiment, 300 members of the 'Black Watch' (armed Baralongs from the 'native stadt') and an extremely limited collection of field guns. But apart from an incident at the very end of the siege, the work of the correspondents was limited to writing and keeping themselves from the acute boredom with which everyone in Mafeking was at one time or another afflicted.

For one month after the siege began, no news came out of Mafeking. Vere Stent of Reuters indulged in the luxury of keeping a daily diary, not with much hope of having it published. However, with the enterprise for which that news agency is rightly famous, Reuters leaped the correspondence gap.

Henry Collins, head of Reuters' Cape Town bureau, engaged the services of a 'bushman', an American citizen called Anderson. He travelled from Cape Town to Hopetown, Kimberley and Fourteen Streams to find a way of getting in and out of Mafeking with the Reuter despatches. Anderson bought a horse and hired the services of a black man in Hopetown. But the going was very rough, he was deserted by the man and the horse had to be destroyed. He found a bicycle and, avoiding Boer patrols, managed to reach the environs of Mafeking.

Under cover of night he crept into the town, relieving Stent of his diary, which now amounted to 10 000 words. Anderson left the same night, and the following day Reuters telegraphed a complete record of the siege to London, where it was avidly read.

Local newspapers were just as anxious to use the material. *The South African News* was one of them and reproduced the Reuters diary word for word, an abbreviated version of which is reproduced here. Colourful, unintentionally funny, and reflecting Baden-Powell's particular brand of pluck, it is a small gem of reporting.

MAFEKING

Diary of the Siege.

Day by Day Incidents.

BY REUTER'S SPECIAL CYCLIST VIA UPINGTON

Mafeking, November 18 — (Reuter's Special Service) — The following are extracts from the official log from the beginning of the siege of Mafeking on Wednesday, the 11th October: The Boer forces under General Cronje, in pursuance of the ultimatum, crossed the border, and a force was despatched to cut out communications with the south. This was accomplished on the morning of the 12th, and during all that day and the morning of Friday correspondents were hard at work endeavouring to get through their wires by the northern route. On Friday afternoon, however, the enemy cut our communications and destroyed our railway line in that direction. The enemy, however, contented himself with burning Kafir huts and looting and foraging at a safe distance from our rifles.

On Saturday morning, just as the grey dawn broke, we heard Captain Lord Charles Bentinck and his patrol.

ENGAGING THE ENEMY

to the north of the town, and there followed on this a fight which I have already described in my despatch of the 14th inst.

After Captain Fitzclarence's fight of this date, the ambulance was sent out to recover two bodies left on the field, and was fired upon by the enemy. Curiously enough that same afternoon a letter arrived from Cronje, in which he suggested that arrangements should be entered into for the observance of the laws of civilised warfare with regard to the wounded. He regretted the war, he said, but if we would not surrender the town he would be forced to shell it. His note was answered with all due courtesy, and it was pointed out to him by Colonel Baden-Powell that his men had already fired upon our ambulance that night. I sent riders to Kuruman, believing it to be the only place open for the transmission of news, and joined the armoured train, which had been ordered to patrol north and south of the town and assist in repelling any attack. Nothing, however, occurred that night, and we slept until sunrise, when we were served up with hot coffee from the galley, or rather the cab of the locomotive.

On Saturday night Colonel Baden-Powell had issued a general order congratulating A and L squadrons, commanded by Captain Fitzclarence and Lord Bentinck, and also the

The hero of Mafeking, Colonel Robert Baden-Powell, depicted shortly after the 217-day siege had ended. Front page of The Illustrated London News, *26 May 1900* (Africana Museum).

crew of the armoured train, under Captain Williams and Lieutenant More, upon their very creditable engagement with the enemy.

Throughout Sunday the town was quiet, and in the afternoon Dr Pirow, of Cronje's medical staff, arrived on the scene in a landau drawn by a spanking pair of greys, and flying the Red Cross flag. He lunched with the staff, and of course was received with every courtesy. He carried a despatch from Cronje, inquiring into the question of

FIRING ON THE AMBULANCE,

in which the Boer General went so far as to say that if anyone had been hurt by the fire he would have had the man who instigated it shot. Dr Pirow was kind enough to take some press wires and private wires back to his camp, while I enclosed my card in a note to Cronje, requesting him to do what he could to forward my news to Cape Town. Whether he did or did not do this I am unable to ascertain.

On Sunday evening I joined fort No. 2 under the command of Captain H. Musson, of the Town Guard, and slept in the trenches in readiness for the expected attack at day-break. So quiet was everything on Monday morning that I breakfasted at Dixon's Hotel, and was strolling round snapping up unconsidered tries in the matter of information when the clanging of the Roman Catholic bell, and the blare of the alarm warned me to be at my post, for, like other correspondents, I had taken up arms, and had been allotted a loop-hole in the trenches, where we expected to need every rifle.

At 9.15 a.m. on Monday, the 15th October, the enemy opened artillery.

FIRE UPON THE FORT

commanded by Colonel Goold-Adams, about 160 yards above us. His guns consist of two 7-pounders and a 15-centimetre Krupp, but his practice was not what might be termed good. It was not until he had fired the fourteenth shell at 9.45 that he managed to strike Riesler's Hotel, in the Market Square, which, it may be noted, was not what he was firing at. The armoured train, moving out upon the rapidly-laid lines to the east, came in for a certain amount of attention, but was not struck, and by one o'clock 63 shells had been fired, and only one dog hit. The Convent, I regret to say, though surmounted by a large Red Cross flag, was struck three times; this after the protestations of the Boers with regard to their intention of fighting on civilised lines. At two o'clock in the afternoon a man named Everett appeared on the rise, bearing an improvised flag of truce. He was met upon the outskirts of the town, blind-folded, and taken to the head-quarters, where he was regaled upon beer and sandwiches. He carried a despatch from General Snyman, to the effect that the General hoped we would surrender in order to save further bloodshed and loss of life; also that we might now, if we wished, leave off. Our reply to this, while courteously worded, was more or less to the effect that, so far as leaving off was concerned, we had not yet begun. This truce lasted until 4.45, and the inhabitants of Mafeking

EMERGED FROM CELLARS,

sandbags, redoubts, bomb-proof shelters, and other places of comparative safety, and a brisk trade was done with pieces of shells lying about the streets, which were sold as trophies for as much as 5s. or 4s. each. At 4.45 Mr. Everett returned with our answer, but the Boers had evidently done enough work for one day, and they retired cautiously on their position on Signal Hill, being evidently suspicious of our silence, as we have not fired a shot in return.

Monday night was a comparatively quiet one, although at eight o'clock an alarm was caused by the advance of the enemy upon the waterworks, which they seized, driving our pickets in on the town. Beyond that and the fact that two jumpy persons either fired at their own men or let their rifles off by mistake, there was no other alarm, and most of us slept the sleep of the tired until dawn. A feature in the siege has been the part played in it by many plucky women, and by boys who may not inaptly be termed children. In our own fort we have a boy named Chiddy, who arrived with a rifle and bandolier, and able to shoot at a man's loophole with the best of us. He amuses himself during the bombardment by recording the number of shells that pass over, and asking any war correspondent who may be about embarrassing questions. At another fort, where they have a machine gun, a boy of 13 is employed in loading the machine belts, while another youth of the same age manipulates the telephone. In the house round which our breastwork is built, all through the shelling of Monday, the 16th, were three ladies, who showed the utmost pluck, and one of them, while the shells were whistling over head, endeavoured to play "God Save the Queen" on the drawing-room piano. It was a little wavery and shaky in places, but the men heard and cheered her, and the spirit of the thing was good.

On Wednesday, the 25th, Hellawell, of the "Cape Times" returned to town, after some exciting adventures during his plucky ride to Kuruman and back with despatches. During the morning the enemy continued his

PRACTICE FROM THE BIG GUN,

and our look-outs on the house-tops and other coigns of vantage warned the men in the vicinity when and where to dodge the projectiles. Going on towards mid-day, the enemy concentrated his rifle fire upon our side of the town, and there followed an experience so unpleasant as I sincerely hope may never fall to my lot again. It was utterly impossible to reply to the enemy's fire in any way, for he was out of the range of our rifles, and pretty well of our artillery. At the same time he was approaching under cover of his shell fire and it was impossible to abandon our loop-hole works for the more genial cover of the bomb-proof shelter. Thus we were kept dodging ignominiously, now under cover of the house to escape the attentions of the big gun, now

CROUCHING IN OUR SANDBAGS,

to avoid the shrapnel and segment which their battery of field-guns, placed directly in front of us, showered upon the fort. Shell fire is said to be more alarming than damaging, and this I can well understand. I must confess to never having met anything more alarming. During the attack a 1 000-lb. shell struck the ground within ten yards of our works. Had it been ten yards to the right, scarcely one of us would have lived to tell the tale. As it was, great lumps of earth, thrown up by the impact of the shell, fell upon us, one striking my foot. Needless to say, this was more alarming than ever. At the end of about four hours' dodging backwards and forwards between the work and the house, one began to get remarkably tired of this novel and undesirable experience. The Boers' infantry advances are infinitely less to be feared than their shelling. They contented themselves with entrenching at about 2,000 yards distance. We could plainly see them demolishing the Grand Stand, and using it to provide themselves with cover from the inclemency of the weather.

On 8 December, *The South African News* published the second part of the diary, described by them as 'the highly interesting diary of the siege of Mafeking forwarded by Reuters Special

Correspondent by special cyclist via Upington'. The first entry in Vere Stent's diary had been dated 25 October. By now the siege was fully in effect. Although there was, at this stage, adequate foodstuff, the population was later strictly rationed. If one discounts the deaths from starvation — most in the black population — the siege was a relatively gentlemanly affair, with no firing on Sundays and, by special arrangement, messages passing between Baden-Powell and General Cronje.

Sunday, of course, was again observed as

A DAY OF REST

by mutual agreement. There is but little question that this day off is a remarkable boon to the inhabitants. Our outposts converse in a curious but friendly manner with those of the enemy. We ourselves indulge in baths, shaves, clean shirts, polished boots, and other luxuries unknown during week days. One is able to go to church, if he be among the faithful, for the celebration is regularly said each Sunday by the rector and Roman Catholic priest. You may eat breakfast in comfort, and during the morning wander round snap-shotting, happy in the knowledge that shells or Mauser bullets will not interfere untimely with your comforts. Your lunch need not be gulped down in fear of a 100-pounder bursting through the dining-room window, and in the afternoon we play cricket matches, and the Volunteer Band discourses music in the Market Square. Let no one imagine that, because we have those interests of comfort, the siege of Mafeking is a picnic. So far we have not been hurt seriously, because we have had the advantage of a man of great knowledge to command us, but as the days wear on, and the enemy more closely invests us, we begin to wonder whether the end may not be really serious.

On Sunday, the 29th, the Colonel Commanding expressed his opinion that the

A 100-pounder Boer gun at Mafeking. General Piet Cronjé, with riding whip, stands beneath the gun. Reproduced in The Illustrated London News, *14 April 1900* (Africana Museum).

174

defences of Mafeking were now so secure as to render it impossible for the Boers to carry the place by storm. He thought further that the enemy's shells would continue ineffective as long as the inhabitants were careful to keep under cover. The following curious extracts from the orders seem worth reproducing, as the enemy's form of bombardment sometimes consists in shelling at long and irregular intervals. It is proposed to keep a

WATCH ON THE BIG GUN,

and as soon as she is laid to fire in the direction of the town or women's laager, a horn will be blown from Wells yard, or the western heights respectively, so as to warn every one to take cover. Immediately the warning must be obeyed, as the enemy lay their gun on one point or another to fire a shot after dark, or after sundown into the town, or at the western heights. The warning is to announce to the people of the town, or of the laager respectively, that the big gun has been laid, and it is pointing in their direction.

On Monday, the 30th, we were led to expect from the messages of Cronje a general concentrated attack, which I may say did not come off. As for myself, finding it impossible to work in any comfort or safety upon the outskirts of the town, I accepted the invitation of Mr Ben Well to share his very excellent bomb-proof shelter, and there work up my diary of events in security, which it was impossible to obtain in the more exposed parts of the town.

There were, of course, deaths in the small community: some, like the officers and men killed on raiding parties were regretted but not unexpected. Some, like the death of Parslow of the *Chronicle* were not expected.

Parslow was an ambitious young man intent on making a name for himself in journalism — and there's nothing like a good war for achieving that. Unfortunately for Parslow, one night in the heat and boredom of Mafeking, he irritated Major Murchison, a half-pay artillery officer, beyond endurance. To everyone's horror, the major, whom some thought was quite mad, pulled a gun on the correspondent and shot him stone dead. Murchison was sentenced to death by Baden-Powell, but because of the acute manpower shortage, his sentence was deferred. When Field-Cornet Eloff and his men attacked Mafeking towards the end of the siege, Murchison, who was languishing in the town gaol, was handed a gun and told to defend the town. For his services on this event he was released.

With a fine eye for pathos (and, in the case of the officers' funeral, a good memory for *The Burial of Sir John Moore at Corunna*), Vere Stent of Reuters described both funerals:

FUNERAL AT NIGHT.

The funeral of the officers who fell took place the same night, and such ceremonies as we, upon the edge of the Empire, fighting to maintain Britain's prestige among her outposts, were able to give were given. Together with the men they were carried to their graves on a trolley, for we had need of all the gun carriages. A Union Jack was thrown over them. The fire of the enemy would not permit us to bury them until the shades of night had drawn in over the cemetery. Then, by the light of a lantern dimly burning, our rector, Mr. Weeks, and the Roman Catholic chaplain read over the graves of each one the service appointed by his Church. Then we lowered them into their long resting-places, and the notes of the "Last Post" wailed slowly and sadly over the veld, reaching perhaps the outposts of the enemy, and that was all there was. No firing of salutes, no booming of cannon, no sounding of the "Dead March" — a soldier's funeral. Then, as

In the trenches at Mafeking: a good shot. Morale under Baden-Powell was extraordinarily high; the trenches were linked to 'headquarters' by a complicated but effective telephone system. The Illustrated London News, *23 December 1899* (Africana Museum).

we wandered back to town, the distant and random guns of the enemy boomed overhead, respecting not even the last ceremonies paid to those who had gone.

A CORRESPONDENT'S DEATH.

On Wednesday, apparently, the enemy had not recovered from their repulse of the day before, and were fairly quiet. On Wednesday night, the death of poor Parslow took place. Of this I will deal in a separate despatch.

On Thursday little of importance happened, and I was appointed executor in the estate of Parslow, who was buried in the evening. He was given such honours as an officer might claim in these lines, for we made him a coffin, and covered him in that last journey to the graveyard with the Union Jack. He was carried to the grave by Major Baillie (of the "Morning Post"), Mr Angus Hamilton (of "The Times"), Mr Hellawell (of the "Daily Mail"), Mr Riley (of the "Pall Mall Gazette"), and your correspondent. The funeral was attended by many members of the staff, who came to show their respect for one of the most promising and gallant young war correspondents ever sent into the field.

The diary for that week was concluded with rousing and fulsome praise for Colonel Baden-Powell, whose considerable organisational and leadership abilities were fully stretched during the duration of the long siege.

The Town Guard have fought well and manfully. It requires more courage to sit right under a bombardment than to go out in the open and tackle the enemy in a battle that lasts perhaps two or three hours. Our battle has lasted 2 months, and we have been

UNDER FIRE EVERY DAY.

We have not been able to eat our meals in peace, and sometimes not to eat them at all. We cannot move about in our own town, and every now and then someone is hurt. However, there is no question of surrender in Mafeking to-day. You must move from shelter to shelter; you must dodge down lanes, having always an eye to the direction in which you expect to be fired upon. From our Market-place the tents of the enemy are plainly visible to the east, and upon the outskirts of the town you cannot cross the road, or leave the house, without being subjected to a smart volley of sharpshooters, watching and waiting all day to get a shot at someone. Our water supply, thanks to Captain Hepworth is sufficient. As to food, we have also sufficient, for that well-known firm of contractors, Messrs. J. Weill and Co., have, with admirable forethought, seen to it that we shall be well fed.

Commanding us we have a man than whom we could have none better experienced. The

COLONEL IS ALWAYS SMILING,

and is a host in himself. To see "B.P.," as he is affectionally termed, go whistling down the street, deep in thought, pleasing of countenance, cheerful and confident, is cheering and heartening. Nay, I would say far more cheering and heartening than a pint of dry champagne. Had any man in whom the town placed less confidence been in command, disaster might have befallen Mafeking, and if we are able to place our name upon the renowned outposts of the Empire which have fought for the honour and glory of Britain, it will be chiefly because Baden-Powell has commanded us.

'This horrible noise was the Dutchmen cheering'

Lady Sarah Wilson inside Mafeking, 1900

If Lady Sarah Wilson, aunt to Winston Churchill, thought there was anything untoward in being captured by the Boers, swopped for a horse thief and sent packing into Mafeking, she didn't display it.

Nor, when a 94-pound shell burst on the luckily sandbagged roof of the Mafeking convent where she was talking to the Assistant Commissioner, sending two tons of bricks and mortar between them and entirely demolishing one wall of the room, did she do much more than blow the dust out of her eyes. She remarked later in the London *Daily Mail*, 'We were absolutely none the worse, the bricks in this country being of a very soft, crumbly nature.'

Charming, attractive and imperturbable, Lady Sarah had been living in semi-hiding in Setlagoli, not far from Mafeking, where she reported on Boer movements until the Boers caught up with her. She joined the five correspondents confined to Mafeking for the duration, and was the London *Daily Mail*'s special correspondent.

There was no shortage of copy in Mafeking and, in any event, Lady Sarah was to mix it with a great deal of socialising, holding little parties in her white-painted bomb-proof shelter and gathering material, not only for the paper but also for her book, *South African Memories,* which was published in 1909.

Her reports, coming from a besieged town which still maintained excellent communications with the rest of the world (Lady Sarah's runners went north, to Rhodesia, whence her despatches were telegraphed to London), were lively, informative, and chipper. Thus, in the *Daily Mail* of 6 March 1900, Lady Sarah describes an increasingly hungry Mafeking, but does not go into all the details, which were quite distressing:

NOW EATING STRAY DOGS.

SIGNS THAT MAFEKING HAS NONE TOO MUCH FOOD.

(From Our Special Correspondent, Lady Sarah Wilson.)

Mafeking (Feb. 19) (via Plumer's Camp, Feb. 25).

We have had a fairly quiet time here since the removal last week of the big gun from the east of the town to the south-west. The position has been apparently chosen as a convenient one from which to shell the native staadt and the women's laager, which was done last Friday and Saturday.

The Dutch women in the laager are writing a protest to General Snyman.

While the shelling of the town is slightly less severe, bullets are much more plentiful, and are a constant source of danger. It is impossible to walk from the convent to the hospital without having two or three shots fired at one, and women and children are deliberately aimed at.

For this reason Colonel Baden-Powell is having a net-work of trenches dug all over the town for pedestrians. There are now miles of these, but in wet weather they are impassable, so risks must be run by all.

The questions of food-stuffs is engaging the attention of the authorities. The natives are feeling the want of food, as the allowance is necessarily very small. They have plenty of money earned by trench digging and working at the defences.

A soup kitchen is therefore being organised, and horses, stray dogs, and the heads and feet of oxen are being utilised for this purpose. The soup kitchen should be a great boon to all.

The town is on strict rations. Oats are procured too with bread meal, and rejected husks for the horses.

Yesterday (Sunday) passed quietly. Cycle sports took place in the recreation ground, but all were aware that the Boers might open fire on us, for General Snyman had intimated that the Boers did not approve of our ways of spending our only holiday, and fault was especially found with the cutting of wood by the natives.

The Boers themselves were, however, busy in digging new advance trenches.

February 22 being Colonel Baden-Powell's birthday, this auspicious occasion will be celebrated as a holiday by the town.

At 04h00 on the morning of 12 May 1900, Mafeking was woken by the sound of gunfire and shouting from the Baralong village on the outskirts of the town.

To the sound of bugle calls, the ringing of church bells and running feet, Baden-Powell's garrison and the correspondents got themselves into battle order. Pulling on clothes in the confusion and dark, the defenders cut unprepossessing figures, dressed as they were in under-clothes and pyjamas. Lady Sarah, dressed but not groomed, climbed through the window of the hotel dining room for a quick cup of coffee before making her way through an uncomfortable hail of bullets to the hospital to help with the wounded.

The cause of the alarm was Field-cornet Sarel Eloff, a grandson of President Kruger, who had launched a determined attack on Mafeking with a force of 240 men. Getting as close as 730 metres from Baden-Powell's headquarters, Eloff was nonetheless beaten off, and retreated with a portion of his men into the old police barracks, where a furious battle ensued.

Angus Hamilton, *The Times'* man, wandered too close to the barracks and was promptly captured. He was not the only prisoner: 32 others, including one severely wounded man and one with dysentery, were placed in a small, fusty room to await the outcome of the battle. It gave Hamilton a different view of the battle, and he was able to despatch his story three days later, after the siege had been lifted.

Lady Sarah's report for the *Daily Mail* was printed on 19 June.

THE LAST FIGHT AT MAFEKING.

HOW LIEUT. ELOFF'S PLANS WERE UPSET.

(By Lady Sarah Wilson.)

Mafeking, May 17

The siege of Mafeking was raised at 10 a.m. on Thursday, May 17. This is the official time. The relieving forces consisted of Colonel Mahon's column and Colonel Plumer's Rhodesian Regiment and Mashonaland B.S.A.P., accompanied by Queenslanders, Canadians, and a Canadian artillery battery.

It is impossible to express our feelings of relief, thankfulness, and delight.

Mafeking, May 14

"The Boers are in the Stadt!" Such was the ominous message that was quickly passed from mouth to mouth on Saturday morning as day was breaking.

One must have lived all these weary months in Mafeking and have frequently wandered through the labyrinth of rocks, trees, and huts to grasp the dread import of this short sentence in its entirety.

I do not exaggerate when I say that in an instant a set, hard, determined expression came over the face of every man as he heard it, even of those who, but a few moments before, had been disposed to joke at the terrific fusillade that was going on to the east, i.e., in the opposite direction, and made contemptuous remarks anent the Boer method of thoroughly awakening the whole town by rifle fire when they meditated a night attack.

A DETERMINED ONSET

As the murmured message became louder and was acknowledged to be the grim truth, the most callous realised that this was no sham onslaught such as we have experienced since General Cronje went south with his invincibles, but that we were face to face with the most critical state of things imaginable — a situation that would try the nerves and the resisting powers of trained regiments to the utmost — how much more to be dreaded with the garrison principally composed of civilians (among whom were many Dutch), and of excitable natives, and the whole community reduced in strength from want of proper nourishment.

But I must hark back a little and relate what occurred before the situation assumed so serious an aspect. At 4 a.m. we were awakened by terrific rifle fire; in an instant one knew it was something more important than the usual volleys the Dutchmen give us when anything startles them during the night. I opened the door on to the stoep and the din was terrific, while swish-swish — came the bullets just beyond the canvas blinds nailed to the end of the wooden verandah to keep off the fierce sun. Now and then the boom of a small gun, a 5-pounder, made itself heard above the noise — but the rifles never ceased for an instant. To this awe-inspiring tune I dressed, by the light of a candle, carefully shaded to avoid giving any mark for our foes to aim at. All the while it was pitch dark but for the stars, and very cold. Now one heard the town was moving — hurried footsteps passed to and fro — lanterns flashed for an instant, intensifying the blackness, and of a sudden the sound I had been waiting for added to the weird horror of the situation — the alarm bugle, winding out its tale clear and true to the furthest alleys, the

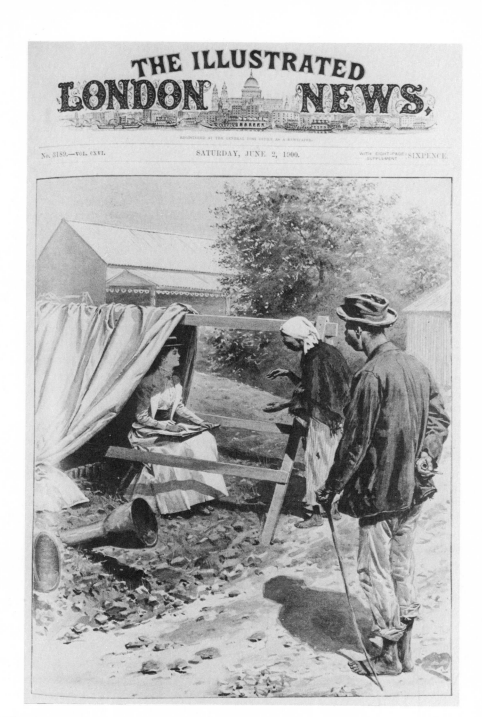

THE ILLUSTRATED LONDON NEWS

No. 3189.—VOL. CXVI.   SATURDAY, JUNE 2, 1900.   WITH EIGHT-PAGE SUPPLEMENT SIXPENCE.

Lady Sarah Wilson writing a despatch outside the entrance to her bomb-proof. Much of her entertaining was done here. The front page illustration appeared in The Illustrated London News *on 2 June 1900* (Africana Museum).

most remote shanties, followed by our tocsin, the deep-toned Roman Catholic bell, which was the signal that a general attack was in progress.

WHEN MINUTES SEEMED HOURS

But a few minutes had elapsed since the firing had commenced, yet it seemed years, and one knew a good hour had to be got through before there could be a glimmering of the new day, so disagreeably ushered in. I went out to the front facing south-west and looking towards the Stadt, sheltered from the hail of bullets coming from the east.

Some one came up who had been at headquarters and reported to the colonel and staff cheery and confident, drinking hot coffee and prepared for any emergency; the colonel, it was stated, was positive the eastern attack was but a feint, and that the real business was shortly to begin round the Stadt. But I doubt if even he anticipated the serious turn matters had even then assumed. And now just as we were noticing that objects could be discerned on the road that before were invisible, forked tongues of lurid light shot up into the sky in the direction where, snug and low by the Molop River, lay the native stadt. Even then one did not realise what was burning; someone said: "A big grass fire commenced yesterday." At the same time a din of confused cries, unmistakably native ejaculations, was borne to us by the breeze along with the smell of burning thatch and wood. "The Boers are in the Stadt." This dread sentence seemed to grow in volume, till to one's excited fancies it became a sort of chant, to which the faint yells of the natives, the unceasing rattle of musketry, the ping-ping of the bullets, formed an unholy accompaniment.

THE HOARSE CHEER OF THE ENEMY.

Hark! What was that? was the universal exclamation of the few folk, mostly women, among whom I was standing; a curious hoarse cheer such as I have never heard before and devoutly pray I may never hear again arose — not in the stadt, half a mile away, but nearer, close by, only the other side of the Railway Buildings. This horrible noise was the Dutchmen cheering — as unlike an English cheer as night to day.

There was no panic. I could see every man walking to the nearest cover of any description and settling himself down with his rifle. A gentleman of the Town Guard came down the street telling us what we already knew, that the Dutch had rushed the fort, only held by fifteen men; "but," he continued, "we will keep them there — they will never get out." He also said the Town Guard were out to a man, even old men of seventy among them, one stone deaf who had been roused by the rifle fire, another minus several fingers, only recently blown off by a shell — all were in their places, there was scarcely a vacancy.

A MEMORABLE WALK.

But my quarters were getting too hot. I bethought me even novices might be useful at the hospital, where there would be surely work for all, so I decided to get there somehow or other. The question was how. The rifle fire was slackening to the east, but from the fort came a most deadly fusillade, and the way to the hospital lay through the most open part of the town, due north. I shall never forget that walk as long as I live; it was broad daylight now, and never had the road seemed so wide and bare, the houses so few and far between. Luckily the bullets were flying high, but they seemed to come from every side.

Twice I had to stop and wait for a lull before going on. At last I reached the hospital trench, and the last 500 yards of the journey were accomplished in perfect safety.

Here my experiences end, for the rest of that dreadful day I spent in the friendly safety of these walls, sheltering so much suffering and sickness, that were, alas, by evening crammed to their fullest capacity. Even here the bullets flew at times thick and fast, and all through the weary hours of that perfect summer day the rifle fire never ceased. Sometimes a regular fusillade for ten minutes or so, then, as if tired out, sinking down to a few single shots, while the siren-like whistle and sharp explosion of the shells from the high velocity gun kept on intermittently and added to the dangers of the streets.

A MELANCHOLY PROCESSION.

From the earliest hours commenced the slow, sad stream of wounded men; sometimes an ambulance wagon would arrive with three or more; again we described a stretcher party moving cautiously across the recreation ground towards us with their melancholy load. Presently three wounded Boers were brought in, the first prisoners Mafeking can claim, then a native with his arm shattered to the shoulder and who, it was whispered, had been one of the guides of the attacking party. All were skilfully and carefully attended to by Major Anderson, P.M.O., and his staff, and in a marvellously short space of time were comfortably installed in bed. All the time the wildest rumours pervaded the air; now the Boers had possession of the whole stadt; again they were murdering the women and children in the laager; a little later they would never surrender the seized fort which was amply provisioned; and as soon as night fell large Boer reinforcements were to force their way in. Of course we knew the colonel was all the while maturing his plans to rid the town of its unbidden guests, but what these were never leaked out. Several times during the afternoon there were furious musketry outbursts followed by ominous silence. Towards sunset came a telephone message that the Boers in the stadt had been surrounded and taken prisoners, the few survivors being in full flight, and after a final burst of rifle fire, just as the moon had risen, came British cheers from the town, and the joyful intelligence that the fort had surrendered to Colonel Hore, who, with his officers, had all the day been in the curious position of captive in his own fort, and that over a hundred Boers, including Commandant Eloff, had given up their arms and ammunition to him.

BRITISH COOLNESS AND MARKSMANSHIP

The events which brought about this glorious finale will be told by such as were on the spot. I am told it was the coolness of our men during the whole day and their wonderful marksmanship that brought about this satisfactory result, sooner even than the most sanguine had dared hope.

A little later that same evening I went to the Masonic Hall to have a peep at the prisoners, and it is a fact that not till I had seen them with my own eyes, did I realise the marvellous success the Mafeking garrison had had. A motley crew they were — in the dim light of a few oil lamps — the greater part laughing, joking, singing even — all smoking the inevitable pipe — representatives of tardy nationalities, the few Boers "pur et simple" holding themselves somewhat doggedly aloof, but the whole community giving one an idea of a body of men who knew they had got out of a tight place and were devoutly thankful still to have whole skins.

AT BREAKFAST WITH ELOFF.

The next morning at breakfast I sat opposite to Commandant Eloff, who, with three other officers, had been accommodated for the night by Mr. Weil, and on my right was a most polite French baron, who could not speak a word of English, Dutch, or German, so it is difficult to understand how he conversed with his present friends. In strong contrast to this affable and courteous gentleman was the Commandant Eloff, of whom we have heard so much, and of whom but a short three weeks ago we in Mafeking were disposed to speak contemptuously, after the half-hearted attack he organised on April 25, which we now know to have been but a sort of preliminary canter to the real business.

Never again, say our soldiers here, can we call that young man a braggart, a man of words and not deeds. That he was brilliantly assisted by his French and German allies is as equally certain as the fact of his having been more or less left in the lurch by his own countrymen, when they saw, that to get into Mafeking was one thing, but to stay there or get out again quite another.

A typical Boer of the younger generation, with curiously unkempt hair, literally standing on end, light sandy whiskers and a small moustache, and wearing on this occasion a solemn, dejected expression on his by no means stupid, but discontented and unprepossessing face — the President's grandson did not scruple to air his grievances and disclose his intentions with regard to the action of the day before.

ELOFF TELLS HIS STORY.

In a few words he told us how it had been posted up in the laager. "We leave for Mafeking to-night, we will breakfat at Dixon's Hotel to-morrow morning"; how he had sent back to instruct Reuter's agent to cable the news that Mafeking had been taken so soon as the fort was in their hands; how he left with 400 followers, mostly volunteers, of whom, when he stopped to count them by the light of the blazing Stadt, only 240 were found to have stuck to him; how the 300 additional men who were to push in by the brickfields when the signal fires were seen absolutely failed him, as did also the real forward movement plans for an attack all round the town simultaneously, instead of merely senseless volleys from the trenches, which was all the help he got from outside.

All this and much more he told us with bitter emphasis, while the French officer conversed unconcernedly in the intervals of his discourse about the African climate, the weather, and the Paris Exhibition, and observed with heartfelt emphasis that he wished himself once more in his native France, which he had only left six weeks ago; while the Dutchmen, not understanding what he was saying, kept on the thread of their arguments in broken English, interrupting him without any compunction.

It was one of the most curious meals I have ever assisted at; the same afternoon the four officers were removed to safer quarters in gaol while a house is being prepared for their reception.

This letter is now sent forward for the second time. The Boers had taken it from my runner, who was shot. When the laager was so hurriedly evacuated on the advent of the relief force, it was found exactly as I sent it. You will see that the Mafeking siege stamps have been carefully cut out.

When the war ended, Lady Sarah went home. She and her husband, Lieutenant-Colonel Gordon Chesney Wilson, were good friends of Edward VII and Queen Alexandra and, until the 1914-1918 conflict, lived typical society lives.

Although she was not the only woman journalist to cover the Boer War (Reuters employed Miss Maguire), she was the most celebrated.

Lady Sarah's husband was killed in the Great War, and she threw herself into nursing. She died in London on 22 October 1929, vice-president of the Society of Women Journalists, a Lady of Grace of St John of Jerusalem and, for her hospital work during the Second Anglo-Boer War, holder of the Royal Red Cross award.

'Partners in quite another game'

Dr Arthur Conan Doyle and his war effort, Bloemfontein, 1900

Arthur Conan Doyle is acknowledged as the father of the modern detective novel. The creator of Sherlock Holmes, Dr Watson and the infamous Moriarty, he was not only a gifted narrator, but a man of exceptional memory and powers of deduction. A writer, doctor, patriot and spiritualist, Conan Doyle was born in Edinburgh on 22 May 1850.

The impecunious young doctor (his salary for his first year in medical practice was £154) sat down to write a book in order to supplement his earnings. The book, *A Study in Scarlet*, was published in 1887. It was an enormous success for the publishers, but not for Conan Doyle, who had sold the copyright outright for the sum of £25. From 1887 until his death in 1930, he wrote one book a year.

When Dr Arthur Conan Doyle, on a lecture tour of Canada, heard about Black Week (the Boer victories of Magersfontein, Stormberg and Colenso) in December 1899, he immediately decided to join the war-effort.

Although over 40, he was determined to enlist as a fighting soldier, fibbing about his military experience to the colonel of the Middlesex Yeomanry. 'Two white lies are permitted to a gentleman,' Conan Doyle quipped, 'to screen a woman or to get into fight when the fight is a rightful one.' Convinced that the fight was indeed a rightful one, but believing that once victory had been achieved the Boers should receive unstinting help to re-establish themselves, Conan Doyle finally joined a unit as a supplementary medical officer, and arrived in Cape Town on 21 March 1900.

He stayed at the Mount Nelson Hotel — full, he said, of wounded officers, adventuresses and cosmopolitans — before entraining for Bloemfontein. When he reached the town, swollen with Lord Roberts' troops, he was put in charge of a 50-bed hospital erected on the cricket field. He immediately faced a severe epidemic of typhoid fever. A sensitive man, he was appalled by the losses. 'Victims died on the way to the lavatories,' he wrote, 'coffins were out of the question and the men were lowered in their brown blankets into their shallow graves at the rate of 60 a day.'

Rejoicing in the company not only of medical friends but in the more colourful society of journalist stalwarts such as Bennet Burleigh of *The Daily Telegraph* and the 'extraordinary queer little Melton Prior who looked like a prim headmaster' and who was the mainstay of *The Illustrated London News*' team of war artists, Conan Doyle contributed to the *Bloemfontein Post* a curious mixture of Kiplingesque poetry and patriotic gung-ho journalism, of which 'A First Impression' is but a short example. It appeared in the *Post* on 6 April 1900.

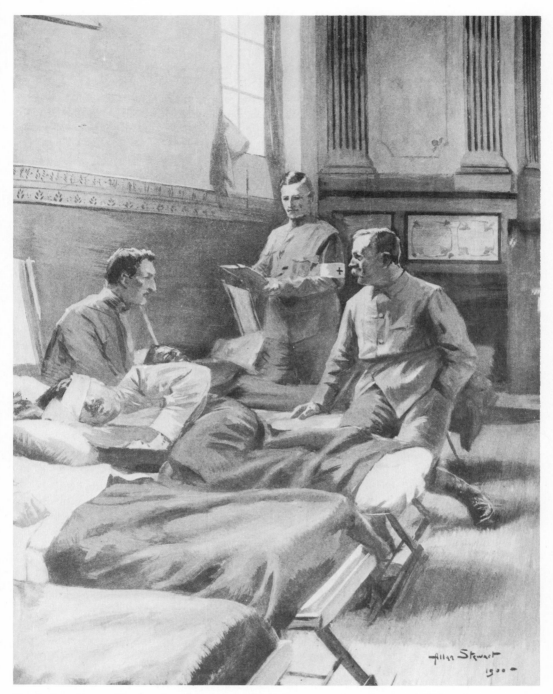

Dr Arthur Conan Doyle, already a successful writer, attending to wounded Canadians in Langman Hospital, 1900. The illustration, based on a photograph, appeared in The Illustrated London News *on 2 June 1900* (Africana Museum).

A FIRST IMPRESSION.

BY A. CONAN DOYLE

It was only Smith-Dorrien's Brigade marching into Bloemfontein, but if it could have been passed just as it was, down Piccadilly and the Strand it would have driven London crazy. I got down from the truck which we were unloading and watched them, the ragged, bearded, fierce-eyed infantry, straggling along under their cloud of dust. Who could conceive, who has seen the prim soldier of peace, that he could so quickly transform himself into this grim, virile barbarian? Bulldog faces, hawk faces, hungry wolf faces, every sort of face except a weak one. Here and there a reeking pipe, here and there a man who smiled, but the most have their swarthy faces leaned a little forward, their eyes steadfast, their features impassive but resolute. Baggage waggons were passing, the mules all skin and ribs, with the escort tramping beside the wheels. Here are a clump of Highlanders, their workmanlike aprons in front, their keen faces burned black with months of the veldt.

It is an honoured name that they bear on their shoulder-straps. "Good old Gordons!" I cried as they passed me. The sergeant glanced at the dirty enthusiast in the undershirt. "What cheer, matey!" he cried, and his men squared their shoulders and put a touch of ginger into their stride. Here are a clump of Mounted Infantry, a grizzled fellow like a fierce old eagle at the head of them. Some are maned like lions, some have young, keen faces, but all leave an impression of familiarity upon me. And yet I have not seen irregular British cavalry before. Why should I be so familiar with this loose-limbed, head-erect, swaggering type; of course it is the American cow-boy over again. Strange that a few months of the veldt has produced exactly the same man that springs from the western prairie. But these men are warriors in the midst of war. Their eyes are hard and quick. They have the gaunt, intent look of men who live always under the shadow of danger. What splendid fellows there are among them!

Here is one who hails me; the last time I saw him we put on seventy runs together when they were rather badly needed, and here we are, partners in quite another game. Here is a man of fortune, young, handsome, the world at his feet, he comes out and throws himself into the thick of it. He is a great heavy-game shot, and has brought two other "dangerous men" out with him. Next him is an East London farmer, next him a fighting tea-planter of Ceylon, next him a sporting baronet, next him a journalist, next him a cricketer, whose name is a household word. Those are the men who press into the skirmish-line of England's battle.

And here are other men again, taller and sturdier than infantry of the line, grim, solid men, as straight as poplars. There is a maple-leaf, I think, upon their shoulder straps, and a British brigade is glad enough to have those maples beside them. For these are the Canadians, the men of Paardeberg, and there behind them are their comrades in glory, the Shropshire Light Infantry, slinging along with a touch of the spirit of their grand sporting colonel, the man who at forty-five is still the racquet champion of the British army. You see the dirty private with the rifle under his arm and the skin hanging from his nose. There are two little stars upon his strained shoulders, if you could see them under the dirt. That is the dandy captain who used to grumble about the food on the P. and O. "Nothing fit to eat," he used to cry as he glanced at his menu. I wonder what he would say now? Well, he stands for his country, and England also may be a little less coddled and a little more adaptive before these brave, brave sons of hers have hoisted her flag over the "raad zaal" of Pretoria.

Arthur Conan Doyle returned to Britain in August 1900, the first draft of his book *The Great Boer War* already complete. Published in that year, it sold 30 000 copies.

Knighted in 1902, Sir Arthur's last twenty years were focused on his writing and an increasing interest in the occult, which impelled him to travel and lecture internationally. He returned to South Africa in 1929 on a lecture tour.

Keen to revisit the site of his first (and only) hospital, Sir Arthur travelled to Bloemfontein. He was shown the Women's Memorial, the monument erected in memory of the Boer women and children who died in the British-run concentration camps. Doyle, who genuinely did not believe the stories of British complicity in the running of the camps or of behaviour unbecoming to a British gentleman, turned red in the face and shouted: 'It's a lie! It's a lie!' The incident was reported in *The Friend* and, that night, an angry mob besieged Sir Arthur's hotel. He was ed, for his own safety, to leave town. He never returned.

'London has been stark raving mad ever since'

The Relief of Mafeking, 15 May 1900

With the possible exception of Edgar Wallace's famous despatch to the London *Daily Mail* announcing the signing of the Treaty of Vereeniging and the end of the Second Anglo-Boer War, the briefest and the most celebrated despatch to come out of that conflict was the Reuters cable telling the world that Mafeking had been relieved.

The day before Field-cornet Sarel Eloff's attack, Vere Stent of Reuters obtained an interview with Colonel Baden-Powell. The smell of relief was in the crackling, dry air as Stent's 'special' despatch, sent at 11h53 on 11 May 1900 and printed in the second edition of *Reuter's Journal* at 13h15 on 23 May illustrated.

MAFEKING, May 11

Now Sir, continued Reuter's Correspondent, here is rather a dangerous question. There are one or two persons in the town who think that you are not doing as much as you might to hurry on the relief.

The General smilingly replied: "Yes, I know, but no one would be more glad to meet the Relief Column this afternoon than I. Of course, it is not much use rushing things. My great endeavour is to prevent the officers of the Relief Force from endeavouring to rush into the place before they are ready and strong enough to do so. It would be better to make certain of relief in two months time than to be beaten in an attempt at relief in one." After a moment's pause, as though to recall old memories, B.-P. remarked: "You remember it was said in the old days in Zululand, that the natives called me, curiously enough "Umhlala Panzi."

I nodded. "Umhlala Panzi" means a man who does not rush things, or, summing up its whole meaning in a phrase which the General is fond of using himself, it describes a man who "sits tight."

"Well now," I resumed, "with regard to the many pleasant things that have been said about us by the newspapers at home?

The Colonel's face brightened. "You have no idea what the praise of the English people has done for the garrison. The knowledge that the whole Empire is watching with appreciation the good fight which they have fought has been worth an extra pound's rations per day to the garrison. It has helped to encourage the good feeling which has existed throughout the siege between everybody, and which has made men pull together under a tremendous strain."

"Now, Colonel," I said, "just one last thing. There has been a good deal said about yourself by the newspapers and the English public. They have sent you more than one message. We Pressmen are the plenipotentiaries of the people. Can you not give me a message to send to the people of England?"

The Colonel looked embarrassed. "Well," he replied, "You see these chaps have got an exaggerated idea of the importance of my personality, whereas I look upon myself as the figure-head of the good ship Mafeking. It has been her stout canvas and the shape of her brave hull that has really shoved the ship along and brought her safely through her stormy cruise, so whenever I read the nice things people say about me, I take it that they said them inasmuch as I am the head and the representative of the garrison. Anything more?"

"No thank you, Sir."

As I stepped out again into the winter sunshine, I heard "Click, Click" of the Colonel's typewriter. He was at work again at once.

At 19h00 on Wednesday, 15 May, nine horsemen of the Imperial Light Horse rode into Mafeking, their arrival almost unnoticed. Major 'Karri' Davies and eight troopers, the advance guard of the Southern Mafeking Relief Force had been travelling, according to a Reuters report on 19 May, at the rate of 20 miles a day in its bid to relieve the dusty little town.

Before dawn, the relief of column itself entered Mafeking. Relieved the town may have been, but it was still cut off from the rest of the world. The correspondents who entered town,

The London Stock Exchange hearing the news that Mafeking had been relieved. The Illustrated London News *26 May 1900* (Africana Museum).

together with those who had survived the siege, were frustrated by the lack of communication: the telegraph lines, cut by the Boers, were still down.

It was the Boers themselves who sent the news to Pretoria that Mafeking had been taken by the British. They were confident that the news would be contained within the capital city until they had time to regroup themselves. But they reckoned without W.H. MacKay, the Reuters correspondent in Pretoria.

A man of considerable charm and diplomatic skill, MacKay had persuaded the Boer authorities that he was harmless and there was no need for him to be interned. Furthermore, he successfully argued, government censorship was so good that even had he wished to evade it, he would undoubtedly fail. Thus, he was left at large, an amiable and seemingly content figure.

The moment he heard the news — and MacKay's sources were excellent — he was determined to break the story of the year. Undetected, he leapt onto the next train leaving for the Portuguese East African border. Once there, he wrote out the momentous news and, for a £5 bribe, persuaded the engine driver of a train leaving for Lourenço Marques to place the despatch inside his sandwiches and, when he reached the town, to take the despatch to the offices of the Eastern Telegraph Company, from which offices the historic despatch could be telegraphed immediately to Reuters head office in London.

The engine driver safely negotiated the border, removing the despatch from his sandwiches once he was clear and duly delivered the piece of paper at 19h00 on 18 May.

Dickinson, Reuters chief editor, was smoking his pipe and watching a game of chess in the London office, news being rather slack that night, when a boy appeared with a telegram. Dickinson opened the telegram at 21h16. One minute later — 21h17 — the news had been received by every newsroom in London. At 21h18, Reuters had telephoned the news to the Lord Mayor and the House of Commons. By 20h20 it had gone to Queen Victoria, the Prince of Wales, the Viceroy of India and the War Office, as well as the whole of Europe, China and Japan, the West Indies, West Africa, North and South America and Australia — and South Africa, where it would take another two days for the Reuters message to be confirmed.

At 21h30 *Reuter's Journal* was on sale on the streets of London. A huge crowd, shouting and waving flags, rushed jubilantly through the city, the subsequent celebrations exceeding those which marked the end of World War I. 'London has been stark raving mad ever since and has not yet recovered,' a delighted Dickinson wrote to his son. Everyone was 'mafficking,' thanks to Reuters. The scoop, of which the news agency is even today justifiably proud, allowed Reuters its proud boast: 'Reuters has cabled great news and it has cabled it first.'

MacKay's despatch read as follows:

PRETORIA, May 18 (11.35 a.m.)

"It is officially announced that when the laagers and forts around Mafeking had been severely bombarded, the siege was abandoned by the Boers. A British force, advancing from the South, then took possession.

The Reuters despatch reached London two days ahead of the official War Office telegram. The War Office had perforce to issue the following despatch as an official communique:

FROM LORD ROBERTS TO SECRETARY OF STATE FOR WAR
Kroonstad, May 30, 3.30 p.m.
No official intimation has as yet been received, but REUTERS state that the relief of Mafeking has been effected.

'1,000 Rand Collieries 40s. 6d.'

Edgar Wallace, 1902

'For God's sake,' Kipling said to the young Edgar Wallace after a dinner at the City Club, Cape Town, 'don't take to literature as a profession. Literature is a splendid mistress, but a bad wife.'

But for Wallace, the illegitimate Greenwich-born son of a part-time actress, journalism and literature were a way out of a humdrum world. In 1896, at the age of 21, he sailed for South Africa as a second-class medical orderly in the British army.

Based at Simonstown Hospital, Wallace began writing poetry and, after a year in South Africa, bought himself out of the army. He wrote reports on municipal dinners for the *Cape Times* and, by dint of much persuasion, was appointed Reuters second correspondent with the Western Division of the British Army in South Africa.

With £100 for expenses and a war correspondent's pass in his pocket, the 24-year-old Edgar Wallace travelled to De Aar to begin his new career. Once there, he bought the correspondent's standard equipment: a horse, a Cape cart drawn by mules, clothes, camera, bedding, and a servant.

Wallace had worked assiduously at his writing, having virtually no experience. Of a 700-word leading article in the *Cape Times* he was later to write that 'there were twenty words I did not understand and eleven sentences which conveyed nothing to me'. His solution was to rewrite every leader for six months, reducing them to understandable terms — and then condense them to exactly 40 words.

Wallace's despatches for Reuters were well received. After six months with the agency, he was appointed the London *Daily Mail*'s South African correspondent, a telegram from the editor giving him 'the freest of free hands'.

His despatches were lively, refreshing and, although he followed the conventional view of the war from the average Briton's point of view, highly original.

In De Aar Wallace met some of the other correspondents: G.W. Steevens, also of the *Daily Mail* who was to die of typhoid during the siege of Ladysmith, F.W. Knight of the *Morning Post,* his arm shot away after the battle of Belmont, Bennet Burleigh of the *Daily Telegraph,* who snubbed him — and Winston Churchill. A quick learner, Wallace no doubt noted Churchill's propensity for making the most out of any given situation, in this instance writing not only despatches for his newspaper but weaving a book out of the despatches and thus greatly increasing both his income and his reputation.

Wallace was to do this successfully with his *Unofficial Dispatches,* published in Britain shortly after the war ended and from which the following story is taken.

THE REBEL AND THE PSALMIST

Port Elizabeth, Cape Colony

I have been to church — to a church in a little dorp on the Port Elizabeth-Graaff Reinet line, a white-washed, square-cut kirk, and ugly.

A village where a handful of khaki-clad militiamen play at guarding a bridge, and the stories of Transvaal atrocities are believed as the Gospel.

What I heard there can be heard in any Dutch Reformed church in South Africa — in Graaff Reinet, in Uitenhage, in Somerset East, even, it is whispered in effect, in Capetown.

The dream of a United Afrikander nation is dying hard.

The Dutch colonists are only now grasping the significance of their shadowy ideal, and the vague, shapeless vision of a separate national life has, in the moment of the realisation of its hopelessness, assumed a certain tangibility. Nothing is more patent to the most casual observer than the fact that it is only during the past two

Edgar Wallace: medical orderly, journalist, dramatist, novelist. The first editor of the Rand Daily Mail, *he was to become the most successful novelist of his time* (Africana Museum).

months that the leaders of the "New National" movement in the Cape Colony have seen the impossibility of the fulfilment of their dream.

At the beginning of the war a general rising throughout the colony would have put altogether a different complexion upon matters, but the malcontents were confident of the success of the Republican forces and, at the worst, of European intervention, and so they played that waiting game which so happily fits the back-veldt indolent.

Now it is that, with all the impotent rage of strong men caught napping, platform, pulpit, and Press thunder forth denunciation of the conqueror. Now it is that every method that human ingenuity can devise, every effort that leaders and interested organisers can put forth, every malignant lie calculated to fire the blood of the unlearned and intensify the already existing hatred, is being employed to the undoing of the English.

Curious to see for myself what manner of thing a political sermon is, I attended an evening service not far from here.

The church, grim and bleak, was half-filled. There was no great display of colour, no attempt at anything startling in shape of dress. Black was the hue, and home-made severity the cut. The worshippers sat bolt upright in their uncomfortable pews, and the boot-squeak of the late-comer and the occasional sniff or apologetic cough were the only sounds that broke the silence. There were elderly men in irreproachable broadcloth, with sombre banded hats. There were young men greatly daring in fanciful suits, but lacking originality in cravats. Stout Boer women in brocaded silk, and plump Dutch girls with expressionless eyes! They came in, keeping step to the monotonous clang of the church bell, in twos, singly, in parties, and in families, recognising with a glance such of their friends as were already seated.

The bell stopped, and a little harmonium droningly asserted itself. And then, accompanied by one of his deacons, the predikant himself entered and ascended the pulpit. The organ wailed itself to sleep, and the predikant adjusted his glasses.

There were spirit and life in the hymns, many of which were sung without as much as a glance at the book, for the congregation had beguiled many a long evening on lonely farms and isolated homesteads singing them over, not so much from any great religious zeal or piety as from that desire to kill time which moves the convict to master the contents of his Prayer-book.

Then there were lessons and prayers, chapters from the Old Testament of people in bondage and their delivery, prayers that this Trouble which is in the Land may pass, that the heart of the Oppressor might be softened, that the Vengeance of the Lord might descend and smite the Destroyer, that Israel be delivered from the hands of its enemies, that the Philistines might be swept into the sea — yea, even as the wind sweeps the locust.

The predikant prayed with fervour — with head uplifted, with hands clasping and unclasping in agony of spirit. In his prayers he did not refer by name to the Boer Republics; he simply asked for Divine intervention for the Lord's chosen. He did not speak of England; he said Philistines and Amalekites. He did not refer directly to Sir Alfred Milner nor to Mr. Chamberlain, but with all the passion he could command he called for vengeance on the false counsellors who had initiated the persecution of the people of the land. He prayed, and the congregation punctuated his prayers with deep sighs and "amens", and I, a Philistine in the House of the Chosen, sat and wondered why this fervour, this undoubted earnestness, had not been directed towards Paul Kruger in the days when a word from the Dutch churches in South Africa would have prevented the war.

Then came the sermon. No particular verse of the Scriptures was taken — the text was a Psalm in the whole. There was no "secondly" and very little "lastly". Verse by verse the Psalmist's song was taken to illustrate the depravity of the British. Each injustice to Israel had a parallel to-day. Each passionate appeal of David had application to the case of Chamberlain's victims in the North. It was the fourteenth psalm that he took as a subject. The fool had said in his heart that the cause of the burgher was a lost cause; that the Lord was not behind His people; that the accursed tyranny of the oppressor should prevail.

And what of these oppressors? These people who tried to hide themselves from the rifles of the burghers by arraying their bodies in mud-coloured cloth? The congregation murmured a sympathetic appreciation of this sarcasm. What of these men? Truly, the Psalmist said, they were corrupt, they had done abominable things, there was not one who had done good; no, not one. What of the wasted lands in the North? What of the dishonoured homes and the blackened walls of the once prosperous farmhouse? What of — ? — again that awful story — that Horror, made doubly authentic by reason of the place of delivery.

He told the story, the bald, crude tale, carrying, to a white Englishman, its own refutation in every syllable, and the congregation held its breath.

He told the story, so that a man seated in the next pew to myself half rose from his seat and, like a man who tries to shout in a dream and finds that he can but whisper, muttered: "There is time yet, there is time."

So that a girl rose from her seat, tittering and whimpering, and was led out.

And the sermon went on. The Lord had looked down upon the Oppressor, and had visited him with affliction — with disaster on disaster. Colenso, Stormberg, Magersfontein had come like a thunder-bolt upon the world. It was the Divine warning to turn from the path of oppression, to open the eyes of a blind nation.

And how had the warning been taken?

Had the nation heeded the voice? No. It had persecuted its unrighteous designs, its unholy object. It had gone from worse to worst; it had become filthy.

Had they no knowledge, these iniquitous people, who had brought war and desolation to the country, whose path had been marked by much blood and burning? These people, who are dead to all dictates of conscience, to all honour and pity? Did they not realise that at the eleventh hour the Lord would save His people?

Oh that the salvation of Israel would come out of Zion! Did his brethren understand what the passage meant?

The predikant paused and leant forward over the pulpit, and there was a silence. Did they understand that the people of the captivity looked to their own kindred for deliverance from their bondage?

Another pause, and the congregation shifted uneasily in their seats.

Thus abruptly the sermon ended, and the people dispersed, some walking, some riding, some driving. Group by group they scattered, parting with limp shakes of great horny hands — the elder men in gloomy silence, the younger men with mutterings of threats and hints of startling things to be.

I passed down towards the little village that staggers from the church at one end to the naked veldt at the other, passed by the little camp, answering the sentry's challenge. There was a rattle of wheels behind me. It was the predikant driving back with one of his flock. I stood on one side to allow them to pass. As the trap neared the little roadside camp a bayonet glittered in the moonlight, and the horses were pulled up sharp.

"Halt! Who goes there?"

Back came the answer, prompt, and clear, and glib —

"Friends!"

It fell to Edgar Wallace, an ingenious man with an eye to the main chance, to score the major scoop of the Second Anglo-Boer War and, indeed, one of the legendary scoops of twentieth-century journalism.

The war was obviously drawing to a conclusion and Wallace was determined to get the news of the signing of the peace treaty to his newspaper before anyone else.

In the bar of Johannesburg's Heath Hotel, Wallace met a financier, Harry Freeman Cohen. The two struck up a friendship and Cohen agreed to become the link Wallace needed between the imminent peace conference at Vereeniging and the *Daily Mail* in London's Fleet Street.

Cohen had a stockbroking brother, Caesar, working in London. The plan was simple: Wallace would encode the story in stockmarket jargon, hand it to Harry Cohen, who in turn would cable his instructions to Caesar. On receipt of the message Caesar would relay it to the *Daily Mail* to decode.

Wallace put his plan into effect well before the peace conference. As he had expected, the

THE ILLUSTRATED
LONDON NEWS,

REGISTERED AT THE GENERAL POST OFFICE AS A NEWSPAPER.

No. 3294.—VOL. CXX.

SATURDAY, JUNE 7, 1902.

WITH FOUR-PAGE
SUPPLEMENT SIXPENCE

The Prime Minister, Arthur Balfour, reading the terms of surrender to the House of Commons, London, on 2 June 1902. Wallace's story ran a full 24 hours before anyone else's and incurred Kitchener's fury. The Illustrated London News, *June 7 1902* (Africana Museum).

censors, already irritated by what they regarded as a sensitive story Wallace had written, challenged his first message. In this, Wallace informed Caesar Cohen that he had bought 1,000 Rand Collieries at a certain figure.

But Wallace had anticipated the challenge and had armed himself with a broker's note which confirmed that he had indeed bought the call on the shares. Subsequent 'deals' went unchallenged. Wallace now turned himself to the problem of getting the inside information.

Fortuitously, he had befriended a man working as a guard in the peace camp. The camp, in Vereeniging, was a marquee surrounded by tents, which in turn were surrounded by barbed wire. Kitchener was determined that no news of the debate, which was an agonised one, would fall into the hands of the correspondents, whom he detested, and they were kept well away from the perimeter.

Wallace appeared unconcerned. Indeed, he didn't even bother to billet with the increasingly angry correspondents. He set up home in Pretoria and travelled by train each day to Vereeniging and back again, sometimes two or three times a day.

It seemed harmless enough, if slightly eccentric. Wallace read the paper, glanced at the scenery, got out of the train, changed platforms at Vereeniging, got back into the train and returned to Pretoria.

For a brief stage, the railway line ran along the barbed wire fence that enclosed the delegates to the peace conference. Wallace's accomplice guarding the entrance to the marquee had been given three handkerchiefs; red (nothing happening), blue (making progress) and white (treaty to be signed).

On the evening of 3 May 1902, after a debate that had lasted two days, the Boers agreed to the terms of peace. Wallace's train passed the camp, his informant, out for a breath of fresh highveld air, vigorously blew his nose with a white handkerchief and Wallace wrote his famous despatch.

No one other than Kitchener, his immediate staff and the Boer generals concerned knew that peace had been agreed upon.

While Wallace had a well-earned drink, the *Daily Mail* locked every door to Carmelite House, keeping the entire staff from teaboy to editor within the building for the night lest the news should escape.

The paper ran the story the following morning, 24 hours before the announcement that the peace treaty had been signed was given by Prime Minister Arthur Balfour to the House of Commons.

Kitchener, apoplectic with rage, sent Wallace a telegram withdrawing his credentials as a war correspondent. Wallace couldn't have cared less: cock-a-hoop with success, he had just accepted the job as founding editor of a new newspaper — the *Rand Daily Mail*.

As the *Daily Mail*'s correspondent, Wallace scooped the 1902 peace talks at Vereeniging, became founder editor of the *Rand Daily Mail* in the same year and, nine months later, back in London, began his career as the most successful novelist of his time.

In 27 years he was to write 150 novels, and to make and lose a fortune. When Edgar Wallace died in Hollywood on 10 February 1932 at the age of 57, he owed more than £140 000. But, in Graham Greene's words, he could 'create legends'.

The cable received by the *Daily Mail* and despatched by Wallace within minutes of his return to Pretoria from Vereeniging, read as follows:

'Have bought you 1,000 Rand Collieries 40s. 6d.'

Deciding the terms of peace — a Boer parliament in the veld, the divisions between the Boers graphically depicted in The Illustrated London News, *10 May 1902* (Africana Museum).

The despatch enabled the newspaper to run the news of the Boer surrender on 1 June 1902. On 2 June, true to the time-hallowed tradition of Fleet Street, the *Daily Mail* began to explain, in the simplest of terms to its discomfitted rivals, how it had scooped them:

THE 'DAILY MAIL' PEACE CABLES

HOW WE REPORTED THE NEGOTIATIONS

With the declaration of peace the time has come for the "Daily Mail" to fulfil its promise, made on April 19, to give "details of one of the most interesting achievements in the history of journalism," the achievement being no less than the practical reporting, day by day, of the progress of the peace deliberations in South Africa.

It is a story which we think will interest our readers, while it will, incidentally, allay the puzzled bewilderment of certain respected contemporaries, whose desire to denounce us has barely been kept in bounds by a recognition of the exceeding accuracy of our news.

Indeed, the most pleasing testimony to the value of our achievement is to be found in the daily outpouring of the vials of contemporary wrath. The potent, grave, and reverend signiors of the Press, the "Times" and "Standard," have reproved us after their kind, more in sorrow than in anger; the petulance of the "Daily Telegraph" has been outdone by the street arab revilings of the "Pall Mall Gazette".

SOME OF THE REVILINGS.

Thus, in stern disapprobation, wrote the "Times": —

There are people who tell us (the war is over) with great confidence, and gain thereby the reputation of being exceptionally well-informed. The "Standard" was more lofty and less courteous. It said: —

The statements in Parliament . . . substitute a precise, though limited, account of the present conditions of affairs for the mass of more or less circumstantial inventions, which the public have been asked to accept as authentic information . . . even in the days when the existence of a demand is too often assumed to justify the supply of anything that will sell, it is something of a surprise to find how little the art of the concocter has been guided by considerations of probability.

The "Daily Telegraph's" comment was: —

All the pretended revelations which have been given to the world are the veriest guess-work of speculation, endeavouring to give the colour of plausibility to the rumours evolved from its own inner consciousness. The "Pall Mall Gazette" complained that the man in the street has been informed every morning as he unfolds his halfpenny newspaper of all that occurred the day before at Pretoria.

Thus unconsciously stumbling upon the exact truth, and in reference to the promise of the "Daily Mail" on April 19, alluded to at the outset of this article, the "Pall Mall" wrote: —

Now, what does such a statement as that mean? When does the time come to make so startling a revelation? We may be sure we shall hear no more about it.

Such were the comments of our contemporaries, repeated almost day after day until in the lapse of time fugitive messages from their own correspondents convinced them and their readers that the "Daily Mail" had been able from the outset to secure accurate and reliable news of all that was transpiring in Pretoria.

HOW IT WAS DONE.

Well, the time has now come to explain "how the thing was done." Like most successful operations, it required a little foresight. The "Daily Mail" got news where its rivals got none, because it foresaw the conditions and provided for them, that is all.

Soon after the movement towards peace began there was a break in the relations between correspondents on the spot and their newspapers. Messages came, but these messages obviously did not contain all that the correspondents could have said. The censorship was hard at work. Correspondents had news which they were not allowed to send. A notable illustration of this is afforded by Mr. Bennet Burleigh's telegram, "Returning, tell Lawson." The "Daily Telegraph" rightly interpreted this as an endeavour on their correspondent's part to intimate that peace was assured, a statement which the "Daily Mail" had made already many weeks before on a much less ambiguous foundation.

Foreseeing some months before this state of affairs whenever the question of peace should become imminent, the "Daily Mail" had made certain cable arrangements with two "Daily Mail" correspondents in South Africa, placed so as to be able to command the best possible sources of news, equipped so as to be able to deal with it immediately and with discretion. This latter point was of importance, for no newspaper of standing would publish, or wish to publish, news which might in any conceivable circumstances be against the country's interest, and in several cases in connection with the series of remarkable telegrams we are about to describe, the "Daily Mail" has suppressed many messages rather than run the slightest risk of erring in this direction.

THE FIRST CABLE

In pursuance of the arrangements alluded to, there arrived at an address in London on April 12 the following cablegram, handed in at Johannesburg at 11.40 a.m. (The cables were despatched from Johannesburg to ensure their attracting no considerable attention, the renewed activity of the gold-mining centre making them but few out of many cables dealing with business which were permitted to come over the wires by the censor.)

Here, verbatim, is the first of the long series of cables:—

Regarding purchase gold farm Paxfontein all necessary parties to contract now Pretoria wither Alf gone get better price have every reason believe vendors wish to sell.

The simplicity of the device renders explanation almost unnecessary. Of course, the particular instance was but an isolated success for a scheme devised to meet all possible contingencies, but it worked excellently. It barely needs translation. "Alf" is Lord Milner, the "vendors" are, of course, the Boers, and the Paxfontein gold farm is our correspondent's happy synonym for Peace.

It is impossible to give the whole series of cables, they would occupy too much space; but two or three may be selected as showing how the chances of peace fluctuated, and how the proceedings of Boer delegates were followed in the columns of the "Daily Mail" day by day.

DETAILS IN COMMERCIAL LANGUAGE.

The following cable gave the fullest details of the friction at the time the delegates left to consult their commandoes:—

Directors left yesterday consult shareholders directorate strongly favour selling and a shareholder really forced directors offer mine for sale deal may almost be regarded settled shareholders fear being frozen out next few months vendors hold plenary rights their sleeping partners being discredited here.

Ratification of agreement may take month. Alf leaves today.

During interregnum between now final settlement our business proceeds as usual your London house probably make statement to their managing committee.

Have already advised vendors price which substantially same offered last year by Centre Mountain Finance Syndicate.

"Centre Mountain Finance Syndicate" is a reference to the Middelburg negotiations, the "last year" is a reference to the Klerksdorp terms, "their sleeping partners discredited here" means that Kruger and the Continental Transvaalers were not considered in the peace of deliberations, while the other allusions explain themselves when once an insight into the meaning of the cable is afforded.

Here is the cable which caused us some days later to sound a warning note:—

Vendors exigent unsurprised if sales lapse objection vendors centre round period elapsing before they granted seat board management they want number seats specified.

Again, translation is hardly necessary. The warning is that the Boers are holding out for representative government immediately on the conclusion of peace, and for representation on the Council which it is desired shall be formed.

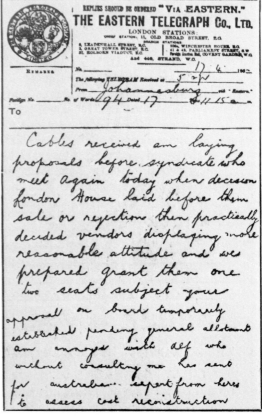

An example of one of Wallace's coded telegrams to the Daily Mail (Daily Mail Library).

When those difficulties were adjusted, there came to the same address in London the following cable:—

Am laying proposals before syndicate who meet again to-day when decision London house laid before them. Sale or rejection then practically decided vendors displaying more reasonable attitude and we prepared grant them one two seats subject your approval on board temporarily established pending general allotment. Am annoyed with Alf who without consulting me has sent for Australian expert from here to assess cost reconstruction.

Stripped of the phrases which are merely there to string together essentials ("am annoyed with Alf" is a picturesque example), it is only necessary to point out that the "London house" is the Cabinet, "cost of reconstruction" means the cost of rebuilding the burned farms.

So, from day to day, there reached the "Daily Mail" offices the latest news from South Africa, and from day to day our indignant contemporaries being newsless, lost their tempers, and sometimes their manners. But it was really very simple after all.

"PEACE ABSOLUTELY ASSURED"

A word may be added on the positive statement made by the "Daily Mail" that peace was "absolutely assured". On this point a separate code had been established. The code word was "Rand Collieries", and favourable news and unfavourable was distinguished by the operations of buying and selling, while the degree of hope or the reverse was governed by the number bought or sold, which ran from one hundred by successive hundreds to a thousand, each variant bearing a different shade of meaning, and a thousand not being brought into use until the deliberations had either been beyond question successful or a failure.

The code itself ran as follows:—

Have bought you:

    100 Rand Collieries 40s. 6d. . . . Situation unchanged.

    200 Rand Collieries 40s. 6d. . . . Situation favourable.

    500 Rand Collieries 40s. 6d. . . . Situation very favourable.

    700 Rand Collieries 40s. 6d. . . . Peace nearly certain.

  1,000 Rand Collieries 40s. 6d. . . . Peace absolutely assured.

Have sold:

    100 Rand Collieries 40s. 6d. . . . Situation unsatisfactory.

    200 Rand Collieries 40s. 6d. . . . Situation very unsatisfactory.

    500 Rand Collieries 40s. 6d. . . . Little hope of peace.

    700 Rand Collieries 40s. 6d. . . . Everything practically off.

  1,000 Rand Collieries 40s. 6d. . . . Everything absolutely off.

To the address — a fresh address — appointed in London came one cable:—

    Have bought you 1,000 Rand Collieries 40s. 6d.

and, with the receipt of this message, the "Daily Mail" knew that the war was over.

'Horror upon horror'

The death of General Koos de la Rey, 15 September 1914

September 15 was a bad day for William Foster. He woke to a quiet morning in the Johannesburg suburb of Regent's Park with his wife Peggy. With them in the small cottage were two friends, a diminutive Dutchman, Carl Mezar, and an American, John Maxim.

By the end of the day, Foster had shot dead Detective Sergeant Charles Mynott, had packed his wife off to safety in Germiston, had the car in which he was fleeing the police break down, and had changed his abode from a cottage to an abandoned mine shaft in Kensington where, with food, drink, a lamp, Mezar and Maxim, he hoped to evade his pursuers.

The police, determined to capture the Foster Gang and deal with them once and for all (Foster, with the help of Mezar, had escaped from Pretoria Central Prison and a twelve-year sentence for robbery and violence in February), threw up roadblocks around Johannesburg. One of the roadblocks was at Langlaagte, on the outskirts of the city.

Travelling towards Langlaagte en route for Potchefstroom in a chauffeur-driven car were General Koos de la Rey and Brigadier-General Christiaan Beyers. De la Rey in particular was a troubled man. He fought with distinction through the first and second Anglo-Boer wars (he was one of the signatories to the Vereeniging peace treaty) and had supported General Louis Botha and the Crown when General J Hertzog broke with the government to form the National Party in 1912.

But, during these early days of the First World War, he felt he could not support Botha's plans to invade German South West Africa (Union troops landed at Luderitzbucht on 18 September 1914). Moreover, De la Rey was sympathetic to the informal agreement among Boer die-hards after the signing of the Vereeniging peace treaty that, when Britain's attention was diverted elsewhere, the struggle for Afrikaner independence would be renewed.

The early flickers of discontent which were fanned into the grassfire of the 1914 rebellion came from De la Rey's stronghold in the western Transvaal, the north-eastern Free State and the north-west of the Cape. No doubt De la Rey, a patriarchial figure with a long, bushy beard, also kept in mind, as he travelled towards Potchefstroom and a meeting with J.C.G. Kemp and officers at the Potchefstroom military camp, the vision of Niklaas 'Siener' van Rensburg of Lydenburg.

Van Rensburg had a graphic vision of a large grey bull, which he took to represent Germany, fighting with a large red bull (Britain), in which fight the grey bull triumphed. He also saw a dark cloud, on which the numerals 15 were stamped, raining blood. Below was a hatless De la Rey followed by a carriage wreathed in flowers. The general took this as a sign that he would be successful in his allotted task.

As the car approached the Langlaagte roadblock, neither Koos de la Rey nor Christiaan Beyers could have been thinking about William Foster or his gang. Reporters from the *Rand*

General De la Rey (South African Library).

Daily Mail take up the story, which was both graphic and extraordinarily detailed. The report of the events which transpired at the roadblock appeared on the morning of 16 September.

HORROR UPON HORROR

GENERAL DE LA REY SHOT DEAD

A most deplorable calamity occurred in the Langlaagte district shortly after nine o'clock last evening, when General Jacobus H. de la Rey, the national hero of South Africa, whilst proceeding towards Krugersdorp in his motor-car was shot through the back of the car by a police patrol and died almost instantaneously. The tragedy, which will be received with poignant sorrow by the whole of the people of the Empire, was directly due to the police precautions which have been taken over the reign of terror launched on the Rand by the bandits in a motor car. The police, both mounted and foot, have been instructed to challenge and hold up any motor car, either by night or day, and, in case of no response from the occupants, to open fire either with revolvers or rifles.

It appears that General De la Rey, who had just returned from his senatorial duties at Capetown, had visited Pretoria during yesterday, and accompanied by Brigadier-General Beyers he left the capital in the afternoon, en route for his farm at Lichtenburg. The party passed through Fordsburg at 9 p.m., and at the top of the rise near Christie's chemist's shop they were called upon to stop by a uniformed policeman, who was armed with a rifle. There was a strong wind blowing at the time, and it is quite evident that none of the occupants of the car distinctly heard the challenge or realised its seriousness. The car proceeded on its way along the road to Mayfair leading to Langlaagte, and the policeman ran to the Fordsburg station, where he communicated what had transpired to the authorities. The number of the car was taken, and the Langlaagte police were warned to hold up any vehicle that came along, and if it did not stop to the challenge to fire.

The orders were strictly carried out as the car passed through Langlaagte village, but again the same sad misunderstanding occurred, due entirely to the heavy wind raging.

The police patrol's warning note rang out in clear accents, but both Generals De la Rey and Beyers and their chauffeur failed to hear the call, and the speed of the car was not checked.

The policeman waited until the car had passed him and then presented his rifle and shot at the back. The bullet passed through the rear and hit General De la Rey, who was seated on the right-hand side of General Beyers, in his back on the spinal cord. To General Beyers' intense horror the aged veteran collapsed and expired almost immediately. The tragedy had scarcely been realised when the car was turned round and driven speedily back to town, where at Fordsburg police station the dead body of General De la Rey was conveyed to the Government Mortuary.

The sadness of the calamity, due entirely to a deplorable accident, will be realised by all classes throughout South Africa.

After the removal of General De la Rey's remains to the mortuary the car remained outside the Fordsburg station, and was the object of morbid curiosity by awed mobs of local residents.

The reporter's facts were not quite correct, but he wasn't to know it at the time. De la Rey was not the only casualty of that night: Dr Gerald Cross was also fatally shot at a roadblock. And the general's death was even more bizarre than anyone guessed. The policeman who opened fire on the car and its occupants was a notoriously bad shot — so bad, in fact, that the bullet missed the car altogether. It hit the road surface, ricocheted upwards and found De la Rey's heart.

The Foster gang was also running out of time. Located by a search party in their Kensington mineshaft, they exchanged angry fire with the police. Reinforcements were called in. A reporter from the *Rand Daily Mail* witnessed the drama that followed — and recorded the following colourful blow-by-blow account.

OPENING UP THE CAVE

FOSTER VISITED BY HIS RELATIVES

There having been no satisfactory sign of a movement in the cave except the shots fired overnight, it was decided by the authorities yesterday morning to open up the entrance again. Detectives Rudd and Martin went down into the cutting to commence the preliminary work of removing the stones, and Sergt. Ling and several constables covered their efforts with their rifles loaded and ready. It was found in the meantime, however, that a crowd was gradually collecting, and the operations on the mouth of the cave was suspended for a while.

Major Douglas, the Deputy-Commissioner of Police, and Mr. H.O. Buckle, the Resident Magistrate, arrived at this juncture. An official of the Public Works Department had been warned to be present, and Major Douglas instructed that a couple of wire fences should be run up, one along the veld parallel with the Kensington tramlines, about 150 yards from the cave, and the other at right angles near the new houses which were being built on the townward side of the cave. Mounted policemen kept the crowd behind these barriers, and the whole work occupied a remarkably short space of time.

It was at 10.30 a.m. that the work of removing the stones from the mouth of the cave was recommenced by Detectives Martin, Rudd, O'Neill and some native police. Crowbars, rakes and picks were used; meanwhile Sergt. Ling, a proven shot, and Detective Fussel lay behind their hastily constructed sangars, ready to shoot if the bandits attempted offence. A dozen constables were also ready, at intervals down the cutting.

While the work was going on a flutter was created by the arrival of a liftman, who declared that there was another exit. He said that as a youth he had often been in the tunnel and versimilitude was given to this statement when he pointed out the old exit to Detective McClymont round the other side of the hill. It was sealed up, however, and had been so for years, and thus perished the last faint possibility of the bandits making their escape.

Progress with the work of removing the stones revealed a small opening into the cave at 11.35, and now the vigilance of the men with the rifles became, if possible, more keen than ever. Not a sound issued, though the detectives listened eagerly at the aperture.

Opportunely at the moment Foster's father made himself known to the police. A sunken faced, slim old man, the elder Foster was obviously highly agitated at the position of his desperate son. He volunteered at once to go to the mouth of the cave. Inspector Hill, who had arrived meantime, ascertained that the father wished to know from his son whether Mrs. Foster and the child were inside. He was given a piece of paper on which he wrote: "Dear Billy: Can I see Peggy or yourself for a moment. From your father — Foster." It was thought possible at the time that Mrs. Foster and the baby might be inside with the murderers, and indeed that was the reason why the police were hesitating to take drastic action.

THE END OF MEZAR

The aperture was made larger by the removal of one or two stones so that the light of day shone strongly into the cave. At this moment — 11.45 — a shot was distinctly heard by those who were close to the mouth, the sound muffled in the tunnel. At the time it was thought that this was a sort of defiance shot, fired when the light shone into the cave, or that in the imminence of his peril one of the desperadoes had pulled the trigger, startled by the phenomenon of daylight in the dark drive.

It is now strongly held that this shot was the end of Mezar, the third and most youthful member of the gang. Whether he was crawling towards the entrance in the hope of escape and was shot by the ruthless Maxim, or whether he shot himself in desperation rather than be caught alive, may never be known. Certain it is that he had been dead some hours when his body was recovered. It was quite cold and stiff.

Meantime the police began their first efforts to communicate with the bandits. There was a prolonged silence after that lone muffled shot. Inspector Leach put his head into the aperture and shouted: "Anyone inside can come out, but come out singly with his hands up. Anyone attempting to come out in any other way will be shot at once."

There was no answer to this, and in view of the fact that the tones were not very loud, it is probable that the bandits did not hear. Inspector Hill took Foster's father to the mouth of the drive and told the old man to shout out his name. In a quavering voice — quavering from agitation — old Foster called out: "Is Foster there? Here's his father, who wishes to see him. Is Peggy there? Can I see either of them? This is Foster's father speaking," he went on in louder tone. "I have got a letter in my hand for you. You will be allowed to come and fetch it. No one will interfere with you."

FATHER CALLS IN VAIN

The old man desisted when there was no answer, and the letter was passed inside on the end of a garden rake. He commenced to speak again in a more assured voice: "William," he said, "is William Foster there? His father wishes to see him or Peggy (Mrs. Foster). There is no betraying about it. I will be allowed to come down or anyone can come up without any interfering." Again there was an interval of silence but apparently Detective Martin heard some whispering, for he shouted: "Foster, are you there?" There was some movement in the drive, and everyone left the cutting except Sergeant Ling, in order to allow of room for any shooting should a rush be attempted. Nothing happened. After a while Sub-Inspector Leach shouted through the opening, using the mouthpiece of a gramaphone as a trumpet, and repeated his statement, that they could come out singly with their hands above their heads. He added: "The police command you to surrender."

Noise was heard in the passage again, and Detective Martin took up the speaking role, using a highly persuasive tone of voice. "I say, Dick," said he, "do you want to come out?" He received some reply at once, for the following words, shouted by Martin, evidently formed part of a conversation.

"Who is that speaking?"

"Is that you, Foster? Do you want your wife to come out? You can come out, but you must come out with your hands up."

"I say, is your wife there, Jackson?"

"Do you want your wife to come out?"

"You surrender?"

"How many of you are in there?"

"Are there three of you?"

"Is Mrs. Jackson there?"

"You're only by yourself?"

"Where is Mrs. Jackson? Whereabouts is she to be found?

"Is that you, Dick?"

RIGHT OH! LAD

"Well, look here, we won't touch you, lad. You march out with your hands up, but there is to be no treachery here. You must not shoot at us while we are pulling away the stones to let her come in. No treachery; will play the game, lad, all right. Right oh!"

"Is that you, Maxim?"

"All right. Good enough."

"Where is she? Is she in Mordaunt Street? Where can she be found?"

"Germiston? What number, lad? 99?"

"Care of Mrs. Doyle, 99, Joubert Street, Germiston. Right!"

"No treachery?"

"All right. That is a fair deal. You will not fire on us while we remove the stones to let her come in."

"Is that Foster speaking?"

"Right, Jackson, lad."

The result of this colloquy was a bustle among the police officials, and Major Douglas's car was sent off to Germiston for Mrs. Foster and the baby. A long silence ensued in the cave, broken only by a faint voice calling for water. It was Foster, who had crept up near the aperture. Detective Martin had apparently received Foster's assurance that he intended to surrender and would not shoot, for he said: "You can have tea if you like."

Two bottles of tea were lowered down on strings and Foster took them. A packet of cigarettes was also thrown through the aperture. While this was going on Foster said that he was wounded in several places. From his ability to move about it would appear that the wounds were not serious. Foster was evidently suffering badly from thirst, but he managed to gasp out a statement to the effect that he was sorry they had had to shoot the policeman. He said that all they were really after was money, not lives.

From one o'clock onwards the crowd grew rapidly. The ground in front of the cave, near the tram lines, soon became black with people, while the kopjes on either side were crowned with dense masses of sight-seers. The place resembled a huge amphitheatre. Yet the crowd could see nothing of the affair, and could only await developments.

FOSTER'S WIFE ARRIVES

Foster's wife arrived from Germiston at a couple of minutes after two o'clock. She stepped down with the child on her left arm — a little girl aged about eighteen months. She had been crying, and hid her face under a faded straw hat. Her clothes had evidently been hastily donned, and she was a pitiful, dowdy little figure. The child on the other hand was wide-eyed with wonder, and not at all abashed. It smiled frequently.

From this time onward the members of the Press and some two score or more detectives and plain-clothes officers were kept away from the cutting and the mouth of the cave. Major Douglas, Sub-Inspector Leach, Sub-Inspector Betts (who came with Mrs. Foster), and Detective Martin, conducted Mrs. Foster, bearing the child, to the mouth of the drive. What ensued in the meantime will be shown elsewhere. At 2.30 the car was dispatched for Foster's mother and sisters, Inspector Giles in charge.

At 2.35 a steel screen was brought in a car. It had been intended to use this as a protection when entering the drive had the bandits proved obstinate rather than suicidal. It was not put into use, because of Foster's apparent willingness to surrender. At 2.40 Foster's father went a little way into the drive, Mrs. Foster being then inside. Foster's mother and two sisters arrived at 3.6 p.m., all three weeping. The two went to the entrance of the drive and spoke with their doomed relative. Mrs. Foster came out of the cutting at 3.40 and climbed into a car weeping. Her two daughters followed ten minutes later, one of them carrying the child. Foster's father followed, and stood near the car.

Four shots were heard, muffled in the depths of the drive, just as the daughter who carried Foster's child was helped out of the cutting. One shot was heard, and then an interval. The two following were fired in rapid succession, and the fourth came after a perceptible pause. There was a stir among the men who were guarding the entrance. The acetylene lights were called for, and Firemaster Hinde hurried along with an electric hand lamp.

After an interval the cave was entered and one emerged with the news that four bodies had been discovered, those of Mrs. Foster, Foster, Maxim, and Mezar.

The snapping open of the breeches of the rifles was the sign that at last police vigilance could be relaxed. The police received the order to unload.

POLICE GO INSIDE

After waiting some time it was decided that a party of detectives should go into the cave. Some thought that the firing of the shots was "bluff", and that Foster and his associates desired to lure some more of the police to certain death. Inspector Hill of the C.I.D., led two other detectives inside.

In a few moments they returned, Mr. Hill carrying two big Mauser pistols. "They are all dead," the officer quietly intimated. Mr. Hill also recovered some ammunition.

Traces of food were found inside, but the bottle of tea which the police had handed in to Foster earlier in the day had vanished.

As dusk was approaching — of course it was quite dark inside the cave — it was quickly decided to carry the bodies out and leave the cave guarded pending a full search to-day.

The melodrama was, if anything, heightened by the description of the scene inside the death cave. Headlined 'The Last Act', the pathos of the scene and the quality of the reporting almost evoked sympathy for the fate of the gang.

After the solemn sound of the shots, muffled as the tones of a funeral drum, there was a prolonged silence; and the armed police turned expectantly to the mouth of the cave. The relaxation of the grip of their rifles indicated the trend of their thoughts. What was anticipated had come to pass. The men had shot themselves.

After the order had been given to discharge the magazines, the guards were withdrawn; and the energies of the police were directed to keeping the crowd always inclined to break through — well away from the cave itself. Nothing remained to be seen but the dead. Why, then, gratify the morbid tastes of the multitude.

Some time elapsed. Presently there came over the veld a solitary motor car, the wheels of which were "shivering" as they sped over the uneven surface, and a yellow dust cloud rose behind. A figure clad in a motorist's overall stepped out, close to the knot of senior police officials. After a few words with Sub-Inspector Miller, he descended the adit; and this very circumstance signified clearly enough that he had come to give formal certificates of death, and to give official sanction for the removal of the bodies. If any doubt remained, the arrival of two mortuary vans, with their coffin-shaped bodies borne on light springs, dispelled it.

Dr. Girdwood made his way into the cave. It was very dark inside. But after making a short journey in he came across the bodies of the dead, revealed in the glare of a pallid light, and making a very ghastly picture. Mrs. Foster lay undermost, a thin slip of a woman, whose soiled white hat and dusty dress bespoke the stress of last hours. She had been shot close to the bridge of the nose, and much mutilation had resulted. Foster, with a dark growth of beard about his chin, his thin, ascetic features, pale with the pallor of death, lay on his back with a bullet wound in the centre of the forehead. His head was resting upon his wife's shoulder; and the assumption is that he killed his wife and then slew himself. It was possible to see that he had been wounded long before in the upper part of the arm; and that the bullet had remained embedded close to the skin. For attempts at excising it were apparent, attempts which had failed possibly owing to the lack of the necessary resolution. His clothes were very dirty; and his face grimy and bloodstained.

Quite close to him was Maxim — the oldest desperado of the party. Curiously enough he had shaved himself quite recently, and the cotton wool bearing the lather lay close to the body. He, also, had shot himself frontally, and the wound was visible in the brow. Very sanguinary the placed looked, and very gloomy — with the shadow of death heavily upon it. Making way further in towards the cul de sac, Dr. Girdwood presently came across Mezar, the youngest and least intelligent member of the gang. He must have been dead for several hours inasmuch as rigor mortis had set in, and his body was stiff and cold. Whether it is correct to say that he shot himself after the cold and the privations of the night, or whether he had expressed an intention to surrender, and had been shot by his confreres (who had sworn never to be taken alive), will perhaps never be known accurately. One suggestion seems as probable as the other, not withstanding Foster's explanation to his father.

After the doctor had said what was necessary to the police, the backs of the mortuary carts were opened, and soon large steel trays were taken therefrom and borne into the caves. They came back with the dead men and woman thereon, covered one and all with blankets. Difficulty was experienced in raising the dead at the horizontal over the rim of the adit; indeed a police officer fell in taking the first stretcher — presumably containing the body of Mrs. Foster. A most unpleasant denouement was thus narrowly avoided. However, the trays were at length safely fixed into the vans, and as they drove off the huge crowds gradually broke up. From kopje, fence and field, people made their way to the Kensington Hill, and soon there was very little left to indicate the dramatic intensity of the happenings in that neighbourhood. The cave was left to the night and to its memories — and the wide vicinity to an experience which is without any parallel in Rand crime.

The *Rand Daily Mail,* intent on wringing as much out of the story as was humanly possible, went on to describe the deaths of William Foster and his gang. The stories are reprinted in their original order.

LAST INTERVIEWS
PARTING SCENES IN THE CAVE

When old Mr. Foster — the father of the young criminal — stumbled back over the rim of the adit after interviewing his son, he seemed to be deeply affected. He was pale and nervous. His hands were alternately moving from side to side, and were then thrust deeply into his pockets. His clothes suggested the following of an artisan, his panama hat was thrust well forward; and his movements in the cave had reflected themselves in the dust of his trousers. His daughter, a young woman, followed him, bearing Mrs. Foster's child, pathetic and conspicuous in its little red cap. She was weeping. All the indications were clearly enough that father and sister had said farewell, not only to Foster, but to Mrs. Foster, and to his companion Maxim.

What had actually happened in the cave? Enquiries indicate the following sequence. The father made his way through the gloom — the darksome place was lit by lanterns — into the middle of the adit, and there saw his son weeping bitterly, with his arm about his wife. The affection which had ever existed between these two, seemed to have been in no wise diminished during the anguish of these last moments — moments literally of blood and tears. It was not fear that caused this weeping — so said the father — but the knowledge that his relatives and particularly his wife, were to see him no more.

Close to where this affecting scene occurred, lay the body of Mezar, stiff and covered over. Foster told his father that the lad had shot himself just before noon, thinking possibly that the removal of the rubble and stones from the mouth of the cave were preliminaries to an attack.

Talk was spasmodic and emotional. In tearful voice the young man spoke to his father of the causes of his downfall, attributed them to the severity of the sentences passed upon him as a lad of eighteen in German South West Africa, and again in Capetown when he was given twelve years for jewel robbery, a sentence which led him to make his attempt to escape from gaol. Close to young Foster stood the swarthy and determined figure of Maxim. "This," said young Foster, "is the man who has stuck to me all through."

"What are you going to do?" asked the father.

"I am going to die," said Foster. "To die here. I have been driven to it," he added with emotion.

After a moment's silence the old man, much affected, said to Mrs. Foster: "You are, I suppose, coming out with me?"

"I don't know," she said after a pause, "I shall see."

Subsequently other affecting scenes took place when Foster's sister arrived, for then the wife of the desperado declared her intention of remaining at the side of her husband and of dying with him.

"For God's sake, come with me," implored old Mr. Foster. "There is nothing against you. The police will only detain you."

"No," she replied. "I am determined to die with him."

'South Africans had experienced their baptism of fire'

The Battle of Delville Wood, 15-20 July 1916

'Shall I ever forget how I jumped over the parapet with my pockets filled with ammunition, my bayonet fixed, and a few score yards away thousands of Germans advancing on us — when behold a deafening explosion took place, and was hurled through space and landed prone on my back, to wake up finding myself confronted by a huge Prussian Guard.

'I gave the matter no consideration but quickly pulled the trigger of my rifle, and he staggered back, shot through the head. Another came in his place, but he experienced the butt-end of my friend's rifle right between the eyes, and as he went down on his knees my pal rammed his bayonet through him.

'I had by this time regained my feet, and like Horatius, I tried to hold them at bay when another shell exploded, knocking me over and landing a hulking big German's body on top of me. There we lay for about 15 minutes, drenched in each other's blood, he dead, and I myself wounded, while several others walked over our bodies.

'I cannot tell you all. Some day when I get home again I will. Dan left for the front this morning.'

Thus wrote Lance-Corporal H.G.H. Kotze of the South African Infantry to his brother at peaceful Oliphant's Kraal in the Cape, after the battle for Delville Wood.

The South African Brigade, made up of volunteers from the Cape of Good Hope Regiment, the Natal and OFS Regiment, the Transvaal and Rhodesia Regiment, the Scottish Regiments in the Union, the 1st and 2nd Transvaal Scottish and the Cape Town Highlanders, reached France on the night of 19 April 1916. Under the command of Brigadier-General Henry Lukin, the brigade took its place in the 9th (Scottish) Division as a fighting unit. On 29 April, the brigade was inspected by Sir Douglas Haig, the new British Commander-in-Chief, and for the following two months was trained in the methods of trench warfare.

On 14 June, training at an end, the brigade was moved to the Somme. It was destined to take part in a summer offensive — attrition on a colossal scale, the aim of which was to crumble the enemy's defence on the Bapaume Ridge by steady, relentless pressure.

John Buchan, an old associate of Sir Alfred Milner, likened this part of France to the high-veld, 'yellow-green ridges and slopes falling away to an infinite distance'. On Saturday, 24 June the main bombardment began, and six days later, at 07h30 on 1 July, the Allied infantry went over the parapets and the battle proper began. On 4 July, Lukin was ordered to relieve the 21st and 89th Brigades, and he and his troops were in position by 03h15 on the morning of 5 July, effectively holding the line between the British and French forces.

Constantly exposed to shelling, sniping and heavy gunfire from front and flank, the South Africans held steady. Brigadier-General Lukin began his pilgrimages along the frontline trenches on that day, steadying his men and encouraging them when they most needed it. He was on his feet for 15 hours.

In spite of losing men (the 2nd Regiment had 200 casualties from shelling alone), the brigade was nonetheless moved up close to the village of Longueval. East and north-east of it stretched Delville Wood, its grassy ridges criss-crossed with German trenches.

Shortly after dawn on 14 July, Lukin was ordered to put his men at the disposal of the 27th Brigade to clear the streets of Longueval of the enemy. When this had been done, he was told to capture and consolidate the outer edge of Delville Wood, the attack to be launched at 05h00, 15 July 1916.

With their shovels the South Africans began to dig themselves in along a 1 200-metre front, with no communication between the units. By 14h30 the wood had been almost taken — now it had to be held.

As darkness fell, the enemy guns increased their rate of fire. Shells were falling at 400 a minute (at Spion Kop they fell at seven a minute), looking like liquid fire against the sky. Holding a wood over half a kilometre square, under intense shelling, bombing and wave upon wave of fresh Germans eager for hand-to-hand combat, the South Africans clung to the south-west corner of the wood against impossible odds.

No food, water or ammunition could reach the increasingly isolated pockets of men; the wounded filled the trenches alongside the dead. Attacked from three sides, from 15 to 20 July, the South Africans held the wood; at 18h00 on 20 July, just as the first eight-cylinder Cadillac in South Africa negotiated Sir Lowry's Pass 'like a bird', their position was relieved.

No reporter was there to describe at first hand the attack: reports of this battle and the five days and six nights of heroism which followed were compiled from military despatches, from interviews with the survivors and the wounded in hospitals in England. Thus, reporters were told rather than having noticed themselves that the men saw larks spinning upwards from the battered and bloodied ridges of the wood and listened, entranced, to the singing of birds in the midst of the shelling.

A Reuters report, printed in the *Rand Daily Mail* and the *Cape Times* of 17 July mentions, albeit briefly, the role played by the South Africans in the overall offensive.

> Sunday — The only references made so far to the share taken by the South African Contingent in the great offensive were contained in a despatch from the "Morning Post" correspondent on July 13 and a message from the Agency's correspondent to-day.
>
> The former merely mentioned that the "South Africans had experienced their baptism of fire," but it is now known through the Agency's correspondent that the South Africans must have been engaged in most desperate assaults, nearly at the extreme right of the British attacking front, and, therefore, close to the French troops.
>
> There is no secret in saying this, for Sir Douglas Haig mentioned the capture of Delville Wood, which is about two miles east, slightly by north, of Combles, which is one of the enemy's most important nerve centres in this region.
>
> It has also been ascertained from the wounded that the men acquitted themselves in a manner of which South Africa may indeed be proud. When the moment arrived to leap over the parapets and enter the zone swept by machine guns, none faltered. There were

Based on rough notes made by an officer in Delville Wood, The Illustrated London News'
*illustration shows 'The gallant South Africans on the Western Front passing over the German
trenches in Delville Wood. The illustration shows the capture of Delville Wood, renamed by the
troops 'Devil's Wood'* (Africana Museum).

just some preliminary handshakes before the leap, and then the South African war cry rang out.

A few minutes later they were at death-grips with the Huns, bayonetting, clubbing and stabbing, but they went on over the German corpses, broken entanglements and man-traps.

A connected story of the glorious part they played is not yet available, just scraps from the wounded, a large percentage of whom are not seriously wounded.

It is no exaggeration to say that the men are very cheery. They feel, as one expressed it, that they had seen and experienced the worst the Germans can do, and that this can be checkmated and beaten by pluck, determination and fearlessness. — Reuter.

On 18 July, South African newspaper readers began to hear more about the battle, although it cannot be said that the news occupied a prominent place in any of the papers in which the Reuters and South African Press Agency reports appeared.

Reuter South African Press Agency.

LONDON

Monday — Conversations with wounded from Ovillers, Bazentin-le-Grand, Bazentin-le-Petit, and Longueval, where the South Africans were engaged, show that the storming of the German second line was characterised by exceptional fury.

The men all knew that it was France's Day, the anniversary of the fall of the Bastille. Some of them had been billetted with Frenchmen, with whom they had become very chummy and could, as an officer said, "parleyvoo like one o'clock."

They rushed from their trenches shouting "La belle France! Vivent les Français!" One wounded officer said that only a few of his men reached the German line unwounded.

Many who were hit went on with the others. Some jumped into enemy trenches weaponless, others turned over when hit like boys turning catherine wheels and then rushed on again with hardly a check.

Said one: "There never was such a scrum. The men did not need Bosche bayonets. They were just like raging devils with their 'Français for ever.' They tackled the Bosches with bare hands. One section commander, like a terrier with rat, grabbed one Bosche by the slack of his breeches and neck, chucked him over the parapet yelling: 'Fall in there.' When that trench was finished, the men cleaned out the dug-outs with German bombs."

In one short despatch from Reuters, the name of Delville Wood appeared for the first time, although it is doubtful from the sketchy reports whether the South African public could have gained any idea of either the battle or the South African role in it.

Monday — Delville Wood, where the South Africans distinguished themselves, lies 300 yards ahead of the village of Longueval. The South Africans co-operated in smashing the Prussians in Longueval, the capture of which in 25 minutes is described in Paris as one of the most brilliant operations seen up to now in the Battle of the Somme.

Our men then pushed on to Delville Wood, which was stormed after an obstinate resistance. The Germans suffered heavy losses.

Here, as in Trones Wood, the Germans fought to the death, many being bayonetted. Duels were fought in which both combatants were pierced and thus fell dead. Every other tree bore machine gun men. The latter when shot fell to the ground or their bodies were caught and suspended in the branches.

A similar toll was taken of the enemy in the grim fighting in all the captured woods, but special praise is bestowed on the South Africans, than whom, says a correspondent, he never saw finer and fitter men. — Reuter.

'No historian's pen can give the memory the sharp outline and glowing colour which it deserves,' wrote John Buchan. 'Only the sight of the place in the midst of the battle — that corner of splinters and churned earth — could reveal the full epic of Delville Wood.' It was only on 26 July that something of what Buchan described as 'an epoch of terror and glory scarcely unequalled in the campaign' began to reach South African newspapers.

Tuesday — The Agency's Special Correspondent at the British Headquarters says the story of how the South Africans fought for mastery in Delville Wood against overwhelming odds will go down as a great epic in South Africa.

The correspondent says the South Africans for several days remained in their fire-swept fastnesses. Their slogan was: "If the South Africans do not gain their objective it will be because there are no South Africans left."

How they took Delville Wood and how they were finally driven back to the confines of the shell-wracked clump has already been related, but what has not been told is the tale of valour filling the teeming interval between the two facts.

From behind innumerable stockades, from many batteries shrapnel, lachrymatory and high explosive shells screamed and crashed among the splendid South African troops who toiled strenuously to consolidate their position, but the task of digging themselves in on ground porous as a sponge from the interminable pounding of shells proved well nigh hopeless.

Yard by yard the depleted remnants were forced to yield ground that nothing living or breathing could hold. When it seemed that the men could no longer cling to the spot a Colonel rallied the remnants of his battalion and for two solid days defied the Germans.

Finally when relief came the pipers of the South African Scottish headed the blackened and weary warriors to rest at their quarters, skirling the pibroch as though at a review, whilst the lads roared the refrain.

Tuesday — Details of the terrific fighting in which the South African Brigade was engaged in the battle of the Somme are still being published.

Correspondents to-day state that the South Africans, in conjunction with the High-landers, were, in Delville Wood and in Longueval, subjected to a fire which, those competent to speak on the matter agree, was worse than anything previously experienced.

As already known, the South African Contingent by their dashing attack seized Delville Wood and were called upon to face the whole might of the enemy, who launched fierce counter-attacks.

These were pressed with such strength and determination and in such force that the South Africans were driven back. They were then joined by some battalions of High-landers.

Presently, by battalions, companies and platoons, the Scotsmen and South Africans rallied, and together they charged from a half-destroyed improvised trench and drove back the advancing masses of the enemy.

This heroic exploit of shell-shocked, wounded, sleepless and battle-worn troops saved our thin line.

217

A precious reinforcement of South Africans, with guns, arrived at the critical moment and assisted this mixed force to capture their original objective, which they still hold.

Monday — Fresh batches of wounded members of the South African Contingent are arriving in England from the Somme battle. The result is that the staff of the South African Hospital at Richmond is kept exceedingly busy. All cases are making progress, and up to the present there have been no deaths among the patients there.

On 29 July more details began to emerge. On that day, the *Cape Times* quoted extensively from the London *Daily Mail* beneath the headlines 'How South Africans Fought' and 'Stirring Story of the Battle of Delville Wood':

Friday — In the course of a stirring despatch, which describes the Longueval—Delville Wood sector as "almost the grimmest battlefield of the whole war," Mr. W. Beach Thomas, the "Daily Mail" correspondent, writes:

A group of South Africans, who had already borne the brunt of the fighting, asked that they should not be relieved. They fought unceasingly for a week, few sleeping. One company became separated in the night and found themselves in possession of a trench, against which they heard the enemy approaching from both east and west.

The South Africans did not respond to the enemy's bombs, but waited till the Germans were close up. The Springboks then hurled themselves on the Germans, whom they fiercely attacked with rifle and bomb, driving them back in a panic.

In this grim business some of the South Africans were at one time fighting literally back to back, some facing east, some west. The remnant finally escaped, only to attack once more with other troops.

"The history of Delville Wood has not yet reached a climax," concludes Mr. Beach Thomas, whose despatch was written before Sir Douglas Haig's gratifying announcement that the wood is now wholly in our hands.

What the despatch omitted, however, were the figures. At midnight on 14 July 1916, when Lukin received his orders, the brigade stood at 121 officers and 3 032 men. When the first remnants emerged from the wood on 20 July, the Brigade stood at 143 — three officers (two of whom were wounded) and 140 other ranks. When everyone was finally assembled, the total number of men was no more than 750.

Brigadier-General Lukin, who had been slightly gassed, stood bareheaded, with tears running down his cheeks, as the remnants of his brigade paraded past.

'This Pentecost of calamity'

The influenza epidemic of 1918

The Spanish Influenza had arrived unobtrusively in South Africa in September 1918, on board two ships, SS *Jaroslav* and SS *Veronej.* The ships, both of which had stopped at Sierra Leone, where the epidemic was raging, had sick men on board. The patients were taken from Cape Town harbour, where the ships had docked, to the military hospitals at Rosebank and Woodstock. By 23 September 1918, the influenza had begun to spread.

Influenza had been reported on the Transvaal mines on 18 September. Kimberley, which was to be particularly hard hit, began to succumb on 23 September, Cape Town on 25 September and Ladysmith and Pietermaritzburg on 30 September. The symptoms were unpleasant but tolerable: headache, pains in the chest, back and limbs, giddiness and high temperatures.

Pooh-poohing the epidemic, *The Cape Argus* (now *The Argus*) discounted the 'scare' rumours on 24 September in an authoritative and somewhat pompous article which stated that the only record in Cape Town of an influenza death in the last two months had been that of 'a coloured man from Natal'.

But within two weeks of that article's being printed, the deaths began. People did not, in fact, die of influenza, but of pneumonia, which struck with horrifying speed, favouring men over women and people in the 25–45 year age group. By Friday, 4 October, 5 000 people in Cape Town had 'flu; by 31 October, nearly 123 000 had gone down with it – and the deaths had reached a total of 6 342. Reports of the calamity began coming in from all over the country. Local correspondents were roped in from all over the place and, as they fell ill, others stepped into the breech. The *Cape Times* of 24 September 1918 carried a brief Reuter South African Press Agency report of the epidemic on the mines, sandwiched between press agency news of the dying days of the Great War.

SPANISH INFLUENZA

Many Cases Among Rand
Mine Natives.

Reuter South African Press Agency.

JOHANNESBURG.

Monday — A serious epidemic of what is believed to be Spanish influenza has broken out among the natives employed on certain mines in the central areas.

The disease first made its presence known on Sunday, when a number of natives were taken ill.

To-night it is ascertained that 110 natives are affected on the Village Main Reef out of about 2,000; on the City and Suburban 204 out of about the same number, and on the Ferreira Deep a much smaller number. Several Europeans are also affected.

It is presumed that the germs of the disease were brought by some person or persons from England by the last mail.

So far there do not seem to be any dangerous cases, although all the cases are distressing.

By 24 October, the epidemic was rife throughout the country. Brief despatches, some refreshingly homely, were printed in *The Cape Argus* of that day.

HAVOC WROUGHT BY EPIDEMIC

Pretoria, Wednesday

There have been up to date close upon 500 deaths in Pretoria from the epidemic, probably a third of these being European deaths. While the local arrangements for visiting and accommodating the sick are now almost perfected there is yet no justification for assuming that the situation has reached its gravest point.

Yesterday, Dr Barry, Superintendent of the Hospital, succumbed to the complaint, while early this morning the death occurred of Mr A.H. Mortimer, of the first of Tindall and Mortimer, solicitors, one of the best known and widely respected men in the town and late Chairman of the Pretoria Club.

A considerable number of the cases now under treatment at the hospital are of a grave character, pneumonia having succeeded a too early attempt at convalescence on the part of victims to mild attacks. The Government officers are suffering considerable inconvenience as a result of the illness of a great number of the staffs.

Graaff Reinet, Wednesday.

The number of fresh cases shows a decrease, and the opinion is guardedly expressed that the epidemic is yielding to the efforts to combat it. The death-toll is steadily mounting, the total registrations up to last night being 227, consisting of 190 coloured and 37 Europeans.

Aberdeen, Wednesday.

The epidemic is increasing here. On Saturday Miss de Kock, the newly-appointed teacher from Van Wyk's Vlei, succumbed, and two European deaths were reported from the district. On Tuesday there were two European deaths in the town. Mr. Piet du Toit, a well-known farmer of Wynberg, in this district, died last night. Mr. J.A. Vosloo, secretary to the School Board, and Mr. Willie Clarkson, have also passed away. There have been about 10 coloured deaths in the last few days. There are about 300 European and 250 coloured cases in town, and about 100 in the district. Everything possible is being done by the local official bodies and the relief committees to cope with the sickness. All business houses are closed each day from one o'clock. The morning markets and schools are closed until further notice.

Caledon.

A correspondent writes that up to October 22, 976 cases had been reported, and there had been nine coloured deaths and one European. The European hospital has been opened but the difficulty lies in securing workers. The organisation to cope with the epidemic is very good. Not many cases have been notified from the district, but the epidemic seems to be getting hold there. In Caledon the matter is well in hand, and they appear to be over the worst.

Stellenbosch, Wednesday.

The Mayor (Mr. P.D. Cluver) and Sir Thomas Smartt to-day met representatives of the local licensed victuallers, who, in the interests of combating the epidemic, consented to close all bars, canteens and bottle stores for the supply of liquor to Europeans and coloured people alike until November 1. Exception will, however, be made for liquor required for medicinal purposes, which will be supplied on certificate. The licensed victuallers having been thanked for their action, the hope was expressed that other districts would follow the public-spirited example set by the licensed victuallers of Stellenbosch.

Thirty-four deaths were reported at the Magistrate's office on Monday representing deaths on Sunday and Monday. Twelve were reported yesterday and four to-day. The epidemic appears to be abating.

The University of Stellenbosch will remain closed till December 2.

Worcester, Wednesday.

The epidemic here is still at its height, and it is estimated that fully two-thirds of the total population has been affected. Numerous fresh cases are daily reported to the visiting committee. Thirty deaths (mostly those of coloured people) were registered to-day, and 18 yesterday. Both temporary hospitals are now full of cases.

Tulbagh, Wednesday.

The community has sustained a very great loss through the death of Mr. Jan W.L. Bonthuijs, who has for several years been carrying on a successful general dealer's business here. The death, which took place yesterday afternoon, was due to an attack of Spanish influenza.

Kimberley was particularly hard hit. *The Diamond Fields Advertiser,* jammed with stories, filled page after page with tightly written copy. On 5 October, between stories headlined 'Austria on the Bulgar Surrender' and 'Italian Thrust on Albania', *The Advertiser* declared that Kimberley was in the grip of the epidemic.

KIMBERLEY IN THE GRIP OF THE "FLU."

Epidemic Continues With Serious Consequences.

YESTERDAY'S HEAVY DEATH TOLL

112 Succumb at Dutoitspan Compound.

More Voluntary Helpers Needed in Hospital and Town.

Nursing and medical staff, Kimberley, towards the close of the 1918 flu epidemic which decimated the town (McGregor Museum).

The strain at the Hospital having become so acute, owing to the excessive numbers of cases being admitted, suffering from the prevailing epidemic, the Board strongly appeals to any (either ladies or gentlemen) who are willing to assist in relieving the pressure at present being borne by the Nursing Staff. All information may be obtained from the Matron or the Secretary.

ARTHUR J. GREEN,
Chairman.
J. R. BOOTH, Secretary.

Kimberley continues to be a big sufferer from the ravages of Spanish influenza, which yesterday had a firm grip of nearly half the population, the death rate amongst the native element being nothing short of appalling. The serious nature of the menace which has taken toll of a further large number of native lives is giving cause for grave concern, especially in view of the shortage of medical men and nurses, but despite this handicap every effort is being made to fight the disease and prevent its spread. Among the mining natives, in particular, the epidemic has continued to rage upon a most alarming scale, and so numerous have been the native deaths that the number registered during the four days of the present month already greatly exceed the average rate for any one month in the year. We are informed by an old resident that a similar disease was prevalent in Kimberley some 26 years ago — during the months of August and September, 1892 — although the outbreak on that occasion was not merely half so severe.

Yesterday's death roll was a heavy one. So far as we have been able to gather, it may be estimated that somewhere about 150 natives succumbed, making to date a total of approximately 210. The malady has been especially virulent in the Dutoitspan Mine Compound, where 112 natives had died yesterday — up to the time of enquiries made late in the day — but so far the cases at the Wesselton and other compounds have been comparatively few. From enquiries made yesterday afternoon we were glad to have the assurance that as the day progressed there had appeared to be indications of a slight decrease in the rate of infection at Dutoitspan. Reports from the other compounds also appeared to indicate that the situation there was improving rapidly, but it was, however, considered too early to make any definite statement as to what the course of the epidemic in those compounds might be. A very large number of the white employees of De Beers Company have also been affected, as well as other European residents, but generally speaking the severity of the attacks is much less than in the case of the natives.

Apart from the compounds, 26 deaths were registered from the locations and other places. This total also included three deaths of Europeans, among them that of a mounted policeman named Roeloff Petrus Oelofse, who had been ill for four days. The deceased was buried yesterday afternoon at the West End Cemetery, and was accorded a military funeral, a firing party consisting of twelve of his comrades being present at the graveside, together with Inspector C.C. Baines and Sub. Inspector Ball.

Five further cases from the Kimberley Gaol are included in the figures given above, as well as five from the Convict Station. The military authorities report that one coloured corporal succumbed to the disease yesterday.

The virulence of the disease, the rapidity of its development, and the rate of mortality, amongst the compound natives, have been far in excess of any similar conditions that have ever obtained on the Diamond Fields, or, it is safe to say, anywhere else in South Africa. The whole of the De Beers staff and workmen able to render service in any capacity in connection with the outbreak have been at work night and day from the first. The most valuable assistance has been freely given by employees in every department. The Constance Williams and Loveday Smith nursing divisions of the S. John Ambulance Association have worked magnificently. The most highly trained nursing organisation could not have done better. The great value of first aid training has rarely been more conclusively shown. The work that has been done by these ladies would need to be seen to be adequately realised and appreciated. The members of the organisations named are entitled to the gratitude of the whole community. We should particularly emphasise the splendid efforts of Miss Tyre and Nurse Knight. The work is necessarily carried on under the most distressing conditions. In all respects, however, the requirements have been most efficiently met, and the volunteer nurses are sticking to their task with a degree of zeal and devotion which could not be exceeded, even on the western front.

As emphasised elsewhere, more assistance is urgently required, and in particular at the Kimberley Hospital. We are asked to bring this matter to the notice of ladies and other potential helpers, in the strongest and most emphatic terms. Men as well as women are asked to come forward and assist. The appeal is to all, whether Europeans, coloured, or native. The Hospital staff is working under the most strenuous conditions of stress and strain. If the present and prospective needs are to be provided for, it is absolutely imperative that an adequate measure of voluntary assistance should be forthcoming. Those who are willing to give their services, to whatever extent their circumstances may enable them to do, are earnestly requested to communicate with the Secretary to the Hospital Board, Mr. J.R. Booth. There is accommodation for further patients, but it would be futile for the doctors to send them there unless there were adequate means of attending to their needs. The Hospital authorities are not, of course, asking for trained nurses. They want the assistance of anybody who is prepared to come forward and help in whatever direction their services can best be utilised. The Board will welcome the help of any who have the time to give, and who are prepared to make themselves useful. They need not be trained and qualified ambulance workers. If there is any considerable increase in the number of white cases — and it is necessary to be prepared for anything that may happen — it goes without saying that there will be still further demands upon the Hospital resources. The doctors cannot possibly attend to so large a number of patients at their own homes. Those who require personal medical attention must needs be sent to the Hospital. Already there are numerous cases for which the doctors are seeking admission. There must, however, be adequate provision for nursing and attendance. We hope, therefore, that the appeal under notice will be responded to as it deserves, and that those of the public who are so fortunate to escape infection will co-operate generally with the authorities in whatever measures may be found practicable for fighting the disease. It is only by prompt and adequate attention, including medical aid and careful nursing, that there can be any hope of coping with such an epidemic.

The locations are also heavy sufferers, and the death-rate within these municipal areas does not appear to diminish. Excellent work, however, in connection with the distribution of soup, and the supplying of medicines and medical comforts, is being continued, and a further appeal is made for more volunteers to assist. The military authorities have been communicated with, with a view to securing the services of more nurses for Kimberley. Mrs. Teychenne, Mrs. Calder, and Miss Gore-Browne are helping Father Blackman to render yeoman service, while Mr. J. O'Brien and his willing staff energetically continue to assist in combatting the disease.

The outbreak continues to further dislocate the customary business activity of the city, whilst many forthcoming fixtures and events have had to be temporarily cancelled. Business generally is at a standstill, if only from the fact that the majority of assistants in the stores have been taken ill, or have consented to render voluntary aid in coping with the malady. The medical profession and chemists are, of course, working at high pressure in their efforts to meet the many demands made upon them, some of the chemists finding it necessary to keep their doors open until a late hour.

There was no Court work (either civil or criminal) at the Government Buildings yesterday.

Owing to the outbreak it has been decided that the town schools under the control of the Kimberley School Board will not be reopened until further notice.

We understand that the big drapery and boot stores in the city will close at 6 o'clock this evening, instead of 9 o'clock, in consequence of the epidemic.

The Acting Mayor desires to notify that families suffering from the present malady, and who are unable to prepare their own soup, can obtain supplies of soup between the hours of 11 a.m. and 12 noon, and 5 and 6 p.m. daily, at the City Hall Kitchen (adjoining the Market Hall — on the eastern side), on presentation of a recommendation from either a doctor, clergyman or members of the committees of the European or coloured benevolent societies. The Acting Mayoress, Mrs. Colin W. Lawrence, and Mrs. G.J. Boyes will be in charge. Applicants must provide their own receptacles.

It will be seen that the Acting Mayor notifies through our advertisement columns that the services of a capable woman are required for visiting and assisting families suffering from the disease. Applications in this connection should be made to the Town Clerk. It is also desired that ladies will offer their assistance in attending households in town which are in need of such help. Those willing to assist in this capacity are asked to notify the fact to the City Hall. Residents who know neighbouring households so badly placed in consequence of the epidemic that they have no one to attend to their comfort and physical requirements are invited to communicate with the City Hall authorities in order that soup and, if necessary, nursing assistance can be supplied to such households.

On 2 October, there were 630 cases in the main convict station, 2 000 at the Dutoitspan Mine. One woman, a voluntary helper giving out milk and brandy (food was running short) told a reporter that 'a man would stretch out his hand for the cup and drop dead before he could take it'.

By 7 October, nearly half the population was in bed: streets were deserted, the trams silent, businesses closed. On 10 October, 10 000 whites, 6 400 coloureds and 23 000 blacks were down with 'flu. Kimberley was like a giant hospital.

Of the 10 doctors in town, only six were well enough to do anything. Because the numbers were so overwhelming, only families whose members had all gone down with 'flu were visited. The signal to the doctors was anything red displayed outside. Hot-water bottle covers, red bathing trunks, ties, and unmentionable items of underwear were all used.

By the time the epidemic abated, 4 861 were dead, 3 743 of whom were black.

In De Aar, terrified blacks refused to bury their dead, so railways staff did it for them. In Beaufort West there were only two able-bodied railwaymen left – one acted as slaughterer, the other as the undertaker. In Oudtshoorn an old Bushman remedy, Ysterbosch tea, was being hailed as a cure. Of a total staff of 75 000, 35 000 railway personnel were ill. But the railways somehow continued to operate, delivering food, medical supplies and materials.

In Cape Town, coffins were unobtainable. Deaths rose to 300 a day. Nigerian troops, lent by the military command, dug graves. A special correspondent, writing in *The Cape* on 26 October, told the story of how voluntary services were organised in the midst of fear and chaos.

THE WOMEN AND THE CITY.

WHAT THEY HAVE DONE TO FIGHT THE SCOURGE.

(By A Special Correspondent.)

On Saturday, October 5th, we were still mildly chaffing about "flu," teasing those whose families were down with it and laughing at the inconvenience we, in common with all our friends, were suffering. On Monday, the 7th, we had realised that we were in the grip of a deadly epidemic, which was taking such toll of the town that hundreds were dying daily, that the supply of coffins had run out, and that all ordinary arrangements for attendance on the sick and the dying and the dead had broken down. Furthermore, the situation was complicated by the discovery that the whole normal life of the town had come to a standstill; that no food shops had been open since Saturday and there was no probability of any food being distributed through the ordinary channels for some days. In other words, a large part of the population of Capetown was faced with starvation unless drastic steps were taken — and taken at once. The realisation of this was due to three women; the Mayoress (Mrs. Thorne), Miss Mabel Elliot and Mrs. Hartnoll. To these three women the salvation of the town is due, and if, later on, some measure of acknowledgement is made, the names of these three women must head the list.

How the Work Began.

At the meeting called by the Mayoress on Monday, the seriousness of the position was explained, and the whole population, with the exception of those themselves in the throes of the disease, came forward with offers of personal service, and before the day was over 24 depôts (afterwards increased to 42) were opened, and by 8 o'clock on Tuesday morning soup was made and ready for distribution. These depôts were at first simply stations for the distribution of soup, milk and medicine, but as time went on their functions were increased until, with the closing of the City Hall on Saturday, the 21st, they became the chief organisation for dealing with all distress.

The task of coping with the disease outside, arrangements for efficient medical control, disinfection of streets, houses, etc.; transport of supplies, and of the sick and dying; making and disposing of coffins, etc., were left to strong men's committees and must be spoken of elsewhere. This article only deals with the women's share — by one who was inside the City Hall and was able to appreciate the extent and wonder of the work done.

The Controlling Executive.

A small executive, consisting of the Mayoress, Miss Elliott, Mrs. Hartnoll, Mrs. van der Byl, Mrs. Abdurahman, and Mrs. Marshall, was formed, and the various steps necessary for dealing with the multitudinous problems which presented themselves were taken in hand at once. Mrs. van der Byl unfortunately fell a victim to the disease at a very early stage, and it was realised that Mrs. Marshall and Mrs. Abdurahman were faced with such urgent calls in their own districts that they could give no time to executive work, so Mrs. Zoutendyk and Mrs. C.B. Martin, who were both in attendance at the City Hall, were co-opted to share the responsibility of the executive.

By Wednesday morning most of the depôts were in full working order, and the numbers appealing to them for help were so great that it had been realised that all supplies must be delivered in bulk, and the central organisation had set itself to the task of getting together the huge quantities of meat, groceries, milk, vegetables, etc., necessary for supplying the various depôts; and before long the huge hall presented the appearance of a big provision store. Later on, as the quantities requisitioned became greater and greater, it was realised that the thing was getting a little out of hand, and Mr. Stuttaford and Mr. Cartwright, responding instantly to S.O.S. signals sent out by the Mayoress, came down to the City Hall and, continuing on the lines already indicated by Mrs. Zoutendyk and her colleagues, brought order out of what was threatening to become chaos.

The Appeals for Help.

It must be remembered that all this organisation, so hurriedly brought into being, was created in the midst of the most appalling calamity that Capetown has ever known. No one had time to sit down and think out the best methods of working, and each one had to act on his or her own initiative and responsibility in the way that seemed best, and that action had to be taken while the hall was a seething mass of people coming for relief under the most ghastly conditions — fathers, themselves in the throes of death, came begging food and succour for their loved ones; tiny children, often the only survivors of whole families, came for help; wistful mothers, with drawn, haggard faces, begged for the bread and soup which meant life for all they held dear. As the roll of helpers increased and it became possible to send out visitors to the houses, more and more horrible conditions were revealed. Stories of whole families dead and dying, of the urgent need of crêches for the little ones, so suddenly bereft of all help; of the tragedy of expectant mothers with no help at hand in their dark hour; of the impossibility of doctors dealing with the terribly serious cases which were reported — not hour by hour but minute by minute. Crêches sprang into being almost magically; hospitals were opened; the medical services were organised on a panel basis, and the Peninsula divided up into zones and circles, so that each house could be visited and the condition of its inmates ascertained. Mr. Kipps and his helpers, who were in charge in the vestibule, where applications for medical relief were to be made, had a terrible time dealing with the innumerable cases needing help. There were few tears in the City Hall those days — just numb, helpless misery; people were stunned by the suddenness and hideousness of the catastrophe, and the needs of the still living were so insistent that the sorrow for the dead had to be postponed. Those waiting for help for others themselves collapsed while waiting, and the dread spectre walked through the hall, breathing in the faces of those who were trying to stem the ravages of the disease. Many of those who so freely offered their services gave their lives before many days were out, and others became too ill to fight longer, and though as the days went on and it was realised that the disease was more under control the atmosphere lightened, there were many heavy hearts for those who would never return again.

Deeds of Heroism.

Of the individual deeds of heroism that were done it is impossible to speak. Of that brave band of men and women who went from house to house, seeing the most appalling

227

sights, bringing comfort and succour to the stricken homes and returning again and again to the Hall for supplies, no words can speak adequately. Their brave, set faces as they told of the needs of those they were helping will remain with many of us as a deathless memory. Each member of the community nobly did his share, from the humblest boy scout to the doctor and the nurse, taking their lives in their hands as they went on their never-ending rounds, shouldering their burdens and accepting their responsibility in a way that is beyond all praise.

Of the aftermath of all this sorrow there has been no time to speak. That Capetown can ever go back to the condition of filth and overcrowding which this epidemic has revealed is unthinkable. No word of creed or colour or race or class was raised during those dread days, and those of us who love our city, and whose joy in her is one of our dearest possessions, are daring to hope that in this "Pentecost of Calamity" she will find her salvation, and phoenix-like rise from the ashes of her dead past to a cleaner and more beautiful future.

By the beginning of November the epidemic was on the wane. The death notices, sometimes filling two pages of a newspaper, had shrunk to manageable proportions. The official figure of 140 000 recorded deaths is thought to be some 60 000 less than the final total of what is assumed to be 200 000. (Many of the non-registered deaths were those of blacks.)

'Strikers gathered in the main street and sang "The Red Flag"'

The Rand Revolt, March 1922

'It was a day of pitched battle, of very real warfare, carried out under the very eyes of thousands of spectators — men, women and children'

The 1922 Strike, or the Rand Revolt as it is more popularly known, was precipitated by the British government's announcement towards the close of 1921 that it intended returning to the gold standard at the parity enjoyed before the start of the 1914-18 conflict.

The Chamber of Mines, therefore, took steps to accommodate what would be a fall in the price of gold from its height of £6.5 to £4.2 per ounce, the statutory gold standard price, and a fall of 35 per cent.

In order to keep mines in production, the Chamber of Mines decided to bring down labour costs as one way of solving the problem. In order to achieve this, the Chamber reasoned, the number of skilled white mine workers (who could earn up to £500 a year and whose wages had risen 60 per cent to the blacks' 9 per cent) would have to be reduced.

Announcing its intention of ending the Status Quo Agreement (the 1918 agreement ensuring job reservation for white mineworkers), the Chamber of Mines came into direct conflict with its miners. On 31 December 1921 a joint meeting of the unions concerned decided to issue a strike ballot, and came out on strike following an ultimatum from the Chamber of Mines on 10 January. It could have been foreseen that the strike would excite emotions, but no one could have anticipated to what extent it would go before it ended in the middle of March.

Many of the strikers formed commandos and began drilling for what looked suspiciously like an insurrection. Smuts watched the situation carefully but did not interfere. 'Let the two parties fight it out,' he said.

By now 22 000 men were out on strike. Under the leadership of the charismatic Percy Fisher, a member of the newly formed Communist Party of South Africa and a member of the strikers' Council of Action, the more militant among the strikers were urged towards direct confrontation with the authorities.

When police protection was granted to strike-breakers, the mood of the strikers turned ugly. The Chamber of Mines' insulting letter — received by Percy Fisher on 4 March — in reply to the South African Industrial Federation's request for a round-table conference, further goaded the miners. '. . . The members of the Chamber are occupied with the winning of gold and they see no reason why they should discuss their business with representatives of slaughtermen and tramwaymen.'

On 7 March a general strike was declared.

As the situation deteriorated, cars and taxis were overturned, the water supply to Krugersdorp was cut off and Benoni fell to the insurgents. Explosions could be heard. Outside the Johannesburg law courts, police were taken by surprise by a commando and were fired on. At Ellis Park soldiers queuing for rations and temporarily unarmed, were fired on, leaving eight dead and 15 injured. Commandos gunned down blacks on the mines. The Rand was in revolt.

During the following week, as open rebellion boiled all along the Witwatersrand, reporters of the *Rand Daily Mail* filled the papers with reports literally from the battle front. The stories they filed are models of reportage under fire and in great confusion. On 8 March, the *Rand Daily Mail* reported:

QUIET MORNING IN TOWN.

A NEW COMMANDO.

BANNER BEARER LOOKING FOR HIS SHEEP.

In town this morning "all was quiet on the Potomac" except for the voices of the orators who have certainly had great opportunities to cultivate the art during the strike. At the bottom of Market Square a number of strikers were "sitting easy" or as easy as they could on the coping of the fence, and there were no signs of unrest until the Post Office was reached. There at 10.30 had gathered a large crowd of sightseers and through them in silence marched a new commando, of quiet behaviour, well dressed, and of all ages from young boys in knickers to old men wearing glasses. For five minutes they marched by the Post Office to the monotonous order of "right left," wheeled to pass the Town Hall and continued down President Street to take their seats orderly in the Town Hall where they prepared to receive oratory. The passing of this quiet commando left the centre of the town strangely quiet.

All the shops stood open, their windows rich in display of dress goods, jewellery and eatables, and a few ladies absorbed in their morning's commission disappeared into the open doors or emerged with small parcels heedless of the crisis. So calm were they that one is prepared to believe that if Eloff Street were engulfed by an earthquake they would gather at the chasm to pick up bargains.

Restaurants were open. Menu cards announced the fare to be prepared for the luncheon hour, though the words "social revolution" were scrawled across one of them. Another notice announced that those engaged in catering, bars, breweries, wine shops, and mineral water factories were to attend a meeting at 10 a.m. to "discuss the position." Another notice being the contents bill of the strikers' journal announced the birth of a "Revolution in Johannesburg," and the dawn of a "new future," the regular future that comes with each breath having apparently deceased prematurely. Returning to the Post Office "the dreary dribble of deadly declamation" had set in beyond all hope. A gentleman in blue had climbed to the flat top of a square pedestal, and there, reinforced by two glasses of amber liquid, was prepared to hold the fort till breath gave out or his throat cracked. The objects of his attack were the "Capitalists," and though he denounced them with the utmost sternness the logic proved rather dull, and the banner-bearer of the Citizens' Commando, truculent yesterday, set off alone in search of his lost sheep. So the position remained at 11, but there were whispers of something going on at Vrededorp, and there was a complete absence of police, mounted or afoot, beyond the calm points-men, who in the decrease of vehicles enjoyed a rare time of leisure.

A Graver Aspect

About noon a striker carried the news to a commando at the Town Hall that there was a "scrap going on with coolies and Chinese," and immediately the commando broke up and raced down on foot and on bicycles to the nest of small houses fronting Becker, Bezuidenhout and Fox Streets at the lower end of Market Street and adjoining the fruit market. The trouble did not originate with the coolies and Chinese. What happened was that some natives, infuriated by last night's affair at the Cemetery, chased strikers whose identity was disclosed by the wearing of red rosettes. "You see," said one shopkeeper, "the coloured people are growing frightened and angry too. They fear that they will be attacked and they don't know what for. They are getting excited — and we too — and other people in this part are alarmed." In his opinion this was not a "right state of things," and the brown faces framed in coloured head dooks looking out from every door and passage leading to rookeries showed anxiety. One coloured boy, whose wild eyes plainly enough showed that he was near the dangerous state of "running amok," loudly declared that he had a "right to live." He carried with him a thick stick quite as formidable as those carried by the best armed of the strikers. At this stage the vanguard of the racing strikers appeared and a coloured man promptly bolted, though others of his colour remained stoically at the doors and windows. One striker burst open a door leading to a corner house whose upper windows were filled by coloured women. There he stood by and waited for other strikers to rush in and do whatever business was expected of them. Two or three entered and came out at once, not relishing the job. Mounted police appeared at the end of the street and went off at a gallop in pursuit of other strikers who had gone on. Then a body of foot police appeared and for the time there was quiet — a smouldering quiet.

No one likes being pushed around. Operators at the Johannesburg telephone exchange gave short shrift to their more militant sisters and in doing so provided the reporter with some wonderful tongue-in-cheek copy, which was tucked away on a page of a *Rand Daily Mail* filled with the more serious events of the revolt.

PLUCKY TELEPHONE GIRLS

VISIT OF THE PETTICOAT COMMANDO

Slapping, Scratching and Bad Language

Yesterday afternoon about 3.30 an attempt was made by the Petticoat Commando to pull out the girls at the Telephone Exchange, but to their honour, in spite of the most trying circumstances, not a single one left the switchboard.

Work was proceeding quietly both in the clerical department and in the operating room when the main entrance was rushed by a body of women who were accompanied by a few youths.

They were escorted by a troop of the Citizens' Commando, who remained downstairs, telling the women to do the job.

The women rushed up the staircase shaking their fists at the girls they met, calling them scabs, and using language in which "damn" was among the gentler epithets.

Part of the way up there is a restroom where the girls off duty were assembled. For a time the occupants held the door against the intruders who, however, by weight of numbers at last forced it open.

"How dare you be on duty when a general strike has been called?" shouted one lady. "How dare you walk about the streets instead of minding your homes and babies?" was the retort. Hereupon, the invaders began to scratch and slap the girls and bit one girl in the arm, who promptly replied by hitting her assailant over the head with the prong of her exchange headgear, which lay near at hand.

This had a salutary effect, and the commando went higher up. They were met at the head of the stairs by an official, who tried to talk reasonably to them. The ladies replied by slapping his face, and dragging him downstairs, scratching and swearing, and had it not been for the arrival of the police, it is probable that he would have been still more severely handled.

IN THE OPERATING ROOM

Forcing their way into the operating room the women made speeches and sang the "Red Flag" and did their best by way of "moral (sic) persuasion" to disturb the workers. But in vain; the girls stuck to their posts and continued to manipulate the switches. The arrival of the police had a somewhat quieting effect, and an officer in bland tones said: "Ladies, I give you three minutes to disperse."

The air was blue with language that would have reduced a bargee to bitter tears, but recognising that discretion is the better part of valour the ladies departed, promising to call again.

The public may well ask what manner of women are these who, throwing aside every shred of decency and womanly reserve, behaved like wild cats to their own sex and used language of the foulest kind.

Are we to take them as representatives of the womenfolk of the strikers, or are they merely hangers-on in search of excitement?

If it were the former, then God help the South Africa for which the strikers profess to be fighting, but we are justified in assuming that these women represent a very small minority of their sex, and that their menfolk would much prefer them to remain at home.

DAY OF FIGHTING IN FORDSBURG

LARGE NUMBER OF CASUALTIES

PRACTICALLY A PITCHED BATTLE

ROADS SWEPT BY BULLETS

MANY POLICE CAPTURED

HOW THE SHOOTING BEGAN

MUCH INDISCRIMINATE FIRING

70th Day of Coal Strike.

61st Day of Gold Strike.

5th Day of General Strike.

Yesterday was the climax of the industrial war on the Rand.

Early in the morning pitched battles commenced between strikers and police at Newlands and at Benoni.

In the former, the strikers overpowered a small force of police and armed themselves with the captives' rifles and ammunition.

At Benoni there was a battle in the neighbourhood of the Workers' Hall, starting at about dawn, and in the fierce street fighting that followed there were fearful casualties on both sides.

Aeroplanes participated in the fray, and Capt. Carey Thomas, observer of one of the machines, was shot through the heart.

This 'plane, flown by Col. Sir Pierre van Ryneveld, made a forced landing, but Sir Pierre escaped.

At Brakpan an appalling tragedy occurred, 2,000 strikers attacking the Brakpan Mine, where, after the resistance of ten special constables and a number of officials had been overcome, two of the latter were taken on the veld and shot after capture.

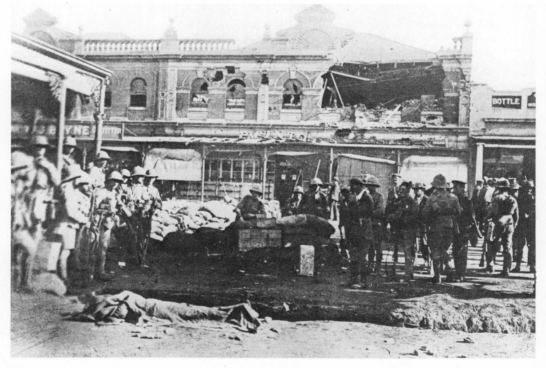

Some of the damage done by shells and bombs in Market Square, Fordsburg. By the time the photograph was taken, the revolt had been quelled (Cape Archives J8175).

There was a blaze of fighting at Fordsburg in the middle of the morning, which continued all day.

The casualties were heavy on both sides, and by evening the strikers had built a sandbag barricade across Main Road, near Market Square.

Probably the culminating event of the whole day was the blowing up of the Benoni Trades Hall by an aeroplane bomb, at 5 o'clock in the afternoon.

Throughout the morning guerrilla warfare raged in Fordsburg, indiscriminate firing taking place and most of the roads being swept by snipers.

The casualties in this street fighting were heavy. The Red Cross afforded little protection; and although a number of dead and wounded were removed throughout the forenoon, there were reported to be many bodies lying in the roads.

During the whole of the morning the sound of fitful rifle fire came from the direction of the operations between the police and strikers.

One of the many fights centred around a group of houses and the Robinson Dump. In or near the houses, which are closely adjacent to the Main Reef Road, a number of men with rifles were located.

POLICE IN THE DITCH

A body of police took up a position in the ditch beside the road, with others some little way up the dump itself.

Nearer town, towards the dip, a big crowd of sight-seers gathered.

The police were fired on from amongst the houses, and replied from the roadside and the dump. Two horses were shot in the road, and the bodies remained where they fell.

About one o'clock shots from the strikers sounded nearer town. Some of the armed men apparently got into the road leading townwards from Ferreirastown and were firing in various directions.

The police holding the roads near Marshall Square seemed to expect a rush in that direction and the horses were quickly taken under cover and the men lay down on the pavements, with rifles at the ready, facing Ferreirastown.

RIFLEMEN ON BUILDINGS

High buildings in the vicinity were also manned by strong parties of riflemen. But the expected rush did not come.

Instead, the firing continued at intervals on the far side of the Fordsburg Dip. Crowds stood about in Commissioner, Fox and Main Streets, in the centre of the town, and stared apprehensively westwards. Ambulances came and went continually. Private cars with big Red Crosses sped towards Fordsburg and returned to town bearing the casualties to the General Hospital.

Thus the terrible affair continued for some hours giving rise to the wildest rumours owing to the impossibility of obtaining detailed information of what was happening.

Fordsburg became the centre of the trouble between 11 and 12 o'clock in the forenoon, and the affair developed into what was practically a pitched battle between the commandos and the police, in which the strikers captured a considerable number of prisoners.

An eye-witness states that no one knew that martial law had been proclaimed during the morning, and that on the sound of the bugle the commando formed up as usual on the Fordsburg Market Square.

234

COMMANDO'S MOVEMENTS

A body of mounted police went up the main street and turned into Park Drive. The commando also marched in the same direction, both bodies of men being in apparently good spirits. The commando went into Park Drive and then broke into smaller bodies, which proceeded down various side streets.

The next thing was that considerable firing was heard. The strikers and police had apparently joined issue near the Robinson and Bonanza Cottages, at the back of Fordsburg, and some distance above the Dip.

Fordsburg was thrown into a tremendous state of excitement, and the firing continued for some while. While it was still in progress, a number of the mounted section of the commando came galloping down the main street with a rifle and fixed bayonet, a bandolier and a horse, which had apparently belonged to one of the troopers.

STRIKER FIRES UPON SIGNAL BOX

A striker armed with a rifle took up a position on some corrugated iron buildings near Cuthbert's and opened fire with deliberation upon the signal box. There was a replying fire from that direction, and the bullets sped across the main street, one of them splintering a window of Messrs. Christie's chemist shop.

About half an hour later there came a lull in the firing, and the bulk of the commando marched back, bringing with them as prisoners eight policemen and about six horses. The policemen had been stripped of rifles, bayonets and bandoliers.

DESULTORY SHOOTING

Desultory shooting continued, and every now and then a report rang out and a sniper's bullet sped down or across the main street of Fordsburg.

About twenty minutes after the first batch of prisoners were brought in, another detachment of the commando returned bringing a few more policemen and horses.

So far as could be seen, none of the prisoners were wounded.

The main battle area at first seemed to have been Crown Road, Mint Road and Central Road, but after the affair had developed there was tremendous indiscriminate firing all over the place.

After the Bonanza fight had died down, the commando took possession of the public lavatory on the Fordsburg Market Square and turned it into a block-house. In the early afternoon they were busily engaged in filling bags with sand — some hundreds of sacks having been procured — and building a barricade around the lavatory and across the road. At this time it was stated that the commando, as the result of its captures in the morning, had a considerable number of rifles and a quantity of ammunition.

29 POLICE PRISONERS

The headquarters of the strike in Fordsburg, the Mine Workers' Union office, is in Market Building, within a stone's throw of the lavatory. This was strongly held, and at 2 p.m. it was reported that inside the strikers had 29 policemen as prisoners.

A rumour widely current in the disturbed area during the day was that the strikers had issued a statement that they would shoot these men if artillery was brought to bear on their strongholds.

Another eye-witness gave the following account of yesterday's extraordinary happenings in Fordsburg:—

235

He stated that at 10 o'clock, when news was received at strike headquarters to the effect that the Trades Hall in Rissik Street had been raided by the police, and that the augmented executive of the S.A.I.F. had been taken away from Goldreich Buildings, trouble began at once.

HOW NEWS WAS BROUGHT

A despatch rider brought the news of the raids, but hardly had he arrived when came the news of the proclamation of martial law. This in itself apparently was to act as a pre-arranged signal for mobilisation by the strikers.

Bugles blew, and in a few seconds men came from all directions, carrying various weapons to the Market Square. Five minutes later shots were heard, and then firing of a more or less continuous character set in.

It was soon seen that the police were firing along the Central Road and across the tram lines. A spectator standing on the corner of the cross-roads outside of the Mynpacht Hotel was seen to stagger, lurch forward, and drop dead. A few minutes later a second individual, a youth apparently, was seen to drop within a yard of the first casualty.

THE CROWD SCATTERS

The crowd by this time had almost wholly disappeared. In fact people vanished round various corners along the road going towards the mines.

Defenders of the barracks, and the police forces on a dump close by, were sweeping the roads clear so far as was possible. The strikers retaliated by firing revolvers and shot guns. Here and there they made use of rifles.

By this time, from the Johannesburg side of the Fordsburg dip, it almost appeared as if a general engagement was in progress extending over a front of almost a mile — across in a straight line from the Robinson Mine dump to Fordsburg in the direction of the railway.

The strikers had protected themselves in sandbag redoubts, and in some cases were making use of bags of sugar and flour removed from a store.

INTERMITTENT FIRE

Experienced shots maintained an intermittent fire up the road towards Mayfair when, it would appear, there was a force of police over the crest of the hill, bullets whistling down the main street from that direction. Commandants walked calmly about signalling instructions up and down Main Street and the various intersecting streets, namely, Lilian Road, Central Road, Mint and Crown Streets.

At all these corners men were stationed.

Firing was kept up mainly at the mine ends of the streets and the spectators were ordered to keep on the sidewalks and under cover.

Main Street, right from the Fordsburg dip to the top of Mayfair, was absolutely cleared, bullets coming not only up and down, but from the cross streets also.

The only signs of activity were the movements of Red Cross ambulances conveying their burdens to the mortuary or the hospital. Orderlies, carrying big Red Cross flags, crossed the fire zones on their errands of mercy, and many had narrow escapes.

WOMAN KILLED

A doctor passed through in a Red Cross ambulance, calling out that he had a woman with him, and upon inquiring it was ascertained she was the mother of a mine captain, and had been shot dead in the presence of the doctor who was talking with her at her own door.

Whether it was accidental or otherwise, or from what direction the bullet came, could not be ascertained, but it was learned that the doctor himself had had a narrow escape from bullets at this spot, although he was wearing a conspicuous Red Cross badge.

About 11 a.m. a squadron of mounted police galloped from Marshall Square, taking the Main Road and going to the support of their comrades, who were holding the approach to the mines.

From this time onwards the firing became more intense, and the police at the barracks also strengthened their crossfire.

FIRE SLACKENS

Fire then commenced to slacken on the part of the strikers. Judging from the difference in the sound of the bullets — the rifles from the police having a very distinctive note. Here and there shots rang out and then a few sharper reports from near the back of the police station. At 12.20 p.m. a shout went up. "Clear out of the way, the police are coming." And there was a mad stampede into passages and shop fronts. The alarm,

A guard of the Transvaal Scottish going on duty outside Park Station, Johannesburg (Africana Museum).

237

however, was a false one, for the galloping patrol proved to be strikers armed with rifles and bandoliers. At the sight of these the strikers set up a lusty cheer, to be repeated when the news circulated that the police had been overpowered at Newlands and that their rifles and ammunition had been taken from them.

The whole situation underwent a complete change. A runner came in from the mine dump shouting: "The police are round at the back and we can get at them."

Other men with rifles quickly appeared on the scene as if by magic and these reinforcements crept up by various ways to attack in the direction of the mine. Shortly after 1 p.m. one of the marksmen on a sandbag emplacement in Macintosh's store, was seen to spring on the parapet and excitedly wave his arms.

POLICE CAPTURED

It seemed a foolhardy thing to do with bullets all round, but the reason was soon apparent when round the corner of Crown Road there appeared a procession of police, fifteen or twenty in number, headed by the Red Cross and escorted by strikers. They had all been captured and disarmed. They went into the strikers' headquarters amid tremendous cheering from the strikers, who, heedless of bullets, crossed into the streets from the sidewalks to witness the remarkable sight. It was stated that their officer was killed before the police surrendered.

Another terrific yell went into the air when round the same corner came another procession of police prisoners, about 30 in number. This made the total captures, as far as could be ascertained, between 40 and 50. With the additional weapons from the captured police, there was no lack of volunteers from among the strikers who hastened to the front along the side streets towards the dump where there was increased firing activity.

There were, of course, casualties, and at the street corners appeared men with white armlets, waving to the ambulance.

There was a lull in the battle from 2 p.m. onwards. Firing died down considerably, but occasionally single shots, and a volley from the dump, rang out. The firing was now mainly towards Fordsburg Dip, and not so high up the hill as previously. Bullets flicked up the dust in the main street beside the tram lines. The news from the front at this time was that the police on the dump were being isolated and surrounded.

At 3.30 p.m. the strikers gathered in the main street and sang the "Red Flag."

During the afternoon a proper military trench was constructed across the main street opposite Macintosh's store, and near the strikers' headquarters.

On Sunday 12 March, Johannesburg residents woke, in the words of the *Rand Daily Mail,* to the 'dull boom of bombs' and lived through one of the most extraordinary days in the by no means dull history of the city. The *Rand Daily Mail* of Monday, 13 March carried an account which could hardly have been bettered had it been a visual television report so succinctly descriptive was it:

WARFARE IN VIEW OF THE PUBLIC

AN AMAZING DAY

SQUADRON OF AEROPLANES IN ACTION

ARTILLERY IN STREETS OF PARKTOWN WEST

HOW THE REBELS WERE BEATEN

The dull boom of bombs, awakening all but the furthest eastern suburbs of the town, roused Johannesburg yesterday morning to one of the most amazing days in its history.

It was a day of pitched battle, of very real warfare, carried out under the very eye of thousands of spectators — men, women, and children.

The people who sought the high buildings, or proceeded to the kopjes near the Fort or the Fever Hospital (writes an eye-witness), saw a wonderful sight. In the bright, early-morning sky, four aeroplanes were wheeling and turning over the kopjes above Auckland Park.

The big Government school on the crest overlooking the tram-line just to the south of Menton Road, was a conspicuous landmark; and beyond it the land rose in a wide green slope to the houses at the top of Vrededorp. The planes had the appearance of an ordinary civilised landscape, such as any part of Johannesburg might present on a clear and bracing Sunday morning.

But the great mechanical-birds buzzing round and round over the school, the kopje, the houses and the open space were birds of prey.

The Brixton kopjes were being bombed from the air.

ALIVE WITH REVOLUTIONARIES

The whole of the landscape was alive with revolutionaries — members of what was known as the Vrededorp Commando, with some of the Newlands men; it is believed, in support.

The school was their stronghold, while the ridge of the kopje was also manned with revolutionary riflemen. Their firing pointed into the Auckland Park police camp in the dip, and this and the post in the Show Ground they had been attacking more or less continuously for two days.

The Government force had held out manfully, and in fact, some of them were actually in the position of having enemies on all sides. When the four aeroplanes came over yesterday the first thing they did was to drop a message of encouragement and congratulations from the Minister of Defence to the besieged police.

The aeroplanes passed over the kopje, and a moment later, the first big explosion sounded.

The revolutionaries are stated to have had a machine gun at the school. At any rate, the dropping of the bomb was followed instantly by machine-gun fire, and a volley from the rifles as well.

This, however, had no effect on the airmen. The 'planes swept around in their great circles, now high, now low, and every minute or two an explosion followed the dropping of a bomb.

CROWDS WATCH THE FIGHTING

A great number of people had by this time gathered on the crest of the hills nearer town or in certain of the streets at Parktown West, from which ordinary residents of the town had the unusual experience of watching a battle virtually over their breakfast.

The bombing went on for about an hour, and in this time 32 bombs were dropped.

The baptism of fire from the air was obviously not to the liking of the revolutionaries holding the kopjes. There were a number of surrenders, and the position of the surrounded police was effectively cleared.

Afterwards there was a lull in the fighting. Between 10 and 11 o'clock there was feverish activity, on the part of the motor transport, and some hundreds of troops were ordered to certain positions. At one time there was a mile of motor cars in one of the Parktown roads, while in another spot three guns of the T.H.A. quietly took up their positions in the middle of the road, close to the houses.

At 11.20 there were five aeroplanes circling over the area held by the revolutionaries. The Government troops were being moved in considerable bodies.

In response to the signals from the sky, the forces nearest to the school took cover, the aeroplanes drew away, and a sharp crash from the battery of guns split the air.

SPURT OF FLAME AND SMOKE

To the spectators it seemed there was simultaneously a spurt of flame and smoke just on the left of the school. The second gun fired a moment later, just over the building, and it was not long before the fascinated spectators saw what appeared to be a direct hit on the corner of the building. A chimney was awry afterwards.

Sniping from the school and from the broken ground on the right was the only reply.

Some rebels came out of the back of the school after a few shells. They could plainly be seen running across the open space — some of them going up to the right towards the ridge, while others went into the compound south of the school.

Shells continued to burst. The guns played on the open space for a while, and presently a party of the revolutionaries seemed to find the school unhealthy, and ran for a sort of hollow on the right.

As soon as the gun-fire died down the fight was taken up vigorously by the rifles, and machine-gun fire was almost continuous.

It was at 11.45 that the infantry made a rush from the police camp on the Show-ground. They advanced at the double, quickly covering the open ground and the Auckland Park tram-line. A fusilade from the kopjes had no effect on their forward rush. They swept the whole ridge with their machine-gun fire and then advanced half way up the ridge.

The rifle duel between the Government forces and the revolutionaries was at its hottest at this point. One body of the strikers deserted the school, skirted the ridges as if to go off in the direction of Brixton. The Government forces came still further up, and came round the corner of the school building — the last of the defenders having apparently cleared out.

The khaki-clad figures spread out like a fan as they passed the school and went higher up the hill. Finally they pushed their way right to the top, and incidentally they cleared out a donga which had been powerfully held for two days.

The strikers who moved to the crest of the ridge and expected to escape that way were mistaken. Excellent use had been made of the motor transport, which had hurried troops to points which the revolutionaries had never suspected. Thus it was that the retreating men found themselves between two fires.

The revolutionaries in this section soon saw that the game was up — and surrendered.

An aircraft on its way over Johannesburg to reconnoitre Fordsburg before the final bombard-ment (Africana Museum).

The final shootout occurred in Fordsburg on 15 March. Smuts, in full control of the situation, ordered leaflets to be dropped, telling 'all persons well-affected towards the government' to leave Fordsburg by 11h00. At precisely that hour a fierce bombardment began.

On 16 March Percy Fisher and fellow conspirator H. Spendiff were dead. In the shattered room in which they died a note was found, saying 'I died for what I believed to be right — the Cause'. It had been signed by both men on 14 March.

The *Rand Daily Mail* reflected on the tumult and violence of the previous day, sketching for readers the devastation which, but one day previously, had been Fordsburg. The revolt had been crushed.

THE RED REIGN

SCENES AFTER FORDSBURG BATTLE

DEADLY GUNNERY

MARKET BUILDINGS' TERRIBLE POUNDING

RIDDLED WITH SHELLS AND BULLETS

HOW THE LEADERS DIED

Deserted, battered, tragic, pathetic — Fordsburg bore very deeply yesterday the scars of the battle of the previous day.

The dull, heavy sky lowered over a scene such as a suburb of Johannesburg has never before presented in all the city's turbulent history, and the atmosphere was gloomy and depressing with the weight of the unbelievable tragedy which had been so lately enacted there. To walk from Johannesburg along the tram route, up the Dip and towards the Market Square was to leave civilisation and to enter a "No Man's Land" of horror and destruction, lawlessness and death. Crowds followed the road yesterday morning, impelled by the fascination which such scenes exercises over many minds. Only a few yards above the Dip they came upon the first signs of the frightfulness of the red reign — the trolley-wire of the tramway pulled down and entangled around the standards at the sides of the street. A little further, and the corner window of a hotel, with 26 bullet holes around and through it, was eagerly pointed out.

The pavement near by was a mass of almost-powdered glass from the window of a shop, whose contents had been looted, the door smashed, and the internal fittings strewn about as if by a mad elephant.

THE WAY BARRED

But here a soldier stood in the middle of the street with rifle and bayonet, barring the way. And the curious sightseers saw no more.

The full horror and tragedy of the ordeal which Fordsburg had undergone at the instance of the "Reds" was hidden from all save those whose business took them further into the place. Behind the sentry the rise of the road swept up bare and deserted to the spot where the barricade still stretched from side to side. A police officer and a few khaki-clad figures could be seen standing or moving in its vicinity. But the rampart had lost its dread defiance it had exhibited before, even when seen through glasses from the town. Its double row of sandbags was sodden and beaten down, and the space between the sentry and the barricade was just — war.

For a distance of a couple of blocks below the Red stronghold — the Market Building, which rises gaunt above everything else — there are the signs of the shattering effect of the shells fired into Fordsburg in Tuesday's battle. The left of the road as one proceeds westward has escaped surprisingly. The upper window of a corner hotel, pierced with bullets and with others bespattering the plaster all round, shows where a sniper had drawn a burst of machine-gun fire; on "snicks" in roof or doorway show the track of a revolutionary bullet from the Market Buildings. The real damage here is confined to the right-hand of the road.

EVIDENCE OF ARTILLERY FIRE

Above the spot where a bottle-store and a boot-store have been smashed in and looted, the observer reaches the spot where the direct bits of the big guns were registered on the roofs and frontages of shops in the block next below the Market Hall. A shell dropped on the roof of Messrs. Conry's pharmacy, reducing it to splinters. An iron girder which had supported the verandah lay torn and bent in front of the store, while several of the verandah-poles had been snapped like pipe-stems and lay in the gutter.

The splinters of the plate-glass windows absolutely carpeted the pavement yesterday, and a little higher, when one reached Sack's Hotel, one noted how the scars of the gun-fire became more thick on approaching the Market Buildings. The roof of the hotel was twice pierced by the guns from the southern side of Johannesburg; while a great gaping hole in the gable on the corner of the street tells that the marksmanship of the men on Brixton kopjes had been just as deadly.

On the opposite side of Lilian Road, the clock in the tower of Market Building still ticks the time of day — despite a bullet-hole in the face, and as indifferent as time itself to the tragic events just past. But it seemed almost the only portion of the building which was intact.

A window fronting Sack's Hotel hung splintered from its cords, and a rag of curtain fluttered outside. A chimney had been so pierced that one could see the light of the sky on the other side. In the corrugated iron roof of the eastern wing are two holes where shells had penetrated, while two or three more had gone smashing through the wall itself. The windows which over-looked Main Road are shattered.

EXTENT OF BARRICADE

The barricade stretched from the western corner of the Market Building to McIntosh's grocery store, and there were ample signs that the deadliest work of the whole grim day was done here. A picture of the demolished upper front of the store — where a whole wall was smashed by a direct hit from a shell — has already been published in the "Mail". But one must see the spot to judge of the ferocity of the machine-gun fire which swept the barricade during the attack by the forces of the Government.

Somewhere on the Johannesburg side of the dip there was a machine gun, which literally sprayed the sandbag rampart with lead. The bags show the deadly accuracy of the fire plainly; while the big plate-glass window of MacIntosh's which is exactly opposite, is pierced by nearly 50 holes of bullets. An enfilading fire must have been poured in while the Government forces were advancing on the Market Square of such ferocity that no one could have been left alive on the barricade. Curiously enough, the window is not shattered, but clean pierced by each separate bullet.

TRENCHES ONLY THREE FEET DEEP

The brunt of the shell fire fell on the western side of Market Building, and on the open Market Square and the trench system by which it was defended. The trenches were only about three feet deep and could have afforded little shelter from the hail of shrapnel bullets sprayed around as the shells burst. The probability is that the Reds never intended to make their big stand here, but to retire into the building when threatened; but a peep into the interior of Market Buildings showed how sadly mistaken were the revolutionaries if they expected shelter here.

The Red occupation had left the place indescribably filthy. As the peaceful residents in the many single rooms and flats comprised in the building abandoned the place to their violent neighbours, the latter ransacked everything. Chests of drawers were smashed open; boxes were turned out. Women's apparel lay littered all over the place, beds were broken, and amid the hideous disorder lay the scraps of provisions, tins, and empty bottles left by the revolutionaries. A stale smell pervaded everything.

It was into rooms such as these that many of the shells made their entry. One, on the

His Majesty's Land Ship Union *commanded by Major Briese, an ex-Witwatersrand Rifles Officer, was sent to attack the strikers' headquarters in Fordsburg. But when the tank reached Fordsburg Dip, something went wrong with the engine and only one caterpillar operated, with the result that the machine went round in circles. A steam truck belonging to the municipality was sent to the rescue and towed the tank into the grounds of the power station (Africana Museum).*

second floor, had been turned into a bomb factory. Here, when the soldiers burst in, they found numbers of bombs of all sorts and sizes — crudely made, it is true, but nevertheless capable of doing incalculable injury to property and of inflicting the most cruel of wounds.

ACTIVITIES OF FISHER AND SPENDIFF

Fisher and Spendiff are said to have presided over this department of the Red affairs. They were there on Tuesday — at least, this is the most generally accepted version of their fate — when the bombardment began. A shell entered through the corner of the wall and burst in the middle of the floor. When the soldiers arrived they found Fisher lying just inside the door and Spendiff on the other side of the room — Spendiff having no fewer than five shrapnel wounds. The two men had paid the penalty of their leadership in this appalling affair.

Surveying the whole scene of battle from the vicinity of the Market Square, one sees that the work the guns had had to do was mercifully done. The fire was directed with the utmost skill on the Reds' stronghold, and that alone; and the effort to spare all other property has been surprisingly successful. The whole damage is confined to as small an area as possible. Not a shell fell in Mayfair; and beyond the one devasted area around the Market Building, Fordsburg, despite its hour's bombardment from two directions is just as if the nightmare of the Red revolution had never been.

LEADERS FATE

WHAT HAPPENED TO FISHER AND SPENDIFF

SHRAPNEL SUPPOSED TO HAVE KILLED THEM

DIRECT HIT ON THEIR ROOM

The deaths of P. Fisher and H. Spendiff have given rise to many rumours. One story is to the effect that the men were shot on the roof of Market Buildings, Fordsburg, by machine gun fire while they were engaged in sniping. A second story is that they committed suicide on Monday night when they found that a considerable number of their supporters were wavering and could not be forced into keeping up a determined front even at the point of the revolver. A third rumour is that they were shot by their own comrades who wished to surrender.

In all probability Fisher and Spendiff were killed by shrapnel fire from Marshall Square. Their bodies were found in a room on the second storey of Market Buildings facing the tram lines. The room in question is situated midway between the clock tower and the flag pole, from which the red flag flew until the assault and surrender.

The room in which the bodies were found had sustained a direct hit from the artillery, the shell having pierced the roof and then penetrated the ceiling at the north-eastern corner.

The shell burst in the room itself and the walls are bespattered with bullet marks. Nothing living in the room could have escaped destruction and doubtless the two ringleaders were there together at the time, and both were killed practically simultaneously.

What added a certain amount of support to the theory of suicide was the fact that on

Monday, the eve of the assault, Fisher, knowing the seriousness of the position, made his will.

In this, it is stated, that he left assets worth £2,000 to his wife, and laid a special charge upon her to keep Mrs. Spendiff should the latter need assistance. The terms of the will are stated to be of such a character as to make it perfectly clear that both men fully contemplated death in the immediate future. The will probably was the ordinary precaution of a man of some little means on the eve of great danger from which he would scarcely expect to emerge alive and he wished to put his affairs in legal order before meeting his fate.

The funeral of Fisher and Spendiff will take place to-day (Thursday) from John Swift's funeral parlour at 10 a.m.

The revolt over, a shaken Johannesburg gradually resumed its everyday life. There had been considerable loss of life: the armed forces alone lost 230 men. Over 800 people were brought to trial, 46 of whom were charged with treason and murder. Four were executed. The miners went back to work at reduced wages.

'I am not guilty of poisoning my son!'

The trial of Daisy de Melker, 1932

It took three hours and forty minutes for the judge, Mr Justice Greenberg, to give his findings on the facts on the case of Mrs Daisy Louise de Melker.

Granting the 46-year-old thrice-married Mrs de Melker permission to sit while he delivered judgment, Mr Justice Greenberg reviewed the evidence heard over the sensational 30-day long trial.

The court was filled with spectators, many of whom had queued overnight to get a seat; outside, more than a thousand people waited, hoping to catch a glimpse of the woman whose trial, with its seemingly inexhaustible series of allegedly poisoned husbands (two) and one son, could hardly have failed to catch the imagination of the public.

The Crown's case was that Daisy de Melker had murdered two husbands, Messrs Cowle and Sproat, by administering strychnine to them, and her 20-year-old son, Rhodes, by putting arsenic in his coffee flask. The motive was greed: all three men either had money or, in the case of her son, an insurance policy.

'I am not guilty of poisoning my son,' said Daisy de Melker in response to the Register's request that if she had anything to say before sentence was passed on her, she should say it then.

Covering the trial for *The Star* was Benjamin Bennett (who went on to write many books on murders and court cases with which he had been associated as a reporter). His colourful report of the finale to a dramatic trial was rushed onto the streets of Johannesburg in *The Star*'s City Late edition on Friday, 25 November 1932.

MRS. DE MELKER SENTENCED TO DEATH

GUILTY OF MURDERING HER SON

ARSENIC ADMINISTERED IN COFFEE

THE ONLY PERSON WHO HAD ACCESS TO THE FLASK

COURT REJECTS OTHER MURDER CHARGES

LARGE CROWD WAITS ALL NIGHT TO HEAR VERDICT

247

Mrs. Daisy Louisa de Melker, aged 46, was found guilty by Mr. Justice Greenberg today of the murder of her son, Rhodes Cecil Cowle, and sentenced to death.

The Court found that the death of Rhodes Cowle was due to arsenic administered in a flask of coffee by Mrs. de Melker.

On the other two counts — the murder of her first husband, William Alfred Cowle, and of her second husband, Robert Sproat — she was found not guilty, the Court holding that the evidence of strychnine poisoning was not conclusive.

The courtroom was crowded for the last act in a drama that has lasted for 30 days and many had queued all night for seats. Mr. Justice Greenberg's judgment lasted three hours and 40 minutes, and at the end of it he intimated that the fulfilment of the sentence rested with the Governor-General in Council.

Mrs. de Melker will be transported to Pretoria within the next few days and will be lodged in the gaol there to await the decision of the Governor-General in Council as to whether the sentence of death shall be carried out.

When the Court resumed this morning the judge first dealt with the application made by the Crown yesterday for the calling of further evidence.

"We have come to the conclusion," he said, "that this should not be done, but that the case should be decided on the evidence before us."

"I AM NOT GUILTY OF POISONING MY SON!"

LAST SCENES IN DRAMATIC TRIAL THAT LASTED 30 DAYS

"I am not guilty of poisoning my son!"

In these words, in a voice broken with emotion and the strain of a trial which had lasted 30 days, Mrs. Daisy Louisa de Melker replied to the formal question of the Registrar when he asked her if she had anything to say before sentence of death was passed upon her for murdering her son, Rhodes Cecil Cowle, by putting arsenic in his vacuum flask of coffee.

Mr. Justice Greenberg, in the calm, even voice in which he had for the previous three hours and 10 minutes given his finding on the facts before him, in the course of which he had found Mrs. de Melker not guilty of poisoning by strychnine her first, and second husbands, W.A. Cowle and Robert Sproat, then passed sentence of death, pointing out that its execution or otherwise rested with the Governor-General in Council.

CROWD'S LONG WAIT

The tiny isolated figure in the dock, dressed in black, turned unseeingly towards the steps which led to the cells below.

The crowds which thronged the court, mostly of women, jumped to its feet to see her go, and then swarmed out into the everyday bustling life of Pritchard Street.

It had come early, that crowd, determined not to be cheated of the smallest detail of the closing scene of the spectacle it had mustered to watch with such avidity day after day for six weeks. Some people in it had been there since the night before, and had passed the hours of darkness camping out on the steps of the Supreme Court, with thermos flasks and blankets. Others had crept up in the wan light of dawn to find themselves even then at the end of a long queue.

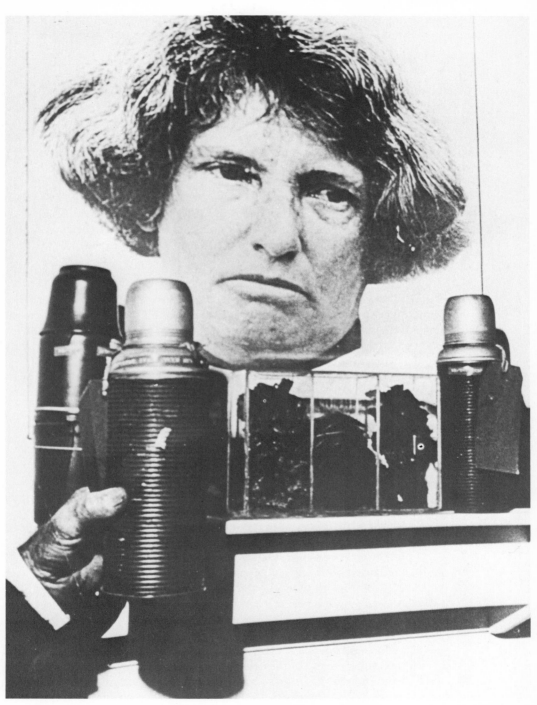

Mrs Daisy de Melker and the vacuum flask of coffee in which she placed the arsenic which killed her son (The Star).

As soon as the doors were opened a mass of humanity surged into court and in a minute or two not a seat was left in that part of the court reserved for the public.

THE COURT RESUMES

Gay laughter and chatter of conversation were momentarily hushed when Mrs. de Melker appeared in the dock to await the arrival of the judge and the two assessors: but broke out afresh when she had taken her seat. Her face looked haggard and drawn and she looked straight in front of her to the small door on the bench through which would issue presently the judge in whose hand her fate lay. She seemed to be almost unconscious of the presence of the crowd, and mechanically sipped a glass of milk handed to her by a warder.

The rustle of the upstanding multitude heralded the entry of Mr. Justice Greenberg and his two assessors, Mr. J.M. Graham and Mr. A.A. Stanford. The tense feeling in the air became tenser still as the judge announced that he did not propose to hear any further evidence, but would pronounce judgment on the facts already before him.

HER FIRST HUSBAND

He proceeded to deal with the case of Mr. W.A. Cowle, Mrs. de Melker's first husband, and his crisp incisive analysis of the evidence was followed with rapt attention. Once someone coughed and the impact of the noise came almost as a physical shock. One by one the judge dissected and examined the relevant facts brought forward by the Crown and the defence.

The sombrely-clad figure in the dock never took her eyes off the judge — they might have been alone in the court together. Only the involuntary clenching of a white handkerchief showed how intense was the strain of this last day of her protracted trial.

"And taking everything into consideration, I find that the charge relating to Cowle has not been proved," came the voice from the bench, and a little colour crept into Mrs. de Melker's cheeks.

Consideration of the death of Mr. Sproat followed. Again the same careful weighing of evidence, for and against, and again: "The evidence for the Crown is not such as convinced me, or to convict the accused, and the verdict on the first two counts must therefore be not guilty."

RHODES COWLE

Mrs. de Melker bowed her head, and an attendant handed her a glass of water, from which she sipped from time to time. As Mr. Justice Greenberg began to deal with the death of Rhodes Cecil Cowle a peal of thunder rumbled overhead, and the court grew gloomy and sombre.

Now and again Mrs. de Melker sank back wearily in her chair, her head resting on the brown coat thrown over its back. At other times she clasped her hands to her head and leaned forward to rest on the rail of the dock.

The voice of the judge in its gravity occasionally dropped almost into inaudibility, particularly when he was dealing with the technical evidence about the properties of arsenic. "There is no escape," he said, "from the conclusion that the deceased died of arsenical poisoning."

250

QUESTION OF MOTIVE

The judge proceeded to examine the theory of suicide put forward by the defence — and to reject it. Such things might be said by a youth, he said, to give him the blasé air of a man of the world, a feeling of superiority, induced in some measure, no doubt, by a recent visit to England.

It was inconceivable that he would poison himself and his friend. Neither was there anything to suggest that the poison had got into the flask accidentally.

Then the judge came to refer to the question of motive. "Where the motive is sentimental or subjective it is difficult to prove and even to discover," he said. "Although the question is of great importance, proof is not always essential."

He recalled how Rhodes was looking forward to a car on his 21st birthday, and how he might well "make himself a nuisance" if he did not get it.

He mentioned Mrs. de Melker's fondness for money, and the woman in the dock shook her head slowly in dissent.

As the judge went on to show that with Mrs. de Melker lay the opportunity of administering the poison her fortitude gave way. She pressed her hands to her face and, bending forward, sobbed bitterly. As she did so some of the women in Court stood up to watch her, but after a drink of water she recovered her composure.

THE LAST ACT

Darkness crept across the Court, and thunder muttered again as the judge came to his final unescapable conclusion.

"I can see no escape from the conclusion that the accused inserted poison in the flask . . . . The only conclusion I can come to is that the accused is guilty of this charge."

The woman in the dock rose uncertainly to her feet and listened, half dazed, to the terrible words of the sentence. A gasping sigh went up from the women in Court, and then Mrs. de Melker was hurried from their sight.

BOOED BY BIG CROWD

SCENES IN STREET OUTSIDE COURT

Mrs. de Melker was loudly booed by a large crowd as she emerged from the High Court buildings to step into the Black Maria. Women predominated in the crowd, which must have numbered over a thousand. She was taken to the Fort within half an hour of the passing of sentence, preparatory to leaving for the Central Prison, Pretoria.

After the sentence Mrs. de Melker walked from the dock down the stairs to the cells unassisted by the police and warders who attended her. Mr. de Melker, her husband, and Eileen de Melker, her step-daughter, and her one sister, were allowed to see her before she was taken to the Fort. She repeatedly protested her innocence.

Arrived at the Fort, Mrs. de Melker requested that she be permitted to see her counsel as soon as possible.

Just over one month after the sentence of death had been passed on her, Daisy de Melker was executed in Pretoria Central Prison shortly after 07h00 on 31 December 1932. There was no last-minute confession.

'He served his country with such distinction that he is surely not unworthy of a short memorial'

Eugène Marais, 1871-1936

Eugène Marais' fame as a naturalist, writer and poet eclipsed his work as a journalist. In all four fields, however, his work was remarkable for its perception, its clarity and its originality.

Robert Ardrey, author of *African Genesis,* described him as 'the purest genius that the natural sciences have seen this century . . . his mind was the first to grasp without inhibition at . . . the evolution of the human soul.' The author of *The Soul of the White Ant* (1937) and *My Friends the Baboons* (1939), Marais was born in Pretoria on 9 January 1871 and, at 11, matriculated in Paarl.

He began his career in journalism in Pretoria and, such was his talent that, by 1890, when he was 19 years of age, he became editor of the important weekly newspaper, *Land en Volk* (established in 1888, the full title of the paper was the imposing *Land en Volk, Waarheid, Vrijheid, Recht.* The paper was suspended from publication from October 1899 to 29 September 1902, and ceased publication on 30 August 1907).

Under Marais' editorship, *Land en Volk* became highly controversial. Marais adopted a strong anti-Paul Kruger pro-General Piet Joubert stance, which earned him the enmity of both Kruger and the Volksraad. His parliamentary reporting so enraged the Volksraad that he was banned from the press gallery. Unperturbed, he continued reporting from the public gallery. He was arrested and charged with high treason and impugning the President's honour (and was acquitted by the Pretoria Supreme Court).

By 1892, Marais not only edited *Land en Volk,* but owned it as well. He married two years later but, in 1895, his wife died shortly after the birth of their son and Marais gave up his career in journalism, although he was to contribute to South African papers sporadically for the rest of his life.

Marais, already a morphine addict — he took the drug to alleviate the pain from neuralgia — went to London, where he studied law and was admitted to the bar at London's Inner Court after the Boer War was declared. For the rest of his life, Marais struggled with his love for the English language and his hatred for what the British had done to his people. 'It was for purely sentimental reasons,' he wrote, 'that I refused to write in any language but Afrikaans, notwithstanding the fact that I am far more fluent and more at ease in English.'

Eugène Marais, editor of Land en Volk, *Pretoria, pictured in 1901* (Transvaal Archives).

He returned to South Africa after the Boer War and gradually withdrew from public life, devoting himself to his pioneering work in natural history, and to poetry. It was in *Die Vaderland* and *Die Huisgenoot* between 1926 and 1934 that a collection of his essays, later to be published in book form as *Burgers van die berge* were first published.

While it cannot be said that Old Leo the War Mule, printed in *Die Vaderland* on 12 August 1933 contained new insights into animal and insect behaviour, it was a warm and humorous tale, a relief from the stark news of hunger and unemployment which filled the newspapers of the time. The story has been reproduced in English.

A few days ago a friend mentioned the death in the far northern parts of the Waterberg of a mule which he suspected to be an animal which, in years gone by, had been well known to most old Waterbergers as 'Old Leo'. For my part, I think he is mistaken, because Old Leo would by now have been in his fiftieth year if he had lived. Although it is not possible, it is unlikely that even Old Leo would have reached such an advanced age.

The history of Old Leo is in many respects so remarkable and interesting, and he served his country with such distinction, that he is surely not unworthy of a short memorial — even if it is not given on the occasion of his actual death.

For ten or twelve years I had the opportunity to study Old Leo at close quarters, and I can say in all honesty that I have never known another animal whose intelligence and character have made such a deep impression on me as this old mule — perhaps precisely because mules are generally not counted among the more intelligent animals, and are seldom admired for their loving character.

When Old Leo was in his fiftieth year, he served in General Beyers's Northern Commando. I have never been able to find out anything about his history before that time. I only know that he was then known by another name which now escapes me. The name Old Leo was a title of honour given to him by the general after an incident which nearly ended the mule's life. It was possibly his closest shave with death, and of these he had had his share, because on the 'field of honour,' Old Leo was a fearless hero. One night, when General Beyers was trekking through the Lowveld, Old Leo was attacked by a lion. He fought bravely and managed to kick his attacker away at least twice. But in the end it was his intelligence rather than his courage which saved his life. Instead of running away into the veld — as most animals would do in the same circumstances — Old Leo ran back to the camp as fast as the lion permitted. When he reached the light of the camp fires he was saved by the sentinels. But his wounds placed his life in the balance for a long time. I think it was the patient personal care of General Beyers that pulled him through. In those days a well-trained mule was virtually worth its weight in silver to the commando, but General Beyers was moved to care for the mule not only by an awareness of the animal's usefulness. There was something more profound than that, because it was quite apparent that Old Leo would never again be useful. Apart from terrible flesh wounds in his hind quarters, his right flank had been put out of joint and mauled by the canines of his attacker. The leg mended askew and was thereafter shorter than the other by several inches. This gave Old Leo a strange gait which proved to be of great service to him.

After his recuperation, Old Leo lived through the whole war. He took part in all General Beyers's battles, and always behaved with valour. The enemy never had the honour of capturing him.

After the war he came into the possession of a certain Gys van Rooyen, of the farm Rietfontein, and there I knew him for about twelve years.

General Beyers owned a neighbouring farm and until his death he never missed an opportunity to visit Old Leo. I think he always intended to pension the old mule off as soon as he could move to one of his farms in the Waterberg. But nothing ever came of this plan. With the outbreak of the Great War, Old Leo was in his thirtieth year and that was the last time I saw him.

On Rietfontein the old mule was regularly used for light work, and I doubt that I have ever seen a more willing animal in harness or under the saddle than Old Leo. Needless to say, after the war no whip ever touched the old mule again; in spite of this we had no horse or mule on Rietfontein that could keep up with him in the traces. I am certain that in town we would not have been allowed to harness him, but we knew exactly what Old Leo could do, and in any case had his war report as guideline.

I have never known an animal to enjoy his work as much as Old Leo. I had not the slightest doubt but that he was proud to be harnessed, and that he would have borne the harness with as proud a mien and curving a neck as any horse if his build and crippled state had made it possible! The reader can decide for himself.

Most of the animals involved in the war acquired odd habits. Horses and mules generally became extremely nervous, and it was not unusual for these animals to react to the first shots of a battle by leaving their masters in the lurch and running off into the veld. In several surprise attacks on outposts of General Beyers's commando, two or even three men were compelled to escape on the back of a single horse because of this acquired habit of the commando animals. There were notable exceptions, and Old Leo counted among the more remarkable of these. As soon as the alarm was sounded, he would immediately rush straight towards the camp with a terrible bellow which was quite unlike the whinnying of a mule. I doubt that any animal under saddle ever made a more dreadful noise than Old Leo — a curious habit which he never lost, and which was always a sign of extreme excitement. So great was his eagerness to get a saddle on his back when the alarm was sounded, that he often sent men sprawling in the camp as he rushed to find his master.

The sound of a gun going off always caused his great alarm and filled him with fear — until his master mounted him. Then his fear left him immediately and he became as calm and tranquil as ever he was at the trough.

He was detached for a few weeks with a number of General Beyers's men to serve under General De la Rey. When Lord Metheun's army was overrun Old Leo achieved glittering honours. He formed part of a detachment whose task it was to attack the English lines across the open veld. In spite of the frantic efforts of his rider, Old Leo led the attack, with a distance of at least thirty paces between them and the next horse. It is said that his odd gait, which resembled a boat on a stormy sea rather than a galloping mule, did much to sow confusion in the English ranks. Without a moment's hesitation, he carried his master at full gallop through the English advance positions right up to the wagons, where the horseman arrived alone and in totally unwanted glory!

This curious habit became so entrenched that Old Leo was not much in demand among the men as a war horse when the commando launched an attack — but then he was much in demand when it became necessary to retreat.

In time Old Leo started manifesting another curious habit, which was to prove a great asset when General Beyers found himself virtually surrounded by the English columns in Waterberg. On reconnaissance missions he often spotted enemy scouts long before his master became aware of them. With a favourable wind he could smell other horsemen miles away, and he showed this by stopping dead in his tracks, pricking up his ears and uttering one or two suppressed bellows (the noise which he emitted could not be described as whinnying). When this happened, neither spur nor sjambok would induce him to move one pace in the direction of the peril. Whenever he crossed the tracks of other riders, he was wont to lower his head to the ground, and then to turn to the side and halt. It is said that Old Leo never once gave a false alarm!

It is wonderful how deeply remembrance of the war had been etched into the memory of this 'mindless' animal. Ten years after the war we inspanned Old Leo for the first time as the leading mule in a team of four on a hunting trip to the Bushveld. We trekked into an uninhabited, untamed and forsaken part of the Waterberg — not without good reason. I might as well admit it: two members of the party lacked the necessary licences, and we were going after unlawful quarry. This was so common in the North in those days that I make this confession without much shame. High government officials were the worst culprits!

From the very first day Old Leo revealed certain habits which often gave rise to great unpleasantness — to say the least. One thing he did was that as soon as we made up our beds at night (on the ground), he took up a position between us as close to one of us as he could get. And there he stood the whole night through without as much as stepping on the corner of a blanket. I remember awakening several times during the night with my view blocked by the expanse of Old Leo's belly — his forequarters on one side of my face and his hindquarters on the other! Neither cajolery nor abuse had the least effect on him. We often tethered him far from the camp, but this also proved futile. We would barely be beneath the blankets before Old Leo took up his watchful nightly vigil. Another far more pleasant habit of his was that he came of his own accord to take up his place as soon as we started loading up and preparing the traces. Thus it was never necessary to tie him up.

I do not know whether his nightly seeking of asylum in the camp was the result of his adventure with the lion. It may of course have been the result of the war during which he had come to associate the camp with a general sense of protection and safety. But I wish to relate one incident which took place during the same hunting expedition, and which is much easier to explain psychologically with some degree of certainty.

As I have already admitted, we were not at all eager to come into contact with the police. One day, on the return trip, we were camping near an old overgrown hunting track on the banks of the small Magalakwen. The river was stagnant, with deep pools here and there. Opposite and not far from our camp there was an island, covered with green grass and a thicket of reeds. Nearby the river was waterless, and the veld on the river bank was dry and sparse, so we immediately herded the mules onto the lush island. We hung biltong and skins on the trees to dry. Here we were as safe as we would have been in the middle of a desert. The police were as unlikely to pass this way as any other travellers.

While we were sitting around the fire without a care and at peace with the world, the silence was suddenly rent by a terrible noise as if a bomb had gone off in our midst. There was a bellowing racket quite unlike anything we had ever experienced before. All three of us grabbed our rifles!

Soon the cause of the noise became visible. From the opposite bank Old Leo came charging over the sand bank at full gallop with his head held high, his mouth gaping wide, and his throat emitting a loud trumpeting bellow the likes of which has surely never been heard from the throat of a mule. He tore through the camp and came to a dead stop against the wheel of the buggy, suddenly tranquil as if nothing had happened.

What had come over him? We immediately and carefully inspected him from all sides. All three of us wondered if he had been bitten by a snake, for we knew that the river was crawling with mambas, but we could not find any marks on Old Leo, and he was by then so quiet and calm that he was obviously not in pain.

Not one of us was thinking of the war, which had ended ten years before.

At last a member of the party came up with an explanation that we had to accept. He suggested that Old Leo must have wandered away from the other three mules on the island and found his way onto the opposite bank, where he took fright when he suddenly realised that he was alone and his companions nowhere to be seen.

We sat down again while Old Leo remained standing at the wheel of the buggy without a movement.

More than half an hour later he again startled us with a smothered repetition of his trumpeting bellow. He was staring across the river with pricked ears; a minute later we heard the noise of breaking branches in the hunting track and saw a cavalcade appearing on the opposite bank. The cavalcade was led by four armed men on horseback — all four dressed in khaki — followed by a wagon drawn by four mules, the coloured drivers of which were also in khaki uniforms. 'Police!' we cried. Happily we were wrong. They were surveyors engaged in marking a stock disease line. They were just as wary of us as we of them, for their wagon was also laden with poached game. However, it did not take long for us to come to an understanding, and we became fast friends. There was no doubt but that it was the approach of this cavalcade that Old Leo had announced. The reader must remember that this took place ten years after the war, and that during those ten years the fear of armed horsemen had become extinct. But in the brain of Old Leo, this war-time memory had never been extinguished during ten long years!

Eugène Marais died an unfulfilled and bitter man, his natural history work plagiarised and his own research unrecognised until after his death. He committed suicide at Pelindaba on 29 March 1936. His posthumous legacy, however, would have exceeded his dreams.

'Only one 5 in 26 holes'

H.B. Keartland on Bobby Locke, 1934

Herbert Bert ('HB', 'Bert' or 'Keart') Keartland arrived in South Africa in 1909 and became one of the country's finest and most professional sports journalists. Born in London on 20 October 1887, Keartland began his writing career in Britain on local papers, moving rapidly to the editorship of *Athletic Field,* but it was to be in South Africa that he was given his major opportunities.

Shortly after his arrival, he joined the staff of the *Natal Advertiser,* the precursor to *The Daily News.* In 1912 Keartland himself made the headlines when, as manager and trainer of the South African Olympic team, he went with it to Sweden, where it walked away with no less than six medals — five gold and one silver — an achievement that has never been bettered.

Keartland served in the South African Defence Force in the 1914-18 war, mostly in East Africa. On his return to South Africa, he was unable to get a job in journalism and accordingly became a PT instructor on the West Rand, writing in his spare time. His account of a murder was judged to be so outstanding by *The Star* that he was immediately employed by them as chief reporter of the newspaper. His employment with *The Star* was to last from 1918 until his retirement in 1947.

In 1922 Keartland was appointed *The Star*'s first sports editor and took the then revolutionary step of insisting that sports coverage be accommodated on one page and not all over the newspaper. He was renowned as a golf writer, but reported on all sports in his clear, articulate style.

H.B. Keartland is credited, if not with the discovery of the amazing Bobby Locke, at least with his promotion and with substantial encouragement. His affectionate, articulate report of Locke's 1939 Transvaal open golf championship was used in *The Star* on Monday, 30 January 1939.

SPELLBINDING GOLF BY BOBBY LOCKE

TRANSVAAL OPEN WON BY 26 STROKES IN FOUR AMAZING ROUNDS

RECORD 72 HOLES' SCORE

When Bobby Locke, fresh from his overseas triumphs, played the first two rounds of the Transvaal open golf championship in the low figures of 66 and 69 on Saturday it was thought that he touched the peak of his form and set a new standard of play in the Union. But remarkable as these scores were, he eclipsed them yesterday with another 66 in the morning and a positively astounding last round of 64.

This gave him an aggregate of 265, which, on a course of 7,031 yards, is probably not

The young Bobby Locke, 1938 (Fox Photos).

merely a South African record, but without equal in the whole history of golf on championship courses.

The significance of his extraordinary brilliance is the fact that in a field of first class players he won by the huge margin of 26 strokes, and that no other competitor managed to beat 70 in the whole of the four rounds.

23 STROKES UNDER FOURS

There was a time in world golf when Bobby Jones declared that level fours was good enough to win any championship. But the youthful South African Bobby has set a higher standard than that with his score at Glendower.

This young golfing wizard from Brakpan was 23 strokes under fours for the four rounds and 35 strokes under the standard scratch score.

Merely for the sake of comparison it may be mentioned that W. Lawson Little set up a record of 271 in the Canadian Open Championship in 1936 which amazed the golfing world, and Jim Ferrier did 266 in the New South Wales "Open" in 1935, while listed among the outstanding American performances is Emmett French's 274 in winning the Ohio "Open", but that over a course only 6,400 in length. The South African record was Locke's 277 in the South African "Open" at Maccauvlei last Easter.

Bobby Locke with the Transvaal Open Championship cup which he won with a record-breaking score at Glendower in January 1939. Others with him at the prize-giving (left to right): *Dr L. Braun, captain of the Glendower Club, Percy Barker, C.T. Elliot, honorary secretary of the Transvaal Golf Union* (standing), *Dr P. Hamilton, president of the TGU, Mrs Braun, Tilson Barry KC and W. Caldwell* (The Star).

259

DOMINATING FIGURE

From the first hole he played, a glorious three at a somewhat easy par five, Bobby simply dominated the championship, but remarkably as he played on Saturday he showed yesterday that he was capable of greater things.

His play need not be described since it would merely be a monotonous record of flawless strokes. He kept swinging his club in that wide-grooved arc with the mechanical efficiency of a robot and had the large gallery spellbound with his length and his accuracy.

The figures of his morning round of 66 tell their own story better than any description of play can do.

He played the round without a five and without a two on his card, which is just about perfect golf — he had 31 putts. It was thought that this performance in the critical third round might leave him exhausted in the home stretch, but so far from leaving him jaded, it merely inspired him to greater heights.

He strolled round the course, seemingly oblivious to the hundreds of excited spectators milling around him, a stooping figure with his boyish features lined with concentration.

H.B. Keartland, still writing — on his 90th birthday (The Star).

ONLY ONE 5 IN 26 HOLES

From the second hole of the afternoon round, when outdriven some 20 yards from the tee by his partner, A.W. Rolfe, he took his shallow-faced spoon and hit the ball high in the air 5 ft. past the pin to hole his putt for a three at a 500 yards hole, everybody anticipated the sensational. He just failed to get his two at the short third and at the fourth (461 yards) he used a five iron to hit the ball at the flag with the accuracy of a rifle shot. He only had to hole a 4 ft. putt for another three.

Such was the amazing accuracy of his shots to the pin that he made putting easy, but he showed his delightful putting touch in trickling down a ten-yarder for a two at the sixth and at that stage was five under fours. He had his first five in 26 holes of play at the eighth, where he slightly pushed out his second into a drain at the side of the green at this 520 yards hole. Unruffled, he chipped out to about 7 ft. of the pin, and his putt for a four hovered on the edge of the cup.

260

He was out in 32 and started back with three fours, but after a superb second at the 490 yards thirteenth he holed a 12-footer for a three. He took a five at the long fifteenth, but two more threes was followed by his smashing a mashie niblick shot, his 63rd of the round, on to the green at the eighteenth (440 yards). With his usual deliberation he proceeded to hole the nine-foot putt for another three and a round of 64.

THE WONDER OF THE ROUND

Bobby had 29 putts in the round, which reflected exceedingly fine putting when it is considered that several more putts might have dropped. But the wonder of the round was the accuracy of his shots to the green, which gave him so little putting to do.

Great golfer that he is and greater golfer that he may become, Locke may never again play four rounds in such amazing figures.

Sid Brews, in paying a graceful tribute to the winner at the prize presentation, remarked that the other competitors were so far behind Locke that they scarcely deserved to get any prize money.

H.B. Keartland died in February 1981.

'The German tanks, seven abreast and ten deep . . .'

Carel Birkby on losses in the 5th South African Brigade, Sidi Rezegh, 1941

'There is battle in the air; I swear there is. It lies thick on the palate,' wrote Captain Sean Fielding shortly before the biggest and most violent tank battle of the North African campaign — Sidi Rezegh.

Battle was indeed in the air. At 21h00 on 16 November 1941, General Sir Alan Cunningham, Commander 8th Army, told his officers, 'I am going to seek old Rommel out and destroy him and his armour.'

The basic plan of 'Operation Crusader' was to move 8th Army forces forward and engage Rommel's Panzers, drawing them towards the Sidi Rezegh escarpment and subsequent destruction. The Tobruk garrison would then break out and join the advancing 8th Army.

A new formation was created for this purpose: the 30th Corps, comprising the 1st South African Division, the 22nd Guards Brigade and the 7th Armoured Division — essentially it was a mobile armoured force.

The odds were ostensibly with the British: 477 front-line tanks, 250 behind the lines and another 200 on the way from Britain, to Rommel's 390. Rommel had no hope of reinforcements. Moreover, the RAF had 550 aircraft to the Luftwaffe's 342.

The confrontation had been well planned: the water supplies alone necessitated building nine reservoirs, laying 259 km of pipe and seven pumping stations.

On the evening of 16 November, and throughout 17 November, troops taking part in the offensive moved to their assembly points. On 18 November Operation Crusader was launched, the 30th Corps advancing into enemy territory with surprisingly little response from Rommel.

It was this very lack of response which threatened Operation Crusader. In order for the offensive to work, Rommel had to send his tanks in strength to meet the British. Cunningham decided to divide his forces and look for Rommel.

On 19 November, as the 7th Armoured brigade reached Sidi Rezegh — the most signal feature of which was a square tomb in the midst of the desert — the 1st South African Brigade moved towards Bir el Gubi. The Germans then began to respond, their tanks engaging the British in a series of huge, sweeping, chaotic engagements.

The 7th Support Group was ordered to secure and hold the Sidi Rezegh ridge (the airfield was already in British hands) early on 21 November, and the 5th South African Brigade to the south was told to supply support.

262

Carel Birkby, one of South Africa's finest war correspondents.

At 10h30 on 22 November the Brigade began to move north in support of 7th Support Group. But Rommel, in one of his characteristically unexpected moves, outflanked the British, the 5th Panzers attacking Sidi Rezegh airfield from the west. In the confusion and mêlée which followed, the 7th Armoured Division was ordered to fall back and join up with the rapidly approaching South Africans.

The South Africans met not with the retreating 7th Support Group but with the impeccably drilled mobilised infantry and armour of the Afrika Corps under General Ludwig Crüwell. Almost 70 German tanks were destroyed, but the 5th South African Brigade, fighting valiantly, lost 3 394 men.

Covering the desert war as a war correspondent for the South African Press Association (SAPA) was Carel Birkby. Carel Birkby's career in journalism had been marked by his penchant for action stories. As a reporter for *The Cape Argus* in the 1930s, Birkby set off in a single-engined aeroplane for the Congo in a vain effort to find a missing Swiss pilot; in 1939 he left South Africa for the Far East, where he observed the Japanese at war with Chiang Kai-shek's Chinese. And in the 1970s, when he was well into his 60s, he crossed the Drakensberg in a hot air balloon.

As the Argus group's general war correspondent, Birkby went to Roberts Heights (now Voortrekkerhoogte), Pretoria, where he did an officers' training course before being seconded by the Group to SAPA as a war correspondent.

It was in this capacity that Birkby reported on the Sidi Rezegh battles. He missed capture by a hairsbreadth and, after evading the Germans, reported from the battlefront, his despatch appearing in South African Associated Newspapers (now the Times Media group) on 28 November 1941.

EPIC SPRINGBOK STAND IN DESERT BATTLE

FULL STORY TOLD

FIFTH BRIGADE HEROISM

FOUGHT TILL LAST SHOT WAS FIRED

MANY ESCAPE TO JOIN OTHER UNITS

The story of the epic fighting by South African troops in the western desert battle is fully told for the first time to-day. The Fifth Brigade bore the brunt of a heavy enemy tank attack. Hour by hour more encouraging news is arriving of men at first reported missing.

EIGHTH ARMY CONTROLS SITUATION

(Sapa's War Correspondent)

Battle Headquarters, Friday.
(Delayed.)

As fast-moving and shifting as an elaborate series of naval actions, the Libyan desert battle is now raging over an area of 5,000 square miles of desolation.

The situation is obscure, as is understandable in warfare so fluid. It is impossible at the moment to give an accurate picture of the operations as a whole or to assess the relative importance of successes or setbacks in any one particular phase of the great battle.

The precise intentions behind Sir Alan Cunningham's strategy are naturally secret, and no observer is in a position yet to assess how this strategy is working out. It can be said, however, that the Eighth Army has control of the complicated situation.

ENEMY'S STRENGTH

It has been clear from the beginning that the Axis forces in Libya — roughly 100,000 strong — would be a tough nut to crack, particularly in view of the considerable German tank strength.

British and American tanks have been engaged almost ceaselessly for a week in a series of tank battles in which they have wrought great destruction.

The losses on both sides have been heavy.

British, New Zealand and Indian troops have all been involved in heavy fighting, and so have the South Africans. They have all been sharing in the successes and sacrifices inevitable in such a ferocious struggle.

A NATURAL CHOICE

The Springboks expected fierce fighting and they wanted to be in the thick of it. The extreme mobility of the South African formations made them a natural choice for tasks that required speed and hard-hitting power.

As the South African public has already realised, it is impossible for our forces to go through a struggle of this magnitude with losses on a negligible scale as sustained in the Italian Somaliland and Abyssinia campaigns.

There are no clear facts yet of how all our formations have fared. As might have been expected, the Springboks have been fighting magnificently.

GRIM BATTLE

Some units have been involved in the most intense fighting of the battle, and at first it seemed that there must be a tale of disaster to tell concerning one South African brigade — the Fifth — who fought a grim battle at Sidi Rezegh on Saturday and Sunday.

But hour by hour there is more encouraging news of various units of this brigade, and one must await developments and the ultimate fate of the rest of the brigade with courage.

In this fluctuating, fast-fought type of battle a man may be a prisoner one day and free the next day as our mobile units strike or carry out speedy encircling movements. For this reason there should be no despondency nor credence in early and exaggerated rumours.

In the belief that the people of South Africa have a right to an early and undistorted account of what has happened to this brigade, I give the facts as they are known up to the present time, gathered from men who have escaped. It is a dispatch which requires fortitude to write as well as to read, but let it be repeated that better news will come of more and more of the Springboks who are now missing.

The Fifth Brigade was part of a South African force which crossed the frontier on Tuesday of last week. It was an integral part of, and was working with the full support of, British armoured forces throughout the operations which followed.

Under Brigadier B.F. Armstrong it moved north in the direction of Tobruk.

South African soldiers cheering General Sir Claude Auchinleck, Commander-in-Chief of the forces in the Middle East, when he came to visit them at an oasis in the desert before the Great Push — and the Sidi Rezegh battles — began (South African National Museum of Military History).

ITALIANS TURN TAIL

On Friday morning the brigade first encountered enemy tanks, when it was attacked by Italian armoured forces at 9 o'clock. The brigade's anti-tank guns and field guns knocked out eight of the Italian tanks in an engagement that lasted one hour.

The Italians withdrew, but returned to the attack at noon. They were met with intense fire and turned tail without giving battle. British tanks ran into these Italians, and, it is stated, destroyed 16 more.

Meanwhile German forces had re-occupied Sidi Rezegh, an important aerodrome on the El Adem-Fort Capuzzo track, 20 miles from Tobruk town.

Sidi Rezegh was the scene of the first encounter between British and German tanks on Tuesday night, November 18, and here British forces captured an entire German squadron, complete with planes and personnel.

SPRINGBOKS MOVE FORWARD

The South African brigade moved forward and deployed to attack Sidi Rezegh from the south. They had first to take the ridge of an escarpment overlooking the aerodrome.

They were met by heavy machine-gun fire, and despite an attempt to outflank the Germans no progress could be made.

British tanks also went forward on the left.

The afternoon wore on without the South Africans being able to secure the ridge, for the moment they showed their heads above the skyline they were met with intense fire.

Towards dusk the brigadier withdrew them to a position just in front of their supporting artillery, where they consolidated in a perimeter camp.

The brigade had up to this stage already sustained casualties.

On Sunday heavier fighting developed.

The brigade was reorganising its perimeter early in the morning in conjunction with a small British armoured formation which had been holding high ground to the east of the aerodrome the day before.

At 7.30 a.m. three German tanks unexpectedly broke into the rear of the brigade, where the supplies and workshops' vehicles were dispersed. These tanks raced right through the brigade, being shelled as they went. Two were knocked out but the third got away. These tanks were probably refugees from a swaying tank battle which was now going on all around the brigade.

The South Africans were cut off from their comrades to the south and from their ration and ammunition columns.

ARTILLERY DEFENCE

Swiftly the South Africans reformed their lines after the brief disorganisation caused by the wild career of the tanks, and they arranged a strong artillery defence to meet the threat of a strong enemy force which was reported to the south.

An enemy infantry attack threatened to develop on the right flank during the morning, but the South African guns checked it.

Intermittent tank battles were now raging to the south and west of the Springboks. An armoured car crew came in with a report of a force of 80 tanks and 500 motor vehicles to the south and west, and a further force of 500 trucks with some tanks a little further away, but the South Africans' sound artillery defences and the British tanks in the vicinity seemed capable of dealing with anything that might develop.

FIERCE ENEMY BOMBARDMENT

At 1.30 p.m. the Germans started an intense artillery bombardment from the north, which grew steadily in fierceness.

At 2.45 p.m. the Transvaal regiment which was forward in the brigade's northern line reported that a strong German infantry attack was developing from the north and north-east.

Preparations were being made to deal with this attack when an enemy tank and artillery attack developed simultaneously from the west. South African artillery and British tanks fought off this thrust.

At 3.30 there was a distinct lull in the battle, though shelling continued. The three Springbok battalions all reported that they had the situation in hand and that the German infantry attack had been beaten off.

THE REAL TANK PUSH

But within a few minutes the Germans made their real tank push at the south-western corner of the brigade's camp. Our field guns hammered at them valiantly, knocking out one after another, but they still came until the guns had spent every round of ammunition

The tomb of Sidi Rezegh. The only landmark in the area, it gave its name to the battles which took place in its vicinity. South African graves lie in the foreground (South African National Museum of Military History).

they had. The anti-tank gun crews fired until they too, had not a round left. The German tanks, seven abreast and ten deep, swept through the supply and auxiliary transport lines, past the brigade group's headquarters, forcing the retreat of the Springboks' riflemen who had fought so long and so valiantly.

The brigade commander, who had been with a liaison officer in a tank from another formation, got out as it was too crowded for action. The tank made off, fighting its way out.

The Brigadier was taken prisoner, and when last seen was under officer escort.

GERMANS RATTLED

The brigade major and several other officers and men were lying under the command vehicle and escaped notice, but an incendiary shell set it ablaze and they had to emerge.

The Germans were rounding up prisoners when a few British tanks broke through and rattled the Germans badly. They ran for cover wherever they could find it, and dived into the slit trenches the South Africans had dug. In this confusion a considerable number of South Africans made a break for liberty.

The British tanks, however, were not in sufficient numbers to turn the tide — the main forces were apparently to the north-east, and had failed to make contact with the German main tank force before it attacked the brigade.

The South Africans who got away were not impressed by the German troops who had broken on them so unluckily. Dressed mostly in Italian uniforms, they were an undersized lot and they were confident only when they were sure of their screen of armour. When the few British tanks showed up they appeared to lose their course.

Groups of men constantly escaped.

BRIGADE MAJOR'S ESCAPE

The brigade major's escape was typical of many. With several other officers, including the officer commanding a brigade of artillery, he lingered near the rear of the line of prisoners which was being formed. As dusk was approaching he and his followers made a bolt for it. They walked nine miles.

Once three German trucks stopped within ten feet of where they were lying in the open sand without concealment. Twice enemy tank columns passed them. After walking nine miles they came upon the brigadier's equipment truck.

On this they drove back to join another South African formation.

An infantryman who also got away had the experience of lying in a slit trench while a tank came straight at him and drove over him. "It seemed to take a year to come those 20 feet," he said later.

GOT AWAY IN TRUCKS

Individuals and groups of men stealthily jumped into trucks and drove off under fire. Groups of as many as 50 men got away and rejoined other units. Even now many parties of escapees are streaming across the desert, either linking up with other formations or crossing the frontier wire. The large numbers who have already got away will be swelled steadily by many more.

Among the auxiliary units which suffered from the German tank attack on the Fifth

Brigade was the Eleventh South African Field Ambulance. Many of the personnel were captured and ambulances and other vehicles were set on fire or destroyed by shellfire. They had done magnificent work tending the wounded.

AMBULANCE ATTACKED

The Tenth South African Field Ambulance was also attacked by German tanks on Saturday morning early. A tank formation broke through the ambulance, firing at it. Some officers and men escaped, but the majority of the personnel were captured and their vehicles destroyed.

Among the missing — some of them were seen by escapees to be prisoners — are five South African war correspondents, Messrs. Conrad Norton and Uys Krige, observers of the Bureau of Information, E.A. Hinds, a cinematographer attached to the Bureau of Information, J.C. Lamprecht, Afrikaans announcer and Roland Sinclair, recording engineer of the South African Broadcasting Corporation's mobile recording unit.

Brigadier Dan Pienaar (holding shell) talks to the crew of a South African armoured car in the Western Desert. The car, an SA Marmon-Herrington armed car, had been modified by the crew to carry a two-pound anti-tank gun with an improvised shield. They frequently used guns abandoned by the Germans and the Italians in the same manner, their sole difficulty being the likelihood of running out of ammunition. Pienaar was killed in December 1942 in an aircrash at Kisumu, on his way back to South Africa from the Western Desert (South African National Museum of Military History).

Carel Birkby was determined, as far as official censorship would permit, to write the full story of the Sidi Rezegh battles, and revealed the full extent of the casualties, far in excess of government figures. For this he earned a stern rebuke from General Smuts, who thereafter cold-shouldered him (in contrast to David Friedman, reporting the war from Fleet Street, to whom Smuts confided the news of the Normandy landings on the morning of 4 June 1944, two full days before the landings took place. Friedmann went on to become editor of SAPA).

Birkby's subsequent career was varied. He reported from Abyssinia and North Africa. Accredited to the Royal Air Force, he was a front-line correspondent in the Middle East and Italy. After the war he edited a paper in the Sudan for four years, resuming his career in South Africa on *The Daily News* in 1948. (He joined, on that paper, an extraordinarily talented group of journalists who were to become, in the years that followed, eminent in the newspaper world: cartoonist Jock Leyden; John O'Malley, who went on to edit the short-lived *Sunday Chronicle, The Daily News* and *The Argus;* G.L. Hutchison, who in due course became editor of *The Sunday Tribune;* Hubert Huxham, who edited the *Sunday Express;* David Brechin, who edited *The Diamond Fields Advertiser;* the great sports writer Louis Duffus; the columnist who had more fire in her belly than almost anyone, Molly Reinhardt, and Laurence Gandar, the almost legendary editor of the *Rand Daily Mail.)*

Keeping his hand in as a war correspondent, Birkby covered the conflicts in Katanga, Angola and Biafra for the *Rand Daily Mail* and the *Sunday Times.* After his retirement in 1975, he wrote for *To the Point.* Birkby died in February 1987.

'Kom aan, Jerry!'

Reporting the desert war, 1942 (1)

In the months that followed the battles around Sidi Rezegh, the South Africans took part in the mobile, confusing desert war which led up to the Battle of El Alamein in October 1942. There were incidents aplenty, as this lively SAPA despatch, sent from Cairo to South Africa, illustrates. It was used in the *Cape Times* and *Rand Daily Mail* of 3 June 1942.

SPRINGBOK LINE UNBROKEN

MAGNIFICENT STAND IN LIBYA BATTLE

CASUALTIES VERY LIGHT

Sapa's War Correspondent.

CAIRO, Tuesday.— Both South African Divisions in North Africa have been involved in the fighting of the past week.

They have held vital positions in the Gazala-Bir Hakheim line, fighting off attacks from both front and rear with conspicuous success, and suffering few casualties.

Twice they smashed enemy tank onslaughts against their positions, and wherever South African artillery and infantry have been at grips with the enemy tank forces they have taken heavy toll of his men and equipment.

BATTLE CRY: "KOM AAN!"

The men of one South African division held off German tanks in the Acroma 'box' and played a great part in foiling the German drive on Tobruk.

They have received the highest praise for this stand which is considered comparable with the decisive stand made by a famous British regiment at Knightsbridge.

The casualties suffered by this division have been remarkably light.

The other division, which has been successfully holding positions in the Gazala line, saw the start of the German offensive when it was heavily dive-bombed on the opening day.

They have suffered little damage from dive-bombing attacks, and they shot down nine Stukas in one afternoon. Since then they have not been much troubled by dive-bombers.

ENEMY PRISONERS

Regiments from all parts of the Union are engaged in the fighting, and a number of enemy prisoners have fallen into their hands.

An account of the part played by the two South African Divisions was given to me to-day by a senior officer who was at the front when Rommel launched his attack.

He described the performance of the South Africans as magnificent and their spirit as invincible.

Every branch of the considerable Springbok force up forward has been called upon to make its contribution, and there is nothing but praise for the ready response given in each instance. The two divisions are in close contact with one another and co-operating without a hitch.

The South Africans have already dealt the enemy some nasty blows. They helped appreciably to prevent Rommel from carrying out his programme of reaching Tobruk in four days, and Major-General Dan Pienaar's gunners meted out severe punishment to the German panzer forces when they tried to establish a bridgehead to assist the battered Afrika Korps.

The South Africans are fighting over a wide area. In the main line down from Gazala they hold several vital positions which the enemy tried in vain to penetrate. The Italians suffering in particular. Farther back, Rommel encountered several concentrations of South African forces and in each encounter the South Africans gave much more than they received.

PLANES BROUGHT DOWN

Giving his impressions of the reactions of South Africans when the offensive started last week, the senior officer said he arrived in the Gazala area just in time for a dive-bombing attack on the South African positions. They were being shelled at the same time, but he saw little result from this attack.

South African anti-aircraft guns fired away at the dive-bombers, and the officer himself saw two Stukas hit. They dived behind our lines and one crashed within view.

In this sector the South Africans destroyed five Stukas and in another sector four more dive-bombers fell to the South African Ack-Ack.

The spirit of the men while they were being attacked was "simply grand," the officer said. Everybody was calm and collected. Even the natives watched the dive-bombers coolly, cheering and shouting "They've got him" each time a plane was hit.

"KOM AAN, JERRY"

The South Africans were equally unperturbed when they heard later that day that the enemy had attacked Bir Hakheim in force. They were all in readiness when the enemy formed up for what seemed like a frontal attack on our line, and gave the enemy such an enthusiastic reception that the attack melted away.

Our artillery, firing with uncanny accuracy, threw up such a barrage that the enemy thought better of it and retired.

At another point in our line three tanks survived the first belt of our minefields, but they got no further, for they found a formidable force of South Africans sitting with set jaws and shouting: "Kom aan, Jerry, we're waiting for you." The tanks were driven back.

One party of Germans infiltrated through our positions on the escarpment, but they were rounded up and captured without much difficulty.

BACKDOOR SHUT

On Thursday when reports were received that an enemy armoured column was approaching from the east, the South Africans braced themselves for what looked like a really serious threat.

Our armoured cars, for whose work, the officer said, no praise was high enough, were out keeping a close vigil and reporting back on the enemy's every move.

An armoured column comprising elements of both 15th and 21st Panzer Divisions, was reported to be moving behind our positions.

At the time Major-General Pienaar did not know where the British armoured forces were. All he knew was that his positions were being attacked by a formidable force of enemy tanks and, with his line already being attacked from the west; he prepared dispositions to meet this menacing array of German armour.

When we intercepted an order to the German panzer forces telling them to clear all in front and drive to the north-west, General Pienaar's only comment was: "I have closed my backdoor. Let them come."

"SEE THE FUN"

The coolness with which the South Africans went prepared to meet this attack greatly impressed the officer. Everyone remained calm, and a senior staff officer was heard telephoning the brigades, informing them that "there might be some trouble", and the General Officer Commanding wanted them to make dispositions to meet the expected attack.

Then suddenly they received a message that British armoured forces were being moved up to give the enemy battle, thus diverting his attention and frustrating his plan.

The officer said he had to leave this South African unit, but General Pienaar tried to persuade him to "stay and see the fun."

When General Pienaar received information that British forces were forming a position to the rear of his troops, he said: "That's fine. Now we will fight together."

An enemy frontal attack was smashed up, and the 90th light motorised division which, supported by Italians, attacked our positions from the east, was also thrown back, the South Africans suffering only a few casualties.

INFANTRY'S JOB

General Pienaar inquired from the artillery commanding officer how much ammunition he had fired. On being told, he said to the officer: "Don't waste ammunition on the Italians. Keep your shells for the enemy's armour, and let the infantry take the Italians on with machine-guns."

There was a good deal of shelling and bombing that night but the South Africans did not suffer.

The officer left in an armoured car during the night. He slipped through the enemy forces on the escarpment in the moonlight, and passed South African supply columns which were being sent forward to General Pienaar.

On his way he met South Africans who had taken part in a gallant stand which checked an enemy tank column west of Acroma.

He found the South Africans in the Second Division "in great heart." This force was holding another important line ensuring supplies for the First Division and constantly harassing the enemy.

Prisoners taken by the South Africans included both Germans and Italians.

'Gallant deeds
and sheepish apologies'

Reporting the desert war, 1942 (2)

'Here are a clump of Highlanders, their workmanlike aprons in front, their keen faces burned black with months of the veldt. It is an honoured name that they bear on their shoulder-straps. "Good old Gordons!" I cried as they passed me. The sergeant glanced at the dirty enthusiast in the undershirt. "What cheer, matey!' he cried, and his men squared their shoulders and put a touch of ginger into their stride.'

Conan Doyle's description of Smith-Dorrien's Brigade marching into Bloemfontein in 1900, printed in *The Friend,* 14 April 1900, is strikingly similar in tone and treatment to South African war despatches written before and since. Patriotic, cheery, quick to praise and never to condemn, accurate whenever possible, noble in the face of fire and with just the right amount of emotion to elicit a tear from an anxious and supportive public, war correspondents are a strikingly similar breed, be they Norris-Newman writing about the horrors of the Isandhlwana battlefield, Conan Doyle in Bloemfontein or Christopher Buckley and Ronald Legge in the Western Desert.

The indefatiguable Legge and Buckley, who had squared up with the Eighth Army for defeat (Tobruk, June 1942) and success (El Alamein, October 1942) wrote this particular piece of gung-ho journalism for the *Cape Times* of 2 November 1942. Biggles would have loved it.

FRONT LINE TALES FROM EGYPT

"FEAR OF DEATH IN THE HUN NOW"

From CHRISTOPHER BUCKLEY and RONALD LEGGE,
Cape Times Special Correspondents.

WITH THE EIGHTH ARMY, Sunday. — One of the company commanders of a battalion which captured a powerful Axis position and has been in some of the heaviest fighting said: "We've got the fear of death in the Hun now. Whenever we got near enough to do some damage the enemy walked out with hands up."

"They are only boys," he added. "Some of them cannot be more than 16 or 17.

"Now we are just waiting for the word to advance again before the Jerries can scram out of it."

He paid tribute to German snipers, who, he said, are used throughout the day to guard guns, and are difficult to locate.

Illustrating the magnificent spirit of this battalion, one leading company commander described their advance through minefields in which forward companies ran into enemy fire.

INSPIRED BY DANGER

"Shells and mortar bombs were bursting around us, and 500 yards from the starting point we had our first casualties," he said. "It was extraordinary how the fact that they were in danger seemed to inspire the men. They laughed, joked and carried on steadily."

One young soldier who was made a lance-corporal the day we went into action, was wounded and losing blood badly. He refused treatment, however, and carried on, keeping his section properly dispersed and controlling their movements. Then the company ran into four machine-guns. One was knocked out by a mortar but the other three kept our men pinned to the ground. The lance-corporal was hit again.

"This chap is dying," said a sergeant-major, but the lance-corporal struggled to his feet saying: "I am all right, but I think with your permission I'll move back to a first aid post."

The company commander did not know whether he got there, but commented: "It was a grand show."

MEDICAL ORDERLY

Attached to this battalion was a little medical orderly, 5 ft. 1 in. in height and weighing seven stone. He was called "Johnny" by everyone.

Johnny always said he was no hero, and that bombs and shells scared him stiff. Then came the night of the advance. During the following afternoon the enemy plastered the entire front and Johnny knew such heavy shelling must have caused casualties.

He had no orders, so waited until the medical officer was asleep and then started out with his kit to attend the wounded. Throughout the afternoon and night he trekked along the front line bandaging, dressing and succouring the wounded. By next morning he had covered 20 miles, and returned with sheepish apologies for acting on his own initiative.

Afterwards he accompanied the battalion to a strong point captured from Italians. A few hours later an officer and two men went out to try to get a sniper who had been causing trouble. The sniper saw them and shot them down. They lay wounded in no-man's-land. Without saying a word to anyone, Johnny gathered up his kit, slipped out and began crawling to the wounded men.

The sniper saw him coming, too. A shot rang out and Johnny died. But his name is still on his colleagues' lips and the memory of his gallant deeds and fulfilment of his duty as he saw it, will live with them.

'Springboks' last laager'

The fall of Tobruk, June 1942

On the night of 20 June 1942, Winston Churchill discussed the development of the atomic weapon with his American counterpart, President Roosevelt. After a late, leisurely breakfast the next day, Churchill went to see Roosevelt in his White House office. Roosevelt was handed a telegram, read it silently and without a word passed it to Churchill. 'Tobruk has surrendered with 25 000 men taken prisoner', it read.

Four days later, in the British House of Commons, a vote of no confidence in the British government was tabled. For Churchill in particular it was a bitter blow, relieved only by Roosevelt's ordering the transfer of 300 new Sherman tanks to the Middle East, which were greatly to assist General Montgomery in the El Alamein campaign.

Approximately 19 000 British and over 13 000 South Africans (the correct figures) had been taken prisoner at Tobruk. Into German hands fell 5 000 tons of food, large quantities of ammunition, 2 000 vehicles and 2 000 tons of fuel. Taken prisoner with his men was Major-General H.B. Klopper, who had been in command of Tobruk, and 2nd SA Division, 201 Guards Brigade, 11 Indian Brigade, 32 Army Tank Brigade, three field artillery regiments, an anti-tank regiment and two medium artillery regiments.

With a landward perimeter extending over 43 km (originally laid out by the Italians before the war) and strongposts 800 metres apart, an incomplete and silted-up anti-tank ditch, missing records of the state and location of the minefields and almost free access to the harbour, Tobruk had hardly been a stronghold when Major-General Klopper took command on 14 June 1942.

Although it was not envisaged that Tobruk should withstand a second siege (36 000 men, including the Australian 9th Division, had been besieged for six months by the Germans from 11 April 1941), Eighth Army supremos saw the town resisting a German attack and providing a base for forces taking part in operations against the enemy, particularly in the El Adem area.

But El Adem duly fell, and it became apparent early on that it would be difficult for the army to defend both the frontier and Tobruk. 'Have no intention of giving up Tobruk, which I hope is only temporarily isolated,' General Sir Claude Auchinleck, Commander-in-Chief of the Allied forces in the Middle East, cabled Smuts from Cairo on the afternoon of 19 June.

Klopper was confident he could hold Tobruk and, should he be attacked by Axis forces, drew up no fewer than six counter-attack plans. But by 19 June the whole area between the Tobruk perimeter and the frontier was empty of British forces and the enemy's strength was building.

Rommel launched his attack on the town and its defences on the morning of 20 June. Early that morning, Klopper received a signal from Eighth Army which stated that as soon as the enemy attacked on the south-eastern sector, a mobile force would seize a prominent ridge and feint towards Sidi Rezegh. At 15h50, Klopper, his defences penetrated and 60 German tanks within sight, sent a message to Eighth Army, but it was not acted upon.

By the time dark fell, Klopper had decided the situation was hopeless. Just after 20h00, he reported to Eighth Army, 'My headquarters surrounded, infantry on perimeter still fighting hard am holding out but I do not know how long.'

He followed this message with another one, 'All my tanks gone. Half my guns gone. Do you think it advisable I battle through?'

At 02h00 on 21 June, he sent a further signal, 'Am sending mobile troops out tonight. Not possible to hold tomorrow. Mobile troops nearly nought. Enemy captured vehicles. Will resist to last man and round.'

Just before dawn on the morning of 21 June, Klopper received a signal: 'Whole of 8th Army has watched with admiration your gallant fight. You are an example to us all and I know South Africa will be proud of you. God bless you and may fortune favour your efforts wherever you be.' The white flag of surrender was raised shortly afterwards.

News of the surrender of Tobruk, although not the details of the battle itself, was received in South Africa later that day, the stories running on the morning of 22 June 1942. The Sapa-Reuter report, short on information, appeared in the *Cape Times*:

OVERWHELMING BLOW AT TOBRUK

ADVANCE BASE NOW IN ENEMY HANDS

PRISONERS MAY BE 25,000

CAIRO, Sunday. — It is officially announced that Tobruk has fallen, earlier Axis reports to this effect being thus confirmed.

The German claim to have taken 25,000 prisoners is not considered unlikely, states Sapa's war correspondent in Libya.

The attack on Tobruk yesterday, which was on a bigger scale than anything the enemy attempted last year, began, he says, with an aerial bombardment. Then Axis tanks made a breach in the perimeter in the El Adem area, through which infantry followed. Then the tanks attacked again. Rommel sent in two columns, supported by tanks. One of them made for Divisional Headquarters, established about four miles from the harbour, and the other attacked the town itself.

The loss of Tobruk, which deprives the British of a valuable advance base, involves the sacrifice of huge stores.

The Allied forces in the triangle formed by Halfaya, Sollum, and Fort Capuzzo are preparing for Rommel's next blow, which may be launched against the Egyptian frontier.

Great activity is again going on in this area, which has already been the scene of much fighting. The triangle is Egypt's western gateway, and unless the enemy can subdue its fortifications the road to the Suez will remain barred.

ROME ANNOUNCEMENT

The Axis announcement of the capture of Tobruk was given by the Rome radio this afternoon in the following terms:

"After yesterday's bitter fighting, which smashed the enemy resistance an authorised British official presented himself at seven o'clock this (Sunday) morning to the commander of our 21st Army to surrender in the name of the commander of the Tobruk stronghold. Axis troops have occupied the stronghold, city and port. Twenty-five thousand prisoners have been taken, including several generals. Booty is overwhelming and cannot be given in detail."

In similar terms a German High Command communiqué also announced the capture of Tobruk, adding that "in a stubborn pursuit of a beaten enemy" towards the east Bardia and Bir El Gobi, the latter about 40 miles south of Tobruk, were captured.

GERMAN BATTLE STORY

The German Radio to-night gave the following account of the battle for Tobruk:

"In most bitter fighting in torrid heat, the resistance of the British 8th Army was broken, and the advance of the Axis troops against Via Balboa began.

"One part of the 8th Army was encircled in the Tobruk area. An attempt by the British forces to break out of the ring, supported by strong tank forces, was repelled. German and Italian troops then began the assault of the fortress, with decisive support from the air.

"The Luftwaffe played a large part in the capture of Tobruk. Numerous bombers, in ceaseless attacks on the fortress wrought great destruction in fortifications and other military works in port and town. The air above Tobruk was dominated by German fighters."

Major-General H.B. Klopper (centre, pointing at map) together with Major-General I.P. de Villiers, MC, shortly before Klopper took over command of Tobruk (South African National Museum of Military History).

LOOSENED DEFENCES

In the absence of details from Cairo, it is perhaps too early to attempt to assess the causes which have cost Britain the loss of the Tobruk citadel.

Certain considerations are, however, fairly clear. The defences had been loosened to a certain extent to facilitate the flow of supplies to forward areas, and it is doubtful if their efficiency could be fully restored in the brief interval in which the British troops were forced back into the stronghold.

The attack seems to have been made with an overwhelming weight of armour, which crashed right through the perimeter from the east and the south-east, where the lines are nearest to the fortress harbour.

The garrison seems to have been smaller than it was last year. A perimeter of more than 20 miles could not easily be held by 25,000 men, especially against such a massive blow concentrated in a limited space.

On Tuesday, 24 June, the *Cape Times* ran a colourful report by Sapa's war correspondent, Carel Birkby, which put together first-hand reports from some of the men who had managed to escape the fall of Tobruk.

ROMMEL MASSING FOR NEW ATTACK

IMPENDING BATTLE OF FRONTIER

SPRINGBOKS' LAST LAAGER

Following the fall of Tobruk, there are signs of an imminent new clash between Rommel's and Ritchie's forces. Axis tanks are massing in front of the Allied positions, which now rest on the Egyptian-Libyan border.

The prisoners taken by the enemy at Tobruk include two brigades of the 2nd S.A. Division under Major-General Klopper and two composite battalions and four batteries of artillery from the 1st S.A. Division. These grievous losses are referred to by Mr. Attlee in a sympathetic telegram to General Smuts, who replied: "Our sorrow will but harden our determination."

From Cairo come the first eyewitnesses' accounts of the struggle in the Tobruk perimeter. The South Africans are prominently mentioned. They formed a laager for a last stand and gave vent to shouts of disappointment and anger when they saw the flag of surrender being slowly hoisted on the mast of a wireless van.

HOW TOBRUK FELL

Sapa's War Correspondent.

EIGHTH ARMY HEADQUARTERS, Tuesday — Rommel was reported tonight to be massing his main forces opposite Fort Capuzzo, in the centre of the Eighth Army's new frontier line. Other enemy units are in position further south towards Sidi Omar.

A very strong column of enemy tanks and lorries of infantry has been moving rapidly east from Tobruk along the Bardia road, just past Gambut, some 20 miles from the frontier.

At Eighth Army Headquarters it is expected that Rommel's attack will be launched as soon as his forces are all in position. Last night this artillery engaged our advanced forces, apparently attempting to feel the strength of our defences.

ESCAPED FROM TOBRUK

Although there was no organised evacuation from Tobruk some troops managed to get away by sea. There were only a few naval units and one small schooner in the harbour when the town was attacked, and practically all of them got away. A few men managed to fight their way out.

To-day's Italian communique says that over 28,000 prisoners were taken at Tobruk.

LAST HOURS IN TOBRUK

FIRST-HAND STORIES OF SURRENDER

Sapa's War Correspondent

CAIRO, Tuesday. — Grim hand-to-hand fighting under the heavy pall of a German smoke-screen marked the last hours of the struggle for Tobruk, according to stories told by soldiers who have reached safety after taking part in the fighting around the fortress.

The fall of Tobruk was preceded by mass Stuka raids and a very heavy artillery barrage.

A number of South African dispatch riders told how the South Africans resisting the Axis attack gave vent to shouts of disappointment and anger when they had to surrender.

SPRINGBOK SPOKESMAN

Travel-stained, unshaven, uncombed and weary-eyed, the dispatch riders sat in the quietness of a South African headquarters office listening to their self-appointed spokesman as he told of the fighting for Tobruk and of their escape.

"On Friday afternoon," he said, "the enemy put out a feeler towards the south-west side of the Tobruk perimeter, but later withdrew.

"On Saturday morning they attacked heavily opposite the South Africans on the west side but were repulsed. Then, in the afternoon, they went round to the eastern side of the perimeter and put everything they had got into a fierce onslaught.

"First, they made an attack on the Indian infantry, but were beaten off. Later, 60 German tanks attacked, followed by German and Italian infantry, who advanced under cover of a heavy smokescreen laid by the German artillery.

"It was a very still, windless day, and the smokescreen hung over the stronghold like a mist. The screen was so heavy over Tobruk that when night came it blotted out the moon and the stars.

"After storming the eastern perimeter, the German tanks went straight for the harbour.

"The garrison was heavily dive-bombed all the time and on Saturday there were continuous air raids. Our artillery fought back but the enemy was too powerful and our people slowly withdrew, fighting all the time.

"Once the enemy tanks had got to Tobruk harbour they cut up towards headquarters on the top of the escarpment to the west. Here our forces held them for about an hour in hand-to-hand fighting. We then withdrew towards the west, where we formed a laager at about 5 o'clock in the afternoon.

"We had more than a dozen tanks, a number of 25-pounders and two dozen armoured cars in the laager, besides infantry.

"At first it was decided that we should try to break out after darkness, towards 10 o'clock. Later, it was found that the enemy was too strong and we spent the night in the laager, where the enemy did not trouble us."

FLAG OF SURRENDER

"But early on Sunday morning the shelling started again. Using anti-aircraft guns for level shooting the Germans kept up a constant bombardment. Dive-bombers joined in quickly, and by 8.45 we had had numerous air raids.

"At that time I saw the flag of surrender being slowly hoisted on the mast of a wireless van. There was a moment of silence among us as we watched the flag go up. Then there were shouts of anger and disappointment from all around."

A sapper lieutenant from London, who was evacuated from Tobruk by sea, described the heavy Stuka raids on the anti-aircraft defences of the fortress and heavy artillery barrage which followed them.

Members of the Native Military Corps holding a white flag and talking to the Allies after Tobruk had been retaken by the Allies on 12 November 1942. The Native Military Corps had been kept in Tobruk after the rest of the garrison had been sent into captivity by the Germans. They helped maintain the harbour, the roads and the little town in general (South African National Museum of Military History).

GUNS FELL SILENT

The anti-aircraft gunners fired gallantly at the Stukas for half an hour and shot down many planes, but it was an unequal struggle, and one by one the guns fell silent.

The lieutenant continued his account as follows: "The enemy artillery then opened up from the south and east on positions held by troops who had already seen a great deal of fighting in this campaign. They were troops from the United Kingdom, South Africa and India. This barrage made it impossible to send an ambulance up the road to evacuate the wounded.

"At the same time the enemy's infantry were thrown against the South Africans, but this attack was held up. In some places the gunners joined the infantry battle with rifles.

"Then German tanks crashed through the eastern sector, followed closely by lorries filled with German and Italian infantry. The tanks dashed straight through to the town itself, ignoring our fighting troops. Just outside the town, on the slope of a slight hill, they halted and turned about with their backs to the sea and their guns facing our forces between the town and the escarpment.

"After the tanks had come from the Bardia road the Germans sent in mobile anti-tank artillery. These splayed out inside the perimeter, and tackled our tanks.

"Inside the battered town were various non-fighting troops such as the Royal Army Service Corps, Engineers and non-European Pioneer units. All got to work immediately.

Tobruk harbour after the Allies had retaken it, November 1942 (South African National Museum of Military History).

They formed road blocks and even fought with rifles and any available weapon from ruined houses along the foreshore of Tobruk.

"A sapper lieutenant, who was driving a truck, evaded the German tanks and reached the harbour area, where there was considerable confusion, as by this time the enemy had brought the docks under methodical shell fire.

"In the harbour at the time were a minesweeper, a schooner and two lighters with a mixed party. The lieutenant reached the schooner, which was picking up from the oily waters of the bay, survivors from one of the lighters, which had been hit by a shell."

TIMELY SMOKESCREEN

The schooner then came under fire, but just as it seemed that all was over with those on board, a British motor torpedo-boat dashed into the harbour and circled the entire bay, pouring out a heavy smokescreen. This enabled the schooner and one big lighter to escape.

The last thing the lieutenant saw of Tobruk was a great mass of swirling smoke. The last thing he heard was the rattle of machine-guns and the explosions of hand grenades.

A South African Corporal from Bloemfontein who was with an ammunition column, escaped on the lighter.

Describing the fighting as he saw it, he said the South Africans, who were holding the western sector of the perimeter, were in great fettle and did not seem to be worried by the initial artillery bombardment on their positions, which was not as heavy as that on the east.

Soon after 7 a.m. on Saturday, between 10 and 20 enemy tanks attacked the South African defences from the south-west, moving in the direction of the Pilastrine track.

POINT-BLANK AT ITALIANS

"I saw eight tanks knocked out in five minutes by the fire from a 25-pounder," the corporal said. "I was at that time busy getting more ammunition up under fire to our guns. Next I saw Italian infantry attacking our gun positions from the rear. The South Africans immediately turned their guns and fired on the Italians point-blank."

At this stage the corporal was wounded and put in an ambulance which was heading for the harbour when it was hit by a shell.

The corporal crawled some distance until he was picked up by an officer of the R.A.S.C., who took him to the town, where he was put on the lighter.

Five months later, on the morning of 12 November 1942, in heavy rain, No. 40 Squadron SAAF sent a reconnaissance aircraft over Tobruk. The town was unoccupied. On the evening of 12 November, 'A' Squadron of the 4/6 SA Armoured Car Regiment was the first Allied unit to enter Tobruk after the German withdrawal. They captured 12 Germans and released a large number of the Native Military Corps, held as labourers since the fall of the town almost five months before.

'A great salvo of cheering'

The royal visit to South Africa, 1947

In March 1946 came a brief announcement from Buckingham Palace: 'The King and Queen have graciously consented to accept the suggestion of the Prime Minister of the Union of South Africa that they should visit South Africa in the early part of next year. Their Majesties, who will be accompanied by the Princess Elizabeth and Princess Margaret, hope to reach Cape Town some time in February 1947.'

When they did arrive — on the morning of 17 February 1947 — it was to a Cape Town already showing signs of insidious royal fever. Crowds estimated at 50 000-strong lined the streets of the mother city; a blind veteran of the Boer War claimed he 'saw' the King; the temperature on the Parade in Cape Town was 38°C in the shade, 45°C in the sun; the Red Cross dealt with 1 000 casualties; nurses on duty at Groote Schuur Hospital brought in their own radios to listen to the commentary; 12 people were trapped in a lift on their way to the top storey to see the Royal Family — and saw nothing at all.

The Cape Argus, in a special edition which sold for 2d, filled its front page with news of the arrival of George VI and his family — the first time a reigning British monarch had set foot on South African soil.

By the end of the two-month visit, the Royal Family had travelled approximately 16 000 kilometres. Princess Elizabeth turned 21 on 21 April and made her 21st-birthday speech to the Commonwealth from Government House, Cape Town. (Five minutes after she completed the broadcast, all the lights fused, leaving the royals, not for the first time, in the dark.) She received many gifts, the most notable of which were a blue-white diamond of six carats, a diamond brooch, 87 diamonds suitable for a necklace, and, presented to her at the State Ball in Cape Town by General Smuts, 21 pure white diamonds from the people of South Africa.

With the notable exception of Dr H.F. Verwoerd, editor of the Pretoria-based newspaper *Die Transvaler,* who refused to acknowledge the presence of the Royal Family, journalists made the most of the visit. The team of reporters from *The Argus,* dotted strategically around town, were no exception; the story of the landing and drive through the city fell into their 'time', *The Argus* being an afternoon newspaper. Syndicated to other papers in the Argus group, they made the most of the occasion. Although clearly admiring, they avoided, for the most part, too much gushing.

ARRIVAL OF THE ROYAL FAMILY

SOUTH AFRICA'S WELCOME

Proudest Day in the City's History

A new and gracious chapter in South African history began to-day as King George VI, his Queen, Elizabeth, and the two Princesses, Elizabeth and Margaret, came to Cape Town.

And the brightest page of that brilliant chapter was written at one minute to ten o'clock precisely when an erectly handsome figure stepped off the gangway of H.M.S. Vanguard on to South African soil.

That moment is all-significant. It can never be recaptured. So far as the Royal tour is concerned, everything that took place before and that which is to come, date from that dramatic moment of actual landing.

Until it struck, a multitude of eyes had wandered from point to point, trying "to take in everything at once," but as the King's feet touched South African soil every eye was fixed, every throat mute.

For the briefest instant there was silence. . . .

Then the King raised his hand in a naval salute, guns from Signal Hill thudded out, the National Anthem blared, a great cheer arose and the spell was almost broken.

But not quite broken. That gesture of the King's — the formal Service acknowledgment of a compliment — is destined to be repeated many, many times within the next eight weeks, but it, too, made history, for it was the "first."

The stiff salute was something more than an acknowledgment; it was the initial, personal greeting of George VI as King of South Africa to his "well-beloved people" of this Dominion, symbolised by the few thousands gathered at the dockside and so privileged to witness it.

If the first salute of the first reigning British monarch to set foot in this country is set in bold type in this chapter of our country's history, then the first glimpse of the King's ship as she hove majestically in sight over the Eastern Mole likewise deserves emphasis.

For those people gathered at the foot of Kingsway, in the amphitheatre embracing J berth, this was the opening scene in the coming drama.

The curtain rose upon it at 8.30 — 90 minutes before the moment of the landing.

Just 12 minutes later a burst of cheering from the crowds clustered at the ends of A berth and the Eastern Mole indicated that Vanguard's bow has cut through the entrance to the Duncan Dock.

With an air of excitement so intense that it could literally be felt, those who were seated rose to their feet and those afoot stood on their toes as the King's ship swung her stately bows in the direction of her berth.

And there, with the ship's bugles sounding over the placid surface of the water, we must leave her for a moment.

Day of Pageantry

This day of pageantry dawned as the first rays of the sun touched the city with pearly fingers and H.M.S. Vanguard was but a speck on the far horizon.

And as usual, the first sight to greet the royal visitors was grand old Table Mountain.

Not since the day Antonio da Saldanha first scaled its heights just 444 years ago has the mountain provided a more sublime setting for the second oldest city in the Empire — and never before has it witnessed such sights of jubilation and excitement as took place in Cape Town this sunshiny February day.

Long before the Vanguard crowded through the entrance into the dock, people began to assemble at J Berth.

The stands were slowly filling when a cavalcade of cars carrying Cabinet Ministers and members of the Diplomatic Corps swept into the amphitheatre to empty their passengers on to the steps of the royal dais.

Stands Adazzle

Around them swept a colourful and constant procession of notabilities in formal morning dress and their wives in gay summer attire.

Three air hostesses in powder-blue uniforms showed people to their seats and the area between the stands was a-dazzle with white naval uniforms, high-ranking officers of the U.D.F. with red tabs and yards of medal ribbon, W.A.A.F.s and "Wassies" in their service khaki, and the rank and file of Cape Town's citizens themselves.

"There They Are!"

How many people watched Vanguard make her stately way to the quayside? Ten thousand . . . 12,000? It is impossible to guess.

They had plenty to watch as the Vanguard made her slow and stately progress towards the quayside. First and foremost every eye was strained to catch the first glimpse of the King and Queen and the Princesses.

And then, a few minutes before nine o'clock, a shout arose: "There they are!"

Under an awning on top of "B" turret, they stood — the King in White uniform, the Queen at his left hand, the two Princesses on his right.

The Queen waved and the first real cheer of the day was born. It was taken up by the people on stands half-way up Kingsway, out of sight perhaps but more than anxious to sound a welcome.

A newsreel cameraman cranked his machine; Press and private cameras were levelled; field-glasses were fixed upon and every eye strained to watch that animated little group on the gun-turret.

Just as the first strokes of the City Hall clock chimed nine a string of coloured flags was suddenly and dramatically raised over the King's ship and a mighty gasp of admiration arose. It was a spontaneous tribute to a naval spectacle never rivalled in Table Bay — the King's ship with the Royal Family in full view.

And at that moment the royal party walked quietly aft from their vantage point and passed out of sight.

The first hint of military pomp to come was provided by the pipe-band of the Cape Town Highlanders.

Marching from the direction of H.M.A.S. Unitie, they wheeled into J Berth enclosure with a fine swing of kilts and a brave showing of bayonets and marched out again — through the triumphal arch on their way to the city proper.

Then came the brass band of the Permanent Force and the South African Air Force combined, led by the most martial figure of the drum major and followed by the Guard of Honour itself — the men of South Africa's "little ships," spotless — in white and marching like veritable guardsmen.

Followed the "snap, snap" of small-calibre guns as ropes were shot from Vanguard's decks to quayside, the mounted police escort arrived — the horses' coats glossy in the sunshine and the accoutrements of their riders jingling — and the battleship came to a standstill.

General Smuts

Perched high up against her after funnel a rating wiggled red and white hand-flags, and the business of hoisting the red-carpeted and green-and-yellow draped gangway began.

No sooner had it touched the quarterdeck with its Royal Marine guard than the crowd turned to watch the arrival, first of the Prime Minister, General Smuts, and then of the Governor-General, the Right Hon. G.B. van Zyl and Her Excellency, Mrs van Zyl.

A continuous roll of cheering from Kingsway heralded their approach, to die away only as they sought the shade of the dais before making their way to the foot of the gangway itself. It was 9.39.

Punctually to the second the Governor-General, Mrs. van Zyl and the Prime Minister trod the quarterdeck at 20 minutes to 10 o'clock and the first royal salute of this momentous day — played by the Royal Marines of H.M.S. Vanguard — brought everyone within earshot to attention.

This was followed by "Die Stem."

And then the three people bringing South Africa's official welcome to His Majesty and his family were escorted below.

The King Lands

After that instant of silence when the King stepped ashore a great salvo of cheering arose, almost drowning in its volume the sound of 21 guns firing the Royal Salute from the top of Signal Hill.

Again the anthem and "Die Stem" were played, and the King moved off to inspect the guard of honour, while the Queen and the Princesses sought the shade of the dais.

It was then, from the Press stand immediately in front of the gangway, that we had our first close-up view of the Royal Family.

The Queen and the Princesses were informally dressed when they stood with the King above the gun turret as Vanguard came through the dock gates.

The Queen wore a plain grey short-sleeved dress and a white straw hat.

The two Princesses wore double-breasted coats and skirts of white crepe with a nautical cut.

Princess Elizabeth let the slight breeze blow through her dark curly hair, but Princess Margaret had tied a gay chiffon kerchief over her hair.

While the ship was being brought alongside the Royal Family went below to change. When they came on to the quarterdeck again ready to land they made a delightfully colourful group.

The King wore the white uniform of an Admiral of the Fleet and the Queen was in mist blue.

Her beautiful crepe dress had panels crossing over the bodice in front and falling from the shoulders to the hem of her skirt at the back. The train-like panels were tipped with ostrich feather fronds to match the feathers on the frothy surge of blue silk net that formed the Queen's turban.

As Her Majesty walked along the red carpet to the dais she unfurled a blue silk parasol.

Princess Elizabeth's charming dress of pinky-beige silk had a plain bodice with the fullness gathered on the shoulders with bows of the material and the wrap-over skirt was draped at the left side.

288

Her hat, trimmed with veiling of the same soft shade, was bonnet-shaped and worn well back on her head.

Princess Margaret wore a silk dress in an enchanting shade of apricot. The plain bodice was embroidered at the neck and short sleeves and the full skirt hung in unpressed pleats. Her bonnet of the same shade was worn well back on the head and trimmed with a full bow falling below her shoulders at the back.

Standing under the dais on a carpet of royal blue, General Smuts presented to the Royal Family those dignitaries privileged to shake hands with the King and to bow or curtsy to the Queen and the Princesses.

They included the foremost men and women in the country — Cabinet Ministers and their wives, members of the Diplomatic Corps and their wives, Vice-Admiral Sir Clement Moody, Commander-in-Chief South Atlantic, and Lady Moody, Mr. J.G. Carinus, Administrator of the Cape and Mrs. Carinus, and the Mayor of Cape Town and Mrs. Bloomberg.

At 10.15 — a full half-hour before the scheduled time of departure — the royal car drew up alongside the dais and, smiling, bowing and looking supremely happy, the King, the Queen and Princesses Elizabeth and Margaret, drove off behind their escort, under the triumphal arch and into Kingsway and the waiting multitudes.

The royal tour had begun. . . .

The Royal Family (HRH Princess Elizabeth obscured by George VI) in Cape Town. They covered thousands of kilometres by rail during their South African tour (The Argus).

Crescendo of Cheers

As the car of royal blue containing the King and Queen passed slowly under the triumphal archway cheering and clapping broke out and rippled down the packed stands lining both sides of Kingsway.

The first burst of applause was a signal which fired the enthusiasm of the crowd, and the welcome grew from clapping and flag-waving to a crescendo of cheering as the royal party progressed towards the city.

Kingsway itself presented a magnificent sight. Troops with fixed bayonets lined both sides of the street, and above the packed stands, standard, flags and bunting fluttered gaily.

The morning mist that earlier on had shrouded and partly hidden the city had almost lifted as the royal procession moved off on its historic drive.

A pilot-car headed the procession, with the first file of 20 mounted police in khaki uniform 20 yards behind.

Then in an open touring car came the King, with the Queen seated at his right hand.

His Majesty was composed and grave, with attentive eyes searching every part of the thronged grandstands, and his hand came repeatedly to the salute in acknowledgment of the cheering. At points where the welcome was exceptionally warm he smiled his appreciation.

The Princesses

At his side the Queen, happy at the enthusiastic reception from the Mother City, raised her right hand and bowed slightly in a gracious gesture.

The two Princesses travelled in a semi-closed car a dozen yards behind Their Majesties, with Princess Elizabeth seated on the right of her younger sister.

Half-way down Kingsway the crowd lost the reserve and self-consciousness which confined its first welcome principally to vigorous clapping.

People rose to their feet shouting and cheering, and dozens of young men and boys broke from the stands and, despite the dust and heat, ran to keep pace with the royal cars until their way was blocked by crowds flocking from the stands to the rope barrier guarding the roadway.

A second file of 20 mounted police followed the Princesses car, and behind them came the Governor-General and Mrs. van Zyl and Mrs. Hugo Brunt, lady-in-waiting to Her Excellency.

The order of the procession was then as follows:

The Prime Minister, Field-Marshal J.C. Smuts; Sir Alan Lascelles, private secretary to the King; the Lady Harlech, lady-in-waiting; Surgeon Rear-Admiral H.E.Y. White, medical officer to the King.

The Administrator, Mr. J.G. Carinus, and Mrs. Carinus.

The Lady Delia Peel, lady-in-waiting; Lady Margaret Egerton, lady-in-waiting; Major M. Adeane, assistant private secretary to the King; Capt. L. Ritchie, Press secretary to the Royal Household.

The Mayor of Cape Town, Mr. A. Bloomberg, M.P., and Mrs. Bloomberg; Major T. Harvey, private secretary to the Queen; and an equerry.

Commissioner of South African Police, Major-Gen. R.J. Palmer; Deputy-Com. L.

Burt, of Scotland Yard; Inspector A.E. Perkins, the Queen's police officer; and Mr. Donald Spies, manager of the royal tour.

In Adderley-street

The throng in Adderley-street, close on 50,000, represented all sections of South Africa's European and non-European community.

They lined the barriers 15 to 30 deep and crammed every available position on the balconies and at the windows of gaily decorated buildings.

For hours the crowd had waited and with the thermometer rising to the 90 mark, newspapers and handkerchiefs were used by the hatless as protection against the hot sun.

There were cheers a few minutes before 9 a.m., when the mounted police escort passed on their way to the docks.

At 9.30 the Prime Minister, and five minutes later the Governor-General and Mrs. van Zyl were applauded as they drove down to the docks.

The firing of the Royal Salute was the signal for the police and cadets lining the barriers to close their ranks.

When the procession rounded the War Memorial the vast crowd gave a full-throated roar. Those in the city's main thoroughfare seemed determined that their demonstration of affectionate welcome should be the loudest.

On the way up the street the King pointed out to the Queen items of special interest on the buildings.

Then, as the procession passed, thousands of people ran to St. George's-street to get another view of the Royal Family.

The procession turned into Wale-street and went down St. George's-street.

When the royal party turned into Adderley-street for the second time police had to link arms and form a human chain to hold back the pressing people.

Coming past the railway station the King was seen to be chatting animatedly to the Queen. Smiling, she waved graciously.

As the procession went down Castle-street to the ex-servicemen lining the route on the Parade, the crowds broke through the police ranks and rushed after the cars.

Ex-Servicemen

Veterans of the wars and campaigns of the last 55 years were among the 5,000 ex-servicemen, commanded by Brig. W.D. Hearn, who lined the route in the Grand Parade area.

As the head of the procession turned on to the Parade the order was given to "off hats," and Brigadier Hearn led the bemedalled and beribboned men in three, thundering cheers.

Outside the City Hall the route was lined by 500 former members of the Cape Corps from both world wars under the command of Major G.A. Wood.

As the royal procession moved slowly past, the years seemed to drop off the old campaigners and their backs straightened to vie with those of the younger generation on parade.

One of the oldest men there was 78-year-old Sgt.-Bugler R.I. Camb, wearing the old-pattern red-tunic uniform of the Duke of Edinburgh's Own Rifles, and pinned to his chest the medals of the South African War and the Bechuanaland Campaign.

The Corps of Commissionaires, under Capt. Alf Button, turned out 28 men, ten of them over 70 years old and 12 over 60.

But probably the oldest man on parade was a veteran of 84 who proudly wore on his chest the medal of the bombardment of Alexandria in the Egyptian War of 1882.

A splash of colour amid the sober suits of the ex-volunteers was provided by the pipe band of the Caledonian Society and the Christian Brothers' School.

The Royal Family, after a hugely successful trip, left South Africa from Cape Town in HMS *Vanguard* on 27 April 1947. Less than five years later, George VI was dead and his daughter, Elizabeth, was Queen. Under the premiership of Dr H.F. Verwoerd, South Africa's links with the Crown were formally ended when the country left the Commonwealth on 31 May 1961.

'Last ball of the day, one run for victory'

The first test, Springboks v MCC, 1948

It would be unusual for sports editors not to have a keen interest in the subject. But Cyril Olliver Medworth, sports editor of *The Natal Mercury* for 23 years, was a considerable sportsman himself. He played both rugby and cricket for Stellenbosch between 1923 and 1925. He played for the junior Western Province team in 1925 and played rugby for Natal between 1928 and 1929.

Medworth, a teacher by profession, joined *The Natal Mercury* in 1946. An all-round sports writer, he nonetheless specialised in his favourite sports of rugby and cricket. What better match could he have reported on than the first test match of the MCC tour in Durban in the week before Christmas 1948? This particular cricket international was decided with the last ball of the last over — one of the most exciting ends to a test match this century.

The excitement of the match was nicely reflected by Medworth in his report which was printed on Tuesday, 21 December 1948 in *The Natal Mercury,* and syndicated to other morning newspapers.

DRAMATIC TEST VICTORY FOR ENGLAND

Leg-Bye Off Last Ball Ends Thrilling Match

McCARTHY WAS HERO OF SPRINGBOK ATTACK

In the most dramatic finish to a Test match ever seen at Kingsmead, or possibly anywhere else — England yesterday won the first of the series by two wickets, to become one up and four to play.

The final two hours' cricket yesterday afternoon were so packed with incident that it is difficult to know just where to start.

England needed one run for victory as Tuckett ran up to bowl the last ball of the day. Gladwin was facing and he meant to get that run somehow. He did.

As Tuckett bowled Gladwin was down the wicket swinging his bat in the general direction of the ball.

MISSED THE BALL

He missed the ball, which hit his pad. But Gladwin and Bedser were on their way to their respective ends and "Tufty" Mann, fielding at silly mid-on, could just not get to the ball quickly enough to roll it on to the wicket for a run out.

There was a wild scramble for wickets as souvenirs and admirers rushed on to the ground to chair Gladwin. McCarthy, South Africa's young fast bowler, too, was hoisted on high.

He had brought his side to the brink of victory. How near South Africa had come to achieving the seemingly impossible! How gallant they were in defeat, how glorious England were in victory they richly deserved!

This Test will ever live in the memory as cricket in excelsis. "This is the best possible Christmas gift we can send our folks back home," seemed to be the first thoughts of the England players.

Never have I seen a crowd at a cricket match so charged with excitement as the 7,000 were yesterday afternoon. Had the Springboks held their catches, then who knows, they might have been the ones cheered to victory.

Olliver Medworth, sports editor of The Natal Mercury *for 23 years (*The Natal Mercury*).*

Game Of "Ifs"

But this has, right from the start, been a game of "ifs" and, with the excitement of the crowds communicating itself to the players, it is easier to make excuses for catches not held with a greasy ball than it is to apportion blame to players who so nearly brought an amazing victory to South Africa.

Many there were who felt, after the excitement had died down, that perhaps in a game of that nature a tie would have been the best possible result.

If there is one criticism to be made it is on the question of appeals against the light. Yesterday afternoon, when the game had reached an unexpected climax, play continued long after the light had deteriorated.

In better conditions on other days of the Test, appeals had been lodged and upheld.

Magnificent

In the pre-lunch session yesterday Begbie and Wade fought such a magnificent rearguard action that it almost seemed they had put South Africa safely out of danger of defeat, particularly as it was realised that with dark clouds looming overhead rain was likely.

This partnership of 85 in 82 minutes showed the ability of the middle batting to bring substance to the innings.

It showed determination and courage and the desire to score runs when possible. Their effort was as meritorious as any in this game of gallant deeds.

Rowan and Wade carried on the good works, but in a slower tempo.

Now time mattered more than runs and South Africa was fighting for breath.

Priceless Runs

Quite unexpectedly Wade went, employing his own typical leg sweep, but one from Jenkins broke enormously to bowl Wade round his legs.

What a glorious innings Wade played. His 63 runs were priceless and beyond compare.

Both Tuckett and Rowan hung on grimly. Even Mann subdued himself for quite some time.

But slowly then wended their way back to the pavilion and then England had 127 minutes left to make 128 runs.

Washbrook and Hutton showed right away that they meant to make the runs and make them quickly. But a major tragedy nearly overtook South Africa when the first ball of the innings was bowled.

Hutton late cut McCarthy. Nourse, fielding in the gully received a severe blow from a rising ball on the side of the knee cap and dropped like a log. Players clustered around him in sympathy, medical aid was rendered and, after eight minutes, precious moments for England, the South African captain arose and there was a sigh of relief when it was seen his directive on the field was not to be lost after all.

Heavy Drizzle

A heavy drizzle set in almost immediately and the players trooped off the ground without any appeal being visibly made by anyone.

This further interruption of 12 minutes made England's task the harder, but also that of the South African bowlers, who now had a slippery ball to handle.

Washbrook was most severe on anything off his wicket and he smote Tuckett high and deep towards long leg, where Wynne waited for the high lofted catch, but he did not get under it properly and Washbrook escaped.

But when Tuckett induced Hutton to spoon up an easy catch to Dawson at silly mid-on, the crowd cheered to the echo.

Mann came in and it was more obvious than ever before that the object was to accelerate the rate of scoring at any price.

Washbrook almost turned a ball into Rowan's hands at backward short leg.

Then Mann lashed out at his namesake and McCarthy waited patiently in the deep field. The catch dropped from his cupped hands accompanied by the groans of the crowd.

But "Tufty" Mann trapped Washbrook into a leg before decision and the crowd hummed with excitement.

Keyed Up

Compton was keyed up for the situation and then Nourse made a strategic move. He brought back McCarthy as much to suit South Africa's ends as to give the young player a chance of forgetting about that catch he had dropped. How wonderfully the young lad responded.

Mann swung on one and Mitchell at first slip made the catch appear easy enough.

Next McCarthy bowled Watkins as he played back and when Simpson off the next ball offered Eric Rowan at silly mid-on a simple catch the crowd could hardly believe this change in fortunes.

But there was more to follow. The tall South African fast bowler completely beat and bowled Evans and with the score 70 for six wickets it looked as though England would have to fight desperately to avoid defeat.

Rolling Gait

It was here that Jenkins, of the rolling gait, stepped into the breach and, with Compton gathering confidence in his partner, they set about steadily mounting the score until it seemed as though they would easily reach their target in the time left.

It meant a run a minute still, but they were going remarkably well and safely.

Just then McCarthy struck another blow for his country by bowling Compton, and when Wade, standing yards back, yelled to high heaven for a catch at the wicket as Jenkins swept round to another express delivery and the umpire raised his finger, it really did seem as though a last-minute victory would accrue to South Africa.

So much happened so quickly in that final five minutes that it became difficult to keep count.

One last ball — a dramatic end to a dramatic match (The Star).

Dropped Catch

As Gladwin quickly joined his partner at the wicket, he lashed at the next ball from McCarthy, but Tuckett in the mist and rain misjudged the catch which should have been an easy one and again it dropped from the fingers.

It was stark tragedy, all this, viewed from South African eyes, but a slice of luck for England.

Came the last over and 8 runs to make.

Nourse reset his field and Gladwin lifted one just over Eric Rowan's head at deep mid wicket to the rails.

Bedser was almost run out trying to sneak another as the over drew to a close.

Breathtaking

By this time nearly everyone was standing, though some turned away, the excitement being too much for them.

Then that final sweep, the frantic run and victory for England.

It had been breathtaking cricket all through and it will surely be many a long year before one will be privileged to live through another game of such intense excitement.

' "Oubaas" passing'

The funeral of General Jan Smuts, 15 September 1950

General Jan Christiaan Smuts spent the day before his 80th birthday on 24 May 1950 driving through the streets of Johannesburg and a crowd of 300 000 to receive the Freedom of the City. Outside the City Hall, albeit one day early, he was greeted by a giant birthday cake encircled by 80 electrically lit candles.

Three days later, on 27 May, Smuts suffered a coronary thrombosis, which was followed by pneumonia, and was ill for seven weeks. His family kept his heart condition a secret from him, and he spent the weeks after his recovery driving around the country. On 9 September, Smuts was photographed sitting in the garden at Doornkloof playing with his grandchildren. On 11 September he took a drive with his wife, Isie, and, after dinner, went to his room. Sitting on his bed he lapsed into unconsciousness and died that night. South Africa lost not only a brilliant mind, but one of the few South Africans of genuine international stature.

The nation, so frequently divided, came together for his funeral on Friday, 15 September 1950, when he was accorded a state funeral with full military honours. Dignitaries from all over the world paid their last respects to him. But none were so heartfelt as the vast, silent crowds of South Africans that gathered to say farewell to a great and much-loved man.

It was a day filled with poignancy, from the bent Boer War veterans who stood in silent tribute as his cortège passed, to bemedalled men who had fought in North Africa and Italy and who struggled, and sometimes failed, to hold back their tears.

Those who were unable to line the route of the funeral procession in Pretoria and then in Johannesburg, or stand in little knots to watch the train with his coffin travel between the two cities, listened to the proceedings on radio. Broadcast by the SABC on the 'A' and 'B' programmes, the funeral service at the Groote Kerk, the procession to the station and scene at the station itself were covered by no fewer than twelve commentators.

Like his friend and ally Winston Churchill's funeral, which was to take place more than a decade later, the final part of Smuts's funeral was a family affair and the press was not privy to the proceedings.

But the public part of the day, from the Groote Kerk service to the slow journey to the crematorium in Johannesburg, was minutely covered by the press. It was difficult for any newspaper reporting the event not to lapse into occasional sentimentality, and *The Star* was no exception. But its reports on the day which, like other newspapers, entirely filled the front page, were well written and, even today, bring a lump to the throat. *The Star*'s reports, two of which are printed here, appeared in the Stop Press edition of the newspaper on Friday, 15 September 1950.

Nation Pays Last Honours to General Smuts

GREAT OF THE LAND AND SILENT CROWDS JOIN IN HOMAGE

"OUMA," LONELY ON HER FARM,
WAITS FOR A FINAL GLIMPSE OF FUNERAL TRAIN

Funeral bells tolled through all South Africa as Field-Marshal Jan Christiaan Smuts, patriot, soldier, statesman, was laid to rest to-day.

Victorious even in defeat in the last great fight of all — against death itself — his body received the final rites of Church and State — and his spirit entered the hall of heroes of the Western world.

Although Pretoria and Johannesburg saw the last great obsequies, the whole country was in truth one vast cathedral shrine for an hour or two to-day.

And people of all races, colours, creeds, in city, town, remotest dorp and farm, formed the vast congregation of his mourners in such a show of homage and of grief as South Africa has never seen before and is not likely soon to see again.

Not least among the mourners everywhere were the dwindling band of his old comrades-in-arms, the oudstryders and the hosts of bemedalled and beribboned men and women who in one or two great wars have been proud to "fight for and with Jannie Smuts."

Staunch Friend

But while the nation mourned the passing of its greatest son, and representatives of kings, and queens, and presidents of the Western world joined with his own compatriots

*Jan Smuts' funeral procession, Pretoria (*The Star*).*

to pay a last tribute to so great a man, the smaller, sadder band of family, servants and friends, paid homage to the revered father, beloved grandfather, kind master and staunch, gay, gallant friend.

Lonelier even than these in her bereavement was the widowed "Ouma" at the farm. As the guns thundered in salute and battle planes dipped among the hills that hid Pretoria from her sight, she sat sadly on the verandah of the Doornkloof home, waiting to catch a last glimpse of her husband's bier as the funeral train sped by on the last journey to Johannesburg.

The thoughts of all South Africa and all her friends far overseas go out to-day and in the days to come to that lonely figure, whose last tribute to a husband who was among the great ones of the modern world carried among its wreathed Cape heath and wild veld flowers a message of grief and yet of hope, "Totsiens, Pappa."

Scenes He Knew

The day broke doleful with grey clouds. As the first light glanced across the eastern hills on lovely Doornkloof farm, it fell on a house of grief. Who there but felt the pangs of loss at the Oubaas's passing?

Poignancy breathed in everything that stirred the memory. Never again would family, servant, friend hear his cheery early morning call for coffee.

They would never see him striding masterfully along the fields and hills, admiring in these golden springtime days the kafirboom with its epaulettes of scarlet blooms, the wild pear trees in clouds of misty flowers white, the fresh green oaks and willow trees that he had planted long ago.

African hoopoe and fiscal shrike flashed among the branches of his favourite avenue. They called to him in vain. Never would he identify the song or species of some favourite bird.

Sad it was to look at the flowering grasses and shrubs and trees which he had loved so much. Even the first veld flowers that came before the rains were barbed with pain.

In his room on a table by the untouched bed lay a well-thumbed copy of his favourite book, the "Wuthering Heights" of Emily Bronte, which he preferred above Shakespeare's grandest play.

It has a special mark against the paragraph that brings it to a close surely one of the loveliest passages in all English literature. Thus it runs: "I lingered round then under that benign sky; watched the moths fluttering among the heath and harebells, listened to the soft wind breathing through the grass, and wondered how any one could ever imagine unquiet slumbers for the sleepers in that quiet earth."

Only a few days before his death he had murmured those wistful words. Could he have known then that his own restless spirit would so soon be at rest like the people in his favourite book?

Mourners Gather

At Doornkloof, on this saddest of sad days, the breakfast is soon over and the family set out for the great church in which the body of the soldier-statesman lies.

The mourners begin to gather in the streets. The church doors yawn. The congregation of friends and dignitaries take their seats.

Along the funeral route outside the soldiers, sailors and airmen of South Africa assume their posts. The generals and diplomats assemble. The organ music sounds forth. Flags mourn at half-mast everywhere.

The hymns are sung, the funeral orations are delivered. The cortege rolls, and as the gun-carriage with its tragic load comes into view sighs break from the sad multitudes.

Saluting Guns

The defenders of South Africa pay homage to their old Prime Minister and Commander-in-Chief.

Pall-bearer generals convey the bier from grief-lined streets to waiting train. The planes dip overhead. The thunder of saluting guns rolls and reverberates among the city and its rolling hills.

TWO THOUSAND PEOPLE PAY HOMAGE IN GROOT KERK

DISTINGUISHED COMPANY OF MOURNERS

Two thousand people representing half of mankind filed softly into the Groot Kerk, Pretoria, this morning to pay homage to Jan Christiaan Smuts.

The coffin, covered with the Union flag, lay before the pulpit. On it were a Field Marshal's cap, Sam Brown belt and sword, and a wreath of purple, white and scarlet Cape heaths, tied with the United Party colours from Mrs. Smuts, bearing the words "Totsiens, Pappa."

From this church, whence General Smuts set out on his last earthly journey, he had, barely two years ago, with his face set like steel, followed the coffin of his beloved friend, Jan Hendrik Hofmeyr. Here, he brought the King and Queen to worship. From here, flushed and solemn, he had followed the coffin of his own leader, General Louis Botha.

Behind the coffin was a bank of arum lilies and white watsonias, and around it walls of wreaths, including those from the Smuts family, the King, Queen Juliana of the Netherlands, the King and Queen of Greece, the President of the French Republic, the President and members of the Senate, the Speaker and members of the House of Assembly, the Government of Canada, the Diplomatic Corps, the Eighth Army Commander and all ranks, Rhodesian military forces, the Border Command, the Memorable Order of Tin Hats, the Empire Press Union, and the people of Irene.

FORMED PHALANX

Half an hour before the service began people started to come in. Representatives of the armed forces occupying pews in the centre of the church behind the five seats reserved for the family mourners formed a phalanx of khaki, scarlet and blue.

The eight warrant officers who were to be bearers sat on their right; the eight South African generals who were to be pall-bearers sat on their left.

The Right Hon. N.J. de Wet, representing the King and the Governor-General, took the first seat on the right of the coffin. Next to him was the Prime Minister and Mrs. Malan and seven Cabinet Ministers. Behind them sat members of General Smuts's Cabinet.

Opposite on the left of the coffin, five diplomats representing kings or presidents, sat in black and gold braid, holding their white-plumed hats. Among them was Sir Evelyn Baring in a morning suit.

Then entered General R.J. Palmer, Commissioner of Police, Mr. F. Boltman, Railway Commissioner, Mr. Douglas Mitchell, M.P., and Senator Heaton Nicholls.

Mr. O.A. Oosthuizen, general secretary of the United Party, and Mrs. Oosthuizen took their places in the mourners' pews.Then came Mr. Henry Cooper, General Smuts's private secretary for many years, and Miss E. Raath, his typist, in uniform with orange flashes.

Mr. J.G.N. Strauss, acting leader of the United Party, and Mrs. Strauss took their places. Mr Strauss sitting with folded arms and motionless face.

DEAD MARCH

Just before 10.30 a.m. the members of the Smuts family, accompanied by five of General Smuts's nurses, came into the church. The congregation stood as the organist played Beethoven's Dead March and "Lead, Kindly Light." The great bell tolled. The doors were shut.

Up to this point the proceedings were smooth and impersonal. Then the Rev. J. Reyneke, accompanied by the Rev. Dr. J.B. Webb and the Rev. Mr. Louw came into the pulpit and Mr. Reyneke announced the poignant Afrikaner sacred song: "Just as the landsman who has ploughed greets with joy the evening shadows."

There was a fluttering of papers and the congregation stood and began to sing, their voices swelling to great volume. The people had begun to take a personal part in the service.

A breeze began to stir outside and drift into the church through the high windows.

With all the men standing and the women sitting, the Rev. Mr. Louw read a prayer, and then Mr. Reynecke, his voice trembling now and then, gave his funeral oration.

"BID YOU FAREWELL"

The high moment of the service was reached when Mr. Reyneke raised his hands at the end of his address and said: "We bid you farewell, Oubaas. Amen."

The congregation then sang "Lead, Kindly Light," which Mr. Reyneke said was General Smuts's favourite hymn and the Rev. Dr. Webb gave his address.

Psalm 146, "Salig hy wat in die lewe," was sung and the blessing given. The congregation all standing, the bearers and pall-bearers formed up on either side of the coffin. The bearers raised it to their shoulders, and followed Mr. Reynecke and Dr. Webb down the aisle while the organist, Miss Sarah Mullers, played Handel's Dead March in "Saul," fading softly into "Lead Kindly Light."

The family and mourners left their seats. The procession moved slowly from the church.

Outside there was a sharp command as the armed forces prepared to take charge of the cortege.

"SLOW MARCH"

At 11.20 the great crowd outside the church tensed as the various military units came to attention. Crowds which had been watching the church entrance began to make their way into the square. Then came the order "Slow march."

'Will you be my turtle dove, or not?'

Todd Matshikiza, 1953/1955

Todd Matshikiza, wine steward, messenger, bootlegger, razor blade salesman, barber's shop sweeper, music teacher, composer, music critic and journalist, first played the piano at the age of seven and was involved with music one way or another all his life.

A teacher by profession (he graduated at Lovedale Institute), he was commissioned in 1956 to write a choral work for the Johannesburg Festival and, in 1959, wrote the lyrics for the musical *King Kong* (described by critic Bernard Levin of the London *Daily Express* as 'tunes weaving around the hypnotic volume of noise').

Matshikiza joined *Drum* in the early Fifties and wrote a regular daily column, 'With the Lid Off', as well as regular jazz articles. His writing formed part of the 'Jazz Age' in South Africa, a veritable explosion of talent among black writers in the 1950s and 1960s. His articles on jazz are musical pieces in themselves — brief, snappy exercises rich in humour, rhythm and the smoky atmosphere of the clubs he loved to frequent, and a salute to the Sophiatown in which they flourished. 'Dam-Dam!' was published in December 1953 and 'Jazzing the Blues' in March 1955.

JAZZING THE BLUES!

Then said Louisa Emanuel to Isaac Peterson, "Will you be my turtle dove, or not?" Isaac replied (in the English used in Show biznes), "No I ain't no turtle an' I ain't no durv. So I cain't be yo' turtle-durv."

Louisa said, "I'm looking for a man to sing with me. He must coo as I purr. Coat as I fur. In other words, his voice must match mine."

Says Isaac, "Baby I'se got ze voice. Dunno if I'se got ze match. We'll figure it out. I reckon you'se got ze figure anyhow."

That's how this partnership started.

I was interested in that conversation as I listened through the stage curtain. Louisa was nervous. The lights were on. Bright. Very bright. Isaac wasn't nervous. Not very. If stage fright got him, Louisa's pretty, confident smile would hide his fright. Louisa. One hundred and twenty pounds of vocal dynamite packed in four yards of lace and taffeta . . . Or four yards of nylon-net and sequins across the chest. Louisa. Pearly white teeth that grace the mouth that lets out the voice that thrills from Johburg to Rustenburg. Even listening to her speak. I wasn't listening. I was hearing, hearing, hearing . . . and hoping she wouldn't stop.

And Isaac. Son of Peterson. Bound by ties of brotherhood to American clothes.

Commanded by a little birdie inside of him to sing . . . sing . . . sing to save the sorrows of ten million black voices.

You wouldn't know him if you met him at home in Vrededorp. Sits around the corner looking lazy like a lord. Slumps down in a chair like he was waiting for some luck. Looks at you with black beady eyes like he's blaming you for it all. And thanks you for his gift of song as if you gave him all.

These two little kids, Louisa Emanuel (aged twenty), and Isaac Peterson (twenty-three), surprised me once by saying, "We two see things the same way. We met and we're tied hand and foot to the stage. And what showbiz puts together, let no man put us under. We want to stay at the top all the time."

Todd Matshikiza

They love a song called "Confess." In fact it's one of their most famous items. The people say, "We wish those two could fall in love each time they sing, 'Confess'." But Louisa and Isaac take love right out of their musical profession. In fact Louisa is "still in mother's care," (as she says), and love will begin to come to her, a little later than now. Meanwhile, Louisa and Isaac are proudly your very own Lord and Lady of Song. They might find time to talk to you between factory hours. Or if you'd like to meet Louisa, her Mom lives with her, and Dad and a fiery dog "Danger," in Vrededorp.

DAM-DAM!

I said to Dam-dam yesterday: "Dam-dam, I bet you my last shirt you're the biggest playboy going on."

He said: "Blow you, Toddie-boy, I'm still looking for my dream gal!"

I said: "What happened to the juicy berries I've seen hanging on you?" For Dam-dam knows a nice dame when he sees one.

He said: "Skip them. You wouldn't bet your dough on a donkey on the racecourse, would you? I dream at the pace of a racehorse. They dream at the pace of a lame donkey."

"Belladonna," he went on, "the Boksburg blondie that dazzled scarlet earrings and bronze brooches and things, she was running me and another mug on alternate days. My love is not for sale. I quit her.

"Valentenia, the nut-brown babe from Westcliff. She dressed like a Parisian goddess. I discovered it was her mistress's wardrobe. I shook her off like coal dust on my feet.

"Tantalusia, tall, tan, terrific. She wanted to attend every show with me. She wanted me to herself. Well, show bizness is my bizness and not my hunting ground for love.

Dam-dam himself, 30 year-old Nathan Dambuza Mdledle, leader of the famous Manhattan Brothers. His troupe averaged £250 a week; their greatest pride was that they were the best-dressed musical troupe on and off stage. With the exception of Contentment Daku, who died at a tribal initiation school, the Manhattan Brothers had been together since they were eight years old (Bailey's African Photo Archives).

"I'm an artist. I belong to the people, and to one woman, body and soul. I belong to Miss Music."

I asked: "Ever broken anybody's home, Dam-dam?" He looked daggers at me and said: "Toddie-boy, never; nix. But I've known men to beat up their women for bringing home one of my records. If that's breaking up a home, I've broken up a thousand homes."

Then Dam-dam looked at his slender well-groomed figure and said: "D'you know why my future wife must be a dreamer? 'Cause I'm a dreamer myself. A thinker. I've no time to eat. Good Gawd! No thinker has time to eat. My future wife will have a home to look after. I've recently spent £110 on the fence alone.'

"Money is not my object. But if I can make it, my future wife must be prepared to enjoy it with me . . . and MaNdlovu, my darling mother, the apple of MY eye. Now scram!"

Which I scrammed.

Matshikiza rose to become chief reporter of *Drum,* but left South Africa for London in 1961. He returned to Africa, working for Malawi Radio as an announcer and, in 1963, joined Zambia Radio. He died in Lusaka in 1965.

'Sniff of victory, tide of defeat'

Louis Duffus and the 1953 Springbok tour of Australia

A team of youthful 'no-hopers' left South Africa in the spring of 1953 to tackle the might of Australian cricket in its own backyard. With total dedication to the task in hand, the team developed into an unexpectedly formidable combination of cricketers and by the end of the tour had earned the unqualified respect of the cricket world.

Reporting on the tour was Louis Duffus, the legendary cricket writer. He was, so to speak, on home ground reporting the tour: he was born in Melbourne on 13 May 1904, and arrived in South Africa as a boy of five. Duffus covered every cricket tour to and from South Africa after 1929 until his retirement as *The Star*'s sports editor (he succeeded H.B. Keartland) in 1967.

The 1953 Springbok tour of Australia was one of the last international sporting events free of demonstrations against apartheid. Perhaps the finest performance of this tour came when the Springboks won the second test in the week between Christmas and New Year. Louis Duffus, in his warm, affectionate style (prone to over-enthusiasm, he was once rebuked by telegram by Keartland and told to report on the game at hand and not the verbiage) described the final day's play for newspapers in the Argus group. His report was used in *The Star* and *The Daily News* on 30 December 1953.

Australia beaten by eighty-two runs at Melbourne

Melbourne Cricket Ground, Tuesday.

Just after 3.30 on a thrilling, sunny afternoon, South Africa dismissed Australia for 290 and won the second test match by 82 runs.

They jumped about the field in jubilation as 14,000 spectators rose to acclaim them and made way for 24-year-old Hugh Tayfield to pass first through the gate after achieving South Africa's greatest feat in a test match.

Today he took 7 wickets for 81 runs and, with his 6 for 84 in the first innings, totalled 13 for 165 in the match to surpass J. Snooke's 12 for 127 against England in Johannesburg in 1905-6.

Tayfield bowled Miller early in the day for 31, and though Benaud (45) and Ring (53) played admirable, aggressive innings Tayfield claimed them both after a remarkable spell of bowling which included taking four wickets for no runs in 103 overs. It was the second time he had taken seven wickets in a test match.

It is only the second time in 31 matches that South Africa have beaten Australia — the other victory being by 38 runs at Adelaide in 1910-11. Jack Cheetham and his young inexperienced team probably accomplished the greatest and, at one time, least expected triumph in the country's cricket history.

The crowd hurried into the ground buzzing with expectation as Hugh Tayfield bowled up the slope to Miller to start his remarkable spell of overs. The wicket was still good — by no means a cause for collapse. Innes fielded for Funston, who had an injured leg and the score was 132 for four, Miller 23 and Langley 0.

Tayfield at once settled into a mechanically accurate length. Cheetham had debated this morning whether to use Melle or Mansell from the top end. He used Melle and seven were scored off an erratic over. When Tayfield took over again Miller streaked up the pitch as Langley cut and had to dive to recover his ground from McLean's return.

Louis Duffus, South Africa's great cricket writer (The Star).

SNIFF OF VICTORY

With the third ball of his second over, Tayfield bowled Langley who appeared to play for spin that was not there. The ball gently removed the bails. The South Africans had a sniff of victory. They flung themselves at shots that were impossible to save and threw to the wicket with violence of keyed up energy.

The "night watchman" had gone for four with only seven runs added. Cheetham changed Mansell for Melle after Melle's one over, but the slow bowler's first eight balls cost nine runs.

Then came the feat that was the theme of the South Africans' excited minds through a restless night. As he came through the turnstile this morning, Miller exclaimed: "I think I'll stop you boys today. I'm seeing them well."

After 16 minutes of tense, quiet play, he attempted a vigorous off-drive and was bowled by Tayfield. Like Langley, he appeared to anticipate a break from a ball that went straight through. Two wickets had fallen for 17 runs. Miller, the chief obstacle to victory, was out for 31, and Tayfield was in the midst of an extraordinary spell of maiden overs.

TIDE OF DEFEAT

As Hole and Benaud formed their partnership, Mansell settled down to a steady length and Australia battled grimly to halt the tide of defeat. Hole drove a lovely cover stroke off

Mansell for four and, as he turned a single to leg Innes threw eagerly to concede two overthrows.

It was 157 for six when Hole tried to swing Tayfield to leg and was so nearly bowled that Watkins and Tayfield spun round and raised their arms to their heads. When they had added 33 to take the score to 181, Hole, who batted 19 minutes, again swung to leg and was gently bowled.

The South Africans showed no emotion but, if their nervous excitement before the game was any guide, a lot of twitching was going on out on the field. When the first run was eventually scored off Tayfield he had bowled nine overs and three balls today and taken 3 for 0. With his final over last night, his figures were 10.3/10/0/4. He had surpassed "Tufty Mann's" feat of starting his test career by bowling eight consecutive maiden overs at Nottingham.

Benaud batted with sound judgment. When Lindwall had settled down he lifted two high fours off Tayfield and received a pat on the back from the bowler who had taken five of the seven wickets.

INDIGESTIBLE LUNCH

For the first time in the match the crowd's sympathy turned towards the game fight of their own players. They warmly applauded the 200. At 1.15 p.m. Cheetham gave Melle the new ball but Lindwall and Benaud played it confidently and we went to an indigestible lunch with Australia 207 for 7.

Melle beat Benaud when play resumed but he was erratic. His full tosses were becoming a cause for lament when suddenly one of them broke the dangerous partnership.

Lindwall played forcefully at the gift from the bowler but hit the ball on to his stumps. He had batted an hour for 19 with three fours. It was a lucky dismissal for South Africa. Australia were 216 for 8.

Benaud, in his second test, was playing an innings of superb control and, when the explosive Ring joined him, South Africa faced their last but by no means easy hurdle.

Benaud's stand developed into a bold masterly innings. He used his feet and hit the ball hard and, with Ring using equal force, the pair put on 45. Then Benaud, at 41, was dropped. He drove powerfully to deep mid-off, a position to which Cheetham had moved from the on after the previous ball. The ball passed through his hands, struck him in the midriff and he doubled up in pain. Players gathered round and there was a pause before he continued.

A LITTLE ANXIETY

The Benaud-Ring partnership developed into the best of the match and, when Australia's margin was reduced to 99 runs, a little anxiety crept into South Africa's position.

The partnership was broken after adding 61 in 72 minutes by a brilliant catch by Melle who ran behind Tayfield to take a ball which passed very close but did not touch Tayfield's upraised hand. Benaud had batted splendidly for nearly three hours and hit four boundaries.

As the last man, Johnston, came in. Ring him out lustily and, to South Africa's dismay, he was dropped off Murray by Innes near the fence when he was 46. Innes sank to his knees and tried in vain to hold the ball a second time.

Fortunately, the lapse was immaterial for Ring hit high over Tayfield's head and Melle

309

took the catch and tossed the ball high into the heaven. Australia were all out for 290 and South Africa had won a great victory by 82 runs.

Duffus was an outstanding sportsman. An accountant by profession, he played baseball and cricket for the Transvaal in the 1920s, initially as wicket keeper, but later as opening batsman. He played hockey for Johannesburg and participated in soccer, rugby, golf, boxing, tennis and squash — an astonishing record, the more so because he was a haemophiliac.

Louis Duffus came to journalism early, writing on sport for *The Star* when he was a school-boy. He gave up accountancy in 1929 to travel with the South African cricket team to England as a freelance writer. In November of that year he joined *The Star* as a sports writer. His coverage of cricket was occasionally controversial: in 1935, reporting on the Springbok tour of the United Kingdom, he was called out of the press box at a match in Swansea and asked to field for the Springboks.

In 1949, Duffus succeeded Keartland as sports editor of *The Star*. He was the author of five books, four of them on sport. And he was a fanatical gardener. It was his boast that he once supplied the people of Sandton with 906 kg of home-grown Brussels sprouts — a boast subsequently immortalised by Jock Leyden, the veteran *Daily News* cartoonist.

'Jeez, Mr Drum, that was a good job'

Henry Nxumalo's great jail scoop, 1954

Under the innovative editorship of Anthony Sampson, *Drum* became a major force in local journalism in the Fifties and early Sixties. In 1952 'Mr Drum' was created with 'the great, gallant Henry Nxumalo' in the role.

Nothing in Nxumalo's past had indicated a career in journalism. His first job was working in a Durban kitchen; his second in the South African army during World War II (he served in the Middle East and England). After the war, Nxumalo returned to manual labour, working for a Johannesburg boilermaker for 50 shillings a month. Nxumalo found his home when he began working for *Bantu World* as a messenger, writing poetry for the publication at the same time. He was made sports editor, and it was in this capacity that he joined the newly launched *Drum* in 1951.

With no experience in news reporting, Nxumalo produced some outstanding investigative journalism, most notably in a series of eight articles on farm labour in the Bethal area where he worked as a labourer to get his stories, and on the conditions endured by black prisoners inside the Johannesburg Fort.

After his exposure of the farm labourers' plight, 'Mr Drum' got himself arrested on a pass offence and was sentenced to five days in the Johannesburg Fort (it had been known as a fort during the Second Anglo-Boer War), known to blacks as 'Number Four'.

Nxumalo wrote the story as soon as he was released from jail and, after it had been scrutinised by a lawyer, it was printed in *Drum*'s third anniversary number, March 1954.

MR. DRUM GOES TO JAIL

Last month DRUM published an article on "My Time in Jail" by Manilal Gandhi. Mr. Gandhi described how prisoners at Germiston Jail, Transvaal, were knocked, kicked, slapped and "treated like beasts."

Mr. Gandhi's allegations in DRUM were widely publicised in the Press, and were supported by a number of statements from ex-prisoners, and also by a former warder. The allegations were, in turn, denied by magistrates, by the Director of Prisons, and by the Minister of Justice.

Many people have called for a commission of inquiry into conditions in prisons. The Director of Prisons has agreed to conduct an investigation. But that is not enough.

DRUM decided to conduct its own investigation. We believed that only by sending a member of our own staff to jail could we be certain of an accurate report.

311

So Mr. DRUM went to jail. The account below is an accurate, carefully checked account of five days spent in Johannesburg's Central Jail. Everything described was seen by Mr. DRUM in person. There is no hearsay, no second-hand description. And the facts contained in this account can be supported by witnesses. The story speaks for itself:

I served five days' imprisonment at the Johannesburg Central Prison from January 20 to January 24. My crime was being found without a night pass five minutes before midnight, and I was charged under the curfew regulations. I was sentenced to a fine of 10s. or five days' imprisonment.

Two constables arrested me at the corner of Rissik and Plein Streets. I was taken to Marshall Square Police Station, charged, searched, given two blankets and locked up in the cells together with 37 others. The night was long. The prison doors kept clanging as more prisoners trickled in during

'Mr Drum' — Henry Nxumalo (Drum).

the night. The cell itself was dark. I couldn't tell the day from the night. Only the familiar shout of the young constable carrying a noisy bunch of prison keys told us it was morning.

We had roll-call, breakfast, got back our personal effects and were packed like sardines — over 40 of us — in a truck and delivered to the cells below the magistrate's court. When we got off the truck into the cells below the courts, one elderly-looking prisoner was a little slow to climb off. The prisoners were jostling to get off at once and blocking the way, and when the old man reached the ground he nearly missed the direction the other prisoners were taking. He looked about and S. saw him. He hit him with his open hand on the temples and told him to wake up.

Before we appeared in court I asked one of the black constables to allow me to phone my employers and my family. He said: "Go on, voetsek!" Meanwhile white prisoners in the opposite cells were phoning their families and their employers without trouble from a wall telephone near the warder.

After our cases had been heard by the magistrate, we were sent back to the cells. Convicted prisoners who couldn't raise enough money to pay their fines employed various methods to get money. They either borrowed from those who had much less or bartered their clothes, promising to release their benefactors as soon as they were out. Discharged prisoners took messages to relatives of convicted prisoners.

This lasted about two hours; we were checked and taken to Johannesburg Central Prison by truck. We arrived at the prison immediately after one o'clock. From the truck we were given orders to "shayisa" (close up), fall in twos and "sharp shoot" (run) to the prison reception office. From then on "Come on, Kaffir" was the operative phrase from both black and white prison officials, and in all languages.

Many of us who were going to prison for the first time didn't know exactly where the reception office was. Although the prison officials were with us, no one was directing us. But if a prisoner hesitated, slackened his half-running pace and looked round, he got a hard boot kick on the buttocks, a slap on his face or a whipping from the warders. Fortunately there were some second offenders with us who knew where to go. We followed them through the prison's many zig-zagging corridors until we reached the reception office.

Pen taken

The reception office had a terrifyingly brutal atmosphere. It was full of foul language. A number of khaki-uniformed white officials stood behind a long cement bar-like curved counter. They wore the initials "PSGD" on their shoulders. When they were not joking about prisoners, they were swearing at them and taking down their particulars. Two were taking fingerprints and hitting the prisoners in the face when they made mistakes.

Five long-term prisoners attended to us. One came up to me and said he knew me. I didn't know him. He asked for cigarettes, but I didn't have any. Another told us to take off our watches and money and hold them in our hands. These were to be kept separate from our other possessions. Another asked me for 2s. 6d.; but I had 5d. only and he wasn't interested. He noticed I had a copy of "Time" magazine in my hand and asked for it. I gave it to him. He hid it under the counter so the warders couldn't see it. Later he asked me what paper it was, how old it was and whether it was interesting. After we had undressed, one long-term prisoner demanded my fountain pen.

"That's a fine pen you've got, eh?" he asked. "How about giving it to me?" I said: "I'm afraid I can't; it's not my pen, it's my boss's pen." "Hi, don't tell me lies, you bastard," he said, "what the hell are you doing with your boss's pen in prison? Did you steal it?" he asked. I said I hadn't stolen it. I was using it and had it in my possession when I was arrested. "Give it here, I want it for my work here; if you refuse you'll see blood streaming down your dirty mouth soon!" I was nervous, but didn't reply. "Look, you little fool, I'll see that you are well treated in prison if you give me that pen." The other prisoners looked at me anxiously. I didn't know whether they approved of my giving my pen or not; but their anxious look seemed to suggest that their fate in prison lay in that pen. I gave it away.

Hit on mouth

We were called up to have our fingerprints taken by a white warder. Before taking the impression the warder made a loud complaint that the hand glove he uses when taking impressions was missing. He swore at the long-term prisoner who assists him and told him to find it. The other white prison officials helped him find the glove. He was a stout, middle-aged man, apparently a senior official. He took my impression, examined it and then complained that my hands were wet. He hit me on the mouth with the back of his gloved hand. I rubbed my right thumb on my hair and he took another impression.

From there I ran down to the end of the wide curved desk to have my height taken, and stood beside the measuring rod, naked. The long-term prisoner taking my height asked for my name and checked it against my ticket. He asked for my address and tribe. He then recited something very long to the white official who was writing in a big book opposite him.

My surname and address were wrong. But I dared not complain at that stage for fear of getting more blows. The only words I recognised throughout the recitation was my first name and "five foot, baasie," which is three inches below my actual height. Though I was near the measuring stick, he hadn't measured me; nor did he measure the other prisoners. He merely looked at them and assessed their height at sight. When finished with a prisoner, he would throw his ticket on the floor for the prisoner to pick it up and get on with the next one.

We were then taken to the showers in another room. There was neither soap nor a towel. After a few minutes under water we were told to get out, and skip to get dry. Then our prison clothes were thrown at us — a red shirt and a torn white pair of short pants. They looked clean; but the side cap and the white jacket which were issued to me later were filthy. The jacket had dry sweat on the neck.

From then on we were bare-foot, and were marched to the hospital for medical examination in double time. Another long-term prisoner lined us up, ordered us to undress and turn our faces to the wall, so that we would not pollute the medical officer with our breath when he came to examine us. While we were being inoculated, another prisoner, apparently being hit by someone for some reason, suddenly ran into the others at the end of the queue and there was a general shuffling round of places. We were then told to face front and make urine. Three prisoners were detained and sent to the hospital as V.D. suspects. Whether the white official in khaki uniform was a doctor or not, I was unable to tell. He didn't examine me. There was a mix-up of prison clothes after that shuffling round and changing of places, so that many prisoners couldn't find their clothes. Everyone picked up the clothes nearest to him. Some said the clothes they were wearing had been worn by the prisoners detained for V.D.

Kicked in stomach

After this we were marched down to the main court of the prison in double time. Here we found different white and black warders and long-term prisoners, who took charge of us. Again we undressed and had our second shower in 30 minutes. I was unable to make out my own clothes after the shower and the skipping. The African warder kicked me in the stomach with the toe of his boot. I tried to hold the boot to protect myself, and fell on my face. He asked if I had had an operation to my stomach. I said no. He looked at me scornfully. I got up, picked up the clothes in front of me and ran to join the others squatting on the floor.

After another roll-call we were marched to the top of the court to collect our food. The dishes were lined in rows and each prisoner picked up the dish nearest to him. The zinc dishes containing the food were rusty. The top of my dish was broken in three places. The food itself was boiled whole mealies with fat. We were marched to No. 7 cell, given blankets and a sleeping mat and locked in. We ate. The time was about 4.30 p.m. Clean water and toilet buckets were installed. But that water wasn't enough for 60 people. The long-term prisoners warned us not to use the water as if we were at our own homes. An old man went to fetch water with his dish at one stage and the long-term prisoner in charge of the cell swore at him. The old man insisted that he was thirsty and continued scooping the water. The long-term prisoner took the water away from him and threw it all over the old man's face.

There was a stinking smell when prisoners used the toilet bucket at night without toilet paper. At 8 p.m. the bell rang and we were ordered to be quiet and sleep. Some prisoners who had smuggled dagga and matches into the cell started conversing in whispers and smoking. The blankets were full of bugs; I turned round and round during the night without being able to sleep, and kept my prison clothes on for protection against bugs.

Filthy hands

We were up at about six o'clock the following morning. I tried to get some water to wash my dish and drink. The dish was full of the previous night's fat, and I didn't know how I was going to do it. But the long-term prisoner shouted at me and ordered me to leave the water alone. I obeyed. He swore at me in Afrikaans, and ordered me to wipe the urine which was overflowing from the toilet bucket with a small sack cloth. I did so. He said I must wipe it dry, but the cloth was so small that the floor remained wet.

He told me to find two other prisoners to help me carry the toilet bucket out, empty it

Bob Gosani's photograph of the inside of Johannesburg Central Jail. It shows the daily searching of prisoners returning from work. Prison regulations demanded that searching should be conducted 'with due regard to decency and self-respect'. (Bailey's African Photo Archives)

315

and clean it. It was full of the night's excrement. There were no volunteers, so I slipped to a corner and waited. He saw me and rushed at me. "What did I say?" He slapped me on my left cheek with his right open hand as he spoke. He said he could have me put in solitary confinement if he wished. He could tell the chief warder that I had messed the floor and I would get an additional punishment. I kept quiet. I had done nothing of the sort. Finally he ordered two other prisoners to help me.

We emptied the bucket and washed it as the other prisoners were being lined up in readiness for breakfast. One of my colleagues tried to wash his hands after we had emptied the bucket. The white warder saw him and slashed him with the strap part of his baton. The dish containing my porridge — and many others — still had the previous night's fat. It had been washed in cold water. The breakfast itself was yellow porridge with half-cooked pieces of turnips, potatoes, carrots and other vegetables I could not recognise. No spoons are provided; so I had my breakfast with my stinking soiled hands. I didn't feel like eating, but feared that I would be inviting further trouble.

'Tausa'

After breakfast we were divided into many work spans (parties). I spent my first day with a span cutting grass, pulling out weeds with my hands and pushing wheelbarrows at the Johannesburg Teachers' Training College in Parktown. We walked for about half a mile to our place of work, and I was one of two prisoners carrying a heavy, steel food can, which contained lunch porridge for a party of 16. Two warders escorted us: one white and one black. Once I slackened because we were going down a precipice; my fingers were sore and the burden was heavy.

The old white warder who was carrying a big rifle slashed me on my bare legs with the strap of his baton and said, "Ek donder jou, Kaffir."

We returned to jail at 4. We were ordered to undress and "tausa," a common routine of undressing prisoners when they return from work searching their clothes, their mouths, armpits and rectum for hidden articles. I didn't know how it was done. I opened my mouth, turned round and didn't jump and clap my hands. The white warder conducting the search hit me with his fist on my left jaw, threw my clothes at me and went on searching the others. I ran off, and joined the food queue.

Hit every day

One night I didn't have a mat to sleep on. Long-term prisoners in charge of the cells sometimes took a bundle of mats to make themselves comfortable beds, to the discomfort of other prisoners. In practice, a prisoner never knows where he will sleep the next day. It is all determined by your speed in "tausa," food and blanket queues. Invariably a prisoner is always using another prisoner's dirty blankets every night.

In the four days I was in prison — I got a remission of one day — I was kicked or thrashed every day. I saw many other prisoners being thrashed daily. I was never told what was expected of me, but had to guess. Sometimes I guessed wrong and got into trouble.

Long-term and short-term prisoners mixed freely at the prison. For example the famous A— D—, of Alexandra Township, who is doing a 10-year sentence for various crimes, was one of the most important persons in prison during my time. He was responsible for the in and out movements of other prisoners and respected by prisoners and warders. Though I was a short-term prisoner, I, too, took orders from A—.

It was a common practice for short-term prisoners to give their small piece of meat to long-term prisoners on meat days for small favours such as tobacco, dagga, shoes (which are supposed to be supplied to Coloured prisoners only), wooden spoons — or to ensure that they were always supplied with sleeping mats.

Many other prisoners shared the same fate. There are no directions or rules read or posted in prison. At least I didn't see any. Thrashing time for warders was roll call and breakfast time as well as supper time. For long-term prisoners it was inside the cells at all times. Long-term prisoners thrashed more prisoners more severely and much oftener than the prison officials themselves, and often in the presence of either white or black warders. All prisoners were called Kaffirs at all times.

On the day of our discharge we were mustered in a big hall at breakfast and checked. There was an open lavatory at the corner of the hall. Six men used it, and when the seventh one went a long-term prisoner swore at him and told him to keep his stomach full until he reached home. He said the man belonged to a tribe he detested: a tribe which killed his brother. After that none of us could use the latrine.

We were then marched to the Reception Office for our personal effects and checking out. The long-term prisoners officiating there told us not to think that we were already out of prison. They kicked and slapped prisoners for the slightest mistake, and sometimes for no mistake at all; and promised them additional sentences if they complained. In the office there was a notice warning prisoners to see that their personal belongings were recorded in the prison's books correctly and exactly as they had brought them. But I dared not complain about my pen which was commandeered on my arrival, lest I be detained. Even the prisoner who took it pretended not to know me.

'Any complaints?'

Before we left prison we were told the Superintendent would address us. We could make complaints to him if we had any. But the fat Zulu warder who paraded us to the yard for the Superintendent's inspection said we must tell him everything was all right if we want to leave prison.

"This is a court of law," he said; "you are about to go home, but before you leave this prison the big boss of the prison will address you. He will ask you if you have any complaints. Now I take it that you all want to go to your homes — to your wives and children — you don't want to stay here. So if the big boss asks you if everything is all right say, 'Yes, Sir.' If he says have you any complaints say, 'No, Sir.' You hear?"

In a chorus we said "Yes."

Just then one prisoner complained that his Kliptown train ticket was missing from his things. It was a season ticket. The Zulu warder pulled him aside and said, "You think you're clever, eh? you'll see!" He put him at the tail-end of the parade. The Superintendent came and we answered him as instructed. Most of us were seeing him for the first time. The Zulu warder said nothing about the complaint of the man from Kliptown. Later as we were going to collect our monies from the pay office, the man from Kliptown was escorted to the Reception Office to see the famous fierce discharge officer, C. C said the man's papers showed that he was charged at Fordsburg and not at Kliptown. He was not entitled to any ticket. But the man insisted that he was arrested at Kliptown, charged at Fordsburg and appeared in Johannesburg. The fat Zulu warder said in broken Afrikaans: "He's mad, sir." He gave the man a hard slap in the face with his open hand and said: "You're just wasting the boss's time, eh? On your way . . . voetsek!" And the man sneaked out.

One by one we zigzagged our way out of the prison's many doors and gates and lined up in two's in front of the main and final gate. We were ordered to leave prison quietly and in pairs when the small gate was open. If we blocked the gate we would be thrashed. We were to come out in the order of the line. The man on the left would go out first and the one on the right would follow. The gate was opened. We saw freedom and blocked the gate in our anxiety. If they thrashed us we couldn't feel it . . . we didn't look back!

There was an immediate outcry following the publication of the story. Due to public pressure, the humiliating 'dance' of the prisoners was stopped, warders were demoted and conditions improved, if only marginally.

The photographs which accompanied the story also caused a storm, with accusations that they had been faked. But they were part of a carefully planned operation. *Drum* editor Anthony Sampson and photographer Bob Gosani had wandered around the Johannesburg Fort trying to see how they could photograph inside it. They found a tall building — it was, in fact, a nurses' home — which overlooked not only the jail but the inner courtyard. Sampson contacted the supervisor of the nurses' home and asked for permission to use the roof of the building to photograph Johannesburg. Knowing that a black photographer would excite suspicion, he asked his secretary, Deborah Duncan, to go along as the photographer, with Gosani posing as her assistant.

Duncan distracted the superintendent, walking to the other side of the roof and taking shots of the city's skyline, while Gosani photographed the warders and prisoners within the jail. The prisoners could see him and began grinning; after a while Gosani was spotted by one of the warders who, frowning, called another warder to view the proceedings on the rooftop of the nurses' home. Gosani packed the cameras away; he had the pictures, and Mr Drum had the story.

There was an unexpected sequel to 'Mr Drum goes to Jail'. In Orlando, delighted *tsotsis* threw a party for Nxumalo. 'Jeez, Mr Drum,' one of them said, 'that was a good job, cleaning up Number Four for us.' For Nxumalo, it was the greatest of accolades. Two years later, Henry Nxumalo was found stabbed to death in Sophiatown on 31 December 1956.

'Swarming, cacophonous, strutting, brawling, vibrating'

Can Themba's requiem for Sophiatown, 1955

'He walked like a township drunk . . . but talking like a scholar,' wrote a friend after Can Themba's death in Manzini, Swaziland, on 12 September 1967.

Stan Motjuwadi, editor of *Drum,* described Can D'Orsay Themba as an erratic genius. 'Sartorially he was a disaster. No tie, a cheap baggy grey workman's gaberdine trousers, a khaki shirt, shoes that had an overdue date with the repairers and the kind of jacket a fussy student would not be seen dead in.'

No one wrote about Sophiatown the way Themba did; no one loved Sophiatown like he did. Indeed, Themba, falling from one shebeen to another, staggering home, evading the American look-alike gangsters on his way to the House of Truth, his corrugated iron shack, *was* Sophiatown. He came to the attention of *Drum* when he won a short story competition in 1953. Themba left his job as a school teacher and joined *Drum* and became, in time, associate editor of both *Drum* and *Golden City Post.*

Can Themba wrote in elegant, if world-weary prose. He chronicled life in Sophiatown, calling it 'swarming, cacophonous, strutting, vibrant' in a series of articles, but none more poignant than 'Requiem for Sophiatown', printed in *Africa South*, September 1955.

REQUIEM FOR SOPHIATOWN

Realism can be star-scattering, even if you have lived your whole unthinking life in reality. Especially in Sophiatown, these days, where it can come with the sudden crash of a flying brick on the back of your head.

Like the other day when Bob Gosani and I sneaked off towards our secret shebeen in Morris Street. We were dodging an old friend of ours whom we call the Leech, for he is one of those characters who like their drink — any amount — so long as someone else pays for it.

Well, this secret shebeen in Morris Street was a nice place. You take a passage through Meyer Street over haphazard heaps of bricks where houses have been broken down, you find another similar passage that leads you from Ray Street into Edith Street, where you find another passage, neater, having always been there between the Coloured School and Jerusalem-like slum-houses, you go down a little, and suddenly there it is.

Quite a fine place, too. A little brick wall, a minute garden of mostly Christmas flowers, a half-veranda (the other half has become a little kitchen) with the floor of the veranda polished a bright green.

Inside, the sitting-room may be cluttered with furniture, it is so small, but you sink comfortably into a sofa as one of the little tables that can stand under the other's belly is placed before you, and you make your order. Half-a-jack of brandy!

How often have Bob and I not whooped happily, "Yessus! The Leech will never find us here." So, though there were more direct routes to this place, we always took the passages. They say these people can smell when you are going to take a drink.

But that day, as we emerged into Morris Street, it was as if that brick had just struck us simultaneously on our heads. That sweet little place was just not there. Where it should have been was a grotesque, grinning structure of torn red brick that made it look like the face of a mauled boxer trying to be sporting after his gruel. A nausea of despair rose up in me, but it was Bob who said the only appropriate thing:

"Shucks."

Can Themba, the life and the soul of Sophiatown (Drum).

Here is the odd thing about Sophiatown. I have long been inured to the ravages wreaked upon it; I see its wrecks daily, and through many of its passages that have made such handy short-cuts for me, I have stepped gingerly many times over the tricky rubble. Inside of me, I have long stopped arguing the injustice, the vindictiveness, the strong-arm authority of which prostrate Sophiatown is a loud symbol.

Long ago I decided to concede, to surrender to the argument that Sophiatown was a slum, after all. I am itchingly nagged by the thought that slum-clearance should have nothing to do with the theft of freehold rights. But the sheer physical fact of Sophiatown's removal has intimidated me.

Moreover, so much has gone — veritable institutions. Fatty of the Thirty-nine Steps, now, that was a great shebeen! It was in Good Street. You walked up a flight of steps, the structure looked dingy as if it would crash down with you any moment. You opened a door and walked into a dazzle of bright electric light, contemporary furniture, and massive Fatty. She was a legend. Gay, friendly, coquettish, always ready to sell you a drink. And that mama had everything: whisky, brandy, gin, beer, wine — the lot. Sometimes she could even supply cigars. But now that house is flattened. I'm told that in Meadowlands she has lost the zest for the game. She has even tried to look for work in town. Ghastly.

There was Dwarf, who used to find a joke in everything. He used to walk into Bloke's place and catch us red-handed playing the music of Mozart. He used to cock his ear, listen a little and in his gravel voice comment, "No wonder he's got a name like that." There was nothing that Dwarf loved more than sticking out his tongue to a cop and running for it. I once caught him late at night in his Meadowlands house washing dishes! He still manfully tries to laugh at himself.

And Mabeni's, where the great Dolly Rathebe once sang the blues to me. I didn't ask her; she just sidled over to me on the couch and broke into song. It was delicious. But now Dolly is in Port Elizabeth, and Mabeni, God knows where.

These are only highlights from the swarming, cacophonous, strutting, brawling, vibrating life of the Sophiatown that was. But it was not all just shebeeny, smutty, illegal stuff. Some places it was the stuff that dreams are made of.

I am thinking of those St. Cyprian's schoolboys who, a decade ago, sweatingly dug out the earth behind the house of the Community of the Resurrection, in order to have a swimming pool. It still stands, and the few kids left still paddle in it. Some of those early schoolboys of St. Cyprian's later went up to Father Ross or Father Raynes or Father Huddleston who wangled a bursary for them to go to St Peter's, then on to Fort Hare, and later even Wits, to come back doctors.

Their parents, patiently waiting and working in town, skimped a penny here, a tickey there, so that they might make the necessary alterations to their house, or pay off the mortgage. And slowly Sophiatown was becoming house-proud.

Of course, there were pressures too heavy for them. After the war, many people came to Johannesburg to seek for work and some hole to night in. As they increased they became a housing problem. As nobody seemed to care, they made Sophiatown a slum.

But the children of those early Sophiatonians — some of them — are still around. It is amazing how many of them are products of the Anglican Mission at St Cyprian's. I meet them often in respectable homes, and we talk the world to tatters.

Mostly we talk of our lot in life. After all, too often we have been told that we are the future leaders of our people. We are the young stalwarts who are supposed to solve the problems of our harassed world.

"Not political unity, we need," one would say; "Our society is too diverse and unwieldy for that. Just a dynamic core of purified fighters with clear objectives and a straight-forward plan of action. That is all."

Another, "No! We must align ourselves with the new forces at play in Africa today. There is already the dynamicity. The idea of a one Africa has never been put as power-fully as at Accra recently. You see, Africans, wherever they are, have not a territorial, a local loyalty: they don't feel that they belong to a South Africa, or a Federation, or a Tanganyika, or a Kenya, or a West Africa; but with Africans in the whole of Africa. In fact, many of us are wondering if Arabs and Egyptians are also Africans. They probably are."

Still another, "But if the boys in the North are getting busy, shouldn't we start some-thing here ourselves?"

"Waal, you see, our ANC here has been caught with its pants down. The Africanists are claiming that Accra has proclaimed their stand. And the ANC representative there could only discuss the tactical difficulties of the ANC in South Africa with her special conditions."

"Ya. But this African Personality idea, what does it mean to us? What does it mean, anyway?"

"I'll tell you. In the world today are poised against each other two massive ideologies:

of the East and of the West. Both of them play international politics as if we're bound to choose between them. Between them only. We have just discovered that we can choose as we like, if we grow strong in our own character. But there's more to this. The West has had a damned long time to win us. Win us over to Western thinking. Western Christian way of living. Their ideas of democracy and their Christian ideals were wonderful, but they did not mean them.

"Let me explain. We are quite a religious people. We accept the idealism of Christianity. We accept its high principles. But in a stubborn, practical sense we believe in reality. Christian Brotherhood must be real. Democracy must actually be the rule of the people: not of a white hobo over a black M.A.

"To us, if a witchdoctor says he'll bring rain, we not only want to see the rain fall, but

Dancing at the Ritz, Sophiatown (Bailey's African Photo Archives).

322

also see the crops sprout from the earth. That's what a rainmaker's for, nay? If the bone-thrower says he'll show up the bastard who's been slinging lightning at me, I expect him to swing that bolt of lightning right back. So if the priest says God's on my side, I'd like to see a few more chances and fewer whiteman's curses.

"But, in any case, Christianity is now an anaemic religion. It cannot rouse the ancient in me — especially the Chaka instinct I still have. Now, you and I are educated guys. We don't go for the witchcraft stuff. And we don't want to go for the juke-box stuff. But much as we deny it, we still want the thrill of the wild blood of our forefathers. The whites call it savagery. Ineradicable barbarism. But in different degrees we want the colour, and vigour and vibrant appeal of it all. So the *tsotsi* seeks in the cowboy the way to strut across the streets with swaying hips and a dangerous weapon in each hand. So the zionist thumps his drum and gyrates his holy fervour up the streets. So you and I and these guys here discuss politics, teasingly dancing around the idea of violence.

"All it means is that in wanting to express her demand for democratic self-deter-mination, Africa is also releasing her ancient-most desire to live life over the brim. That's how come we sometimes seem to talk in two voices."

"Wait a minute," another shrieks, "Wait a minute. We're not all like that. Some of us would like to get things right, and start anew. Some piece of social engineering could get things working right, if our moral purposes were right, not just vengeful."

"Sure, but our masters have taught this damned thing violence so well by precept — often practice — that they get you to believe that it's the only way to talk turkey to them."

We do not talk about this particular subject only; our subjects are legion. Nkrumah must be a hell of a guy, or is he just bluffing? What about our African intellectuals who leave the country just when we need them most? But is it honestly true that we don't want to have affairs with white girls? What kind of white supremacy is this that cannot stand fair competition? What will happen if a real topmost Afrikaner Nationalist gets caught by the Immorality Act? In fact, all those cheeky questions that never get aired in public.

But it always ends up with someone saying, "Aw shut up, folks, you got no plan to liberate us."

Somewhere here, and among a thousand more individualistic things, is the magic of Sophiatown. It is different and itself. You don't just find your place here, you make it and you find yourself. There's a tang about it. You might now and then have to give way to others making their ways of life by methods which aren't in the book, but you can't be bored. You have the right to listen to the latest jazz records at Ah Sing's over the road. You can walk a Coloured girl of an evening down to the Odin Cinema, and no questions asked. You can try our Rhugubar's curry with your bare fingers without embarrassment. All this with no sense of heresy. Indeed, I've shown quite a few white people 'the little Paris of the Transvaal' — but only a few were Afrikaners.

What people have thought to be the brazen-ness of Sophiatown has really been its clean-faced frankness. And, of course, its swart jowl against the rosy cheek of Westdene.

'A legend in the shebeens . . . people travelled miles to hear him talk deep into the night,' Can Themba left South Africa for Swaziland and exile in 1963. Banned from being quoted or from publishing in any South African publication, he died in 1969.

'If you cannot move, throw coal at my voice'

The Coalbrook mine disaster, February 1960

In late January/early February 1960, three items of news dominated South African newspapers: on 20 January, during the no-confidence parliamentary debate, the prime minister, Dr Hendrik Verwoerd, announced that a referendum on the establishment of a republic would be held.

Two weeks later, the papers still full of the forthcoming referendum, the visiting British prime minister, Mr Harold Macmillan, made his historic 'winds of change' speech in Cape Town, the implications of which were far-reaching and which occupied many columns of newspaper space.

But the item which dominated every newspaper in the country for no less than 11 days was the disaster which struck the Clydesdale Colliery, Coalbrook, shortly after 19h30 on the evening of Thursday, 21 January 1960.

The night shift of 945 men, together with 80 pit ponies, had gone underground without incident. There had been a subsidence at 16h30 that day and, more alarming, cracks had appeared in the nearby Sasolburg-to-Heilbron road. But, after inspection, it was decided that it was safe to send the miners down for their long night shift.

At about 19h30, miners who were 150 m from the lift in the northern section of the mine found that the gas content was rising rapidly, alarmingly increasing the chances of an explosion.

As the mine captain ordered his men to get out of the mine — but not to panic, not to run — the mine began 'talking', audibly creaking and groaning. There was a sudden blast of air, followed by an explosion. The lights went out, the vital ventilation system was destroyed and debris flew about the mine.

A stunned Archie Schonken staggered towards the lift. Mr G.S. van der Merwe turned his helmet light on and looked around him in disbelief. Men, some stunned, all shaken, escaped either by lift or by crawling up the incline ramp to the surface, 150 m above.

News of the disaster, although its extent was still unknown, reached the nation through the SABC that evening. The following morning the *Rand Daily Mail* team of reporters broke the story. It was the first of a series of dramatic front pages which were to run in almost every newspaper in the country, both morning and evening dailies, for the following two weeks. Almost without exception, they are fine examples of lucid, factual despatches. The first story ran in the *Rand Daily Mail* on 22 January 1960.

COALBROOK
207 Trapped in Free State mine

Staff Reporter

At least seven White and 200 non-White colliery workers were trapped last night by subsidence of the old surface workings of the Clydesdale North Colliery, in the northern Free State.

The situation was aggravated by the blast of air which was forced through the old into the new workings. The blast caused a further subsidence.

Mr C.M. Brothers, managing director of Clydesdale Collieries (Transvaal) said last night that he had received a report of a serious explosion at the colliery.

Representatives of the management were underground, conducting rescue operations. Mr Brothers drove to the colliery himself at about 1130 pm.

The Star team had been working through the night and had had more time to get details than the morning paper. Mine officials, never forthcoming when there is an accident or disturbance at a mine, were unco-operative and, for almost 24 hours, genuinely unable to determine how many missing men there were. At one stage they called in the police to issue a statement to reporters in an effort to keep them away from the rescue operations.

The Star on the afternoon of 22 January noted that hope had begun to fade for the trapped miners.

UP TO 2 P.M. TODAY NOBODY HAD BEEN RESCUED, AND THERE WAS NO "PIPE TALK" (MESSAGES TAPPED ON PIPES) TO INDICATE THAT MEN WERE STILL ALIVE BEHIND THE ROCK FALL.

The men were trapped by two great subsidences late yesterday afternoon. They are thought to have just over half a mile of narrow workings in which to move.

Nobody knows how many hundred yards of rock and debris separate them from the proto (rescue) teams who are working in two-hour shifts.

Proto teams use oxygen

The rescue teams are fighting to get an air-pipe through to them. There is a water-pipe still through. But the air in the blocked half-mile is contaminated with deadly methane and carbon-monoxide gases.

Some experienced miners here say the gas proportion could be as high as 90 per cent.

The rescue teams themselves are having to use oxygen breathing apparatus, and have to be very careful not to do anything that might touch off an explosion of the methane gases. And there is no direct communication with the entombed men.

There were two falls — a small one at half-past four and the serious one at about 7.30 p.m.

The gravity of the latter fall can be gauged from the fact that roads in the area cracked up to a foot wide and some road surfaces have subsided several feet.

The fall drove the air through the shafts and blew up a fanhouse with a noise like an explosion. This fanhouse has now been repaired, and is pumping air underground again.

Five of the six Europeans entombed are married men, and are all South Africans. The other is a young Hungarian, Gabriel Zabo, who came out only about three years ago.

The other men are a shift boss, Piet du Preez, a fitter, C.J. Prinsloo and three miners, Theodorus de Koker, Daan Marais and 'Boet' Smit.

With their families

Many of the Natives are long-term employees who have their wives and families living with them in the mine compound. Most of the others are Basutos.

While their husbands and fathers gasp for life in the black depths below wives and children are sobbing the hours away without news from the management on whether they can still hope — or resign themselves.

An official said: "If a statement is to be issued it will be done through the mine office."

Up to noon the office had made no statement.

After the first fall at 4.30 p.m. in No. 10 section, most of the miners, White and Black, left hurriedly. But they returned — only to be trapped by the second fall.

Rescue teams, who have been underground, are despondent. There has been no "pipe talk" — the method of striking pipes running through a rock fall to tell rescuers that there are still men alive beyond the rock barrier.

Hundreds of people and dozens of cars are thronging the area round the mine shaft, and the headgear is still and silent.

Sapa quotes the Department of Mines as saying that the ventilation fan which was damaged by the collapse of the ground has been restored to working order.

But the restoration of a satisfactory supply of air will be difficult because of damage to the pumping machinery.

The five South Africans are married. Mr. Prinsloo has two children, Mr. de Koker has one, Mr. Marais has three and Mr. Smit has four.

Clydesdale Collieries belong to the South African General Investment and Trust Company, Ltd., usually known as "Sagit." Head offices are in Johannesburg.

And on the front page, which was almost entirely devoted to the disaster, were little vignettes which were to capture the hearts of the population as, day after day, they were faced with grim pictures and grimmer news.

VACANTLY THEY STARE —
SENSING THE UNFOLDING OF A TRAGEDY

By a Staff Reporter

Relatives and friends of the trapped men kept vigil all morning at the Coalbrook pithead.

They wait and pray — but inwardly they sense the mounting feeling that little can be done to prevent the unfolding of a tragedy.

A wife with a child aged four vowed she will not leave until she sees her husband again.

Others huddle in cars with grandmothers, uncles and nephews deriving from them what comfort is possible.

Natives stand in large groups, dazed by a disaster they can only dimly comprehend. Isolated twos or threes talk excitedly, but most stand staring vacantly into the middle distance.

By contrast the rescue work is characterized by briskness. Mr. E.C. Wood, in charge of rescue operations, is in his twenties. His face, blackened with dust and seamed with sweat, pushed away an offer of coffee and sandwiches.

With an impatient gesture he strode back towards the pithead.

Many races are concerned in this epic rescue bid. Hungarians, Portuguese, other newcomers to the Union, work away desperately with Englishmen, Afrikaners and Natives.

A tired, grim-faced young man who was one of the last to emerge last night, said he had crawled up a 2,000 ft. incline. He was almost at the end of his tether when he got out.

He is Louis Nagy (24), a fitter who came out from Hungary three years ago. He is married with a child of three.

He staggered and crawled up through coal dust and fumes.

"I hardly knew what I was doing at times, or where I was going. I can still barely remember how it started."

But, in spite of indications to the contrary, there was still hope for the trapped miners: 223 from Basutoland, 206 from Moçambique, eight from South Africa. In other parts of the world men had survived entombment for as long as ten days. It was hope, in the end, which kept everyone going, from the Proto teams clearing a passage at the rate of two metres every three hours, to the Salvation Army ministering to the families at the pithead, to the reporters battling for

Workmen hurriedly shore up the collapsed fan house at the Coalbrook North Colliery. The photograph was taken by a staff photographer who flew over the colliery on the morning of 22 January and was used on the front pages of most Argus newspapers (The Star).

information from an unco-operative mine management to the witchdoctor throwing bones in their midst. 'All dead,' he said, but no one believed him.

The Star's Saturday, 23 January edition carried the headline 'At dawn: Air gets through to miners' and then continued:

Some hope — but it is faint

500 MAY BE TRAPPED

By a Staff Reporter

The first glimmer of hope in the 36 hours since the subsidences at the Coalbrook Mine buried several hundred people — estimates vary between 350 and 525 — came with the first break of dawn today.

The hope is no more than a flicker for the relatives of the trapped men who spent the night at the colliery pithead, huddled in blankets against the chill Free State wind.

Air is getting through to the section where the men are entombed. There has still been no communication with them but that is no longer considered necessarily a bad sign. It is now known that the pipe line along which "pipe talk" could have been passed, was broken in the rockfall.

The air pipe means no more than that if there are still survivors they will be able to breathe air less contaminated by lethal methane gas than it was.

New hazard: rising water

But time is running out fast. If there still are living men down there they must have fresh air, water and food — and the knowledge, to keep their will to live strong, that help is near.

To the contaminated air has been added a new terror. Proto teams tell of walking chest deep through water that might be filling the lower workings.

Yesterday the teams were coming up from below with their faces dull with despair and exhaustion. They spoke gloomily of several days, perhaps a week, before they could hope to break through from No. 5 level — which they have now reached — to No. 11, where the men are trapped.

Then at 4 a.m. one of the men in a team said that air was getting through past the obstruction. At that time, he estimated, the proto teams had managed to work about two thousand feet from the shaft in the direction of the rock fall.

They are trying to work their way round the obstruction through disused workings. Maps are going down to help them to plan the advance. In the meantime other working crews are inching their way along the main haulage shaft, at the rate of 2 ft. an hour.

Since the air first started getting through all other sections of the mine have been cleared to force the utmost quantity past the obstruction. Pit ponies from those sections were brought up early this morning — by 8 a.m. about 30 had come up in the skips.

Still unknown

There is still no official figure of how many Natives are trapped with the six Europeans. Surface officials did not keep accurate figures of how many returned to the mine on Thursday evening after they had fled from the first subsidence in the afternoon.

328

A statement issued at 3.45 p.m. yesterday spoke of "about 400". There are at least 350 and the latest estimate from a surface official is 525, made up of five sections of 65 each and 200 in the main east haulage way. There are also about 70 horses trapped with them.

Teams of miners from the Transvaal and the O.F.S. arrived at short intervals during the night.

Many reported that they had lost their way because all the direct routes were cordoned off by the police.

The only road still open is a roundabout route over badly corrugated roads from Sasolburg.

The police are allowing only cars carrying people on official business through, to prevent the roads being blocked by sightseers.

The tense sequence of operations continues endlessly. One group of rescuers emerges undoing breathing apparatus. There is a momentary flicker of hope amongst the anxious waiters, but only for a moment.

Still there is no official statement — and there has been none since 7.15 this morning.

A giant oxygen lorry comes into the yard with fresh supplies. If it cannot be conveyed to the trapped men, it can at least be used by the proto team.

This spirit hangs over all operations. Anything that gives fresh hope must go forward — anything likely to bring better news to the anxious and tearful wives and children.

They are the passive heroes of this disaster; they can only wait.

After another fall inside the mine, the Proto teams had to withdraw. Iscor offered the mine the use of a huge diamond drill which could bore faster than any other in the country. But the drill was at Ellisras, 500 km away. It began its journey to Coalbrook at 06h45 on Saturday, 23 February, travelling at a speed of 30 km an hour. While the country, seldom so united, held its breath, traffic police cleared its path. The drill reached Sasolburg at 01h00 the following morning and within two hours was in operation. The miners had been entombed for 53 hours.

Within sight of the 10 000 trippers with hampers and drinks who arrived on Sunday, 24 January for a day's entertainment, the drill continued operating, penetrating one metre every three hours.

DRILLING MAY BRING A FLICKER OF HOPE TO TRAPPED MINERS

From a Staff Reporter

All hope at Coalbrook is now centred on the drill. The area at the mine headquarters itself wears a strange air of shocked silence. All thoughts are on the men one and a half miles away who are driving the 13¾ in. borehole down through the earth. There has been no contact with the men below since Thursday afternoon, but today's flicker of hope came from a former mine captain who said that the sound of the drill biting through the dolerite will travel along the rock layers to the men below.

They may recognize the significance and be heartened for the next two days until the drill breaks through.

Tension will mount until Thursday. The drill crew will know they have broken through when the water which circulates down the bore shaft stops coming out at the surface. They will know then that the 2,000 gallons of water in the borehole will have found a way through to an empty space below.

Some hours after they have lifted the hundreds of tons of steel driving the bit, they will put a microphone down. They may hear the noise of rock settling. They may hear the noise of running water. They may hear nothing — or they may hear sounds of human voices.

The drilling crew lost six vital hours early today when gearbox trouble brought them to a stop at 131 ft. By 11 a.m. they had restarted and are now going through rock a little less hard than the dolerite they struck yesterday.

At the emergency shaft half a mile away the atmosphere is optimistic. Such good progress has been made that Mr. D.N.J. Walton, manager of the construction company doing the preliminary work, is confident that he will break his schedule of 10 days.

Instead of waiting, as is usual, for a proper headgear and winch house to be built, they will convert one of their mobile cranes for the shaft sinkers to use for a few days while riggers erect the headgear.

DREAD OF RAIN

Their one dread is that rain will bog down their heavy machinery in the soft black soil. Tons of coal waste is being brought in to make a hard standing.

Last night there was some rain, though not enough to delay the work. Today's heavy rain on the Reef reaches south only as far as Vereeniging, but anxious eyes are watching the skies.

This morning Escom technicians were marking out the route the power line will take from the mine headquarters to the new shaft. They too are hopeful of breaking their seven-day deadline.

By 2 p.m. today it was 115 hours since 435 miners — the official figure is now six Europeans and 429 non-Europeans — were trapped by rock falls 515 feet below the surface.

By Monday night, 100 hours into the disaster, the underground works had to be sealed off to prevent fire. A team went down to build a double wall, sealing the mine permanently. The only hope of rescue lay in the Iscor drill and a new shaft being sent down in a nearby field of mealies.

TIME-TABLE OF DESPAIR IN A MEALIE FIELD

From a Staff Reporter

This is the scene in the mealie field, just off the Sasolburg, Heilbron Road, as the clock ticks off its race with death:

There are 100 men, some at one drill rig and the others 150 yards away, watching the other, while a few women are serving tea.

The rigs are strung with electric lights. In the small circle of light no more than a dozen men strain and curse with impatience when a momentary delay interferes with the rhythm of their work.

With faces to the light stand the doctors, the mine officials, the reporters and the photographers.

FOR 60 HOURS

The clothes of the drillers are oil-spattered, their faces grease-stained and lined with fatigue. They have been working at top pressure for 60 hours.

At 9.30 p.m. No. 3 leads by five feet. Then soft shale clogs the diamond teeth and it must be lifted to replace the bit.

11 p.m. — No. 2 is at 484 ft. The men positively snatch out the lengths of rod to remove the core.

11.06 — A loose joint sprays water over the crew. The drill is stopped for several precious seconds while a worker taps with a hammer to free it and another throws all his strength on to the handle of a huge spanner.

MINUTES LOST

11.25 — The steel rope fouls the sheaf and more precious minutes are lost to free it.

11.30 — A piece of core has jammed in the barrel. The drill is at 485 feet. The core is removed, and a geologist inspects the core minutely and goes to a parked car to discuss his finding with mine officials.

11.35 — There comes a whisper that No. 3 is at 499 feet and there is a minor stampede of newspapermen. But the crew are pulling up the rods. At 11.50 the drill restarts.

Midnight — An official says it will be at least another hour or two, but nobody leaves the drill sites, though the night has become chill.

NO AIR

12.24 a.m. — No. 3 at 509 feet, just the height of a tall man from the level where the break-through can be expected. It is soft ground, and the drill lowers quickly, although it is now being rotated more slowly.

1.50 — No. 3 is at 521 feet, and the geologists say that instead of at 515 feet the break-through should come at 522. An official tests the borehole for up draught, but there is no sign that air is moving either up or down the shaft.

2.23 — No. 2 is at 505 feet in shale.

2.57 — The water pressure at No. 3 drops suddenly, then fluctuates. This might be a sign that the drill has broken through and the water is finding a way to seep from the drill point instead of returning in the close circuit to the top of the hole.

MISSING 5 FT.

3.55 — No. 2 is at 526 feet. The barrel contains only 10 feet of core, though the drill went down 15 feet. Can the missing five feet have been the break-through into an empty shaft?

Then starts the reluctant realisation that both drills are well past the intersection level, and there have been no signs of life. They both continue until they come up with several feet of foot-wall — the shale under the coal seam — showing in the core.

Now everybody knows they are through the coal seam in which runs the working galleries and through to the dyke below. There are just a few minutes left to hope, before the electric plumb kills it.

Fresh drills were flown from Houston, Texas, via London. By Wednesday the men had been trapped for six days. But, said mine management, ever hopeful, the men had water (Proto teams had waded waist-deep through it) hopefully they had air and, *in extremis,* they could eat the pit ponies.

On Saturday, 30 January, armed police with teargas kept the trippers away from the mine and the vital access roads. By 23h00 on Sunday, 31 January, the tenth day after the disaster, one of the drills was 145 m down. Knowing that the final story was about to break, the SABC, which normally closed transmissions at 23h00 on Sundays, kept its transmitters on the air throughout the night to give news of the progress of the drilling.

On Monday, at 08h00 in front of a small, tense audience of rescue workers, management, medical teams and reporters, a pipeline was passed down one of the boreholes, and pumped up water.

The Star, in a running story that had left neither the front pages of the paper nor the hearts of its readers, ran the now-inevitable headline: 'All 435 at Coalbrook Are Dead'.

BOREHOLES SHOW END CAME SUDDENLY

CRUSHING ROCK — THEN FLOOD OF WATER

By a Staff Reporter

The 435 miners trapped at Coalbrook are dead. Those who by some miracle escaped the first violent blast must inevitably have been crushed to death by the millions of tons of earth falling into the working passages.

Finally, to remove even the faintest hope that one or two might have escaped, it was established at 8 a.m. today that one of the test boreholes had water 94½ ft. from the surface and the other at 133½ ft.

So ends South Africa's worst mine disaster — and South Africa's most valiant attempt to pluck men from the jaws of death.

The six European and 429 Native miners lie in a common grave 522 ft. below the surface, perhaps never to be found and brought to the surface to be reburied in separate cemeteries.

The men were buried at 7.30 p.m. on Thursday, January 21. The 9 in. Iscor bit has reached a level of about 207 ft. It is expected that excavating will continue at the emergency shaft, now at 65 ft, as long as rising water does not make it impossible to continue.

The two small boreholes reached and passed the critical level — established today at 522 ft. — shortly before dawn. All the probes revealed was that there was crushed ground in the working shafts.

Then at 7 a.m. a pipeline was passed round that the Welkom to pump air from below for testing for impurities. It pumped water, not air.

An electric plumb was sent down. It showed the water level at 94½ ft.

Then the other borehole was tested, and it showed water at 133½ ft.

Nobody looked

At that very moment Mr. Macmillan's party flew over and circled the site in two aircraft. But nobody looked at the sky.

The end: the cord which lowered the microphone into the cavern in which the miners lay recorded nothing but the dripping of water (The Star).

The bitter realization that all rescue efforts were in vain turned the men's eyes downwards.

Already at 4.44 a.m., when word passed round that the Welkom borehole had holed through into crushed ground, the urgency had gone from the rescue work.

Since Friday morning the drillers had laboured to drive down the two 3-in. holes that might have brought air and food to the miners.

At 4 a.m. they were still working at top pace.

One — two

By 5 a.m., however, they were going through the motions of changing bits like a team of surgeons who work on to complete an operation though the patient has long since died on the operating table.

Even when the first borehole showed water at less than 100 ft., they did not entirely lose heart.

Perhaps, they argued, that borehole might have been blocked so that water pumped into it during the drilling operations would not escape.

But no optimism could withstand the second reading.

Hope, that had lingered for 11 days, died at 8 o'clock today.

But that was not the end of the drama. As rescue workers began to pack up, the Salvation Army to go home, the country to go back to work and new pages to be filled with other events, a final effort to communicate with the miners was made by lowering a microphone down the Iscor drillhole. Sapa reported the final, most heart-breaking scene of all:

COALBROOK, Friday.
There were moving scenes here last night when efforts were made to communicate with possible survivors of the Clydesdale mine disaster by means of a microphone which was lowered down the Iscor drillhole.

The microphone had been lowered 500 ft down the borehole and it hung in a chamber, magnifying only the sound of running water.

A Basuto mine boss-boy, weeping, pleaded with his two brothers trapped below to respond to his calls.

"Come to my voice and speak," he said. "If you cannot move, throw a coal at my voice. Do not be afraid, we want to help you.

"Wherever you are, talk back to me. There is lots of meat and food here for you."

But there was no reply.

A helmeted European miner, a voluntary rescue worker, took turns with the Basuto boss-boy to shout down the microphone in Afrikaans, English and Basuto.

The miner, Mr Johannes Mocke, said: "You down below answer. Just speak. There is nothing else to do. If you must speak where you lie or sit, we will hear you and answer you.

"There are no buttons to push — just answer back. Come closer, there are no rockfalls here. Just a drillhole. It is faith. Come closer. We are waiting to help you."

The waiting women were advised to go home. The news would be brought to them as quickly as possible, they were told.

"We can't sleep," they replied.

A woman sobbed: "They are so young, I can't believe it."

But the microphone brought no reply and in the early morning they went home. — Sapa.

'I am a Government servant and cannot comment'

The Sharpeville massacre, 21 March 1960

On Monday, 21 March 1960, residents of black townships on the Witwatersrand (Soweto, Orlando, Bopholong, Sharpeville) offered themselves to the police for arrest. Under the leadership of Robert Mangaliso Sobukwe, president of the newly formed Pan Africanist Congress, they had defied the law and left their pass books at home.

Had the action gone according to plan, police stations, courts and prisons would have been overflowing with the resulting arrests. Sobukwe had been explicit in his instructions: there was to be no violence — merely peaceful protest on a huge scale. The Pan Africanist Congress slogan for the campaign, coined by Sobukwe, a graduate of Fort Hare and a lecturer in Zulu at the University of the Witwatersrand, was 'No bail, no defence, no fine.'

Late that morning, reports began to come through that the police had opened fire on protesters at the Bopholong township near Evaton. The press had been out since the early hours of the morning covering the protests and, almost with one accord, set out for Bopholong. Benjamin Pogrund, the reporter covering black politics for the *Rand Daily Mail,* together with photographer Jan Hoek, were among the press contingent.

No sooner had they reached Evaton than they came upon a convoy of Saracens and armed police. They were, the police said, going to a place called Sharpeville, near Vereeniging. No one had even heard of Sharpeville.

Ignoring orders to stay outside the township, Pogrund and Hoek, followed by another car carrying *Drum* reporter Humphrey Tyler and photographer Ian Berry, tucked themselves in behind the Saracens and so entered Sharpeville.

All was confusion, with crowds of between 5 000 and 20 000 milling around. 'Suddenly,' recalled Pogrund, 'there were sounds like firecrackers going off, and one of us shouted: "My God, they're shooting!"' The car in which Pogrund and Hoek were driving was attacked and they escaped in the Ford Prefect from the township over the open veld, but not before they had caught a glimpse of Ian Berry. He was, said Pogrund later, standing up 'amidst the bullets, and his pictures, published around the world, showed people fleeing and policemen with sub-machine-guns standing on Saracens in the background.' Sixty-nine people died and 178 were wounded.

Out of this chaotic and almost happenstance visit to Sharpeville came some fine journalism, some of it angry, some of it restrained, but little that was not, in some way, moving. James Ambrose Brown's report, written not from Sharpeville but from Baragwanath Hospital, fell into the latter category.

Ambrose Brown's career in journalism had been distinctive. As a soldier in the Transvaal Scottish, he served in the Second World War, writing an eye-witness account of the Battle of

335

Alamein which was published by the *Saturday Evening Post* and described by that publication as 'the greatest worm's eye view of battle to have come out of the war so far'.

He joined the staff of the *Rand Daily Mail* in 1945 as a reporter, moving to the *Sunday Times,* where he served as feature writer, arts editor and columnist until he left in 1968 to freelance as one of South Africa's most versatile writers.

It was in his capacity as a columnist that Ambrose Brown was contacted by Dr Isadore Frack, superintendent at Baragwanath Hospital. Frack knew Ambrose Brown as 'the angry young man' who wrote the 'I Think Aloud' column in the *Sunday Times.* 'He told me in a voice low and tense that I must come to the hospital,' recalled Ambrose Brown. 'I walked past the police at the gate and at once Frack explained that he would give me full permission to go anywhere in the hospital, speak to anyone I wished — but I must guard his position as a government servant. In other words, he would give me the facts I wanted in the guise of "no comment".

Ambrose Brown noticed that Frack's hand, holding the heavy calibre bullets taken from the casualties was trembling uncontrollably, and he feared that his phone was already tapped. Frack was outraged at what had happened only hours earlier and urged Ambrose Brown to get the story to the outside world.

After walking through the hospital and speaking to people through the ward sisters, Ambrose Brown wired London's *News Chronicle* for permission to send his story by cable. On receipt of the story, the editor cabled back: 'Congratulations. Your story in best traditions of journalism.' The story ran on Saturday, 26 March 1960 under two lines of double type across the entire front page under the headline:

WOUNDED TELL STORY OF THE MASSACRE

Police turn hospital into prison

JOHANNESBURG, Friday.

The coloured people's hospital at Baragwanath, Johannesburg, already filled with 140 victims of Sharpeville, is standing by for the arrival of a fully equipped 100-bed military field hospital — in anticipation of more bloody clashes this weekend in the African townships around Johannesburg.

Baragwanath Hospital is a hospital under siege. Its superintendent, Dr. Isaac Frack, is virtually a prisoner.

I know Dr. Frack as a dedicated man devoted to healing the African. He has always been open with information. Today he was a changed man.

His hospital swarms with uniformed and plainclothes policemen. I saw senior police officers using his personal office as a conference room. And he had nothing to say.

Dr. Frack, the man who recently showed his superbly equipped wards to Mr. Harold Macmillan, has been gagged. A doctor told me: "We believe his personal phone is tapped."

Hiding the facts

Outside and inside each of the five wards and a hall where men, women and children lie with bullet wounds, are groups of armed police. Their orders are to prevent the escape of any of these citizens of Sharpeville. The wounded believe that they are to be jailed as soon as they leave their beds.

336

Such injuries as they have suffered are normally seen only after a battle. The most experienced surgeons and doctors have been shocked by these multiple gunshot wounds — bone powdered by heavy calibre slugs, limbs so mutilated by bullets tearing through that amputation is necessary, a great number of wounds inflicted from behind. These facts cannot be denied, but they are not available from official sources.

My impression is that every effort has been made to keep the world ignorant about the Sharpeville wounded. I saw and spoke to them — unofficially.

I asked Dr. Frack's permission to visit the wards. He replied: "I have to refuse. My instructions from the Minister of Justice are that no Press men and no lawyers are allowed to visit casualties." I asked permission to ask the surgeons, who worked 60 hours non-stop, about the nature of the wounds. He said no.

I asked Dr. Frack if it was true that many of the wounds were caused by copper-nosed .45 bullets. He replied: "No comment." I asked was it true that detectives seized all bullets as soon as they were removed from the wounds? "No comment."

I asked was it true that many of the wounds were so grave that immediate amputations were necessary, that bones were shattered and powdered by the impact and there was gross mutilation of flesh? Dr. Frack said: "I cannot comment."

More are dying

I asked Dr. Frack if he could show me one of the bullets removed from a wound. He said he hadn't one.

The scene outside the Sharpeville police station shortly after the massacre (South African Library).

I asked him what it felt like to be superintendent of a hospital in which the staff, from himself down to the medical orderlies, are under strict orders to say nothing. He replied: "I am a Government servant and cannot comment."

I asked him how long his patients would be under guard. He told me: "Some may be three or four months on their backs. Some are dying now." He said that 143 casualties were admitted to this one hospital. Three were dead and were removed at once to a police mortuary to join 65 more. There are 110 wounded men, 29 women and four children.

I left Dr. Frack hunched at his desk. My impression was that this doctor had facts that could shock the world, that he was nauseated by what he had seen, but stood staunchly to his silence.

I went to the guarded wards, walked past guards and interviewed wounded in four of them. In the fifth I was challenged by an African sister. Her orders, she said were "No interviews." She rang for the chief matron and said to me: "I am sorry, who will tell the people now?" When I told her that I had already spoken to many patients, she smiled.

Hit again and again

The first patient I spoke to (they all begged not to be named) was under a saline drip. This 47-year-old showed me his wound. A bullet hit him in the lower back and left through the groin. "I was running away," he said.

Next was a mill worker, aged about 20. He had five wounds. He said: "I had been at an all-night church service. On the way home I saw crowds. The first shot hit me in the foot. I walked away. I was hit again and fell. I crawled and was hit again. My friend was dead. I began to pray."

Another bed held a teenage lad with a belly wound. He said that the police called the Africans forward and then fired. "Some of us were still sitting on the ground waiting for them to speak."

I spoke to two women with leg wounds. One said: "I went to look for my husband. He was dead." The other turned her face to the wall and said she would not speak to a detective.

A boy of nine told me that he and his brother of 10 had gone out of his father's shop when the firing began. Bullets sprayed the wall. His brother fell dead. "I was lucky," he said and smiled.

Strangely — laughter

Every ward I visited looked like a military hospital after a battle. Bottles of blood and saline, traction splints, plaster casts spotted with blood. And silence. The astonishing stoical silence of the African. Strangely, there was also laughter. These amazing people were able to laugh as they told me of Sabre jets "swooping to frighten us".

I met families who had come 20 miles to visit their wounded. They had been allowed to see them for the first time four days after the shootings. The order is visits only on visiting day.

A truck driver aged 50 told me: "My son of nine is here and my brother. Thank God they are recovering.

"I went to the square to take my son away before the trouble started. I got there in time for the shooting. The people were running." He pointed out a man. "My friend there has been searching two days for his wife. He found her just now — in the mortuary."

A well dressed wife of a professional man said: "Don't write what my husband does. It would come back on us." I met a man who described a wound he had seen on a man crawling from the square. "The bullets took away whole pieces of flesh." He made a fist. "I wanted to help but I became too sick."

Yet no hatred

Yet, astonishingly, I met neither hatred nor bitterness. I met only black men and women (wounded and unwounded) who cried: "This is a terrible thing. We pray that it can never happen again, that good will come out of it."

I met, also, blank official silence. But I can tell the people of Britain that South African white opinion is deeply shocked. I know that moderate police officers are horrified.

Unfortunately, some Africans believe that the Sharpeville massacre was a deliberate police reprisal for the Cato Manor killings of police. I spoke to some who said: "The police shouted before they opened fire, 'Now we are killing you Kaffirs.'"

Ambrose Brown's story was also used by his paper, the *Sunday Times,* on 27 March, changing the *News Chronicle*'s headline to: 'In hospital where men, women and children lie with bullet wounds . . . It's "No Comment!"' and omitting the final paragraphs, together with the last sentences of the penultimate paragraph.

For the *News Chronicle,* Ambrose Brown's story was one of the last South African events it was to carry on its pages. The 114 year-old paper, founded by Charles Dickens as the *Daily News,* ceased publication in October 1960.

For South Africa, the massacre marked the end of an era of carefree journalism and ushered in a new epoch: ground-root as well as liberal protest against the rule of apartheid. Journalism became coloured in almost every facet, from sport to women's pages and drew increasing attention from the international media in response to foreign interest in the country.

James Ambrose Brown, prize-winning journalist, writer and playwright.

'Do you see this too?'

Laurence Gandar, Rand Daily Mail, 1962

To reporters in the newsroom of the *Rand Daily Mail,* Laurence Gandar was an austere, un-approachable figure. To those who knew him better, Gandar possessed a steely intellectual centre, displaying emotion in attacks of asthma. To those who read his work over the course of his career, which stretched from *The Sunday Tribune* in 1936 to the *Rand Daily Mail* in 1966, Gandar was a writer of almost intuitive political perception, with a warmth which, running through the cool logic of his words and the precision of his argument, was at times heart-wrenching.

It was Laurence Gandar, 42 years' old when he became editor of the *Rand Daily Mail* in 1957, who gave to his paper its identity as a liberal, crusading, fiery journal, one where the quality of writing genuinely mattered, but which quality was, nonetheless, secondary to the quality of caring. Under Gandar's editorship, the *Rand Daily Mail* attracted some of the finest journalists in the country, published some of the most outstanding journalism and, probably from the day in 1957 when he became editor, began to die, very slowly. It was said that the *Rand Daily Mail* was the country's conscience; alas, as the years of unrest deepened into years of conflict, fewer and fewer people wanted a conscience over the breakfast table.

In 1953, while he was assistant editor on *The Daily News,* Gandar began writing a weekly political column under the pen-name of 'Crossbencher'. Four years later, as editor of the *Rand Daily Mail,* Gandar wrote a similar column — 'Political Viewpoint' — under his middle names, Owen Vine, changing subsequently to his own byline.

Like his powerful series, 'The Nation that Lost Its Way', 'Political Viewpoint' contained many fine articles. Gandar's writing was distinguished by its extreme clarity, its elegance and, in hindsight, by its prescience. 'Towards White unity — on a war footing' is a fine example from 'Political Viewpoint'. It appeared in the *Rand Daily Mail* of 14 March 1962.

TOWARDS WHITE UNITY — ON A WAR FOOTING

Those who have tears for South Africa, prepare to shed them soon. For inexorably we are moving into that twilight that precedes the night.

In these early months of 1962 we are nearing the culmination of a long process, a fateful concatenation of events and forces that seem from the start to have conspired against a peaceful solution to our unique and forbidding problems.

If I were asked to state at what point I believed the forward approaches of disaster came into view, I would say it was the Government's announcement of its Transkei independence plan. All the indications are that this was to be the great symbolic act of sacrifice designed to justify in the eyes of the world and the hearts of South Africans the policy of separate development of White and Black. This was to be proof positive. And all

340

Laurence Gandar, the crusading editor of the Rand Daily Mail (Times Media Ltd).

the considerable apparatus of State publicity was employed to show to the world this wondrous thing demonstrating beyond further doubt or argument the moral basis of apartheid.

But the world was not impressed, and the increasingly militant power of its opinion continues to bear upon us. Yet this was the last card, the very last, that the Government had to play. The Transkei was the biggest and best African homeland, the only one that formed a coherent geographic entity. If the Transkei has failed to convince the world about apartheid, then the Government has nothing left with which to turn the flanks of humanity's wrath. There is no further demonstration of its faith that it can make; there is also no further concession it is prepared to offer.

Today its attitude to the world is this: "We have made our gesture and it has not persuaded you. You wish to compel us to change our policy? All right, now we stand and fight." This, in a nutshell, is the South African situation today — an overwhelming force bearing down on an unyielding object. The only questions to be resolved are how irresistible is the force and how immovable is the object.

Within the setting of this impending clash, in South Africa itself, there is a curious and growing lightheadedness, the kind of morbid elation that soldiers experience immediately before encounters of immense peril. The anxieties of planning, the anguish of decision-taking are over — the ground is chosen, the die is cast and the men are irrevocably set upon whatever lies ahead.

And so Afrikaner Nationalism, impelled by the death wish of its own race mythology, leads the country into a thundering re-enactment of its own history — the struggle of a tiny, White self-righteous people against the evil of Black barbarism — first the Bantu impis, now the Afro-Asian hordes. Surely, the Nationalists believe, there can be no more glorious fight, no more heroic downfall if downfall there must be.

And so, by committing the nation to battle as it were, they have made, in the holy name of patriotism, comrades in arms of every White who lives here, like it or not. It is all for one and one for all.

In this they have, ironically enough, been greatly aided by those who are their traditional political enemies at home.

The reasons for this are worth examining because they are at the root of the South African tragedy. It is a story of human failure on a grand scale, of mass surrender by stealth. Here it is.

341

Down the years the main political opposition to Afrikaner Nationalism, the United Party, has been saying to the people of South Africa: Be anti-Nationalist and you can consider your political duty well done. Just be against the Nationalist, it matters not greatly what you are for. You do not require to have a definable political philosophy based on recognised moral principles; any policy, be it vague or fatuous, will do just so long as it is anti-Nationalist.

While there were still historical causes in this country for anti-Nationalism as an emotional force, this policy worked well enough, but with the growing estrangement of South Africa from the rest of the world and especially the coming of the Republic and the break with the Commonwealth last year, those grounds have been crumbling away. Anti-Nationalism, *per se* is almost a spent force today and the United Party finds itself with too narrow an area of disagreement with the Nationalist Party on the fundamental race question to sustain itself.

Worse still it has helped to destroy its own future by making conservatism in race matters respectable among anti-Nationalists. ("White leadership with justice," "White leadership for the foreseeable future" and so on). It has not merely failed to educate its own followers to the acceptance of some substantially different and higher set of values in race matters: it has actually helped to condition them to a concept of White domination close enough to that of *wit baasskap* to make the transition from one to the other relatively easy.

Thus the anti-Nationalist following of the United Party stands dressed and ready for complete capture, at some suitable psychological moment for the Nationalists. This the Government perceives well enough and it is now busy manoeuvring into position for the great takeover.

The next state of emergency will be the time, and there will surely be another state of emergency, perhaps even this year. When it comes and assuming that the stress is considerable, the White population of South Africa will go streaming into the Nationalist laager, stripped of the power of resistance which some genuine moral principles might have given them.

And when that happens, standing at the entrance to the laager and waving the people in, with the United Party — playing out its role as a "responsible Opposition". It happened during the last state of emergency and it will happen again.

During the past 48 hours United Party Senators have been rehearsing this very role.

After the Minister of Defence, Mr Fouche, had told the Senate that some Afro-Asian countries had secret plans for an invasion of South Africa, Senator Sutter pledged the United Party's full support to the Government in its plans to build up South Africa's military power.

And so the tragic story unfolds. South Africa, abandoning hope of persuading the world that apartheid is just and workable, moves steadily on to a war footing — call-ups, rearming, munitions making, research and, of course, including pistol clubs. The conditions are created for a new kind of White unity — backs to the wall, our country right or wrong, patriots all.

The process is far advanced, the stage is set. We may act out our differences for another year or so, but there is no mistaking where all the signs are pointing. Do you see this too? Or is there something that I have not understood? If so, tell me now, for my heart is breaking.

In 1966, in one of the editorial putsches that were such a depressing feature of South African Associated Newspapers' management, Laurence Gandar was removed from his position of editor and was appointed editor-in-chief, a position which effectively removed him from most spheres of editorial influence. Or so the directors thought.

But Gandar, with an almost biblical sense of continuity, had imbibed his disciples with his own brand of political philosophy and thus Gandar's spirit, although not his hand, could be discerned through the editorships of his successors (all, in one way or another, fired by management): Raymond Louw, Allister Sparks, Rex Gibson.

'Therein lies my identity:
I am a South African'

Nat Nakasa, 1964

'What happens to the writings of a man when he is dead and gone?' asked Nat Nakasa. It was a poignant question from a man, talented, witty, ironic and compassionate, denied the right to return to his homeland, who died tragically young in New York in 1965.

Born in Durban in 1937, Nakasa was the first black South African to write a weekly column in a white newspaper. 'As I See It' appeared each Saturday in the *Rand Daily Mail* under its editor, Laurence Gandar. The column was a wry, gently sarcastic read which shared its page with the likes of regular writers such as Allister Sparks — the last but one editor of the doomed paper — and Laurence Gandar.

Nakasa was a subtle writer and avoided openly angry pieces, preferring instead to write dry, atmospheric articles, rich in irony. He was awarded the prestigious Nieman Fellowship in 1964 to read journalism at Harvard. Nakasa was refused a passport and was granted, instead, an exit permit which prohibited his return to South Africa.

It was with the knowledge that he was to leave his country, never to return, that Nakasa wrote 'It's difficult to decide my identity'. It was a classic, moving piece of journalism and appeared in the *Rand Daily Mail* on Saturday, 20 June 1964.

IT'S DIFFICULT TO DECIDE MY IDENTITY

A small audience in Germiston was told this week that the Afrikaans Press and Broadcast House had elevated "kaffirs" to "Mr." and "Mrs." instead of keeping "savages" in their place by traditional apartheid. This was said, according to the report, by Dr. L.E. Beyers, provisional Transvaal leader of the Nationaliste Bond.

There is one thing I like about Dr. Beyers and men who think like him. Such men are honest men. They have the courage of their convictions. It is unfortunate, that there aren't many of them left in the 20th century. We have, to be sure, more than enough people who think like Dr. Beyers, but few of them have the courage to speak their minds.

As a journalist, I sincerely hope that men like Dr. Beyers will still be going strong when we get television in this country. I would encourage Dr. Beyers to say some of these things to a wide audience on television. I would volunteer to be used by the doctor as a sample of a young savage.

But then this country may not get TV for a long time. For the present, we have no choice but to allow such rare television material as Dr. Beyers to be wasted on small Bond audiences in Germiston.

Meanwhile, however, Dr. Beyers has set me thinking. In his talk this week Dr. Beyers was only contributing to a discussion which has been going to the Afrikaans Press debating whether it is a sin against apartheid to drink tea with Africans. Chief Kaiser Matanzima has just voiced the opinion that the people of the Transkei should be called Africans and not "Bantus" or "Natives", let alone "kaffirs" and "savages".

To my mind, the importance of this discussion is that all the questions asked relate to the question of my identity. Who am I? Where do I belong in the South African scheme of things? Who are my people?

Negroes in Harlem are asking themselves the same question. Some have tried to answer it by forming "Back-to-Africa" movements. Others have formed organisations like the Black Muslims.

I have the same problem on my hands. It often pains me to realise that even my speech cannot really be called me. This becomes worse, in my case, because I am more impressionable than most people I know. I am the sort that speaks like an American after meeting one or like an Englishman after interviewing a peer.

I am supposed to be a Pondo, but I don't even know the language of that tribe. I was brought up in a Zulu-speaking home, my mother being a Zulu. Yet I can no longer think in Zulu because that language cannot cope with the demands of our day. I could not, for instance, discuss negritude in Zulu. Even an article like this would not be possible in Zulu.

I have never owned an assegai or any of those magnificent Zulu shields. Neither do I propose to be in tribal wear when I go to the U.S. this year for my scholarshp. I am just not a tribesman, whether I like it or not. I am, inescapably, a part of the city slums, the factory machines and our beloved shebeens.

I'm not even sure that I could claim to be African. For if I were, then I should surely share my identity with West Africans and other Africans in Kenya or Tanganyika. Yet it happens to be true that I am more at home with an Afrikaner than with a West African. Some of my friends who have been abroad say they got on best with Afrikaners they met in Europe instead of Englishmen or West Africans.

We saw some evidence of this when a number of Nigerian students passed through Johannesburg once. We took them to a party in Soweto where they were welcomed like long lost brothers. After marvelling at their flowing robes and talking some politics, we didn't know what to do with them.

Being Moslems — and millions of Nigerians are Moslems — they did not drink. We could not offer them meat because that also would have gone against their faith. They raised a laugh when they told us that some of their friends at home were polygamists. "We must explain," someone quipped, "that you chaps will have to make do with one girl each in this country. We can't fix you up with a lot in one shot."

Once we were through with this kind of talk, our visitors were abandoned in one corner of the room and nobody had much to say to them. They were perfect strangers, more so than the many South African Whites who spend some of their time in the townships. To speak of those Nigerians as "My people" would not make much sense, even though we all had flat noses.

I don't see that there is any justification in calling me a non-European either. That is as silly as this business of South African Whites who insist that they are Europeans. Some of them have never set foot in Europe. Nor did their grandfathers.

It is the insistence of the Whites that they are "Europeans" which has, in part, inspired such silly slogans as "Africa for the Africans". The Africa of today is simply not the product of assegais and rain queens. Johannesburg was built by the White technical knowhow and enterprise plus the indispensable co-operation of Black labour. To that extent, this city will never be Black or White. Black men cannot look at the tall buildings of Johannesburg and say "this is ours" without being fraudulent. Nor can the Whites.

If I am right, therein lies my identity. I am a South African like Dr. L.E. Beyers. "My people" are South Africans. Mine is the history of the Great Trek. Ghandi's passive resistance in Johannesburg, the wars of Cetewayo and the dawn raids which gave us the treason trials in 1956. All these are South African things. They are part of me. So is Dr. Beyers inescapably a part of me. And I refuse to think that part of Dr. Beyers is a "savage".

Nat Nakasa. 'If I should leave this country and decide not to come back, it will be because of a desire to avoid perishing in my own bitterness.' (Times Media Ltd).

Nat Nakasa left South Africa for good at the end of 1964, after writing a poignant and satirical article, 'A Native of Nowhere'. 'When I write next week,' he said, 'it will be as a former South African.'

Nakasa travelled to New York. (In addition to his work on the *Rand Daily Mail,* he had contributed to *The New York Times,* worked on *Drum* as assistant editor and founded *Classic,* a magazine whose objective was to encourage writers with causes to pursue.) Two days before his death he confided, 'I can't laugh anymore and when I can't laugh I can't write.'

On 14 July 1965, Nakasa fell to his death from the seventh floor apartment he shared with his wife. At his funeral, Miriam Makeba sang Zulu laments, the congregation joining in with Zulu hymns.

'The battle on the prayer front'

Schalk Pienaar on the Stellenbosch students, circa 1940

One of the few editors to transcend the great divide of the Afrikaans vs English press was Schalk Pienaar, editor respectively of *Die Oosterlig* (1946), *Die Beeld* (1965-1974) and *Beeld* (1974-75). He was, in fact, the founding editor of *Die Beeld,* Nasionale Pers' first Sunday paper. Within five years, the paper had achieved a readership in excess of one million. And he was also the founding editor of *Beeld.*

The son of a dominee in Merewille, Cape Province, Pienaar was brought up in the Karoo and in Stellenbosch. An outstanding scholar, he was awarded a Rhodes Scholarship to study in Oxford. In 1937, after his return to South Africa, Pienaar joined the staff of the Cape Town newspaper, *Die Burger,* breaking his service in 1941 to study history at Stellenbosch University, where he completed three courses in one year.

From then on, Pienaar remained in journalism. It is said, with some justification, that the route to an editorship must include a stint either as a parliamentary reporter or a political correspondent. Pienaar's interest in politics was undoubtedly fostered by his appointment as parliamentary reporter for *Die Burger* in 1941.

It was during his tenure as editor of *Die Beeld* that Pienaar wrote a much acclaimed weekly column which ran in the newspaper from 1965 to 1970. Its range of subject matter was catholic and it was distinguished by Pienaar's succinct style and warm, wry humour.

EK WAS EEN VAN DIE BASTARDS

In die afgelope dekades het dit dikwels aan ons Engelse universiteite gebeur. Witsies of Ikeys word kwaad oor iets wat die owerheid gedoen het of nie gedoen het nie, storm in optog waar die owerheid hulle nie wil hê nie, die polisie gryp in . . .

Waar is die dag toe die Stellenbossers dit reggekry het om op een enkele Saterdag die polisie te laat mobiliseer, eers in Kaapstad en toe op Stellenbosch!

Dit was, om presies te wees, 27 Julie 1940. En ek was daardie dag 'n deel, 'n berekende deel, van die moles.

Eers gou 'n stukkie agtergrond vir mense wat onbekend is met die hoogspanninge wat ons almal in die oorlogstyd vasgegryp het. Die burgemeester van Kaapstad het kans gesien om te verorden dat elke dag (Sondae, verbeel jou, uitgesluit) presies om twaalfuur twee minute lank vir 'n Geallieerde oorwinning gebid moet word.

Op die klokslag blaas 'n beuel. Dan staan mens botstil en bid. Ná twee minute blaas die beuel weer. Dan mag jy weer loop.

Nou was daar darem heelparty van ons mense wat geen duiwel omgegee het van wie die Britte 'n pak slae kry nie. Gaan staan en bid dat die Britte wen? Nooit gehoor nie. Maar as jy stap — praat van vryheid en demokratiese regte in Kaapstad — dan word jy gemoker.

Dit was in sulke omstandighede dat ons op Stellenbosch kans gesien het vir 'n ding. Van die heilige reg om te betoog en al sulke hoë woorde het ons toe nog nie geweet nie. Ons het sommer maar net besluit om 'n ding te doen. Ons sal Kaapstad toe gaan en in die bidpouse stap. Die hel haal die man wat aan ons probeer slaan.

(Koddig hoe die godsdiens altyd daarby is. As dit nie Sint George se katedraal is waar die Ikeys sedertdien moleste gemaak het nie, is dit die bidpouse. Nes die Iere. Ons pleeg graag ons onheilighede in die naam van God.)

Natuurlik kies ons toe vir ons operasie Adderleystraat uit. Ons sukkel nie met systraatjies nie.

Die spulletjie het uit die Ossewa-Brandwag gebore geraak. Laat my militêre roem nooit misken word nie; ek was destyds adjudant van 'n generaal. Vir die generaals en goeters het ons niks van ons planne vertel nie. Hulle kon dalk onverantwoordelik genoeg wees om ons te verbied om onverantwoordelik te wees.

Toe ons die Saterdagoggend in Kaapstad opdaag, sommige per motor, die meeste met die trein — dit was nog in die dae voordat ons ryk geword het — toe weet Kaapstad klaar van ons. Adderleystraat staan dik van die mensdom. Die polisie is daar. Die koerante is daar. Almal wag vir iets. Mense — en daaronder moet jy studente seker ook maar reken — kan mos nooit hul groot monde hou nie.

Sake word erger. Matrose kom opdaag, duidelik nie toevallig nie. Net voor twaalf kom daar militêre vragmotors aan en soldate met geweers klim uit. Ons ouens, om seker te maak dat ons mekaar nie pak wanneer die groot baklei begin nie, het elkeen as kenteken 'n viooltjie in die knoopsgat op die Parade gekoop. Dit was nie 'n baie slim plan nie. Die mense sien dit raak en begin ons uitken. Die spanning kon gevoel, gehoor en gesien word.

Maar 'n mens het darem tog jou ydelheid. Hiervoor het jy Kaap toe gekom en dit gaan jy nou doen, of daar nou soldate, matrose, konstabels, duisende mense — veral dan ook vroumense — is of nie.

Die sekondewyser stap aan.

Die plan is soos volg. Net twee man stap. Daantjie Barnard was die een. ,,Pienaar, you are his friend. Tell him that only funk can keep him out of a Springbok team." Só het oubaas Mark Markótter op 'n dag aan my gesê.

As die Oubaas hom daardie dag sou gesien het, sou hy sy opinie oor Daantjie se durf moes wysig. (Dit is ander dinge, onder meer 'n Wêreldoorlog, wat verhinder het dat Daantjie losskakel of senter vir die Springbokke speel.) Die ander stapper was Umtali Joubert, bokser vir sy universiteit in 'n mindere gewigsklas.

Daantjie is lankal dood. Umtali, hoop ek, leef nog. Maar dit terloops.

Toe die beuel op die sekonde van twaalf blaas, begin die twee manne stap. Daantjie van duskant, Umtali van anderkant. Die oorlogsmanne kan nie dadelik inspring nie. Hulle moet eers bid. En ons kan ook niks doen voordat hulle inspring nie.

As iemand onder al daardie duisende ooit daardie dag gebid het, was dit waaragtig met oop oë. Die duiwel het in die lug gehang, en wie wil dit waag om 'n kans te mis om die duiwel te sien?

Umtali en Daantjie sê agterna: Ek het nie geweet twee minute is so lank nie.

Schalk Pienaar (Die Burger).

Hulle was lankal oor die straat en weer op pad terug, toe blaas die beuel eers vir die tweede maal. En toe gebeur alles gelyk.

Die soldate spring in, met die kolfkante van hul geweers darem. Umtali slaan die eerste man skoon onder sy geweerkolf uit. Ruggelings ontmoet hy Adderleystraat behoorlik. Die polisiesersant wat sy oog op daardie komende ding gehad het, vat Umtali aan sy skouer en sê: ,,Nie 'n sleg hou nie, boet, maar dis jou laaste een, hoor.''

Van gebeurtenisse om hom, behalwe dat dit 'n algemene gefoeter was, kon Daantjie agternooit mooi vertel nie.

In elk geval, almal het ingesak. Die blote gedrang het gemaak dat groot skade nie aangerig kon word nie. Dit het bietjie minder as 'n halfuur geduur. ,,Die slagveld aan die bidfront,'' is dit daarna in 'n oorlogstydse woordspeling genoem.

'n Goeie ou vriend wie se naam ek nie waag om te noem nie, want hy staan te hoog aangeskrewe, is deur 'n vrou dwarsdeur sy gesig geklap. En wat is 'n man se antwoord daarop toe? Vroue is altyd die gevaar by sulke geleenthede.

Die Burger het daarna berig — die verslaggewer het op 'n balkon gestaan soos dit uit die oogpunt van verstandige beriggewing en eie veiligheid gewens was — dat die volgende gilstemme gehoor is:

,,Kill the damned Dutchmen!''

,,Wipe out the Dutch bastards!''

,,Put our soldiers on the Dutch hooligans!''

,,Chop off the rebels' heads!''

,,Down with the bastard Nationalists!''

Nou ja, ek kan nie ontken dat ek een van daardie bastards was nie.

In die omstandighede het die polisie 'n baie goeie stuk werk gedoen. Hul knuppels was uit, maar is nooit in werklike erns gebruik nie.

'n Paar manne is gegryp, maar kort daarna weer gelos. Die een en ander kon agterna spog met blou kolle en dergelike meer, maar niemand is hospitaal toe nie. Ten spyte van die hele gewalt.

Die einde was eintlik 'n gewapende vrede. Soldate het die polisie naderhand gehelp om die orde te herstel.

Die studente het 'n afmars gemaak met die sing van ,,Afrikaners Landgenote''.

Die soldate en matrose het geantwoord met ,,Britannia Rules the Waves''.

349

Die teen-antwoord was „Die Stem".

Agterna is as feit gestel dat die destydse Eerste Minister, genl. Jan Smuts, die bidpouse in belang van die goeie orde wou laat beëindig; ons Stellenbosse onhebbelikheid het dit vir hom politiek onmoontlik gemaak om dit te doen.

'n Pragtige storie wat verband hiermee hou, word van die ou Generaal vertel. Op 'n dag was hy op die punt om 'n gebou te verlaat. Sy aide sê vir hom: „Generaal, wag net 'n bietjie."

„Waarom?"

„Die bidpouse, Generaal."

„Wat, is hierdie geneuk nog aan die gang?"

Nou 'n nasleep van die Slag van Adderleystraat voordat ons by die vervolg kom — net om aan te toon hoe studente daardie tyd met sukses gehanteer is.

Oubaas Mark Markötter nooi Daantjie en my na sy huis. Daar was 'n derde man ook, maar ek kan om liefdeswil nie onthou wie hy was nie. Daardie ou Christenmens wat in sy tyd van soveel onchristelikhede beskinder was, skink vir ons elkeen 'n bier en vir homself 'n whisky. Hy sê vir ons:

„Kyk. Ek self vermy dit om in Kaapstad op straat te wees as dit twaalfuur word. As dit gebeur dat ek tog dan daar betrap word, dan gaan ek in 'n telefoonhokkie, al het ek geen oproep te maak nie. As die bidpouse my nietemin op straat sou vang en iemand molesteer my, dan moker ek hom." (Die Oubaas se kierie was beroemd.) „Maar ek gaan soek nie moeilikheid nie. Is dit nodig dat julle moeilikheid gaan soek?"

Ten spyte van al ons moerigheid was dit die einde van ons storie. 'n Wyse ou man — ongeag sy rugbywysheid — het gepraat en ons het begryp.

Nou die vervolgverhaal.

Ná afloop van die Slag van Adderleystraat het ons nêrens gaan bid of ween nie. Ons het op gepaste plekke 'n bier of twee gaan drink en onder mekaar oor ons heldedade gespog. Toe gaan koop ons in Andringastraat op Stellenbosch ons laat-Argus. Ek meen, daar is seker ander dinge op aarde ook, maar 'n mens moet tog darem weet wat van-middag op Nuweland gebeur het.

Net daar begin toe die Slag van Andringastraat.

Dit was daardie tyd die enigste plek op Stellenbosch waar jy Saterdagaand koerant kon koop, en die tou was altyd lank. Daar was lankal ergernis oor die indring van mense in die tou. Vol moed en gloed oor Adderleystraat word oor die laaste bier besluit dat sulke dinge vanaand na behore gehanteer sal word. The great house of Tarquin will suffer wrong no more!

Sal dit dan toe nie so gebeur dat dieselfde Daantjie Barnard daardie aand 'n Kleurling pak nie. Die destydse advokaat — die latere hooggeroemde regter — Theo van Wyk het hom in die Stellenbosse landdroshof op 'n aanklag van aanranding kom verdedig. Dit was eintlik 'n baie ligte aanklag; die landdros was verbaas en die aanklaer ontsteld dat 'n advokaat kom opdaag het. Daantjie was klaar skoon los, toe word hy voor die magistraat volgens ons destydse oortuigings heeltemal onbehoorlik eerlik. Toe sit hy natuurlik vas.

Theo van Wyk wou nie geld hê nie. Dis mos vir 'n vriend. Maar daarvan wou ons niks weet nie. Die hoed is omgestuur en Theo se koste en Daantjie se boete was dadelik daar.

Dit in die verbygaan.

Dieselfde Saterdagaand breek die duiwel op Stellenbosch los. Die Kleurlinge groepeer en maak 'n teenaanval op wat in die tou voor die koerantwinkel gebeur het. Eiendom en voertuie word op 'n streep beskadig.

Daar kom 'n teenmobilisasie van studente uit die koshuise. Kleurling-eiendom word op 'n streep beskadig.

Dit alles duur voort tot diep in die Sondag. Polisieversterkings word ingeroep van die Paarl en van Kaapstad. Daar word geskiet — darem net met loskruitpatrone. Maar die nodige resultaat word bereik.

Ou prof. Gawie Cillié, ons buurman destyds, wat vir ander dinge as sy uitbundige liefde vir my beroemd was, kyk oor die draad en sê vir my: ,,Schalk, ek het 'n pistool. Ek bring dit vir jou vir gebruik as dit nodig word."

Ek sê: ,,Doktor, dankie, maar ek dink nie dit sal nodig wees nie."

Op een van die pilaartjies van Dagbreek se ingang staan ou prof. E.C. Pienaar. 'n Indrukwekkende figuur met sy silwer hare. Hoe hulle hom daar bo gekry het, sal ek nog altyd graag wil weet. Hy sê: ,,Kêrels, as dit nodig word, ja. Maar hou julself in toom."

Op die ou end bedaar alles toe, soos alles geneig is om te bedaar, behalwe soms.

Maar in die hele proses gryp darem ook die Universiteit amptelik in. Die destydse rektor, prof. Bobby Wilcocks, het 'n paar van ons bymekaar geroep. (Ek het die onfeilbare vermoë om op plekke te kom waar ek nie werklik hoort nie en waar ek nie graag wil wees nie.)

Dit was nadat die distrikskommandant van polisie, kol. J.A.V. Mentz van die Paarl, by hom was. Hy het toevallig — as 'n mens in verband met polisie-optrede van toevalligheid kan praat — die rugbyman Hannes Morkel met 'n bloekomstompie in sy mou betrap. Met watter onskuldige bedoelings kon Hannes tog 'n bloekomstompie in sy mou gedra het?

Flappie Lochner het vir Hannes in die polisiekantoor gaan lospleit. (Ek sou kon sweer Flappie was die derde, of altans dan die eerste van ons drie die aand by oubaas Mark, maar hy sê nee, dit was nie hy nie. Hy was in elk geval by geeneen van die twee veldslae betrokke nie, want Flappie is 'n vreedsame man — behalwe op die rugbyveld.)

Hoe ook al, prof. Bobby het in alle redelike billikheid vir ons 'n paar dinge gesê en gevra. Dit was die einde van die tweede en laaste hoofstuk.

Oor net een ding skaam ek my in die hele dubbele episode. Dit was toe heeltemal agterna 'n paar van ons gevra is om met die hemel weet nou meer wat, maar dit moet iets soos die Universiteitsraad gewees het, te praat. Ou dominee Affie Louw het gevra of ons studente nie as gebaar die hoed onder mekaar sal rondstuur om die skade wat in Kleurlinghuise aangerig is, te help vergoed nie.

Ek het geantwoord nee.

Daar was pyn in die liewe ou man se oë, maar hy het niks verder gesê nie.

Al verskoning wat ek vandag kan aanvoer — as 'n mens dit 'n verskoning durf noem — is dié wat Churchill gegee het toe aan hom gevra is watter verskoning hy eendag voor die Regterstoel kan gee vir die gooi van die atoombom op Hirosjima. Sy antwoord was dat hy sal sê: "Lord, at the time I was awfully angry."

Naskrif aan Ikeys en Witsies: As julle iemand wil oortuig dat julle met betogings en sulke dinge nie moedswillig is nie, moenie na my toe kom nie. En as julle seer kry en 'n bietjie meer simpatie wil hê, probeer om 'n bietjie minder skynheilig te wees.

I WAS ONE OF THE BASTARDS

These past decades it has often happened at our English-speaking universities. Wits or UCT students get mad about something the authorities have done or have not done, charge in to demonstrate where the authorities don't want them, the police move in . . .

Ah, for the day Stellenbosch students on one single Saturday twice managed to mobilise the police, first in Cape Town, then at Stellenbosch!

It was, to be exact, on 27 July 1940. And I had a share in the rumpus, deliberately so, that day.

First, a bit of background for those unfamiliar with the high tension that gripped us all that wartime. The mayor of Cape Town saw fit to ordain that every day at twelve noon (Sundays, you can imagine, expected), they had two minutes of prayer for an Allied victory.

On the stroke of noon a bugle blew. Then one stopped in one's tracks and prayed. After two minutes the bugle blew again. Then you could proceed.

Now there were quite a couple of our Afrikaans people who didn't care a damn from whom the Brits got a hiding. Stop dead and pray that they win? That'll be the day! But if you kept on walking — there's freedom and democratic rights for you in Cape Town — you got hammered.

It was in circumstances such as these that we Stellenbosch chaps saw a gap. About the holy right of demonstration and all such high falutin' goings-on we hadn't then yet heard. We just decided to do our thing. We would go to Cape Town, and keep on walking in the pause for prayer. And the devil take whoever tried to hit at us.

(Funny how religion is always involved. If it isn't at the St George's cathedral that the UCT students have since raised hell, it's a pause for prayer. Just like the Irish. We love to perpetrate ungodly things in the name of God.)

Of course we chose Adderley Street for the operation. We don't bother with little side streets. The business was conceived in the Ossewa-Brandwag. Never let my military fame be underestimated; I was at the time adjutant to a general. To generals and the like we didn't breathe a word about our plans. They might just have been irresponsible enough to forbid us to be irresponsible.

When we arrived in Cape Town that Saturday morning, some by car, and the majority by train — those were the days before we got rich — Cape Town already knew about us. Adderley Street was thronged. The police were there. The newspapers were there. Everybody was waiting for something. People — and I suppose you have to include students here — never can keep their big mouths shut.

Things got worse. Sailors came along too, obviously not by chance. Just before twelve, military trucks arrived and soldiers with guns got out. To make sure that we didn't tackle one another, we chaps each wore in the buttonhole a violet bought on the Parade. That wasn't very clever. People noticed this and began to identify us. The tension could be felt, heard and seen.

But one has, after all, one's vanity. For this you have to come to Cape Town, and this you're going to do, whether there be soldiers, sailors, police constables, thousands of people — especially womenfolk — around or not.

The seconds tick by.

This is our plan. Only two fellows are to walk. Daantjie Barnard was one. "Pienaar, you are his friend. Tell him funk can keep him out of a Springbok team." So Oubaas Mark Markötter said to me one day.

If Oubaas Markötter saw him that day, he would have changed his mind about Daantjie's courage. (Other things, among them a World War, kept Daantjie from playing centre or scrum-half for the Boks.) The other walker was Umtali Joubert, boxer for his university in a lesser weight class.

Daantjie has long since died. Umtali, I hope, is still around. But this is by the way.

When the bugle blew, on the second of twelve, the two men started walking. Daantjie from this side, Umtali from that. The pro-war chaps can't jump in immediately. They have to pray first. And we can't do anything either, before they do.

If one of those thousands prayed that day, I swear it was open-eyed. The devil hung in the air, and who would miss a chance of seeing the devil?

Umtali and Daantjie later said: "I never knew two minutes was such a long time!"

They were across the street and back again before the bugle blew a second time. Then everything happened at once.

The soldiers jump to, with the butts of their guns only, let be it said. Umtali hits the first fellow right out from under his gun butt. Reeling, he falls flat on his back in Adderley Street. The sergeant of police, who had his eye on what was coming, lays a hand on Umtali's shoulder and says: "Not a bad blow, brother, but it's your last, you hear me?"

Of what happened around him, except that there was a free-for-all, Daantjie could later never give a good account.

In any case, everybody joined in. The press of the crowd prevented serious damage from being done. It lasted a little less than half an hour. "The battle on the prayer front" it was later called in a wartime play on words.

A good old friend whose name I daren't mention because he is too highly thought of, was hit across the face by a woman. And what did he say to that? Women are always the danger at times like these.

Die Burger later reported — the reporter was up on a balcony, as sensible reporting and personal safety dictated — that the following yells were heard:

"Kill the damned Dutchmen!"

"Wipe out the Dutch bastards!"

"Put our soldiers on the Dutch hooligans!"

"Chop off the rebels' heads!"

"Down with the bastard Nationalists!"

Well, I can't deny I was one of those bastards.

In the circumstances the police did a very good job. Their batons were out, but never seriously used.

A couple of fellows were seized, but freed shortly after. This one and that could afterwards parade their bruises, but nobody went to hospital. In spite of the whole furore.

The end was really an armed peace. Soldiers later helped the police reinstate order.

The students marched off singing "Afrikaners Landgenote".

The sailors and soldiers retaliated with "Britannia rules the waves".

The reply to that was "Die Stem".

Afterwards it was stated as a fact that the then Prime Minister, General Smuts, had wanted to end the prayer pause in the interests of good order; our unruly Stellenbosch prank made this politically impossible for him.

A lovely story in this regard is told of the old General. One day he was on the point of leaving a building. His aide said, "General, wait a moment."

"What for?"

"The pause for prayer, General!"

"What, is this darned business still around?"

Now, an aftermath to the Battle of Adderley Street, before we come to its sequel — just to show how students were successfully handled at the time.

Oubaas Mark Markötter invites Daantjie and me to his house. There was a third man, too, but I can't for the life of me remember who he was. That good old Christian, who in his day was blamed for so much unchristian behaviour, poured us each a beer, and a whisky for himself. He says to us:

"Look here, I myself try not to be in a Cape Town street at twelve. If I happen to be caught there, I go into a telephone booth, even if I don't have a call to make. If the prayer pause still overtakes me in the street, and somebody molests me, I'll hammer him." (The Oubaas's walking stick was famous.) "But I don't go looking for trouble. Did you have to go looking for trouble?"

Despite all our anger, that was the end of our story. A wise old man — let alone his rugby wisdom — had spoken, and we took his point.

Now for the next chapter of the serial.

After the Battle of Adderley Street we didn't go anywhere to pray or to weep. We had a beer or two at suitable venues, and bragged to one another about our deeds of derring-do. Then we went to buy the late edition of the *Argus* in Andringa Street in Stellenbosch. I mean, I guess there are other matters of import too in the world, but one has to know what happened at Newlands that afternoon.

Just there began the Battle of Andringa Street.

At the time that was the only place in Stellenbosch where one could buy a paper on Saturday night, and the queue was long. There had long been bad blood about people jumping the queue. With us all full of courage and glory about Adderley Street, it was decided over the last beer that this matter would be properly taken in hand. The great house of Tarquin would suffer wrong no more.

What but that same Daantjie Barnard that evening tackled a Coloured fellow. The then advocate and later famous judge Theo van Wyk defended him on an assault charge in the Stellenbosch magistrate's court. It was really a very slight charge and the magistrate was surprised and the prosecutor put out when an advocate turned up. Daantjie was virtually already acquitted hands down, when he became in the view we held at the time, quite indecently truthful in front of the magistrate. That cooked his goose, of course.

Theo van Wyk wanted no fee. It was for a friend. But we wouldn't hear of it. The hat was sent round, and Theo's fee and Daantjie's fine were found in no time.

This is in passing.

That same Saturday night all hell breaks loose at Stellenbosch. The Coloured group together and launch a counter-attack to what happened at the front of the queue at the newspaper shop. Property and vehicles are damaged left, right and centre.

There is counter-mobilisation of students from the university hostels. Coloured property is damaged left, right and centre.

All this continues till well into Sunday. Police reinforcements are called in from Paarl and Cape Town. There is shooting. Only with birdshot, but it has the desired effect.

Old Professor Gawie Cillié, our neighbour at the time, famous but not for his exuberant love of me, looks over the fence. "Schalk," he says, "I have a pistol. I'll bring it for you to use, if it becomes necessary."

I say, "Doctor, thanks, but I don't think it will be necessary."

On one of the little pillars at the Dagbreek men's hostel stands old Professor E.C. Pienaar. An imposing figure with his silver mane. How they got him up there, I've always wanted to know. He says, "Fellows, if it comes to the worst, yes. But control yourselves."

In the end, it all subsides, as everything always tends to subside, except sometimes.

But the University did after all also officially take some steps. The then principal, Professor Bobby Wilcocks, called a couple of us in (I have the unfailing knack of getting to places where I shouldn't really be and where I have no wish to be).

That was after he'd had a visit from the District Commandant of Police, Colonel J.A.V. Mentz of Paarl. He had by chance — if one can talk of chance in connection with police action — found the rugby player Hannes Morkel with a length of bluegum wood up his sleeve. Now with what innocent motives could Hannes have had a length of bluegum up his sleeve?

Flappie Lochner got Hannes off at the police station (I could have sworn Flappie was the third man that night at Oubaas Mark's but no, he says he wasn't. He wasn't in any case involved in either of the two battles, for Flappie is a man of peace — except on the rugby field.)

Be that as it may, Professor Bobby, in all reason, had a couple of things to ask us and to tell us. That was the conclusion of the second and last chapter.

Of only one thing am I ashamed in the whole double episode. It was when a few of us, after it was all well and truly over, were asked to talk to goodness knows what, it must have been something like the University Council. Old Dominee Affir Louw asked whether we students would not, as a gesture, send round a hat, to help repay the damage done to Coloured homes.

I said no.

There was pain in the dear old man's eyes, but he said nothing further.

All I can say today in mitigation — if one dare call it mitigation — was the reply Churchill made when asked how he would one day before the Seat of Judgment justify Hiroshima. He said his answer would be, "Lord, at the time I was awfully angry."

Postscript to UCT and Wits students: If you want to convince anybody there's no mischief to your demonstrations and the like, don't come to me. And if you get hurt and would like a bit of sympathy, try to be a little less sanctimonious.

Dogged by ill health, Schalk Pienaar left the editorial chair of *Beeld* in 1975, retiring to Frans-kraal. In 1977 he was back on *Die Burger* as book editor. He died on 12 October 1978, but not before he had accumulated an impressive list of awards. In 1973 he was awarded the Markus Viljoen Medal for journalistic achievement, the first time this award had been given to a working journalist. In 1975 he was awarded South Africa's highest award for journalistic achievement, the Pringle Award and, in the year of his death, both the SA Instituut van Vertalers and Talke award for outstanding service in the field of practical language, and the D.F. Malan Erepenning Award from the National Party of the Cape Province.

'Verwoerd has been stabbed — story follows'

The assassination of Prime Minister Hendrik Verwoerd, 6 September 1966

Dr Hendrik Verwoerd, prime minister of the Republic of South Africa, took his seat in the House at 14h13 on Tuesday 6 September 1966. Verwoerd, the architect of apartheid, was two days off his 65th birthday; he had been premier for eight years and 10 days.

Stanley Uys, political editor of the *Sunday Times,* had also taken his seat in the press gallery. From where he sat, he had a clear view of most of the House. Uys' seat was directly above the Speaker's chair; to the right of the Speaker sat the Prime Minister. From his seat, Uys was aware that the press gallery was slowly filling up. He noted Tertius Myburgh — who became editor of the *Sunday Times* in 1975 — taking his seat (in this respect, Uys' memory was incorrect, as were so many others on that confusing, dramatic September afternoon: Myburgh, then political correspondent of *The Star*, was not in the press gallery at all. He had come from a good lunch at the Mount Nelson Hotel with the Australian Ambassador, George Oliver of the *Rand Daily Mail* and John Geordie of *The Star* and had not yet reached the door of the press gallery).

Bob Steyn, political editor for the Argus group (whose papers included *The Cape Argus* (now *The Argus*) and *The Star*, was sitting in front of a closed-circuit television set that had been installed in the press common room. He expected it to come on any second: Verwoerd was expected to make his first speech of the session and *The Cape Argus,* being an afternoon newspaper, *The Star* and *The Daily News*, had to publish news of the speech almost as it occurred. The time was 14h13.

The lobby bells were ringing as Myburgh walked towards the press gallery. As he put his hand to the mahogany door, it burst open and he was knocked out of the way by journalists rushing for the lobby. Myburgh dashed into the almost deserted press gallery.

Steyn, looking at the blank closed-circuit television set knew something was wrong. The House of Assembly ran to time and by now the set should have been on. He glanced at his watch, got to his feet and ran down the corridor towards the press gallery. He recalls the ashen faces of the correspondents as they ran for the lobby.

Stanley Uys really noticed Tsafendas only when he was actually on Verwoerd. Uys, like the other political and gallery correspondents, knew Tsafendas. He was 'a strange looking man with silver-capped teeth' who kept a long, sharp knife in the messengers' room which he used for cutting bread. Tsafendas leant over the prime minister and began stabbing him. Verwoerd did not utter a sound. Uys sat in his chair and watched in complete disbelief, momentarily numbed. By now, most of the correspondents had rushed out of the press gallery. Myburgh ran in and, aghast, looked down on the confusion below. Both men recall B.J. Vorster, then Minister of Justice, standing detached from the scene, quietly watching, and then walking purposefully away.

Without fully grasping what had happened, the Argus News Service had sent out a flash: 'Verwoerd has been stabbed — story follows' within one and a half minutes of the assassination. The journalists by now were mostly in the lobby, in time to see Verwoerd's body carried, on a stretcher, out of the House of Assembly, a dazed policeman holding the bloodied knife.

Bob Steyn and his team now had the story of the year. With few facts at their disposal, unaware of whether the prime minister was alive or dead, they sat down to write the dramatic report. Tertius Myburgh was the first to begin writing: he had to make the City Late editions of Argus newspapers.

As the correspondents wrote the story, Steyn, standing at the telex machine, edited each piece, put it into a coherent whole (he remembers writing one paragraph himself) and sent the story on the wires. By the time they had finished writing, the news had come through: Verwoerd was dead. The story, as it appeared in the City Late edition of *The Cape Argus*, 6 September 1966:

VERWOERD STABBED TO DEATH IN THE HOUSE OF ASSEMBLY

Dagger attack by messenger of Parliament

CERTIFIED DEAD AT HOSPITAL

The Prime Minister (Dr. H.F. Verwoerd) died of stab wounds inflicted on him in the Houses of Parliament this afternoon by a man wearing the uniform of a parliamentary messenger.

The S.A.B.C. announcing the death of Dr. Verwoerd, gave the name of his assailant as Dimitri Tsafendas.

Ministers, other Government members and members of the Opposition rushed to the aid of the Prime Minister, after he had been stabbed in his front bench seat.

The Leader of the House of Assembly, Mr. B.J. Schoeman, said that the Prime Minister was certified dead when he reached the Groote Schuur Hospital.

Mr. Schoeman said Parliament would meet at the usual time tomorrow for a motion of condolence in the death of the Prime Minister.

Two members of the Sapa's parliamentary team, who were in the Press Gallery at the time, saw the man walking up to Dr. Verwoerd where he had just sat down in his bench.

He suddenly lurched forward, half jumped on to Dr. Verwoerd's bench and stabbed at him with a long dagger.

Dr. Verwoerd tried to ward off the blows. The man was seen to strike at Dr. Verwoerd's throat and chest more than once.

Four times

The Prime Minister was stabbed four times. Dr. E.L. Fisher, M.P. for Rosettenville, who attended to Dr. Verwoerd, immediately after the stabbing, said he received four wounds — one through the heart, one in the carotid vessels in the left neck, one in the region of the right lung and one in the region of the left lung.

357

Mr. Jannie Rall, M.P. for Harrismith, said he saw the man walk quickly into the Chamber from the direction of the lobby.

As he walked he thrust his hand under his jacket. Mr. Rall said he observed to a companion that the man was behaving strangely, but they concluded that he was hitching up his trousers.

Mr. Cas Greyling, Nationalist M.P. for Carltonville, who was one of the first to reach Dr. Verwoerd's assailant and pull him off the Prime Minister said he became suspicious of the man when he saw him walking into the debating chamber towards Dr. Verwoerd.

Mr. Greyling dashed from his seat in the cross-benches some 30 yards away and he saw the man raise his hand and plunge the knife downwards into the breast of the Prime Minister.

It took everybody in the House a few seconds to realise what was going on. Several Ministers and members from both sides of the House then jumped up and pulled the man off Dr. Verwoerd.

Violent struggle

He put up a violent struggle and it seemed as if he was trying to stab some of them, too. They took hold of him, however, dragged him away from Dr. Verwoerd and pinned him down on the floor.

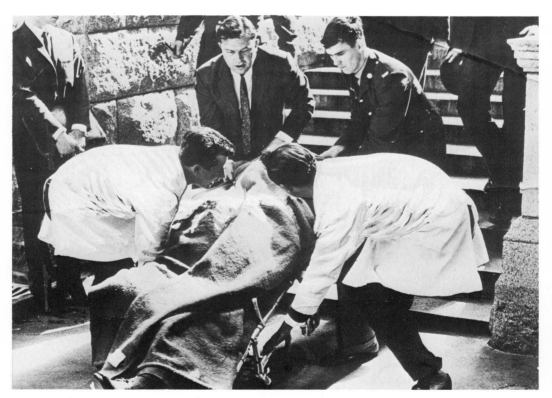

Verwoerd's body being removed from the House of Assembly after the assassination (Die Burger).

358

Other members, including several medical doctors, attended to Dr. Verwoerd. The front of his shirt was bloodstained and blood flowed on to the green carpet where it quickly formed a large pool.

'Kiss of life'

Dr. C.V. van der Merwe (Nat. Fauresmith) gave Dr. Verwoerd the 'kiss of life'. He was assisted by Dr. E.L. Fisher (U.P. Rosettenville), Dr. A. Radford (U.P. Durban Central) and Dr. G. de V. Morrison (Nat. Cradock).

Dr. Verwoerd had an ashen colour and sagged limply in his bench. At one stage the Minister of Foreign Affairs (Dr. H. Muller) brought a cushion and put it under his head.

Not only members but also other Parliamentary officials, Dr. Verwoerd's personal bodyguard, the Commissioner of Police (Lt.-Gen. J.M. Keevy) and other people were at this stage on the floor of the House round the Prime Minister.

Messengers and police cleared the public and Press galleries.

The assailant is believed to have had three knives on him.

The incident took place just before the House was due to reassemble after the long weekend, to deal with the Prime Minister's Vote in Committee of Supply.

During the weekend the Prime Minister had had his historic meeting with the Prime Minister of Basutoland (Chief Leabua Jonathan).

```
PARLY 32.


FLASH ---- FLASH


HOUSE OF ASSEMBLY.


                          PRIME MINISTER DEAD ++


ENDS FLASH.      1530/RJP/6.9.66.
```

Carried out

The Prime Minister was carried from the Chamber on a stretcher about 2.30 p.m. and taken to hospital by ambulance.

While he was being put into the ambulance outside the main entrance to Parliament, a large group of Parliamentarians and their wives and members of the public watched. Many of them wept.

When Dr. Verwoerd was taken away by ambulance a doctor M.P. who attended him said his condition was critical. He said the Prime Minister had three stab wounds. One had penetrated Dr. Verwoerd's heart.

Graaff's shock

The Leader of the Opposition, Sir de Villiers Graaff, speaking to Sapa from his office, said he was 'shocked at this ghastly tragedy.'

Sir de Villiers said he had nothing further to say at this stage, but would probably issue a statement later.

A man's hand

Mr. John Wiley, M.P. for Simonstown, said: 'I just saw a man's hand with a dagger. He was apparently standing behind the main door from the lobby. He was in messenger's uniform. I saw the hand plunge down and stab Dr. Verwoerd and saw him fall.'

Dr. Verwoerd had walked into the Chamber from the direction of the lobby. He was smiling and chatting to M.P.s on the floor of the House.

As he turned to sit down in his front bench to the right of the Speaker — the time was almost exactly 2.15 p.m. by the chamber clock — the man ran from across the floor and stabbed him high up on the left side of his chest.

He turned to move towards the door leading to the lobby. But, he was soon jumped upon by scores of M.P.s from both sides of the House.

The drama took place as the bells were ringing for the Assembly to meet for one of the high points of the session — the debate on the Prime Minister's Budget Vote.

The spectators' bays were packed. There were dozens of schoolchildren in the bays.

Dr. Verwoerd was to have celebrated his 65th birthday on Thursday.

He was born in Holland in 1901.

MRS. V.'s LAST KISS

The Argus Political Correspondent

Mrs. Betsy Verwoerd kissed Dr. Verwoerd while doctors were battling desperately to save his life in the Assembly Chamber this afternoon.

She went down into the Chamber from the wives' gallery and was led away after kissing her husband.

The City Late Argus group deadlines having being met and, for the morning group of papers (SAAN), the first stories written, Myburgh and Uys realised that they had obligations to the international newspapers for which they were stringing (they included *The Guardian, The New York Times, The Observer* and the *Christian Science Monitor*).

Telephoning their respective wives to say they would not be home for a considerable while, Uys and Myburgh hunted out a typewriter with the loosest carriage they could find. Jamming in as many sheets of paper and carbons as they could, the pair set out to write the story for the world's newspapers. One typed, one dictated in turns and, as the story ended, they divided the copies between them and sent the despatches off.

It was not, of course, the end of the story. The papers carried news of the assassination for many days. The following morning's *Rand Daily Mail* carried a front page leader by its editor-in-chief, Laurence Gandar, under the headline: 'A heinous crime'. George Oliver, political correspondent of the *Rand Daily Mail* (who had a colourful subsequent career, having the dubious distinction of being expelled from the House of Assembly during the 1969 parliamentary session for two weeks for writing a report in which he alleged that certain parliamentarians had taken wagers on the results of a by-election; he left journalism to stand as a United Party candidate for Kensington in the 1969 election and, after serving as a MP and the UP's Director of Information and Publications, joined the New Republic Party and was appointed property editor of the *Sunday Express*) wrote a detailed report on the assassination on the front page of his newspaper, his story running beside the poignant picture of the prime minister being carried out of the House of Assembly.

'Dominee, dit is my krag en my sterkte'

Rykie van Reenen and Mrs Verwoerd, 1966

Dr Hendrik Verwoerd's body was rushed from the House of Assembly to Groote Schuur hospital. He was stabbed, at 14h14, with four blows of the knife to his heart, chest and throat. The body arrived at Groote Schuur at 14h55, to be met by three surgeons, two doctors and five medical students. He was declared dead at 15h05.

Rykie van Reenen, general reporter and columnist (her column, 'Op die Randakker' gained a considerable following) for *Die Beeld,* was telephoned on 7 September by Elize Miller, sister-in-law to the NG predikant of Malmesbury, Herman Kinghorn. Elize Miller recounted to Rykie — then based in Johannesburg — how her husband, visiting Groote Schuur hospital on the afternoon of 6 September, had become involved in the drama following the prime minister's death.

Confirming the story with the predikant, Rykie wrote the story. It appeared in *Die Beeld* on 11 September 1966.

Ouderwets, miskien, maar ek glo dat daar tye is wanneer iedere mens — al is hy ook al wie, en al is hy ook al watter openbare figuur — die reg het op privaatheid. Dat selfs nie die vernames in hul smart en persoonlike droefheid voor die mensdom oopgespalk mag word nie. Dit glo ek.

Tog wil ek u die verhaal vertel van hoe mev. Betsie Verwoerd Dinsdag die nuus van haar man se dood gekry het, en hoe sy dit ontvang het. Daar is iets hier wat úitstyg bo die persoonlike, en praat van 'n geesteskwaliteit wat ons trots en dankbaar kan wees om nog onder ons te vind.

Die verhaal van hierdie aspek van die noodlotsmiddag begin gewoon genoeg met die N.G. predikant van Malmesbury, ds. Herman Kinghorn, wat vir die dag stad toe kom, met sy vrou en met die eggenote van een van sy gemeentelede wat siek lê in die Volkshospitaal.

Die pasiënt klaar besoek, eet hulle die middag in die stad. En as ons huis toe ry, sê die dominee onder die ete, kan ons gerus darem net gou op pad aanry by die Groote Schuur-hospitaal, waar 'n ander gemeentelid siek lê.

By die hospitaal bly sit die twee vroue in die motor en ds. Kinghorn, terwyl hy wag om toegelaat te word by die pasiënt, sit gesels in die kantoor van die onder-superintendent van Groote Schuur, sy jeugvriend, dr. Krisjan Viviers, wat op Uitenhage nog in sy C.S.V.-kring was.

Die telefoon lui. Dr. Viviers luister. Nee! Dit kan nie wees nie! Hy spring op. Met sy

*Rykie van Reenen (*Die Burger*).*

hand oor die mond van die gehoorstuk gedruk, sê hy versteld: "Hulle sê dr. Verwoerd is gesteek!" Ds. Kinghorn kom ook met ongeloof en ontreddering op die been. Deur die venster sien hy hoe TP 1000 voor die hospitaal stilhou, hoe mev. Verwoerd met mev. Tinie Vorster by haar, uit die Premier se ampsmotor klim.

"Dit is waar," sê hy met ontsetting, en toe hy oomblikke later die kantoor verlaat, kom dr. Viviers reeds met mev. Verwoerd en mev. Vorster die gang op. In die oomblikke van verdwaasde konfrontasie steek hy hand uit. Hy is ds. Kinghorn, sê hy, en wens mev. Verwoerd sterkte toe.

"O ja," vind sy nog die selflose krag om te sê, "my kinders se predikant in Pinelands mos gewees!" (Ilsabeth du Bois en haar man was voor hul vertrek na die buiteland in sy gemeente.) Toe hulle aanstap, en hy trap-af gaan, roep mev. Vorster hom terug. "Dominee," sê sy, "jy moet my nie nou los nie. Doktor is reeds oorlede, maar mevrou weet dit nie."

Minute later, terwyl mev. Verwoerd in die kantoor wag, wenk Krisjan Viviers, wat intussen die toedrag van sake gaan vasstel het, vir sy vriend: Hy moet ingaan, hy moet vir haar die tyding gaan neem. Dr. Verwoerd is inderdaad heen.

Hy het ingegaan, en langs haar stoel gekniel. "Dominee, wat wil u vir my sê?" vra sy. Hy bly stil. Woorde kom op so 'n tyd swaar. "Wil u vir my sê hy is heen?" Herman Kinghorn het net sy oë bevestigend geknip.

"Die Here maak nooit 'n fout nie," was haar woorde.

Ná 'n kort gebed — "Wat sê 'n mens in so 'n tyd? Ek het maar net vir die Here gevra om haar sterk te maak" — het hy aangebied om saam te ry na Groote Schuur, die huis. Sy was bly daaroor. Kalm, baie kalm, het hulle daar tee gedrink. Rondebosch se twee predikante, di. J.F.N. O'Kennedy en Willem de Vos, was ook daar, en mevv. Hobbie le Roux en Joyce Waring het kort daarna gekom.

"Mevrou, dis nou nie 'n tyd om vir mekaar te preek nie," het ds. Kinghorn vir haar gesê in die verslae stilte wat in die middaguur in die groot vertrek gehang het. Maar hy wou net daaraan herinner dat iemand, die dag toe Lincoln ook aan die hand van 'n sluipmoordenaar gesterf het, gesê het: "Alles is wel, God regeer."

"Dominee," het sy met 'n stil, vaste stem gesê, "dit is my krag en my sterkte."

Watter krag, watter sterkte, getuig die feit dat dit in hul verstelde oomblikke van aankoms by Groote Schuur, mev. Verwoerd was wat voorgegaan het met 'n kort gebed om berusting en kalmte. "Sy vir ons, plaas van óns vir háár," vertel mev. Vorster, met 'n uiting van die bewondering en agting wat die hele land gevoel het vir die skraal, klein vrou wat met soveel dapperheid die diepste denkbare water deurwaad het.

Ds. Kinghorn sê my agterna hy beskou dit deur en deur as bestiering dat mev. Verwoerd daardie Dinsdagmiddag 'n vrou van die kaliber van mev. Vorster aan haar sy gehad het: kalm, beheers, in eie reg 'n kwaliteitsmens. Ek wil met hom saamstem. Vir dié, egter, wat vir hom op sy beurt ken, in sy onpretensieuse en innige menslikheid, is dit ook 'n troos dat dit juis hy was wat vir haar die finale bevestiging moes bring van die hartsvrees waarmee sy al hoeveel lange jare moet saamgeleef het.

Toe Herman Kinghorn ná die uur of wat by die CK-motor by die hospitaal terugkom, sit en gesels sy twee passasiers nog heerlik. Wéét julle nie wat vanmiddag hier gebeur het nie?

Nee, wat? Hulle het wel die ambulans voor die ongevalle-deur sien stilhou, en mense daar sien maal, maar so gaan dit mos maar by 'n hospitaal se ongevalle-afdeling, dan nie? vra hulle.

Translation

Old-fashioned, perhaps, but I believe that there are times when every person is entitled to privacy — whoever it is, including any public figure. That even prominent people should not, in their grief and personal sorrow, be spreadeagled before the world. This is my belief.

Nevertheless I would like to tell you how Mrs Betsie Verwoerd on Tuesday heard the news of her husband's death, and how she took it. There is something here that goes beyond the personal and which testifies to a quality of spirit which we can be proud and thankful still to find among ourselves.

The story of this aspect of the fateful afternoon starts quite ordinarily, with Malmesbury DRC minister Dominee Herman Kinghorn coming to Cape Town with his wife and the wife of a member of his congregation who was ill in the Volks Hospital.

Having visited the patient, they lunch in town, and, says the dominee over lunch, on the way home they really should just drop in at the Groote Schuur Hospital, where another member of his congregation lies ill.

At the hospital, the two women remain in the car, and Dominee Kinghorn, while waiting to be allowed in to the patient, sits chatting in the office of Groote Schuur's vice-superintendent, Dr Krisjan Vivier, a friend from his youth who used to be in his SCA group way back in Uitenhage.

The telephone goes. Dr Viviers answers. No! It can't be! He jumps up. With his hand over the mouthpiece he says in dismay: "They say Dr Verwoerd has been stabbed!" Dominee Kinghorn starts to his feet in incredulous bewilderment. Through the window he sees TP 1000 coming to a halt in front of the hospital and Mrs Verwoerd, accompanied by Mrs Tinie Vorster, getting out of the Prime Minister's official car.

"It's true," he says, appalled, and moments later, as he leaves the office, Dr Viviers is already coming up the passage with Mrs Verwoerd and Mrs Vorster. In the moment of stunned encounter he holds out his hand. He's Dominee Kinghorn, he says, and wishes Mrs Verwoerd strength.

"Ah yes," she finds the selfless strength to say, "you used to be my children's minister in Pinelands!" (Ilsabeth du Bois and her husband were in his congregation before they left for abroad.) When they move on, and he starts down the stairs, Mrs Vorster calls him back. "Dominee," she says, "you can't just leave me now! Doctor has already died, but Mrs Verwoerd doesn't know yet."

Minutes later, while Mrs Verwoerd waits in the office, Dr Viviers, who has been to find out what the situation is, beckons to his friend. He's to go in, he's to break the news to her. Doctor Verwoerd is indeed gone.

He went in, and knelt at her chair. "Dominee, what do you want to tell me?" she asked. He made no reply. Words do not come easily at times like these. "Do you want to tell me he's gone?" Herman Kinghorn could only blink his eyes in affirmation.

"The Lord never makes a mistake," she said.

After a short prayer — "What does one say at such a time? I just asked the Lord to make her strong!" — he offered to drive with them to Groote Schuur, the residence. She was glad of that. Calmly, very calmly they had tea there. The two ministers of the Rondebosch congregation, J.F.N. O'Kennedy and Willem de Vos, were there too, and Mrs Hobbie le Roux and Mrs Joyce Waring arrived shortly after.

"Mrs Verwoerd," Dominee Kinghorn said in the stunned silence that hung over the big room that afternoon, "this is no time to be preaching to one another." He just wanted to recall, however, that on the day Lincoln, too, died at the hand of an assassin, someone had said: "All is well, God reigns supreme."

"Dominee," she said in a quiet, even voice, "that is my strength and my support."

What strength, what support, is borne out by the fact that, in the bewildered moments of their arrival at Groote Schuur, it was Mrs Verwoerd who initiated a short prayer for resignation and calmness. "She, for us, instead of we for her!" Mrs Vorster recalls, voicing the admiration and respect the whole country felt for the small slip of a woman who with such fortitude went through the deepest waters imaginable.

Dominee Kinghorn later remarked to me that he saw it as absolutely providential that Mrs Verwoerd that Tuesday afternoon had had at her side a woman of Mrs Vorster's calibre: calm, composed, a person of quality in her own right. I have to agree. But for those who know him, in turn, in his profound and unpretentious humanity, it is also good to know that it was he, of all, who had to bring her the final confirmation of a deep dread with which she must have lived for so many long years.

When, after an hour, Herman Kinghorn got back to his Malmesbury car at the hospital, the two women were still happily chatting. Don't you *know* what happened here this afternoon?

No, what? They did see the ambulance stopping at the door of Casualty, and people milling around, but isn't that just how it goes at the casualty department of a hospital? they asked.

Rykie van Reenen was a warm, unconventional figure. Her first job in journalism was as a women's page reporter towards the end of the war. She insisted on travelling by motorbike, to the dismay of her more conventional sisters. In 1973 she was appointed deputy editor of *Rapport,* the first woman to be so honoured in the Afrikaans press. Now retired, she was awarded an honorary doctorate of literature from the University of Stellenbosch in 1986. And she remembers Mrs Verwoerd with warmth. 'She was a gutsy lady.'

'The surgical equivalent of Mount Everest'

Death of the world's first heart transplant patient, 21 December 1967

At 15h45 on Saturday, 2 December 1967, Mrs Myrtle Darvall and her 25-year-old daughter, Denise Ann, stepped off a pavement in Main Road, Observatory, Cape Town. Both were knocked down by a car. Myrtle Darvall died instantly; her daughter was still alive but brain-dead.

Just before 06h00 on 3 December, Denise's heart was transplanted into the body of Louis Washkansky, a 53-year-old Sea Point businessman in an operating theatre of Groote Schuur Hospital. The five-hour operation, carried out by a meticulously well-rehearsed team of 30 surgeons, anaesthetists, technicians and nurses led by Professor Christiaan Barnard, was the first of its kind in the world and made medical history.

The team, which had performed Groote Schuur's first kidney transplant a scant two months before, had been on 24-hour standby for the previous four weeks. At midnight the team was assembled and at 01h00 with the bodies of Denise Darvall and Louis Washkansky on heart-lung machines, the operation began.

There were four stages in the operation: the coupling of Darvall and Washkansky to their respective heart-lung machines; the removal of the donor's heart, the circulation of which was kept going by pump; the removal of Washkansky's dilated heart and, the fourth and most intricate stage, the placing of Denise's heart into Louis Washkansky's chest cavity. Once arteries and veins had been connected, electrodes were placed against the walls of the heart and a current was switched on for a fraction of a second. 'It was like turning the ignition switch of a car,' commented Professor J.H. Louw, head of Groote Schuur's division of surgery, later describing how the heart began to beat strongly.

The main Cape Town newspapers had been informed that a heart transplant would be performed within the next few weeks, so when the newsrooms were told that the operation was in progress, they were prepared to handle the story which made international news. Splashed across the newspapers of the world, and with both foreign and local newsmen vying for copy (on Washkansky, on the Darvalls, on Professor Barnard, on Groote Schuur, on the morality of the operation, on the reaction of churches — the list was endless), the story was a dramatic one which ran to front pages for the 18 days in which Louis Washkansky lived.

Seconds after the respirator tubes had been removed from Louis Washkansky at 20h39 on 5 December, 24 hours after the operation, he spoke to Chris Barnard: 'I am much better. What kind of operation did I have? You promised me a new heart.'

Barnard replied: 'You've got a new heart.'

366

Surgeon Chris Barnard shortly after the announcement that the world's first heart transplant had taken place at Groote Schuur, Cape Town (Cape Times Collection, South African Library).

Washkansky, whose dry sense of humour was much enjoyed by the press, found himself the centre of what he considered to be an inordinate amount of attention. Even details of his food were reported: on 11 December, a presumably breathless world was told he had eaten his favourite meal of steak and eggs. But on 16 December Washkansky developed pneumonia. Although there was a brief improvement in his condition, he failed to respond to treatment and there were signs that his body was rejecting the new heart. Louis Washkansky died in Room 283, Groote Schuur, at 06h45 on 21 December 1967.

Roger Williams (holder of the 1976 Settlers Prize for Outstanding Journalism and the first journalist on an English-language newspaper to be so honoured) and John Scott, gallery correspondent and columnist, covered the Washkansky story from the beginning. To Scott went the honour of breaking the story, to Williams the chance to write about the death of the man whose every heartbeat had been listened to worldwide.

Although Washkansky died in *The Cape Argus'* 'time' (the *Cape Times* was the morning paper, *The Argus* hitting the streets after midday), the *Cape Times*, working to a tight deadline, brought out a special edition at 11h00. Taking pride of place in that special edition was Roger Williams' story, which nicely summed up the momentous days of life and death that particular summer.

'BLEEP' FADES AS BRAVE LOUIS DIES

The high-pitched 'bleeps' of the electro-cardiograph monitor that echoed across the world from a room in Groote Schuur Hospital with the message that Louis Washkansky was winning his fight for life with the aid of a young woman's heart have stopped forever.

The little light that flashed on and off beside his bed in reassuring unison with the 'bleeps' has gone out — but for 18 glorious days it was the centrepiece of one of the greatest human stories ever told. It blinked out the saga of a man's extraordinary courage and will to live — and what *Time* magazine has termed "the surgical equivalent of Mount Everest."

It was also a reminder of the courage of the medical men and women who scaled this 'Everest' and of the grief-stricken man, Edward Darvall, whose unfaltering decision made the historic heart-transplant operation possible.

There have been few comparable occasions in recorded medical history in which people from all walks of life and of all races and creeds throughout the world have been so concerned about the progress and welfare of one man, who was described by a close relative as "just an ordinary guy — with tons of guts". The entire civilized world hung on every phrase he uttered, and on every bulletin issued on the condition of this once obscure Woodstock grocer who overnight was immortalized by medical science.

Millions laughed at his wisecracks, and marvelled at the news that he was sitting up in bed, dining on his favourite dish of steak and eggs, and even talking of throwing a party when he went home "before Christmas".

Roger Williams

Golden hands

They admired the way he repeatedly denied his unsought fame and pointed to "the man with the golden hands" — Prof. Chris Barnard, leader of the transplant team — as the real figure of fame in this surgical drama.

Soon after the operation, I moved among people who knew Louis Washkansky intimately — and the picture I formed of him was of a man who loved life, but never feared it; a man who was tough and outward-looking but who was also extraordinarily kind and generous, in an undemonstrative way. A man who served with him in the SA Engineering Corps in World War II told me: "Louis was the kind of man who would forgo his leave-pass to enable a fellow soldier to visit a sick wife, or see his children."

Louis Washkansky knew before the operation that without a new heart, the odds were heavily against him, and that he was certain to die 'within a few weeks'. Even so, it is testimony to his courage that when Professor Barnard gave him two days to decide whether he wanted to be the world's first heart-transplant patient, he took only two minutes to reply: "Go ahead." He knew, as Professor Barnard did, that like Leigh Mallory on Everest, Scott in the Antarctic and Yuri Gagarin, the first man to be shot into space, he was about to venture into the Great Unknown.

After four agonizing weeks of waiting, during which the transplant team was on constant 24-hour standby for the "ultimate operation", he was wheeled into an operation theatre about midnight on December 2, to receive the heart of 25-year-old Denise Darvall, an accounting-machine operator at a Cape Town bank, who with her mother had died after being knocked down by a car earlier in the day.

After an intricate five-hour operation, two electrodes were placed on each side of the transplanted heart, which was shocked into renewed life in Mr. Washkansky's chest. The shock also electrified the world — and Professor Barnard, his team, the Darvall family

368

and Mr. Washkansky became headline news and the leading topic on the major television networks. Journalists besieged Groote Schuur Hospital, and Professor Barnard's achievement became the cover-story in the leading international news and pictorial magazines.

Last fight

Officials at Groote Schuur Hospital found themselves at the receiving end of an endless succession of telephone calls and cables from towns and cities in widely-scattered parts of the world.

High spirits and optimism over the progress being made by the man they called 'Washy' in the desert and the Italian campaigns of World War II turned to foreboding last Sunday when it was disclosed that he was being treated for what at first appeared to be pneumococcal pneumonia in both lungs. The millions of people who had seen the Groote Schuur operation as the opening of a door to new life found themselves willing Mr. Washkansky into renewed health and vigour as he fought his last great fight with the aid of what must be one of the most dedicated medical teams in history. As the 'bleeps' of the electro-cardiograph faded, and finally stopped yesterday morning, there were many who recalled Professor Barnard's remarks soon after the operation: "This man's will to live is most fantastic."

The Washkansky saga has ended with no immediate evidence of organic rejection — and nothing can reject the events and the achievements of the past 18 days. The medical Everest has been climbed in Cape Town, and it is now a matter of finding how to climb down again. The newly-formed Chris Barnard Fund for research into heart and organ transplantation may well form a vital stepping-stone in this next part of the journey towards complete success in heart transplantation.

• For Louis Washkansky, the journey is over, but he will always be remembered as the man who was there at the beginning in the fantastic story of "new hearts for old".

'With love and hisses'

The incomparable Molly Reinhardt

'If I were asked to say what I consider to be one of my more notable achievements, I would not be at a loss for an answer. Offering Molly Reinhardt a job as columnist on the *Sunday Times* would be my prompt reply,' wrote the ever-gallant Joel Mervis, editor of the *Sunday Times* from 1959-1975.

Reinhardt had spent considerable time on two Natal newspapers — *The Natal Mercury* and, more significantly, *The Daily News* — before she approached Mervis with an idea for a weekly column. The convent-educated Molly Reinhardt already had a considerable reputation in Natal as a biting wit and a hell-raiser. She told (she did not ask) Mervis that she would like to call her proposed column 'With Love and Hisses', and promised faithfully that it would be sharp, original and (sometimes) funny.

Molly Reinhardt fulfilled all three promises and more for the 13 years in which her column ran in the *Sunday Times* (1962-1975). When she finally gave it up in order, she thought, to write a novel, Reinhardt had become something approaching a national institution.

Compared by the unimaginative to Dorothy Parker, Reinhardt was an original from her style of dress to her idiosyncratic column and her strongly-held beliefs. If her hallmarks were her cigarette holder, her turban and her whiplash tongue, the success of 'With Love and Hisses' was due, apart from its innate style, to an honesty of approach which invariably drew a reaction from readers.

Molly Reinhardt's wit, like her observations on the contradictory country in which she lived, were allowed full rein in 'With Love and Hisses', which occupied a unique position in South African journalism. Her columns were later collected and published in book-form: *With Love and Hisses* and *With More Love and Hisses.*

The following examples of Molly's work were used in the *Sunday Times* of 25 August 1968, 21 January 1973 and 7 April 1973 respectively.

Krugersdorp is in a tizzy over torsos

Top spot this week goes to Krugersdorp, jewel of the West Rand, where no girl over the age of seven may wear a bikini. With one bold stroke Krugersdorp has wrested the idiocy crown from Aliwal North, where the age limit for bikini-wearing babies is nine.

I apologise to readers of this column for the tardiness of this vital intelligence. It came to me in a letter from a chum whose hobby it is to study the lesser lunacies in this mad and sunny land.

He wrote: "A few weeks ago you mentioned that all females, except for girls under

Molly Reinhardt (Sunday Times).

ten, are banned from wearing bikinis in Aliwal North. Get with it, kid. As the young say, you are hopelessly switched off. Read the enclosed and long live the Saint Tropez of the Western Reef."

Attached was a cutting which announced that the Krugersdorp Town Council is to enforce its ruling on what the correctly dressed young miss will wear at the municipal swimming bath.

A prize of 13 pairs of smoked glasses goes to the reader who correctly interprets the following passage:

"No girl over the age of seven may wear a costume whose top and bottom sections are not permanently joined by a piece of material which, in its average width, is less than a third of the width of the wearer's torso."

Struth! This decision to enforce the regulations follows a request from the general commission on public morals of the Nederduitse Gereformeerde Kerk, whose letter said: "The human body is a temple of God and should not be unseemly displayed."

The letter continued: "Not only do these skimpy fashions degrade a woman in the eye of man, but they dull the moral feeling of our Whites and promote the immorality which caused the decline of many cultured nations in the past."

I have never heard such poppycock in my life. It is doubtful if at any time there has been a healthier attitude to the human body than at this precise moment. South African beaches are littered with beautiful bodies wearing the minimum of covering and presenting a picture of vitality and a wonderful zest for life.

I'll bet a dusty crinoline to a mini-bikini that the attitude of these young people is far healthier than that of many of their elders. The day when sex was shrouded from head to toe might have made the female more intriguing but I wouldn't like to know what the boys were thinking as they stole glances at the provocative upholstery. What could be more obvious than the idea behind the bustle? And what more coy than the "now you see it — now you don't" attitude as an ankle came into view?

The Church's letter continues: "The impression that unseemly displays of the female body must make on non-White men, many of whom are only half civilised, need not be mentioned."

On the contrary, I think it most definitely should be mentioned. This kind of insensitive remark must be extremely distasteful and hurtful to black men, carrying with it the implication which it does.

This is the kind of thinking that clapped Mother Hubbards on the joyous Polynesians and destroyed innocence with hypocritical — and highly profitable — cotton.

But away with Tahiti and back to Krugersdorp. What I want to know is who on earth thought up that enchanting description of a bikini in the Council regulations. And what lucky Krugersdorper has landed the job of measuring the piece of material which "in its average width is less than a third of the width of the wearer's torso."

Can't you imagine a conversation between a wearer and a measurer? It would go something like this: "Pardon me, Miss, but I want to measure your torso."

"Not while I'm conscious."

"It's the regulations, Miss. Are your top and bottom sections joined by a piece of material?"

"That's for me to know and you to find out."

"Come a bit closer, Miss, I've got to take your measurements."

"Tell that to the Marines. I've met your kind before."

"Excuse me, Miss. I'm only doing my job. I just want to measure that little bit between the top and bottom section."

"I bet you do. You're not the first one. If you touch me, I'll scream."

"Hang it, Miss, I've got to find out if the average width is less than a third of the width of your torso."

"Drop dead — and what's wrong with my torso anyway."

"Now, Miss, there's nothing wrong with your torso. I only said that I had to measure it. I think you've got a lovely torso. The only thing wrong with your torso, Miss, is that it's in Krugersdorp — and for a torso like yours, Miss, Krugersdorp is the wrong place."

BOTTOMS UP WEEK

This is bottoms-up week in this outpost of *The Sunday Times.* If any reader thinks this is the end, he couldn't be more right. The bottoms under review belong to 10-month-old baby Sharon Sterrenberg of Bellville, and of disco dancer 21-year-old Susan O'Dea. The only thing these two bottoms have in common is that they both caused a sensation.

Miss O'Dea has insured her behind for R100 000. The lady, who comes from Sydney, Australia, reports that when she goes into her dances the customers "just stand and stare".

They have told her she has the finest bottom in London. This decided the dancing doll that she had been neglecting a good thing. She told a reporter that she decided to insure her bottom when she realised it was her most valuable asset.

I do not for one moment discount Miss O'Dea's concern that she had left her bottom without suitable security, but it is an incontestable fact that she got her posterior view into most Fleet Street news sheets. Miss O'Dea stuck out for R100 000 and I presume it was the rock bottom price. This fast-thinking lady says she is insuring her bottom against "disability or injury". Anyone for a free kick?

Ten-month-old Sharon Sterrenberg's bottom has been banned from the baby pool in the municipal swimming baths of the enlightened town of Bellville. This vanguard of Cape culture and enlightenment frowns on skinny-dipping among babies, and quite right too.

One thing leads to another, and a naked baby could easily degenerate into a topless teenager or the cover on a pantihose packet.

The superintendent of the baths, whose name unfortunately I do not know, asked the baby's mother to clothe Sharon, who was romping in the altogether. Not surprisingly Mrs. Sterrenberg removed herself and her offending baby from the scene of the crime.

The Mayor of Bellville, Mr. M.D. Meyer, said he fully supported the superintendent in his action and pronounced these momentous words: "Why should one draw an age limit to skinny-dipping?"

Why indeed? From what I have seen of Bellville, a little skinny-dipping might introduce a note of gaiety to that petrified forest off the Cape Flats.

Mr. Meyer, the Mayor, warned: "If one encourages children to indulge in nudity, they may well carry this inclination into later life." Wise words. A 10-month-old baby encouraged to "indulge" in nudity is obviously doomed to a life of disgusting permissiveness. There are no limits to the depths to which a baby paddling brazenly without clothes could sink as the years roll on.

It might take off its clothes at the drop of a hat — if it wore a hat — and debase the nation's womanhood, which is so sacred a charge. It would also undermine our decent, clean, pure, undefiled, hypocritical and traditional way of life.

My own opinion is that any mayor who talks about a baby "indulging in nudity" needs to have his chain pulled to let in a little fresh water to the civic septic tank.

QUESTIONS ON TV EFFECTS

I read with a high-pitched scream of laughter that South Africa's eventual TV viewers are to be quizzed on politics, race, sex, art, morality and family life. A survey to discover the effects of looking at the box is being conducted by the SABC, and a questionnaire has been sent to 2 500 people. Their answers will reflect attitudes in the pre-TV era and the same questions will be asked in another survey after the introduction of TV.

In case readers of this column missed the original story in *The Sunday Times,* here are a few statements which appear in the questionnaire. People are asked whether they definitely agree, disagree, or definitely disagree that:
• Dancing is sinful.
• The world is in need of a religious revival.
• There is nothing wrong with the use of rude four-letter words in plays and books.
• South Africa's national flag is the most beautiful in the world.
• There is nothing wrong in principle with marriage across the colour line.
  And it asks:
• Do your children play with Afrikaans-speaking friends? (I am unable to report whether this question is also phrased: Do your children play with English-speaking friends?)
• Have you ever tried to frighten your children by using the police as bogey-men?
  I think the SABC quizkids have left out some absolutely essential questions if they want to fathom South African thinking. My survey would include the following:
• Do you think Michaelangelo's statue of the boy David would look more decent in baggies than as originally made?
• Do you think rugby Springboks should have sex before, during, or after a test match? Would this improve the game as a spectator sport?
• Do you think multi-racial sporting teams are okay provided there are separate trials, separate dressing-rooms, separate lavatories, and separate aircraft?
• Do you think the green and gold and the Springbok symbol should be reserved for Whites? On the other hand, do you think that this is sacred-cow thinking, or just plain bull?
• Do you think that the choice of the all-Black opera, "Aida", is hilarious for the all-White Old Nick Opera House? Or would you prefer to see Othello in white-face instead?
• Do you cross the border to buy Playboy, or to play, boy?
• Do you think it is more immoral to bathe in the nude on Monday than to dance on a Sunday?
• When TV comes, do you believe that tennis trials should still be held in secret or seen to be believed?
• Do you associate the Continental Sunday with a licentious orgy, or with decadent drinking on pavements and then going to see a blue film?

- Do you prefer fully clothed statues of male politicians to female nudes? If so, would you care to explain why?
- If mixed rugby were allowed, do you think this would lead to the collapse of our traditional way of strife?
- Would you rather see "Lady Chatterley's Lover" on TV or Gary Player reading Current Affairs?
- Have you ever tried to frighten your children by using Helen Suzman as a bogey-woman?
- Do you think South African TV is going to throw up a bright political star? Or are you just going to throw up?

' 'n klein Nuwe Jerusalem'

Petrus Johannes Cillie, Die Burger, 1969

When is a despatch not a despatch? Probably when it is a speech first and a despatch second. Petrus Johannes Cillie, now chairman of Nasionale Pers and holder of the first chair of journalism at Stellenbosch University (1977-1983), was asked to speak to the pupils of Hoër-skool Jan van Riebeeck, Cape Town, on the occasion of Republic Day, 30 May 1969.

Cillie was then editor of *Die Burger* (1954-1977), the paper founded on 26 July 1915 as the official mouthpiece of the National Party. As editor of the paper through the Verwoerdian era, Cillie trod a difficult path between, on the one hand, purist apartheid and, on the other, the dawning of a degree of reality, harsh though it was beneath the hand of Prime Minister B.J. Vorster.

Cillie (with a degree in mathematics and physics) spoke with a certain old testament flair; his writing style was similar, and developed, on occasion, a kind of biblical majesty. Having delivered his speech on 30 May 1969, Cillie sat down to rework it for *Die Burger,* in which paper it appeared at the beginning of June. It is almost moving and, with its cautious references to the need to love a country warts and all, a sign that the times were gradually changing. The article was also printed in a collection of Cillie's work by Tafelberg in 1980 under the title of *Eet jou rape eerste.* Cillie's sense of humour was always dry.

Hoe het 'n mens Suid-Afrika regtig lief?

Woorde wat 'n mens dikwels hoor en gebruik, slyt naderhand af. Jy raak doof vir hulle.

Dan is dit goed om weer 'n slag na te dink en te vra wát beteken so 'n woord eintlik? Daardie woord moet weer blink geslyp word, sodat hy opnuut skyn in sy regte betekenis.

Wát bedoel ons as ons praat van vaderlandsliefde? Wát sê ons wanneer ons sê ons het Suid-Afrika lief? Hoe het 'n mens 'n land lief?

'n Land is nie 'n mooi meisie of 'n gawe seun nie. Dit is nie 'n babetjie of 'n moeder of 'n vader nie. Dit is 'n yslike uitgestrekte lap aarde tussen die oseane, en die grootste deel daarvan het ons self nog nooit gesien nie, en sal ons miskien nooit sien nie.

Is dit was ons liefhet, hierdie grondgebied wat ons Suid-Afrika noem en maar so half ken?

Of is dit die miljoene mense wat hier woon, van baie volke en tale? Is hulle die Suid-Afrika wat ons liefhet? Kan ons sê ons het hulle lief as ons net 'n paar honderd van hulle op hul naam ken?

Of is dit die berge en vlaktes van Suid-Afrika wat ons liefhet, die dorp en die buurt waarin ons woon, ons huis en die strand waar ons vakansie hou?

Bedoel ons, as ons sê ons het ons land lief, eintlik dat ons ons familie en vriende liefhet wat saam met ons in Suid-Afrika lewe?

In ons liefde vir Suid-Afrika, die liefde waarvan ons partykeer so maklik praat, is daar seker iets van al hierdie dinge. Daar is mooi mense, mooi plekke, mooi gebeurtenisse hier in ons land, en dit wek 'n gevoel van liefde op, en dan sê ons sommer samevattend op 'n dag soos Republiekdag: ons het al hierdie dinge lief, ons het Suid-Afrika lief — alles wat mooi is in ons land, van 'n mooi nooientjie tot 'n pragtige skildery wat 'n Suid-Afrikaner gemaak het.

Dit is die Suid-Afrika wat ons liefhet: al die groot en goeie dinge en mense in die land. Ons noem dit sommer alles tesame Suid-Afrika.

Tog, as dit ál is wat ons wil sê as ons sê ons het Suid-Afrika lief, dan is dit nog nie die regte vaderlandsliefde nie. Ons liefde moet nie net die mooi dinge omvat nie. Ons moet nie net die mooi dinge in Suid-Afrika uitsoek en sê: dit is die Suid-Afrika wat ons liefhet nie.

Dit is maklik om net mooi dinge lief te hê. Dit eis nie veel van ons nie. Dink maar aan 'n vader en 'n moeder met 'n feitlik volmaakte kindjie: 'n sterk liggaampie, 'n skerp verstandjie, 'n gesonde inbors. Dit verg nie baie van hulle om só 'n kindjie lief te hê nie.

Die eintlike toets vir ouerliefde kom wanneer die kindjie nie volmaak is nie, soos die meeste kinders maar ver van volmaak is: wanneer die kindjie 'n liggaamsgebrek het, of 'n skreeulelike gesiggie; wanneer hy maar dom is, of 'n nare streep in sy karakter het; wanneer hy geneig is om te lieg en te steel, en dwarstrek en die hele huis omkrap. Dit is dan wanneer ware liefde in die spel kom en beproef word.

Dit is egte liefde om so 'n kind nie te verstoot nie, om hom te help om sy gebreke te bowe te kom; om uit die lelike mensie wat hy is, iets moois en skoons te probeer haal; om te glo dat daar onder al die lelikheid iets edels is wat met liefde en dissipline, met wysheid en inspanning te voorskyn gebring kan word. Dit is ware ouerliefde.

Ware vaderlandsliefde is iets soos dit. Egte liefde vir Suid-Afrika is nie net liefde vir wat goed en aangenaam is in ons land nie. Daar is veel, veel wat sleg en onaangenaam is. Ware liefde is om nie daarvan weg te hardloop nie, maar om dit reg in die oë te kyk, en om ook dieper te kyk na 'n visioen van 'n Suid-Afrika sónder daardie gebreke: 'n beter en skoner Suid-Afrika wat met ons liefde en arbeid te voorskyn geroep moet word uit die werklike Suid-Afrika wat ons rondom ons sien.

Wanneer ons sê ons het Suid-Afrika lief, moet dit beteken: nie net Suid-Afrika soos hy is nie, maar soos hy kan word — 'n land van ons eie en ander se hoogste drome.

'n Man van 'n ander land, 'n Engelsman, het vir sy land só 'n liefde gehad, wat hy uitgestort het in 'n bekende gedig. Hy was William Blake, 'n man wat gesigte gesien en drome gedroom het. Hy het gelewe in die tyd toe Engeland 'n industriële land geword het, teen die einde van die agtiende en die begin van die negentiende eeu.

Daardie industrialisasie het afskuwelike vorme aangeneem. Hulle het nie mooi, lugtige fabrieke gebou met ruskamers en ventilasie en verwarming in die winter nie. Dit was nare, rokerige plekke, met kieme besmet, vinnig saamgeflans om die meeste geld in die kortste tyd te maak. Die woon- en werkstoestande was allervreesliks, veral vir die heel jong kinders wat feitlik in slawerny deur lange ure daar moes swoeg.

Dit alles het in William Blake 'n vurige verontwaardiging en 'n heilige woede losgemaak. Hierdie dinge, so het hy in sy siel gevoel, mag in Engeland, sy Engeland, nie gebeur nie. En hoe was "sy Engeland" dan? Dit suggereer hy in die gedig "The New Jerusalem", waarin hy sy visioen, sy ideaal vir Engeland stel: 'n plek waar die Here tuis sou wees — 'n Nuwe Jerusalem waar Christus graag sou wil wandel:

And did those feet in ancient time
Walk upon England's mountains green?
And was the holy Lamb of God
On England's pleasant pastures seen?

And did the Countenance Divine
Shine forth upon our clouded hills?
And was Jerusalem builded here
Among these dark Satanic mills?

Bring me my Bow of burning gold!
Bring me my Arrows of desire!
Bring me my Spear! O clouds, unfold,
Bring me my Chariot of fire!

I will not cease from Mental Fight,
Nor shall my Sword sleep in my hand,
Till we have built Jerusalem
In England's green and pleasant Land.

P. J. Cillié (Die Burger).

Dit is egte vaderlandsliefde: 'n vaste voorneme, 'n dure eed dat wat verkeerd is in sy land — "these dark Satanic mills", die vreeslike euwels wat industrialisasie en geldgierigheid sonder gewete oor die land gebring het — dat dit uitgeroei sal word, en dat Engeland 'n groen en lieflike plek sal word waar die Seun van God oor die velde sal kan stap.

Mense met egte vaderlandsliefde het só 'n vlam in die hart, só 'n dwingende droom en visioen van 'n beter en gelukkiger land waarvoor hulle sal werk sonder om te rus, totdat die Nuwe Jerusalem gebou is.

Nou sal jong mense kan sê: "Ons het ook so 'n droom en so 'n visioen êrens in ons hart van 'n beter Suid-Afrika, 'n land waar die Here self sal wil wandel. Maar hierdie sake is in die ou mense se hande. Ons is jonk en magteloos. Ons kan die land nie hervorm en regmaak wat in hom verkeerd is nie."

Hulle het gelyk. Baie moeilikheid word in die wêreld veroorsaak deur jong mense wat dink dat hulle alles wat lelik en sleg is, of wat hulle as lelik en sleg beskou, met geweld kan afbreek, en dat 'n nuwe wêreld, 'n Nuwe Jerusalem, só gebore kan word.

Dit kan nie gedoen word nie. Hulle het nie beheer oor die wêreld nie, hulle het nie beheer oor Suid-Afrika nie. Maar die jong mense het nou al verantwoordelikheid vir 'n hoekie van Suid-Afrika, en dit is hulleself, hul liggaam en gees, en hul verhoudinge met hul familie en vriende en onderwysers. Dáár kan hulle nou al 'n klein Nuwe Jerusalem begin bou; dáár kan hulle aan 'n beter Suid-Afrika begin werk. En naderhand, namate hulle ouer word, kan hulle breër kyk.

Die man wat oor ons velde ry en die diep erosieslote in die kosbare grond sien, en wat daar besluit dat dit end moet kry: dat dit in sy Suid-Afrika nie langer mag gebeur nie, só 'n man het die regte vaderlandsliefde. Hy word 'n beskermer van die onvervangbare

Suid-Afrikaanse aarde. Hy veg met 'n goue boog en pyle, met 'n vurige oorlogswa, vir die Suid-Afrika van sy drome.

Of die man wat sy oë oop hou in 'n stad soos die Kaap, en die baie sukkelende ou mense raaksien, feitlik verstote op hul oudag, wat in koue agterkamertjies sommerso rondwoon, en dan werk daarvan maak om hulle lewe te verlig en te veraangenaam — hy bring Suid-Afrika 'n bietjie nader aan 'n land waarheen die Here en sy engele met vry-moedigheid genooi kan word om oor ons berge en deur ons vlaktes te kom wandel.

O, ons is nog ver van 'n Nuwe Jerusalem af. Daar is baie werk vir ons elkeen in sy eie hoekie van Suid-Afrika. Egte vaderlandsliefde beteken nie om ons rug te draai vir ons land se gebreke en foute nie, maar om hulle onder die oë te sien, soos 'n goeie ouer die foute van sy kind, en om reg te maak wat binne ons mag is om reg te maak.

Dan eers wys ons ons het Suid-Afrika regtig lief, wanneer ons hom nie net liefhet om wat hy is nie, om wat ons uit hom haal aan skoonheid, rykdom en plesier nie, maar wanneer ons hom liefhet om wat hy nog kan wees, wat hy behoort te wees: 'n land wat waardig is om deur die voete van die Here betree te word.

Kom ons dink aan Suid-Afrika só, soos William Blake gedink het aan daardie Engeland van sy tyd met donker, sataniese fabrieke wat sy aangesig geskend het: as 'n land wat met werk en stryd 'n Nuwe Jerusalem kan word. Jonk soos ons mag wees, laat ons ons voorneem om ons in te span so lank as wat ons asemhaal, en om nie te rus voor-dat ons ons volle deel gedoen het om só 'n Suid-Afrika te bou nie.

Dit is vaderlandsliefde, en dit is wat ons eintlik belowe wanneer ons sing dat ons sal lewe, dat ons sal sterwe vir Suid-Afrika.

(Translation)

What does Love of South Africa really mean?

Words heard and used often get blunted in the course of time. One becomes deaf to them.

Then it is a proper time to stop and think, and ask what a particular word really means. It should be sharpened and polished to shine anew in its true sense.

What do we mean when we speak of love of one's country? What are we saying when we claim that we love South Africa? How does one love a country?

A country is not a pretty girl or a fine boy. It is not a baby or a mother or father. It is an enormous stretch of earth among the oceans — the major part of which we have never seen, nor are likely to see.

Is it *that* which we love — this subcontinent that we call South Africa and only partly know?

Or is it the millions of people living here, of many nationalities and languages? Are they the South Africa that we love? Can we say we love them if we know only a few hundred of them by name?

Or is it the mountains and plains of South Africa that we love, the towns and the neighbourhoods where we live, our homes and the stretches of coast where we spend our holidays?

When we say we love our country, do we really mean that we love our families and friends living with us in South Africa?

In our love of South Africa, the love of which we sometimes speak so glibly, there may be an element of all these things. There are fine people, fine places and fine events in our country, arousing a feeling that moves us to state all-embracingly on a day like Republic Day: we love all these things, we love South Africa — everything that is beautiful in our country, from a pretty lass to a magnificent painting by a South African.

That is the South Africa we love: all the great and fine things and people in the land. All of them together we call South Africa.

Still, if this is all we mean when we say we love South Africa, it is not yet the right love of one's country. Our love must include not only the fine things. We must not select merely the fine things in South Africa and say 'this is the South Africa we love'.

Because it is easy to love fine things. It does not demand much from us. Imagine a father and mother with an almost perfect child — a healthy body, a quick mind, a fine character. It is not a burden to them to love such a child.

The real test of parental love arises when the child is not perfect — as most children are far from perfect — when the child has a physical defect or an unattractive face; when he is mentally dull or has an ugly trait in his make-up; when he tends to lie and steal, and to upset the whole family through his perversity. It is then that true love is tested.

It is real love not to spurn a child like that, but to help him to overcome his failings; to try to evoke something good and noble from the little brat that he is; to believe that behind all the ugliness there is something fine that can be brought to light by love and discipline, by wisdom and effort. Such is true parental love.

Real love of one's country is like that. True love of South Africa is not merely love of what is good and pleasant in our land. There is much — a great deal — that is bad and unpleasant. True love is not to run away from it, but to face it squarely and to look deeper for a vision of South Africa without these defects: a better and finer South Africa that can be brought into being out of the existing South Africa that we see around us.

When we say we love South Africa, it must mean: not only South Africa as it is, but as it *can become* — a country of our own and other people's finest dreams.

A man of another country, an Englishman, had this kind of love for his country, which he poured out in a well-known poem. He was William Blake, a man who saw visions and dreamed dreams. He lived at the time when England was becoming an industrial country, at the end of the eighteenth century and the beginning of the nineteenth.

Industrialisation assumed some horrible forms. People were not building beautiful airy factories with restrooms, ventilation and central heating during winter. They were disgusting, smoky places, infested with germs and hastily built to make as much profit in as short a time as possible. Living and working conditions were appalling, especially for young children, who had to toil for long hours virtually like slaves.

All this moved William Blake to fiery indignation and a holy rage. Such conditions, he felt in his very soul, should not be occurring in England, his England. And what was 'his England' like? He describes it in the poem 'The New Jerusalem', in which he states his vision and ideal for England as a place where the Lord would feel at home — a New Jerusalem where Christ would like to walk:

> *And did those feet in ancient time*
> *Walk upon England's mountains green?*
> *And was the holy Lamb of God*
> *On England's pleasant pastures seen?*

And did the Countenance Divine
Shine forth upon our clouded hills?
And was Jerusalem builded here
Among these dark Satanic mills?

Bring me my Bow of burning gold!
Bring me my Arrows of desire!
Bring me my Spear! O clouds, unfold,
Bring me my Chariot of fire!

I will not cease from Mental Fight,
Nor shall my Sword sleep in my hand,
Till we have built Jerusalem
In England's green and pleasant Land.

Now that is true love of country: a firm resolve, a solemn oath that what was wrong in his land — 'these dark Satanic mills', the frightful evils that industrialisation and avarice without conscience had brought on the country — that these had to be removed, and that England was to become a green and pleasant land where the Son of God could walk through its fields.

People driven by true patriotism have a flame in their souls, a compelling dream and vision of a better and happier country, for which they will work without rest until the New Jerusalem is built.

Young people may reply: "We do have such a dream and such a vision of a better South Africa in our hearts, of a land where the Lord Himself would want to walk. But these matters are in the hands of the old people. We are young and powerless. We cannot reform the country and put right what is wrong."

They are right. Much trouble in the world is caused by young people who believe that they can break down violently everything that is ugly and evil, or which they regard as ugly and evil, and that a new world, a New Jerusalem, can be created like this.

It cannot be done. They do not control the world; they do not control South Africa. However, young people do already bear responsibility for a small corner of South Africa: their own selves, their bodies and souls, and their relationships with their families, friends and teachers. There they can start building a New Jerusalem in a small way. There they can start working for a better South Africa, and as they grow older, their vision may broaden.

A man who drives through our fields and observes how erosion has eaten away the invaluable soil, and immediately resolves that this must stop; that in his South Africa such things must no longer be, that man has the right love of South Africa. He becomes a protector of the irreplaceable South African earth. He fights with a golden bow and arrows and a chariot of fire for the South Africa of his dreams.

Or a man who keeps his eyes open in a city like Cape Town, and sees the many struggling old people, virtual outcasts living in cold and cramped back rooms scattered all over, and then accepts the challenge to lighten and sweeten their lives — he brings South Africa a little nearer to the ideal of a land to which we may invite the Lord and His angels to come and tread our mountains and plains.

We are far from being a New Jerusalem. There is plenty of work for each of us in his or her own corner of South Africa. True love of our country means not to turn our backs on our country's defects and faults, but to face them like a good parent facing the shortcomings of a child, and to mend what is within our power to mend.

Only then do we show real love of South Africa, when we love it not only for what it is, for what we receive from it by way of beauty, riches and pleasure, but when we love it for what it can still be and ought to be — a land worthy of being trodden by the feet of the Lord.

Let us think of South Africa as William Blake thought of the England of his times — with dark, satanic factories disfiguring it — as a country that by labour and effort can become a New Jerusalem.

Young as we may be, let us resolve to exert ourselves as long as we breathe, and not to rest before we have played our full part in building such a South Africa.

This is love of country; this is patriotism — and this is what we actually vow when we sing that we shall live and die for South Africa.

'Good honest graft in the tight'

Neville Leck's report on
Western Province's victory at Ellis Park, 1969

Provincial rugby is the lifeblood of the sport in South Africa, and Currie Cup clashes between giants such as Western Province, Transvaal, Northern Transvaal, Natal and Orange Free State have an emotional intensity equalled in few other sports. Neville Leck, sports reporter for the *Cape Times,* captured some of the excitement in an evocative report he filed immediately after the Currie Cup match between Transvaal and Western Province at Ellis Park on 5 July 1969. It was published in the *Rand Daily Mail* and *Cape Times* on 7 July.

FINEST HOUR!

JOHANNESBURG. — He was choked with emotion. And tears of pride streamed unashamedly down his cheeks as his burly form filled the dressing-room doorway.

This was Hennie Muller, the Western Province coach and task master, when he confronted his 15 triumphant heroes as they slumped down, leg-weary, beneath buzzing Ellis Park's grandstand on Saturday.

This was a man overflowing with pride after watching a dream come true. Momentarily he was lost for words, but he did not have to speak. "We all knew how he felt, because we felt the same," one of the players told me.

When Muller and manager Dave Stewart led their Western Province rugby team into Johannesburg on Friday, cock-a-hoop Transvaal supporters gave them no chance of victory over their own new "giants of the North".

"We whipped Northern Transvaal. Now we'll whip you," they boasted.

But, only 24 hours later, blushing bright pink, those same supporters were hurriedly swallowing their words as their one-time supermen were crushed 28-9 by "Tiny" Neethling's inspired band of Province cavaliers.

Mesmerized crowd

If you have seen a slick entertainer take a decidedly cool audience, slowly warm them and finally mesmerize them, then you know what Province did to the crowd at Ellis Park on Saturday.

And if any one man won them over, it was dark-haired H.O. de Villiers.

De Villiers scaled the heights of true greatness on Saturday. Find a better fullback on this performance and you will have found a rugby genius.

Maturity has brought a brilliant balance to this young superstar's game. On Saturday he tamed that wild, adventurous spirit just sufficiently to ensure he never once put his team in danger.

But at the same time, he never allowed caution to stop him from bursting away on attacks that gave his harassed opponents a pocketful of trouble.

Some dismal jemmies have suggested Transvaal fly-half David Attwood-Smith made H.O. look good by booting the ball down his throat. Forget it. Attwood-Smith kicked well.

Neville Leck, sports writer.

Uncanny play

In actual fact it was quite the reverse. H.O.'s uncanny positional play made the Transvaal pivot look bad. His biggest mistake was to kick at all.

The Cape Town Springbok capped his game with a brilliant try-making break and a goal-kicking display that thoroughly vanquished his early-season kicking hoodoo.

His break started about 35 yards out. Scrum-half Des Christian whipped the ball back to him from a set scrum. He lined up for a drop-kick, but then, with the defence flying at him, he flashed to the right, beating Transvaal's star flanker Piet Greyling with a powerful outside swerve.

The ball went on to Eben Olivier and finally back inside to Alistair Thom who raced in untroubled for the first of his two tries.

De Villiers's boot was "grooved" to perfection. Five times it swung into conversions — two from wicked angles — and five times it found its mark. It was also responsible for booting Province into a three-point lead after only 50 seconds — this time from 40 yards out.

For his efforts, De Villiers was chaired off, tugged at and back-slapped like a pop idol, but Province were by no means a one-man team.

Except for Christian, whose service was easily his worst this year, every man-jack of the team came up with his best as they welded together to produce all that has been best in Western Province rugby down the years.

Honest graft

Good honest graft in the tight, tireless support and cover defence in the loose and imaginative and determined running reduced powerful Transvaal to the levels of mere mediocrity.

384

The 'Vaal were just never given a chance to get into the game, either up front or behind the scrum. They never clicked because they were never allowed to.

Splendid leaping

In a grinding front-row duel that at times had both hookers' heads only inches from the ground, Transvaal's new strongman, Martiens Louw, gave Neethling as torrid a time as Gert Kotze gave Piet Bosman. And it helped Robbie Barnard edge Charlie Cockerell 5-4 in the tight-head count.

But that was where the home side's superiority began and ended.

Hennie Muller's assertion that the dropping of giant Springbok lock Piet Botha by the Transvaal selectors was a major blunder was proved correct.

Without him, Transvaal's expected domination of the line-outs never materialized, thanks to some splendid leaping by WP's Andre de Wet and to a lesser extent, Neethling at number two and Thom at number seven.

In the loose, stocky Boland Coetzee has never played with more fire — it earned him a punch on the nose from Transvaal's Sakkie de Klerk — as he combined with wide-ranging Thom and "Kat" Smith to form a loose trio that completely outplayed their opposite numbers.

Yes, in spite of the fact that individually Greyling and eighth-man Cyril Els were the best of the Transvaal forwards.

Ample evidence

Smith and Thom covered miles, following the ball like guided missiles, always ready to haul down an attacker or carry on a Province attack. Their two tries each was ample evidence of their superb support.

Of course the Province loose forwards' task was made so much easier by the power-charged support their tight forwards gave them in the tight-loose — Neethling was outstanding here, completely vindicating any tight-heads he may have lost — and because their incisive backs so often ripped through the defence to cross the advantage line.

Those magnificent backs and their flying boots, they were a sight to see.

They weaved magic spells as they combined pace, finesse and mountains of inspiration to punch holes in a defence that is solid by any standards.

Barnard started quietly, obviously conscious that he had just returned from injury, but once warmed to his task, he was back to his brilliant best.

Twice he laid on tries for "Kat" Smith with that bewildering jink; his fingers were seemingly coated with glue and on the rare occasions he kicked, it was done wisely and well.

Playing against his old province and men who know best how to contain him, Barnard made a mockery of that cruel tag someone once gave him — "the youngest ex-Springbok".

Darting Eben

And Olivier, darting, weaving and elusive as ever, teamed up to form a twin-pronged fork of destruction. His finest moment was when he engineered Gert Muller's try.

Given the ball with no apparent way through, he used a hand-off and blazing acceleration to run out of a Hugh Bladen tackle before giving Muller an overlap.

Not as spectacular, Mike Lawless nevertheless brought important solidarity to the line both on defence and attack, while Muller and Andrew van der Watt always probed strongly when given the chance.

Muller made a meal of Transvaal's Springbok hope, Tobias du Toit. If Jannie Engelbrecht misses the first Test against the Wallabies, his replacement looks sure to come from Stellenbosch.

On the opposite wing, neither Van der Watt or Syd Nomis had much chance to use their tremendous speed, but it was clear that Nomis is South Africa's first-choice wing right now.

Once, and only once, the ball came to him quickly by way of his feeble-fingered backs. And he used it to power through so close to the line — only a jarring De Villiers tackle stopped him dead — that Attwood-Smith was able to scoop up the ball and dive over.

Lack chances

Bladen, the other speedy Transvaal back, looked as if he too could have been dangerous, but with Attwood-Smith kicking away too much precious possession and Davies fumbling too often, he, like Nomis, lacked the chances they needed.

After it all, a stunned Toy Dannhauser, the Transvaal skipper, said: "We were walloped by a far better team, but watch out next time. We can only improve."

He was right, of course, Transvaal will improve. Greyling for one is going to be a tower of strength. On Saturday he was playing in only his second game in more than three months and already he looked a sure Springbok flank.

But it will not be enough. If Province continue to play the rugby they played yesterday, they will be bringing the Currie Cup home again this year.

For the record, Transvaal's points on Saturday came from a try by David Attwood-Smith and two penalties by Jannie van Deventer, Kat Smith (2), Allistair Thom (2) and Gert Muller scored tries for Province with De Villiers landing a penalty and all five conversions.

Neville Leck, who began his working life as a copper miner at Anglo American's Rhokana Mine in Kitwe, Zambia and who crossed into South Africa driving a scarlet Austin Healey 3000 sports car, did not stay in journalism, although it remained his first love.

After covering most of the international rugby tours to and from South Africa in the late Sixties and Seventies and writing three books (*Nice Boys Come Second, H.O. — A Biography of Courage* and *SA Sport*), Leck left the *Cape Times* for a job as sales and marketing director of a sports goods company, the victim, as so many journalists have been, of indifferent salaries.

'A battered Springbok team'

Barry Glasspool on rugby and demonstrations, Leicester, 1969

With the increasing publicity given to South Africa's policy of apartheid and the consequent international opprobrium, South African sportsmen, travelling under the Springbok banner, found themselves, quite literally, in another ball game altogether.

South Africans had already been barred from the Olympics (they last participated in the Rome Olympics, 1960); now, any Springbok team travelling beyond the borders of South Africa was subjected to sometimes violent, sustained demonstrations. It became impossible to separate sport from politics.

Under captain Tommy Bedford, the Springbok rugby team which left for Britain in October 1969 returned chastened in February 1970. They had not only failed to win one of the internationals, but had had to cope with demonstrations so violent that, at one stage, they threatened to abort the tour altogether.

It was the second major international tour Barry Glasspool, sports editor of the *Sunday Times,* had covered. But instead of writing about sport, he found himself in the midst of one of the most dramatic news stories of the year.

The Springboks, confined to their hotel in the midst of tight security, were bussed to and from the rugby ground. On one occasion, their bus was hi-jacked just before a game; fortunately, none of the team was in it, but for the first time on a tour there was a real fear that members of the team could be seriously hurt.

For a reporter, it was difficult to keep a balanced perspective. Glasspool, writing his despatch immediately after the match, wrote two stories — one to cover the news angle, the other to cover the game itself. In spite of the difficulties in covering the game, Glasspool said the tour had been a marvellous experience in journalism for him. Both his articles, filed from Leicester, appeared in the *Sunday Times* of 9 November 1969, the news report appearing as the front page lead, the report on the match itself falling further back in the newspaper.

300 demonstrators fight with constables outside Leicester ground

POLICE IN RUGBY CLASH

THE TOUR IS IN JEOPARDY

But Springboks fight back to win match 11—9

LEICESTER, Saturday. Policemen clashed violently with anti-apartheid demonstrators outside the Leicester ground before the Springbok rugby match against Midland Counties East at Leicester today. Police helmets went flying as about 300 demonstrators burst through a police cordon about 300 yards from the entrance to the ground.

Police then drove a wedge of constables behind the mob who had broken through, cutting off about 2,000, mostly students, who foundered against another line of policemen.

In the end it was victory for the Springboks and Leicester's police force. As the Boks were hammering their way to an 11-9 win, the strongly manned police force was winning the battle with the demonstrators trying to break through the cordons to carry out their threats to disrupt the match and end the tour.

Barry Glasspool (The Star).

Half a dozen demonstrators did manage to escape the tight police cordon. They sat down and they were removed with no great delay. Others were intercepted by police as they came over the fence and were carried or escorted from the ground.

The "Sieg heil" chants from outside the ground, where the long-haired students had massed, were drowned by the lusty cheers of the estimated 12,000 crowd. The match was an all-ticket affair and the careful vetting by officials had much to do with the match being played with a minimum of fuss.

Rugby stewards placed strategically in the crowd were also an effective measure. They acted as "spotters".

As soon as they saw the threat of trouble, a quick word was passed to two police and the demonstrator was led away.

Organisers of the Stop the 1970 Tour Committee had widely circulated that they intended to wreck this match. It was considered the make or break point of the tour.

The effective police control here will be taken at all matches and confirms the view that some pre-tour reports of "thousands of militant demonstrators" have been grossly overplayed.

The demonstrators erupted into violence after an uninterrupted march through the town chanting anti-racialist slogans.

The police had been assured that they would peacefully enter a car park immediately opposite the ground, but this is where their tactics overruled promises of non-violence.

As the slogan-carrying mob approached a double line of police, Black activists, carrying posters of the Black Power and Black Panther movements, started a chant of "No, no, no", "Zimbabwe, Zimbabwe", "Smash apartheid", "Get the Fascist coppers", "Sieg heil" and "Springboks, go home".

A mounted police inspector said: "Move back now, or we shall have to force you back."

The surging crowd refused and over a dozen mounted police pushed their horses into the demonstrators' ranks.

In a scene of wild confusion, policemen, demonstrators and Saturday afternoon shoppers could be seen forced against walls, in pain, or doubled up in the road writhing in agony.

Face down

One young constable was doubled up outside the ground entrance after a kick in the groin.

Suddenly a flurry of policemen burst from the side of the road scattering the demonstrators and pushing many of them, facedown, in the road.

Two newspapermen were thrown against a brick wall, suffering cut arms and faces. An ambulance took away eight casualties.

Shaken housewives returned to their homes near the ground weeping. Some of them lost their shopping under thousands of thudding boots, and many spent 20 minutes struggling through police and demonstrators to reach safety.

A police superintendent on his own came face-to-face with four breakthrough students and, as he grabbed two by their necks, he was thumped by the others until a sergeant and two constables came to his aid. The breakaways were forced back through the police lines into the 2,000 howling and screaming crowd.

A police spokesman said: "There has never been such security here for either a soccer, or a rugby game. Well over 1,000 policemen were involved, many of them brought in from outside Leicester."

After the demonstrators had turned back, they still ignored police appeals to gather in the park.

Face-to-face with the police lines they hurled abuse at the officers.

About half-a-dozen members of the National Front, a Right-wing organisation, who carried pro-South African banners, beat a hasty retreat when the demonstrators snatched their posters and smashed them.

The police were screening the crowds going to the entrances to the ground, allowing through only those who had tickets. There were long queues at the entrances formed by people wanting to see the rugby match.

Leaflets attacking apartheid were being handed out at the entrances by students who were not part of the march. Streets near the ground were sealed off, and traffic was diverted as a security measure, while the police dealt with the demonstrators.

The police had kept an all-night guard on the rugby ground in case of sabotage but the only mark left by apartheid opponents were two-foot high slogans daubed on the wall outside.

The demonstrations inside the ground were much quieter. The match was interrupted five times in the first half as the odd demonstrators wandered on to the field, but they were mostly escorted quietly off.

Perhaps the demonstrators became bored, but in the second half they showed little inclination to disrupt the match as the Springboks piled on the pressure.

During the match itself, less than a dozen managed to get on the pitch. They were quickly removed by police and stewards.

The near-capacity crowd booed the demonstrators loudly and enthusiastically shouted, "Chuck him out", "Let him have it" and other advice to the stewards. At half-time there was loud applause for a member of the crowd who held up a banner saying "Welcome Springboks."

Two injured policemen and seven student demonstrators who collapsed during the march were taken to hospital just before the match started.

Nine demonstrators were arrested and charged with either committing a breach of the peace or disorderly conduct. They will appear in court on Monday. All except one of the 10 demonstrators who were led from the ground went peacefully.

In the 39th minute of the game one demonstrator decided to pit his strength against a burly policeman. His effort was fruitless and he crashed to the ground to be dragged away by the scruff of his neck.

Some of the most dangerous moments of the day erupted as the game ended. The demonstrators, whittled down to about 800, regrouped and charged against the police cordons screaming "Fascist bastards" and "racialist swine".

Tempers among the rugby-going crowd snapped. A man with his little boy lashed out at a bearded face and demonstrators pinned him against a wall.

Another man wearing a Springbok rosette clashed with a placard-bearing demonstrator. Police managed to stop the fight as the two groups came angrily towards each other for what could have been an ugly battle.

Demonstrators started throwing pennies at the crowd, but the crowd was moved away quickly.

A chanting group of about 300 demonstrators then marched to the Springboks' hotel. Outside, they shouted "Springboks, we want you". They dispersed after 10 minutes.

Then Glasspool, with obvious relief, got down to the real task in hand:

PHEW! BUT IT WAS SO CLOSE

LEICESTER, Saturday.

Phew! It was close, mightily close. But a battered Springbok team bounced back from a half-time deficit to score the first win of the tour over Midland Counties East here today.

Victory by 11 points (goal, drop goal, penalty goal) to nine (two tries, penalty goal) is a satisfactory result, but there are still too many creaking joints in the Boks' machine, which will need some oiling before they begin to look and play like great Springbok sides that have toured Britain.

It is a tribute to the mental resilience of today's side, however, that they were sufficiently flexible to meet the unexpected complications brought about by the injuries to Jan Ellis and Hannes Marais.

Marais went off after only 12 minutes limping badly and Ellis was taken off after 22 minutes with no apparent shoulder injury. The loss of the South West African flanker's driving was sorely felt. Hard though reserve hooker Don Walton tried, it required Herculean efforts from Piet van Deventer and Tommy Bedford to match the considerable talents of the Counties' trio of Taylor, West and Matthews.

Van Deventer gets my award as the Boks' man-of-the-match.

390

The darkhaired Griqua forward was always in the thick of things, smelling the ball out, and he was on hand to take Piet Visagie's inside pass to crash over for the first try of the tour.

Priceless effort

Van Deventer could not have chosen a more appropriate time than this priceless effort for, although the Springboks were starting to assert themselves with the strong swirling wind at their backs, they were unable until Visagie's neat cut through in the 67th minute to convert good scoring positions into points:

The Boks, mainly through the individualistic attempts of Dirkie de Vos, attacked principally through kick-and-chase tactics. There's no doubt that De Vos at scrumhalf has the ability to pinpoint his tactical kicks but today I'm afraid the little Western Transvaal player overdid the kicking.

He was battling to gauge a tricky wind and twice kicked away a clean rucked ball. It makes a mockery of having exciting runners like Andrew van der Watt and Renier Grobler cooling their heels out in the cold.

Both wings showed when they went hunting for the ball on their own that they had the pace to beat their opposite numbers.

Fine goal

In between the irritating first-half stoppages — the stuttering breaks did not help the Springboks' concentration — Visagie dropped a fine goal, just on the stroke of halftime, to cut the lead to 9-6.

After only two minutes, the Bok flyhalf had slotted a difficult penalty into the wind from 48 yards, only for the lead to be neutralised a minute later when big lock forward, Peter Larter, slammed one over from the centre spot.

It was during this period of reshuffling in the Bok pack with Mof Myburgh coming on for Marais and Walton for Ellis, that the Counties almost grabbed an unassailable lead via tries by wing Glen Robertson and centre Peter Sweet.

Sloppy defensive work was at the root of both tries though, for the first, one must excuse skipper Tommy Bedford, who sensed the move and fell back. He was beaten by a capricious bounce yet recovered and just missed his tackle on the wing as he raced over.

Fluffed kick

The centre David Small, grubber-kicked through into the gap and, once Bedford's clutches had been eluded, Robertson's path to the line was unobstructed.

This try came in the 31st minute and Larter, who also missed two other reasonably goalable kicks, also fluffed this conversion. Sweet's try in the 40th minute was a by-product of a frightful pass by Johan van der Schyff in trying to clear a rolling ball. Up flashed Bob Taylor, who was with the Lions in South Africa last year, to pouch the ball and switch the direction left.

With a three-man overlap, Sweet had only to run in the try, though, from my spot, the final pass looked slightly forward.

Second gear

Pat Briggs at flyhalf played with decreasing composure as the game ran its course and Van Deventer was able to hustle and harry him into mistakes.

Yet, sadly for the Boks, that necessary edge of speed to the breakdown point is still missing and, even in the first half, some of the big men were still coming over the horizon to the loose scrums.

Andre de Wet, Van Deventer and Bedford excepted, the Boks' mobility around the field has still to shift out of second gear.

Behind the scrum Visagie, who cleverly took the tackle to set up Van Deventer's try, was sound while Eben Olivier and Grobler could not be faulted on defence.

There is still a lot of work to be done but this victory has put the tour on the right road.

So it's little wonder that the players' spirits were high tonight.

'A sorcerer and his apprentices'

Stanley Uys on the Herstigte Nasionale Party, 1969

Under the premiership of B.J. Vorster, the 1969 election was declared on 16 September. The results of the election, like those of virtually every one since the 1948 election which swept General Smuts' United Party aside, were more or less a foregone conclusion. Not only was the National Party clearly on the ascendant, but the main opposition party was in disarray.

Under the conservative leadership of Sir D.P. de Villiers Graaff (he finally resigned as Leader of the Opposition on 28 June 1977 after leading his party for 21 years), the party had seen the breaking away of the left, most notably Helen Suzman, Colin Eglin and John Cope, and the subsequent formation of the Progressive Party.

With 149 seats at its disposal, white South Africans voted the Nationalists into 111 seats, the United Party into 47 (this was the last election in which that party featured significantly), one to the fledgeling Progressive Party (the vote went to Helen Suzman) — and none at all to Albert Hertzog's Herstigte Nasionale Party. Writing about the latter, in an otherwise routine general election campaign proved almost pleasurable, so disorderly and tumultuous were its political meetings.

Stanley Uys was political editor of the *Sunday Times* as well as running the paper's Cape Town bureau. One of the most experienced political writers of the day (Uys had been appointed political correspondent of the *Sunday Times* in 1949) and one of the most respected, Uys wrote an article stating that the United Party was under the control of a 'verkrampte mafia', which helped with the demise of the party. Writing with almost apparent relief, and a small degree of glee, Uys reported on the colourful election campaign of Dr Hertzog. The despatch appeared in the *Sunday Times* on 16 November 1969.

Stanley Uys (Times Media Ltd).

393

Watching Dr. Hertzog stump the country with Mr. Jaap Marais and Mr. Louis Stofberg in tow, like a sorcerer and his apprentices, one cannot help but admire the sheer physical fitness of this 70-year-old man. Even if he wins no seats on April 22, he will be able to claim some kind of endurance record.

Between them, the three men have addressed, or tried to address, nearly 18 meetings since their party, the Herstigte Nasionale Party, was founded. With one exception, and that actually was a meeting addressed by the fourth Herzogite M.P., Mr. Willie Marais, in Pretoria North, all the meetings have ended in disorder.

This in itself must be an emotionally exhausting experience for Dr. Hertzog and Co., but they are undaunted. They are able to sit, as they did on a Paarl stage this week, ankle-deep in fruit and vegetables, with the light of commitment still gleaming undimmed in their eyes. Some people, I suppose, would call it fanaticism.

This week, Dr. Hertzog staged the H.N.P.'s much-publicised invasion of the Cape. The scene was Worcester, home town of the Hertzogite M.P., Mr. Stofberg, and the venue was the narrow, inadequate agricultural hall. Politically, I found this meeting more interesting than the meeting the following night in Paarl, where the Battle of Paarl was fought.

At the Worcester meeting, the Nationalist audience, although noisy, was good-humoured, and there were no fisticuffs and flying projectiles to distract one's observations. Certain important conclusions can be drawn from the Worcester meeting, I think, if it is seen in the context of all the other meetings.

The immediate conclusion is that, by taking over H.N.P. meetings, the Nationalists are stunting the growth of the new party. They are literally inhibiting it out of existence, or nearly out of existence.

Dr. Hertzog cannot get his message across in calm to audiences, and in view of the disturbances, I would be very surprised if the H.N.P. is able to put as many candidates in the field in the general election as it had hoped to do.

Terrified

Some of the prospective candidates must be too terrified to appear on a platform. Why should they — to get a blow on the head or a tomato in the eye?

Another obvious effect of these riotous H.N.P. meetings is that they are serving to mobilise Nationalists behind their own party. The apathy about which Nationalist Party organisers were complaining recently must be dissolving rapidly now as the call goes out to man the barricades. The appeal is not only to the loyalty of Nationalists: it is also to man's latent aggression. The gladiators are on display — roll up! roll up!

It's crazy politics, of course. If you shut your eyes and listen to Dr. Hertzog speaking, you could swear that, for 90 per cent of his speech at least, you were listening to Sir De Villiers Graaff. The issues are the same — criticism of the Government's mis-management of the economy, a plea for the farmers, the pensioners, the struggling wage-earner, etc., etc. It is all good sound stuff.

For the remaining 10 per cent, though, you could swear you were listening to Genghis Khan. You look at Dr. Hertzog, on the surface a kindly old gentleman, and you ask yourself: What bugs him?

It is only when you catch the glint of his eyes behind his glasses that you realise that here is a flat-earthist, as rare a specimen as would be found anywhere in the world today. No wonder Dr. Hertzog collects antiques; his most priceless possession is himself.

The ease with which Dr. Hertzog switches from advocating the cause of an exclusive, dominant Afrikanerdom, grinding everyone else's face in the dust, to a protest against Mr. Vorster's "tyrannical" methods, makes one blink.

BOSS law

Explaining with almost child-like simplicity to his Worcester audience the implications of the Bureau for State Security (BOSS), Dr. Hertzog said: "If one of BOSS's authorised officials in Worcester is cross with you, he can lock you up for as long as he likes. This is one of the most tyrannical laws ever passed."

Whereupon, one of the tiny band of Hertzogite supporters who were clustered around the platform, shouted "Stalin Vorster." One felt like interjecting: Look who's talking!

Dr. Hertzog's obsession with BOSS is intriguing. Obviously he is firmly convinced that BOSS is going to be used against the H.N.P., and as an ex-Cabinet Minister with contacts still in high places, he is probably right.

I don't think we realise fully yet just what an important part BOSS is possibly designed to play in White politics in the country.

Another significant development taking place in Nationalist politics as a result of the emergence of the Hertzogites, and a healthy one at that, is that Nationalist audiences, in establishing the contrast between their outlook and the outlook of H.N.P. speakers on a platform, are committing themselves to policy directions over which they have been lukewarm in the past.

For example, the whole question of the Nationalist Party's relationship with the English-speaking section is being raised at H.N.P. meetings. The H.N.P. wants to have nothing to do with English-speaking South Africans, and it says so quite openly. This forces Nationalist audiences to make up their minds where they stand, and almost automatically, if only to fix the distance between themselves and the Hertzogites, they come down on the side of the English.

Similarly with immigrants: the Hertzogites simply don't want immigrants unless they can be assimilated immediately into Afrikanerdom and become card-carrying members of the H.N.P. Confronted with the issue, Nationalist audiences have jeered at the H.N.P. outlook. They have shown they do not fear "swamping" by immigrants.

And so, bit by bit, as the differences between the H.N.P. and the Nationalist Party are defined, the H.N.P. is pushed a little more to the Right and the Nationalist Party a little more to the Left. This will not happen on all issues, of course. Over matters like Black diplomats and visiting non-White sportsmen, the Nationalist Government may still, for some time, unavoidably be the captive of H.N.P. propaganda.

There is another way in which Nationalist audiences are being pushed into taking a stand — behind the leadership of Mr. Vorster. Not until the H.N.P. appeared on the scene and presented Dr. Hertzog as an alternative Messiah to Mr. Vorster, has Mr. Vorster enjoyed such popularity. The mere mention of his name at H.N.P. meetings now brings deafening applause from the Nationalist audience.

The H.N.P. intention was to undermine Mr. Vorster: in fact, they are making him unassailable.

The obverse of the coin is that the rousing of the Nationalist rank and file out of its apathy, the whole emotional mobilisation of the Afrikaner nation, is generating political intemperance and intolerance, and all the Opposition parties, not only the H.N.P., will feel the backlash of this.

Meanwhile, the H.N.P.'s immediate future looks bleak. At this rate, it is not going to win a single parliamentary seat on April 22, and its share of the total vote cast may be minimal. In that event, the only damage it can cause to the Nationalist Party in the election will be to split the vote in Nationalist-held marginal seats, and let in United Party candidates. Both Dr. Hertzog and Mr. Jaap Marais have admitted this will be done.

It seems to me that, if this is the pattern of events — of course, the situation is so fluid that the pattern could change quickly — the H.N.P. is not going to be an important factor in the election itself, except as a catalyst.

Instincts

The reason I say this is that I am convinced that Dr. Hertzog has miscalculated the political situation. He appears to be under the impression that there is an essential "verkramptheid" in Afrikanerdom which needs only to be unleashed and brought to the surface to ensure victory for the H.N.P. As the election campaign proceeds, so he is discarding the mask, and appealing unashamedly to the electorate's basest instincts.

He presents the H.N.P. as the only God-ordained party; he says openly that English must be a second language; he declared that the country does not want immigrants (and one of his lieutenants, Mr Willie Marais, adds that the H.N.P. itself does not want Jews); he denounces "American money power", and his programme of principles envisages tampering with the parliamentary system.

Dr. Hertzog is living in the past. How many rank-and-file Afrikaners, I wonder, care two hoots about "American money power?" The issues Dr. Hertzog conjures up are ghosts from the 1930s. They are not real issues for Afrikaners today.

The whole verkrampte concept, therefore, is founded on a misappraisal of the political mood of the country. We are no longer living in the days of hundreds of thousands of poor Whites, or of an oppressed Afrikanerdom.

No, the really interesting situation is the one that will arise after the election, when the Nationalist Party takes stock of itself and discovers that the unity and solidarity which is being forced upon it now is artificial.

If one looks at the Nationalist Party's parliamentary caucus, the seat of power, one sees that it is composed of verkramptes (who pulled out of the verkrampte breakaway at the last moment), semi-verkramptes, semi-verligtes and verligtes. These are polarities, rather than two clear-cut groups. They will find living with each other an exacting experience which will tax their discipline to the utmost.

The verkramptes and semi-verkramptes are not going to like the idea of being verligte captives, which is what they are at the moment. They resent intensely this total verligte victory over Dr. Hertzog and the other three Hertzogite M.P.s — and herein lies a situation of potential conflict.

The Nationalist Party, in fact, is undergoing some deepseated change, the nature of which it is difficult to determine at this stage. Certainly, it will never be the same party again. It is too late simply to repair itself, like a self-sealing tube.

Stanley Uys' ironic style, appreciated by many international papers (he was, at one time or another, a stringer for the *News Chronicle, The Sun, The Observer* and *The Guardian* as well as the BBC) together with an increasing restlessness with the South African scene, led to his accepting the job of London editor of the South African Morning Group (now Times Media) in 1977. He retired in 1985 to freelance, specialising in African Affairs.

'Greater frankness and greater permissiveness'

The editors' debate: Joel Mervis and Dirk Richard, 1969

There has long been a great divide between the English and Afrikaans Press. The days of bilingual papers in the tradition of early country newspapers (with the notable exception of the *Paarl Post,* successor to *Die Afrikaanse Patriot*) and the wonderfully innovative, if slightly dotty *Die Volkstem* (published originally as *De Volksstem* in August 1873) have largely passed.

But in 1969, in the run up to the general election, an interesting experiment in bridging the divide was made by Joel Mervis, editor of the *Sunday Times,* and Dirk Richard, editor of *Dagbreek.* (*Dagbreek,* no longer in existence, was formed in 1947 as the first Afrikaans Sunday newspaper, amalgamating with *Die Brandwag* in 1962 and, once again, merging with *Die Beeld* in 1970 to form *Rapport.*)

At the annual Chamber of Mines dinner in 1969, Dirk Richard sat next to R.S. Cooke, that year's president of the Chamber of Mines. The talk got round to the divisions between the English and Afrikaans-speaking Press. What a pity it was, said Cooke, that Afrikaans views weren't represented in English newspapers and vice versa.

The following morning, Richard picked up the phone and spoke to Mervis. Why not write a weekly column, he suggested, in which each would reply to the other's subject, taking it in turns to choose the topic? (Mervis remembers it slightly differently: in his version, *he* picked up the phone. Moreover, he claims that Richard had to go to Cabinet level to get the project approved. Richard recalls discussing it only with his managing director, Marius Jooste. They are both agreed that Mervis discussed it with no-one.)

The routine, once it was established, was simple: one week Richard would write his column and send it over to Mervis, who would write his response. The roles were reversed the following week. The articles were published simultaneously in both Sunday newspapers. As the following debate illustrates, *Sunday Times* political editor Stanley Uys was not the only one to write about the contentious issue of the Hertzogites. Richard's gentle style of writing contrasts strongly with the caustic pen (and wit) of Mervis.

THE EDITORS' DEBATE

COMMENT BY DIRK RICHARD

Why all this publicity for Hertzogites?

After our rendezvous last week with the pugnacious Afrikaans editors, we can today take a look at the SUNDAY TIMES and the Hertzog group.

Judging from the enthusiastic publicity given to the Hertzogites by your paper, there must be a close relationship between them and the Times. The Prime Minister said at Nigel on Tuesday evening: "I do not know why the Hertzog Group wants to start a newspaper — they get enough publicity in the SUNDAY TIMES."

Why do you do this, Mr. Mervis?

As a newspaperman I know, of course, that a newspaper must publish news or political views, even though its editor does not necessarily agree with it. News is news, and the journalistic test is always this: Would the reader find it interesting and newsworthy? Would he look for another newspaper if mine suppressed or neglected that news?

I will even make this admission: the Afrikaans newspapers have been too one-sided and too alike, and they allowed too few views or news reports, which differed from the official Party policy, to be published.

The Afrikaans readers then turned to the English language papers "just to see what the Opposition said and thought." The situation is changing, and a greater frankness is penetrating the columns of Afrikaans newspapers.

But even after this admission about the greater 'permissiveness' of the English Press, I return to my initial question: why do you promote the Albert Hertzogs and the Barry Bothas in this way?

There is a great difference between normal news coverage and exaggerated publicity. The Hertzogites get more attention in the SUNDAY TIMES than in any other English language newspaper.

Motive

Do the other editors exhibit poor news sense? Or do they preserve the balance between news coverage and newsworthiness, and the SUNDAY TIMES not?

The motive of the SUNDAY TIMES sticks out like a sore thumb: the more the Hertzog group is pushed and built up, the greater the potential danger to the Vorster Government.

Between you, Mr. Hennie Serfontein and Mr. Barry Botha there exists a continuing contact. Even Dr. Hertzog has now become a zealous informer of the English language Press — the same Press which he, until recently, condemned venomously and contemptuously as the liberal minded Press which was planning the downfall of the White man.

Now you and the Hertzogites are allies in the battle against Mr. Vorster. These people want to force South Africa back to the time of the ox-wagon, which is long past; they are against co-operation between English and Afrikaans-speaking people; their leader even asked recently: Do you want your daughter to dance with a Maori?

If people with this mentality must achieve success, it would retard South Africa's progress and impede the unavoidable role which the country must play in southern Africa.

Why do you not condemn them in your opinion columns with the same fervour with which you report their activities in your news columns? Indicate your displeasure, draw attention to the consequences of the course followed by Albert Hertzog.

But no, that you do sparingly. The Times even tries to cast suspicion on other

Nationalists by subtly and cunningly associating them with the Hertzog Group.
Do not build something which can only harm South Africa, colleague.

REPLY BY JOEL MERVIS

...BECAUSE WE'RE A NEWSPAPER

Mr. Vorster and Mr. Richard, in their assessment of what constitutes news, apply a subjective test. That is to say, if they do not like the news, then they apparently prefer to see it suppressed or, better still, slanted. Neither Mr. Vorster nor Mr. Richard has complained about the accuracy of our news. What they object to is the volume of it.

The SUNDAY TIMES applies an objective test. We give publicity to the Hertzog Group because their breakaway movement is NEWS. The fact that we disapprove of verkramptes is quite irrelevant.

The best way to test Mr. Richard's complaint is to take an actual case from real life.

Let us look at Dagbreek and the SUNDAY TIMES of last Sunday — the day following the official establishment of the Herstigte Nasionale Party.

Both newspapers made the new party their main report on the front page. The SUNDAY TIMES headlines read as follows: "1,000 Verkrampte Delegates Cheer Historic Political Move: New Nat Party Formed: Herstigte Nasionale Party to Fight Over 100 Seats."

Joel Mervis, Sunday Times *editor 1959– 1975. Under his editorship the paper expanded from being a Johannesburg Sunday to a national one* (Times Media Ltd).

Dirk Richard: too verlig *for the Afrikaans Establishment.*

Those headlines are reasonably factual and objective, giving a fair picture of the previous day's events.

Now let us take a look at Dagbreek's front-page headlines. This is what they said: "Hertzog-party Born Full of Imaginary Complaints (skete): Weak Leader: Weak Management: Weak Name." (The word "skete" also has another meaning and one would not use the word in polite society).

These headlines, in my view, are tendentious and slanted. They are not news headlines at all, but sheer propaganda.

In its issue last week Dagbreek gave virtually as much publicity to the Hertzog Group as the SUNDAY TIMES did. But Mr. Vorster complains only about us. The explanation probably is that our reports were fair and objective, while Dagbreek's were loaded with snide comment and angled presentation.

What really seems to be wrong with the SUNDAY TIMES is that it gives the facts about the verkramptes in a balanced way.

Perhaps this is the moment to remind Mr. Vorster that on August 14, 1966, in Dr. Verwoerd's lifetime, the SUNDAY TIMES first revealed the existence of a "Hertzog Group" and it gave it that name. Ever since, we have constantly exposed the activities of the Hertzog Group; and we have warned Mr. Vorster many times to take action against this verkrampte danger.

He ignored our advice and our warnings; he has got himself into a first-class jam as a result; and now he complains that we are giving too much publicity to the Hertzog Group! It is certainly hard to please a Prime Minister these days.

May I remind Mr. Vorster also that in 1967 Dr. Hertzog issued summons against the SUNDAY TIMES for R100,000, alleging that we had accused him of being disloyal to Dr. Verwoerd.

Dangers

Mr. Vorster watched this in silence although he knew that Dr. Hertzog (to use Mr. Vorster's own words) had been *grossly disloyal* to Dr. Verwoerd.

If we accept Dr. Hertzog's version, the SUNDAY TIMES was the first to accuse him of disloyalty to Dr. Verwoerd. Mr. Vorster did not get round to making that accusation until three years later.

For Mr. Richard to suggest therefore, that I am an ally of the Hertzogites in the battle against Mr. Vorster is the height of absurdity.

Nevertheless, I could foresee the dangers ahead. For three years, while Mr. Vorster was twiddling his thumbs, doing nothing, and talking about "holiday episodes", the SUNDAY TIMES was waging Mr. Vorster's battle, often singlehanded, against the verkramptes, exposing them, flushing them out, and constantly warning Mr. Vorster of the peril.

On March 23, 1969, we wrote: "Mr. Vorster's failure to act firmly against the verkramptes a year ago makes it more difficult for him to deal with them now; and his dilly-dallying today will make his position still more difficult a year hence.

"If Mr. Vorster is not careful, he will earn himself a reputation as a modern Nero, with this minor difference, that while Pretoria burns Mr. Vorster plays chip shots."

And now, after all this, Mr. Richard has the audacity to ask me why I do not condemn the verkramptes with the same fervour as I report their activities.

It is too late now for Mr. Richard to come to me for help. I did my best, for more than three years, to get Mr. Vorster to stamp out the verkrampte movement before it had a chance to spread; but neither he nor Mr. Richard took any notice.

Warning

The harm and the damage have been done; and I predict that the verkrampte will steadily and inexorably gnaw the heart out of the Nationalist Party.

If only Mr. Vorster had paid some attention to what the SUNDAY TIMES was telling him, he would not have this kingsize political headache today.

As for the verkramptes — not least Dr. Hertzog himself — who have for so long condemned the SUNDAY TIMES, perhaps they will now appreciate what it means to have in South Africa a powerful newspaper which is free, independent and reasonably objective.

Joel Mervis retired as editor of the *Sunday Times* in 1975 after a tenure of sixteen years. One of the most respected of editors, Mervis practised at the Johannesburg Bar for five years before moving into journalism. Under his editorship, the paper acquired its glitzy image, whilst reflecting his insistence that good law originates in the minds of men and has to be supported by an informed public. He still freelances.

Richard had a more chequered career. In 1972 he became editor of *Die Vaderland.* Regarded as too *verlig* by the Establishment, Richard was relieved of his editorship in 1979 and retired in 1981. Since his retirement he has written books (one of them, *Moeds willig die Uwe,* recounts the history of the Afrikaans Press of the north), short stories and one-act plays.

'Just a tickle here and there'

John Scott, in (and out of) parliament, 1972

If he had not been able to write 'Notes in the House', averred John Scott, he would have quite simply gone mad, sitting in the House of Assembly day after day for over 17 years. As it was, 'Notes' provided the antidote he needed to leaven the heavy dough of a parliamentary debate.

Syndicated to all SAAN newspapers, the satirical column was reproduced daily in the *Cape Times*. During that time, 'Notes in the House' amused thousands of South Africans, including the parliamentarians themselves, and, to a lesser extent, Scott himself.

The former medical correspondent for the *Cape Times*, which he joined in 1966, Scott broke the news of the world's first heart transplant in December 1967, before becoming the paper's political correspondent. For 17 years, from 1969 to 1986 he wrote 'Notes', unquestionably the country's most successful parliamentary column. In 1972, Scott began a satirical column, 'PS'. It ran three times a week from 1972 to 1986.

A man given to mild eccentricity, Scott found his 'Notes', like his column 'PS' easy to write because the raw material was before him every day. The most favourable response to his columns came from the government benches. Other parties, says Scott, expected too much and were therefore always disappointed, whereas the National Party expected nothing from his pen and occasionally allowed themselves to be pleasantly surprised.

'Just a Tickle Here and There' was published in the *Cape Times* on 6 June 1972 and referred to an event which had taken place four days earlier, when baton-wielding police charged passive student demonstrators on the steps of St George's Cathedral, Cape Town. 'Two Who Tried for the VC', also published in the *Cape Times* in June 1972, is an ironic example of Scott's 'PS' column.

JUST A TICKLE HERE AND THERE

All those who were battered and beaten by the police last Friday will be gratified to learn they were not actually hurt. The truncheons that bounced off their skulls were made of soft rubber.

The good news was announced in the Assembly yesterday by Mr. Jimmy Kruger, one of the Nationalist Party's legal experts.

The victims must regret not having been informed of this earlier. It would have saved unnecessary trips to the hospital and unnecessary treatment by doctors.

The Government's consideration for those who might have got in the way of a charging policeman only began to manifest itself in the debate.

For instance, when Mr. Lourens Muller, the Minister of Police, was asked why teargas was not used last Friday, he said it might have harmed people near by.

"You just hit them," said Mr. Hennie Van Eck.

But Mr. Van Eck was forgetting about the softness of the rubber truncheons.

"In these circumstances I believe that the police acted with great tolerance," said Mr. Muller.

Just a tickle here and a tickle there.

"If the police had used no violence, can you imagine what would have happened?" asked Mr. Muller.

Yes. There would have been no violence. And the Prime Minister would have been disappointed. He said so.

"If the police didn't take action in the way they did, I personally would have been disappointed," Mr. Vorster told the House.

John Scott, whose story on the world's first heart transplant made international news.

I am so glad for Mr. Vorster's sake.

Sir De Villiers Graaff asked if someone had to be beaten to death before Mr. Vorster appointed a commission of inquiry.

"That is a senseless interjection," replied Mr. Vorster powerfully.

"Why?" asked an Opposition member.

Mr. Vorster did not say. But it was pretty obvious. If you ask hypothetical questions about someone who is beaten senseless, they must be senseless questions.

In any case, whoever heard of anyone being beaten senseless with soft rubber?

Mr. Lourens Muller said the students should rather have had their demonstration on Rondebosch Common. It would be quiet there, and newspapers would be able to take their pictures without disruption.

This is another example of Mr. Muller's consideration, one that may be overlooked by people who are so quick to criticize him.

There seemed to be doubt, still, about how many police saved Cape Town from the students, and how long they continued to beat them with their soft rubber truncheons.

Mr. Vorster said "twenty or more".

"Double that number," said Mrs. Cathy Taylor.

"In the region of 60," said Mr. Mike Mitchell.

"About 30," said Mr. Muller.

Any more offers? Going at thirty. Going, going . . . gone to that dapper Minister with consideration for others.

Members were similarly agreed on how long the police beat people. Sir De Villiers suggested that police violence continued twenty minutes after the first baton charge.

"Did you have a stop-watch?" asked Mr. Hennie Smit, of Stellenbosch.

Later Mr. Muller said that the charge lasted five minutes.

Mr. Vause Raw: "Did the hitting last for only a few minutes?"

Mr. Muller: "Yes. My information is that the charge lasted only five or six minutes."

"Your clock stopped," said Mr. Jack Wainwright.

Either that, or people who thought they were beaten up twenty minutes later were gravely mistaken. We all make mistakes. You think you're being chased up the road by a baton-waving man and then wake up in the gutter fooled by a mere nightmare.

Mrs. Suzman wondered why the Government got so upset when students sang "We Shall Overcome", a Negro spiritual.

"It's an accepted student song," she said.

"Nonsense," shouted Government members.

"They sang it at Harris's funeral," said one.

"They will sing it at your funeral, too," said another.

"Yes, they will," said Mrs. Suzman. "So what!"

Mr. George Oliver of Kensington kept careful note of all the Government members who had laughs on their faces. He said the MP for Harrismith, Mr. J.J. Rall, and the MP for Stilfontein, Mr. Koeks Rossouw, laughed their heads off when Sir De Villiers Graaff spoke about the pregnant woman who was beaten.

When Mr. Rall noticed that Mr. Oliver was looking at him, he "straightened his face", said Mr. Oliver.

"But the honourable member for Stilfontein still thinks it is a great big joke."

Mr. Oliver said Mr. Rossouw had encouraged the police by shouting: "Slaan hulle, slaan hulle."

Mr. Oliver said he also saw Dr. Piet Koornhof laughing when the debate started.

"Come off it," said Dr. Koornhof, without a flicker of a smile.

"The honourable member can laugh in this House if he chooses," said the Speaker.

But for the moment, no one did laugh.

TWO WHO TRIED FOR THE VC

Ever willing to obey my political overlords, I have been looking round for a place where I can indulge in "open-hearted voluntary conversation" with black and brown fellow South Africans.

Mr. Louis le Grange, Deputy Minister of the Interior, feels I am not having enough of it. Open-hearted vc, that is.

He told the central youth executive of the National Party near Bloemfontein last week that there was a "pitiful lack of communication" across the colour line. Why, many white South Africans had never even been into a black township, he said.

It just so happened that I met a coloured acquaintance rushing to catch a train the other evening. I too, was on my way home.

"Ho ho," I said to myself. "Here is an excellent opportunity for a bit of the old open-hearted what-not."

Then I called across to George and said: "What's the hurry, old chap?"

"Ag, they've stuck us so far out in the bush that unless you get a move on you never get home," he replied.

"Look, let's have a quick little drink somewhere before you disappear into the bush," I said. "The deputy minister says we must make with the communication."

"A cold beer would go down well," he said. "But where?"

"You got a point there, George. We'll have a dry voluntary chat on the way home."

But almost immediately we arrived at the Cape Town station entrance, the one that says "Whites only" and "No dogs allowed".

"At least we can catch the same train," I said. "You go down the road and enter the station your end, then come back along the platform to the point where the black coaches end and the white ones begin. I'll meet you there and we can talk about how the different races are finding one another."

"That's a wonderful idea," said George, and he hurried on down the road while I took the short cut to the place we were both headed for.

I got to it first, naturally, and waited for him to reach it from the opposite end of the platform.

"At last," I said. "Let's have a seat."

George coughed discreetly.

"There's a bit of a problem," he said. "Either you sit on that seat there and I stand, or I sit on this here and you stand."

"I know what, let's both stand," I suggested.

"Why didn't we think of it in the first place?" he agreed.

And we were just about to converse voluntarily with each other in an open-hearted manner when the whistle went and we had to jump into our respective coaches which were very close together, back to back you might say, but not quite suitable for communication unless we stuck our heads out of our windows and shouted.

"I'll get out at your station," I yelled.

I did. He was very appreciative of my attempts to keep the dialogue going.

"Come down to my place and I'll run you home in my car," he said.

"That'll be marvellous," I said. "We can communicate on the way."

At this point we were interrupted by his going down one subway while I went down another. There was a long queue at the bus-stop.

"Whites downstairs," shouted the conductor.

"I'll see you at the township," said George, going upstairs. "Lucky I'm not a bantu, hey!"

"Why, George?"

"Because you haven't got a permit to go into a bantu township. It's difficult to socialize with the bantu, man."

And he disappeared on to the top deck.

John Scott resigned from the *Cape Times* in February 1987 to stand as the Progressive Federal Party candidate in Simonstown in the May 1987 election and, although he was not returned to parliament, he was the only PFP candidate to reduce an existing National Party majority.

'The whole bloody world will rejoice'

Donald Woods replies to the Minister of Defence, 1972

Donald Woods, editor of *The Daily Dispatch,* was due to play golf at 11 am on the morning of 16 October 1972. There was an editorial for the following day's paper to be written and Woods had to write it. The subject of the editorial was not a problem: the Minister of Defence, Mr P.W. Botha, had posed an interesting question. 'Who,' he asked, 'would rejoice if the Nationalist Government was toppled?'

In no more than 20 minutes, Woods, who was later to be banned and flee the country, largely over the stance he took following the death of activist Steve Biko, wrote his editorial from his large office in East London.

The editorial, one of the most celebrated in South African journalism, was published in *The Daily Dispatch* on 17 October 1972 and reproduced the same day in the *Cape Times.*

'The Cape leader of the Nationalist Party, Mr. P.W. Botha, asks who will rejoice if the Nationalist Government is toppled. Dar-es-Salaam will rejoice, he says. Lusaka and Peking and Moscow will rejoice, he says.

'He asks who else will rejoice. Here is an answer for him: Cape Town will rejoice, Johannesburg will rejoice. Durban will rejoice. Port Elizabeth, East London and Maritzburg will rejoice. Germiston, Springs and Benoni will rejoice. Every single South African city of any size — apart from Pretoria and Bloemfontein — will rejoice.

'Mdantsane will rejoice, Soweto will rejoice. Langa, New Brighton and Guguletu will rejoice.

'And outside the country, too. Nairobi will rejoice, Cairo will rejoice, Jerusalem, Tel Aviv and Bagdad will rejoice. Algiers will rejoice. Lagos, Luanda and Lourenço Marques will rejoice. Addis Ababa will rejoice, Marrakesh and Rabat will rejoice. Timbuktu will rejoice.

'London, New York, Paris, Bonn and Berlin will rejoice.

'Chicago, Los Angeles, San Francisco, Washington, Boston, New Orleans and St. Louis will rejoice.

'Ottawa will rejoice. Toronto, Quebec, Vancouver and Winnipeg will rejoice.

'Dublin and Belfast will rejoice. Glasgow, Edinburgh and Aberdeen will rejoice.

'Bristol will rejoice. Cardiff and Swansea will rejoice. Birmingham, Manchester and Leeds will rejoice.

'Marseilles will rejoice. Bordeaux will rejoice. Amsterdam, The Hague and Rotterdam will rejoice.

'Stockholm, Oslo and Helsinki will rejoice. Madrid will rejoice. Lisbon will rejoice. Rome, Milan and Naples will rejoice.

'Vienna will rejoice. Athens will rejoice. Belgrade, Budapest and Warsaw will rejoice.

'Calcutta will rejoice. Bombay, Madras and Karachi will rejoice.

'Bangkok will rejoice, Singapore, Hong Kong and Jakarta will rejoice.

'Sydney will rejoice, Melbourne will rejoice, Adelaide, Perth and Brisbane will rejoice.

'Auckland will rejoice. Wellington, Christchurch and Dunedin will rejoice.

'Can Mr. P.W. Botha be serious when he asks who will rejoice when the Nationalist Government is toppled from power? Surely he knows the answer:

'The whole bloody world will rejoice.'

Donald Woods (The Daily Dispatch).

Following his banning order, Donald Woods, his wife Wendy and their children, fled South Africa for Lesotho and then Botswana in 1978. The family arrived in Britain to start a new life in June 1978. An active political writer, Donald Woods still concerns himself with South Africa. The film, *Cry Freedom,* banned in South Africa, was based on his books *Biko* and *Asking for Trouble.*

• *Donald Woods is a listed person and cannot be quoted in South Africa. Special permission to reproduce his editorial was obtained from the Director of Security Legislation.*

'We hate the language and we hate the owners of it'

The Soweto Riots, as reported in The Times, 1976

This is how it went on that 16 June 1976:

07h00-09h30: High school children move from school to school demonstrating against the use of Afrikaans as a teaching medium. They carry placards and urge passive pupils to join them.

09h30: A crowd 5 000-strong confronts policemen in the vicinity of Orlando West High School. The police try to halt the march and remove the placards. The police are stoned; a 13-year-old boy is killed and seven children injured by gunfire. Sociologist Dr Melville Edelstein is killed. Police are withdrawn from the area.

10h00: Youths collect in the area of Orlando West High School. A West Rand Administration Board official is clubbed to death nearby, the black municipal policeman accompanying him is knocked unconscious and is burned to death in his vehicle.

10h00-12h30: Police take up positions near Orlando station and call for reinforcements. Army helicopters and ammunition are requested.

13h30: Teargas is dropped by helicopters on Orlando West High School to disperse crowds of youths. Vehicles are set alight. The riot squad moves into the Morris Isaacson High School area.

14h00: More police reinforcements are sent in as fires break out near Phefeni station.

14h20: A heavily armed column of police vehicles leaves Orlando police station for the hill overlooking Orlando West High School where huge crowds of youths have been gathering. The crowd has dispersed.

15h30: Reports come in of large groups of youths moving at random, stoning cars. A beer lorry is set alight near the Jabulani police station. Thirty-six other vehicles are reported burning. The West Rand Administration Board buildings in Dube and Jabulani are fired. An anti-terrorist force from Johannesburg moves into the area of the Phefeni station. They are dressed in camouflage suits and carry light machine guns.

15h00-16h00: Police use teargas around the burning WRAB buildings in Dube and Jabulani. Crowds of youths disperse temporarily. More armed police reinforcements arrive at Orlando police station.

17h00: New fires break out.

20h00: Twenty buildings are burning, including the Urban Bantu Council building. Widespread looting of shops and bottle stores. More armed police reinforcements arrive.

20h30: Attempts are made to set fire to a garage and bottle store on the Soweto-Noordgesig boundary.

22h00: Fourteen Hippo armoured personnel carriers arrive and are immediately deployed in the most volatile areas.

Nicholas Ashford

Reporting for *The Times* as its southern Africa correspondent, was Nicholas Ashford. Together with a colleague from Associated Press, he drove into Soweto. Shortly after they had passed Orlando Football Stadium, their car was forced off the road by a car driven by blacks. Although Ashford was no stranger to war or to riots (he had covered both the Arab-Israeli war in 1973 and the Portuguese revolution and its aftermath in 1974-5), he nonetheless feared the worst. Getting out of his car, he discovered that the car which stopped him was full of journalists from *Drum.* They told him not to go any further — Melville Edelstein lay dead a few blocks away — and they urged him to turn the car around and leave Soweto.

Although Ashford covered the Soweto riots from beginning to end, he found it was the unpredictability of the rioting that made it difficult for him, and other journalists, to report. 'The main problem was that you had a police force which at that stage was fairly frightened, because as far as I could see, they hadn't coped with an upheaval of this magnitude before, and of course, they weren't properly equipped with helmets, or trained to deal with the situation.

'On the other side, you had an often very angry crowd, and although they could see that you were not in uniform, the fact that you had a white face, at least initially, made you the enemy.' It took quite a lot of persuasion to convince a crowd that they were not only journalists but foreign journalists.

His first report for *The Times* on the Soweto riots was carried on the front page of the newspaper and appeared on 17 June 1976.

SIX DIE AFTER SOUTH AFRICAN POLICE OPEN FIRE ON RIOTERS

The worst outbreak of civil unrest in South Africa for 16 years claimed six lives yesterday. More than 60 people were injured in the rioting at Soweto, the African township outside Johannesburg. The rioting began during a march by black students protesting against the use of Afrikaans in lessons. Police opened fire and cars and buildings were set on fire. Two of the dead were reported to be white motorists and another two were black children.

ARMY REINFORCEMENTS ARE CALLED INTO SOWETO

Johannesburg June 16

Army reinforcements were called into Soweto, Johannesburg's huge African township, tonight after a day of rioting which left six people dead and more than 60 wounded.

Late tonight the township was still in turmoil with roving bands attacking and looting buildings and setting fire to shops and vehicles while hundreds of armed police and anti-terrorist units attempted to restore order.

The riot, which began as a protest march by 10 000 black students against the use of Afrikaans in lessons, is the worst outbreak of racial unrest in South Africa since Sharpeville, 16 years ago. Police opened fire on the students who had started pelting them with stones after police had tried to intercept their demonstration.

The full extent of the death and violence involved so far is unclear because ambulance drivers trying to reach the riot areas were being hampered by stone-throwing crowds of angry blacks. However, the dead are said to include two whites and three blacks. The final toll may be considerably higher.

One of the whites, Mr Melville Edelstein, was a senior official of the West Rand Urban Bantu Administration Board which is responsible for running Soweto. A man of known liberal views, he was the author of a book entitled 'What do young Africans think?'

The other white was also a board employee. He was dragged from his car and then clubbed and stabbed to death. Later a banner was placed over his mutilated body saying: "Beware — Afrikaans is the most dangerous drug for our future".

Two of the blacks killed were schoolchildren. Both died of multiple injuries and gunshot wounds. The third black to be killed was an elderly man. Unknown numbers of policemen as well as four white women were injured, and two police dogs were hacked to death.

Tonight Soweto was illuminated by fires of burning buildings. Among the buildings set on fire was Soweto's "town hall", the Urban Bantu Council Chamber, the township showpiece.

In the first move by the Government since black students started boycotting classes over the Afrikaans issue more than four weeks ago, it was announced that Soweto's schools would be closed until the weekend. All bus services have also been suspended. Meanwhile, the inhabitants of Soweto are planning to organize a "stay at home" campaign tomorrow.

In Parliament, Mr James Kruger, the Minister of Justice and Police, said the situation in Soweto was still fluid and the police were trying to move the rioters away from residential areas and into open ground. The Army reinforcements which included armoured cars and armoured vehicles, were expected to take part.

Mr Kruger said he believed the police had used as little force as possible. They had first used tear gas to try to disperse the crowd but this had not been successful. They then fired warning shots and this stopped the students for a while and then they advanced again. Blacks who were present at the scene denied that warning shots had been fired.

When I visited Soweto this afternoon a thick pall of smoke caused by tear gas and burning vehicles hung over a small hill where the riot was taking place. Two Army Alouette helicopters made repeated sorties over the riot area as reinforcements of armed police moved there. Eyewitnesses said the helicopters were dropping tear gas canisters.

All available police in Soweto, as well as detachments from Johannesburg, including anti-terrorist units, have been sent to the township.

The mood of the inhabitants was very hostile towards all whites. At Orlando police station two women were dragged away by the police for shouting: "Kill the whites." As I drove to the riot area a car full of Africans waved me down and warned me that if I went any farther I would be killed by rioting students.

The riot started early today when high school pupils began congregating at several points in Soweto to march on Phefeni junior secondary school, the focal point of the protest against the use of Afrikaans as a medium of instruction.

The protest march of up to 10,000 students started peacefully, although the mood was tense. Students carried banners with slogans denouncing the use of Afrikaans such as "Down with Afrikaans", "We are not Boers" and "Viva Azania" (the name given to South Africa by black nationalists). They also sang the black anthem, *Nkosi Sikeleli Afrika* (God Bless Africa).

Armed police tried to surround the pupils as they converged on Phefeni school which lies on a small hill not far from the huge Orlando power station which dominates the rows of barrack-like houses where more than one million blacks live. At one stage the entire hill was covered with chanting and shouting pupils.

What happened next is still unclear. According to a senior police official at Orlando police station, his men were forced to open fire when the students started stoning the police and their vehicles. Asked whether the police had first fired into the air he said: "No, we fired into the crowd. It's no good firing over their heads."

According to Miss Sophie Tema, a reporter from *The World*, a newspaper for black readers, the rioting started when children taunted the police, a policeman threw a teargas shell and the demonstrators then replied with stones.

She said a crowd of several thousand students had gathered in front of Phefeni school when about 10 police vehicles containing about 30 policemen, mainly blacks, arrived. A section of the crowd then began taunting the police and waving placards at them. A white policeman replied by hurling what appeared to be a teargas shell.

Miss Tema said the crowd immediately became angry and began throwing stones and any other objects they could find. At no stage, she said, did the police warn the students to disperse. She then saw a white policeman pull out his revolver, point it and fire. Other policemen then began firing.

The students then started running and she saw one hit in the chest and fall. She then saw a boy of about six or seven years old fall with a bullet wound. "He had a bloody froth on his lips and he seemed to be so seriously hurt so I took him to Phefeni clinic but he was dead when we arrived", Miss Tema said.

Brigadier R. Le Roux, who is directing operations in Soweto, described the situation as "very bad. Everything is in such an upheaval it is impossible to say exactly what is going on." Later in the day he refused to make any statements to the press and made it clear that action would be taken against journalists unless they left the area. Black journalists warned their white colleagues they would be lynched if they tried to approach the rioters.

All the injured blacks were taken to Baragwanath hospital on the outskirts of the township. A hospital spokesman said 19 of them had bullet wounds.

The boycott of Soweto schools began in mid-May and last week an estimated 5,000 children were on strike at seven schools. Their complaint goes back to a ruling two years ago by the local Bantu Educational Department that instruction in black schools in

The most historic of all the photographs to come out of Soweto 1976: Sam Nzima's stark picture of 16 June's first casualty: Hector Peterson. It was used on front pages all round the world (The World).

southern Transvaal should be carried out in both English and Afrikaans on a 50-50 basis.

The students, and many sympathetic teachers, have protested that this ruling is unfair and discriminatory. White children can still choose between either language, whereas blacks have to be taught in both in addition to their own home language. They are particularly opposed to the use of Afrikaans, which they regard as the language of apartheid.

Although their protest is basically about the language issue it also reflects the growth of militancy and sense of "black consciousness" among young Africans. Many of the rioting students, as well as some adults who joined them, were giving Black Power salutes today.

Mrs Winnie Mandela, wife of the imprisoned nationalist leader Mr Nelson Mandela, said today: "The language issue is merely the spark that lit the resentment that is building up among black people. Every car that looked like a white man's car was burned. That was nothing to do with Afrikaans."

The riot, only a week before Mr Vorster, the Prime Minister, sets out for Germany, for talks with Dr Henry Kissinger, the United States Secretary of State, could not have come at a worst time for the South African Government. Dr Kissinger is expected to tell Mr Vorster that South Africa must change its race policies if it is to count on Western support in helping to solve the problems of southern Africa.

On 18 June, *The Times,* in a front-page story, enlarged on the previous day's rioting. In a leader headed 'From Sharpeville to Soweto', the newspaper pointed out that an explosion had long been predicted: 'the wonder has rather been that — in spite of many strikes, demonstrations and protests which have taken place with occasional casualties — the South African police have so long managed to keep the lid down.' On 19 June *The Times* carried another front-page story from Ashford:

MR VORSTER ORDERS POLICE TO USE ALL MEANS TO END RIOTS

Tough action to stop rioting in South Africa's black townships seemed certain last night after a statement by Mr Vorster, the Prime Minister. He told Parliament the Government would not be intimidated. Nor would it hesitate to act because of his coming talks with Dr Kissinger. Unofficial figures put the death toll in three days of rioting at around 97 with 1,000 hurt.

97 reported dead in three days of clashes

Johannesburg, June 18

As violence and rioting spread across the Rand like a veldt fire today, Mr Vorster, the South African Prime Minister, issued a warning in Parliament that the Government would not be intimidated by the three-day-old explosion of violence in the black townships.

With rioting continuing in Soweto and eight other areas tonight, the unofficial death toll rose to around 97 with more than 1,000 people injured. Police and hospitals were refusing any further official figures.

Tough Government action seems certain following the Prime Minister's statement and an announcement by Mr James Kruger, the Minister of Justice and Police, that all public outdoor meetings are banned until June 29.

414

Mr Vorster told a tense House of Assembly that the police had been instructed to use all means at their disposal to protect lives and property. They were to act without regard to persons. He said the riots were obviously not a spontaneous eruption, but a purposeful attempt to polarize people, the object of which was to create large-scale panic. He added that the police were busy restoring order and there was no reason to panic.

The Prime Minister said it would be a mistake to think that the Government would hesitate to take action because of his coming talks with Dr Kissinger, the United States Secretary of State. However important these talks were, the public order in South Africa was more important to him.

Mr Vorster is expected to leave tomorrow to meet Dr Kissinger in Germany.

The most serious new outbreak of violence today was in Alexandra township, a small isolated black area in the north-eastern suburbs of Johannesburg. At least 25 people were shot, some of them fatally, as police opened fire on protesting crowds of Africans.

Among those shot was a 23-year-old man, Mr Felix Mtlhongo, who was killed when police fired into a crowd that was taunting them. He was not among the crowd but was visiting a friend in the area.

Violence spilled into the neighbouring white suburbs with the stoning of cars and an attack on two white women. It caused the partial closure of Louis Botha Avenue, in Johannesburg, one of the main arteries leading into the city from Pretoria.

It is unclear how the violence started in Alexandra except that students began marching early in the morning in support of their counterparts in Soweto who have been protesting against the use of Afrikaans as a medium of instruction in black schools. When I arrived there shortly after 9 am, at least one building was ablaze, cars had been overturned, shops looted and, as in Soweto, a strong element of hooliganism had been injected into the demonstration.

New fires broke out in Alexandra this afternoon and sporadic shooting continued. The coloured primary school was set on fire and this was followed by two explosions in the middle of the township where the business area is.

According to first official estimates at least 84 buildings have been burned out or badly damaged during the Soweto riots. They include three schools and nearly all administrative buildings as well as beer halls and liquor stores owned by the West Rand Urban Bantu Administration Board. More than 120 vehicles have also been wrecked.

Outside Johannesburg the rioting was most serious in the township of Tembisa, not far from Jan Smuts international airport.

Other East Rand townships affected by rioting included Katlehong, near Germiston, Vosloorus, near Boksburg, and Daveyton, near Benoni. A total of seven Africans were killed on the East Rand today. On the West Rand one student was killed when schoolchildren tried to attack an administrative officer at Mahlakong township near Randfontein.

Tonight Brigadier J.F. Vissier, Assistant Police Commissioner for the Witwatersrand, said that Navy, Army and other defence force units were on standby and were ready to move to key points if necessary. "We have forces at all trouble spots and all potential trouble spots," he said.

There were few reporters, whether British, German, French or South African, who did not have some kind of tension-filled experience during their reporting of the Soweto riots. *The Star* photographer Alf Chapman had the unnerving experience of facing a mob head-on, camera in hand; his car was rocked by rampaging students but he was able to drive off and his picture made *The Star*'s 16 June front page. Harry Mashabela, also of *The Star,* was telephoning his newspaper from Dr Aaron Mathlare's house when he shouted into the phone: 'They are burning the house down. I have to go,' and ran out of the house, leaving the receiver dangling.

Reporter Fanyana Shiburi heard a shout: 'Here is a White!' saw a mob hurl a rock through the hapless driver's window, pull the man out by his hair and stone him to death. Lucy Gough Burger, photographing pupils at Phefeni School, was pinioned against her car by a student mob. 'Get out, white woman,' they chanted. Derrick Thema, *Rand Daily Mail* reporter, saw a mob pull a man from a car and stone him to death. Another reporter staggered into his newsroom, his shirtfront wet with the blood of a dying child he had held in his arms.

Nicholas Ashford, like many other reporters during those tense days, had to place himself in potentially dangerous situations to get his story. He wrote the following calm despatch, which appeared in *The Times* on 19 June, after a nerve-wracking drive through the accessible parts of a burning and tense Alexandra.

'GO BACK OR THEY WILL KILL YOU' WARNING

Alexandra Township
Johannesburg, June 18
Today it was the turn of this black enclave on the north-eastern fringes of Johannesburg to suffer the agony which Soweto has been experiencing for the past three days. While buildings burned and shops were looted, men, women and children were being felled by police bullets.

This morning I and two colleagues visited Alexandra shortly after trouble broke out and before the area was sealed off by armed police. In the centre of the township smoke and flames billowed from a burning building. Men, who had returned home from their jobs, eyed us suspiciously but not with the same hostility I experienced in Soweto two days ago. Carloads of excited Africans drove past, cheering and giving clenched fist Black Power salutes.

Unlike Soweto, which is several miles from Johannesburg and can be quickly isolated, Alexandra is uncomfortably close to white areas.

The neat, spacious white homes with their manicured lawns and double garages are little more than a stone's throw from the mean, unmade streets of Alexandra where blacks live up to seven to a room in houses without electricity or water. It is because of its proximity to white areas that the township is gradually being demolished and its inhabitants moved to other areas.

On the perimeter of the township a group of young policemen, dressed in camouflage uniform, nervously clutched rifles and automatics. In nearby factories we could see groups of white civilian vigilantes armed with rifles surveying the scene in the township.

One of the soldiers ran towards us. "Go back, go back, or they will kill you," he cried. In fact, the Africans looked considerably less menacing than he did, so we decided to talk to them. When they heard we were British journalists they became friendly and talked openly to us, expressing their hatred of the system under which they were forced to live.

They admitted there was a hooligan element behind the violence, but said it was the only way of expressing their pent-up emotions of bitterness and despair. The issue of compulsory Afrikaans language lessons in schools which started the Soweto rioting was a symbol of a much more deep-seated resentment. "We hate the language and we hate the owners of it," one said.

Another, a qualified motor mechanic, said he earned only £14 a month whereas white apprentices were paid four times as much. "There are no jobs and the people are just rotting here. There are men here who have degrees but cannot work."

The group talked about the hated pass law system. They said the police raided their homes late at night, kicked in their doors and dragged away those who did not have permits to be there. "What does a youngster think if he sees a relation or a friend being taken away in handcuffs just because he does not have a permit?" one said.

All agreed that the present unrest was going to continue and probably get worse. "The whites are stupid if they think they can get away with the present system," the mechanic said.

While we were talking we suddenly heard a burst of gunfire from the group of policemen who by that time were about 200 yards away down the road. First there were single shots and then automatic fire. One of my colleagues saw one of the policemen fire, apparently unprovoked, into a crowd of Africans. Certainly we saw no sign of any stones being thrown at the police.

Shortly afterwards the dead and wounded started arriving at a clinic nearby. Two men and a woman came in with gunshot wounds in their legs. Another woman was brought in the back of a lorry with a bullet in her chest. An old lady had blood pouring from her head. There was blood everywhere.

Alf Chapman of The Star, *at some risk to himself, took this photograph of a mob of schoolchildren running through the streets of Soweto. The photograph, which was widely duplicated in other papers, made the front page of* The Star *on the day it happened: 16 June 1976.*

The clinic was unequipped to deal with this type of injury. Black and white doctors and nurses patched them up as best they could and then waited for ambulances to take them to hospital. "Please help us," pleaded Sister Teresa, who was in charge of the clinic. "We do not have sufficient transport. Can you take some of them to hospital?"

A young boy was loaded into the back of my car. He was completely unconscious from a huge bleeding wound over his left eye. "Oh, my God, this is terrible," said one of the Irish sisters at the clinic.

We were told to take the boy to the General Hospital in Johannesburg, which is supposed to be for whites only, but will take blacks in an emergency. When we arrived at the casualty entrance a doctor looked at the youth, took his pulse and then said, politely, but firmly: "Would you mind taking him to the non-European hospital nearby."

There the injured from Alexandra were already starting to arrive. "We have received at least 10 already and we have run out of stretchers," said the sister. The boy was dragged unceremoniously from the car by two orderlies and heaved bodily into the hospital. There was a hoot from behind and I moved on as another car came to unload its bloody cargo.

Although the rioting was by no means over, it had abated, and reporters began to write wrap-around stories: why and how Soweto 1976 had happened. Full analyses would come later. *The Times,* sober and factual to the last, carried this report on the riots by Ashford on 20 June, after which date Soweto, although frequently mentioned in the paper, moved off the front page.

SOUTH AFRICANS ASK WHAT WAS THE REAL CAUSE OF BLACK TOWNSHIP RIOTS

Johannesburg, June 20

Like a person recovering from a gigantic hangover, a sullen and uneasy calm settled over the black townships of the Witwatersrand this weekend after a three-day orgy of rioting which left an estimated 100 dead and probably more than 1,000 injured.

While black and white leaders started to take stock of the millions of pounds worth of damage done by the rioters, questions began to be asked as to why the Government had failed to anticipate the trouble and how such a catastrophe could be prevented in future.

The upheavals ended almost as abruptly as they started. After sporadic outbreaks of looting and violence yesterday morning in Soweto and some of the east Rand townships, order was restored during the afternoon and the townships enjoyed one of their quietest Saturday nights in months. Today a police official said the situation was calm but that police were remaining on the alert.

A shortage of food and liquor caused by looting, together with a sudden cold snap which sent mid-winter temperatures well below freezing point, contributed to the swift subsidence of violence. Rioters also appear to have heeded the warning by Mr Vorster, the Prime Minister, on Friday that the police would use all means at their disposal to quell the disturbances.

Probably of more importance, however, was the reaction of moderate black opinion in the townships against the continuation of senseless violence by young hooligans. For, as the smoke from the burning buildings and vehicles began to clear, it became evident that what had begun as a protest against discrimination had been used by hooligans and vandals as an opportunity to plunder and loot. By no means all who died were innocent victims.

418

In some townships black vigilantes armed with knives and sticks formed their own patrols to protect people and property from the marauding bands of *tsotsis* (young hooligans). Taxi drivers were offering to help police clear the streets and in Tembisa, north-east of Johannesburg.

In Alexandra the damage seemed to have been even greater though it had suffered only one day of disturbance. A large clinic had been ransacked and every window smashed. Smoke was still smouldering from some burnt out shops, the charred skeleton of a bus was smashed into the wall of a house. Some shops in the neighbouring white suburbs had also had their windows broken.

Mr Sam Moss, a member of the Transvaal Provincial Council, said at least 25 years work, in terms of public buildings and amenities, had been destroyed. He estimated that the damage in Soweto alone could total as much as £20m and probably £30m in the Witwatersrand as a whole.

Yesterday the Government, after three days of procrastination, took its first positive step to defuse the situation when Mr M.C. Botha, the Minister of Bantu Administration, held talks in Pretoria with Soweto leaders.

A communiqué issued after the meeting said 11 Soweto delegates had pleaded with the minister to reconsider the so-called fifty-fifty principle under which black school-children are supposed to be taught in both English and Afrikaans. The riots began when police opened fire on a demonstration by schoolchildren protesting against the use of Afrikaans in lessons.

For his part, Mr Botha explained that the fifty-fifty principle was not a hard and fast rule and schools could apply to deviate from it. He said the "tragic occurrences in Soweto were caused by misunderstandings and confusion". Two more meetings between Soweto leaders and Government officials have been arranged for later this month.

The question now being asked is: What was the real cause of the riots? Were black feelings deliberately excited by political agitators? as the Government seems to think. Was Afrikaans the real issue or was it merely the spark that ignited the whole powder keg of urban African grievances?

According to Mr James Kruger, the Minister of Justice and Police, there was every reason to suspect there had been some organizing factor behind the riots. A certain section of blacks was seeking a confrontation with whites, he said.

The Minister claimed that Black Power movements were linked with communists and were working for unrest within the country. The movements were working in co-operation with organizations and individuals in London and elsewhere overseas. He had been expecting trouble for some time, which was why the Government had armed itself with new internal security legislation.

However, black school teachers remain adamant that teaching in Afrikaans was the principal cause. One of Soweto's most respected headmasters, Mr Wilkie Kambule, of Orlando High School, said in a newspaper interview: "The main reason is that young blacks these days tend to be radical and they see Afrikaans as the language of the people in authority. The continuing refusal of the Government to realize this is the most dangerous factor in the whole situation."

The opposition English-language press today urged the government to recognize the warning signs before it was too late.

But probably the most interesting comment was contained in the pro-Government Afrikaans newspaper *Rapport.* Referring to the Sharpeville shootings 16 years ago, it asked how it was "that this thing from which we so much wanted to spare ourselves, and our children has happened again?"

"Have we really changed so little?"

It urged that the Afrikaans-language ruling should be suspended.

Meanwhile, both blacks and whites have been asking why the police could not have used less lethal weapons than rifles and automatics to quell the riots — such as rubber bullets or water cannon. According to Mr Kruger the police have tried experiments with these and found that "they made people tame to the gun." Rioters must know that when a policeman picked up his rifle the best thing was to get out of the way immediately.

He added that 22 of the people who had died during the rioting were shot with bullets of a calibre different from those used by the police. So far, however, there have been no reported cases of any policeman suffering from gunshot wounds.

'Sweep the evil spirits out of the ring'

Bert Blewett, Sunday Tribune, 1978

For sportswriter Bert Blewett the boxing match between Tap Tap Makhatini and Daniel Mapanya was an interesting but not unusual event. With other sports journalists he took his seat at the ringside in Durban on the night of 2 September 1978 and sat back in anticipation. The two boxers came into the ring and, to everyone's astonishment and Mapanya's visible horror, a sizeable impi of Zulu warriors stormed the ring. In the mêlée, recalls Blewett, no one was certain what was happening.

Makhatini, supported by the Zulus and their battlecry encouragement, almost swelled with confidence. Mapanya, who was later to request that the match be declared invalid because he had been cursed, stood in horror.

In retrospect, it was nothing more than modern boxing hype, but as recently as 1978 it was unprecedented in South African boxing. Blewett, shaken like the rest of the correspondents, wrote this report for the following day's *Sunday Tribune*. Bert Blewett knows what he is writing about: he joined the Natal Boxing Board of Control in 1971 to become a licensed referee and judge, resigning that occupation in 1973 to become a boxing writer.

The night Makhatini's muti man mesmerized Mapanya

'TONIGHT YOU DIE' HE HISSED

The curse of a witchdoctor turned a champ into a chump at West Ridge Park on Monday night — and it happened right there in front of 8 000 people.

As Daniel Mapanya climbed through the ropes to defend his South African middle-weight title against Tap Tap Makhatini he was confronted by an incredible sight.

A Zulu impi in full tribal regalia had been allowed to invade the ring.

As they shouted war cries and brandished shields, their leader stomped his way across the canvas and deliberately bumped into the champion.

"Tonight you die," he hissed — and almost hit Mapanya with the knobkerrie he was wielding.

Mapanya claims he lost the fight there and then. "You should have made them sweep the evil spirits out of the ring," he later told his manager David Smith.

And whether you believe African folklore or not, the fact remains that no fighter should have his concentration broken by such amazing antics only seconds before he is called upon to defend his South African title — and his world-ranking.

Even in the United States, the home of all that is bizarre in showbiz, such incidents are not tolerated. Mentally a fighter is probably at his most vulnerable when he enters the ring and it is common practice to keep him quiet and undisturbed until the first bell rings.

Throughout the day Mapanya's trainers had worked towards that end. Smith even instructed the fighter not to accept any phone calls in the afternoon, insisting that he should have a complete rest.

The Zulu dancing took the Mapanya camp completely by surprise. They were astonished to find the ring crowded with prancing men and looked to the Natal Boxing Control Board to clear it.

But Mr Mike Mortimer, chairman of the Board, later admitted the dancing had got out of control and said it was never intended that the Zulus should enter the ring.

Makhatini meanwhile was walking on cloud nine. He had even joined in the dancing himself and he must have been the most motivated man at West Ridge Park.

It showed in round one when he sauntered out of his corner and dropped Mapanya with a vicious left hook. He never knew what hit him and he was still trying to put the pieces together when Makhatini floored him twice more in the second round.

Nothing he tried worked. His cornermen were imploring him to stand off and box. But there was a complete lack of communication. He just wasn't listening.

The witchdoctor's curse had blown his mind. Makhatini's punches had scrambled his

Tap Tap Makhatini digs a right to the body of Mapanya in their championship fight at West Ridge Park (Sunday Tribune).

422

Bert Blewett, boxing writer, former referee and judge.

brain. He did everything wrong. He went to close quarters when he should have boxed at long range. He walked into one left hook after another. His own punches lacked sting.

But when Makhatini sliced open a deep cut on Mapanya's right eye in the fourth round it momentarily broke the spell. For a brief moment the champion fought back furiously, driving Makhatini to the ropes and bombarding him with an avalanche of punches.

By round six he was back in complete control and he dropped Mapanya with a beautiful combination in the 7th before knocking him out with an explosive left hook to the jaw after 1 min 16 sec.

As Mapanya went crashing on to his back and struggled to regain his feet, my mind flashed back to a conversation I had with Smith earlier in the day.

"Daniel is seldom nervous," Smith had said. "The only thing he ever fears is the unknown. He was worried when he fought Dan Snyder because it was the first time he had met an American. Tap Tap doesn't bother him. He knows what to expect."

But he never expected the ring to be crowded with Zulu warriors. He never expected a witchdoctor to curse him. And he never expected Makhatini to be so supremely confident.

'We howl, bray and beg for the knockout'

Chris Greyvenstein, SA Boxing World, 1980

In the late 1970s, South African boxing fans became wildly excited over the world title aspirations of local heavyweights Kallie Knoetze and Gerrie Coetzee. In the space of 12 months both were beaten and swept from the international scene, Knoetze permanently and Coetzee, who went on to win the championship, temporarily.

Chris Greyvenstein covered both matches for *SA Boxing World.* Although no longer employed as a sports writer (he is managing editor of the *Cape Times*), Greyvenstein entered the tight-knit world of sports writing when he was assigned to help the brilliant but aging *Sunday Express* sports writer, Charlie Lamb. Too old to type, Lamb dictated his stories to Greyvenstein and, too old to see clearly, frequently confused one player with another. Greyvenstein discreetly corrected Lamb's dictated stories before sending them for setting.

Gerrie Coetzee met Mike Weaver at Sun City in a bid to take the World Boxing Association heavyweight title from him. The fight was staged with all the glitz for which the venue is famed, although it raised no enthusiasm in Greyvenstein's elegant despatch. 'It's showbusiness,' he noted, 'but it's showbusiness with blood.' The article was written within hours of the fight and appeared in *SA Boxing World* in December 1980.

THE SUN CITY SHOWDOWN

by CHRIS GREYVENSTEIN

We select the strangest burial grounds for our champions these days. Norman Sekgapane and Kallie Knoetze went down in the dust of Mmabatho while Gerrie Coetzee's heavyweight title hopes are interred, temporarily we hope, in the crater of an extinct volcano in the Pilanesberg hills; not far from where President Paul Kruger once owned two farms in the heart of what I am told is the finest cattle country in the land.

It could be around here, some say, that the Kruger Millions have been hidden for the past 80 years, nearly 65 000 ounces of raw gold worth R320 million at the current price.

Nobody digs for treasure here anymore; most prefer to try blackjack, roulette, chemin de fer and punto banco in the air-conditioned dusk of Sun City's hexagon-shaped casino, braving the shimmering, glittering confusion of mirrors, chrome, glass and artificial waterfalls rather than the Bushveld sun beating down on the surrounding slopes with their forbidding thorn trees.

An 18-hole golf course designed by Gary Player himself, three squash courts, an eight-lane ten-pin bowling alley, a cluster of tennis courts and saunas now stand where long-horned cattle and white-faced goats had once in their turn replaced the lion and antelope which roamed here for untold centuries.

Nearly 20 000 of us undertook the safari, happily following the beat of the publicity tom-toms, to see Coetzee challenge Mike Weaver for the World Boxing Association heavyweight title. For some it was a 30-minute hop by air but for most it was five times as long by road from Johannesburg, through hamlets and villages, past a monastery, a convent, a seminary, a sign advertising the largest platinum mine in the world, and, as a final warning to those about to stand in queues to drool over the uncut versions of "The Happy Hooker" and "The Stud", a revivalist tent on the outskirts of Rustenburg.

A steeply-rising hill and on the other side is hotel entrepreneur Sol Kerzner's answer to Kubla Khan, his own "stately pleasure dome", an ochre-coloured palace which convinces me anyway, that Samuel Coleridge Taylor's Eastern prince is behind on points.

This was to be the central piece, the focal point, for the milling thousands until it was time to trudge the dusty few hundred yards up to the stadium, miraculously constructed from 130 tonnes of steel in less than four months, most of which was spent in planning rather than on building.

A tough old cop with no faith in the Juvenile Court cured me of the gambling instinct some 35 years ago in the backyard of a monumental masonry opposite the Brixton cemetery in Johannesburg. Sun City was not going to succeed where Mar del Plata and Las Vegas have failed. The usual pre-fight wrangles and rumours, the problems of the organisers and the antics of the supporting casts, hold far more fascination than one-armed bandits anyway.

The place is swarming with boxing writers from all over the world, emphasising and justifying their predictions to each other. Big fight predictions are pointless, really, but what will the people do for laughs if the writers stop making them?

Wilf Rosenberg, who has the uncanny knack to solve all problems and consequently is on the receiving end of everyone's hassle, has made his mark in another sport and therefore does not have to be a boxing expert. He is chatting amiably to Mannetjies Roux, also a rugby Springbok but of a slightly later vintage than himself, when Jay Edson, looking for all the world like a king-sized canary in his yellow Southern Sun outfit, comes puffing up with the latest knot to unravel. "Mother Neale wants another seat," he says in a resigned sort of way. "She wants to sit where she can look into Coetzee's eyes. Wants to psyche him or something. Can you help?"

Rosenberg settles it by giving Weaver's guru his own seat and before he goes off on his next mission Edson, a kindly man who has been around the fight business long enough to know every angle, asks if we had heard that Coetzee had turned down an offer of R35 000 to use trunks with a sponsor's name on it. "Can you believe it?" he muses. "Just 'cause he wants to wear the trunks his old lady made? Jeez, I dunno . . ."

The usual exhibitionist pops up. Stark naked he finds a seat and hopes to be noticed. Everybody studiously ignores him and his act is a flop.

Kallie Knoetze is also around and talking, but nobody is listening much, even if he is still a darn good rugby player. All eyes, instead, are on Marvin Hagler, fresh from beating Alan Minter and the only world champion with an undivided kingdom recognised by both the WBA and the WBC. "Marvelous Marvin" is bald and looks menacing, but actually he is a nice man with charming manners.

Floyd Patterson makes his way rapidly through the throng, self-effacing as ever and with the worried expression of someone who is trying to remember what he had done with the car keys.

There is no place for a special social rating in the over-crowded hotel but there are little pockets where the very rich and the very important cluster in the safety of each other's company. They cast bleak looks at the steaming masses around them and pretend that they are somewhere else.

We exchange hopeful handshakes with the men who control boxing in South Africa: Mr Justice H.W.O. Kloppers, cool and comfortable in a fashionable sports shirt, Dr Izak Labuschagne, his usual affable self, Mike Mortimer, Clive Noble and Marcus Temple, clean-cut, confident men, reflecting the new image of boxing, light years removed from the days of James R. Couper and Woolf Bendoff, battling with skintight gloves in a corrugated-iron enclosure. Stanley

Chris Greyvenstein (Cape Times).

Christodoulou's handsome face shows uncharacteristic tension; as the Board's Executive Director, Stan has carried the heavy responsibility of reconciling powerful and conflicting interests.

Somebody must have slipped up. The discs which give us entry into the Gary Player Country Club are blue and white and not the omnipresent Southern Sun yellow — or is it orange? But the hospitality is appreciated and it helps to see old friends like Pat Jackson, the last South African trainer to be in the winning corner in a world title fight. He is under contract to give his comments exclusively to one of the Sunday papers and the example of chequebook journalism reminds old-timers of some of the stunts cooked-up in more original days to get the fight news on the front pages.

There was the time for instance when one of Joe ("Yussel") Jacobs's fighters lost a close decision to Young Stribling in the Deep South. Jacobs earned himself acres of space by claiming that the Ku Klux Klan had influenced the officials because he was a Jew. Before the return fight in Newark, New Jersey, an enterprising fellow hired a couple of bums, put flour sacks over their heads, and ordered them to chase Jacobs down the street. It nearly caused a race riot but it also made a good front page story.

It is time to go and we scuffle through the dust to the stadium gates. There are the ones who obviously went into training with a bottle to defend honour and country, but generally this is an unusually quiet and well-behaved crowd who queue patiently to be screened by the guards with their metal detectors.

426

Every possible security precaution is meticulously observed and I cannot help but think of the night so long ago when I took a bus with the late Jack Kukard to a tournament in Johannesburg's Olympia Ice Rink. I was hoping to sell programs and Jack was scheduled to fight an Irish immigrant called O'Connor in a four-rounder and I recall his dimpled smile when he thanked the gatekeeper for letting him in without a ticket, while I slipped in on his boxer's pass.

The leather-lunged Rufus Papenfus, making a welcome comeback as a Master of Ceremonies and still the best in the business, helps us through the uninspiring preliminary contests and between rounds he is assisted ably by the long-legged show-girls who hip-sway seductively around the ring with the cards announcing the number of the upcoming round.

Welile Nkosinkulu beats a wizened Argentinian bantamweight but disappoints as he seems to be under the mistaken belief that he is Tickey the Clown. Harold Volbrecht, who is a good fighter, struggles against a game and competent Coenie Bekker and Reuben Pardo and Al Styles know what it is all about but simply cannot put it together.

The ring is cleared and a dozen plumed and sequined dancers are swept through the ropes on a wave of ear-splitting music. Trim and high-stepping members of the Sun City Extravaganza show, these are really beautiful girls who glide through their act with lithe and sensuous grace.

The music shudders to a halt, the dancers freeze into pretty poses, and we know that the big moment has come.

The challenging theme from "Star Wars" thunders from what seems like a hundred amplifiers to bring Gerrie Coetzee into the ring; the music from the unforgettable "Rocky" accompanies the arrival of champion Mike Weaver. ("Mike has seen the movie 17 times", the man in the next seat whispers).

The flags are carried by tall and shapely beauties ("The one with the South African flag calls herself Christién Ling, but she is really a Miss Engelbrecht from Standerton", I am informed, unasked, by my neighbour) and soon everyone is standing to attention for the ceremonial rendering of the anthems.

It is all in rather poor taste, I feel. Girls in G-strings holding aloft the flags so many have died for, like a scene from a World War II Hollywood musical re-shot in the permissive 1980s. The patriotic prelude to big fights is becoming dangerously overheated; so stirring when it is a spontaneous crowd reaction as it was when Pierre Fourie met Bob Foster, so embarrassing when it is presented as a part of the entertainment package.

Sitting behind Coetzee's corner, I cannot see the challenger's face but Weaver is totally without emotion as he stares fixedly ahead, his bandaged hands folded in front of him, his red and blue gown with the Everlast tab comfortingly traditional. In the viewfinder of my camera he is framed on his right by manager Don Manuel, on his left by trainer Ray Barnes and the all but bare bottom of the lady brandishing the "Stars and Stripes".

Bophuthatswana's lovely anthem is played with considerable dignity, but a choir recording of "Die Stem" is deemed necessary to guide the crowd. It is followed by an American cabaret singer giving his quivering version of "The Star Spangled Banner" and with the opening bar, Weaver, the ex-Marine who saw action in Vietnam, stiffens to full attention and his right fist is clenched and held tight against his chest.

The side-show is over and Jesus Celis, the Venezuelan referee who represented his country as a featherweight in the 1950 Olympic Games, calls the fighters to the centre for brief and final instructions. This was to be the first and last time in the fight that Mr Celis, a drably-dressed, plump individual, appeared to have any control over events.

Weaver looks like a statue chipped from black marble by a Michelangelo; Coetzee is bulkier, soft and pink in comparison, his face chubby behind three-day old bristles.

But he is not the timid challenger of the John Tate debacle. He goes into the attack immediately and he lands hard and often, stopping the champion in his tracks and making him blink with shock. This is the pattern in the early rounds. Coetzee is scoring with clean, stunning punches to the head; blows which would have sent the average heavyweight crashing to the canvas. But Weaver is no ordinary heavyweight. He takes his punishment stoically and retaliates with unspectacular but murderous rips to the body. It is a good start for the challenger, however, and a female member of the champion's entourage faints and has to be carried out of the arena.

Coetzee is beginning to breathe through the mouth in the fourth round. He is standing back when he should be following up, he is not using his left-jab effectively and too often he bulls his man to the ropes only to lean on him in what seems like a futile attempt to tire him with his greater weight. No matter, I think to myself, he is ahead on points and he will regain his rhythm soon enough.

In the eighth round he does indeed and for a few precious seconds Gerrie Coetzee is the best heavyweight in the world. Weaver is in desperate trouble as an exquisitely-timed

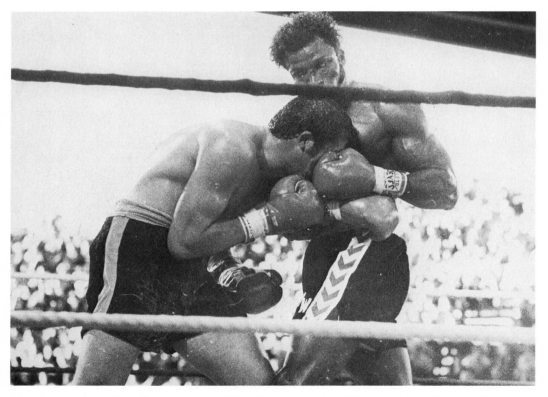

The fight at Sun City: Coetzee meets Mike Weaver head on (South African Boxing World).

428

right explodes on his chin, flinging him into the ropes where he hangs like a laundered shirt on a washing line.

We go back to the primeval urge for the kill of our hairy ancestors as we howl, bay and beg for the knockout. But somehow, Coetzee cannot get through the protective shield of those muscular arms, somehow Weaver survives until the bell.

Memory will preserve a good many things about this merciless encounter, but most vivid of all will I remember the faces of champion and challenger as they come out for the ninth round.

The light of battle has died in Coetzee's eyes and has been replaced with a look of despair, if not resignation. On Weaver's face there is an expression of serene confidence; he knows that he has survived the crucible.

"Coetzee ahead on points, but he is going to lose the fight," I scribble in my notebook and it takes no great perceptiveness to see that his punches have lost their speed and sting. He leans heavily on Weaver at every opportunity and the champion's cornermen are hurling abuse at the inept referee.

Coetzee is no quitter and he keeps trying, keeps landing rights and left-hooks to the patiently-advancing Weaver's head, but there is a jerkiness in his movements which drives the last bit of hope out of my heart.

The champion has all but made up the leeway when the 13th round starts. Coetzee is now on the defensive, flicking left-jabs and trying to keep his body out of range from those rib-busting hooks. Suddenly he jumps in and hits Weaver with jarring force to the head. The champion sweeps him back with a left; Coetzee retreats along the ropes and straight into the path of a right-hook which lands rather high but slams him heavily to the canvas.

He makes it to his feet, swaying dizzily, defenceless. The referee continues the count and Weaver celebrates his knockout victory by hurling himself into the air, triumphantly flinging his arms high above his head.

No use trying to see what is happening in the ring, now filled by officials, police and pushing, mauling photographers, all of them frantically buzzing about like flies discovering an abandoned picnic basket.

Coetzee, his gallant bid over, climbs out of the ring and he passes a few feet from me, his mother hugging him tightly. Someone is asking him something and he replies with a resigned tilt of the head, an almost imperceptible shrug. Surrounded by relatives and seconds, he disappears to the loneliest place on earth, the loser's dressingroom.

We linger on for a while, hardly noticing Charlie Weir forcing Ray Hammond to retire and Robbie Williams losing to one of Weaver's sparring partners. Instead we share with each other our disappointment at the fall of yet another South African champion. Blessed with the gift of hindsight we deplore the doleful errors and sigh over what might have been.

Back at the hotel it looks as if they are preparing to shoot a crowd scene for a disaster movie; a nightmare of noise and confusion.

We drive back through a pall of smoke caused by a veld fire, past hardier souls trying to grill their sausages and chops as forks of lightning and rolls of thunder warn of impending rain. Silently we listen to Trevor Quirk describing a Springbok rugby victory in faraway Santiago.

For no particular reason I remember the old fable about the frog who tried to jump out of the well. Last I heard the frog was still in the well.

'The chance to wear our beloved Springbok colours'

Dan Retief, Rand Daily Mail, 1981, Cape Times 1983

In his capacity as the SAAN group rugby writer, Dan Retief travelled with the Springbok rugby team under the captaincy of Wynand Claasen for the 1981 test series in New Zealand.

Previous South African internationals, marred by anti-apartheid demonstrations, were as nothing compared to the campaign which faced the Springboks on their arrival. The tour was marred, not merely by the demonstrations all Springboks had become depressingly familiar with since the mid-Sixties, but by violence. One game was called off altogether, another game was halted when a low-flying aircraft flour-bombed the field. The tour, which was a fiasco, ended with matches being played within barbed wire and police cordons and the Springboks isolated behind a tough security screen.

If it was not a happy tour (Claasen recalls it with a shudder), it was at least an interesting one. For Dan Retief, rugby writer for the *Rand Daily Mail,* this tour was arduous. Not only did he have to write about rugby, he also had to cope with reporting the demonstrations and the political manoeuvring which perforce dogged the tour.

His copy, filed late at night and early in the morning to meet his newspaper's deadlines, was a mixture of both sport and politics. Although Retief was concerned about what was happening to rugby itself, he was more concerned with the cost of the tour to New Zealand society.

Retief reported on the games with his usual distinctive style and, momentarily putting the anti-apartheid demonstrations aside, filed this brief piece on the kicking skills of a member of Claasen's team: Naas 'The Boot' Botha. It ran in the *Rand Daily Mail* and *Cape Times* on 4 August 1981.

Botha's boot upsets Kiwis

WANGANUI, New Zealand. — When New Zealanders hear the name *Naas Botha* they subconsciously whisper the opening phrase of their world-famous haka: "Ka mate, ka mate — it is death, it is death."

According to the legend the words of the haka were uttered by a Maori warrior as he lay cowering before a threatening enemy.

Fortunately for him the danger was dispelled and he was able to give joyous voice to the rest of the haka, sung in praise of the sun, who, he believed, was the god who had saved his life.

"Ka ora! ka ora!
"It is life, it is life.

Dan Retief

"This is the hairy person,

"Who caused the sun to shine!

"One upward step! Another upward step!

"One last upward step! The step forth!

"Into the sun that shines!"

Kiwis are cringing at the thought of facing the boot of Botha.

And, in the land of the long white cloud where it rains so often, you can't blame them for being pessimistic about the chances of the sun driving away the golden boy of Pretoria.

In just two games Botha has advanced from 13th to fourth place on the list of the points scorers while playing in a Springbok jersey.

Botha's 34 points in the matches against Taranaki and Manawatu advanced his total from 134 points to 168 in just 14 games, an average of 12 points a match.

He has now skipped ahead of Basie Vivier, Dougie Morkel, Ian McCallum, Jannie Engelbrecht, Gerald Bosch, Freddy Turner, Wynand Mans, Okey Geffin and Roy Dryburgh, and only Gerrie Brand (293), Piet Visagie (240) and Keith Oxlee (201) are still ahead of Botha.

Consider, however, that Brand played 46 games to register his points, Visagie 44 and Oxlee 48. The Springboks flyhalf can also lay claim to being the greatest drop kicker the game has seen. In his 14 games in the green and gold he has registered 13 drop goals.

Nearest to him are Visagie (eight in 44 games) and Bennie Osler with eight in 30 games.

Botha is already second on the list for points scored in test matches and needs to score 28 points in the three tests against the All Blacks to surpass Visagie's record of 130.

Botha and his likely opponent, Doug Rollerson, fought a keen and sometimes petulent battle in the Manawatu game.

Rollerson, who also possesses a skilled boot, started the psychological warfare when he 'nudged' Botha early on after the Springboks had kicked the ball.

Botha chased after his protagonist and though the purists would have liked him to keep his cool, Botha at least showed Rollerson that he is not to be intimidated.

They taunted each other for the rest of the game, but Botha had the final word with 16 points to the 11 kicked by Rollerson.

It was pleasing to see the two of them settling their dispute immediately the final whistle went.

Doubtless they will resume the argument in Christchurch in two weeks and only time will tell who'll be shouting: "Ka ora! Ka ora!"

Morné du Plessis (The Argus).

Springbok rugby captain Morné du Plessis retired from rugby in the middle of 1983. Dan Retief wrote a tribute to the man who captained the Springboks in the days before official rugby tours ceased, one of South Africa's finest captains and a player of stature. The article appeared in the *Cape Times* on 27 May 1983, on which paper Retief was working as sports editor.

'Your captain is a great guy . . .'

When I sat down to write a tribute to Morné du Plessis, the man who personified the spirit of Western Province rugby, a single sentence, spat out by an angry Irishman, welled up in my mind.

The words were uttered by Syd Millar, one of the great men of rugby, at a cocktail party after the second test between the 1980 Lions and the Springboks in Bloemfontein.

I remember the moment clearly for it epitomized the esteem in which Morné du Plessis is held wherever rugby is played. The day was June 14, my birthday, and the Springboks had managed a stirring, try-scoring 26-19 victory over Bill Beaumont's team.

"Your captain is a great guy . . ." That's all Syd Millar said and as I look back on the career of a man who captained Western Province in 103 of his 112 matches I can't think of a finer tribute, for the words were spoken with such respect and honesty.

The incident that led up to this little episode in the life and times of Morné du Plessis had started at breakfast on the morning of the test.

The Lions were bitterly incensed over a morning newspaper report quoting Springbok manager Butch Lochner as saying that "the difference between the two sides is that they cheat and we don't" — or something to that effect.

Now Syd Millar is not a man to be trifled with. A prop forward in his day, he knows only the language of front-row forwards and that is to pile straight in without fear or caution.

And he told that gathering at Bloemfontein just how upset his team had been at the remark attributed to Lochner, particularly in the light of the sacrifices the Lions had made to come to South Africa.

Some of the Lions later admitted that there had been talk of their returning home.

And that is where Morné stepped in. He paid tribute to the Lions for having come; he paid tribute to their brand of rugby and many a gruff man in the room swallowed hard when he thanked them for "having given us the chance today to wear our beloved Springbok colours."

"I hope that we can learn to win as graciously as you have lost," continued Morné, "and, even if it may not be my station to speak, I trust that one newspaper article, perhaps it was a misquote, will not spoil your tour for you."

It was after that that Syd Millar walked up to Lochner and said: "Your captain is a great guy."

Bill Beaumont, a 'great guy' himself, told me later: "I could never have done that; repudiate the chairman of the selectors."

Late that night there was another glimpse of Du Plessis's inherently humane touch. There he stood, arms linked with big Fran Cotton, as they lustily sang some long forgotten song. Du Plessis had led the whole of the Springbok side to the Lions' hotel to exchange friendship and memories with the vanquished visitors.

Morné du Plessis possessed what has been called the common touch. Perpetually

433

stooped forward in a concerned way, his brow wrinkled with concentration, Du Plessis radiated sincerity and honesty.

He was by no means a great orator. The quality he transmitted was not stunning eloquence but earthy truthfulness.

It was this part of his personality that enabled him to win over any number of hyper-critical British journalists during that 1980 Lions tour and which probably moved Naas Botha to remark on the aircraft home from New Zealand in 1981: "If only we had Morné with us. I'm sure we would not have had half the trouble we ran into and on top of it we would have won all three tests."

Coming from Botha that is a tribute indeed; seeing that he is the 'demi-god' of the crowd who most liked to hate Du Plessis — a hangover of that famous tackle incident.

One says "liked to hate" purposefully for by the end of Du Plessis's career there could not have been a more revered figure in South African rugby.

He had managed to transcend the bitter feelings which marked his early career when even his politics were drawn in, in an attempt to discredit him in the northern press.

By the time the Lions arrived he was probably the most popular choice as Springbok captain in the history of the game.

On the playing field he left a legacy of having captained the Springboks to 13 victories in 15 internationals — a record which will stand, and probably improve, with the test of time.

He was also the prime mover in the establishment of the Chris Burger Memorial Fund for Players; an organization born out of his deep shock when team-mate Chris Burger died during a game in Bloemfontein.

This incident had a profound affect on Du Plessis. It is to his credit that the fund may one day come to be seen as his greatest memorial.

A glaring omission in his career for Western Province is that the team never won the Currie Cup outright, coming closest in 1979 when they shared it with Northern Transvaal.

His 'decade' however coincided with the finest era of Northern Transvaal rugby and one wonders whether his concentration on the importance of enjoying the game and the free rein he allowed himself and his team did not count against him.

Often reckless as a skipper, but equally likely to be brilliantly inventive, Morné du Plessis became the embodiment of the spirit of Western Province rugby.

In a province which produced so many great names Morné du Plessis will be remembered as a giant.

'Oh God! It was like war'

The Pretoria bomb blast, 1983

Pretoria's 'Bloody Friday' began seconds after 16h30 on Friday, 20 May 1983. A bomb, concealed in a 1982 cream Colt Gallant parked in Nedbank Square, and consisting of nearly 60 kg of military explosives and shrapnel, exploded prematurely, killing 19 and injuring 217 in a scene of indescribable carnage.

Not only did the bomb kill the innocent: it also killed the two perpetrators, Bakayi Maseko and Freddy Shongwe, one of whom was in the car when it exploded, the other standing on the opposite side of the road.

Although police cordoned off the area and refused to allow anyone, including the press, access to Nedbank Square, teams of reporters were able to put together a story containing the facts, many of them eye-witness accounts. With terse, one-sentence paragraphs which accentuate the urgency with which the main report was written, *The Star* compiled the most dramatic front page in the country, its headline being particularly memorable. The story of the Pretoria bomb blast appeared in *The Star* on Saturday, 21 May 1983.

'OH GOD! IT WAS LIKE WAR'

Pretoria carnage as huge bomb explodes

The horror of the Pretoria bomb blast which left 15 dead and more than 150 injured was summed up by a young and stunned national serviceman as ambulances roared through the city street: "There was just blood and glass everywhere. And bodies — I am in the army but I have never seen dead people or people injured like that before."

A shaken member of the Permanent Force, near tears from shock, said: "Oh God! It was like war."

South Africa's most horrendous terrorist attack took place just after 4.30 pm when a huge car bomb exploded outside the Nedbank Square in Church Street.

The rush hour turned from a scramble to get home into a time of horror as the blast tore through hundreds of people.

Bleeding and dismembered bodies, both dead and alive lay scattered along the pavement, in shops and in the street, flung outside by the explosion.

A red hot flashing light was the first workers in Nedbank Square's ground floor shops observed of the explosion that shook Pretoria's city centre.

Ambulances, riot police, detectives and virtually the whole of the traffic department dashed to the scene.

The dead and injured were carried away by ambulances as police flung a cordon around the area. Some of the injured were taken to the SADF's Number 1 Military Hospital in Pretoria.

Forty-three blacks were treated at Pretoria's Kalafong Hospital. One woman died on admission. Among the critical was Mr Abraham Mashile, who had severe injuries to his neck and pelvis and had both his legs broken.

The dead and injured included more than 70 members of the armed forces.

Mr Louis le Grange, the Minister of Law and Order, was on the scene shortly after nightfall.

"There is no doubt in my mind who is responsible for this despicable attack this afternoon," he said.

"The leader of the ANC (African National Congress), Mr Oliver Tambo publicly warned that in 1983 they would increase their operations against South Africa and attack us.

"This is the biggest and ugliest incident of its kind."

He said the bomb exploded at a time when thousands of people were walking on the pavement.

Reporter Arnold Kirkby, on the staff of the Pretoria News, *was walking down the street when he heard the explosion. Although a reporter and not a photographer, he usually carried a camera. Without thinking, he ran towards the sound of the explosion, taking photographs as he ran. His arrival coincided with that of the police, and his were among the first photographs to be used* (Pretoria News).

436

The photographs, showing shocked bystanders, were published in Argus *newspapers (*Pretoria News*).*

"Among those killed were Air Force people, uniformed people and civilians, both black and white. Quite a number of blacks were killed."

Mr le Grange told newsmen it was believed the bomb had been in a blue Alfa Romeo motor car which had been parked in front of the building.

It was suspected that more than one bomb had been planted, and bomb experts had combed the building looking for more devices.

The entrance to Air Force Headquarters was littered with the bodies of airmen caught in the direct line of the explosion, barely metres away.

The soldiers lay over each other, their blue uniforms in shreds with broken limbs protruding, bleeding and shattered.

Three cars were aflame outside the entrance, sending black palls of smoke high above the terror scene.

From inside screams of agony and help mingled with the sound of the crackling flames and the oncoming police and emergency vehicles.

People were running around in a daze, bouncing off one another in their haste to get away from the burning cars.

Shop windows lay shattered, shards of glass with splatters of blood told of the impact of the blast.

A young soldier his face a charred ruin sat rocking back and forth in the window of the Golden Egg Restaurant, his eyes unseeing and the sounds from his throat like those of a wounded animal.

A young girl, one of three people laying in a cluster, looked blankly at the destroyed scene, crying softly for her mother.

Another woman her face and body a bloody mangle of flesh pointed a distorted finger to the sky and groaned her agony.

An engine block from a motorcar, possibly the one in which the bomb was placed, lay further down the street, while nearby the gearbox and a fender told of the force and size of the blast.

The first police and ambulances arrived within minutes, to assist people on the scene to administer to the worst of the injured.

Curtains from the Standard Bank across the street were brought to cover at least six people in the street. In the bank itself, badly mutilated people lay on bloodstained carpets.

Mrs Sarah Mabene sat looking out at the scene from which she had escaped.

"I was in the cafe, when the bomb exploded. I don't know how I got across the street."

Her back and neck had strips of flesh ripped off, and she looked at the ambulance personnel who came to take her away as though they were aliens.

A Pretoria traffic officer, his clothes smeared in blood, told how he dragged a badly injured man out of a burning car and desperately tried to extinguish flames enveloping several victims caught in the blasts.

"There were five explosions," Mr George Alison said.

"I saw people on fire and others literally flying through the air."

The chief officer of Civil Defence in Pretoria, Mr Mynard Beukes said his people were immediately mobilised and on stand-by with manpower and equipment to help the police and other emergency services.

"It was heartening to see civilians, who volunteered to do this work, so well prepared and prompt," he said.

'Blood is thicker than water'

Joe Lelyveld on Lieut-General Charles Sebe's arrest, July 1983

Joseph Lelyveld joined *The New York Times* in 1962 as a 25-year-old copy boy. In 1986, the former copy boy became foreign news editor of his paper, and won a Pulitzer Prize for his book on South Africa, *Move Your Shadow.*

Lelyveld travelled extensively during his two tours as *The New York Times'* southern Africa correspondent. At the end of his last tour, Lelyveld obtained a Guggenheim Fellowship and wrote his Pulitzer Prize winning book. Two classic chapters emerged from it, both redolent with imagery and Lelyveld's emotional (another correspondent, covering a treason trial with Lelyveld, was appalled to see tears trickling down his face as the accused were sentenced) but velvet-deep prose: 'Forced Busing' and 'Generalissimo'.

'Forced Busing' is a haunting description of an early morning bus ride in kwaNdebele; 'Generalissimc an interview, it sucn it can be called, with Charles Sebe, late of the Ciskei. He is wickedly, if ironically observed by Lelyveld. The germ of the chapter is to be found in a despatch he wrote for *The New York Times.* It was published on Sunday, 24 July 1983.

AFRICAN HOMELAND ARRESTS A GENERAL

Head of Ciskei Police and Army is Seized on Orders of His Brother, the President

By JOSEPH LELYVELD
Special to The New York Times

JOHANNESBURG, July 23 — Until he landed this week in one of the jails that had been part of his expanding domain in the nominally independent homeland called Ciskei, a case could have been made that Lieut. Gen. Charles Sebe was the most powerful black man in South Africa.

As Director of State Security, which gave him control of Ciskei's police and fledgling army, the flamboyant former sergeant in the South African security police seemed to be growing steadily more powerful with the active backing of his old employers. Ciskei, an impoverished tribal area for Xhosa-speaking blacks, was carved out of the eastern part of Cape Province, a region that has long been a crucible of black resistance to white rule.

General Sebe's role in countering the influence of the underground African National Congress was shown in various ways in the year and a half of Ciskei's nominal sovereignty; in a campaign of harassment against black trade unionists whom he and the South African security police saw as agents of the underground, and in the steady expansion of the resources at his command, which jumped by 90 per cent to $27 million this year to support the homeland's security forces of more than 3,000 men.

Training a Parachute Unit

South African officers were even helping train a small parachute unit for General Sebe at a secret base on the Indian Ocean coast. In recent interviews he readily acknowledged that he was in close liaison with the divisional commanders of the South African security police in the industrial ports of East London and Port Elizabeth.

But when he was arrested on Tuesday at his heavily guarded home outside of Zwelitsha, a black township that is the seat of Ciskei's government, two South African security policemen — his own former colleagues — were in the detachment sent to take him into custody. For the 49-year-old officer, who saw himself as an anti-Communist crusader, the involvement of the South African police in his arrest probably hurt as much as the fact that it was being carried out on the orders of his own elder brother, Lennox L. Sebe, Ciskei's President for Life.

Arrested at the same time was a white adviser to General Sebe named Tallefer Minnaar, who had a series of foreign assignments for South Africa's National Intelligence Service.

Spokesmen for President Sebe, a former school inspector and Congregationalist preacher who is said to be subject to spells of tension and depression, denied that he had purged his own brother to head off a coup. But they offered no other explanation for the shake-up and the arrest of at least 16 people, including three of the President's nephews and the son of his Vice President, which occurred after he rushed home from his second visit to Israel this year.

South Africa's Stake

South Africa's stake in the security situation in an area that is considered to be potentially the least stable in the country, was underscored within 48 hours of General Sebe's arrest when Pretoria's two highest-ranking police officials, Gen. Johan Coetzee and Maj. Gen. François Steenkamp, the new head of the security police, arrived in Zwelitsha to meet with President Sebe.

Officials in Pretoria have been exceedingly circumspect in discussing the upheaval in Ciskei, pointing out that South Africa regards President Sebe as the head of a sovereign nation. But official sources indicated that South Africa had no confirmation of any plotting by General Sebe against his brother and that the participation of South African officers in the general's arrest should not be read as a judgment by Pretoria that he had become unreliable.

Rather, it was said, with the arrests of General Sebe and his top officers, the homeland's security apparatus was in need of emergency help.

It seemed evident that the moves President Sebe made for his own security undermined the efforts South Africa has been making to promote an effective black-led security force in Ciskei. In the other homelands the key security officials are all whites, either South Africans or former Rhodesians. But Charles Sebe, who did undercover work for the South African security police, exercised real authority. His nominal replacement, a Methodist minister who served as army chaplain, will be supported by a white brigadier.

Joseph Lelyveld, former southern Africa correspondent for The New York Times *(The New York Times).*

Stormy Cabinet Session Reported

The City Press, a black weekly, reported that President Sebe and his brother argued recently at a stormy Cabinet meeting at which someone had the temerity to question the legitimacy of one of the brothers — the lack of physical resemblance is striking — and an ashtray was hurled across the table, gashing the Foreign Minister.

In an interview last month General Sebe spoke of the obligations of a security officer who disagrees with the political leader he serves. "He is the one appointed by God to lead the people," he said. "You are not appointed by God to lead the people. You are pursuing a profession. You are pursuing a trade.

He then said he could imagine a security matter on which he would "put my foot down up to a point that they kicked me out or on a point of principle I stage a walkout."

Asked whether he could imagine a situation in which he could do the "kicking out," he replied: "I can't do it. I can't kick them out." A smile then spread slowly across his face and he continued: "No, you see, if he was not my brother. Blood is thicker than water. Blood is thicker than water."

'It is a state of mind'

Allister Sparks on the high walls of apartheid — and mampoer, 1984-85

On 2 November 1983, white South Africans went to the polls to vote on a controversial new constitution, masterminded by the prime minister, P.W. Botha. The famous 'Yes/No' referendum attracted a vote of 63,3 per cent, with two-thirds of that number voting in favour of a 'yes'. The referendum was fiercely contested and was remarkable for the division of opinion it created among English-language newspapers. *The Star* alone remained neutral, urging, almost on the eve of polling, its readers to make up their own minds ('*The Star*'s indecision is final', noted one reporter).

Covering South Africa for *The Washington Post* and *The Observer* was former *Rand Daily Mail* editor Allister Sparks. Like his immediate predecessors, Raymond Louw and Laurence Gandar, Sparks had been fired by the management of his newspaper.

A protégé of Gandar's, Sparks had succeeded to the editorship in 1977. If management thought that they finally had a tame editor they were rapidly disabused. The most astute political commentator since Gandar, Sparks filled the paper with his own brand of intellectualism and a surfeit of politics which saw white readers forsaking the paper for less liberal journals. As the readership profile shifted from predominantly white to predominantly black, and as advertising support was withdrawn, management shifted uncomfortably.

But Sparks, described by a peer as 'a mixture of sensitivity and gross insensitivity', failed to heed the unease. Under his controversial and aloof editorship, the *Rand Daily Mail,* together with its sister newspaper, the *Sunday Express* (edited by Rex Gibson), played a leading part in exposing the government's role in the great Information Scandal involving the improper use of public funds by the Department of Information for media manipulation and secret buying of influence.

Allister Sparks was dismissed as editor of

the *Rand Daily Mail* in 1981 following a decision by the newspaper company's board of directors to make the paper appeal more to the white than the black community. Sparks, exhausted and emotional with strain, flew down to Cape Town to address the annual congress of the South African Society of Journalists.

His face red with suppressed tension, Sparks walked into the large conference room in which the congress was being held. With one accord, every journalist rose to his feet as Sparks, his hands trembling and tears in his eyes, struggled to compose himself and deliver a fiery speech.

By the end of 1981, Sparks had been appointed correspondent to both *The Washington Post* and *The Observer.* It was undoubtedly in this field that he found his métier. His copy was lucid, biting and, for foreign readers, deceptively low-key. Using the 'Yes/No' referendum as the theme for his despatch, Sparks wrote an eloquent article for *The Observer.* It was published ten months after the referendum, on 20 September 1984.

H.G. Wells might have invented such a place: a country where people occupy the same space but live in separate time frames, so that they do not see one another and perceive different realities.

The gulf between white and black in South Africa has always been there, of course, but it has acquired a new dimension of late, as the whites take what they regard as a bold step towards reform, while the blacks react to it with anger and a deepened sense of alienation.

Ten months ago, the whites voted by an unprecedented two-thirds majority to endorse a new Constitution that gives limited parliamentary representation to the Coloured and Indian minorities. One month ago, the Coloured and Indian communities showed by an unprecedented 87 per cent boycott of their elections that they spurned the reform, because of its exclusion of the African majority, while in the weeks since then the African townships have erupted with the angriest outbreak of violence since the 1976 Soweto riots.

Yet even such palpable evidence of black rejection of the new deal seems not to penetrate the white time frame. It is not as though the whites are bewildered or hurt or even surprised by the reaction to what they thought was a generous gesture. They have simply not taken it in.

Some of the new Coloured and Indian parliamentarians won their seats with a slenderness of voter support that might qualify them for a place in the 'Guinness Book of Records.' But white South Africa has watched on television as they have been sworn in with a medieval pageantry inherited from Westminster, with trumpets and wigs and a solemn procession through historic corridors.

It hears them being interviewed and quoted on the news. It does not hear the mocking remarks of the communities they supposedly represent. Memories are short and perceptions selective. With incredible speed, the derisory voting figures are forgotten, and the pretenders take on an aura of legitimacy.

As for the black ghettos, they are out of town and out of sight. Little of what happens there penetrates to the affluent tranquility of white suburbs. Except when an occasional police vehicle drives through a white area, or an employee fails to turn up for work, the trouble might be in another country.

Probably no more than 5 per cent of white Johannesburg has ever been to Soweto. Most could not even tell you how to get there, although it is one of Africa's most populous cities in its own right.

Newspaper coverage of the unrest has been low key. After a week in which 38 people were killed and more than 300 injured, the story did not make the front page of any of South Africa's national Sundays. News bulletins on the semi-official radio and television services have been blatantly censored, with none of the footage of police action that viewers have seen abroad.

But the lack of perception across the colour line is more than just a matter of separation, censorship or inhibited reporting. It is a state of mind. Life for the whites here derives its essential character from the idea that they are not in Africa, or, if their physical presence in the continent is too much to deny, that they are not really *of* Africa.

As the world knows, this idea finds its legal expression in statutes which have proclaimed 83 per cent of the land area to be 'white' South Africa. Other races may live there only in designated areas under a law called the Group Areas Act. The admission of Africans is strictly controlled to limit their numbers to the minimum needed to run the economy.

Yet for all the efforts of the white administration over 36 years of apartheid, the idea remains an ideological illusion, a gigantic act of self-deception. Although 20 per cent of all South African whites live in metropolitan Johannesburg, they account for only one-third of the city's population of 2,8 million. The Coloured and Indian minorities account for another 7 per cent. The rest are Africans, and it is they who provide the workforce that keeps the city running. As consumers, they account for more than 60 per cent of its purchasing power. Johannesburg could not survive one day without them. The same is true in varying degrees of every other town and city in the country.

Much of white South Africa's energy, as a political and social entity, is devoted to trying to obscure this fact. Its peculiar incognizance of the black masses all around it seems to be an extension of the same imperative.

This special kind of apartheid colour-blindness manifests itself in many strange ways. According to the law, no black person may own a business in a 'white' city, not even a shoeshine stand. Yet a whole population of small-time entrepreneurs exists in 'white' Johannesburg as a kind of visible underworld that goes unnoticed. Unlicensed drinking establishments, known as shebeens, thrive in alleyways and on vacant plots. Lottery operators ply their trade on the pavements. A barber runs his *al fresco* business beside an overpass on the M1 motorway that slices through Johannesburg.

I have just completed a building alteration to my white suburban home. The work was done by a black contractor, whose existence is known to scores of satisfied clients, but whose identity must remain concealed. He lives with his woman in the servants' quarters of a convent, from where he conducts his substantial business operation. Though his very presence in the 'white' city is illegal, his workmanship is inspected and approved by officials of the local authority.

It is on Sundays that the separate existence of the two populations of the same city is most apparent. There are some 120 000 black domestic servants living in rooms in the backyards of white suburban homes and on top of apartment blocks in Johannesburg. It is the population of a sizeable city within a city.

On Sundays, this other city has the day off — but nowhere to go. There are no public facilities in the suburbs for blacks, on the assumption that they are there only to work and are not real residents.

They gather on pavements, building sites, parking lots and in the smart shopping centres which are closed on Sundays. They gather at bus stops, these thousands known only as Martha, Mary, Jane or Betty, to meet grannies who bring in their children from the 'homelands' for a day's visit.

Many are dressed in flowing white gowns with blue or green trimmings, and they walk through the streets carrying religious banners. Millions of blacks belong to sects which have broken away from the white denominations, and they gather for their services along the banks of suburban streams. That, too, is part of their separate existence.

The whites, meanwhile, are gathered around swimming pools and tennis courts in spacious suburban gardens. It is pleasantly languorous there in those secluded surroundings, sipping chilled white wine in the summer sun. Soweto and Sharpeville might be a thousand miles away.

This presents a visual paradox that highlights South Africa's separate time frames. Never does Johannesburg look more black than on Sundays, with the thousands of servants on the streets. Yet never do the whites feel more securely alone and at ease than on those days when they gather with their friends behind their high garden walls.

Mampoer is more than just a drink — it is almost a way of life. As befitting his rural Cape childhood, Sparks was more familiar with the fiery witblitz than with the upcountry mampoer — but he learned to appreciate the intricacies of the brew very quickly. Sparks' affectionate report on the 1983 brew ran in *The Washington Post* of 26 March 1983.

KOPERFONTEIN FARM, South Africa — It was like people returning to their roots. About 300 Afrikaner families gathered on this arid cattle farm in the Groot Marico district of western Transvaal to celebrate the art of making moonshine liquor handed down to them from their *voortrekker* ancestors who opened up the country 150 years ago.

The voortrekkers made the moonshine not because regular liquor was under prohibition but because none was available in this remote and hostile hinterland into which they trekked in ox-wagons to escape British rule at the Cape of Good Hope.

They gave the name *mampoer* to the fiery distillate that they boiled out of fermented peaches, apricots, wild berries, the fruit of the prickly pear cactus, or whatever was on hand. When they used grapes they called it *witblitz,* or white lightning, which was the strongest of all.

It was a tough liquor for a tough frontier people, and it was to become interwoven with Afrikaner folklore. This hillbilly region in particular was made famous by Herman Charles Bosman, a writer of folksy tales that brought out the inner warmth and often unconscious humour of a people whom the world and most other South Africans see largely as stiff-necked racists.

The making of mampoer was in danger of dying out because of laws prohibiting the passing on of distillers' licenses from father to son. The number had dwindled to 109 when the law was changed last year to permit the inheritance of licenses again.

The liquor still cannot be sold or moved off the maker's farm, but the change means that at least the tradition of mampoer will live on.

Saturday's celebration was occasioned by the decision of the mampoer-makers, or *stokers* as they are called, to form themselves into a guild appropriate to their new status.

They were invited to perform this ceremony here at Koperfontein by its owner, Oom Apie van Staden, a rotund 74-year-old father of 10 who is a connoisseur of mampoer and a stoker himself.

445

Oom Apie even invited a Cabinet minister, Oom Hendrik Schoeman, the minister of Transport, to give the occasion a touch of class.

"Oom," it must be noted, means uncle, and everybody in these parts is called either uncle or aunt as a term of respect. The proper mode of address is in the third person. "Good morning, uncle," says the youngster in short pants at the farm gate. "Will uncle please drive straight up the road and park uncle's car under the black wattles."

They came, many of the "ooms" and "tannies", in Mercedes-Benzes, for the Afrikaner is no longer the underdog in South Africa that he once was. His National Party has been in power for 34 years. It has looked after him well — and he is determined not to let any of that power slip away to the black majority.

Most of the burly men wore baggy shorts and open-necked shirts, but the women came dressed to the nines with bouffant hairdos and high-heeled shoes that had them tottering over the rough ground to Oom Apie's big iron shed where the ceremony was held.

They were a little stiff and formal to begin with, and it took them a little time to unbend. But the warmth of country folk and pioneer stock lies only a sip or two beneath the surface.

So it came to pass that the great mampoer booze-up began with a reading from the Bible and a prayer. Dominee Daniel Jakobs, of the Hervormde Kerk, the sternest of South Africa's three Dutch Reformed churches, quoted from Genesis to warn the assembled stokers of the evils of liquor.

Then he also noted that the Bible is abundant in its approval of the preservation of a people's cultural heritage — and mampoer, after all, is a piece of Afrikaner culture. So the minister pronounced it all right.

The celebrants thus reassured, a band struck up, featuring a concertina and guitar, playing the bouncy waltzes and quicksteps of traditional *boeremusiek,* the music of the voortrekkers.

Barbecue fires flickered to life under the wattles, and in a hut a short distance away some stoker got the furnace going under Oom Apie's big copper still.

Proudly the old uncle watched as the colourless liquid began to drip from a pipe at the bottom of a 44-gallon oil drum filled with water. When the liquor ignited at the touch of a match and poured in a flaming stream to the floor, Oom Apie pronounced it ready to drink.

"Damned healthy stuff," he declared. "I've been drinking it every day for 34 years and I've never seen a doctor, never taken medicine."

He recommended it particularly for toothaches, snake-bites and corns. For the corns, just dab it on with cotton. If necessary, he added, you can also fuel a tractor with it.

Meanwhile, back at the shed, entries rolled in for a competition to choose the champion mampoer-maker.

The variety was as mind-blowing as the liquor. Green, red, yellow and brown bottles. Spirits distilled from every fruit imaginable. Others sweetened and flavoured to make them into liqueurs: orange, banana, honey, apple, coffee and aniseed flavours.

A crimson "Cointreau". A thick, white substance was called "mother's milk". Another, made of cream, chocolate and mint with an apricot spirit base, bore a label advising: "shake before pouring".

By evening the place was swinging. The two ministers, Cabinet and religious, had left, taking the last inhibitions with them. Oom Piet van Vuuren's concertina trilled louder as he skipped about the floor in his baggy khaki shorts, and Tant Sannie's shoulder straps came adrift.

The champion stoker turned out to be Oom Daniel Yssel of Ventersdorp, an amiable giant with a Stetson hat.

Oom Daniel was overwhelmed by his success. "*Bliksem* — bloody hell," he kept muttering as he sat with his family around their barbecue fire.

He had not even entered his best mampoer, he confided, because some dumb judge thought it was burned. In fact he had matured it in an old wine vat.

"My worst mampoer won the prize," he marvelled, grinning under the Stetson. "Bloody hell, bloody hell."

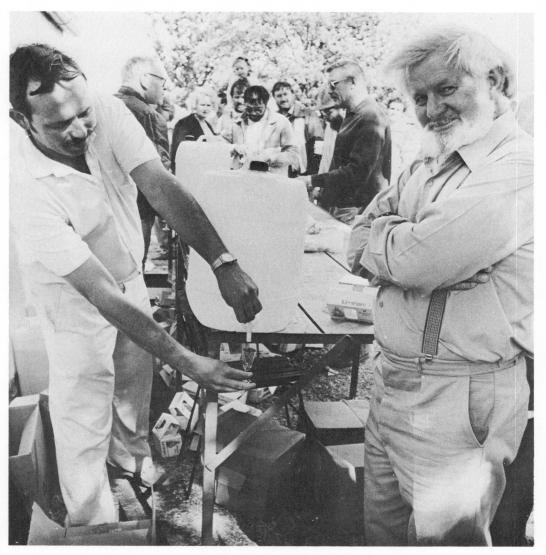

*The Mampoer is made: the 'ceremonial' tasting begins (*The Star*).*

'Tears for Maki, tears for the beloved country'

David Beresford, The Guardian, 1985

Other than her family and her friends, no-one knew who Maki Skhosana was until she died, horribly, at the hands of a 500-strong mob. An appalled television team filmed her stoning, her beating and, finally, her necklacing. Maki's death, on 20 July 1985, was shown in every detail to a shocked world.

David Beresford, southern Africa correspondent for *The Guardian,* was not at the scene of her death; he visited Maki's mother in her Duduza home a few days later. By anyone's standards, it was a heart-rending occasion. In writing the story, which appeared in *The Guardian* on 26 July 1985, Beresford broke one of his cardinal rules — never to include himself in one of his own articles.

'I was so moved I broke my rule and brought myself into the last line. I felt I had come face to face with Paton's tragic reality of South Africa,' he later commented. 'In a way I wanted to identify with the article. It was the most terrible, heartbreaking story.'

From DAVID BERESFORD
DUDUZA

It was a plastic carry-out bag from a local supermarket. Mrs Diana Skhosana tipped the bloodstained contents on to the table: a piece of faded blue T-shirt, a head-scarf, handfuls of earth and some broken sticks. She was keeping them for burial with her daughter, Maki Skhosana, a name which is not well-known, although the last minutes of her life were witnessed by millions of television viewers around the world.

Maki was the girl who was beaten and burnt to death in front of cameras at a funeral in the township of Duduza on Saturday. The story behind her death is a long and complex one: of eight young men who died trying to 'strike a blow against apartheid; of their Russian grenades which did not work properly; of a mystery man 'from Lusaka' who supplied them 'and who may or may not have been a provocateur and of Maki who may have been his agent or may have died simply because of her name.

It seems to have all started sometime early in June, when a mystery man made his appearance in the townships of Duduza and nearby Kwathema and Tskanane. He apparently introduced himself to student leaders belonging to the Congress of South

David Beresford (Ellen Elmendorp).

African Students (COSAS), as having come from Lusaka and being a member of Umkhonto We Sizwe, The Spear of the Nation — the military wing of the outlawed African National Congress, South Africa's main liberation organisation.

He said he had a supply of weapons and he had come to arm the COSAS executives in the townships. He seemed flush with money. He said he had 10,000 Rand for them and would pay the commander of a proposed operational unit 2,000 Rand and others 1,000 Rand apiece.

After a number of delays the students agreed to co-operate. But they decided they would not all take part — for fear if anything went wrong it would wipe out the entire leadership — instead deputing some of their more militant members.

On Monday, June 24, a group of them were collected by the 'ANC' man in a minibus and driven off to a derelict mine in the bush. He produced two grenades and explained how they should pull the pins, count to three and then throw them. They threw them and they exploded.

Duly satisfied, they returned to the township, agreeing to meet again the next night at three collection points, including a church in Duduza and a shebeen (illegal drinking den) in Tsakane. The targets were to include the homes of two security policemen in Tsakane and Kwathema and the limpet mine was to be used on a power sub-station at Kwathema.

At their collection points the 'ANC' man distributed the grenades, reminded them again how to use them and left after instructing them to try to coordinate the attacks at midnight. In Kwathema three of the students headed for the policeman's home. They were early, so they went to a friend's house nearby and waited. Then at about midnight they marched out and, as they approached the target house, heard the blast of the limpet mine in the distance.

The first student took out his grenade and pulled the pin. It exploded immediately, killing him. Police appeared down the street and the other two students ran for their lives. It is not known what happened in Tsakane, where two died in similar explosions, or at the power station, except that the limpet mine obviously exploded prematurely.

In Duduza the picture is confused. By one account a group of students were seen talking outside the church, inside a security gate. Then police were seen at the back of the premises and the students began to run. As they bunched to get through the gate there was an explosion. One dropped dead and several appeared to have been injured.

The survivors ran for it, taking refuge at a house some distance away. More police

449

arrived at the house and in a melee which followed there were further explosions in which another three students were fatally injured.

In Duduza the bodies were left lying in the street and a large crowd began to gather. The scene was described by a black journalist, Rich Mkhondo, in a report subsequently published in the Johannesburg daily newspaper, *The Star*: 'We joined about 2,000 residents who had gathered around the bodies of the youths who had died at about midnight. The most horrifying moment of my life was when I was shown the bodies of the youths. I had never before seen the body of a man without a head. Nor had I seen pieces of human flesh scattered around and people trying to put them together again.

'As I was trying to gather information about the deaths of the youths I noticed more hippos (armoured personnel carriers) and police vehicles had arrived. I heard residents shouting, refusing to allow police to take the bodies to the government mortuary and saying they had their own mortuaries.

'As I ran into a house with a number of residents I felt a burning pain on my right shoulder. I had been struck with birdshot. On looking outside I saw the bodies being loaded into police vans. Some parts fell to the ground. A person inside the house said: 'Look. They are throwing the bodies inside the vans like sacks of potatoes.' A woman standing next to me was crying.'

It has been confirmed that the grenades were Russian made RGD5s, an egg-shaped grenade packed with TNT and with a fragmentation radius of 15 to 20 metres. The firing mechanism is quite simple. It has a conventional grenade lever, anchored by a split pin. When the pin is pulled out and the lever released, it unleashes a spring-loaded pin which hits a percussion cap, igniting a chemical fuse which takes three to four seconds to burn before exploding the detonator.

They could have been doctored, simply by replacing the three to four second fuse with an instantaneous one. But accounts of the one explosion taking place as the pin was pulled suggests that if they were doctored it was done more elaborately.

It is possible that these particular grenades were adapted, at the manufacturing stage, for use in booby traps — with a tripwire — and were supplied in error by a genuine representative of the ANC. Incidents have been reported of SA security personnel being injured in a similar way while testing such grenades.

But of course in the townships the residents have no doubt that the entire episode was a scheme hatched by police to wipe out the student leadership. And, whatever the truth of it, the events fuelled the hatred which led to the death of Maki.

Maki's precise relationship with the 'ANC' man is not clear. What is known is that he was originally introduced to the students by a girl and that by some accounts he did have a girlfriend called Maki, although it appears she was not Maki Skhosana — she just had the same christian name.

Whatever the circumstances, the story began to circulate in Duduza that Maki Skhosana was a police agent. She heard the rumour — she even went to a local priest and told him about it. But she insisted she was innocent of any involvement in the hand grenade deaths and that she was not going to acknowledge guilt by running away.

Maki was a simple girl, aged 24, an unmarried mother with a five-year-old son, working in a nearby glove factory. She lived with her mother, a 54-year-old domestic servant, a brother and a cousin in one of those little four-roomed matchbox houses characteristic of South Africa's townships with their concrete floors and ceiling-less iron roofs. And, stubbornly, she not only insisted on staying in that house, but went to the funeral of the Duduza grenade victims, and to the funeral of those killed later.

Apparently there was an attempt, by one or two student leaders, to get her away from Saturday's funeral. But she refused again. And so the fury of Duduza was unleashed upon her.

They chased her across the veld, they beat her, they stoned her, they tore her clothes off, they set her on fire, they put a huge rock on her so that she couldn't get up and they rammed a broken bottle into her vagina.

Her mother was crying uncontrollably. The two black clergymen with me couldn't take any more and one of them lumbered to his feet and said: 'Let us pray.'

And so we stood there with heads bowed, around a plain kitchen table in the township of Duduza in the middle of the Transvaal. And her mother wept on and there were tears in all our eyes; tears for Maki, tears for the beloved country.

The story of 24-year-old Maki Skhosana, as it appeared in *The Guardian*, formed part of a portfolio which earned Beresford the award of International Reporter of the Year 1986. Almost one year later, he turned his attention to the Cape.

In June 1986, following the unrest which had erupted through the black townships of the Witwatersrand like lava bubbles, the ramshackle, sprawling squatter complex of Crossroads, outside Cape Town, experienced its own brand of violence. In what amounted to an orgy of terror, inexplicably uncontrolled by police, *witdoeke* vigilantes burned more than 70 000 people out of

Crossroads (Cape Times).

their miserable homes, leaving them to find emergency accommodation in temporary charity shelters.

Declared an emergency camp in 1976, the State had been trying for more than three years to persuade Crossroads residents to move to Khayelitsha. The *witdoeke,* under the control of its self-styled mayor, Johnson Ngxobongwana, attempted to establish control over both Old and New Crossroads by blatant force.

The destruction of the squatter communities in the cold, wet Cape winter of May and June 1986 was marked by violence, anguish and official indifference. The Press, trying to cover the violence, were more or less unprotected. George D'Eath, a cameraman, was mortally wounded by assailants within shouting distance of the police. Beresford travelled to Cape Town, and with the assistance of Stephen Wrottersley, crime reporter on *The Argus,* was taken into Crossroads at the height of the fighting in a police Casspir.

His vivid report was published in *The Guardian* in late June 1986.

From DAVID BERESFORD
CAPE TOWN

A respectful silence fell in the 10-ton armoured personnel carrier as a police radio controller announced that he had a message from South Africa's Minister of Law and Order, Mr Louis Le Grange.

He wanted to congratulate his men on the good work they were doing; they were to keep it up and he would handle all the questions at the top.

Looking out of the window of the Casspir, at the battlefield of Crossroads, it was difficult to understand what the minister was talking about.

The huge vehicle was surrounded by hundreds of blacks seemingly unaware that carrying a dangerous weapon is a criminal offence.

Waving their pangas, spears, knives, axes and clubs, the vigilantes — their characteristic 'witdoeke' or white scarves wrapped around arms and weapons — surged backwards and forwards, trying to whip themselves and each other into a killing frenzy, to attack the crowd of 'comrades' facing them a few hundred yards down the road.

Police and troops watched curiously from their mobile forts, then roared off in search of the source of nearby gunfire, leaving the two mobs to get on with the killing, if they could get up the courage.

In all directions mute testimony was offered to a conspicuous failure of Mr le Grange's men. It was a surreal landscape of corrugated-iron sheets sticking out of the ground at crazy angles, interspersed by twisted beds, lopsided poles, and smoking debris — the homes of the KTC squatters, flattened in a terrifying, 48-hour rampage by the witdoeke.

The police and troops ran across open ground and leaned out of the open-top Casspirs and Buffels, with an easy insouciance which belied the danger behind the crack and thump of nearby guns.

The danger was brought home when an elderly officer pointed out a man on a distant hill: "He's got a gun," he said. We gazed and then dived for the floor as a shot clanged off the armour plating.

As we clambered back to our feet and grinned ruefully at each other, a reporter, Bert van Hees, looked down and, mildly astonished, watched the blood pouring from his forearm. The shock of the impact had numbed the nerves that should have told him he had been hit. Police tore at his shirt and bound a rough tourniquet as we roared out of the camp.

Outside the police station in the nearby township of Guguletu there was an ambulance, but the medical attendants had little time for an arm wound. They were desperately bandaging and setting up a drip for a critically injured television cameraman George D'Eath who had been found badly hacked.

Our Casspir roared off back into Crossroads. The radio, crackling in Afrikaans, reported that a 'white' sniper had been spotted and that another gunman was firing at Casspirs from some sand dunes. We arrived at the dunes and three officers leapt off, the colonel in charge shouting after them as they loped off into the sand to watch out for 'Barnard'.

Warrant Officer Barrie Barnard is the subject of an unpleasant legend on the Cape Flats. A figure who features prominently in stories of police atrocities. He was apparently hiding in the dunes, waiting in ambush for the sniper.

The setting was wrong, but it all smacked of Starsky and Hutch. The policemen — some even clad in the sneakers and black bomber jackets favoured by the American television duo — playing out a cops and robbers fantasy while civil war raged around them.

The station commander at Guguletu is a long-distance runner and there is a picture of him racing on his office wall. The photograph carries the legend: 'Blessed is a man who perseveres under trial, for he will receive the crown of life'. But the misdirected perseverence shown by Mr Le Grange's men offers only more deaths in South Africa.

'Life to the death'

Rex Gibson, Rand Daily Mail, 1985

In 1979, Rex Gibson received South Africa's most prestigious award for journalism — the Pringle Award, given by the South African Society of Journalists. In 1985 it was his dubious honour to receive the award for the second time, on behalf of the staff of the *Rand Daily Mail* on the occasion of its closure.

Like other members of the staff of the newspaper, Rex Gibson, editor from 1982 (following a nine-month interregnum by *Sunday Times* editor Tertius Myburgh) after the firing of Allister Sparks, knew the *Rand Daily Mail*'s situation was parlous.

It was not just the losses that were causing grooved foreheads amongst both management and the admittedly more sanguine editorial staff. (In 1982 the paper's losses were estimated at R7 million; in the first half of the 1983 financial year, earnings plunged by 30 per cent) in 1984 Jim Bailey, the founder of *Drum* and a descendant of mining magnate Abe Bailey, sold a substantial block of South African Associated Newspaper shares to Johannesburg Consolidated Investments, then under the chairmanship of Gordon Waddell. Suddenly, the majority shareholding changed from a family to a giant business.

Even then, Rex Gibson, who had accepted the position as editor of the *Rand Daily Mail* against the advice of his friends, believed the paper could survive, given efficient management, support from shareholders and brighter editorial. Indeed, there were signs, late in 1983, that things could slowly be coming right. But it was too late.

It was only three weeks before the board meeting which sounded the death-knell for the paper (the meeting is now known as the

Rex Gibson: 'It has always been my dream to edit the Rand Daily Mail. *In the last days I was tense with fear that somebody might say that the* Mail *had closed because I had failed to protect it adequately. Thank God no one ever said that.'* (The Star).

Ides of March, 1985) that Gibson was able, intellectually, to accept the fact that his paper was going to be closed. Emotionally, however, he was unable to come to terms with the closure: he kept hoping against hope that the paper would, somehow, survive.

At about 15h15 on 15 March, Gibson was called from his office to address the board. 'They were all excessively friendly,' he recalled later, 'which made my heart sink.' Ian McPherson, chairman of SAAN, said to Gibson: 'You have asked for the opportunity to speak to the board. The floor is yours.'

Gibson, on his feet, looked around. 'I have this small problem. I'm not sure exactly what alternatives the board is considering, so I don't know on what to address you.' There was complete silence. Gibson: 'It would be easier for me and simpler for you if I knew on what I should address you.' The silence continued. Gibson: 'In the absence of any information from the board, I will address you on the rumour in today's *Financial Mail* which said the *Mail* was to be closed.' In the continuing silence, Gibson addressed the board.

One of the directors — the only one in the entire meeting to speak — said to Gibson: 'You have argued that to close the *Mail* will irreparably damage SAAN. Some of us believe the opposite to be true — that not to close the *Mail* will destroy SAAN.'

'I knew in that moment they had decided to close the *Mail*.' Fifteen minutes later, Clive Kingsley, managing director of SAAN, telephoned Gibson, now back in his office. Kingsley showed Gibson a typed memorandum — which Gibson believed must have been written prior to the board meeting — saying that the 83-year-old newspaper was to be closed. 'The whole thing was a charade, a despicable charade,' said Gibson.

On Monday, 29 April 1985, Rex Gibson wrote the final leader ('Go in peace,' it was headed, closing with the final paragraph: 'We who have loved this newspaper, and worked joyously on it, take our leave of you now, in trepidation and in hope'). When he had finished the leader, Gibson wrote his own, personal lament for the death of a paper he loved and which closed, with the services of the last, like the first editor, (Edgar Wallace) being dispensed with. It appeared in the last issue of the *Rand Daily Mail,* 30 April 1985.

Life to the death on our Mail . . .

It is the beginning of the day on which the Rand Daily Mail is going to put itself to death, the quiet time before the first shift comes on duty. Across the mezzanine floor which accommodates newsroom and sub-editors' department, electronic screens blink out an insipid green cast over a forlorn landscape of cluttered desks and cardboard packing boxes.

The glass partition that separates the sports department from the rest has become an informal noticeboard. Scrawled notices invite retrenched journalists to seek jobs in Australia, on other newspapers, in public relations. The Southern African Society of Journalists provides its latest advice on what to do now that the worst has happened. An enterprising soul has offered a souvenir: framed, the last front page of the Mail, the first front page of Business Day, R20 the lot.

There is nothing special about this big, ill-proportioned room; nothing that invites fancy. Ghosts do not lurk in flimsy partitions and walls of glass and steel. This is not the heart of the Mail, although all physical evidence points to the contrary. The room is empty and it is the emptiness that is intolerable.

Soon the journalists will arrive bearing the heart of the Mail and, because they are hurt and bewildered and bitter, there will be laughter and bantering until they leave for good.

Down the years, the Mail refused to die. I remember being part of the deputation that went to see the chairman of SAAN when Laurence Gandar was fired the first time. We won a reprieve, but he went in the end. Then came Raymond Louw, and I remember the day he came into my office and said: "I want you to be the first to know. I have just been fired." But he was not fired, simply removed from the editor's office and transferred to management. Later he was fired, and he came again into my office and said: "I want you to be the first to know that I have just been fired — again."

I remember Allister Sparks, on the fateful day when the board met to discuss his future, saying to me: "They are going to fire me today." And I, with my customary pre-science, saying: "Nonsense, they wouldn't do that."

And through all those tumultuous years, the real heart of the Mail did not stop beating. Its spirit seemed unquenchable.

All journalists are loyal to their papers. From the people of the Mail there was some extra quality, a quality capable of giving extreme offence and intimidating outsiders, who called it arrogance. But it was not that; at least, not entirely. It was the spirit of the underdog. The Mail would have been an all-time loser had it not been an all-time fighter. Successive editors imposed style and form and content on it, but there was one thing they could not do: betray the principles for which it stood. The journalists saw to that.

And a funny lot they were, too, to be laying down unspoken rules like that. There were more eccentrics than is generally regarded as desirable; more mavericks than anyone should have to cope with. They disagreed with each other interminably on every possible subject. Their political allegiances ranged from card-carrying Nationalist to radical Left. And, despite their differences, they all had this quaint notion about newspaper integrity. The Mail repaid them. Its proudest boast to itself was that anyone of any political persuasion could work on the Mail because the paper never demanded anything more of them than honest journalism.

In the last six weeks, the journalists of the Mail have faced a task more daunting than any outsider could realise.

Normally when a newspaper is closed down it is a sudden thing — here today, gone tomorrow, wounds cauterised by adrenalin. It is very rare that a paper is required to drag itself into posterity step by painful step. This was what was demanded of the Mail staff.

And, unwitting though it may have been, it provided the best tribute that the company could offer to Mail journalists.

Not once did it cross the mind of board or management that the journalists might be unequal to this cruel task; that they might leave the body of their paper to whimper and die while they saw to their own futures. It is so easy to stop trying, to snuff the spark today, since it will surely die tomorrow anyway.

But no one did.

They determined to produce the best newspapers they could in the time left to them. Readers will judge whether they succeeded, but at least they tried, professional to the last. Perhaps only journalists will know what it demanded of them.

And so, now, it is 10 am on the last day of the Mail and the large room on the mezzanine floor is beginning to fill. The heart is beating again. The emptiness has gone away for the moment.

On the evening of 30 April, the *Rand Daily Mail* held its last party. Gibson issued instructions that, because feelings were running high, only presently-employed staffers were to be allowed into the *Rand Daily Mail* offices. Affronted, former RDM staffers held an alternative closing-down party at 'The Fed', the infamous journalists' bar which had soothed the spirits of many a reporter. Back at the *Rand Daily Mail*, Gibson had assembled all living former *Mail* editors: himself, Allister Sparks, Ray Louw, Laurence Gandar. The following morning, Gibson and his deputy editor, Benjamin Pogrund, took their secretaries out to lunch. None of them can remember it.

'Walking blindfold through a mine field'

Tony Heard and the Tambo interview, 1985

On 4 November 1985, readers of the *Cape Times* (frequently mistaken for South Africa's oldest paper — that honour belongs to *The Natal Witness* — the *Cape Times* was founded on 1 January 1840, closed on 29 April 1840 and re-established on 27 March 1876) were astonished, on opening their morning daily, to find a 3 600-word verbatim interview with the banned president of the African National Congress, Oliver Tambo.

Publication of the article caused an outcry in government, police and newspaper worlds. The editor of the *Cape Times* and author of the article, Anthony Heard, was promptly charged under the Internal Security Act on 8 November for quoting a banned person, but was not held. His newspaper came under siege by the international media, he was almost swamped by letters from supporters the world round and, for his courage in defying the restrictive laws governing the Press in his country, was awarded the 1985 Golden Pen of Freedom and, in 1986, the Pringle Award.

Before leaving for a trip to the United Kingdom in October 1985, Heard asked the then SAAN London editor, John Battersby, to arrange a meeting between himself and Tambo. Battersby was not initially aware that Heard intended not only interviewing the ageing president and long time friend of the imprisoned Nelson Mandela, but, in defiance of South African law, of publishing the interview.

The interview was recorded and transcribed as soon as Heard stepped off the plane in Cape Town. His sub-editors were incredulous when they read the copy. Heard insisted on the publication of the now historic interview and sat back to wait events (not the least of which was a rash of pro-Heard graffiti on Cape Town walls, the most memorable of which was 'Tambo should be seen but not Heard'). But he had calculated the mood of the authorities correctly; after much huffing and puffing, charges against him were quietly dropped.

Asked to explain why he ran an interview which was bound to cause official reaction and which could have led to his imprisonment, Anthony Heard wrote a piece for the *Los Angeles Times.* It was subsequently republished in the *International Herald Tribune* on 12 November 1985.

> CAPE TOWN — A prominent South African newspaper editor once said that editing was like walking blindfold through a mine field. That was in the 1950s. He should try editing now.
>
> The government has spent 38 years finessing a form of press control that places on newspapers the onus to publish at their peril, but severely limits our leeway to inform

Tony Heard, editor of the Cape Times, *1971-1987* (Cape Times).

readers on vital matters. It is a twilight world of press freedom. The conventional wisdom among South African journalists has been that if you are light on your feet, lucky and work hard, the public can still be informed with a degree of adequacy.

The ordinary process of simply publishing news as it breaks is foreign to South African conditions, particularly now.

A prime example is the provision in the Internal Security Act that forbids publication of any utterance by a person who has been banned by the state. Banning has been described as civil death, since it restricts a person's movements and associations. Although there are more excessive forms of dealing with dissent in the "less-free" parts of the world, the South African banning system is, to my knowledge, unique.

Anyone who quotes a banned person is in big trouble. The penalty is up to three years in prison, with no statutory provision made for a fine, although sentences can be suspended. Editors maintain up-to-date file boxes in their offices to check whether people are banned.

It is not difficult to quote a banned person by mistake in the production of a daily newspaper, which has the equivalent length of a medium-sized novel. It happened to me some months ago when Zollie Malindi, an African activist politician, was inadvertently quoted in an obscure report in the Cape Times — purely by error.

I was summoned to court with the reporter who had written the story. In that case, after we made several appearances in court, the charges were dropped without explanation and I was free to continue walking through the mine field.

Now I am again the subject of police investigation, this time for publishing a 3,600-word interview on Nov. 4 with Oliver Tambo, president of the African National Congress. It would be novel but futile to argue in court that 3,600 words could get into a newspaper inadvertently.

There were compelling public-interest reasons for the publication. Prominent South Africans have been queuing up to see Mr. Tambo and his senior aides as the South African crisis of unrest and economic downturn bites hard into white confidence and as support for the ANC among blacks remains strong. Gavin Relly, chairman of Anglo American Corporation, the giant mining industrial organization, has seen Mr. Tambo. The leader of the liberal Progressive Federal Party, Frederick Van Zyl Slabbert, and senior party members also have met with the ANC. The government frowns on these contacts, and is now denying passports for such visits.

It was ironic and unsatisfactory that influential South Africans were contacting the ANC and yet, because of the government's restrictions on the press, almost all South Africans were being denied the opportunity to hear the ANC's positions on the most important issues of the day.

Since I was in London recently at the same time as Mr. Tambo, I took the opportunity to see him in his Victorian home in North London. I was struck by his essential moderation: he favours a mixed economy (here he appears to stand almost to the right of the Labour Party in Britain), a role for free enterprise, respect for home ownership and the security of whites as well as blacks. His views on communism, his clear dislike for violence and his keenness for talks with the government strike a moderate note.

Mr. Tambo seemed to be a black African moderate in the mould of a Kenneth Kaunda or Julius Nyerere. A 68-year-old grandfatherly figure, he looked to me more like the last white hope in South Africa than the Communist-terrorist demon presented to South Africans by the government-controlled broadcasting services. I described him as a reluctant revolutionary.

The key point is that it would be far easier for whites to settle with a man like him than with the bitter young militants who are rising through the ranks of the ANC. So the deal is urgent.

Even making due allowance for a measure of tactics (he was clearly out to impress his London audience with his moderation), the view emerged of a man quite unlike the one presented to South Africans through misleading quotes selected by the government and its supporting media. The interview was presented to our readers as part of the mosaic of viewpoints, ranging from far right to far left, that the Cape Times publishes.

It was as simple as that. Since I had had brushes with the law about quoting banned persons, I knew the possible consequences.

Publishing Mr. Tambo's views can only contribute to the inevitable peace process: A greater understanding of mutual positions can only help black and white to find accommodation. The incident could even serve to move the government to amend its cumbersome and oppressive ways, so that, unlike the white Rhodesians — who were kept in the dark until the day Robert Mugabe took over — white South Africans at least will know what they are up against.

So if the price to be paid for trying to serve the public's right to know is a measure of personal difficulty, that will have to be borne.

Heard became editor of the *Cape Times* in 1971. In August 1987, after 16 years as editor (he was then the longest-serving editor of a major South African newspaper), Tony Heard was dismissed by Times Media Ltd.

'I looked like a monster, but my God, I was happy'

Glynis Horning on Tandie Klaasen, jazz singer, 1986

Thirteen years ago, soul and jazz singer Tandie Klaasen had acid thrown in her face. To this day she doesn't know why. Horribly disfigured, she forced herself to sing in front of a 60 000-strong Soweto audience only one year later. On a working visit to Durban in 1986, she was interviewed by Glynis Horning, woman's editor of *The Natal Mercury.*

Horning recounts that she was so moved by Tandie Klaasen's story she had tears running down her face as she made her notes, the drops wrinkling the notepaper. Klaasen, recalling in detail the attack, also began to sob. The story, affecting but understated in Horning's clean, immaculate style, appeared on *The Natal Mercury*'s woman's page on Thursday, 8 May 1986.

The article provoked what Horning said was the most moving response she received from a feature she had written: a letter from a reader seriously contemplating suicide until she read about Tandie Klaasen's courage in the face of daunting odds. Reading about Tandie had given her the strength to continue with her own life.

This was the Big One.

After the long years rising from Sophiatown church choir to Swaziland casino cabaret and the stages of most South African capitals, two Japanese impresarios had come up with a formal invitation to tour the Far East with . . . NINA SIMONE.

"I tried not to be excited, I had had too many disappointments in life."

Tandie Klaasen gives a characteristic grimace-grin and lights one of many cigarettes.

"Too many failed promises of help from international stars I supported on tour, like Percy Sledge and Eartha Kitt and Dobie Grey. But this was a concrete offer. Too wonderful to be true!"

She just had to share it with a friend.

SUPPORT

And her closest friend was delighted with her, with the prospect of her beauty and talent finding fulfilment abroad, with her new riches (R6 000 for a six-month contract), and with her immediate plans to channel a substantial portion of that into building a creche for the children she adored.

Like Tandie's other friends, this one rallied around, giving her clothing and suitcases and urging her to "sock it to the world for us Tandie, sock it to the world!"

And she invited her to supper on the eve of her departure.

Tandie was stepping into the lounge when she heard the strange cry.

"Haak! That was it: Haak! It was my friend urging someone to go for it."

Someone did. One of two boys Tandie had barely noticed standing at the gate.

He threw petrol and paint thinners into her face.

"I remember they were playing my album, *Love is Strange.* And I remember thinking this is the end of everything. And wondering why, why, why. And the pain. Oh, the pain . . ."

Thirteen years on, *Love is Strange* remains her only album. But it hasn't been the end of everything.

She still doesn't know why ("Jealousy, who knows? I've seen that woman once since, at a garage, and she dropped her shopping parcels . . .").

Glynis Horning (The Natal Mercury).

And the pain is finally healed, although the scars will always remain.

"I remember the day I first took off the bandages and looked at myself in the mirror. The doctors didn't want me to. They stood around with their hands stretched out to support me, and as the bandage came away with the smell of a dead person, I saw the anguish in their eyes reflected in that mirror.

"I thought: accept it Tandie, accept it. But then the bandage fell, and there was really no face. No mouth, just a hole. And only a muscle on one side of where my throat had been to hold my chin to my trunk.

"What was I? What was I going to be?"

She doesn't know if it was then, or during the three weeks she slept standing up, strapped by her side to a support after graft operations removed the skin from her thighs — "Sometime, though, I began telling myself, you've got to make a go of it, Tandie. You're alive!"

But then her husband broke down at her bedside, and told her he couldn't live with her 'like that'. He was leaving.

"It was as though I had been burned for the second time. And he wasn't the only one. Friends who had loved me for my face and my fame left me too, and too often I would feel pity in those that stayed."

But Tandie found strength in the love of her 12-year-old daughter — "she kept saying, 'Dad, let's love Mummy now, she needs it,' but he got the divorce" — and in the realisation that there is real truth in the saying that beauty lies below the skin. "My husband was a very handsome man . . .

"From him, then, I learned that real love is when you don't have an arm, or a leg, or an eye, and your man still says, this is my woman."

She's found such a man in the intervening years, but he's married: "We're like brother and sister — I have great respect for him, and for his wife."

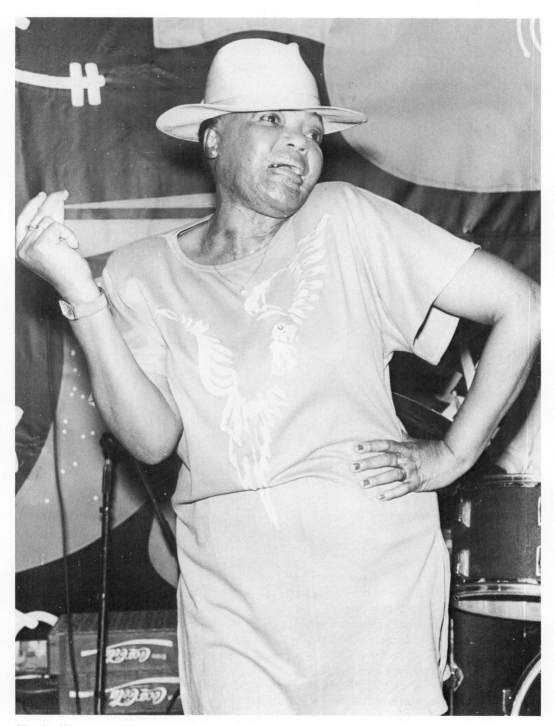

Tandie Klaasen: still singing (The Natal Mercury).

Her career, too, when compared with its early promise, remains largely unfulfilled, in spite of tours of Israel and Greece.

"I don't think my record company pushed the album. And there's still this feeling that South African artists are not as good or important as those from overseas. But I'm working at helping to change that, so things will be better for other generations of singers — like my daughter Lorraine, who is now married in Canada."

RETURN

Tandie's first return to the stage was before 60 000 people at Soweto's massive Emphi stadium a year after the burning.

"Ken Gampu announced me: Ladies and gentlemen, he said, the lady of songs is back. The people went wild, they screamed and ululated. And I sang *The First Time Ever I Saw Your Face* . . .

"The tears were pouring down the people's faces, even the press men taking pictures.

"And I forgot I was burned. I sang, and my mouth cracked, and the blood oozed down my face and dress. I looked like a monster, but my God, I was happy.

"I felt beautiful."

'This is something I've got to see'

Peter Younghusband's report on a Paarl rugby match, September 1986

A former special correspondent in southern Africa for *Newsweek,* Peter Younghusband is something of an expert when it comes to reporting zones of conflict. Before his return to this country from Washington, where he was the London *Daily Mail*'s White House correspondent, Younghusband had covered the Congo violence, the Zanzibar revolution, the conflicts in Biafra and the Sudan, as well as the Vietnam war, Israel's six-day war and the guerrilla war in the Aden protectorate — but nothing like the Paarl rugby match.

It is a fallacy that foreign correspondents spend all their time writing shock-horror stories about their host country, especially if that country happens to be South Africa, as Peter Young-husband's report on a Paarl rugby match nicely illustrates.

RUGBY MATCH CHISELS A CRACK IN APARTHEID

The bar in the Picardie Hotel in the town of Paarl in the Western Province of South Africa is not exactly the cultural centre of the community. But it is a place where national issues of great importance are frequently debated with both eloquence and vigour — so much vigour in fact that on occasions the debaters move outside into the High Street so as to address each other in more robust fashion.

It is at occasions like these that the police sometimes join the debate, whereupon the venue switches once more this time to the Charge Office and cells of the Paarl Central Police Station.

The final speeches are usually heard in the Paarl Magistrates Court, where the magistrate gives the final ruling on who was right. Invariably he rules that the police were right.

It was here, in this vibrant forum of the Picardie Bar, that one Johannes Vermaak, a railway shunter of honest repute, entered dramatically and announced the shattering news that the town's elite white High School, Paarl Gymnasium, was going to play the local Paulus Joubert coloured High School at rugby.

There was a long pause of total silence as the shock of this intelligence seeped into the embalmed minds of the Picardie assembly. All around the bar pints of Lion beer and tots of Old Buck gin and Commando brandy paused on their way to parched throats — in itself a rare interruption in the Picardie Bar.

465

Then Frans Esterhuizen, a farmer, shouted: "Jee-sus Christ. You mean our boys are going to play Hotten-tots?"

Dirk Malan, a long-distance lorry driver, said: "They'll also be playing Coolies. They've got Coolies at that Paulus Joubert School."

"But at least they won't be playing Kaffirs, they've got no Kaffirs there," said Bokkie van Jaarsveld, an agricultural implements salesman.

Bokkie van Jaarsveld was regarded as the liberal of the Picardie Bar, and his comment was ignored.

"Well," said Frans Esterhuizen, grimly, "this is something I've got to see." Everyone agreed that this would be a rugby match not to be missed.

As the news reached other parts of town it drew similar reactions of surprise, some of it more sophisticated than in the Picardie Bar, and some of it even less sophisticated.

Peter Younghusband: first ashore on war-torn Zanzibar.

By and large the reaction was disapproving. At best it was doubtful.

"I know things are changing in this country," said a middle-aged lady in Checkers supermarket, "but isn't this going too fast?"

To understand more easily the nature of this doubting it should be known that Paarl is a very conservative town. It is where the Afrikaans language was first formed and spoken, and a monument to the language stands proudly on a nearby hill to remind all of this important fact.

The town is white-walled and beautiful, situated among vineyards. Its rural, mainly Afrikaner community would like to keep it white-walled and beautiful — and white.

That a white and a coloured school had decided, among themselves, to play rugby together, was disturbing to this tranquillity — and proved once again that there was dangerous liberalism in learning and books.

It was true that multi-racial sport had arrived in South Africa, but it was not yet acknowledged in Paarl, sacred shrine of the language of Afrikanerdom.

For these various reasons a large crowd came to watch the rugby match between Paarl Gymnasium and Paulus Joubert High School last week.

Dr Danie Craven, grand chief and high priest of South African rugby, was there to give his blessing. "This is a breakthrough to a better South Africa," he said.

But old Paarl residents shook their heads sadly. Oom Danie van Niekerk, aged 80, and who had hoped to reach his grave without seeing such a terrible thing, said to his younger brother, Oom Johannes van Niekerk, aged 77: "Yerrah, yerrah, Jan, what has become of our town?"

Oom Johannes scowled. "It's all this damned television from America," he said.

The Picardie Bar debating society was there, with pint flasks in their pockets and prepared to be nasty, but feeling inhibited under the cold-eyed gaze of several members of the Paarl police force who came to stand purposefully close to them.

Elders of the Dutch Reformed Church, dressed in black, watched the scene with folded arms and narrowed eyes, intent on reporting back to God.

The coloured spectators who came to support and cheer for the Paulus Joubert team, stood separately from the white spectators.

The coaches of the two teams spoke last anxious words to their players. "If I hear any of you call any of them a Hottentot or a Coolie, I'll beat his brains out," said the Paarl Gymnasium coach.

The coloured coach of the Paulus Joubert team told his boys: "By inviting us to play them, these honkie Boers are behaving nicely — so no kicking or swearing at them. Now take off your boots, I want to make sure no one's got a knife in his sock."

The match was watched mainly in silence, although cheer teams from both schools worked valiantly at infusing some gaiety into the scene.

Privileged by years of better training and facilities, the white team began to pile on the score, and some white spectators smiled or nodded cynically.

The Picardie Bar contingent made snide comments.

Then, quite suddenly, a centre three-quarter on the coloured side found a gap in the Paarl Gymnasium defence and streaked through in a weaving, storming run. He ran like a person obsessed, as if pouring all his energy and determination into this one feat of excellence.

His brilliant burst took him forty yards and within five paces of the white line before he was pulled down.

The crowd — all the crowd — went mad with delight. In that instant the great South African love of rugby, which is more important than religion, more important than politics and knows no race barrier, eliminated all prejudice and made the crowd as one.

In that one electrifying moment apartheid was forgotten and South Africa moved a little further out of the shadows here in Paarl where Afrikanerdom has its roots.

"Yerrah, Jan, but these Hottentots can play rugby," said Oom Danie van Niekerk.

Which summed up an unfamiliar feeling among many of those present that perhaps such games were not a bad thing after all.

Younghusband is a master of the snappy introduction so much valued by editors the world over. Writing on one occasion from the twin hills in Swaziland known as Sheba's Breasts, his despatch began, simply: 'I like it here.'

On a quiet day in the Congo war in 1960, Younghusband persuaded a Belgian pilot to fly him over a position held by hostile troops. On returning to base a bullet hole was found in the plane's fuselage. In his despatch to his newspaper that day, Younghusband wrote: 'I was shot at today as we flew low over enemy lines . . .' (As a result of this mild exercise in hyperbole, the correspondent of a rival newspaper also covering the Congo story was sent a cable from his foreign editor, which tersely enquired: '*Daily Mail* says Younghusband shot at. Why you unshot at?')

But Younghusband's best effort was reserved for Zanzibar. When the revolution erupted in the early Sixties, all outside contact with the island was lost. While frustrated correspondents milled around in Dar es Salaam on the Tanganyikan mainland, Younghusband secretly hired a dhow, which slipped out of harbour at night and reached the island late the following afternoon.

Such was the intensity and noise and apparent danger of the battle ashore that the dhow crew refused to land and anchored indecisively several hundred yards offshore.

Angered and frustrated at being so close to the story yet unable to get there, Younghusband stripped to his underpants and swam ashore against an ebbing tide, almost drowning in the act. On reaching the harbour jetty, exhausted, he was immediately arrested by armed guards, who locked him, dripping wet and all but naked in a customs shed, failing to observe that it contained a telephone.

Younghusband lifted the receiver, dialled zero and to his amazed relief got an immediate response from an operator who had been trapped in the central telephone exchange by the fighting. He placed a call to the *Daily Nation* in Nairobi, was put through immediately and dictated his despatch, which was promptly relayed to London.

An ecstatic *Daily Mail* trumpeted the scoop in typical Fleet Street popular newspaper style: '*Mail*'s man first ashore on war-torn Zanzibar. Exclusive report'. The report included an account of the epic underpants swim. This moved the satirical journal, *Private Eye,* which regularly features the escapades of Fleet Street's popular press, to headline its own account of the event: 'First transvestite lands on spice isle'.

Peter Younghusband's affectionate report from Paarl on an epoch-making rugby match was printed in the *Washington Times* on 9 September 1986.

'It is just one more African conflict'

Al J. Venter on the Angolan border, 1986

Like many war correspondents before him, covering conflicts the world over has a special fascination for Al J. Venter. There is the whiff of personal danger, the challenge of writing up a story, frequently under arduous conditions — and getting the story out. It is a situation with which Archibald Forbes, Charles Norris-Newman, Winston Churchill, Carel Birkby and the correspondents who came after them were well familiar.

The Angolan conflict stretched long across southern Africa. From 1975, when South African forces invaded the country, until 1989 when a peace of sorts came to the vast territories, war spilled across the land. Correspondents from all over the world covered the battles, the forays and the incursions into Namibian and Angolan territory. Venter was no exception.

A correspondent, in the late 1960s and early 1970s for NBC (News) New York, the BBC, the London *Daily Express* and *Sunday Express,* United Press International (UPI) and *International Defense Review*, Geneva, Venter has made a life's work out of conflict and in particular the Angolan war. The author of the first book to appear on guerrilla warfare in southern Africa (*The Terror Fighters,* 1969), Venter took into the bush with him as many creature comforts as he could. In this he emulated, although not in quite such a lavish way, Winston Churchill, who travelled the length and breadth of South Africa with his wagon a metre deep in London supplies.

Venter's luxuries include gin (and tonic), a couple of bottles of claret, salami and (on occasion) Beluga caviar. 'If I'm going to die in the bush, I might as well do it on a full stomach,' he once remarked. Blown up by a landmine in Angola without suffering any notable after effects, Venter enlisted with the FNLA in order to get a story. After six weeks' fighting, he deserted and, together with the correspondent from *Le Monde* (who was carrying Marxist literature with him) was arrested and charged with desertion in the face of the enemy.

The pair were held initially in a Lubumbashi whorehouse. Aware that the discovery of the Marxist literature would probably mean a very rapid death sentence, the two correspondents slashed open a much worn mattress in the room in which they were being held and stuffed the offending papers into it. They smuggled out a note, written on lavatory paper, to Agence France Presse, who in turn contacted the French and British authorities. The pair were eventually driven to the Zambian border, after being thoroughly beaten up.

Venter's despatch, covering a sortie with South African troops, was printed in July 1986 in the American publication *The Best of SOF,* which featured 20 of the best articles on war reporting internationally over the previous decade.

THE BOYS IN THE BUSH

by Al J. Venter

Peter Dreyer could have been a combatant in any fighting man's army. Wiry, like a terrier, he could march for days at a stretch and often through the night if the trail was "hot".

His appearance — torn fatigues, bush hat tucked in on the sides to allow for, as he put it, "better hearing", T-shirt with sleeves ripped off and looking as if it had been on his back for a month, buckle-down webbing and R4 automatic carbine — belied his origins. A seven-day growth of beard, sparse in parts, could not conceal Dreyer's youthful features. The South African turned 19 on his last 11-day patrol along the Angolan border.

A decade and a half earlier, he probably would have been indistinguishable from the thousands of young

Al J. Venter, war correspondent, TV documentary maker and author.

Americans and Australians serving in 'Nam. He enjoyed the same kind of home life as they before coming to the front. He had folks and a girl back home. Evenings, when he was bedded down in his narrow slit trench that had taken half an hour to dig in the dark, he would spend time reflecting upon what he would probably be doing at that moment were he not in the bush. Dreyer's thoughts were the stuff of a hundred wars before him and countless thousands of soldiers on patrol in wartime.

But, in Vietnam, the terrain and weather were different, for South West Africa is a dry, often dusty land, especially in the north where the terrain gives way to almost desert conditions for some months of the year.

The common denominator is the enemy. Like the Viet Cong, SWAPO — or *Swaps,* as its members are referred to by Dreyer and his pals — receives most of its moral and material succour from the Soviets.

While I was with Dreyer in the bush, he fought his own war, usually with animated vigour. His mind was tuned to absolutes; there was no middle way. It was either for or against — and SWAPO was definitely against — especially in a conflict so close to home. As the crow flies, Ovamboland is about 650 miles from the red brick municipal house in which Dreyer was born and bred in Mafeking (of Boer war siege fame).

It takes a couple of days to get into the routine of spending more than 12 hours a day walking through some of the most inhospitable country on any continent. It's not easy going. The sand in this region is soft and for much of the distance it's a punishing "uphill" struggle, like walking on the seashore. It's interesting that throughout Ovamboland there are no stones; if you run out of ammo you haven't even got rocks with which to defend yourself. The only comforting aspect is that the enemy is faced with similar problems.

Certainly, one of the lasting recollections from this remote bush country is of the

470

sounds encountered en route, noises — a symphony of the African night — to which most city people never become accustomed.

So it was, in early April 1981, during that second two-hour watch after the cries from the nearby kraal had settled to a monotonous murmur that the bush baby suddenly screamed above our heads like a woman raped. In less time than it takes to sound a general alert, we were all on our elbows at the ready. It's astonishing that a tiny animal which would fit comfortably in cupped hands can create such mayhem. But it happens. Routinely.

Few of the men slept easily that night. An hour earlier, most of the 30-man patrol had been roused by the sharp call of a jackal, barely 50 yards from where we lay in a calcite depression. It was an ominous, hollow cry; to the superstitious among us, it spelled disaster.

The outer sector had reported back briefly by radio. But the young lieutenant, barely a year older than Dreyer, wasn't satisfied until he'd checked out the direction of the call himself. The lieutenant — called "Horse" by his men — returned 20 minutes later not entirely convinced that the sound could not have been human, though at the time he said nothing.

Then most of us fell into a fitful sleep, punctuated occasionally by Africa's discordant uneasiness. No doubt there were others out there in the dark watching, too.

Other sounds, like the sharp screech as one of the animals of the night made a kill woke some of the men after midnight. It seemed that there was something remorseless about the cry, futile and helpless, like the war which raged sporadically in this vast, arid African basin fringing the cold Atlantic.

We would probably have been more alert had we known that we would encounter — at first light — the tracks of a 50-strong enemy insurgent force headed southward out of Angola, barely a mile from where we slept. They could as easily have chosen the narrow tracks on this side of the Odilla watershed. Then, at least, some of the men would have been able to justify this fruitless seven-day march for a spoor of blood.

The possibility of contact is real enough on all these patrols. But in reality, a firefight rarely materializes in its conventional, accepted form. More likely, we — like the enemy we sought — would spot a couple of dim figures moving among the sparse mopani trees and sound a challenge. Shots would follow. Then a search. Nothing. Another 12-hour chase, often at the double, with Airborne leapfrogging ahead in an attempt to set up a stop group. Then maybe a kill. Maybe . . .

The enemy is hungry. In Ovamboland this year they're killing 50 000 head of cattle because the rains have been so sparse. Locals have little enough to keep themselves alive, not to mention feeding the units of an insurgent force.

Few of the men complain about the rigours of the bush, for the majority are still young enough to adapt quickly. In any event, these are the same kinds of hardships which have been weathered by a full generation of southern African fighting men before them — Rhodesia's included.

It is just one more African conflict. In the past, the continent left its mark on French, British, Portuguese, Spanish, Belgian, German, Italian and American troops, as it is now doing along the borders of an ebullient Angola.

The average South African operational patrol can last — according to demands or circumstances — anywhere from a few hours to several weeks. On average, though, periods between seven and 11 days are the norm, although long-range penetration groups do, on occasion, go out for months at a stretch. Those are the Special Forces . . . the "Recces".

Special forces prepare for demolition of a Soviet PT-76 amphibious tank lying half sunk in the Kunene River. A South African Air Force Alouette gunship hovers in the background (Al Venter).

472

In a land as arid as Ovambo, the men try to carry as much water as possible. It might not always be feasible to resupply, though it is possible to "chopper" water in, in an emergency. During dry seasons, available water is usually covered by a green bacterial slime, but the majority of troops appear (with the help of purification tablets) to cope with it astonishingly well. One sortie with a mounted patrol in 1978 left me in the hospital for a fortnight after I was obliged to drink bad water to stay alive. You need to understand real thirst under tropical conditions to appreciate that predicament.

On average, troopies pack six one-litre water bottles. A "rat-pack" a day containing a fairly adequate supply of provisions makes for more weight, though after the second or third time out, men are less likely to haul as many cans of food. Dog biscuits can make as good a meal as a steak when you're really hungry, though few modern soldiers are likely to believe it.

With weapons, ammunition, spare batteries, mortar bombs, mines, additional food, water and a dozen ammo clips each, the average South African troopie can count himself lucky if he sets out from base carrying less than 80 pounds. Packing this weight, he is expected to average 25 miles a day through the soft sand, which can be hell to anyone experiencing it for the first time. It could be *Beau Geste* all over again, though the terrain lacks the sparseness of the Sahara.

The radio "mech" invariably marches heavier; he rarely settles for less than 100

Action against Swapo elements in a forward base on the Angolan border with Namibia (Al Venter).

473

pounds, including his rifle. The heavyweight prize patrol usually goes to the machine-gunners. On our seven-day sortie, Number One Bren, loaded down with additional magazines and three belts of 7.62mm ammo, each containing 200 rounds, topped 114 pounds, but the bearer appeared to manage comfortably, although his muscles stood out like brown cords. Better him than me . . .

No patrol works along any set pattern in the bush regions adjoining Angola. The object, each time, is to search for the enemy and, if possible, destroy him. And while some foreign observers — notably the Israelis — have been critical of this form of military methodology, routine patrols do serve the purpose of preventing ground saturation of much of Ovamboland by SWAPO cadres. Vacate any area for a period and SWAPO will exploit it before long. The Rhodesians learned that hard lesson in December 1972, when *Operation Hurricane* was initiated.

Tracking in this war has become something of a science. Some of the more experienced scouts — many of them city-bred white folk — can tell, from a short series of spoors, a man's pace, weight, and his height as well. It's also possible to "read" whether the subject was alert, his mood and whether he was carrying a heavy load (the heels dig in deeper).

An interesting comment made by one of the experts attached to South West Africa's Special Operations Unit was that very often city boys become better trackers than farmers' sons. Some are even better than locally born Africans, though even the enemy has to concede that the primitive little yellow-skinned Bushman has no peer in this field on the African continent.

Put a Bushman on the spoor of a SWAPO contingent and, all things being equal, contact is usually made if pace and light allow. That's one of the reasons why SWAPO will usually shoot on sight any Bushman civilian — male, female or child — it finds in the Operational Area.

It's tragic sidelight of a continuing war.

'A scar on the soul
of our communities'

Percy Qoboza on the lessons of Soweto: ten years after

The tenth anniversary of the Soweto uprising, 16 June 1986, was marked not merely by a State of Emergency, rumours of unrest in Soweto and a worker stay away, but by a series of articles commemorating the historic event.

With the hindsight of a decade, Percy Qoboza, editor of *City Press,* looked back on the days leading up to the explosion of violence and mob rule in an article published in the *Sunday Times* on 15 June 1986.

According to the *Sunday Times* of that date: 'a picture of Hector Peterson lying mortally wounded — and which came to symbolise 16 June — was planned for this space, but was withheld by the *Sunday Times* to comply with the restrictions imposed on the media in terms of the emergency regulations. Mr Qoboza's article, written before the emergency was declared, has also been drastically edited to comply with the regulations.'

Although angry about the censorship, Qoboza, a Nieman Fellow and holder of the Pringle Award and The Golden Pen of Freedom, was philosophical about it. The article, as it appeared in the *Sunday Times,* is printed here. Notwithstanding the required censorship, it makes good, angry reading and provides an insight into the actions of some of the principal figures in an unforgettable drama, seen through the eyes of the late Percy Qoboza.

'Of all the horrors experienced, none will obliterate the memory of that 11-year-old boy falling under the hail of police bullets. He was the first casualty of the unrest . . .'

For many of us who lived through the trauma of June 16, 1976, it was a nightmare that has left a deep scar on the soul of our communities.

And what patently shocks me is that the three men history will indict for the hundreds of lives lost, thousands of men, women and children maimed, remain obscure in the public mind as this nation continues to count the cost of the conflict they began.

Topping the list of the people whose short-sighted actions launched this country into the bloodiest decade is the leader of the Conservative Party, Dr Andries Treurnicht.

As Deputy Minister of Bantu Education, he introduced the controversial directive that forced black schools to teach 50 percent of classroom subjects in Afrikaans. There was an immediate outcry from parents, teachers and students.

It is well worth noting that there had never been any resistance to or even talk of

475

Afrikaans being taught at our schools. So there was no question of any resentment towards Afrikaners as people like Dr Treurnicht would like us to believe.

The anger was sparked by the sheer fact that black education, inferior as it is at the moment, would deteriorate even further. Black teachers were not proficient enough to teach in Afrikaans, let alone as a subject.

But to expect them to extend their already limited use of the language by teaching such subjects as history, mathematics or science in Afrikaans was merely to add another terrible roadblock against people struggling for liberation.

While the debate and argument was going on, the whole issue became violently politicised. More so when one took into account the time spell it was allowed to occupy in the national debate.

This time spell became deadly.

I know that the ox wagon occupies a cherished place in the history of some people in the land.

But the ox wagon mentality that accompanies decision-making in this land is lethal. To illustrate what I mean:

When my wife and I left South Africa in August 1975 to study for a year at Harvard University in the States, the question of Afrikaans in the schools was already a boiling issue.

When we got back from the States in June the following year it was becoming a volcano in its intensity.

I was so shocked by the public anger that I took it upon myself to go to Parliament and get Dr Treurnicht to suspend the directive. I met him for an hour and he was unmoving and determined.

Nothing I could say to him could convince him that violence could threaten in the townships. His last words to me were as devastating as his directive:

"Surely, Mr Kwabusa, if my people are paying for your children's education as we are, then we surely have the right to decide what they must be taught and how they must be taught."

It was the most tragic display of insensitivity I have ever come across.

Later on that day, with the help of friends such as Rene de Villiers, Helen Suzman and John Patten, the second figure in the whole tragedy was persuaded to see me. That was John Vorster, then Prime Minister.

He saw me in his parliamentary office that afternoon and I very much repeated what I had told Treurnicht, but this time with all the sense of urgency I could master.

He was half-listening to me, his eyes fixed on a TV screen following proceedings in Parliament. At the end he turned to me with the icy, cold-blooded look that only Vorster could produce in moments of high agitation.

He gave me the assurance that his Government intended proceeding with the implementation of the directive in spite of what anybody else said.

He gave me another assurance. This time spine-chilling.

"Law and order," he said, "will be maintained at all costs."

I left Cape Town a very disillusioned but also a very angry man. These people were sitting there in their ivory towers without an inkling of what was happening to the country.

As everybody knows, exactly six days after my trip, Soweto exploded.

I knew, or I thought at the time, the very deep sense of anger and outrage. But even I was not prepared for its ferocity.

Naked power caused it all. I knew on that day the kids were going to hold a mass meeting at Orlando stadium.

I knew because I am a father of five children and they told me they were going to discuss the whole education crisis at that meeting. All fathers and mothers knew that.

At about 10 that fateful day came the phone call from one of my reporters, Sophie Tema, that thousands of students were approaching the Orlando stadium for the meeting.

Yes, they were peaceful. No, they were not carrying any placards. I asked her and photographer Sam Nzima to keep an eye on the event. Exactly an hour later she was back on the phone.

With a shaking voice she announced that Soweto had gone up in flames. From her vivid account of the events that led to that violent outbreak, it seems the police confronted the marching students and gave them five minutes to disperse.

But before she could even count up to 10, the police opened fire on the students.

For Sophie the horror of it all will follow her to her grave. Of all the horrors experienced, none will obliterate the memory of that 11-year-old boy falling under the hail of police bullets. He was the first casualty of the unrest.

Percy Qoboza (City Press).

His name, Hector Peterson, has become a living symbol of youth resistance in South Africa.

That day Soweto was covered by a dark, menacing cloud. Fathers and mothers downed tools as rumours filtered through about the problems of the townships.

They hurried back to Soweto to see if their children were still alive. For me and my reporters it was the beginning of hell.

A hell we have gone through and were to go through for a decade to this very day.

School buildings went up in flames. Administration buildings were brought down. Bottle stores were burned down. Any building that represented officialdom did not survive the fury.

It is worth noting here that none of the schools that were put up by the Teach Fund suffered even a scratch.

For in spite of the blind fury that engulfed people, they still distinguished between buildings put up by the State and those by private enterprise.

At this stage, the third of the three musketeers emerged. His name: Jimmy Kruger, then Minister of Police. His men were dispatched from all over the country and far from containing the unrest, the fires were simply fanned.

Sad to say, they did not learn their lessons.

Jimmy Kruger, however, was unrepentant in the defence of the police force and police methods. In the same way that his successor, Louis le Grange, does today.

Mr le Grange may well take note that 10 years later, even the Nats, so notorious when coming to defend each other, are distancing themselves from Jimmy Kruger and refer to him in the most contemptuous terms for his handling of the police.

Kruger's response to the escalating violence that spread across the borders of Soweto into every town and village in South Africa was to declare war on the Press. The media has always been the whipping boy of South African politics.

By that October, Kruger demonstrated that he meant business in his declared war against the Press. In one day his police arrested and imprisoned without trial four of my senior reporters.

They were photographer Moffat Zungu, writers Z B Molefe, Willie Bokala and Joe Thloloe. They were kept in Modder Bee Prison for periods ranging from three to five months under Section 10 of the Security Act.

They were not in jail because they were criminals. Neither did they instigate violence or in any way behave in a manner that could cast aspersions on them as professional journalists.

A year later he was to close down *The World* and *Weekend World* and topped that dastardly action by coming for me and my news editor and also tossed us in jail for nearly six months without trial.

This had the desired impact as far as the Press was concerned. Over-cautious editors began to look at copy more often. Sometimes to a stage of near self-censorship.

But the troubles of South Africa did not vanish from the face of the earth. They simply did not find their way into editorial pages of many newspapers for fear of victimisation.

This nation has never known real peace since 1976.

Instead of violence diminishing, it is growing in leaps and bounds. Not surprisingly.

We have never learned the lesson of '76.

The Government still believes it can solve political problems by using force.

Until such time that it comes to the realisation that the security forces can never replace sensible negotiation with the true leaders of our communities, that violence will continue.

At the end it must come face to face with the reality that it is dealing with a new generation of black men.

Brutalised by a society that has given violence a dubious credibility it does not deserve, and fired by the spirit of wanting to live in a free and just society, that generation has shown an amazing capacity to suffer pain.

The State President would do well to reflect on the words of the late Dr Martin Luther King Jnr:

"The ultimate weakness of violence is that it is a descending spiral, begetting the very thing it seeks to destroy. Instead of diminishing evil, it multiplies it.

"Through violence you may murder the liar, but you cannot murder the lie, nor establish the truth. Through violence you murder the hater, but you do not murder the hate. In fact, violence merely increases hate.

"Returning violence for violence multiplies violence, adding deeper darkness to a night already devoid of stars. Darkness cannot drive out darkness; only light can do that. Hate cannot drive out hate; only love can do that."

This whole nation is suffering from the negative paralysis of a sense of hopelessness.

White people are scurrying out of the country and black people are bracing themselves for what threatens to be the worst winter of their discontent.

This cycle of violence must be broken by honest negotiation carried out by people who must accept the inescapable truth that unless they learn together as brothers, then they will perish together as fools.

The Government must accept that gradualism such as it espouses is not on. Not as a negotiating starting point. What we need now is a bold, unequivocal statement of intent.

A commitment to demolish all the structures of apartheid. A programme of action, based not on the perceptions of the National Party but on the broad aspirations of all our people.

It's the only way. The only choice between peace and chaos.

'"Comrade Nico Smith", the Calvinist minister'

Michael Parks, Los Angeles Times, 1986

In 1986, Michael Parks sent 255 by-lined stories to his newspaper, the *Los Angeles Times*. On average, he sends eight to nine articles a week, a mixture of the longer pieces required by the *LA Times* and daily stories. 'There's no shortage of stories in South Africa,' Parks once noted. 'A lot happens in the country.'

It was for that very reason that Parks, who has served as foreign correspondent in Vietnam, Moscow, Cairo and Peking (he speaks both Russian and Chinese) asked to be posted to South Africa when he joined the *Los Angeles Times* in 1980.

Among one of Parks' many assignments was an interview with the Rev. Nico Smith of Mamelodi. The article, which appeared in the *Los Angeles Times* on 24 October 1986, was in part responsible for Parks' winning the 1987 Pulitzer Prize for international reporting.

WHITE PASTOR JOINS BLACK 'REAL AFRICA'

By MICHAEL PARKS

Times Staff Writer

MAMELODI, South Africa — The moving van's journey from the white, middle-class Pretoria suburb of Meyer's Park to this black ghetto township on the outskirts of the South African capital was less than three miles and took only a few minutes.

But for the Rev. Nico Smith, it was like emigrating, leaving the country of his birth and entering another, stepping out of his own world to discover a strange one.

Smith, the pastor of Mamelodi's Dutch Reformed Church, and his wife, Ellen, a child psychiatrist, had just become the first whites to move into an urban black township with official permission since the South African government formally segregated residential areas in 1950.

Leaving Ancestral Home

"It was a very strange emotional experience, wrenching but exhilarating," Smith said recently. "You realize that you are moving out of your father's house where you were born and bred and where you have lived for 57 years and are moving out of a culture to which you belong into Africa, the real Africa.

The Rev. Nico Smith of Mamelodi (Reuters).

"There was uncertainty, there was excitement, there was anxiety as we realized we were entering a totally different world . . . We had worked here for 4½ years and thought we knew it well, but without living here we were just visitors, day-trippers almost, from another country. It's only now, by moving here, that I feel I have said farewell to apartheid."

For Smith, the different sounds of a black township — dogs barking but no birds singing, heavy traffic already at 5 a.m. but an almost eerie stillness after 9 p.m., cocks crowing before dawn — have been vivid reminders of what he calls "our emigration" from white South Africa.

Neighbours in Bed Early

Lying awake in bed the first night in his new home, Smith suddenly thought how quiet densely populated

Michael Parks (Reuters).

Mamelodi was, much quieter than his old white suburban neighbourhood. And then he realized that Mamelodi's 300,000 residents go to bed early because so many of them rise at dawn to be at work across town by 7 a.m.

Later, he awoke to crowing roosters instead of the singing birds he was used to — and realized "how few trees there are here in which birds can nest" and that many black families still keep poultry in their small yards because supermarket prices for eggs and chickens are beyond their small incomes.

Even more than before, Smith said, he realizes how separate are the worlds of South Africa's 25 million blacks and its white minority of 5 million.

"We whites have built a Western world at the southern tip of Africa," Smith said. "If all this were quietly cut off, towed away and attached to Europe, few people would notice the difference. We think we have become Africans, but we haven't. We are pretending. Until whites stop pretending and truly become part of Africa, we will not resolve our problems. . . .

"The terrible thing is that apartheid has worked! It has divided this country so completely into separate worlds that uniting them again is a Herculean task even when it only takes, as it did for us, a drive down the road."

After only a week in Mamelodi, Smith says he finds himself "moving away, more and more, from the white world."

"The news on the radio sounds like it is from another country," he remarked. "The news of white South Africa might be that of Switzerland or Sweden, a place I've visited but don't live. A few days ago, when I listened to President P.W. Botha on the radio for the first time in the township, he sounded more aggressive than I remember him being, and I was really frightened, in fact, that he was going to come kill the people. . . .

"Our perspective obviously began changing years ago, but moving into Mamelodi seems to have accelerated the process and really made us feel part of the people."

Smith and his wife decided to move to Mamelodi to be closer, physically and spiritually, to his congregation of nearly 500 families, but getting government permission took two years, and building their new house nearly as long.

Although the Anglican and Roman Catholic churches frequently assign white priests to black parishes, their bishops do not, as a matter of principle, seek government permission for the white clergy to live in the townships. The government, rather than risk embarrassing clashes with the churches, ignores such apparent violations of the 1950 Group Areas Act and other laws enforcing racial segregation.

"We decided to try to do it legally, with government permission, because we wanted that official acknowledgement that we were members of this community and entitled to be so," Smith said, sitting amid the disorder of half-unpacked boxes and furniture not yet in place.

As a pastor, Smith felt that he could not remain in Meyer's Park but had to move across the railroad tracks into Mamelodi to be true to his Christian faith.

"Christ as the son of God through the incarnation became part of the human race," he said, "but he did not become flesh among the rulers or the upper class but as the son of a carpenter in Nazareth. . . . I tell whites that if Christ came today, he would be born somewhere in Mamelodi."

The Smiths' home was designed so that it would not overwhelm the township's small, four-room, red-brick "matchbox" houses, yet give them enough room to live and work comfortably.

About a fourth the size of their Meyer's Park home, it has an open-plan downstairs, where the lounge leads to Smith's "study corner" and then to the dining room, across from a modern kitchen, and a small guest bedroom. Upstairs, under a geodesic dome modeled on the design of the American architect Buckminster Fuller, there is a bedroom and a study for Smith's wife. The backyard is surrounded by a brick wall to give a bit of privacy, and in front there is the start of a modest lawn, rare in black townships.

"We decided we needed to get out of the Western concept of a house, and I thought that the dome, though it is very unusual for South Africa, was in the image of the round top of an African hut," Smith said. "Remembering that sometimes there are 25, 28 or 30 persons living in the little matchboxes down the street, we felt we had to have the maximum space in something not so big."

The house was largely financed by foreign donations. Members of the Bel-Air Presbyterian Church in Los Angeles donated $20,000 or three-quarters of its cost.

"Our congregation could not do it — they are too poor," Smith said. "White congregations that might have helped wouldn't because they thought I was mad. Thank God the Americans understood and helped."

Construction was complicated by the unusual design, by the continuing civil unrest and, most of all, by the maze of laws and regulations that govern almost every aspect of life in South Africa's black townships.

"What a struggle we had," Smith said, recounting battles over conflicting construction codes, zoning regulations and other rules meant for blacks that now applied to him as well. "When I describe all the permits I had to obtain and the laws I had to get around and the regulations I had to comply with, blacks really enjoy it. They say, 'Now you're really becoming a black man — that's what we go through from birth to death.' "

Since moving into the new house, they have received a warm welcome from Mamelodi residents, Smith said.

"This is the South Africa they want to see — blacks and whites living together, getting to know and understand one another, helping each other — and perhaps we represent a bit of hope that it might be possible some day," he added.

But the Smiths are regarded with considerable disdain, often disgust and sometimes suspicion by many South African whites, particularly other Afrikaners, who regard the couple as renegades.

" 'Aren't you afraid?' is the first question whites ask," Smith said. "White fear is one of the great barriers to understanding and progress in this country, and the thought of living among blacks seems to arouse concern even with our liberal friends. . . .

"Fear of the unknown is always great, of course, and then the large number of blacks compared to whites is another factor. But over the past two years there has been an increasing realization by whites of the depth and the degree of black anger — some people are seeing they may well have reason to be afraid in the future. . . ."

Smith confessed that he was apprehensive the first day when he had to leave his wife at home alone until late in the evening while storing the rest of their furniture at a farmhouse outside Pretoria.

"I was very tense, thinking of my wife as the only white among 300,000 blacks," he recalled, "but when I got home she was her normal relaxed self and I saw I had no need to worry."

A few days later, he got a lesson in township violence and crime.

"I had been visiting a neighbor and, coming out of his house, we saw two young men with long knives robbing a third right in front of us," he said. " 'Let's go help,' I said, but my neighbour said, 'Don't go near those boys — they will kill you in an instant.' Unfortunately, he was right, and I thought that, if only the police would deal with this sort of crime instead of driving up and down intimidating honest people, the community would be so grateful."

The next question whites ask is simply, "Why?" Smith continued, "and the attitude behind it is, 'Well, it is all right perhaps for a white clergyman to work among blacks and bring them the Gospel, but wanting to live among them is incomprehensible.' The reason is that we whites don't regard blacks as 'our own people, our own kind.' "

When permission was granted for the Smiths to move to Mamelodi, it was doubly shocking because they are Afrikaners.

"I went from being an outcast to a traitor," he said in an interview at the time. "To my people, what we wanted to do was unfathomable, and that it was a deliberate decision was unforgivable."

While probably 75% of the white adults in Pretoria have been abroad, Smith said, "perhaps 1% have been to Mamelodi, and maybe 10% know where it is. And whites regard this as perfectly natural. That is what I mean when I say apartheid has succeeded in dividing us and making it seem normal."

Most white South Africans, according to recent public opinion surveys, do regard their racially segregated "own residential areas" as essential, and oppose any reforms that would change present laws and bring integrated neighbourhoods.

Addressing a recent meeting of his ruling National Party, President Botha reaffirmed his commitment to the basic principle of residential segregation while saying that the government might allow a few areas to become multi-racial and permit wealthy blacks to move into upper-class white neighborhoods.

"You will have to get rid of me first before you get rid of this principle," Botha said, describing segregated residential areas as a "cornerstone" of government policy.

To Smith, the repeal of the Group Areas Act and related laws is nearly as important as full political rights for blacks in ending apartheid and establishing "a just and democratic system" for the country.

"The changes up to now have not been real changes," he said of Botha's step-by-step reforms. "They are attempts to remove the abnormalities that the Nationalist government imposed in what it thought was a solution — a way to keep a tight grip on blacks. . . .

"When they removed the pass laws," he said, referring to the repeal this year of legislation that required blacks to have government permits to enter urban areas, "I thought that was something, because they had caused so much misery to so many millions of people over the years.

"But then a black friend told me it was actually like a big bully grabbing your arm and twisting it behind your back and hurting you more and more until the pain seemed unbearable and then letting go and telling you to say, "Thank you, boss, thank you.' "

Such views have made Smith, a former missionary and theology professor, controversial for more than a decade, and he has become even more outspoken — some would say radical — as a result of the civil unrest of the last two years.

"If the government does not negotiate with the African National Congress and the Pan Africanist Congress, there will be more and more trouble," he warned. "The longer they wait, the more that human relationship will be damaged, and perhaps damaged to such an extent that it won't be safe for a white person to live anywhere in South Africa."

Smith, who is often the only white at the scene of confrontations with the police and army who is not in the security forces, says he has seen "frustration, anger and alienation" growing among blacks here and in the other ghetto townships around Pretoria, where political violence has frequently been intense over the last two years.

"Instead of developing the human relationships that we need to save us from a catastrophic conflict, we seem to be destroying them, almost deliberately," he said.

Introduced at black funerals and political rallies as "Comrade Nico Smith," the Calvinist minister has won the trust of even militant black youths, who have asked him to mediate with the police and government on occasion and who clearly regard him as part of "the struggle", as they call their fight against apartheid.

But all this also brings intense police surveillance. Police and army patrols pass his house regularly. Daughters of a white colleague at the University of South Africa, where Smith is a part-time lecturer in theology, were picked up on a visit to Mamelodi and questioned for four hours about their relationship with him. A foreign television crew filming his move to Mamelodi was quickly told to leave. When Smith asked why, he was told, "Orders are orders."

"You then understand the brutality and aggression that blacks experience day after day in this society," he commented.

Smith hopes nevertheless that his house will become a "contact point" between blacks and whites.

"I hope my white friends, particularly the conservative ones, will come to visit and that they can meet my black friends here," he said. "I want to be a bridge, if I can, and I hope I can, but many of the gulfs in this country appear to be getting wider and deeper."

'A decaying smell of the past'

Ken Owen on the 60s, liberalism and the shadow of a giant, 1987.

Controversial, provocative, scathing, unrepentent, Ken Owen has enlivened South African journalism for over 20 years, but no more so than in the three years he has edited *Business Day.*

His perversity is legend; so, too, are his writing skills. His editorials and leader-page articles (his Monday column in *Business Day* is fast becoming a cult) are filled with a rich imagery and biting prose which make his work both formidable and elegant. Not since the days of Laurence Gandar has an English-speaking editor written with such passion, style and power. 'He writes,' noted a contemporary, 'like a nightingale'.

Journalism, Owen said once, has always been discussed as though it was some kind of absolute. But it's not. 'You say what you have the courage to say in the form that is available to you. It has nothing to do with the State.'

Owen first met Alan Paton in the 50s. New to journalism (he was a failed miner and bank clerk), he was unable to fully understand Paton's philosophy. The decade Owen spent in the United States — from the late 1960s to the late 1970s — fashioned his own liberalism. When he returned to South Africa, Owen embraced the ageing Alan Paton's liberalism. 'It seemed to me that he, more than anybody else, was a civilised voice in a barbarous country.' Indeed, the very future of journalism in South Africa, Owen believes, depends on how many journalists display the same high courage as the late Alan Paton.

In the days after what many people, nationally and internationally, believed would be the last white election in South Africa, Owen, in a ruminative, poignant piece of journalism linked to Paton, wrote a despatch which appeared on the leader page of *Business Day* on 25 May 1987.

The shadow of Alan Paton

Viewed from the Press gallery in Parliament, the political scene has been changed almost beyond belief but there is an atmosphere about it — a decaying smell of the past — that is disturbingly familiar.

The outward, visible changes have been reduced already by journalistic hype to a cliché: apartheid attacked from the right, the NP defending the cause of reasonableness like an ogre in a pretty mask, and so forth.

And indeed it is hard to avoid comparing Connie Mulder's praise for Zulu nationalism with old Daan de Wet Nel's lyrical talk in the Sixties of the "ox-wagon culture" of the Xhosas.

486

Editor Ken Owen: he enjoyed one of the shortest editorships in South African history when he assumed the editorship of Business Day *in 1985. It lasted three days before he was removed. In 1986 he was reappointed editor of the paper* (Business Day).

The CP's talk of partition is a re-run, slightly out of focus, of the Odendaal Plan for Namibia, which sent veteran observers of the Sixties reeling down the corridors, helpless with laughter.

Where's your map?" cry the Nationalist backbenchers, just as the old UP backbenchers used to cry out for a map. And, of course, no map comes forth.

But behind all this, in peripheral vision, lies something else which is even harder to bring into focus: a shadow of the Sixties when the political debate inside Parliament was even farther removed from the realities in the streets than it is today; when Verwoerd's astonishing flights of fancy seemed less comical than Andries Treurnicht's Boerestaat, or whatever it is to be called, and when the dreamer was not in Opposition but in power.

Then, as now, the country had been through a period of convulsive violence, culminating in the Sharpeville massacre, then, as now, the currency had crashed as foreign confidence collapsed and exchange controls were imposed to defend the national treasure. Foreign correspondents were clawing their way into the country lest they miss the revolution, and the middle-class whites were clawing their way out.

The Progressive Party had been slaughtered at the polls, reduced to Helen Suzman alone, and the Rand Daily Mail became — for friend and foe — a revolutionary symbol because it refused to continue calling Africans "natives". That gentle old liberal, Chief Albert Luthuli, was honoured abroad like Archbishop Tutu, and banned at home.

That was the time when John Vorster, an implacable young man with wartime connections to Nazism (through the Ossewabrandwag) that seemed to us much worse then than the political pedigree of any of the CP members seems today, took command of the extra-parliamentary forces which Parliament controls: the police, the secret agencies, the security apparatus, the Department of Justice, the law.

And he fashioned them into a machine that ground the extra-parliamentary opposition to dust.

He began by finding his own version of the "total onslaught" in the form of an atavistic tribally-based off-shoot of the Pan Africanist Congress called Poqo. In a chilling funeral oration at the grave of two white youngsters beheaded in a night time Poqo attack

487

in Paarl, he named the liberation movements "the forces of darkness". He went from the graveside to demolish the rule of law, introducing 90-day detention (which turned out to be indefinite detention in practice), and he gradually, systematically, wiped out the extra-parliamentary opposition.

When it comes to extra-parliamentary politics, government holds all the cards, but he did not even use the army.

That was a time when left-wingers gleefully pronounced liberalism irrelevant, and set to helping young liberals make bombs in order to "prove their commitment to the cause".

John Harris blew up an old woman on Johannesburg station, and left a young girl to live out her pitiful life behind a mask of terrible scars. Adrian Leftwich, a little weasel of a man, sponsored a conspiracy of violence among his UCT friends, and ratted on them after only an hour in the hands of the security police.

He dragged down with him Bill Hoffenberg, one of the finest medical scientists of our century, who was innocent, but left the country to escape a banning order imposed because Leftwich had named him as being sympathetic; so his marvellous skills were lost to this country, and the medical students at UCT who might have learned from him are today deprived.

When I saw Leftwich later in New York, as haunted as Judas Iscariot, he was a shell of a man but he survived while his friends served their prison sentences, the lone coloured man among them serving the longest of all.

The active communists, having derided the liberals for their ineffectuality, fled abroad. Albie Sachs, who had helped to shape Leftwich's revolutionary fantasies, was

The late Alan Paton (Business Day).

quick to go, along with Brian Bunting, who now counsels SA draft evaders in London, and Frennie Ginwala, now a leading Marxist theorist for the ANC. The Slovos left, and Wolpe and Goldreich, and many others slid out of the struggle, leaving their gullible liberal recruits behind. Within a few years, SA had become a political graveyard, sterile and silent.

Through it all, however, one liberal stood like a giant. Alan Paton never flinched, not when the rule of law crumbled, nor when the communists fled, nor when his fellow-liberals betrayed him and their own cause by turning to violence, nor even when his close friends and associates were banned, leaving him standing alone, diabolically untouched.

Alan Paton's liberal convictions are not a springtime thing, to be cast away when the heat rises. He does not say truth has become untrue because it has lost utility. He does not lose compassion nor abandon principle. He does not abandon either hope or struggle.

The PFP Members of Parliament sit bleak and gloomy below the Official Opposition. Their liberal support has fled, either abroad or into extra-parliamentary allegiance; one constituency counted 1 500 voters abroad; in another, a man of 70 was given the task of putting up posters because no younger help was available. They are mocked from both sides and they are lonelier than Helen Suzman in 1961 because their hopes were higher, and their intellectual support groups inside Parliament are weaker.

There is one comfort: it has been almost 40 years since the values of Alan Paton's world were rejected by the white electorate, and we have gone from Graaff to Botha, from Verwoerd to Treurnicht, but still Alan Paton, the extra-parliamentarian, does not flinch.

From the Press gallery, as the smell of the Sixties rises again, a thought takes shape: the communists fled, and Iron Man Vorster broke in the end, and liberals betrayed their heritage, but Alan Paton stood his ground, and we are fortunate, in this faithless century, to live in the shadow of such a man.

'I am furious'

Aggrey Klaaste, 1987 and 1988

A journalist of much experience, Zola Aggrey Klaaste was offered the editorship of the *Sowetan* early in 1988, assuming his position on 1 May. An already controversial, but relatively unknown journalist, Klaaste almost immediately began to put into action what he had long hinted at in his increasingly highly regarded weekly column On the Line — the building of a new nation.

The 1978 Nieman Fellow at Harvard and former detainee, Klaaste's vision of the future of the country in which he lived was of necessity a mixed one. He was, after all, one of the victims of apartheid. But Klaaste, whilst acknowledging his debt to the past also acknowledged a commitment to the future. Writing with a welcome frankness and, as a colleague remarked, 'sometimes brutally', Klaaste came out, late in 1987, with what was described at the time as one of the strongest condemnations of black political violence to have appeared in any black newspaper. Klaaste had begun to make waves.

His despatch appeared in the *Sowetan* on 26 October, some seven months before he became editor.

FRATRICIDE WILL NOT SET US FREE

Early last week I thought it was about time someone said something nasty about the violence in Natal. I thought it was about time someone had the guts to read political gangsters the Riot Act.

We have been treating the violence sparked by political opportunism with kid gloves for just too long. Most of us were too damned frightened to say anything about the phenomenon that is both ugly and shameful.

In the end some of us who are presumed to be opinion-makers are faced with the impossible task of defending our people for doing the indefensible.

It has been almost impossible to explain the necklace thing away. In fact there is no way we can hold our heads up after that thing.

Now we have the savagery in Natal which puts us right back into the Dark Ages.

I am furious. The cause of this is the way in which a child was beheaded by hoodlums, murderers, near Maritzburg last week. I don't care what the magnitude of your political passion is, you don't do such things.

What makes me even more furious is that those involved in the battle — and I am cowardly enough not to call them by name — are fighting for power they have no chance of wielding. One could understand black political organisations fighting over a prize that was already in the bag. For God's sake liberation is not even in sight and those who are busy fighting for such high stakes are setting the struggle back by years.

Irony

The irony of this type of butchering going on in a lovely place in Natal is unnerving. Natal has the Valley of the Thousand Hills. Natal boasts a host of laughing streams gurgling between tree-clad hills, so beautiful they make you ache inside. Natal has one of the most regally gentle people in the country, the Zulu nation.

King Shaka Zulu who has been insulted by South African historians, must be turning in his noble grave when things that had been said about him are being perpetrated today.

Natal is a fairly homogeneous province where most of the Africans are Zulu. Natal has had its faction fighting which many of us excused because it looked like a traditional feud usually associated with such ancient people. Natal has now put us into deeper shame.

The awful thing is that the political parties that are tacitly or helplessly behind these murders presume themselves to be future leaders of South Africa. I cannot see how we will accept such leadership which is partly responsible for such horrible acts long before it assumes its place at the helm.

We cannot accept the inability of the leaders to control the passions that have been unleashed because of the ignorant, senseless, reckless political opportunism from some people who think they have the monopoly to the truth.

What makes matters worse is that these same people are forever moaning to the world about their innocent democratic structures. They are always telling the world they abhor violence. Better for a man to say he is for violence and then commit such acts.

I must say that I don't think this sounds angry enough. It is also bizarre for me as we are at the moment dealing with the human drama of two lovely kids who have been taken to the heart by most people — the Mathibela twins.

We have been running stories of black children in detention who have been tortured and whatnot. How can we possibly point a finger at faceless butchers when we murder children, chop their heads off with an axe, in broad daylight.

We must simply shut up, we blacks.

The hypocrisy in the struggle is having a grave effect on honest committed people who are honestly fighting for the freedom of the people of South Africa.

Struggle

Perhaps it is just as well the struggle has been set back by 20 years. We are simply not ready. I don't care what you think.

It is not as if this kind of savagery, bad as the latest is, is confined to Natal. We had people being butchered, being burnt, we had old men and women being set on fire, we have had people decapitated with cheerful abandon for almost four years now.

If this is the type of retribution that will become common when blacks rule blacks, then perhaps we need a great deal more oppression to make us humble, responsible, dignified in our anger against oppression.

I am not saying we should visit such horrors on other people. But the world is completely surprised that blacks should be doing this kind of thing to other blacks. It does not make sense.

Believe me, I have tried to defend the necklace phenomenon. I have told people as to how we have been forced by the system to become this way.

I have made a passionate plea for children who have been brutalised, turned into monsters by the evils of apartheid.

In the end I could see the cynical disbelief in their blue eyes, those chaps from across the sea.

I could actually hear them sniff caustically at my lame defence. I could see how the brain tells them we are indeed a barbaric, even cannibalistic, people.

I don't know when this will end. I have said it before. Come the day of liberation I will take my kids and make a beeline for Beirut. Perhaps it is tough there, but not so primitively savage.

Klaaste espoused the concept of 'Ubuntu', the rough translation of which is 'humanity'. Interviewed by *New York Times* southern Africa correspondent Christopher Wren, who described him as a 'gentle crusader', Klaaste expanded on his vision of Ubuntu. 'It was to people, you must become actors in your life.'

Shortly before he became an overnight celebrity with his Nation Building scheme, Klaaste wrote 'I am 48 years old and have lived through 40 years of National Party rule. It has been a daunting experience, full of despair, helplessness, tempestuous bouts of anger, grief and very little hope.' But it was the hope he concentrated upon.

In a speech in Johannesburg in October 1988, Klaaste launched his Nation Building scheme. He spoke of the need to put past wrongs behind; of the need for hope and the necessity for communication; of the promise of the future. In short, he said, it was time to stop crying. Klaaste's dramatic and powerful vision of the future captured the imagination of a country in turmoil — anxious about the future, but determined to achieve a settled and equitable future. Klaaste put into words what many South Africans had been thinking.

His article, on the subject of building a nation of the future appeared, initially in the *Sowetan,* and subsequently reprinted in major newspapers, on 26 October 1988.

TODAY: THE MOVE

While our rivals and some of our detractors wish to make believe that nation-building is a flash-in-the-pan idea by a new editor anxious to sell newspapers, or perhaps his name, I can say without equivocation that the idea took years to manifest itself.

This manifestation was, in fact, the result of a combination of personal, political, historical and other factors that have impacted on my life for 30 years.

In other words, this is no obscurantist idea. It is no fly-by-night notion plucked from the air. The timing for it is, frankly, profound.

Nation-building is many things. In the final analysis it is something like a unilateral declaration of independence in style, in shift of thought, and in the crucial role that blacks will play in this country's future.

I am 48 years old and have lived through 40 years of National Party rule. It has been a daunting experience, full of despair, helplessness, tempestuous bouts of anger, grief and very little hope.

I have lived, likewise, through three historic watersheds in the country's history: Sharpeville, March 21, 1960; Soweto, June 16, 1976; and September 4, 1984 onwards. I have been chastened by these events, as they showed me, singly and jointly, the best and the worst in the human experience. As a journalist — almost this entire period — I have been placed somewhere near the centre of these events.

After Sharpeville in 1960, the first paradigm towards a phenomenon I have been able to

Aggrey Klaaste, editor of the Sowetan, *the 'gentle crusader' (*Sowetan*).*

identify began. After the first shock of the tragedy, we were thrown into uncontrollable anger, which was ruthlessly smashed by the State.

The aftermath of the tragedy saw the banning of the ANC and PAC and the systematic destruction of almost all political dissent.

The newspapers, the artists, commentators and all opposition political organisations stridently opposed the Government. Day after bitter day we wrote, spoke and acted out the evils of the apartheid system.

Unwittingly, we were fanning and reinforcing the deep, but impotent anger, in the hearts of blacks. I am not saying there was anything wrong in that. It was a natural reaction. The uncanny thing is we were planting the seed for the next explosion.

Meanwhile the white communities were being told a different story. Lulled into a sense of false security by the Government and its powerful organs, white South Africa was made to believe everything was under control. Even those whites who have been close to the black struggle gave themselves a silent hug of comfort. Things were under control. The Government and its media reinforced this view. The people were told over and over again that the few radicals who had inflamed a gullible black population had been smashed.

The next terrible explosion was 17 years later — 1976. This time the cost was much higher. People were seriously beginning to question the legitimacy of the apartheid system. Our children caught most of the flak and became the heroes and martyrs of the struggle. It hurt badly.

A few businessmen, perhaps bothered by plain self-interest, perhaps out of badly battered consciences, decided to do something. The thinking then was to form a black middle-class, a kind of buffer between the raging masses and the whites. But, generally, the delusion was being perpetrated that this killing of children was also just another historical aberration. That if something was done quickly to patch up the cracks, all would be well.

Blacks lost many things. Worst of all, we lost the innocence of our children. We also lost their respect for us.

As if we were a nation accused, there was a swing to the right in white politics which is perhaps as frightening as the necklace phenomenon of the Eighties. It is, in its own appalling crudity, fanning race hatred. Apartheid is not dead at all. No, it is about to stalk the streets of our townships in all its dreadful menace.

There is, therefore, a holding of the angry breath in the black community. It is probably unconscious, but I can feel it in my bones. There is the silent preparation from blacks for the next inevitable explosion.

Quite clearly, somebody has to do something to stop this madness. Or at least cushion the blow.

But obtaining a political kingdom is not the means to an end. For political kingdoms to be effective, lasting and particularly democratic, they need all sorts of power structures to underpin them. They need a back-up of strong people who have economic and academic clout, who have strength to recognise the value of a free Press, who have a spiritual or religious foundation. Such kingdoms, sadly, also need a strong defence system, a respectable system of justice, a strong security system.

It has been difficult to shift the focus from the political struggle.

But we had to do something. It seemed to us with the fractious nature of black politics, even the vocabulary — for instance, talk about black unity — had become jaded. We had to look for a new vocabulary. We had to be able to use that vocabulary in ways that would not lead to confrontation with a highly suspicious Government.

We also had to develop a lateral type of thinking, a thinking that would in the end lead to black unity. We thought of nation building. It is ideologically a neutral label. It also tells the majority of people who had retreated from political activity that they count.

And, for heaven's sake, how many good people are there who should, by all definitions, be accorded the label of leaders? In the end we are saying to our brothers and sisters who are actively involved in the struggle, they need to build strong people. A strong following of thinkers and doers. Not simply a vast number of angry and plainly dangerous people.

We say the political kingdom will look after itself if it has strong people behind it.

We should start building now. The economy is depressed and there are many frightened and unhappy people. All it needs is a match to the dynamite for things to blast off.

Why, you could well ask, is the need for building now? For years we have been obsessed by politics. We have said to ourselves, to our children and to the world, that the only leaders who are of consequence among us are the political leaders. That has been shameful in many ways.

Those who are politically active had to bear all the attacks from the state. Many of them have died. Many of them are in exile. Many of them are in detention.

We are asked in times of crisis, *aphi amadoda?* Where are the men? The answer, almost pathetically, has always been: they are in jail, in detention, in exile.

What an insulting thing to say to the many black men and women who are doing excellent work who could easily wear the cap of leadership!

Nation-building is about the recognition of such leadership. My sons need to know I have the potential of being a leader, that I can handle a school boycott, that I can understand and explain the profundity behind "liberation before education" while at the same time stressing the desperate necessity to acquire knowledge and power.

We are still looking for that essential chemistry that will convince my sons and their peers that they are the leaders of tomorrow.

We need to have the type of black leadership that will decrease the fear in the hearts of the young Afrikaners. They are afraid of our numbers. They are convinced by the perception that we are a vast population of gullible people easily swayed by communists and other radicals. We have to show those people that when we talk of building, we include them in that happy future. We have no secret agenda.

We will start helping to rebuild the structures in all forms in our societies. When we run out of ideas, out of money, out of managerial skills, we will ask for help from our white friends. We are prepared to go to Pretoria and Stellenbosch universities for such help.

The ultimate ideal is that we, who are the majority, will build ourselves, by seeking help internally, and externally, for that matter, to build South Africa for all.